A LIFE IN PROGRESS

CONRAD BLACK

KEY PORTER BOOKS

For Jonathan, Alana, and James

Copyright © 1993 Conrad Black

All rights reserved. No part of this work covered by the copyrights hereon may be reproduced or used in any form or by any means — graphic, electronic or mechanical, including photocopying, recording, taping or information storage and retrieval systems — without the prior written permission of the publisher, or, in case of photocopying or other reprographic copying, without a licence from the Canadian Reprography Collective.

Canadian Cataloguing in Publication Data

Black, Conrad
    A life in progresss

ISBN 1-55013-520-1 (bound)   ISBN 1-55013-618-6 (pbk.)

1. Black, Conrad – Biography.   2. Businessmen – Canada – Biography.
3. Capitalists and financiers – Canada – Biography.   I. Title.

HC112.5.A53A3 1993   338'.092   C93-094662-6

The publisher gratefully acknowledges the assistance of the Canada Council, the Ontario Arts Council and the Ontario Publishing Centre.

Key Porter Books Limited
70 The Esplanade
Toronto, Ontario
Canada M5E 1R2

Design: Scott Richardson
Typeset in Adobe Janson Text 11/14 by Indelible Ink
Printed and bound in the United States of America

94 95 96 97 98 6 5 4 3 2 1

Contents

Prologue / v

1. An Unconventional Youth
   1944–1967 / 1
2. Quebec from the World's Fair to the War Measures Act
   1967–1970 / 42
3. Pathways to Manhood
   1970–1972 / 70
4. The Twilight of *Bonne Entente*
   1972–1974 / 107
5. Closing the Nursery Door
   1974–1976 / 138
6. Financier in Waiting
   1976–1978 / 173
7. Rebuilding Argus Corporation: From Tractors into Oil
   1978–1981 / 217
8. Financial Engineering: From Oil into Iron Ore
   1981–1983 / 269
9. Argus Becomes Hollinger: From Groceries into Newspapers
   1983–1986 / 309
10. A Trans-Atlantic Newspaper Company
    1986–1989 / 351
11. Spanning the World from Quebec to Australia
    1989–1991 / 398
12. Domestic Upheavals and a World View
    1991–1993 / 460

Index / 517

Prologue

There may not be any acceptable excuse for a person of my age and position to write a book principally about himself. My explanation for writing this book now is that it is largely a comment on Canada, which is at a difficult stage in its political evolution. I owe my countrymen a statement of why I am not now mainly resident in Canada and of my hopes and concerns for that country.

Much of what is recounted here has been the subject of extensive public comment in several countries, often somewhat inexactly. In a number of cases the record is better set straight as soon as possible.

Finally, I dare to hope that someone facing one or more of the obstacles encountered by the author in this narrative may derive some encouragement from it.

I wish to thank several people for their collaboration and help with this volume, especially my wife Barbara Amiel Black, with whom I fell profoundly in love when the original manuscript was nearing completion and who married me as it was being revised. I am also grateful to my friends Peter Atkinson, Emmett Cardinal Carter, Dan Colson, Max Hastings, George Jonas, Michael Levine, Charles Moore, Anna Porter, Brian Stewart, and Peter White for their care and advice.

Most authors know the feeling of wanting with pen or typewriter to get something off their chests. That is what I have done. The act is its own reward and really seeks none other.

CHAPTER ONE

AN UNCONVENTIONAL YOUTH
1944–1967

I WAS BORN IN MONTREAL, AUGUST 25, 1944, to comfortable parents. Canada's large expeditionary force in Europe, composed almost entirely of volunteers and a huge mobilization of natural and industrial resources, had secured the country's graduation from British dominion to rather more autonomous American protégé. Traditionalists would be irritated by the de-emphasis of Britain, and they and the gentle Canadian left were wary of the United States, but this was progress well-earned and welcome as such.

Montreal was Canada's premier city, a felicitous combination of English-Canadian solidity and discretion and French-Canadian kitsch and panache. The prosperous and Britannocentric English-language community largely ignored the surrounding French majority, whom they generally considered to be pleasant, slothful, and priest-ridden. The French were tacitly assumed to be destined, not altogether improvidently, to roll the tennis courts and manicure the greenswards of the Anglostocracy in the bucolic English resting places of Knowlton, Murray Bay, Tadoussac, Cacouna. Apart from a few politicians, clergymen, and hockey players, the French attracted little notice from their English-speaking compatriots. A week after I was born, the occasionally demagogic "autonomist," Maurice Duplessis, was re-sworn as premier, having spent the previous five years in opposition and infirmity.

Before I was a year old, my parents moved to Toronto. The Great Depression had convinced my father that prosperity, a fortune in fact, was essential to happiness. He lived, he often said, "in a pecuniary society." He wound down and retired from the aircraft propeller manufacturing company he headed to become assistant to the legendary beer baron E.P. Taylor.

My father, George Montegu Black, Jr., was six feet, five inches tall, slender, cultured, humorous, enigmatic, and in his later years, rather melancholy. He had intellectual aptitudes and ambitions and was a Rhodes scholarship candidate when the financial crisis gradually eliminated the wealth of his father who, in the summer of 1929, had been an affluent real estate developer and insurance dealer in Winnipeg.

My father developed marital as well as material ambitions in the early 1930s and, after graduating in arts from the University of Manitoba, qualified himself as a chartered accountant, a profession in which he never, as far as I could discern, had the slightest interest. After completing his accountancy program in 1937, aged twenty-six, he married his fiancée of six years and joined his father in the modest brewing and bottling business where the original George Montegu Black had fetched up to try to recreate his evaporated fortune.

They toiled together in this task almost until the birth of my brother, the third George Montegu Black, in the summer of 1940, by which time the war had attracted my father to Ottawa. His eyesight barred him from the active military, but he eventually became an assistant deputy minister of National Defence for Air, helping to organize a pilot-training scheme in Canada for the whole British Commonwealth, before repairing to Montreal in 1941 to manufacture propellers on a prodigious scale.

My grandfather had represented the Harmsworth family in Western Canada, in particular the original Viscount Rothermere. He was the junior partner in a variety of real estate and financial investments they had in the western provinces. He took my father and my aunt Margaret to Europe several times in the twenties, and they spent most of 1923 there. My father had a monosyllabic exchange with Rudyard Kipling while on a Mediterranean cruise that year, once glimpsed Georges Clemenceau, and listened credulously while Rothermere recounted his son's candidacy as king of the Versailles-created state of Hungary.

My father acquired a passable acquaintance with French, with the cities and countryside of France, Germany, Italy, and England, and, for someone just entering his teens in the Canadian prairies in the mid-1920s, an untypical worldliness.

My mother, Jean Elizabeth Riley, but universally known as Betty, was a natural, convivial, and altogether virtuous person. She was as straightforward as my father was complicated and sophisticated, as affable as he was prone to be aloof, as constant as he was temperamental. Apart from youthful athletic prowess, she as a champion figure-skater, he as a pro-level golfer, and an appreciation of each other's high and sharply different qualities, it was never obvious to me, when I became experienced enough to judge such things, what they had in common.

In Toronto, they evolved from the attractive young couple from the West via Montreal, to a picturesque, almost improbable pair whose private conjugal abrasions were sometimes saddening, often hilarious, but almost never such as to mitigate my goodwill and gratitude. They became gradually more eccentric, she often going to bed right after dinner, he sitting up much of the night, rarely unfortified by a generous spirit issue, "brooding" as he said, and reading. She read extensively also, and had an almost encyclopedic knowledge of modern fiction. She preferred British and French novelists to the gloomy and overwordy Russians and Americans such as Steinbeck and Caldwell "who always had a fly in the pie or the coffee."

He sometimes conceived that the house was beset by intruders or that mallards were improperly trespassing in his swimming pool and on several occasions blew the glass out of the storm door in the garden room and brought plaster down on his shoulders while mistakenly demonstrating to himself that a shotgun was unloaded. As a gesture of resistance to the Canadian winter, he always kept his outdoor swimming pool heated to almost 85 degrees until December 1 although his fuel bills became astronomical and the propane tank had to be changed almost every day in November.

Even their Christmas presents to each other became rather colourful. One year he gave her "a driveway," i.e., a re-pavement of one, as she left the house almost daily and he was rather reclusive, and she gave him a splendid camera. He wrestled it out of its wrapping, fidgeted aggressively trying to load it, offering a hilarious narrative as he did so, concluding, "You wrench it open, and jam it closed" as pieces flew in all directions, and sent it back for extensive repairs on December 27.

Whenever asked what he wanted for a Christmas or birthday present, he invariably replied, forlornly, "A few kind words." When, as not infrequently happened, he was apprehended being overly histrionic, he would resignedly ask, "What is the use of repining?"

Despite his often proclaimed methodicalness, he frequently had difficulties with gadgetry, and on one twenty-fourth of May, when we still lived in Forest Hill in central Toronto, he purported to give us a ballistics lesson before firing off a sky-rocket. Between ignition and lift-off, the launch-pipe slipped and the rocket followed an almost horizontal trajectory, went through a neighbour's open bedroom window, buzzed about the walls like a giant bumble-bee, and blew up with a spectacular report. The wizened old face, surmounted by a crown of pin-curlers, that thrust itself out the same window a few moments later did not appear to be amused.

On another occasion, after spraining a finger, he set out to carve himself a splint and gave my brother and me a woodworking lesson. He wasn't far into it when he almost severed another finger with the knife he was using and commended himself to a serious doctor.

In those early years, my brother and I saw him mainly on weekends and holidays; Saturday and Sunday lunches were the only meals my brother and I took with our parents. They were usually the occasion for my father's rather esoteric but often riveting monologues, of which he cheerfully tolerated an almost endless series of interruptions. Order was restored to proceedings by his solemn utterance of his original opening line. Some of these are familiar yet: "There were these flying apes of Alinglappalap" was a long-running favourite. "Some have been more vociferous in their criticism of the CBC than I have, but few have been more consistent" always heralded an amusing and discursive harangue against the public broadcasting network.

Like Nancy Mitford's uncle in *The Pursuit of Love* (one of my father's favourite books), "he either loved or he hated, and generally, it must be said, he hated" (at least in his later years). Thus, those who he liked, no matter how unfortunate their appearance, were merely "ill-favoured," while a woman he notoriously disliked was immortalized as "a snaggle-toothed horse Godmother with a tongue that could clip a hedge."

He found *Who's Who in Canada* such "a monument to human vanity" that he sent in his entry one year declaring, as a send-up, his occupation to be "distance friction consultant." This job description was queried and, unfortunately, never published.

He was a considerable verbal stylist, easily irked by the awkward formulations of others. He could hardly endure sports telecast commentaries because of the inelegant utterances of the announcers. Foster and Bill Hewitt's references to "the both" of (two) players and Dizzy Dean's assertion that "he swang at" the ball particularly upset him. He claimed, with some seriousness, that Richard Nixon lost the 1960 election because of President Eisenhower's frequent references to "nukuler" weapons. He never forgave Mackenzie King for warning the Canadian public in 1940 that the prospect of German victory "towers above us like an avalanche" and remonstrated fiercely with Jack Pickersgill on the issue. (Jack, who was King's private secretary, strenuously professed agreement and innocence.) My father was always a hugely entertaining and original raconteur.

His own deliberate malapropisms were usually quite colourful. "I will batten down the hatches, tie myself to the mast, and take to the hills," he once said to a nonplussed Bud McDougald. He always identified an amusing phrase, such as John P. Marquand's: "I only have three friends and the two of them don't like me." He was the only person I ever met who purported to know that Haile Selassie, on returning to his capital cleared of Italians in 1941, proclaimed it "a day of liberation, castration, and feasting."

He had a number of preposterous notions about himself, such as that he possessed "perfect musical pitch" and that he could sleep for a predesignated time and awaken himself precisely when he wanted with a "self-auditory" snore. He had no such talents but his attempts to assert and demonstrate them were unfailingly amusing.

He was a persuasive capitalist, and it was doubtless under that influence that in 1952 I invested my life's savings, $59, in a share of General Motors, which I have never sold. At that time, it was almost a Cold War Victory bond. On one occasion when I slipped outside and several dollar bills in my pocket became muddy, I washed them

[5]

as best I could and was observed doing so, leading to the legend that I made a practice of washing money like Scrooge McDuck.

My father's grandfather had arrived in Winnipeg from the United States, my mother's from Yorkshire, both in the last quarter of the nineteenth century. The Blacks had a little American flamboyance and, when materially ascendant, consumed unselfconsciously, though in a manner that fell well short of ostentation. My mother's numerous family (she had six brothers and a sister), the Rileys, were and generally still are, understated, steady, stoical, and inconspicuous. They were half patrician and half bourgeois, the best, most reliable, and unvarying salt of the Canadian earth. With her great and widely appreciated friendliness, my mother would yet refer to my brother's and my low-budget trips to Europe as "making the grand tour" and to non-relatives who worked for an insurance company of which her family owned 20 per cent as "professional management."

This was my pedigree, honourable and unexceptionable, like so much of Canada, worthy of some pride, and of no embarrassment.

The Toronto of the early fifties was an almost relentlessly drab and tedious place even to the eyes of a seven-year-old. There was no flair in fashion or architecture, no visible spontaneity of any kind, just the dour, dreary earnest and envy of low-church Protestant Ontario. "As quiet as wartime Toronto on a Sunday," wrote Alistair Horne about Algiers at the end of his magisterial work on the Algerian war. My mother and I had a twenty-year contest to identify the most unsightly of Toronto's thousands of creosote-soaked, bowed, heavy-laden telephone poles.

My father came to disparage all travel, even from his suburban home to downtown Toronto, as a life-threateningly inconvenient excursion to nether regions, but in those days, mindful of how interesting European travel had been to him at the same age, he dutifully took us to New York and Montreal often and, in 1953, in a fine monarchist gesture, to England for the coronation of Queen Elizabeth II.

On February 7, 1952, my brother, whose droll qualities developed early and have never deserted him, while accomplishing the perfunctory ceremony of saying goodbye to our slumbering parents on the way out to school, declared the occurrence of two unbidden developments. He had discovered in his breakfast cereal a weevil, whose existence was vehemently denied by my parents' Chinese

AN UNCONVENTIONAL YOUTH

cook despite the production of the insect's sodden corpse. (The cook was the most proverbially inscrutable person I have known; he died ten years later at a great age, leaving an estate of over $500,000.)

My brother's second titbit of news was that the King, George VI, was dead. My father, who usually managed to sleep through this domestic rite, sat bolt upright, baring his undershirt to the new day, and became very animated. This was the genesis of our great visit to England the following year.

My childhood passion was ships, both capital ships of the world's navies and the great liners. I memorized the length and tonnage of the greatest steamships and the main armament of all the world's battleships and laboured acquaintances, and even passers-by, with information of this kind at every opportunity. I wept with sympathy when I was told in 1950 that the last of the four-funnel liners, the *Aquitania*, was being broken up and scrapped.

My reward for this preoccupation was our return first-class passage to Southampton on the world's greatest ship, RMS *Queen Elizabeth* (1,031 feet, 83,673 tons). I can never forget the inexpressible excitement I felt when I saw, and then we boarded, the great ship in New York. My brother and I explored almost every accessible corner and compartment of the vessel. The supreme incarnation of authority I had ever seen to that point was the captain, erect, courteous, distant, and deferred to.

One of the stewards in the promenade deck lounge regaled me endlessly with his transatlantic experiences, extending back through *Queen Mary*, *Mauretania*, *Berengaria*, *Majestic*, and *Olympic*, the *Titanic*'s happier sister. On leaving Southampton for the return to New York after three months, the *Queen* sailed up the centre file of the great deployment of ships for the Spithead naval review. I convinced myself that I saw HMS *King George V*, which had been the Home Fleet flagship in the sinking of the *Bismarck*. We undoubtedly did see Britain's last and greatest battleship, the *Vanguard*, which I had badgered my father a few weeks earlier into having us driven forty miles to Shoeburyness to glimpse fleetingly off-shore through the fog. (Thirty years later, one of the *Vanguard*'s last captains, Sir Alistair Ewing, supervised the installation and removal of my hurricane shutters at Palm Beach, and I heard his reminiscences as happily as I had those of his contemporaries I met on my first visit to Britain.)

I met a few of the other passengers on the ship, including Sir Eric Bowater, and other prominent British industrialists who fulminated on the evils of McCarthyism. In vain did my father assure him that the American political process, in its unfathomable way, would work it out. The British were well-launched in their political leitmotif of doubting the American aptitude for western leadership. As I had for some months been rushing straight home from school to watch the McCarthy-dominated hearings on television, I hesitantly dared to defend the practice of exposing and scorching out communists in Hollywood and the State Department and said that at least it was good entertainment. It is my first remembered try at conducting an adult conversation. (The next best television divertissement was David Brinkley's summary of the dog-fights in the air war over Korea and his narration of the previous day's war footage. Next came "Victory at Sea" with Richard Rodgers's uplifting score. Only after these and a great sporting match and perhaps a political speech came, in my rating system, the comical efforts of Jackie Gleason and, a year or two later, Phil Silvers.)

Britain itself, which I feared might be an anticlimax after so stimulating a sea voyage, was a life-enhancing experience. As we drove into London from Southampton, my father purported to quote Bismarck: "God, what a city to loot!" The majestic façades, splendid palaces (especially Apsley House), the great hotels and clubs (we stayed for a time in Claridge's before moving to Connaught Square), the endless colonnaded porches of the West End, the many categories of richly liveried support people, the Guards, the coronation itself, especially the venerable Winston Churchill in his carriage, the teeming activity of the port and river, the great churches, the country, Windsor, Stratford, Hampton Court, Harrods, even the bomb damage, London's badge of honour in the late war that my elders never tired of refighting, all was magnificent. London did not seem as powerful, of as mighty a scale, as assertively energetic as New York, nor was it or is it, but it was great and fascinating and, in any case, the comparison with Toronto, by the end of the trip, the only city in the world I knew better, was invidious.

I had seen London and New York and thus had experienced the Canadian problem: we were derivative and secondary, good but not great. We were different from the British and slightly distinguishable from the Americans, but the only really important distinction seemed to be that they were greater, more exceptional, more important than we. We were fortunate to be allied to such benignly kindred nations, even though they overshadowed us. We had the Queen and the Americans didn't; we had the French and the British and the Americans didn't, but they were not a human resource highly prized by most English Canadians. I had stood in front of Sunnybrook Hospital with my mother and her father in 1951 when Princess Elizabeth passed, but the Queen was English and came to Canada only for two weeks every few years.

The Americans and British had Churchill, Eisenhower, MacArthur, Marshall, and Montgomery. They had the stars, we had worthies, or so it seemed to me in 1953, when the only great Canadian star I knew of was Rocket Richard.

What I admired about the Rocket was not just his electrifying scoring rushes, but his fierce determination, ever more fanatical as the pressure rose towards and through the play-offs, and, as I eventually came to appreciate, his incarnation of the pride and aspirations of his ethnic group. More impressive to me than his sudden-death overtime goals was the implacable determination that caused him to go through the sleeper train from Montreal to Detroit, during a weekend home-and-home series, tearing open curtains to find, and pummel in his berth, one of his opponents. Assumedly it was the same combative instinct that caused him to leap from behind a pillar in a New York hotel and try to strangle a referee who had recently penalized him.

Here, I reasoned, was the true pride of champions, a refusal ever to accept defeat, not the quavering submissiveness to defeat as eulogized on English and English-Canadian playing fields. The Rocket accepting the Stanley Cup from the unsympathetic Clarence Campbell in Toronto at the end of his last game, Ted Williams hitting a home run in his last turn at bat, Sugar Ray Robinson regaining his middle-weight championship from Carmen Basilio and Gene Fullmer, the triumphant heroism of the human will was what interested me in sport. We had some of that in Canada, but the cry of the loon and the dip of the paddle were no substitute for national greatness.

I was particularly honoured, July 1, 1992, to be summoned to the Privy Council of Canada by Her Majesty The Queen in person with Maurice Richard, an event I couldn't have dreamt of when I listened furtively to my radio in bed in the early and mid-fifties to hear of his nightly Olympian exploits. (Unfortunately, the Rocket couldn't be physically present, but that didn't diminish the honour of being his classmate.)

There would be other "junkets," as my father called them, after that to the coronation, especially a trans-continental train trip in 1955, but it was difficult, come September, to return to the regimentation of Upper Canada College: homework, the frequently encountered aroma of urine and formaldehyde (which I still find unpleasantly evocative), compulsory sports (for which I had inherited no aptitude from my parents), the tedium of the three Rs imparted with increasingly frequent, but more or less gentle, impositions of the hickory stick. Canada's premier private school, like most of Canada's institutions, emulated English progenitors. Lines were written out in detentions, we were made to run around "The Circle," but such lapses into mischievous indiscipline as I was sometimes subject to usually led swiftly to a sore fundament or (more painfully) bruised palms.

In the early years, this involved more sound and fury than pain. In grade two, when we were seven, the school's only woman teacher meted out applications of a wooden spoon to our hands. In grades three and four there was a mixed regime: the arithmetic teacher assaulted our hands with a ruler, the teachers in charge of the forms operated a demerit system. At the end of regular classes on Friday, all those who had assembled three demerits or more (a threshold I unfailingly crossed) lined up facing the wall outside the class door and in alphabetical sequence were more or less good-naturedly paddled on their backsides.

From grade five on, except for those classes presided over by men who didn't fulfil themselves through the beating of little boys' posteriors, there was, as my grades six and eight teacher (I always had problems calling them "masters") put it, "nothing to save you but the seat of your pants." Being slightly perverse, intermittently irreverent, and generally unlucky, I tested that distasteful salvation more often than most students. As we aged and grew and became more physically resilient, the beatings became each year more severe.

One particularly irritating technique was that of the faculty member who described a student's transgressions in pseudo-judicial terms and then called for a vote of the class on whether he should be caned. The vote was always overwhelmingly in favour. My foolish classmates enjoyed and legitimized the system. I voted against until my turn came and all but my closest friends voted for the maximum penalty, which was always carried out instantly and with considerable vigour. Occasionally there were voted selections from among various students, by their peers, of which should be punished, or with what relative gravity, i.e., how many strokes of the cane should be meted out. It was "give us Barabbas," and my outrage at my classmates for their eager participation in this sadistic charade was almost greater than my contempt for its author.

At first I had no opinion of corporal punishment. Order had to be maintained, and this imitative English method was part of our private-school culture. As the years passed, I came to regard recourse to it as often deviant and sometimes brutal. If Shaw was correct that "He who can, does. He who cannot, teaches," then it seemed also that he who can commands and he who can't intimidates. Surely there were better methods of education; I construed it as my duty not to submit to official terror. I evolved progressively from a sceptic, to a rebel, an insurrectionist, an anarchist. (In 1977 I even started a novel about the excesses of the Ontario private schools and the psychological damage to certain alumni, but I gave it up as I have little aptitude for fiction and became concerned that such a work focusing on neurotic after-effects could be in questionable taste, or even thought overly autobiographical.) Like all guerrilla operations, mine would steadily escalate until either the regime changed or the recalcitrant faction was neutralized, cowed, or expelled.

The slavish acolytes of the system, the Sonderkommandos, eventually disgusted me, such as those who observed us as we were herded to the showers after games and, closely observing discolourations, attributed the "zebra" award to the most frequently beaten boy in the junior locker room. (I was runner-up in the winter term of 1955, the only distinction I have ever earned at Upper Canada, except for second place in the junior chess championships in 1959.) All those who, by their docility or obsequiousness, legitimized the excesses of the school's penal system, the several sadists and few aggressively fondling homosexuals on the faculty, and the more numerous swaggering boobies who had obviously failed in the real world and retreated to Lilliput where they could maintain their exalted status by constant threat of battery: all gradually produced in me a profound revulsion.

One of the more enthusiastic flagellators of the time was Laurier LaPierre. Many years later when we became friendly radio debaters in Montreal and he sponsored my thesis at McGill, and still later when he publicly declared his homosexual proclivities, it became possible to imagine some of the socio-economic and psychological displacements that must have motivated this penniless young French-Canadian socialist to assault so violently the comfortable derrières of Upper Canada's scions.

I wasn't opposed to a just use of force, as described by my friend and grades two and six classmate, John Fraser, in his book *Telling Tales*, as a suppression of unintended cheekiness. On this occasion, when a group of grade six students, including me, were noisily cavorting in a corridor, the annoyed invigilator of a senior form examination pointed at the sign "Examination in Progress" and rhetorically asked us if we could read. I instantly replied, not meaning to be as provoking as I obviously was, "No, I'm receiving an inferior education." The teacher shrieked with delight as he dragged me by the scruff of the neck into the classroom and over his desk, bellowed his pleasure at being able to enhance my education, and whipped me with a riding crop he miraculously produced from his desk. The upper classmen looked up languidly from their examination papers to enjoy this divertissement and I was propelled back out into the corridor with the words, which resonated in my thoughts for some time, "Please come back whenever you're feeling undereducated." I have rarely been cheeky since.

I was similarly discouraged from my only attempt at bullying. One day, a few months later, with the Form teacher out of the room, I escalated a minor dispute with the presumed class weakling into a full-fledged tussle. He proved much more formidable than had been anticipated, and my initiative was neither a pugilistic nor a moral success. The teacher returned earlier than we had foreseen and summoned us to the front of the class for the inevitable dénouement. I endeavoured to salvage some dignity from the fiasco by doing the honourable thing and pleading that my opponent should be discharged as "he was only defending himself."

"Rather successfully, too," came the master's reply, as he brandished his swagger stick. He accepted my request for clemency for my doughty opponent. So ashamed was I that I was almost impervious to the ensuing come-uppance, though it was painful, and my apparent philosophical stoicism redeemed me somewhat in the perverse judgement of my classmates. I never engaged in, or was even neutral about, bullying again.

This had been the only unprovoked recourse to physical violence of my school years and was not a success even before the intervention of the teacher. I was engaged in a few school-yard disputes over the years. I always acquitted myself with more distinction than on this occasion but I soon realized I had minimal potential as a pugilist. I never got past the second round of the school boxing tournament and was relieved when dental work prevented me from participating further.

Disciplinary injustices were not infrequent and sometimes chronic, and I was certainly not the most flagrant victim of them. My final struggle with the authorities began in the autumn of 1958. I had a double-gating, a two-hour Saturday detention. At the end of one hour, the duty master called the names of those who were free to go. He inexplicably included me and instead of volunteering that there must have been a mistake, I silently departed assuming a commutation, was recorded as absent, and was summoned the following Monday by the Upper School's disciplinarian-in-chief. (I had graduated from the Preparatory School the previous June.)

I naïvely assumed that retribution would bear some resemblance to the offence. My oppressor, an ancient, arch, and canny schoolmaster looked like the standard description of John the Baptist's executioner. He recognized in me a fundamental subversive, as I had probably become by then, determined upon a pre-emptive strike, and dealt me a ferocious beating. He applied himself so strenuously to his task that both his hearing aids sprang from his elephantine ears and he glowered, flush-faced, after me, like an incredibly aged and demented fugitive from outer space.

This time, I would not, so to say, turn the other cheek. Only my fear of the application of the criminal justice system to juveniles caused me to rule out arson. My father was a subscriber to the English-language edition of *Réalités*, several issues of which were devoted to the Algerian war. Though I found the fedayeen unattractive peasant terrorists and my sympathies were mainly with the French, whose Foreign Legionnaires and paratroopers I thought romantic if severe, I was at least aware of the disruptive potential of covert operations.

I conceived and unleashed a systematic campaign of harassment and clerical sabotage against the regime. The school had been structurally condemned and largely devolved to portable classrooms while the main building was replaced. This facilitated my insurrection. First, I picked the lock of the portable classroom that held the records of the cadet corps, the school's battalion. I removed my card so I became a non-person and subtly altered various other cards to bring inconvenience and unjust charges of being AWOL down on various people who I disliked or found ludicrous. My tampering was not so blatant that the authorities realized there had been a violation, and I happily bedevilled their "paramilitary foolishness," as I called it, for the balance of the year.

For good measure, I lifted my card from the files of the athletic director, thus escaping the obligatory sports program and its sweaty locker-room sequels. (I was sufficiently grateful to John Bosley for being less athletically co-ordinated then and so my performance went unnoticed, while he became the butt of much merciless ridicule, that I always voted for him as my MP from 1979 on. I might have been a less reliable elector had I not owed Bosley so much from those early years.)

Next, I struck more brazenly at the chief disciplinarian's headquarters, picked his lock in dead of night (after my confirmation class, conducted by the school's principal), rifled his desk, and selectively altered some of his records. I managed to have a couple of friends exonerated by removing the denunciations of them and even inculpated one person with whom I had clashed by inciting a denunciation for some truancy. As the end of the scholastic year approached, I prepared my *coup de maître* (not to say *coup de grâce*). The demolition and reconstruction of the main school building necessitated serving lunch in two shifts, and for the first shift, the school's central office was left entirely deserted, but the papers and documents that were frequently handled were left very accessibly in the locked room where three or four of the secretaries worked. I recruited three accomplices, one of whom had a wide range of keys and locks, and he quickly found a key that opened the office door. The moment that the door sprang open, I had a powerful sensation that unfathomable opportunities and dangers were opening also. Whatever happened to me, I knew I had humbled the oppressive system. We removed a large number of the upcoming final examination question papers. As I had already, for my own curiosity and amusement, taken a copy of the academic records of every student in the upper school, I could easily identify those who would be prepared to pay most dearly for them. A brisk, high-margin commerce ensued (a margin of 100 per cent, as I had no cost of sales).

I was going to reduce the school's whole academic system, except for the senior matriculation class, to utter chaos while achieving a spectacular mark for myself having done virtually no work. I am neither proud nor ashamed of what happened. It was an awful system whose odiousness was compounded by banality and pretention, but I was becoming somewhat fiendish and in the end inconvenienced hundreds of unoffending people, students, and faculty.

One supplicant actually knelt in front of me, begging for an examination paper. My research in the school's purloined records revealed that he had scored only 12 per cent in the subject in question at Easter, and I recognized that if I acceded to his request and his mark jumped to 90 per cent, it would be too much even for the dunciad that administered the school, so I affected not to know what my importunate confrère was talking about.

By the last week of the school year, I had almost completely undermined the system. Like the principal figure in the movie of a few years later, *King Rat*, I had more power than our jailers. I penetrated the Masters' Common Room and reassigned the faculty to supervisory tasks by typing up and substituting my own assignment sheet, assuring among other things that our examinations were presided over by the least vigilant people available, the music and printing teachers, as I recall.

It all ended abruptly on June 9, 1959. One of those to whom I had sold a paper was too slow-witted to memorize the answers or even write up a crib sheet that had anything on it but the answers. When he was caught, it was obvious that he had had prior knowledge of the questionnaire, and when interrogated he sang like a canary flying backwards at three o'clock in the morning.

Even the disciplinarian-in-chief realized that things had gone well beyond any possible application of his preferred methods. My fellow plotters and I were expelled and the principal's wife, festering in a hammock in her husband's residence yard, her hirsute face peering gloomily out from under a conical hat of the kind the Vietcong made familiar to the west in the sixties, assured me that my "life [was] over." Since I had never believed a word the desiccated old sorceress had ever said, I didn't see any reason to believe that. (Nearly twenty-five years later, Jim Coutts, running in the Spadina by-election, discovered the principal's widow living in the same old-age home as Maryon Pearson, and amusingly described his unsuccessful solicitation of her vote.)

As a sequel to my casual reading on the Algerian war, I had just read Camus's Algiers-set novel, *The Stranger* (having, for obvious reasons, little need to study my school curriculum). The narrator is unjustly sentenced to be executed and concludes the book by saying that he hoped to go to his death jeered by crowds "howling their execration."

As I left the school I had attended for eight years for the last time, some of my dear colleagues, including a couple who had ardently initiated commercial discussions with me in the preceding several days, bellowed abusively and righteously, like Camus's mob. I thought of the Stranger, though the parallel was tempered by the fact that I could hardly, and never did, claim innocence.

I saw one of my accomplices twice in the succeeding couple of years. The other two I have not seen these thirty-four years. I apologize to them all. I had my own partially defensible motives for seeking to sow bedlam at Upper Canada College and to bring the rafters and pillars down around its imposture. I shouldn't have dragged others in with me, and I have regretted it ever since.

My parents were quite philosophical, almost unflappable in fact, but I felt acute remorse for my former nanny, a saintly and long-suffering woman (to say the least) who wept when she heard of my disembarkation.

My father secured my admission to Trinity College School in Port Hope to the succeeding grade (since my academic performance had been quite passable even before I expropriated the examination papers). T.C.S. was and is another eminent private school. It was less

AN UNCONVENTIONAL YOUTH

academically proficient than Upper Canada, but more progressive, as I saw no sign of the birch, though I was ineffectually threatened with it occasionally.

I liked the students, as I had liked most of the students at my previous school, but I found the extreme regimentation and lack of privacy of a strict boarding school so jarring that I became almost compulsively insubordinate, though not as insidiously so as at Upper Canada. On March 22, 1960, the exasperated authorities in this school asked my father to withdraw me after I half-filled a radiator cap with ink and fired it at a faculty member like a flying saucer. "I'm sorry it's come to this," I said to the venerable headmaster, as I shook hands with him, but in fact I was not at all displeased. The ever resourceful George Black first professed to believe that my "formal education [was] at an end," as he said resignedly when he and my mother drove me back from Union Station in his splendid Packard convertible (which I still own and maintain in mint condition). But his spirits revived when I demurred, and he secured my re-admission to T.C.S. as an "extramural student."

He had retired as president of Canadian Breweries in 1958 and was now more or less a man of leisure. His idleness was not serene and it was a difficult time for him, not only because of me, but he had the time and took the trouble personally to invigilate in the billiard room of our house my examinations for grade eleven. I scraped enough together to pass into grade twelve at Thornton Hall, a pretentious cram school on Poplar Plains Road.

It was run by a neurotic Scottish lady with a penchant for totalitarian politicians, who easily prefigured (The Prime of) Miss Jean Brodie, and by her paramour, a seedy and raffish fop who was the school's founder. Here I met the finest teacher I ever had, Eric Johnson (Latin and French) and struck up enduring relationships, especially with my dear friend Brian Stewart, who has gone on to great journalistic distinction. I have almost uninterruptedly been grateful for and have always reciprocated his indefectible friendship ever since the day we met in September 1960.

I squeezed with excruciating precision through to grade thirteen, despite the harassments of the Scottish female Mussolini (she had the Duce's lantern jaw as well as his ideology). At one point in my final year, my father in one of his many moments of inspired flamboyance offered to buy the school from its founder. It appeared to be a successful business but the overture was declined with thanks. In a final act of defiance to a school system that I had found almost unrelievedly loathsome for a whole decade, I withdrew from Thornton Hall in February 1962 and prepared myself for senior matriculation, which anyone who paid a refundable five dollars per examination was entitled to attempt in the required nine examinations at the old armoury on University Avenue.

My fellow candidates were a bizarre assortment of perpetual students, late bloomers, and self-help enthusiasts. George Black was sceptical and was understandably tired of my educational travail. He guessed that I would finally have to repeat a scholastic year but he and my mother cheerfully took me to lunch between examinations on the opening day, at the Park Plaza. They never really understood what I was so upset about in my school years, nor why I couldn't be more quiescent, like other boys, but they occasionally found my methods slightly intriguing, though that was small consolation for the worry and embarrassment I caused them.

I was as determined to clear the last hurdle out of high school as I had been at times to shake the system on my way through it. In 1962, a matriculation candidate passed all nine examinations or repeated the year. There were no supplementals and no revisions. I had a 50 and a 51 but went up from there. I graduated from high school, though not strongly enough to be admitted by McGill, the University of Toronto, or York University.

On the morning the postman delivered my grade thirteen results, my mother awakened my father, who normally didn't open his eyes until about noon, and then only to have his bath, having usually been up to four or five a.m., reading. On that day, several hours before he would normally "lower (himself) into the bath," he purposefully arose at 9:30, put on his dressing gown, and marched determinedly the length of the house. He extended his hand and said, "I congratulate you" and returned happily to his bed, after I volunteered that he, by his Job-like patience and almost unflagging support, was at least as deserving of congratulations as I. Considering his tenacious attachment to habit, the acidulousness of some of our disputes, and the fact that he had had few and trivial reasons to congratulate me for some years, it was an affecting moment, for both of us.

Upper Canada and Trinity College are apparently good schools now, whether they were then or not. I surmise from the financial appeals I get from both Upper Canada and Trinity, from my sudden inclusion in their old boys' mailing lists a few years ago, and from Thornton Hall's references to me as, in a convocation statement in 1987, a "distinguished alumnus who shows by example the spirit of enterprise learned at Thornton," that all is forgiven. It is by me in all matters where I had any right to be aggrieved.

As I had always suspected, better days lay ahead of these trying years. It had not been an effortless launch into young manhood.

The insufferable poltroon who had been Upper Canada's principal in my time soon retired. His success undoubtedly banished the previous pervasive air of the Waspy, snotty, parochial play-pen for Rosedale and Forest Hill, where the likes of Vincent Massey had appeared every few years to bore a new generation of school-leavers, an inordinate number of them on their way to Bay Street to live somnolently ever after from the avails of the old school tie.

The official history of Upper Canada, written by another former English teacher of mine, described a pastoral student commonwealth I did not recognize.

The greatest lesson I learned from my school days was admiration for those who endured and persevered with quiet dignity in a system that was unfriendly or even unjust to them. The heroes of school days were not those who excelled at what came easily to them, even less those who rebelled, the group of which I was merely a notorious exemplar. The heroes were those who tried, who survived adversity, and who by trying and surviving strengthened their characters. It took me some years to appreciate this.

My parents had moved in 1951 to a commodious house on a seven-acre property at what was then the northern fringe of metropolitan Toronto. There wasn't really anyone my age in the neighbourhood and after my brother was packed off to boarding school in 1954, I became rather lonely and started to read somewhat precociously. Such was now my scepticism about the local Anglo-imitative group-think that I tried alternative views of the late war, starting with the first volume of Charles de Gaulle's memoirs. In the same week in 1955 I read in Hitler's last will and testament that "France is a raddled old strumpet that has never ceased to swindle and confound us and left us to foot the bill" and de Gaulle's famous assertion that he had "always thought of France in a certain way, the Madonna in the frescoes." They couldn't both be right and for romantic reasons at least, de Gaulle's version was preferable.

De Gaulle in the wilderness was a strangely romantic figure, the custodian of French national self-esteem since before I was born, and the only non-communist alternative to perpetuating what he called the "regime of the parties" of the Fourth Republic. I had followed in the newspapers the desperate struggle at Dien Bien Phu (Vietnam) and noted that de Gaulle, though only a retired general and private citizen, summoned his own observance at the Arc de Triomphe. He published his own instructions to the army and police, which was preposterous, but his orders were followed. ("*Le peuple n'est pas tellement là*," he said philosophically as he got out of his car in what is now the Place Charles de Gaulle). I heard Edward R. Murrow's commentary on Malcolm Muggeridge's interview with de Gaulle in 1956, in which the general, who had only five or six parliamentary supporters at the time, declared that the country would undoubtedly call upon him to redeem the nation within a very few years. When the French regime started to crumble in 1958, I followed the return of de Gaulle with the utmost interest and partisanship.

Having read his own account of his defiance of the general staff when he championed air and mechanized war in the thirties, of his defiance of the realities of defeat when he "assumed France" in 1940, and of his defiance of the Anglo-American leaders during the war, I found him, in my stifling little Anglo-idolatrous world, an inspiring and heroic figure. When he re-emerged in 1958, his success, as one of his biographers (Bernard Ledwidge) subsequently remarked, "was so right artistically, it must be right politically."

I had not been uninfluenced by my father's laudations of capitalism and had enjoyed my limited experiences of its benefits. I had always found most of the redistributive left phony, envious, and mediocre bleeding hearts whining and snivelling about meritocratic Darwinism, almost as boring as and much more dangerous than the Establishment drones who aroused their resentment. I accordingly couldn't generate much sympathy for the international left, so de Gaulle was, for me, the great political rebel of the time.

He had famously "declined always to follow the dictates of a false discipline" and seemed, among other virtues, to be a man capable of having resisted an oppressive school had it been his misfortune to be sent to one. I arranged to have a dental appointment when he came to Toronto in 1960 so I could see him and watched his car sweep up University Avenue. As far as I knew he was, except for the British monarch, the only really important person who had ever come to Toronto.

One of the few substantive political differences I had had with my father was over his view that Franklin D. Roosevelt was a socialist, if not a communist. He has always been, next to Abraham Lincoln, the American leader I most admired, not only because he triumphed over a cruel infirmity, over national economic and psychological depression, over "the apostles of war and of racial arrogances," or because he was the chief architect of the United Nations and official creator of nuclear energy, the Manichean poles of world brotherhood and Armageddon, but because he completely suborned, outwitted, and co-opted the American left and delivered the nation from the horrors those forces inflicted on most other advanced countries.

Roosevelt the shaman was one of the great talents of American political history. This was the true Roosevelt whom I commended to my sceptical father, the Roosevelt who had resided between the Astors and the Vanderbilts at Hyde Park and who said, "It's hard for a man with five children and ten servants to make both ends meet." Despite my advocacy, my father's view of Roosevelt did not moderate. When he thought I was playing his speeches too loudly (when I was still in high school), he would appear and demand the volume be reduced. On one occasion he menaced, "If I hear that sewer's voice in this house again I'll smash the records. Do you hear me, damn it?" I did, but he continued to hear Roosevelt's apostolic cadences in his house occasionally.

In 1955 I had seen Sir Winston Churchill on television answer a reporter's question by saying that he sought a summit conference "between the big three . . . or big four": France was a condescending afterthought.

My father had introduced me to the study of Napoleon in 1958 with A.G. Macdonell's marvellously readable, if slightly bowdlerized

Napoleon and His Marshals. I was not attracted by Napoleon's constant war-making or his elevation of his shiftless relatives to the usurped thrones of Europe, squandering the exaltation of soul generated by the revolution. He was never a rival in my admiration to the other great historical personality to whom my father introduced me (on our railway trip to the west coast in 1955), Abraham Lincoln. I was, however, as are almost all acquainted with his career, partially captivated by his attainments as a military commander, aphorist, swashbuckler, and self-mythologist.

By 1962, in addition to being an amateur Napoleon buff, I was a passionate Gaullist francophile in full and systematic rebellion against the smug, prim, Anglo-Protestant parochialism of the Toronto of my youth.

I came to hope, and then to believe, that the Anglo-Americans needed the French, that de Gaulle's resuscitation of the dignity and strength of France was a positive development of which Quebec's Quiet Revolution was a local replication, and that we had in Canada an opportunity to unite the two greatest cultures of the West. We would do within Canada what the Western world as a whole would do when it accommodated de Gaulle's renaissance of France.

It was in this roseate mood that I set off in September 1962 for Carleton University in Ottawa as a freshman, initially in journalism but after one semester, history. Carleton was the best university to which my modest matriculating average could gain me admission. I hoped to find in Ottawa a bicultural haven and the burgeoning capital of an emerging power in world affairs. I confidently told my father I would not live in Toronto again. George Black, having lived in Ottawa in 1940, smiled knowingly (though I would not have returned to the Toronto that I was so jubilant to leave).

Ottawa was a bit of a disappointment and made even Toronto seem exciting. I settled into the Savoy Hotel on Slater Street, a residential hotel favoured by back-bench MPs and senators and transient members of the Ottawa Rough Riders football team. I revelled somewhat to excess in my unaccustomed freedom and spent most afternoons at the House of Commons watching the debates from the gallery, evenings playing cards with senators who were fellow tenants, and stayed up late reading broadly on a wide range of subjects, provided only that they had no connection to the courses in which

I was enrolled. I boycotted the freshman-initiation procedures, which seemed just as juvenile as the fatuities I had recently escaped.

I had had a basement apartment and my window was normally blocked by a parked automobile. I came to accept as an augury of each new day the make of the car whose hub-cap constituted my entire physical world view. A rare Cadillac or Lincoln was a good omen and things went downhill from there.

I rarely appeared at the university that autumn, but became something of an amateur of contemporary Canadian government. I was a parliamentary connoisseur, particularly enjoying the debating skills and bumptious histrionics of Jack Pickersgill and Réal Caouette. The Diefenbaker government had lost its parliamentary majority in June 1962 and was poised on the edge of oblivion, so it was a dramatic political season. I also had the benefit of my card-playing chums in the Senate, an unending source of comical but not very reliable espionage.

My most frequent companions in these poker marathons (on our more intellectually ambitious evenings we moved up to nines or bridge) were Jean-François Pouliot, James Gladstone, and John Robertson. Senator Pouliot had been MP for Rivière-du-Loup-Témiscouata for thirty-four years and was an inexhaustible storehouse of lore about Mackenzie King, Henri Bourassa, Taschereau, Duplessis, Cardin, Lapointe, Power, St. Laurent, and others. It was a marvellous eye-opener and Canadian politics could not have been more entertainingly imparted. Senator Gladstone was the first Canadian Indian senator and was John Diefenbaker's gesture to the native people. Senator Robertson was a retired railway brakeman from Kenora who had run unsuccessfully for Parliament several times. Both men were amusing raconteurs in their slightly coarse ways. On a good night we might be joined by George Nowlan, a redoubtable Nova Scotian who was Diefenbaker's last finance minister, or Walter Aseltine, one of the Conservative Senate leaders, who both lived in the building but usually had other things to do than playing cards. It was not a political primer designed to inspire confidence in the seriousness, sobriety, and statesmanlike aptitudes (or even probity) of all of our legislators.

The Savoy was a little soap opera, an absurdly miniaturized Grand Hotel, with picturesque itinerants coming and going. The manager was a minor but amiable wheeler-dealer who fancied himself a figure of some influence. The chief room clerk was an excellent companion who persevered admirably and at time of writing is a vice president of the Toronto-Dominion Bank. One of the tenants for a while was Rafael Leónidas Trujillo's former police chief in the Dominican Republic, Arturo "the Razor Blade" Espaillat, whose constabulary work had been judged so checkered by brutality and embezzlement that he was under a deportation order. Another tenant was the executive assistant to the then minister of justice, Donald Fleming, and the hotel manager took the minister's assistant to lunch to argue the Razor Blade's virtues. He winked at me as they left the hotel for their power lunch. Two days later, when I surfaced shortly after noon and took in my newspaper, I was astonished to read in bold headlines that the manager was under indictment for attempting to bribe a public official.

He was eventually acquitted, after Espaillat had fled to Mexico. The Razor Blade sometimes joined our games; he was an interesting but very sinister figure. The building was owned by Sam Berger, who ran unsuccessfully for mayor of Ottawa against the famous incumbent, Charlotte Whitton. The Savoy's manager, prior to his legal entanglement, was also co-manager of the mayoral campaign, and I negotiated with him a mitigation of rent in exchange for the performance of minor political skulduggery such as removing Whitton lawn signs. I was in the House of Commons gallery when the Diefenbaker government fell in February 1963 and I did a little minor political work for local Liberals in the ensuing campaign. I briefly entertained some hopes for good government from Mr. Pearson and his colleagues.

It was all a refreshing diversion for an eighteen-year-old so recently escaped from the rigours of strict school discipline. Unfortunately, the academic consequences of such a life were rather negative. In February I received a letter from a woman who proved to have been my History 100 professor since September, announcing that my university career would end soon and ignominiously unless I mended my ways; she invited me to visit her. I did and we have been friends ever since. Naomi Griffiths remains my very favourite professor of all time, an ebullient English specialist in Acadian history.[†]

AN UNCONVENTIONAL YOUTH

When my results caught up with me in June 1963, I was in London on my first autonomous trip to Europe. I was allowed to retain the two credits I salvaged, but bombed the others so completely that I was not allowed to try the supplementals. By the skin of my teeth, I avoided dismissal from the university and was allowed to re-apply for the failed courses. It was a novel and interesting experience to be officially pronounced an academic failure, one fate I had always avoided in my tumultuous school years.

I momentarily considered staying in Europe and relaunching my life there and had an acerbic exchange of letters with George Black, who had fleetingly dared to hope that my academic perils had ceased. After a few weeks of reflection, I concluded that I was really just sulking, that quitting was not the answer, and resolved to make up for wasted time in the following two years.

In the meantime, my tenuous relations with my father dried up my only significant source of income; to stay on in Europe, I would have to find an alternative method of support. My trip to Europe up to this point had been an historical pilgrimage, albeit of esoteric inspiration. I was travelling with my brother and as we circumnavigated France, counter-clockwise like beagles, I dragged him to many and varied stations of French history, from Lourdes to the Vichy Casino where the Third Republic voted itself out of existence, from Marshal Foch's house at Tarbes to Victor Hugo's in the Place des Vosges, from the home base of the French navy at Toulon (where the splendid battleship *Jean Bart*, which had seen action at Casablanca in 1942 and Suez in 1956, was in the roadstead) to the beaches of Normandy and Dunkirk, from the German submarine pens at St. Nazaire to Napoleon's palace at Fontainebleau. His tomb at the Invalides was as uplifting a place to me as it had been to the young de Gaulle, as described in the opening pages of the general's memoirs.

Above all, we explored the ancient and modern invasion approaches to France, at Châlons where Attila had been repulsed, Waterloo, Vimy, Die wacht am Rheim at Strasbourg, Belfort, Colmar,

---

† She motivated me to a salvage operation on my academic year, which ended in April. (Twenty-seven years later, she presented me to convocation, in hilarious terms, for an honorary doctorate. We publicly reminisced over our first meeting.)

and Mulhouse. I looked for the academy at Metz where cadet Foch, in the midst of his graduating examinations in 1871, learned from the booming of the German guns that the city had become part of the German Empire, and for the railway station where he returned, with Weygand, on the evening of November 12, 1918, restoring Metz to France "at the head," as Liddell Hart wrote, "of the greatest host in human history." I even tried, unsuccessfully, to contact the ninety-four-year-old Weygand, to ask him about Foch, the Battle of Warsaw, the Levant, and the shambles of 1940, but he declined to see me.

The most memorable sight of all was the battlefield of Verdun, with the statue of Maginot, the little monument *Ici fut Fleury*, the *tranchée des baïonnettes* where a column of French soldiers had been buried alive, only their bayonets protruding above the ground. We walked around the great fort of Douaumont, where de Gaulle had been wounded and captured, March 2, 1916, and the ossuary containing in its walls the bones of 130,000 French soldiers killed in the great hecatomb around Verdun.

Among the greatest of all sights I discovered that summer were St. Peter's in Rome and Lourdes. I had had a slight experience of the Roman Catholic Church in Quebec, with its ubiquitous clergy, monolithic stone buildings, and spires thrusting heavenwards from countless little parishes, urban and rural. But a church holding 45,000 people, designed by Michelangelo and Bernini, which required 222 years to build and where 172 popes were buried was not something that bore comparison with the churches of Hull and Ottawa, or even St. Joseph's in Montreal.

Even less had the plastic idolatry and tasteless evocations of French-Canadian Catholicism prepared me for Lourdes, where millions of people, many of them whole, intelligent, attractive people, came out of faith to mingle with the infirm. There was a religious schism in our family, as my mother was an agnostic and my father was an atheist. Toronto, or at least the Toronto Establishment, was overwhelmingly Protestant, Quebec was mercilessly provincial though its Church was formidable, to a fault: "Squeeze a fish hard enough and it will get away," Duplessis had told Cardinal Léger.

Lourdes's underground basilica accommodating 20,000; the grotto where worldly people actually believed there had been an apparition; the cultural and material vigour of the Catholic Church in France and Italy where it had been pillaged and oppressed by atheist governments, where popes had been imprisoned and cardinals murdered: these were phenomena for which seeing Cardinal McGuigan disembark from his Cadillac on Bay Street and viewing Brother André's underclothing and pickled heart at St. Joseph's had provided a most inadequate preparation.

Even the supermarkets of religious trinkets around Lourdes, garish and offensive though they were, did not achieve the depths of commercial abasement that are familiar to even casual visitors to religious sites in Quebec.

Never in all my subsequent visits to Paris have I replicated the exhilaration I felt in June 1963, driving into Paris for the first time through the St. Cloud Gate.

In that splendid and inspiring springtime of 1963, the only cloud larger than George Black's hand, apart from my academic *échec*, was my financial embarrassment. My brother, worn down by my marching and counter-marching in unintended re-enactment of Napoleon's campaign of the frontiers of 1814, returned to Canada and sent me some of my own modest savings. But by mid-July there was nothing for it but to sidle up to, if not actually join, the work force, and I managed to land an occasional appointment as a Thomas Cook tour guide in Paris.

I left each of my busloads of tourists at Place de la Concorde with a little homily improvised about the classic façades of Church and State facing each other in La Madeleine and the Palais Bourbon, and the minatory presence of the military, symbolized by the overshadowing dome of the Invalides, with the happy ending that under the incumbent French ruler, the army had been deployed to the salvation of republican institutions. To judge from their glazed faces and underwhelming gratuities, they were no more interested than a group of Missourians had been when I purported to identify (from my imagination to be sure) the rooming house where Captain Harry Truman had stayed on his way back from the First World War. "Boy," said one of my dour customers as he stepped down from the bus, "we're Republicans and we're none too pleased that Harry came back at all."

I lived in what amounted to a garret: a small, clean, fourth-floor walk-up room, fifty feet from the bathroom, in the Hotel Bois de Boulogne, long since demolished, 164 Avenue de Malakoff. It was operated by two ferocious well-travelled Parisiennes, who gradually softened and became rather solicitous, if not maternal. I played pinball with the regular clientèle of The Café des Sports downstairs, ate at the cut-rate Relais des Chauffeurs, and became a recognized member of the neighbourhood. This brief period was my closest simulation of a Bohemian phase. It was quaintly but wholly satisfying and I have never since mocked the efforts of young people sincerely trying to "find" themselves. I didn't see the future with great clarity but I had figured out that the best entrée into the great world I had glimpsed was not to be a drop-out in the only society I knew.

By mid-August, even this trickle of earned money was becoming insufficient, and I moved to Spain, which at that time was a fascist pariah state where it was possible to live in comfort for a fraction of what a comparable standard of living would require in Paris. Brian Stewart was there, indulging his then current interest in bull fighting. We visited the awesome Vallé de los Caidos, monument to the million dead of the Spanish Civil War, strolled in the Retiro Park, browsed in the Prado. We astounded Brian's university residence friends with recitations from Hugh Thomas's magisterial history of the Civil War, which thoroughly debunked the official Franco regime version. It was a splendid wind-up to a great summer, but soon it was time to return to Ottawa, be it ever so humble, and revive my guttering academic fortunes.

Nothing much was required to resuscitate my academic career beyond appearing at the university with some regularity and keeping up with the course work. I did not return to the Savoy, but moved to the eleventh floor of the newer and less central Juliana building and as neighbours, traded in my derelict, gaming senators for the young local newsreader, Peter Jennings; the flamboyant mining promoter, John C. Doyle, who eventually absented himself from the Canadian jurisdiction with not much more decorum than the Razor Blade had; and my father's old associate, Senator M.W. McCutcheon, with whom I had many an entertaining, if often somewhat liquefied, evening.

I attended lectures from time to time and was just settling into my chair for my first philosophy lecture ever (not having got around to attending one in my freshman year) on Friday, November 22, 1963, when the first reports of the assassination of President Kennedy circulated. I sped home and from my balcony watched the flags being lowered on the Peace Tower and across the Ottawa skyline in the metallic grey pre-winter twilight.

Apart from being tragic in itself, the gruesome murder of the president filled me with foreboding. I have always loved the United States; as a youth I was impressed by its power and showmanship. From an early age I had felt that it possessed all of Canada's strengths on a geometrically greater scale without being unoriginal, mean-spirited, or self-conscious. It had seemed a charmed and magic country, but on the day the president was murdered I had dark (and not altogether unfounded) fears that its luck had run out.

I settled into a rather agreeable routine for the balance of my sojourn in Ottawa. I went to the odd morning lecture, most in the afternoon, and often drove from the university directly to Saint-Pierre-de-Wakefield in the Gatineau Hills and affected a revenance from the boulevardier summer of 1963 by sipping wine, smoking Gauloises or Gitanes, and reading *Le Monde*, *Paris Match*, or even *Le Devoir*. My French was a bit unsteady, though I was working on it, so this was a gesture based on aspirations rather than cultural attainments.

By 1966 I was smoking so heavily that I had to take a slug of Slivovitz, the fiery Yugoslavian plum brandy, before retiring, to stop coughing long enough to get to sleep. Eventually I became so alarmed by my catarrh and my brandy intake that I abruptly stopped smoking cigarettes in 1966 and cigars in 1969 and have not smoked (or had a drop of Slivovitz) since.

There were many lectures in the evening, to avoid early mornings, and often I went back to Hull, in the ancient Ottawa student tradition, for several nightcaps, usually at Chez Henri, which had the best and most regular and predictable fights and the most invincible bouncers I have seen. My interest, it need hardly be added, was as a spectator. I usually read for an hour or two after returning home after closing.

In the spring of 1964 I met a friend of one of my cousins who had first moved to Ottawa as executive assistant to Maurice Sauvé, the progenitor of the New Wave from post-Quiet Revolution Quebec. It was the ineffable Peter White, a man of astounding stamina, confidence, and optimism. Bilingual and facile, he appeared a new type of anti-parochial English Canadian. He was so peripatetic and, like most Westmounters, frugal that he suggested that all he needed as an Ottawa residence was a bed and bureau in the back of my kitchen.

The result was an amusing experiment. Maurice was the minister of forestry and natural resources (René Lévesque, then Quebec's natural resources minister in Jean Lesage's government, remarked that the federal government might as well name a "minister of Potatoes"), and he and Peter worked to establish a rural development system that was the basis for the eventual federal effort at regional economic expansion. We were always coming and going at odd times. On one late night, I didn't notice that a passenger, doubtless somewhat waterlogged, had not closed his door of my car when I backed in to my space in the Juliana building's garage. The door was sheered off, undamaged except for its hinges, and we took it upstairs in the elevator, purporting to turn it into a coffee table. Peter and several others of the minister's entourage were attempting to advance the state of their department. Their policy conference swiftly degenerated into an uproarious rout and the worthy cause of Canadian rural development was not much advanced that evening.

Maurice Sauvé was the Canadian head of the Canada-United States Inter-parliamentary Group and he and Peter made plans to attend the U.S. Democratic National Convention in Atlantic City in August 1964 that would renominate President Lyndon Johnson. As the weeks went by, Maurice dropped out and Peter became the delegation head and invited me to accompany him. At the last moment, he was detained on official business and it devolved upon me to represent the Canadian Parliament at the convention. I invited Brian Stewart to accompany me, and as soon as I had finished the summer courses that enabled me to make up the credits failed in my first year, Brian and I started out by car for Atlantic City, on my twentieth birthday.

It was an unforgettable spectacle. To the little spit of land whose town had been slowly going to seed since the crash of 1929 and which had been immortalized by the board game Monopoly, came all the uncrowned heads of the American state. Brian pointed out two policemen taking, as he thought, a pickpocket into custody. In fact, it was Adlai Stevenson, who extended his hand to me in the political style that never came naturally to him, as he was conducted to the hall to eulogize Mrs. Franklin Delano Roosevelt. The other eulogies that night were Robert Kennedy's to his slain brother and James A. Farley's to Speaker Sam Rayburn. Then came the acceptance speeches of Hubert Humphrey and Lyndon Johnson. Finally, as it was his fifty-sixth birthday, L.B.J. went onto a balcony over the boardwalk and the beach with scores of the barons of his party. Tens of thousands of partisans were deafened as night was turned to day by a colossal fireworks display. As he waved benignly down on us, well-launched on what was clearly going to be a mighty landslide over Barry Goldwater, Lyndon Johnson appeared to be a demiurge, unassailable and almost omnipotent, commander-in-chief and legendary master of the Congress.

I could not have conceived that scarcely three years later he would be unable to move around the country, other than to military bases, without provoking violently hostile demonstrations. The next time I saw him, in 1967 in Montreal, he was very beleaguered, and when I actually met him, in 1969, he was in reluctant retirement, unhappy and unwell, a winged and caged eagle. Only a more experienced judge than I then was could have seen that this time of triumph, August 27, 1964, would erode so quickly.

We were the guests in Atlantic City of Congressman Cornelius Gallagher, the American head of the Inter-parliamentary group, and his wife, of Bayonne, New Jersey. They seemed a very attractive and genial couple and he appeared to have a bright career ahead of him. I was startled, therefore, several years later, when allegations surfaced that Congressman Gallagher knowingly tolerated murder in the basement of his home and generally making himself a Mafia pawn. This was a lesser and tawdrier tragedy than Lyndon Johnson's but it was complementary.

One portent of what was to come flared up in nearby Philadelphia; a riot erupted in a poor black district, and Brian and I drove to "the city of brotherly love to watch the race riot." It was not a pretty sight. Several blocks were torched; others had been trashed; hundreds were injured, and large groups of surly and belligerent black toughs milled and roamed about. A brick apparently launched from an upper floor narrowly missed our windshield.

A clairvoyant was not required to foretell that black urban violence could become an American growth industry. Brian wrote our experiences up with great dramatic creativity in the Oshawa *Times*, where he had just started work after graduating from Ryerson.

My admiration was unbounded for Lyndon Johnson when, a few months later, he deployed the full might of the U.S. government against racial discrimination. His championship of civil rights, under-appreciated in the Vietnam era, was one of the supreme acts of modern American statesmanship.

My senior year as an undergraduate was the most serene I had had since I was a pre-schooler. A theatre club of which I was the president staged a "Royal Nonsuch" adapted from Mark Twain. The prurient freshmen of Arnprior and Smiths Falls and environs were enticed in their hundreds to pay $2.50 each to see "1001 Freudian delights," and one of my friends appeared nude, painted blue from head to toe with a rose in his mouth and danced around the stage to a 45 r.p.m. Beatles record. When the music stopped, the curtain came down to generous applause that gradually gave way to restiveness several minutes after the performer had fled to the showers and his co-producers had removed the till and deserted the gate. There was a considerable controversy and the student ethics inquiry was presided over by my chess-playing friend and Canada's subsequent free-trade negotiator, Gordon Ritchie. It was an amusing spoof but was neither a legal nor university rules infraction.

In the autumn of 1965, after graduating from Carleton with a B.A. in history, I enrolled at Osgoode Hall Law School. I couldn't think of anything better to do and had greatly enjoyed my undergraduate years. It was another good social year, but after I sailed through the mid-year examinations I became thoroughly overconfident. A couple of my drinking chums were stock exchange floor traders and I became quite distracted by feverish (and modestly successful) speculations. One of them, Henry Timmins, son of Hollinger Mines chairman, Jules Timmins, ran as an independent candidate for Parliament in Halton in the federal general election of 1965. His was an uproarious far-right campaign, a rough parallel to William Buckley's simultaneous campaign for mayor of New York. Henry died of alcoholism a few years later.

Only when I finally started my end-of-term drive was it clear that I had left the real work too late. I made a further tactical error in attempting all the examinations and not confecting a medical excuse to dodge a couple and focus exclusively on the others. I was uneasy when I departed on my second adult trip to Europe, although my modest stock market winnings ensured that, unlike three years before, I wouldn't have to conduct busloads of tourists about to pay my hotel bills. In Ireland, I stayed with Galen Weston, whom I had met socially in Toronto, and in London with Brian Stewart, who now worked on a suburban London newspaper.

I went to Galen's wedding, and then Brian and I set off on a leisurely air and automobile trip to Vienna, Trieste, Budapest, Zagreb, and Belgrade and were on our way back to Venice, when, by prearrangement, I telephoned George Black to inquire into my law results. I should have made other arrangements; history repeated itself but this time an academic recovery was going to be more complicated. I failed a majority of the subjects, was not allowed to write the supplementals, and, for good measure, was expelled from the faculty and effectively barred from the study of law in Ontario, though I might be permitted to repeat the year after a suitable interval of penitent contemplation of my scholastic turpitude.

On reflection, I had, by my cavalier behaviour, been mocking the profession, or at least those who controlled access to it. They probably engaged in overkill, but it is not altogether surprising that they underestimated my academic potential. The whole episode taught me lessons far more important than those I had neglected to study at Osgoode Hall.

I had never really taken school problems too seriously, irritating though they were; I hated school and moved ahead each year anyway. My first university year had been marred by a tactical error but was recovered.

Humdrum though it might be, it was time to outgrow mischief and debauchery. At twenty-two, I sadly concluded that I had to stop floundering around like a dilettante, vicariously reinvigorating myself reading (but apparently drawing few useful conclusions from) the lives of great men. There was also a question of vanity. I never cared much about being thought insubordinate but I found it deeply humiliating, though in a way that was motivationally useful, to have my basic intelligence judged insufficient even to be a candidate lawyer in southern Ontario. Although I had never had a very precise idea of what it was, I had a more exalted notion of my own destiny than that.

I returned briefly to my parents' house, uttered a Lear-like oath of unspecific vengeance on the Muse, a blood-curdling promise of a reformed sense of purpose, understandably received with incomplete credulity, and went to Quebec to begin again.

In June, the apparently invincible Quebec Liberal government of Jean Lesage had been narrowly defeated by the Union Nationale led by Duplessis's most talented living disciple, Daniel Johnson. I had admired both men since I had watched their debate during the 1962 provincial election. I had read the Quebec press carefully during my years in Ottawa. Quebec politics and the quality of Quebec political leadership were the best in the country, and I had returned from Europe to relaunch myself and discovered that my former subtenant Peter White was Premier Johnson's executive assistant. I telephoned him and said that if it was my lot to be in Canada, it must be in Quebec and it was not one minute too soon to invoke the Union Nationale's legendary penchant for patronage. Quebec was the only part of Canada that appeared to have any sense of mission or even purpose, and in the Lesage-Johnson era, before nationalism turned to separatism, pursued it with great panache.

Peter White, always a magnanimous dispenser of favours within his gift, offered me a half interest in two little weekly newspapers that he owned in the Eastern Townships, forty-five miles east of Montreal, *L'Avenir de Brome-Missisquoi* in Farnham and Cowansville and the *Eastern Townships Advertiser* in Knowlton. The consideration for this investment was nominal and consisted of a balance of sale determined by subsequent earnings, just under $500. Peter and I never entirely agreed on that figure but we resolved the matter by my taking a rug from the cabin I rented from him on a property his father owned on the shores of Brome Lake.

I settled into that one-room cabin with several cases of books and whisky and set about cobbling together a career. Peter also arranged for me to write occasional speeches for Daniel Johnson in his capacity as Quebec's natural resources minister though I'm not sure he ever used any of them. (The Union Nationale was not overburdened with talent and Johnson and Jean-Jacques Bertrand, in addition to being premier and vice premier, between them held the portfolios of Natural Resources, Intergovernmental Affairs, Education, and Justice.)

Apart from forays to Montreal and Quebec, I confined myself to the backwoods of the Eastern Townships. Knowlton is a genteel and pretty town with a few dozen opulent country houses and several hundred more modest weekend homes serviced by a thousand or so canny and avaricious descendants of United Empire Loyalists. It was a strange mélange of Anglo-patrician Montreal nestled among vintage townspeople and virtual hill-billies in a corner of a French province and on the borders of the United States.

To put myself in an appropriately purposeful mood, I read some of the books of Joseph Conrad, starting with *Youth*, with the narrator's description of assuming his "first command" when fire obliged captain and crew to take to the boats, of which his was one. I imagined a tenuous allegory. When I got to *Almayer's Folly* with its description of the Dutch trader looking across the strait at his more successful Moslem rival and occasionally shaking his fist in frustration in the Moslem's direction, I transposed the scene to Brome Lake. I peered enviously across at the country house of John Bassett, Sr., long time publisher of the Montreal *Gazette*, father of the publisher of the Toronto *Telegram*, whom I always admired for his panache and disregard for the rigours of Toronto society, such as it was, and grandfather of lifelong friends.

Another evocative book was *The Life of Lord Strathcona*, especially the description of his thirty years as a factor in Hudson's Bay. I needed snow-shoes to get to and from my cabin in the winter and one night was almost run down by the two-car train that came through between the cabin and the Whites' house several times a week. I found it consoling that Strathcona not only survived his ordeal, but made millions, lived into his nineties, and died a peer and High Commissioner in London. Less encouraging was Carson McCullers's *The Heart Is a Lonely Hunter*, which, with the savagery of the Quebec winter that piled snow up over the roof of my cabin and exploited its draftiness so systematically that it was sometimes almost an igloo, caused me briefly to consider chucking in my hand and resuming the study of the law at Tulane University in New Orleans. My one attempt at skiing, courtesy of an advertiser who owned the Mount Sutton ski area, caused me to break both skis. I was severely disconcerted and took the ski-lift down. I have not tried downhill skiing since.

Finally there came the rites of spring. Our little newspapers and my four helpers on them, one of whom grandly but accurately referred to herself as the "infrastructure" of the company, survived the rigours of winter, too, and were probably more rugged than I was. There were amusing moments, especially when I received almost no response to my aerated editorials on world affairs, which, except for their stylistic excesses, could have been in a serious (arch-conservative) metropolitan newspaper. I followed the precedent of my predecessor, Stuart Marwick, and published a page from the local telephone directory as an editorial, but that elicited no more animated a response than my comments on Vietnam or the Canadian Constitution.

I alienated some of my readers but earned the beatific pleasure of the premier by supporting the bill with which the government of Quebec broke a teachers' strike, and I had a full-scale debate over it in our pages with the principal of the Knowlton High School. On another occasion, I used my trivial knowledge of environmental matters that I had acquired researching speeches for Johnson to question the water quality in Brome Lake. When I was sharply rebuked at a town council meeting, I resolved to show them the power of the press.

Like Orson Welles in *Citizen Kane* saying "People will think what I tell them to think," I launched a violent campaign against the "mis-managers of the dying lake." The amiable septuagenarian mayor and his councillors I reviled as "Mayor Parkes and his Performing Algae." On another occasion, Morgan Knowlton, the last surviving descendant of the town's founder, sent in a classified advertisement beginning "Most of you probably think that I'm dead, but I'm not." One of my more energetic subscribers regularly sought to use my newspaper to refute admittedly unpublished "vulgar gossip" to the effect that he was engaged in "the horse piss business" as he helped extract a medically useful ingredient from pregnant mares' urine. There were several slow news weeks when this was as close as I could come to breaking a story.

One of the most interesting people I met in the Eastern Townships was the brilliant but eccentric rocket scientist, Gerald Bull, who was conducting McGill University's High Altitude Research Project at Mansonville. He became somewhat sociable on a couple of occasions, though he was a slightly morose man; I had no ability to distinguish between scientific insight and charlatanism, but I tried to follow his subsequent career and regretted his murder in Brussels in 1990, while he was allegedly working for Saddam Hussein on his giant cannon.

I first met Daniel Johnson at the Mont Shefford Hotel in Granby in October 1966, and he remains the most charming man I have ever met (narrowly edging out Ronald Reagan). Peter White brought my defence of the premier's legislated end to the teachers' strike to his attention, including my citation from Duplessis that "the right to strike against the public interest does not exist." The premier especially appreciated my enthusiastic support for his threat, if the teachers didn't return to work, to station a provincial policeman in each classroom to maintain order while he and Jean-Jacques Bertrand gave the various lessons themselves over closed-circuit television.

It was a magnificent display of mad French-Canadian panache, like the popular suggestion during the FLQ crisis in 1970 that at seven o'clock on a fixed evening, everyone in the province visit, search, and if needs must, ransack the home of his next-door neighbour in order to find the kidnapped Pierre Laporte and James Cross. Pierre Trudeau's subsequent threat to replace the entire French network of the CBC "with still photographs of Chinese and Japanese vases" had the same general inspiration. My slight but much appreciated reward for my trivial support of the premier was a press pass and quasi-official status at the Montreal world's fair.

As the gentle spring of 1967 liberated Quebec from the vice-grip of winter, Expo 67 opened, and much of the world beat a path to Montreal. I settled into a most agreeable summer of usually ineffectual pursuit of the leggy pavilion hostesses of scores of countries, and of standing friends and acquaintances to drinks at the bar of the Quebec pavilion. Virtually my only officious statement of the whole summer was "*Le chef veut une consommation,*" when fetching a whisky and soda for Mr. Johnson.

The atmosphere in Johnson's entourage was casual and light-hearted but respectful. On one occasion when I delivered a speech to him in his office, his desk was piled high with documents awaiting signature. With a broad smile and a sweep of his hand, Johnson volunteered that "I don't sign what I haven't read and I don't have time to read them."

He sometimes gave me a ride in his official car and it was in these conversations that he inspired my first interest in Duplessis. I had had, until then, the standard English-Canadian view of Duplessis as more or less of a domestic Hitler. I tried to pepper Johnson with questions about de Gaulle, who had taken an interest in him, received him, and like all who met Daniel Johnson, obviously liked him. Although he once acknowledged that he and de Gaulle were amicably trying to use each other for their own political ends, he usually replied with another question, a habit he amusingly intensified when it was pointed out to him. When I asked him the time one day, he launched into an expansive lyric on the theme of "what possible interest could you, a young man assured of a brilliant future, have in the time?" Almost the only way to get a serious answer from him was to ask how Duplessis would have responded to something.

The only blight on these golden months was a spectacular road accident in June. While driving at speed on a rural road near Knowlton, a tire suddenly flattened, the car skidded across the road, hurtled through space for sixty feet, and settled in a gulley. I was knocked colder than a mackerel, and was awakened by cows nuzzling the window. With heavy bleeding from a gashed forehead, I walked half a mile to a farmhouse whose startled occupants drove me to the hospital in Cowansville. After being stitched up in an ante room, my first visual re-acquaintance with the world, when the surgical cloth was withdrawn, was the Orwellian vision of photographs of the town's leading figures, Jean-Jacques Bertrand and the flamboyant contractor and mayor, Roland Désourdy. It was a very close call but I recovered quickly though the forehead scars will always be with me. I found the incident more reassuring of my natural good luck than frightening, but I have been a somewhat cautious driver ever since.

Montreal presented a splendid and enviable spectacle in the summer of 1967. On St. Jean-Baptiste night, June 24, a million Montrealers lined Sherbrooke Street from Delorimier Street all the way into Westmount. The reviewing stand was across from the Ritz-Carlton and Cardinal Léger, Premier Johnson, Mayor Drapeau, and the executive committee chairman, Lucien Saulnier, made an impressive official phalanx in the place of honour. Appearances, I was beginning to learn, could be deceiving; within a couple of years, Saulnier would be retired, Johnson dead, Léger departed to the bowels of Africa, and it would be decades before there would be another large and peaceful St.-Jean-Baptiste-Day Parade.

One month later all was anticipation as General de Gaulle approached the shores of Quebec in the cruiser *Colbert* (a means of travel chosen supposedly to facilitate his visit to St. Pierre and Miquelon, but in fact to relieve him of the protocol imperative of starting his Canadian visit in Ottawa). As his ship steamed past Blanc Sablon and up the St. Lawrence and bulletins of his progress were received in Johnson's office, the premier's entourage cleaned up the quality of their spoken French, and even the most slipshod of them started to sound a little like amateur de Gaulle impersonators.

The recently returned Brian Stewart and I stood patiently in the large and wildly enthusiastic crowd around Montreal City Hall awaiting de Gaulle and Johnson, who arrived in early evening, standing in the back of a Lincoln convertible that had brought them along the old North Shore road from Quebec City, supposedly built by Louis XV but really by Duplessis. The government of Quebec had used the province's school buses to bring in huge crowds to cheer de Gaulle and Johnson all along the 120-mile route. For me de Gaulle incarnated modern European history, as well as the revival of the French-speaking world, and the restoration of geo-political diversity, of alternatives to the bleak and glacial monoliths of the Cold War alliance systems.

As he passed, wearing the simple two-star general's uniform he had earned by his heroism before the Nazi hordes at Abbeville in 1940, I thought of Verdun and Ingolstadt, where he was a prisoner of war in the next cell to the future Soviet marshal Tukhachevsky and learned to speak German; of the repulse of the Bolsheviks from Poland with Weygand; of the flight from Bordeaux; and of the great liberation march down the Champs Elysées on the day after my birth ("One step behind, please, gentlemen," he said to the politicians and servitors who crowded into his instant coterie at the hour of victory).

Less agreeable were the sensations I experienced when he addressed the crowd after prevailing upon Drapeau to reconnect the microphones on the balcony, which the mayor had shut off as reports came in of de Gaulle's steadily more provocative remarks at each stop his motorcade made as it approached from Quebec.

I became very uneasy when he told us "the secret," that the reception the province had given him that day reminded him "of the Liberation," which he soldiered through on Carlton Gardens overlooking the Mall while our Canadian soldiers slogged ashore in Normandy with their British and American comrades. When de Gaulle took up from the placards below and shouted with a great shaking of his huge frame that seemed to bring forth the inspiration from his limbs and through his whole being, "*Vive le Québec libre!*" I had, for the first time, the sinking feeling that my *bonne entente* idyll might not function as planned.

I drove gloomily back to Knowlton and wrote the first anti-Gaullist thoughts I had entertained, urging Pearson editorially to declare our distinguished visitor persona non grata and throw him out. As Brian Stewart said to me that night, half the countries of the world, especially the Americans and the British, envied us our ability to embarrass de Gaulle. Pearson did his best and eventually produced a respectful reproof, but de Gaulle cancelled his visit to Ottawa and was allowed a more dignified departure than I thought he deserved.

It fell to Jean Drapeau to lament that notwithstanding the general's solicitude for Quebec, French Canada had had to persevere alone, "hanging our culture on the barn-door, for 200 years." It was a powerful address, uniting Quebec resentment of French condescension, federalist irritation with outrageous meddlesomeness, and personal respect for de Gaulle. If Canada were a politically stable and self-confident country, that speech would have come from Pearson or Johnson. In the celebrated centennial year of 1967, the only other occasion, apart from Drapeau's response to de Gaulle, when someone succeeded in speaking for English- and French-Canadians was Daniel Johnson's summation at John Robarts's Confederation of Tomorrow Conference in Toronto in December when he enumerated a long but reasonable list of jurisdictional ambitions and said that for decades he and his predecessors back to Taschereau and Duplessis had been asked what Quebec wanted. He had provided the answer, "What does Canada want? *Que veut le Canada?*" It was electrifying but did not elicit a swift or clear reply.

It was time to re-embark on the academic treadmill. It had finally dawned on me that I had been a rather silly and undiscriminating rebel, the student equivalent of an armchair revolutionary, a political type I was finding increasingly distasteful as the Vietnam era unfolded. I concluded that there were higher and more useful callings than invoking great names like de Gaulle's in bucking the false disciplines of the Canadian Establishment, an unintimidating and not overly sinister entity that for tactical reasons at least, was better joined than fought.

CHAPTER TWO

QUEBEC FROM THE WORLD'S FAIR TO THE WAR MEASURES ACT
1967–1970

I N SEPTEMBER 1967, I ENROLLED IN THE LAW faculty of Laval University in Quebec City, well beyond the unforgiving jurisdiction of Osgoode Hall. I never intended to make the law my career, but I thought it might be a useful degree and I declined to allow the faculty at Osgoode Hall to have the last word on my talents as a law student. The day of my "psychometric" entrance examination, I had to come from Toronto and return there as I was a delegate at the Progressive Conservative convention that chose a successor to John Diefenbaker, who retired with the utmost reluctance after badly trailing two provincial premiers and a former cabinet colleague on the first ballot. The MP from Brome-Missisquoi, the indefatigable Heward Grafftey, in whose comfortable Knowlton house I had had many sumptuous meals, invited me to be a delegate and I arrived back from Quebec at Maple Leaf Gardens just too late to vote in the last ballot. I did not have the impression that the new leader, Robert Stanfield, was going to be an epochal figure. (Heward, a high-spirited and unusual man, often astonished visitors by standing stark naked on his stair landing and bellowing "Do you want to see the member's member?")

My three years at Laval were the most fulfilling I had had. Unlike any other academic institution I had attended, it generated a profound and durable sense of camaraderie. The little group of only about twenty English-speaking students in a faculty of perhaps 500 included some exceptionally endearing personalities. I have particularly valued over all the intervening years the friendship of Jon Birks (who went on to lead his family's jewellery business in difficult circumstances), Dan Colson and Peter O'Brien, both of whom actually practised law in different offices of Stikeman, Elliott). The French majority, faculty and students, could not have been more hospitable. There was no hint of personal prejudice, even from our more nationalistic confrères. The few extreme separatists who harangued the faculty with blood-curdling references to "the vampires of English finance" we invariably addressed in English, including their Christian names (i.e., "Andrew" and "John Peter," not André and Jean-Pierre). They were almost as ludicrous in the eyes of the French-speaking members of the faculty as they were to us.

The challenge of properly learning the language while simultaneously grasping the curriculum required an unprecedented level of diligence from me. Examinations could be written in English but a high level of French comprehension was essential and had to be acquired quickly. In my first year, my attendance was faithful, even at eight a.m. In the course of one such lecture, a family law professor fell sound asleep in the middle of one of his interminable droning sentences. (I was in some sympathy with him, but was slightly surprised when, two weeks later, the federal justice minister, Pierre Trudeau, named him an Appeal Court judge.)

In my second year at Laval I attended rather less frequently, but often by my undergraduate standards, and my scholastic performance improved. In October of my final year, I arrived for my first lecture of the term, in the midst of the Bill 63 debate over liberty of choice of language of instruction for all parents in Quebec, to find the atrium of the graduate arts building festooned with a banner six floors deep bearing the elegant bicultural device "F— Les Anglais." I turned 180 degrees and resolved never to attend a lecture in that faculty again. I adhered to that intention and graduated with "distinction" attaining 97.5 per cent on my last examination in international private law.

When I registered at the university in 1967, the Montreal world's fair was still in progress, Johnson was premier, Lévesque was a member of the Liberal Party, and *bonne entente* was still a rising tide. When I graduated in April 1970, the great majority of my confrères were militants of the Parti Québécois, which had been founded by Lévesque only in 1968. The tide was going out.

Most of the women in our faculty, as the 1970 provincial election approached, romped around the campus in crotch-high miniskirts with large buttons, almost breastplates, bearing the single word "Oui." It was the most effective political advertising I have seen.

I had had the habit of listening to U.S. presidential addresses since the middle Eisenhower years and followed Lyndon Johnson's attentively as he spoke on the evening of March 31, 1968. To me, L.B.J. was something of a cult figure, as his predecessor had been and still is, to millions. L.B.J. had eliminated segregation and given millions of blacks the vote they had been unjustly deprived of, he had declared war on poverty, waged an undeclared war on communist aggression, lowered taxes, and briefly balanced the budget. He was in some respects an heroic figure, the more so because of the necessity of overcoming what Dr. Johnson called "the disingenuousness of years," but I appeared to be almost the only person in the world who thought about him this way.

When, on March 31, 1968, he said, "I shall not seek, and I will not accept the nomination of my party for another term as your president," I had a ghastly feeling that not only the communists but the Radical Chic quislings who had kidnapped American liberalism and lionized Ho Chi Minh, who had exalted the Vietcong and debased American martial traditions and strategic interests, had won. Everything I politically believed in, including traditional and tolerant liberalism, was being desecrated by cowards and hucksters. The subsequent assassinations of Martin Luther King and Robert Kennedy and their aftermaths brought orgiastic satisfaction to the international forces of anti-Americanism, including the particularly dreary local Canadian variety, and corresponding dismay for me. A just posterity should not forget how effectively Richard Nixon dealt with the dreadful problems he inherited in January 1969.

The de Gaulle government was shaken to its foundations by the events of May 1968. I listened avidly to my short-wave radio, which I used for French news as the drama unfolded, never doubting that the general would triumph. The BBC happily proclaimed that "day by day the proud façade of Gaullism crumbles into dust." The peculiar French trait that possesses the people of that magnificently rich and comfortable country to tear up the paving stones and hurl them at the police every generation or so, crested with a march in Paris of half a million people demanding that de Gaulle resign.

Then, imperceptibly, their sense of bourgeois avarice returned, the general spoke for four and a half minutes "as the sole legitimate repository of republican power," excoriating the "washed-up old politicians," dupes of "totalitarian communists . . . who would not count more than their weight, which would not be heavy" (in the event of his departure). Three-quarters of a million people marched back up the Champs Elysées demanding that de Gaulle remain (a large number were probably repeat marchers from earlier in the week, returned to their bourgeois senses). De Gaulle dissolved the National Assembly and in June won the greatest electoral victory in 175 years of French republican history. It was the last great tour de force of a great man whose desire to reduce the international influence of the Anglo-Saxon powers was making him sadly inaccessible to my adherence, though not to my admiration. It was gripping drama and inspired leadership.

I was again near the reviewing stand at the 1968 St.-Jean-Baptiste-Day Parade, which had moved several miles eastward to the National Library (of the so-called Québécois nation) at Lafontaine Park. The rioting and hail of projectiles were so intense that I had to take refuge in a police horse van, the horse being heavily engaged in facilitating the vigorous night-sticking of the manifestants. All the dignitaries on the reviewing stand except the new prime minister, Trudeau, and Mayor Drapeau, fled. At one point, the indépendantiste leader, Pierre Bourgault, was chaired past me, as he thought by his supporters, but, in fact, by Montreal's plain-clothed finest, who threw him head first into a police car and "interrogated him aggressively" (*Le Devoir*). There were scores of injuries and several hours of disorderly mobs surging around the east end. It was not a federalist confidence-builder, though Trudeau won a sweeping victory in the general election the following day, partly because of his refusal to be put to flight by the mob.

In a journalists' bar in July 1968, I negotiated a modest commission from the features editor of the Montreal *Gazette* to write political analysis on Latin America. I flew to Buenos Aires to join Jon Birks, who had a summer job there. I was quite impressed with the

Argentinian president, General Juan Carlos Onganía, despite his puritanical flourishes that required unmarried men and women to maintain an "air space of at least six inches" between themselves at all times when in public, a particular sacrifice given the startling pulchritude of Porteña women.

I indicated that if Onganía was generally unsuccessful, Péron could return. "Argentina is one of the world's great Latin countries but is today uneasy," I pontificated. "If Péron was a Sukarno, could Onganía be a de Gaulle?" The answer came two years later when Onganía was sent packing by his fellow generals and left the Casa Rosada in a taxi without even being given cab fare, according to newspaper accounts. I was in Argentina on the anniversary of the death of Eva Péron and observed the flowers piled up at the gates of every cemetery in Buenos Aires. (The authorities hadn't revealed where she was buried.) Péron finally did return in 1973 and died in office a few months later in 1974. (He was preceded by a dentist, Héctor Cámpora, who was elected president on the self-deprecating promise to be "General Péron's obsequious servant.")

I went to Montevideo, where I searched unsuccessfully for the remains of the pocket battleship, *Admiral Graf Spee*, in the Plate River estuary, to Rio de Janeiro, São Paulo and Brasília, Lima, Cuzco, Bogotá, and Caracas. I was impressed by Brazil, despite the political juvenilism. The foreign ministry (Itamarati) was professing to believe in the existence of an American conspiracy to flood the Amazon and fill it with Polaris submarines. In between chasing British Airline stewardesses around my hotel in Rio de Janeiro, I attended a mass rally protesting the Russian invasion of Czechoslovakia, addressed by the histrionic Cardinal Archbishop Câmara. The cardinal paused to draw breath every ten minutes or so and interrupted his tirade by playing a gramophone record of the Czech national anthem.

I also attended a municipal football match in Maracaña Stadium, attended by about 155,000 people. It was an exciting and mysterious though a rather frivolous city, half *Flying down to Rio*; half *Black Orpheus*. "Between the world famous beaches of Copacabana and Ipanema, soldiers in baby blue helmets peer out over the barrels of 15-inch-diameter battleship guns at the South Atlantic horizon that has not been broken by the masts of a hostile armada since the retirement of the Portuguese 146 years ago," I concluded for the *Gazette*. My articles were fairly well received and were a modestly successful début in metropolitan newspapers.

Daniel Johnson died September 26, 1968, at Manicouagan the night before the projected opening of the mighty and graceful vaulted arch dam 660 feet high and a mile long that now bears his name. When I visited the site a few years later, I was as disappointed at the unseemliness of Johnson dying in a camper trailer (*roulotte*) as I was in 1970 when I learned that de Gaulle died of a ruptured aorta, apparently induced by reaching for the television listings! Banal ends to exceptional lives.

The Union Nationale had governed, under Duplessis and Johnson, the only people who had defeated the Liberals in Quebec since immediately after the fall of Mercier (1891–2), by artfully persuading the conservatives and nationalists to vote together. Johnson's death passed the torch of Quebec nationalism to René Lévesque. The conservatism of Duplessis and Johnson (and Henri Bourassa and Lionel Groulx before them) and their respect for existing institutions, courts, Church, and constitution provided a natural brake on their nationalist impulses. I knew Lévesque slightly, and I knew that there would be no such restraint with him. In Quebec City, the academic and political communities often frequented each other, and politically involved members of the law faculty had a good deal of access to most politicians. Lévesque, who had called Johnson "the most sickening (*vomiteux*) man in Quebec" when Johnson was leader of the Opposition, now declared that "Quebec has lost its greatest statesman" and set about usurping his following.

I was back in Latin America at the end of the year when Peter White and I went on a holiday to Mexico and I went on to Cuba. Fidel was still being romanticized by the left as the eradicator of disease and illiteracy, the future that worked for Latin America. I found Cuba horribly depressing; nothing worked, one-tenth of the population was in exile and one-tenth in prison. Half of Havana's external wall space seemed to be taken up by graphic identifications of Fidel with Lincoln, Washington, Jefferson, Bolivar, and other authentic statesmen.

The former captain of the Tropicana had been demoted to our decrepit hotel. Like Malcolm Muggeridge's Paris bistro proprietor after the Liberation, he measured everything by the progress of his business. "I had Gary Cooper, Mr. (Meyer) Lansky, and the entire New York Yankees one night; I made $5,000 in six hours. Batista was elegant. We wouldn't have let anyone who looked like Fidel into the Tropicana. This country has become a pig-sty."

I attended the great rally marking the tenth anniversary of Fidel's accession. Posters throughout Havana urged everyone to "The Revolution Plaza with Fidel," the annoying left-wing emphasis on intimidation by the assemblage of physical masses of people. He spoke for four hours. There were long line-ups for ice-cream cones in Havana, even in January, but Fidel excitedly told his huge audience of every one of thirty-some ice-cream flavours that were now available. "We have strawberry, (applause), we have banana (applause)," and so forth.

A fellow visitor from Quebec translated it for me for about an hour until we gave up and returned to our hotel.

When I left Cuba, the passport control official asked me whether I would be back to see Havana again. I replied, "Yes," and whispered to a British businessman standing next to me, "Through open bomb-sights." It was all so depressing that there was nothing for it but to go, via Mexico, New Orleans, and Miami, to Palm Beach, to take up the invitation of my father's business partner, John A. (Bud) McDougald. It was an efficient antidote to the Cuban sojourn. The huge, splendidly maintained mansions, the swarms of Rolls-Royces and Ferraris and Mercedes-Benzes and Aston Martins, the violently rich winterers in the Everglades, and Bath and Tennis Clubs, even the demented Birchite social prattle of the idle rich, all, even that, seemed to have more of a future than the Spartan, Newspoken, tropical Stalinism of Fidel.

I was again glued to my short-wave radio in the last days of the French referendum campaign in April 1969. The omens were not good. "Whatever may happen," said the tired general in his last address to his countrymen, "the army of those who have supported me will hold in their hands the destiny of the nation." Perhaps, but their numbers were insufficient, and the general, who had approved an absurdly complicated wording for the plebiscitary question, resigned. I had never imagined that so great a career would end so trivially, a referendum over Senate and regional reform, whose result, a narrow negative vote, did not imply lack of confidence in the regime. In conceiving and conducting the campaign as he had, and in staking his presidency on it, de Gaulle was clearly following some obscure psychological motivations. There was a certain grandeur in his resignation statement: "I am ceasing to exercise my functions as President of the Republic. This decision takes effect at noon today."

When it was broadcast, I reread from his memoirs his words on the defeat of Winston Churchill in 1945: "He lost neither his glory nor his popularity thereby, only the adherence he had won as a guide and symbol of the nation in peril. His nature, identified with a magnificent enterprise, his countenance, etched by the fires and frosts of great events, were no longer adequate to the era of mediocrity."

I attended in June 1969 the Union Nationale convention, which officially confirmed the admirable but guileless and unprepossessing Jean-Jacques Bertrand as prime minister of Quebec, but conferred over 40 per cent of the delegate voters on the crypto-separatist imposter, Jean-Guy Cardinal, minister of education. The convention was not just a monument to Johnson's popularity. It was a final demonstration of the Union Nationale's joys of incumbency. Free beer, wine, and liquor were dispensed at the Château Frontenac and in hotels and bars throughout Quebec City to the entire population. It was a rollicking and authentically populist spectacle.

The recently elected leader of the Opposition in New Brunswick, Richard Hatfield, attended. Peter White and I were talking to him as Bertrand's motorcade drove past on its way to the temporary campaign headquarters at the Palace of Commerce in the fairgrounds. When Peter remarked that the convention was costing $25,000 an hour, Richard looked suitably respectful and volunteered that his entire recent successful leadership campaign had cost only $25,000.

In the summer of 1968, Peter White and I had tried to buy the *Sherbrooke Record* from John Bassett who, after the end of his first marriage (his wife was from North Hatley), lost interest in the *Record*. A move to a new building and a new press, the traditional pitfall of the newspaper business, had gone $100,000 over budget and the company was losing money. John Bassett's local manager was able to get backing to assume more of the retained losses than we were prepared to take and bought the *Record* in August 1968. By the following spring, his press was being repossessed and he was ready to sell. The vendor retained the building and escaped with a whole skin, and we bought only some ancient desks and typewriters and goodwill for a total of $18,000, which our little newspaper business in Cowansville and Knowlton produced.

Peter had met a potential third partner in the course of his political manoeuvrings to obtain the Union Nationale nomination in Brome County (which was why he was interested in the *Record* in the first place). This turned out to be David Radler, a business school graduate (McGill and Queen's) who had lived from his wits as a consultant to the Department of Indian Affairs; he was also owner of a native handicrafts shop at the Montreal world's fair and its permanent successor, Man and His World, and a restaurateur. He and his father owned a famous north-central Montreal restaurant that was a Union Nationale meeting place.

When Mario Beaulieu, who had once been a waiter in the Radlers' restaurant and who was now the finance minister, ran in a by-election in the restaurant's constituency, David was in charge of the ethnic polls, i.e., all non-French votes. Where the other poll captains mulled over nationalist slogans, David had two photographs spliced so that there appeared to be one photograph of Beaulieu between Daniel Johnson and Pierre Trudeau, all with arms interlocked, and ran the cutline "Trudeau=Johnson=Beaulieu=même chose" (in ten languages). He swept his polls. Beaulieu had run against Lévesque in 1960 in the neighbouring district, Laurier, with the tacit agreement that he would not call Lévesque a separatist and Lévesque would not call him a crook. Lévesque won narrowly.

Peter met David on election night 1966 celebrating the Union Nationale victory at the Renaissance Club. David had been on his way by car to Kingston resigned to a Liberal victory, but when he learned from his car radio that a Johnson victory was indicated, he turned back to join Beaulieu and the other revellers.

We took over the *Sherbrooke Record* on July 1, 1969, and quickly set about cleaning house. We interviewed all thirty-two employees and concluded that, since the company had lost $180,000 in the previous twenty-two months, over 40 per cent of the work force had to go. We weeded them out over a couple of weeks, dividing the unpleasant responsibilities between ourselves. It was not happy work, but there was no alternative but insolvency and the loss of all the jobs. Peter became so zealous he reached one targeted employee in a cabin at Niagara Falls. Unfortunately it was subsequently discovered to have been her honeymoon and Peter managed an awkward partial recantation; she worked half-days. One of the advertising salesmen came in one of those early days to say he could work only half weeks because of illness and, when pressed, said that his psychiatrist had identified "the new owners of the *Record*" as the source of the illness. We imposed draconian cost controls and turned our first profit after a couple of months.

Since the former owners' press had been repossessed, David determined that the most economical printer, given prevailing exchange rates, was in Newport, Vermont. We thus became the only daily newspaper in world history to be printed in a foreign country. None of us could foresee how far this interesting partnership would lead, but when in less than two years, we started to rack up annual profits at a rate of over $150,000, we determined to expand in the newspaper business. I had a sense that I had started on a career that could be greatly fulfilling. The combination of information, comment, finance, management, and potential influence was very alluring, even at the mundane levels I had experienced them.

On August 27, 1969, I published in the *Record* a long article entitled "A year after Chicago, Homage to L.B.J." It was a violent assault on Johnson's critics, whom I continued to think had overlooked his efforts on behalf of blacks and the poor, misrepresented his objectives in Vietnam, and engaged in "vulgar snobbery." I described Norman Mailer as "the bedraggled warhorse of American blowhardism," asked that "the real Walter Lippmann please shut up," and described the California Democratic leader, Jesse "Big Daddy" Unruh, as a "bovine charlatan." The U.S. information officer in the consulate in Montreal sent it to L.B.J., and he had his followers insert it in the Congressional Record. He wrote me a most gracious letter and we conducted a sporadic correspondence up to his death.

David and I holidayed in New Orleans and Miami just after New Year's 1970, but I returned to Quebec City to represent our interests at the Quebec Liberal convention (that is, to represent that the *Sherbrooke Record* could be of some political importance, a doubtful proposition). Jean Lesage, one of the great figures of Quebec history, had been badgered into retiring by a restive caucus and discontented federal Liberals. Claude Wagner electrified the convention with his address, beginning with the words "*On va se regarder les yeux dans les yeux. On va se dire ce qu'on a à se dire.*" His remarks included the refreshing assertion "*Je suis fédéraliste, point.*" In a serious convention, he would have won, but almost half the delegates were *ex officio* and the Liberal establishment, for its own reasons, rigged the convention.

Wagner came ahead of Laporte, but the winner was Robert Bourassa, an intelligent, courteous, and even rather amusing man whom I had known since shortly after his first election in 1966. He had had an ardent flirtation with Lévesque when, in his post-electoral Damascene self-actualization, deprived of the ministerial perquisites, Lévesque threw down the mask and declared himself a separatist. I spent the convention with the greatly respected publisher of *Le Devoir*, Claude Ryan, an unfailingly thoughtful man who would have been surprised indeed to think he would be Bourassa's successor as Quebec Liberal leader.

Entirely agreeable though my life was, I began to experience worrisome symptoms of tension. Indigestion, claustrophobia in restaurants, airplanes, and other confined spaces, fitful sleep, sudden attacks of perspiring and even hyper-ventilating, all new to me, began to occur with increasing frequency. Finally, on the night of March 1-2, 1970 I was awakened by almost malarial symptoms of anxiety. I was shaking violently, sweating torrentially, even, it seemed, in places where I had not thought there were sweat glands, such as the backs of my hands, and was gasping asthmatically. The physical symptoms were reminiscent of descriptions of historic death throes like those of Henry VIII or Alexander VI (Borgia). Psychologically, it was more like descriptions of bilharzia, with paralysing illogical fears. It was far more terrifying than anything else I have known.

I sweated through the night, walked for six hours on the Plains of Abraham, endeavouring to guess at the origins of this frightful uprising from what must long have been subconscious, and went to the delightful Irish Quebec general practitioner Dan Colson and I used to inflict our hypochondria on and with whom we exchanged intemperate political opinions.

He prescribed some sleeping pills and suggested I go home to my family for a week or so. I went to Toronto for two weeks. My parents were no less encouraging, supportive, and solicitous with the passage of years and the shifting of focus from academic hobgoblins to nervous exhaustion. My mother suggested I have a drink or two from time to time and I assured her that whatever the problem, it wasn't abstemiousness.

My father, through a good friend and medical neighbour, arranged a consultation with the psychiatrist-in-chief of the Clarke Institute of Psychiatry. It was a helpful session. When there were recurrences, as there would be, he said, I should "sweat it out." It had been an anxiety reaction. My suggestions of the possible ultimate causes were probably a good place to start. The problem didn't require a pharmacological solution. What was recommended was psychoanalysis. In order to submit to a treatment which had been so widely stigmatized and stereotyped I required of myself to generate some interest in qualifying as an analyst myself so that my pursuits would not be entirely subjective and it was on that basis that I entered into an analytical program in September 1971.

Only once did the diffuse, paralysing, strangling terror of a full seizure of anxiety return, in November 1972, but there would be a number of secondary recurrences over the next thirteen years, gradually declining in frequency and intensity. I would have to live during most of those years with a vulnerability to occasional bouts of miscellaneous obsessive fear.

For a couple of years I carried a sick bag with me to mitigate unpredictable fears of sudden nausea. I never was sick in those circumstances but that had little to do with my fears, which gradually abated.

The inexorable success of the analytic process was gratifying as well as intriguing as I came gradually to recognize and reduce the sources of the occasional vulnerability to anxiety. Eventually I became wary of too much self-preoccupation and excessive concern with life's most mundane functions and penumbral recollections.

I read a huge number of summaries of analyses and several published diaries of analysands. Any serious study of the functioning of the human mind is interesting, the more so if the mind in question is one's own. After two-and-a-half years of this regime, I concluded that I was a good deal more interested in assuring my own freedom from self-inflicted distraction than in studying, much less endeavouring to minister to, the psychiatric vagaries of others. After a time I couldn't take much interest in other people's early bed-wetting or insufficiency of parental acceptance.

As my increasing means allowed, I became a patron of mental health causes, especially the Clarke Institute of Psychiatry in Toronto. One gratifying occasion in 1989, many years after the last recurrence of my anxiety, and after six years as a trustee of the Clarke Institute, occurred when I was able to bring Henry Kissinger, by then a director of our company, to Toronto for a benefit dinner for the Clarke which raised a sizeable sum.

There was one other cultural development, important to me and partly related to this subject; a latent religious sense, never to be endowed with fervour or even much piety, much less sanctimony, had been kindled. My desperate (usually) silent importunings of providence in the most difficult bouts of nervosity incited me to read some theology, especially the masterfully elegant and persuasive Cardinal Newman.

I started along part of the trajectory traced by Newman and by many others and sloughed agnosticism for a moderate religious practice, without ever losing toleration for other views, including the atheism I for some years rather vigorously and no doubt tiresomely espoused. Once I believed God existed, I found it impossible not to acknowledge, i.e., worship him, discreetly.

I wrote my last examinations at Laval University, finishing April 27, 1970, two days before the Quebec election that consigned the Union Nationale to the dustbin of history and elevated Robert Bourassa, who was to become a sort of French-Canadian Mackenzie King. In my home poll in Sillery, I voted for the Liberal Claude Castonguay at the same polling place and just behind Jean Lesage and the eighty-eight-year-old Louis St. Laurent. I cast about for anything worthwhile written about the Union Nationale that Duplessis and Johnson had led to victory six times in the previous nine elections. Finding nothing suitable, I gradually, over the next year, determined to provide it myself.

In early May, I witnessed an epochal Quebec tableau as the entire government, contrary to custom, attended upon the lieutenant-governor to resign. The first of nearly thirty official black sedans, Duplessis's fleur-de-lis flag fluttering on each right front fender, arrived at its destination before the last had left the National Assembly. Twelve of the ministers had been defeated in their own constituencies. Thus, in a final defile of ministerial privilege, did the Union Nationale pass forever into Quebec history.

Peter White ran in Brome for the Union Nationale and was buried under the Liberal tidal wave. Where Duplessis had been so inflammatory in 1939 that the conservatives deserted him, leaving only the nationalists for support, in 1970 Bertrand lost all the nationalists to Lévesque, and practically all the English-speaking Quebeckers to Bourassa. Peter went down to a defeat rendered rather farcical by his and David's partisan manipulation of the *Sherbrooke Record* which, not surprisingly, backfired.

David was the manager and fought valiantly, but secretly lost faith in the effort early on when he discovered, but didn't tell the candidate, that there were no volunteers, only paid (i.e., by us) employees. After each meeting, in which his remarks were greeted with wild applause, Peter exulted, unaware that each resonance of clapping hands was far from disinterested.

I left in July for a long overseas trip, starting with Jon Birks's wedding in Lima. My real destination was the great theatre of the era, Vietnam. President Lyndon Johnson, remembering the piece I had written about him in the *Sherbrooke Record* the previous summer, graciously asked the U.S. Embassies in Tokyo and Saigon to assist me in gaining interviews. It was a memorable journey.

The demure, stylish, convent-educated young ladies of Lima and their macho, blustery, or esoteric boyfriends or husbands were elegant and hospitable, but lived behind high walls and moved fretfully, darting through the congested streets in their unobtrusive automobiles. Political concern and discord were obvious and it was a troubled country that couldn't live much longer on the old diet of repression by juntas, juvenile sloganeering, and blaming it all on the gringos.

I arrived dishevelled in the mysterious East after a twenty-hour flight from Lima to Tokyo. I stayed a couple of weeks in Japan, fiercely reading potted cultural and political histories and visiting the usual sites, from Kyoto to Hiroshima, cruising on the Inland sea, and particularly studying anything redolent of the so-called MacArthur Shogunate.

In Manila the opportunity to dote on MacArthur's proconsular remnants was much greater. I stayed in the Manila Hotel where the general lived from 1935 to 1941, where, as MacArthur's old aide General Alexander Smith told me, MacArthur's mother was carried through the lobby of the hotel a few weeks before she died there in 1935. I stood on the dock at Corregidor where he left and on the beach at Lingayen Gulf where he fulfilled his promise to return.

In Seoul, I had an interview with the president of South Korea, Park Chung Hee, a compact, tough, dapper man, who recalled polite but sinister prison camp commandants from Pacific War films.

I read large parts of his three-volume autobiography, a very uneven work, at least in translation (various things gave the author "the creeps"), but which contains some eloquent passages on the struggle against communism and under-development. The whole Western involvement in Korea appeared to have been an unambiguous success, especially after a helicopter tour of Seoul I took with the noted Washington columnist, Jack Anderson, which the Korean president arranged. Seoul's relentless expansion, burgeoning industry, and high-rise sprawl were a surprise to me, steeped as I was in descriptions of the dismal, war-ravaged expanse of tentative mud flats that it had been fifteen years before. I was assuming there had been considerable progress. I was not expecting another São Paulo.

Hong Kong was a fantastic city. The women, Westernized orientals in dress and manner and bilingualism, were the most beautiful of any city I had visited, except Buenos Aires and Budapest. The harbour was the most intense and varied I had seen, the natural setting as fine as San Francisco's and perhaps Rio de Janeiro's. The architecture was as exceptionally varied as the cultures it housed, the Hilton Hotel, Bank of China, and Hong Kong Cricket Club were snugly nestling neighbours. The People's Republic representative in Hong Kong had me to lunch at the Peninsula Hotel and gave me a ride in his left-hand-drive Lincoln. Even at the height of the Cultural Revolution, he dressed and talked like an urbane roué, a fugitive from a Charlie Chan movie cast in the fleshpots of the East. Despite his hospitality, I flunked my ideology test for admission to China, which degenerated into a ludicrous shouting match as I defended Nixon and Johnson against Maoist calumnies. At the first apostrophization of a "running dog" (me), I was ready with "Stalinist lickspittle."

Jakarta was a nondescript capital but I had some interesting conversations, especially with U.S. embassy officials. Taipei was a Cold War period piece. I had a rather bland interview with the prime minister Chiang Ching-Kuo, Chiang Kai-Shek's son. As in Korea, American money was clearly buying an economic miracle.

Singapore was an oriental Toronto, clean, prosperous, well-organized, and desperately law-abiding, but lacking flair and spontaneity. It was in transition from the old colonial culture of Tiger Balm and pink gins under whirring fans in the bar of Raffles Hotel to the opportunistic modern city state. I went to the point where the last landsmen to see HMS *Prince of Wales* and *Repulse* would have watched them put to sea in December 1941. "We are looking for trouble and expect to find it" was Admiral Phillips's last signal.

All of this was a mere prelude to Vietnam and Cambodia.

Vietnam had been the story that shaped and enflamed international political discussion for the whole decade from 1965 to 1975. All political protests seemed to refer to it. When his universities and unionized workplaces erupted in 1968, de Gaulle, with the customary French talent for rationalization, blamed the unrest on the debasement of the authority of political leaders and institutions prompted by American policy in Vietnam. When the demonstrations originally against the Vietnam War erupted on many American university campuses, and Grayson Kirk at Columbia, Nathan Pusey at Harvard, and Clark Kerr at the University of California all caved before the forces of nihilistic unrest, I lost the sympathy I had had for the liberal academic establishment since the McCarthy era fifteen years before. These impressions were confirmed when I visited Columbia University with some friends during the disturbances there in the spring of 1968.

The relaxation of the sexual mores, of which I was, in conventional parlance, an active beneficiary, the rise and rise of women's fashionable hemlines, the soft drug culture, which I never touched, having only recently and with difficulty overcome my addiction to tobacco, all this and the stentorian popular music that accompanied it, propagating liberationist and bohemian themes, all were heavily influenced and inspired by disenchantment with Vietnam.

Self-righteous youth seized the screen and the airwaves. "You do your own thing in your own time. You should be proud," said the sophomoric Peter Fonda to a bayou farmer in the gelatinously banal *Easy Rider*. The iconoclasm of overwrought youth abated only at the feet of elderly revolutionaries, thus the adoration of Mao and Ho, and the veneration heaped on superannuated poltroons such as Herbert Marcuse. De Gaulle even tried to exploit this with apparent partial success. In his famous interview in the spring of 1968 with Michel Droit for the parliamentary elections, he asked where these "revolutionaries" had been when he had rebelled against the forces of capitulation and Nazism in 1940, when he had defended the country against putschists in 1962-3, and when he had "obtained the beginning of the liberation of the French of Quebec." There is fortunately no evidence that the French voters were much stirred by this last consideration.

It was bracing to arrive at the source of this great drama in September 1970. Two turns out over the nearer Mekong delta and its inscrutable jungles and dun river banks and we were in Tan Son Nhut, then the world's busiest airport: in a sea of hucksters, moneychangers, pickpockets, petty officials, arriving and departing conscripts, determined emigrants, and a few of the international curious, including me. The oriental pandemonium of overcrowding and ceaseless ant-like movement was transmuted by the corruption of wartime into a tension of decadence and danger. Nothing was really as it seemed.

I had scarcely muscled my baggage through the teeming ramshackle terminal before the Saigon black market materialized in various languages, pigmentations, and currencies. By the time I reached the Caravelle Hotel, whose manageress's true vocation seemed to be moneychanging, I had been offered cameras, typewriters, female and male prostitutes, and a truckload of Budweiser.

When I presented myself at the United States Embassy, a building the Tet offensive of two-and-a-half years before had made familiar to television viewers throughout the world, the marine sentry solemnly picked up his telephone and announced: "Mr. Black has arrived." In a few seconds, an operative clattered down the corridor waving a telegram from the then secretary of state, William P. Rogers, which asked for all courtesies to be extended to me as a "personal friend" of Lyndon B. Johnson and an influential newspaper publisher. The Secretary of State had clearly, but for me usefully, misunderstood the relationship between L.B.J. and me, which had consisted of a five-minute meeting and an exchange of correspondence prompted by my article about him. Even Canada was not especially well-known in official Saigon, much less my modest role there, but the Americans and South Vietnamese were touchingly grateful for anyone whom they thought might be positively disposed to what they were trying to do.

The embassy could not have been more helpful and arranged meetings with virtually every prominent non-communist in the country. After hearing all the anti-war jokes about "blowing Ellsworth out of his bunker," it was a particular pleasure to meet Ambassador Ellsworth Bunker. His serene and courteous confidence, at the age of seventy-eight, was reassuring. I expressed various concerns about the Saigon government's real level of popular support, the corrupt disposition of much of the ocean of American money washing over the country, the tenuous domestic support for the U.S. war effort, the efficacy of American anti-guerrilla tactics, the reliability of the South Vietnamese army (ARVN). The venerable and courtly ambassador avuncularly assured me that all would be well.

The U.S. Commander, General Creighton Abrams, whom I met at his headquarters near Tan Son Nhut, Pentagon East, was more precise and less sanguine. He felt confident that the North Vietnamese didn't want much more to do with fighting Americans, particularly because of the American ability to produce an airstrike in any part of the country and in any weather, in no more than fifteen minutes. He was not so confident of his gallant South Vietnamese allies, confined his praise of the Saigon government to the assertions that it was an improvement on its predecessors and that all evidence was that the Vietnamese were not enthusiastic about communism. He gave me a lift downtown in his armour-plated Chrysler, bearing with scant impersonality four stars on its licence plate. I seem to recall that he smoked constantly and he did die of lung cancer four years later. General Abrams cared ardently about casualty levels and was purposeful without being dogmatic or blasé. He was an impressive man. His predecessor, General William Westmoreland's endless requests for more conscripts interspersed with predictions of imminent victory had dragged the whole war effort into incredulity, if not disrepute. Abrams reminisced modestly and with unfeigned reluctance about D-Day, the relief of Bastogne, the aborted liberation of Prague in May 1945, and his years with General Patton. He seemed, I thought, as I rode along with him, the sort of commander to whom one would be relatively happy confiding one's sons, or oneself.

He was, in every commendable sense, the military head of the American mission. I met many less exalted officials, civilian and military, who were essentially volunteers. They hated every minute they spent in Vietnam and lived for the tapes their families regularly sent from the United States, desperate though the homesickness that each one provoked was. It all reminded me of de Gaulle's visit to Stalingrad in 1944, when he allegedly exclaimed to his Russian military guide: "What a great nation!" His guide assumed he meant the Russians, but de Gaulle is supposed to have corrected him: "No, the Germans. On the Volga, what an indomitable people!"

To anyone who saw how sacrificing, how selfless, was the motivation of virtually every American in Vietnam, the antics of those who admiringly carried the Vietcong flag through the streets of Western, including American, cities, were insolent and contemptible. Much harder to contest, however, were the claims of those well-disposed people who doubted whether the American Vietnam involvement was strategically justifiable. Absorbent, impervious, unfathomable, South Vietnam was hard to envision becoming so Americanized, so secure, as South Korea, much less Taiwan.

I went with Professor Patrick Honey, a renowned Vietnamologist from the University of London, to interview North Vietnamese prisoners of war. Some of them spoke French and I was able to converse with them unassisted. For the others, Patrick Honey was a very capable translator. They effectively confirmed what General Abrams had told me; their countrymen had, in Pentagonese, been severely attrited by fighting the Americans. Several described walking or bicycling down the Ho Chi Minh Trail when the B-52s, flying too high to be seen or heard, unleashed a carpet bombing of earth-shaking intensity, or Phantoms arrived at speed, unannounced, deluging the trail with an instant inferno of napalm. Less lethal, but quite demoralizing, were their encounters with high-frequency sonic devices dropped by the American Air Force, which, at the approach of pedestrians, produced a sound so piercing that it attacked the nervous system and caused a temporary loss of control of the bowels. The description of this, though scatalogical, was fairly humorous.

I settled into a comfortable routine: interviews in the mornings and afternoons, luncheon with officials or other members of the huge international press corps. One of the more engaging was Steve Cowper of the Anchorage, Alaska, *News* with whom I intermittently kept in contact afterwards and was pleased to see, during the *Exxon Valdez* oil spill fiasco in 1990, had become the governor of Alaska. We have met since and his laconic humour, which so enriched my evenings in Saigon in 1970, was undiminished by the passage of twenty years. Two prominent Americans I first met in Indochina but came to know better were columnist Joseph Alsop, and the young diplomat, Tom Enders. I harangued Tom Enders on the need to attack the dykes on the Red River at Hanoi in June when the whole town could be flooded if North Vietnamese aggression justified such an extremity. I met him in my one foray into rural Cambodia and our exchange was rather picturesque, at the edge of a rice paddy. I was pretty exasperated by the American policy of using a conscript army in an undeclared war for an objective less than victory pursued by half-measures.

Dinner was usually in the excellent restaurant on the roof of the Caravelle, watching through the heavily taped windows (to render them shatter-proof) as the U.S. Air Force dropped flares all around the perimeter of Saigon to prevent enemy infiltration. A fairly thoroughly enforced curfew was imposed at twelve o'clock. In the five minutes before every midnight, a plump Indochinese woman walked down Tu Do Street under my window, eerily making music from bamboo sticks and drums. She remains the best-remembered evidence I encountered of the famous Vietnamese *goût pour le merveilleux*, a taste for the fantastic. It was not necessary to do more than listen to her other-wordly music to grasp that there was a scarcely bridgeable gap between the civilizations of Vietnam and of its great trans-pacific protector.

After the passage of her itinerant symphonette, I repaired to my bath and watched a baseball or football game, live (or virtually so), by television satellite from the United States. I had not settled into the bath for more than a few minutes when a very large cockroach emerged each evening and circumnavigated the upper perimeter of the bath-tub, with the self-confidence of a cat.

It was not so large as the immense roach that I saw in Phnom Penh a few weeks later being conducted around on a string leash by a child, but it probably deserved a more ceremonious end than the one that awaited it. I went up-country one weekend but as good hotel rooms were at a premium, I sublet for three days to a visiting CBS crew. (Both CBS and NBC had their offices in the hotel.) When I returned, the roach's head was intact and seemingly alert, but its torso and hindquarters had been smeared against my wall by my CBS sub-tenants. In Saigon, there was no point ringing for the maid.

I can not claim to have seen much military action, but I did often see the spectacle of long rows of American helicopters crossing endlessly over trackless forests and jungles. For all witnesses to it, this will always remain the supreme demonstration of the Vietnam War's incompatibility of civilizations: their objectives and their methods. The U.S. Air Force was invincible but ultimately ineffectual.

I visited all the corps areas and met many prominent Vietnamese. They had made such an agile progress from the French through Diem, Kanh, Big Minh, and Ky to Thieu, that I doubted most of them would be unequal to the task of making their peace with the Vietminh should that be necessary. General Nguyen Be, the Vietnamese counter-intelligence chief, was the most impressive. Saigon was a city girt about with concertina wire and heavily populated by crude military statues. It appeared everywhere to be trying to convince itself of its own courage and belligerent aptitudes, like Hemingway's portrayal of rear-area Italian staff officers, interrogating retreating soldiers and "looking very military in the early morning" in *A Farewell to Arms*. General Nguyen Be seemed an authentic soldier, intelligent, disciplined, determined, brave.

Doubtless there were many others, but the believability of ARVN as a fighting force was not augmented by the habit of the American GIs of referring to their indigenous allies as "zipper-heads," usually preceded by a vulgar and very unflattering adjective. When I visited an American fire base near the famous fortress of Khe Sanh "athwart enemy communications" (as the Pentagon explained the utility of the fortress), the American soldiers sat around at picnic tables while large-bore howitzers automatically fired, reloaded, moved a few degrees to the right, fired again, and so forth, supposedly discouraging a North Vietnamese approach. When I asked the base commander if this was really an effective way to combat the North Vietnamese, he shrieked with surprise and assured me there were no North Vietnamese around. He averred that the only unsubdued enemy in the area were tigers, but he was toughening up his "gooks" (i.e., "zipperheads") by putting them in the outer perimeter at night where they could fight it out with the tigers. It was eery, surreal combat: mechanical war from picnic tables against an invisible enemy whose continued existence was disputed. It was indeed magnificent in its way but was it war?

More convincing, though hardly more reassuring, was the commander of the Korean zone, at the head of 50,000 stocky, hard-drinking troops. He explained to me that his area was entirely pacified. When I asked his secret in being so uniquely successful, he unselfconsciously explained, "Because I kill everything that moves, man, cat, child, squirrel, unless it is wearing a Korean or American uniform." This was not a version of winning the hearts and minds that would play well in Peoria, much less New York, Washington, or Hollywood.

I visited the An Quang Pagoda, centre of Buddhist clerical opposition to the Saigon government, where several monks had immolated themselves. My wary exchanges with some of the An Quang personnel convinced me that Vietnam was an even more unfathomably enigmatic country than I had imagined. I went to Vung Tau, the famous Cap St. Jacques, which retained in its seaside villas the civility of colonial days, to see Nguyen Cao Ky, then sulking in the vice presidency. He was dapper, sinister, shallow. Ky had been pilloried by the U.S. press for his alleged enthusiasm for Hitler. He denied any such predilection to me, but seemed to me a vain and avaricious opportunist, not untypical of many people who survive in a prolonged domestic war, but not a plausible leader of the sort of cause and values the Americans purported to be defending.

Much more interesting was the President, Nguyen Van Thieu. The U.S. Embassy requested an interview for me and it was granted at once. I attended upon President Thieu at the large, modern, and inelegant Tu Do Palace on the morning of October 1, 1970. His immediate bodyguard in his anterooms were the most intimidating looking such group I have seen, narrowly edging out the apes who accompanied Charles de Gaulle to Montreal in 1967.

He held forth for an hour and a half, partly in English and partly in French. It was an astonishing flow of controversial reminiscences and sulphurous reflections on contemporaries. Thieu garrulously assured me that President Kennedy had been behind the assassination of Diem, which had been widely rumoured but never publicly alleged by a comparably highly placed source. The U.S. military Assistance Command had cut off supplies of gasoline pending Diem's resignation or removal in 1963, and Thieu couldn't operate his tanks for the last ten days of Diem's life. De Gaulle he dismissed as "a bitter old man repudiated by his own people trying to recover a lost empire." Sihanouk was "a charlatan, a poseur, a communist stooge." His spluttered hatred of Mao Tse Tung, and the Chinese generally, was the authentic voice of ancient Vietnam. Thieu declined to come altogether to the defence of his most notoriously corrupt generals, Dang Van Quang and Do Cao Tri, saying only that if they really were embezzlers, they would be prosecuted. He gave me the exact date (the following week) of the first deployment over Vietnam of the American B-57s.

His attacks on communism generally, and the Vietnamese version in particular, were vehement and rooted, I sensed after steady prodding, in his Catholic education, even more than political and military combat. There was no ring of hollow expediency or polemical posturing. Tenacious and cunning he certainly seemed, but not a diaphanous manoeuvrer of the kind that swarmed much of every day in Saigon's boulevard cafés. There was nothing opportunistic or bombastic in his confident predictions of victory, including an optimistic timetable and a rather glib but newsworthy sketch of the end game. He thought he represented a superior system and wishfully believed that he would be sustained by his great overseas ally.

The U.S. expeditionary presence was iconically represented by extravagantly autographed photographs of Lyndon Johnson, Richard Nixon, Spiro Agnew, and others identified with the American effort. Unlike President Park in South Korea, he didn't have an industrial or economic vision to illuminate his post-war dreams, beyond vague notions of rice exportation and a nascent manufacturing sector.

"Like Churchill," he said, his policy was "to win the war." Sufficient unto the day was the evil thereof.

I didn't doubt his motivation or his courage, only whether he had a winning hand. But my desire to see the Americans win and the communists and their specious, fadish, loathsome, cheering section in the salons, campuses, and media of the West, mercilessly routed, caused me, even more than my gallant and gracious host, to believe in the victory of America and Vietnamization. When the interview ended, the president's cousin, well described by Henry Kissinger in his memoirs as "the egregious Nha," an aggressive alumnus of the University of Oklahoma, stepped forward and pinned on my lapel an impressive "National Defense Medal." I surmised I had earned it by drinking ten cups of Vietnamese tea without once expressing any curiosity about the whereabouts of the lavatory. (It gave me great pleasure, many years later, after the country had been absorbed by the North Vietnamese Army, to wear the medal to pretentious occasions such as the opening of the Royal Winter Fair in Toronto.)

The summary of the interview was filed by me a few hours later at the AP office and was front-page news throughout the world. It was the highlight of my sporadic career as a journalist, and I was lionized in the principal press hangouts of Saigon over the next several days. Sixteen years later, when I interviewed the *Daily Telegraph*'s embarking Washington correspondent in London, he said that for a month after I bought control of that newspaper, he had tried to think of why my name was familiar and finally remembered my story from Saigon when he had been the *Telegraph* correspondent there. "Who is this guy? How did he get this access and where the hell is Sherbrooke?" were briefly hot questions in the Saigon Press Club.

On the evening of October 1, 1970, I went to dinner at Tan Son Nhut field hospital with Dr. Michael Kent, head of the mental hygiene unit, whom I had met when I went to buy some tranquillizers to assist my sleeping as I travelled around the country. Our dinner was interrupted three times by the arrival of disoriented soldiers, brought in by para-medical MPs after cracking up and becoming catatonic or dangerous to self or comrades. Crippled and maimed casualties of war were everywhere in Saigon, but they were not as affecting as these men whose minds and souls had been shaken by the violences of war. They were lately drawn from the ways of peace and yearned but for return to their lyricized homes. Their government had not succeeded in imparting to many of them the remotest notion of what they were supposed to be doing there. And keeping the men in the combat zone for a twelve-month tour, twice as long as the officers, was one of many unimaginably foolish practices that a Saigon PX the size of Toronto's main Eaton's store would not put right. Dr. Kent and his colleagues confirmed most of the worst fears I had about the condition of the U.S. Army in the field, the extent of drug addiction and demoralization, and the uneven quality of the officers. In all of the circumstances, they had performed admirably but they were heading for the exit.

My enthusiasm for the American war effort did not go to the extreme of approving the insertion of a conscript American army into the trackless, diseased, booby-trapped jungles of Vietnam, nor of the Americans fighting the Vietnamese war on the ground at all. This was why I had rejoiced in Nixon's magisterial Vietnam address of November 3, 1969, in which he revealed the Vietnamization policy, coined the phrase "silent majority," and said he would take responsibility for that policy. "If I am right, what my critics say now won't matter. If I am wrong, what I say then won't matter." I was hopeful of a benign ending to the horrible war when I left Saigon and returned to Canada via Phnom Penh, Bangkok, Honolulu, and Los Angeles. As I deplaned at Los Angeles, I was greeted by headlines in newspaper boxes declaring "Army marches into Montreal." Following the FLQ's kidnapping of the British official James Cross, and Quebec's labour minister, Pierre Laporte, Trudeau had imposed the War Measures Act.

In my absence, David Radler and Peter White had committed the *Sherbrooke Record* to be co-producers in Montreal, with John F. Bassett (son of the publisher of the Toronto *Telegram*, grandson of the publisher of the Montreal *Gazette*), of the libertarian nudist musical *Hair*. It was for us a ludicrously uncharacteristic lapse into Woodstock, prompted, I imagined, by my having vetoed our participation in the play *And Miss Reardon Drinks a Little*, which, despite a banal script, went to Broadway and was a financial and critical success. When War Measures came down, the cast, faithful to their tiresome sixties "commitments," marched out of Gratien Gélinas

Comédie-Canadienne (which my father had subsidized as head of Canadian Breweries in the fifties), into the parking lot of the Hydro-Québec building where the premier of Quebec has his Montreal office and urinated on official cars and mooned the serried ranks of Bourassa's reinforced security unit. Upholding Quebec's highest constabulary traditions, the authorities threw the cast in jail with a minimum of protocol, interrupting the production for two days, as we refused to pay any bail for them.

The War Measures Act was not, in any case, a big boost to nights out at the theatre. One of our associates was the son of Fred Waring, the well-known band leader of The Pennsylvanians. The senior Mr. Waring came to a strategy session in November, drank prodigiously, and slurringly repeated the mantra, as he rocked precariously in his wooden chair, "It's just like the goddam U.S. Army. You have to train these bastards." On the fourth or fifth version of this advice (whose applicability was not obvious to me despite my recent sojourn with that army), he fell majestically backwards, passed out, and sprawled over the floor like an articulated bean bag for the balance of the evening.

Since *Hair* was a self-professed tribal production, the cast "adopted" North American Indians in each city where they played. David Radler, adverting to his days as a counsellor to the Indian Affairs department, produced a band of Abenakis from Sept-Iles, led by their chief, Walter Watso, subsequently famous for his "investment" of a $75,000 Indian Affairs department grant in Las Vegas. The English- and French-language press were unfortunately unable to co-ordinate their timing of group photographs with the cast and Walter's braves and they passed the interval between the English and French newspaper sessions in a neighbouring tavern. When *Le Journal*, *Montréal Matin*, and *La Presse* arrived, the cast and the Indians were too drunk for organized photographs and as Walter pushed and dragged his people on to their buses to take them back to the North Shore, he was audibly disappointed, though he was exhorting them in neither English nor French, and I could only guess at the burden of his reflections. The production folded before Christmas, taking away with it my brief and involuntary career as an impresario.

Another project that had been considered while I was in the Far East and which David and Peter phoned me about in Saigon was an obscure radio station in Oshawa. David and I agreed we would fill the late-night schedule with our own reflections on leftish tendencies in the media, which might have been slightly entertaining, but the deal wasn't completed. We also looked briefly at the purchase of an expansion National Hockey League franchise, but David and I agreed that we wouldn't be able to sign the sort of pay cheques professional athletes were starting to expect.

Under the War Measures Act, we shared a guardian soldier at the *Sherbrooke Record* with the neighbouring Bell Telephone installation, and David was the English-language censor of the Eastern Townships. When the editors of the Bishop's University student newspaper, *The Campus*, which we typeset and sent on to the printers, jocularly challenged his authority, he stripped out the entire contents of the paper except for the date and some sports scores and had it printed in that condition. It was as if I had never left Saigon.

Brian Stewart was now City Hall reporter for the Montreal *Gazette*, and I went with him to the celebration of Mayor Jean Drapeau's crushing victory in the October municipal election. The mayor portrayed his opponents as terrorists and took every poll in Montreal and 92.5 per cent of the vote. The harangue he gave us that night and the general atmosphere of martial law reminded me of the O.A.S. uprisings in Algiers of the early sixties. The mayor philosophically told Brian and me, "It's like baseball. They cheer a player one night and boo him the next. They cheered me in 1954, booed me in 1957, and are cheering me now. It doesn't mean anything. The only popularity that counts is to be popular with oneself." I got the distinct impression that he was, and that there was a kernel of wisdom in his views that deserved to be remembered.

Many friends of mine were incarcerated without real cause but dined out for decades afterwards on their "ordeal." Gently taunting my separatist or soft-left acquaintances was a rather agreeable pastime. The most amusing venue was the Nelson Hotel in Place Jacques Cartier, where the punch-drunk former prize fighter, Reggie Chartrand, who worked there and was one of the leading "*Chevaliers de L'Indépendance*," could always be provoked to a colourful, if incoherent, outburst.

The provincial justice minister, Jérôme Choquette, was photographed peering respectfully up at Duplessis's statue still awaiting a permanent place and stored with seized slot machines in the basement of the provincial police building on Parthenais Street. I busied myself writing rabidly pro-Trudeau and Drapeau editorials in the *Record*, demanding that "all those whose conduct encouraged" the murder of Laporte (whom I had known slightly and whose cleverness I admired) be made "the moral outcasts of the community."

CHAPTER THREE

PATHWAYS TO MANHOOD
1970–1972

T THE BEGINNING OF 1971 I MOVED INTO the main house owned by Peter White's father at Knowlton for which the cabin I had rented in 1966 and 1967 was an outbuilding. Midway between Sherbrooke and Montreal, it was convenient and comfortable. In Sherbrooke, David Radler, Peter White, and I fiercely overmanaged the little newspaper, producing astronomical profits considering we had paid only $18,000 for it. We eventually bought a fishing-tackle warehouse for a building and a press to put in it, but some of the economies we effected must have set records.

Employees were monitored, more or less good-naturedly, but with superhuman persistence. We had a Montreal telephone directory by sequence of telephone numbers and relentlessly hunted down any personal calls from Sherbrooke to Montreal. When one reporter marched into David's office to present a petition of grievances, David fined him two cents, deducted from his weekly pay cheque, for wasting a sheet of paper. When, on the night of NDP leader Allan Blakeney's first victory in Saskatchewan in 1971, the same reporter raised the two-finger V for victory sign, then current among the left, to David, he too raised up two victorious fingers and said, "That just cost you two," and deducted two dollars from his next pay cheque, "for provoking the owners."

One scheme I struck upon for reducing salaries with an impeccable cover of good intentions was to hire a convict under a federal government bonded rehabilitation service, at a modest salary. I went to the Cowansville Penitentiary (one of Roland Désourdy's countless patronage achievements) and interviewed a recommended prisoner. I liked the individual and sincerely hoped the experiment would succeed. After two weeks, he started writing forged cheques and fled to New Brunswick. When news of his conviction and sentencing in Fredericton came across the newswire, the night editor, oblivious to the fact that the recidivist had been his desk-mate, since he never knew his surname, ran the item as a local news story.

I eventually devised what I described as the elastic compensation system for the reporters and debated with them at the end of each week what they "deserved" on the basis of the volume and quality of their journalistic production. It was an outrageous system, of course, but many of our reporters went on to considerable distinction at larger newspapers, and few of them would deny that the *Record*, despite the oppressions of our management, did give them a firm grounding in the journalistic craft.

Not all or even most of our managerial initiatives were capricious. (I, as publisher, dealt more frequently than David or Peter did with the journalists.) Our reporters gave new and atavistic meaning to the word "cub"; none of them had done this sort of work before, and few of them had got much beyond high school. Many had neurotic and familial problems that David and I were always happy to help with if asked (including recruiting a psychoanalyst for one of them), and even I was able to teach many of them something about the English language and how to give an employer value for money. I can remember firing only a couple of reporters at Sherbrooke of the dozens that came through, though most of them certainly gave us cause. When they moved on, it was voluntarily and to a better paying job at a larger newspaper and for many of them, when they sought a recommendation to another employer or a university, David and I gave them some of our stationery and told them to forge our names to any commendation they wanted to compose, no matter how elegiacal.

When the complaints from the reporters became too voluminous, I would invite Brian Stewart to give an impartial professional critique of the editorial product. He was well-known after three years at the *Gazette* as City Hall editor as the most perceptive commentator on the Drapeau regime, a stylish writer, and a local television personality. His judgements of the *Record*, although never stooping to meanness, were usually sobering and often caustic: "What may I ask, is the justification for opening what purports to be a news story with the (apparently rhetorical) question: 'Are you still bothered by discharge?' He was even more scandalized by the salacious implications of the sports headline referring to the hockey victory of the Drummondville Royals over the Sherbrooke Beavers: "Beavers Get Royal Thrashing."

In the spring of 1971, I met the legendary Lord Thomson of Fleet at a Canadian Press function, and he gave me his "rules of thumb" starting with his policy that all building alterations had to be approved personally by him and if it was proposed to make a publisher's office larger than the men's washroom, Roy fired the publisher. We had already, as the condition of our newspaper impelled, instituted frugalities that vastly transcended anything I have seen unearthed in the Thomson organization or elsewhere for use in disputes with employees as a mock source of current wisdom. David kept a copy of a famous early nineteenth-century manual on industrial relations and regularly recited the opening sentence, which asserted that any such study must start from the premise that all employees are slothful, incompetent, and dishonest.

Only the three owners could sign cheques for the company or authorize expenditures above $5. Practically every invoice led to an inquiry worthy of Torquemada. Every conceivable item necessary to newspaper production was rationed, economized, and made the subject of intense haggling. All dispensable personnel expenses were violently pared. David dismissed the bird-watching stringer, unaware that he was an almost lifelong chum of Peter's. When Peter, apprised of his friend's fate, objected, David cried out with incredulity: "Do you expect me to pay $50 a week for four column inches about pink breasted finches in Moe's River?"

We operated from John Bassett's old "uniforms and mail-bag" account what amounted to a modest slush fund for our preferred causes and tenuously business-connected expenses.

Not only the reporters were learning. There could be no better school for newspaper proprietors, nor a stronger motivation than that provided by having one's own modest savings engaged. David and I went out on the delivery routes. We even tried to familiarize ourselves with the photo-typesetting equipment in order to avoid being baffled by our production head who, like most printers, was always bandying about unnecessarily technical jargon. Only we handled the banking, including getting an exclusive interview with our enterprising local Bank of Montreal manager, René Gagnon, when he tussled with a would-be robber. All three of us were known to deliver newspapers personally when irate unserved subscribers telephoned in the evening.

Distribution was the responsibility of an astonishing local Townships character as picturesque as his name: J. W. Wathen Brack. He was five feet seven inches tall, weighed 310 pounds, and walked with a cane because, as he helpfully explained, his knees tended to buckle in the freighted interval between meals and bowel movements. (He usually described the latter part of the digestive cycle with more than a hint of original scatology.) He was a good and well-liked man and when he died of the inevitable coronary in 1977 a fine remembrance by the Brome-Missisquoi correspondent of the *Record* concluded "God rest ye merry gentlemen."

We all sold advertising, locally and to agencies, and we all were known to report, edit, and supervise layout. The *Sherbrooke Record* was a tight ship, and a year after we bought it, it was making ten to fifteen thousand dollars a month, having lost nearly $10,000 per month in the two years before we bought it.

Ten years later when David Radler told the Kent commission on newspapers in response to a question asking what our chief contribution to Canadian journalism had been, "the three-man newsroom and two of them sell ads," he was not telling the whole story. David himself also devised a technique for utilizing the same page, simultaneously, for news and advertising, by jamming an entire page with country correspondence ("Mrs. Bloggs suffered a severe bee sting while visiting Mrs. Jones"), and small stories without any pictures, and then selling a colour ad at half rates over it, i.e., "Shop at Au Bon Marché," in red ink. We experimented with this format, inching up the price to the advertiser by claiming he had thousands of guaranteed readers to whom this would be irresistible subliminal advertising, and so forth.

The submission to the Kent commission was less controversial than my presentation on our behalf to Keith Davey's Special Senate

Committee on Mass Media in 1969. I wrote my opinions of the psychological state and ideological condition of most of the so-called Canadian working press. "There are not adequate safeguards to ensure that those vested with the influence and heady individual exposure of almost the least important by-lined journalist are intellectually and psychologically qualified for their positions."

My view was, and remains, that although most journalists, like most people, are conscientious men and women doing their jobs as well as they can, many are possessed by envious frustration that they are chroniclers condemned forever to report on the sayings and doings of others.

I lamented the abdication of most editors, publishers, and newspaper proprietors, and in words that have often been quoted since, usually out of context, I wrote: "My experience with journalists authorises me to record that a very large number of them are ignorant, lazy, opinionated, intellectually dishonest and inadequately supervised. The profession is heavily cluttered with abrasive youngsters who substitute 'commitment' for insight, and to a lesser extent, with aged hacks toiling through a miasma of mounting decrepitude. Alcoholism is endemic in both groups." (Today, these are by far the most famous words ever addressed to that commission but Keith acknowledged them rather perfunctorily at the time.) I apostrophized the discreet compact that the Southam organization in particular had made by handing its reporters complete control of contents and great budgetary laxity in exchange for basking in reportorial approbation as model owners, thus shortchanging both their shareholders and their readers.

I resorted to extreme strictures against the ubiquitous and corrosive anti-Americanism of much of the Canadian media, focusing on the Montreal *Star* and the CBC as illustrative. I railed against the *Star*'s increasing presentation of notorious Australian communist Wilfred Burchitt's americophobic tracts as balanced and intelligent comments on the Far East without ever touching upon his political affiliations. I recited extensive evidence of the CBC's anti-American biases and generally attacked the Canadian media for lack of rigour, a dreary and impenetrable soft-left group-think, a gross disparity in its aptitudes for dispensing and receiving criticism, insufficient literacy, an almost complete lack of flair, and a predilection for behaving like a rampaging industrial union while pretending absurdly to be a learned profession.

My reflections on the Fourth Estate were based on extensive experience of the Canadian media, socially, professionally, and as consumer-observer. They stirred up strenuous media objections but have never been and, at the time they were made, could not be authoritatively refuted.

Not at all controversial, though perhaps more entertaining, was our submission to the Senate Committee on the Constitution, which held hearings throughout the country in 1971. When it came to Sherbrooke, the hall was packed with separatist students who mercilessly heckled everyone except a member of the public who asked in very laborious French why we as a nationality were "licking the anus of the Queen of England."

I wrote a serious constitutional treatise essentially supporting official bilingualism and an amending formula close to the Victoria Charter that emerged in the summer of 1971. When I got a look at the crowd, I suggested that Peter deliver our paper because of his great bilingual proficiency and linguistic dexterity generally. He translated instantaneously with a panache worthy of Duplessis, emphasized his relationship with the late Daniel Johnson, and magisterially dismissed questioners, from the Senate panel or the audience. It was a boffo performance but as it attracted no interest at all, we would have done better following David's advice on the contents of our brief which was that Canada, as presently constituted, was "a flop."

The editorial stance of the *Sherbrooke Record* was pro-government in Quebec and naturally hostile to the Parti Québécois, reasonably well disposed to Trudeau as Quebec's greatest federalist, despite David's occasional incitement of editorial suggestions that he was a communist because "he signed some document in Moscow," but militantly pro-American in international affairs. Pro-Hanoi anti-war demonstrators were attacked in blood-curdling terms and, faithful to the conclusions I came to in my sojourn in Vietnam, I debated (rather unequally) with both pacifist and pro-communist anti-war correspondents and even columnists.

On one occasion Dalton Camp, whose pieces we took from the Toronto *Telegram* syndicate that we inherited at the *Record*, wrote a very gratuitous offering imputing diabolical motives in Southeast

Asia to successive U.S. administrations. I wrote a polemical and abusive response beside Dalton's column, concluding that it was the last such piece he would write for us, as I had cancelled him. (I replaced him with William F. Buckley, who could be relied upon to produce no such heresies.) Dalton manfully wrote me back, for publication, that now he knew "how those liberated folks in My Lai (site of Lieutenant Calley's infamous massacre) felt."

One day in the spring of 1971, a young recent graduate from Bishop's University sauntered into the *Record* and asked for a job as a reporter. David advised him that the only possible opening was as a sports reporter. When the applicant expressed interest, David gave him the sports quiz he and I had devised of obscure questions about the era that we knew, the mid-fifties, when this candidate would have scarcely been out of his cradle. Our rule was that one correct answer out of five questions would qualify a candidate for a job, but no one, up until then, had answered a single question of the quiz successfully.

David asked who the shortstop of the Detroit Tigers had been in 1954, and when the young man instantly replied, "Harvey Kuenn," David told him to "go to the nearest typewriter and start working." Five months later, when David was in the Arctic advising the native people on behalf of the federal government and Peter was in Guatemala, I pensioned off the deadwood at the top of the editorial department and appointed this twenty-one-year-old sportswriter as editor. He was Scott Abbot, who went on from Sherbrooke to the University of Tennessee, to Canadian Press, to invent the game Trivial Pursuit, to a life of considerable wealth and leisure. He was an excellent editor and a delightful companion and we all rejoiced in his subsequent success.

When we bought the *Daily Record* in 1969, it had no assets except some clapped-out typewriters and office furniture (the reporters routinely described their desk chairs as "death traps") and was on the verge of bankruptcy, the press having been repossessed by the manufacturer. Our methods may have been idiosyncratic and drastic, but the newspaper survived, outlived the *Quebec Chronicle-Telegraph* (now a weekly) and even the Montreal *Star*, and flourishes yet.

In 1945 *La Tribune*, Sherbrooke's French daily newspaper, had a circulation of 9,000, the *Record* 7,000. In 1969 when we bought it, the *Record*'s sale had crept up to 8,000, *La Tribune*'s to 45,000.

Chronically minority, marginal, with tenacious but elderly and not very prosperous readers scattered across a hundred miles along the U.S. border, all within the circulation area of the Montreal *Gazette* and *Star*, the *Record* would not have survived with any management significantly less purposeful than ourselves.

The paper had a little history. Louis St. Laurent had been the Compton correspondent of the *Record* in 1896. John Bassett, having returned from the war to contest the 1945 federal election in Sherbrooke and, with typical courage, after campaigning unsuccessfully in his Black Watch kilt and uniform (in a town with 2,000 military registration evaders in it), was the resident publisher for three years.

John Bassett (Jr.) had been a rather controversial figure in Toronto. His prominence as a flamboyant newspaper publisher and sportsman, chairman of the Toronto Argonauts and Maple Leaf Gardens, founder of CFTO, an unsuccessful federal political candidate in 1962, a powerful physical presence whose abrupt divorce outraged Toronto's more prudish old families in the mid-sixties, had long attracted the hostility of the city's most vocally envious and spiteful people. He had always been generous with his time to me and other young people, and I never thought his critics were his peers. He had an outstanding war record, was a courageous politician, a pioneer in television, a capable sports executive and talented publisher, who had revived the *Telegram* from a long torpor when, with the Eatons' backing, he took it over at the age of thirty-seven, from the estate of his friend, George McCullagh. I have always thought him one of Canada's builders, and a dear friend, as have been his wives and his sons.

In furtherance of a possible offer for the *Telegram*, which was alleged to have become unprofitable, I had spoken with my father's associate, John A. (Bud) McDougald, then president of Argus Corporation, who had mobilized, with the chairman of the Canadian Imperial Bank of Commerce, Neil J. McKinnon, a sizeable possible investment. I was about to call upon John Bassett with whom I had last negotiated when endeavouring to buy the *Sherbrooke Record* three years before, when one Saturday morning in October 1971, Bud telephoned me in Montreal to read John Bassett's announcement in the *Telegram* that he was closing the paper.

It was not a stylistically exemplary announcement ("This decision I have made, it goes without saying that it is the saddest I have had to make in my life in war or peace."). A considerable agitation developed to defer the decision and entertain possible offers for the *Telegram* though John spoke from the outset only of giving it a "decent burial" and had already sold the "subscription lists" to the *Toronto Star* for $10 million, i.e., the *Star* was paying to help make more palatable the euthanasia of its competitor.

It shortly emerged that the *Globe and Mail* would buy the *Telegram*'s building and presses. On balance, John Bassett had scored another coup and made perhaps $20 million for the shareholders, extricating himself from a chronically unprofitable newspaper, and he laid the foundations of the delightfully successful *Toronto Sun* as he did so.

We had a try at keeping a possible sale alive and sent John a telegram expressing "continuing firm interest" in buying the newspaper. Fred Eaton called to say that John's response was "It's fine for these boys to have an interest, but where's their money?" (Certainly a reasonable question.) It was Yom Kippur and David was prepared to "fly to Toronto on an empty stomach" but Fred said, "No thanks, we'll grab the cash and run." Theirs was the correct economic decision and while we would have cut costs drastically, we too might well have had to repair to the launch of a successor like the *Sun*. But we could not have done it as well as Doug Creighton, who swiftly became one of the country's greatest publishers and was always one of Canada's most refreshing people.

Almost a year later, we appeared before the Restrictive Trade Practices Commission in Montreal. It was investigating whether there had been an unlawful restraint of trade in the closing of the *Telegram*. I did not quote Fred Eaton's remark other than in anodyne summary, as I thought it could be misunderstood. The rest of my testimony was essentially character evidence for the Eatons and the Bassetts, and we went to lunch with the head of the commission inquiry, Louis Couture, and had a very agreeable conversation about Duplessis and his most redoubtable opponent, T.D. Bouchard.

At one point, in 1971, we almost bought T.D. Bouchard's old newspaper in St. Hyacinthe, *Le Clairon*, from a colourful separatist veterinarian, Dr. Rajotte, who had known Bouchard. So great had his admiration for him been that he bought his newspaper and launched a mighty effort to revive it, almost going bankrupt raffling off new

Cadillacs. He became so emotional in his desire to divest himself of *Le Clairon*, especially to someone who appreciated the Bouchard legacy, that he climaxed his sales pitch by exclaiming, "I'll give you the equipment!" "What equipment?" I asked. (He had the weekly newspaper printed elsewhere and didn't own a press.) "Waxers!" he shouted. "I have seventeen waxers and they're yours!" and he started to press waxers into my hand (small simple devices, the size of staplers or tape dispensers, worth about $20 each). He was one of the more endearing people I've negotiated with, but it was no deal.

On another occasion Peter White telephoned the owner of the St. John's (Quebec) *News* and asked after the state of his business. "Lousy," came the reply. "For five dollars I'd sell." Peter drove directly to St. John's, met the owner in a bar, wrote the contract of sale on a paper cocktail coaster, and bought the paper for only slightly more than the initially indicated price.

Undismayed by our inability to buy one of Canada's largest newspapers, the *Telegram*, I picked up Keith Davey's Special Senate Committee on Mass Media report, consulted the appendix that listed the daily newspaper owners, and telephoned all the independents, offering fairly explicitly to buy their properties. I received a number of expressions of interest in British Columbia, and David and I flew to Fort St. John and bought from the legendary Ma Murray's son the family newspaper, *Alaska Highway News*. We went on to Vancouver and arranged tentatively to buy the Prince Rupert *Daily News* and the Terrace *Herald*, contingent only upon our visits to the towns. This was easily achieved at Prince Rupert, where the highlight of our visit was a fist-fight between two native (Indian) ladies in front of a liquor store, but at Terrace, the autumn snow was so heavy that we were discouraged from deplaning and we bought it sight unseen.

Prince Rupert had had the same circulation, within a couple of hundred, since it was founded in 1905. Its Andy Warhol-like moment of glory was when Franklin D. Roosevelt came to town in 1944 to visit the Alaska Highway workers, on his way back from meeting MacArthur and Nimitz in Hawaii, and the *Daily News* photo library had a shot of his outsized battleship in the roadstead, habitually plied by much humbler craft.

We paid $240,000 for the Murrays' paper, one-half a balance of sale, half on the borrowing power of the *Sherbrooke Record*. One year's profit from those two papers eliminated that debt. We paid only $150,000 for Prince Rupert and Terrace, half a balance of sale and half as a call loan against the Prince Rupert *Daily News*'s current liabilities. Not much more than a year was required to eliminate that debt, too. The vendor at Prince Rupert was the fabled stockbroker and speculator, W. Binney Milner, whom I visited in his palatial house on Marine Drive. He was then eighty-one.

He was a sly old cove, a survivor of Bay Street from the piping days of George Drew as chairman of the Ontario Securities Commission nearly forty years before, when prospectuses didn't really have to be true and no stock was held in escrow in a new issue underwriting. Bud McDougald told me that in the late twenties, when he used to take the de luxe train to Florida, and put his 16-cylinder Cadillac on board, Binney was a celebrity as he regularly put on two Dusenbergs and was at the centre of the highest stakes card game on the train. Even in 1972, when I saw him last, he was a man of style: he reciprocated Bud's greetings and said, "I haven't seen him since the day Herbert Hoover was inaugurated" (March 4, 1929).

St. Clair Balfour, chairman of Southam, put me in touch with the owners of the (Summerside) *Prince Edward Island Journal-Pioneer*, the province's evening newspaper. My last business initiative of 1971 was to buy this property and its printing division. In order to consult with someone on the merits of the deal, I telephoned my brother from my motel. The building was so flimsily constructed that for fear of being overheard by one of the vendors who was in the next room, I sat with blankets over my head and whispered my thoughts into the receiver until my brother banished my concerns just before I suffocated. At $250,000 down, and $250,000 balance of sale repayable over five years at 5 per cent interest fixed rate on the declining balance, this was another excellent purchase. After a year and a half, the down payment was regained and the balance of sale was not onerous.

We requested a name for our expanding company from Alex Konigsberg, Peter White's very agreeable law partner, and asked for something with "Royal" in it, as the provinces to which we were expanding were so strenuously monarchist, a novelty to Quebeckers. "Sterling" was the closest he could get, so oversubscribed was "Royal" in British Columbia and Prince Edward Island. Sterling

Newspapers Ltd. has been the corporate equivalent of the Little Engine That Could and has carried a huge burden for us these twenty years. Sherbrooke, Prince Rupert, Fort St. John, and Prince Edward Island made a pre-tax cash flow of over $600,000 net of interest in 1972. We continually reapplied variants of our Sherbrooke formula. We now owned newspapers from coast to coast, admittedly with long gaps on the way. It was like stringing fish.

In 1977 when we had all left Quebec and were not in transports of optimism about the province's short-term future, we sold the *Sherbrooke Record* to our friend (and John Bassett's cousin), George MacLaren for $865,000, forty-eight times what we paid for it eight years before, and having stripped out about a million dollars of profit with which we built our newspaper company. John Bassett had parlayed his ownership of the *Record* into a share of the *Toronto Telegram*, the launch of Canada's greatest television station, CFTO, Inland Publishing, and a number of other valuable television and radio licences. George MacLaren sold the *Record* on to Pierre Péladeau at a profit of over $2 million in 1989. It has thus been a talisman to successive owners. What was achieved during our watch in Sherbrooke has since ramified far more widely than any of us, much less anyone else who encountered us at that formative and picturesque stage, could have imagined.

Peter White and I tried our hand at political king-making in the wreckage of the Union Nationale, which had plunged to 20 per cent of the vote in the 1970 Quebec election, from 41 per cent in 1966, and was now the third party in the province behind Bourassa's Liberals (45 per cent) and Lévesque's Péquistes (24 per cent). In a vacuum, we reasoned that anyone can have influence, no matter how far removed they are from real potential power. A quarter of the traditional Union Nationale vote had gone to the Péquistes and a quarter to the Créditistes, (the Poujadist followers of Réal Caouette, farmers, reactionary workers, and petit bourgeois). The party of Duplessis and Paul Sauvé and Daniel Johnson was now, as Jean-Jacques Bertrand's successor, to have Marcel Masse, Mario Beaulieu, or Gabriel Loubier.

Masse, "*un jeune homme prédestiné*," as de Gaulle had publicly described him in an evocative choice of words resembling Churchill's famous description of the forty-nine-year-old general himself in 1940, was an attractive, even slightly glamorous, figure, but severely afflicted by the ultra-nationalist contagion.

David's friend, Mario Beaulieu, was a traditional conservative nationalist who would always try to come up to the verge of separation, to steal, adapting Disraeli's metaphor, the independentists' clothes without getting in the water himself; "*Québec D'abord*" (1966), became "*Québec 100 pour-cent*" (1969) and "*Québec plus que jamais*" (1970), but never "*Québec libre.*"

He had not grasped the message of the death of Johnson and the rise of Lévesque, the passage of the nationalist leadership from the moderate right to the medium left: without a leader who was able to set himself at the head of both the conservatives and the nationalists, the conservatives could no longer compete with the social democrats for the nationalist vote nor with the Liberals for the affections of the moderates.

The nationalists voted for the independentists. The socialist posturings and trappings appealed to the working class and the academics, but above all, it was an intellectually defensible method of redistributing money from the English and the Jews to the French at all echelons. There were no French-speaking conservatives for most of the seventies. The only way to make anything out of the one-third of the voters who had adhered to the Union Nationale or the Créditistes, was to rebuild the Duplessis-Johnson nationalist-conservative alliance, to oppose equally what Duplessis called the "scandal of separation and the marionnettes of Ottawa." Sloganeering alone wouldn't achieve it.

To turn the middle into a position of strength would require a leader of the force, credibility, and tactical dexterity of Duplessis or Johnson (the only people who had defeated the Quebec Liberal Party in seventy-three years).

Peter and I had been equally impressed by Claude Wagner's address to the Liberal convention in 1970, and we assumed he would hear an appeal to return to public life since there was no reason to believe he had forsworn political ambition any more than he had on his previous sojourn on the bench. He had accepted only to become a Sessions Court judge after the trumped-up convention that had elevated Bourassa over him on the votes of *ex officio* delegates appointed by Trudeau, Lesage, and Jean Marchand. His appointment was Bertrand's last act before dissolving the National Assembly, as he had renamed it, thus pulling the plug forever on the Union Nationale. All polls indicated that Wagner, a civilized personification of law and order, enjoyed a great popularity that put him in the electoral category of Trudeau, Lévesque, and Drapeau.

Peter and I wrote to Wagner, whom neither of us knew, beginning our letter with his words to the previous year's convention: "'*On va se regarder les yeux dans les yeux. On va se dire ce qu'on a à se dire.*' You should be prime minister of Quebec." We invited him to lunch, and he came, to a private dining room at the University Club of Montreal in May 1971.

It was a very agreeable occasion, inhibited only slightly by a waitress who appeared to have an obsessive-compulsive aversion to crumbs and was continually bursting in to scoop up the remains of the last five minutes' crackers and toast. Wagner was attractive, good-humoured, reasonably intelligent, very bilingual. His potential as a political candidate was no less obvious in a group of three than it was when he was addressing thousands of conventioners. We were suggesting putting Wagner up as leader of the Union Nationale, rallying the Créditistes, and stopping and then reversing the flow of non-separatist nationalists to the P.Q. and of traditional conservatives to the Liberals. The objective was to prevent an avowedly separatist party from becoming the official Opposition and to shield Bourassa, among whose strong points ability to resist pressure has never figured, from the relentless drift towards sovereignty.

This began a relationship with Wagner that endured until his death in 1979 and peaked with his famous campaign for the federal Conservative leadership in 1976. In 1971 I canvassed a number of prominent businessmen for him, and Peter ascertained that many prominent Union Nationale survivors were very enthusiastic about his candidacy. He eventually decided, however, that he could not leave the bench for something so risky (and, I suspected, underfunded), as the leadership of the bedraggled and shop-worn Union Nationale. Loubier was elected and led the party to extinction in 1973 and Lévesque surged forward to be Opposition leader and, in 1976, premier.

My opinion of Wagner was not strengthened by the spectacle that I observed on several occasions at his home of the sour influence of his wife, Gisèle. When questions about his career were put to him in her presence, it was Madame who answered, almost spitting out her words from her cheese-paring face (her chin and nose slightly approaching each other, like Wordsworth's old Cumberland leech-gatherer). Unpredictable, ill-tempered, and unworldly, though not unattractive in her rather wild way, she was a flaming red-haired harridan whose presence at her husband's side was far from comforting.

Congenial companion and formidable image though Claude was, even in 1971 I had nagging fears that behind his imposing façade and bright but empty eyes, he was a General Boulanger, a Hamlet, irresolute, incapable of risk-taking, and hag-ridden. Even if he were to prove all of these things, it wouldn't have disqualified him from successfully competing for the public's esteem with the first version of Robert Bourassa and with the remnants of Quebec's traditional right.

Claude Wagner was, from 1964 to 1966, one of the leading lights of the so-called *équipe du tonnère* (the team of thunder) who supposedly brought Quebec into the modern age. The members of this team were Jean Lesage, Claude Wagner, René Lévesque, Pierre Laporte, Paul Gérin-Lajoie, and Eric Kierans. If Wagner, in some respects, was an impostor, the same could be said for most of the others. There was a sizeable element of self-indulgent puffery and myth-making in this notion of a Team of Thunder. The first time I had seen Jean Lesage in person was at his arrival at a federal-provincial conference in Ottawa in November 1963; as he strode into the Château Laurier, he flicked off his rubbers without a downward or backward glance, relying on trailing lackeys, who were numerous, to pick them up. This was in stark contrast to Duplessis's famous arrival at the federal-provincial conference of 1945. His car had broken down, and he prevailed upon a farmer to drive him in a jalopy, with his ministers sitting on each other's knees. Duplessis leaped from the car at the door of the Château Laurier in front of the cameras, brandishing his cane and saying, "We are the delegation from Quebec. We are poor as you can see. That is why we want our share of the taxes."

Jean Lesage had never been defeated personally or as leader, until his narrow loss to Daniel Johnson in 1966. After this startling setback, feeling himself diminished and humiliated, he showed some traits of the over-inflated bourgeois his opponents taunted him as being and became more prone to drink. I always considered Jean Lesage, especially in his last years when I saw him often, a sincere Québécois and Canadian and a great figure in the history of both jurisdictions. It was an unkind fate for him to face this supreme crisis of self-esteem near the end of a career whose unbroken sequence of success had given him little preparation to meet such a challenge.

I always thought Gérin-Lajoie's stewardship of the education department was essentially a fraud. Duplessis built the schools and universities but left clerical personnel in them at absurd salaries compared to secular equivalents (thus assuring a balanced budget, low taxes, massive public works, and generous kickbacks to the Union Nationale). Gérin-Lajoie's secularization, achieved amidst ululations of modernization, resulted in the same people teaching the same curriculum to the same students from the same texts in the same buildings, at ten times the cost to the taxpayers.

Pierre Laporte, like his great former mentor Duplessis, was unable to resist the manipulative and unashamedly tactical aspects of politics, but unlike Duplessis, was personally avaricious as well. He was a fox with a Yogi Bear face, whose presence in a leadership group endlessly holding itself out as reformers illuminating Quebec at the end of its dark age, was incongruous.

René Lévesque was a fine intuitive politician. He was the philosophical, likeable corner grocer, with furrowed brow and hydraulic shoulders, who often spoke the truth when he said that when he thought something, he knew that the people of Quebec would be thinking it, too. Although Lévesque was always perfectly courteous to me, he also had a miserable personality and was a rather repulsive little gnome, with a chronic addiction to cigarettes, tar stains up his hands, greasy, twitchy, and specious. (When he won the 1976 election an Anglo-Quebec friend of mine emigrated to Ontario, not out of protest at a separatist government, but because Lévesque wore Hush Puppies to his own installation as premier.) It was irritating to hear Lévesque masquerade as a moderate but explain any act of extremism, including bombings that killed or injured innocent people, as the "understandable results of frustrations."

It was obvious to anyone who listened to Lévesque through the sixties that he was a separatist, but he revealed that fact explicitly only after the defeat of the Lesage government by Johnson in 1966. His genius of glib over-simplification of complex political subjects was well deployed in the selling of his independence option. It was the ultimate gift of the superficial journalist; Lévesque, on his television program "Point de Mire," had introduced French Quebec to the world in the fifties. It was an important but not always an endearing gift.

Eric Kierans was a former shoe salesman, self-made millionaire, head of the Montreal Stock Exchange, and an interesting and pleasant man, several cuts above the average provincial minister. In 1972 and 1973, I debated with him and Frank Scott (co-founder of the CCF and distinguished former McGill law dean), respectively representing the Conservative, Liberal, and New Democratic parties on Montreal's local CBC outlet. (This was nonsense as I preferred Trudeau to Stanfield, Eric was more or less an NDPer and Frank Scott, "after a lifetime of fighting injustice from the right, concluded the greatest threat now came from the left," and was philosophically conservative.) At heart Eric Kierans was always a working-class Irish contrarian, and though able and affable, he was rather predictable and his opinions were humdrum, Studs Terkel blue-collar advocacy with a paper-thin academic alloy.

And there was Claude Wagner, an uncertain trumpet. This was the "Team of Thunder." It had been a very fractious and not very thunderous team. More impressive were some of the senior civil servants, especially Claude Morin. Jacques Parizeau's mandarin service consisted mainly, in my observations, of Daniel Johnson asking him for a statistic and Jacques consulting the innards of his briefcase and responding crisply, "Ten thousand tons, *chef*." He is a most agreeable and civilized companion, but a Molièresque *haut bourgeois*, aspiring to be conveyed in a Citroen DS, with Duplessis's ubiquitous fleur-de-lis flag fluttering bravely on the fender, to a three-martini lunch in a five-star restaurant at the public's expense, with a lackey to apply to and lift from his shoulders the obligatory camel-hair overcoat. If Jean Lesage's self-importance contained elements of tragedy, Jacques Parizeau's is almost entirely comical. I have always liked and respected this amiable and urbane Tartuffe but found it a bit difficult to take him seriously as a political leader.

The *équipe du tonnère* was a rodomontade that Quebec dismissed in 1966 when it elected Johnson. But the myth-makers continued to propagate it in English Canada for many years and were still audible when I assaulted their fortified positions with my book on Duplessis in 1976.

This project percolated slowly through the early months of 1971 as I scoured the existing sources. My friend from Carleton University, Naomi Griffiths, sent me an invitation she had received to a colloquy about Duplessis at the University of Quebec at Trois-Rivières in late May. The well-known nationalist historian, Michel Brunet, chaired a panel of four youthful separatist academics, speaking the precise pedantic lingua franca of the genre and wearing the requisite tweedy uniform, including the rimless spectacles.

For two hours pompous phrases resounded in the university auditorium as Duplessis's memory, in his native city, was given the customary mugging. Finally, an aged, quavering, spare little man arose immediately in front of me and bellowed at the hall for fifteen minutes, waving sheaves of papers that he represented as specimens from Duplessis's inaccessible archives, and systematically refuted everything that had been said.

At the *vin d'honneur* afterwards I commended the intervener, Robert Rumilly, and said that it was high time Duplessis was analyzed seriously and not just treated with cant and bias. He enthusiastically invited me to visit him at his house in the Town of Mount Royal, which I did the following weekend. We sat in his second-floor study in a fine stone house that history built (he had written scores of volumes on Quebec history), with autographed photographs of Action Française leader Charles Maurras, Marshal Pétain, Camillien Houde, and Maurice Duplessis beaming benignly down upon us from the four walls.

Robert Rumilly was a veteran of the Battle of Verdun, a man of the right appalled at what he considered the degeneration of France after the First World War. In 1928 he was participating in an Action Française demonstration (Maurras's non-clerical non-fascist, but arch-conservative and nationalist intellectual movement) when the Paris police opened fire on the demonstrators, killing the person next to Rumilly. He determined then to leave France and come to Montreal, never to return, even as a tourist.

He apparently brought with him enough money to live on, but took up what proved an extremely prolific pen, first as a tractarian and more or less hired biographer (he was trumped as a paid biographer of Mackenzie King in favour of Emil Ludwig during the Second World War). He soon started work on his monumental forty-one–volume *History of the Province of Quebec*, largely culled from newspaper accounts (as Trudeau humorously taxed him with doing when I cited Rumilly as a source for an historical assertion in 1982). It grew over the decades, a new volume being produced every six months or so and ultimately achieved an extent of over three million words. He expanded sections of this immense work to produce comprehensive chronologies of Henri Bourassa, Honoré Mercier, and now, in 1971, Maurice Duplessis. The work was commissioned by the custodians of the Duplessis papers, an organization that rejoiced in the name "*La Société des Amis de Maurice-L. Duplessis, Inc.*"

Rumilly was one of the vanguard of figures from the French right who arrived in Quebec through the thirties and forties, fugitives from rising political disorder, then from the imminence of war, then from the German occupation, and finally, from the liberators' vengeance on those deemed to have collaborated with the Nazis. It was a motley and unrepresentative lot of Frenchmen, driftwood from the Pétainist traditional right, who found this escapee from the pages of Balzac to greet them. The fugitive de Bernonville, whom St. Laurent deported for his alleged collaboration, was one of the more famous. Another, though less controversial, was François Dupré, who owned the Ritz-Carlton in Montreal for some years.

Rumilly re-used envelopes that had come through the mails and had been post-marked; he was the first person through the doors of the well-known clothing store Brisson and Brisson on Sherbrooke Street every year on its special sale day. He shambled about like a walking bundle of rags and when asked how he was, invariably replied, "Not bad for a little old man" ("*un petit vieux*").

When I was trying to contact François Leduc, Duplessis's roads minister in his first term, Rumilly, who had misplaced his telephone number, straightfacedly proposed that I phone all the dozens of F. Leducs in the Montreal directory and open the conversation with "Is that the home of François Leduc, who Maurice Duplessis dismissed as roads minister in 1938?" He read every conceivable broker's report and husbanded his means with a voracious zeal. He had a quick and mordant wit, based on his asperity and French cynicism, but like my French landladies on the Avenue de Malakoff in 1963, he displayed an almost surprising solicitude and camaraderie at times.

Rumilly, having been at Verdun, had a natural loyalty to Pétain and was an authoritarian traditionalist, more of the Salazar school, being insufficiently militaristic or totalitarian to qualify as a fascist, though he was frequently accused of being one. The diluvian watershed of the French world was 1940, which separated the Vichyites from the Gaullists and those who co-operated too whole-heartedly with the English to have much time for the Gaullists or the Vichyites.

In Canada, the Bloc Populaire, Henri Bourassa, *Le Devoir*, and young nationalists like Jean Drapeau (who ran as a Bloc Populaire candidate in 1942 and managed André Laurendeau's Bloc campaign in 1944) were relatively pro-Vichy. So was much of the Canadian foreign service, including the young Pierre Dupuy, who was Canada's representative at Vichy and who ended his career as commissioner general of Expo 67, in which capacity de Gaulle was not enchanted to be greeted by him.

The Canadian and Quebec Liberal parties and many of their wartime and future leaders, such as Jean Lesage and unelected officials like Jules Léger (though not necessarily his brother, the cardinal), were generally assumed to be more interested in British and universal causes than in any restoration of France.

Individuals such as Georges Vanier, who were early and emphatic in their rejection of Vichy and support of de Gaulle were remembered with as much suspicion by one side as gratitude by the other. (De Gaulle prayed at Vanier's grave when he came to Quebec in 1967.)

If the Bloc Populaire and nationalists had been considered pro-Vichy, and the Liberals pro-English, the Union Nationale should, historically, have been de Gaulle's preferred party in Quebec and this was the relationship upon which Johnson built. Almost like ethnic distinctions in other communities, such as different groups of Slavs or Sephardim and Ashkenazi Jews, these arcane political differences still cut deep in the Quebec of the sixties and early seventies, especially while de Gaulle reigned.

Rumilly's principal contribution to political events in Quebec had been his promotion of a reconciliation between Mayor Camillien Houde and Duplessis in time for the 1948 provincial election, in which Duplessis carried eighty-four constituencies out of ninety-two. In gratitude for his role, Houde had championed Rumilly to Duplessis and he was retained as more or less of a pamphleteer for the Union Nationale. Rumilly produced an election book for them in 1956 entitled, with scant impartiality, "Fifteen Years of Accomplishments: The Facts Speak," and concluding with the lyrical cry of jubilation, "O my Province of Quebec!"

On that May evening in his commodious study, I satisfied Rumilly that I was interested in producing something in English (his works were almost never published in English) and that I would "do justice" to Duplessis. To deal seriously with the subject, it was necessary to get into Duplessis's papers, which Rumilly had been citing with such irrefutable reconditeness when I met him at Trois-Rivières. He gave me a letter of introduction to the custodian, Mlle. Auréa Cloutier, who had served Duplessis's father, Judge Nérée Duplessis for three years until his diabetes forced him to retire and he urged her to "go and work for young Maurice." This she did, from before his public career began in 1927, until he died in 1959 after twenty-eight years as a party leader, eighteen of them as prime minister and attorney general of Quebec. She continued through the tragically brief term of Paul Sauvé, but retired when the government, after a rending struggle for power, fell into the incapable hands of Antonio Barrette in January 1960.

Advised that entry to these archives could be accorded only on the recommendation of one of the directors of La Société, I secured a further letter from the ineffable Jean-Noël Tremblay, Johnson's and Bertrand's waspishly acerbic cultural affairs minister, described by Peter Newman as "the best seventeenth-century mind in Ottawa" when he was a Diefenbaker-Duplessis MP from 1958 to 1962). At this time, I had only a vague notion of writing a monograph on Quebec's economic progress under Duplessis, or something to open the door to a more balanced view of him than the one that then obtained throughout English Canada and much of French-Canada's academia.

I attended upon Mlle. Cloutier in June 1971, bringing a bottle of premium champagne with me. It was the first of fifty-five visits to her at Trois-Rivières and of fifty-five bottles of champagne to lubricate my progress through Duplessis's archives.

Duplessis's papers were almost completely unclassified, stuffed into filing cabinets and shoe-boxes in the basement of his house, 240 Bonaventure Street, almost next to the Cathedral. A bill to launder his shirts was apt to be next to a letter from Lord Alexander or Mackenzie King. It was a time warp. Almost nothing had been moved since he had died twelve years before. Once I got a good look at these papers, at how considerable a record they provided of so seminal a career in Canadian political history, I knew I would have to write something substantial. And if it were going to be an authoritative challenge to an unreasonable conventional wisdom, it would have to be thoroughly documented.

The field of French-Canada Studies had been only recently established as a distinct discipline in English-Canadian universities, especially at McGill, Toronto, and York, and the whole process of trying to understand developments in Quebec had become the academic equivalent of a cottage industry.

Most of the Toronto specialists had been appalled at Duplessis-style conservative nationalism and, with undoubted good faith, propounded the view, any dissent from which was attacked with a violence reserved for the most destabilizing form of heresy, that if Quebec would secularize, socialize its economic institutions and public services, and cease being distracted by nationalist totems, we could all co-exist happily in a *bonne entente* social democratic Canadian commonwealth.

Some were more enthusiastic than others about the socialist flourishes, and the more naïve adherents were those Trudeau referred to during the War Measures imposition of 1970 as "Toronto separatists" and "weak-kneed bleeding hearts." The *sine qua non* litmus test of all English-Canadian Liberals and New Democrats commenting on Quebec, whether they had participated directly or only vicariously in the recent history of Quebec, was that Duplessis was unrelievedly bad.

I was coming to the tentative conclusion that French Quebec's interest in social democracy was a preparedness to accept Danegeld from a federal government whose enduring relevance to Quebec was increasingly unclear. It was also a subscription to a fashionable method of redistributing money between socio-economic groups whose lines of demarcation had a providential resemblance to the province's ethnic divisions, i.e., to the French from the non-French, from each anglo or Jewish Quebecker according to his means, to each "authentic" Québécois according to his relative lack of means, with the vocal approval of English-Canada's premier and most fashionable Quebec-watchers.

The conservative nationalists were anti-separatist, anti-socialist, not particularly anti-English and respected Canada's political and social institutions. Further, my research already indicated, as I explained to Brian Stewart and Betty Shapiro in my television début in July 1971, in a local Montreal program that Brian accurately described as a "TV grapefruit league" (of which he was co-host), Quebec had made more economic progress, adopted more useful social programs, including some of Canada's most generous pension, day-care, and minimum-wage arrangements, built more roads, schools, hospitals, and universities, all under Duplessis, than ever before or subsequently. I was gnawing with increasing persistence at the roots of a vast and oppressive orthodoxy, which would eventually respond as all tyrannies do when they feel threatened.

On about my fifteenth visit to Mlle. Cloutier, she produced from the medicine cabinet in the bathroom of Duplessis's basement a bulging accordion file, which, she said as she plunked it down in front of me, contained only items that "M. Duplessis handed me saying 'This is for when we write our memoirs'." It included figures from the famous Union Nationale Caisse Electorale (the party war chest), a copy of the leader of the Opposition's tax returns, bits of gossip from bishops, and so forth.

In order to spur myself through the material, I enrolled at McGill in an M.A. program in the French-Canada Studies program, where I would participate in a few group discussions, conduct research in the library, and eventually produce a thesis on the subject "Maurice Duplessis, 1927–1939 as viewed through his correspondence." This was the sunset gun of my academic career and was designed only to help get me halfway through the work, that I might then have the momentum to finish what was already shaping up as a large tome. After all the vicissitudes of my earlier academic endeavours, I should have guessed that this final chapter would not be entirely without controversy.

From late 1971 for over a year, Rumilly and I conducted interviews together, driving all around the province in the very comfortable and roadworthy Cadillac Eldorado that I then owned, and very agreeably discussing Quebec and French history and current Canadian politics. He prevailed upon me to write to Pierre Des Marais II to ask him to seek the leadership of the Union Nationale after Claude Wagner declined to do so. (Pierre and I subsequently became intimately associated at Carling O'Keefe and then UniMédia when we bought control of that company.)

The historical trips with Rumilly brought me in contact with the last survivors of the old Quebec, *du bon vieux temps* — the ultramontanist Archbishop Cabana, the nonagenarian head of Quebec's Depression-era colonization effort, Ernest Laforce, who had campaigned as a lad for Sir John A. Macdonald in 1891, a huge cavalcade of superannuated judges, politicians, intellectuals, and businessmen. Duplessis had said to Malcolm Muggeridge (whom I also met in this process) that the key to governing Quebec was to keep the Jesuits and Dominicans quarrelling. I interviewed extensively the leading Jesuit Duplessist academic, Father Emile Bouvier, director of industrial relations at the University of Montreal, and the leading Dominican anti-Duplessis scholar, Father Georges-Henri Lévesque, dean of social sciences at Laval University.

One of the most interesting people encountered on these trips was the venerable clerical separatist writer, Father Gustave Lamarche, a less belligerent version of Canon Lionel Groulx. After an intense closeting with Father Lamarche in Joliet, Rumilly engagingly asked, "Who is subverting the other between you two?" Lamarche graciously said that "if all English Canadians were like Mr. Black, there would be no need for Quebec's independence." I replied, "If all prominent French Canadians were like le père Lamarche, all English Canadians would be like me."

The gentility of old Quebec could be addictive; it had, as Duplessis himself used to say, "a savour." Louis St. Laurent, when I interviewed him, seemed nonplussed when I asked why he and Duplessis, despite their strenuous disagreements, invariably concluded their letters with the lawyerly "Confraternal salutations." I had known Jean-Jacques Bertrand since 1966, and after interviewing him several times in 1971 and 1972, I found him so philosophical and altruistic despite the buffetings of a long political life, that I modestly supported his wife financially when she was a successful parliamentary candidate in the eighties. It was the only appropriate remembrance I could think of for this man whom Claude Ryan well eulogized in 1973 as the repository of "the highest civic and human virtues."

In August 1971, I journeyed to Africa on holiday and arranged to include a visit with one of the most illustrious Quebeckers of all, Paul-Emile Cardinal Léger. I had seen the cardinal at many public occasions; he was always a formidable presence, trim, of medium stature, with silver hair combed straight back under his biretta, and deep, dark, quintessentially French-Canadian eyes squinting and flashing with an intensity that faithfully reflected the powerful and original activity of his mind. His most outstanding characteristic was, and remained right to his death, his rich melodious gift of speech in conversation and oratory that conferred upon him, at least in French, an almost infallible eloquence.

When, in 1973, I knew him a good deal better and wrote up a nomination for him for the Nobel Prize for Peace, he gave me both a book and a record of some of his more important speeches, and I was able to study his technique more carefully. His gift for imagery and for dramatic presentation was as great as anyone's that I have heard, not excluding the most celebrated contemporary public speakers such as Martin Luther King, Ronald Reagan, and de Gaulle himself. Cardinal Léger was usually fatigued and often even slightly distracted. As my aunt, who sold him her house on Ramezay Place in Montreal in 1966, said, he had the air of "a fanatic, but a nice fanatic."

My first endeavour to reach the Cameroons was frustrated by the fact, which I discovered when I deplaned at Dakar from New York, that my luggage had been despatched to Berlin. Each day I bought a new change of clothes while spending the nights in *pied noir* bars, but resumed progress was abandoned at Bamako, where onward reservations became impossible and bats crowded into my hotel room through an aperture in the wall that had once been occupied by an air conditioner. I repaired to Paris to regroup.

When I finally arrived at Yaoundé airport from Paris and gave Cardinal Léger as my reference, I was at once treated as a person of great consequence. It was thus obvious from my first moments in the country that the cardinal's dramatic removal to equatorial Africa had been interpreted by the Cameroonese as vested with much of the significance that was attached to it in Quebec. It was an electrifying decision, for so powerful and popular a figure to stand down from such a post in order to fight tropical illnesses in the Third World. Apart from whatever personal motives he may have had, this renunciation could also be seen as a comment on both the future of the Roman Catholic Church and of Quebec. His political acumen was legendary, and I was interested in anything that this brilliant and sensational man might be prepared to reveal about his people, his Church, or himself.

I read Graham Greene's *A Burnt-out Case* on the plane to Yaoundé as I had read his *The Quiet American* when going to Vietnam the year before. Greene was having one of his ecclesiastical crises when he wrote it, and its anti-Catholic tenor, like his relentless anti-Americanism in the other book, mitigated their utility to me.

I stayed in the Yaoundé Inter-Continental Hotel and drove in a taxi fifteen kilometres into the bush to the former German colonial mission at Nsimelon. The cardinal entered as we were about to start dinner, closely followed by a fluffy, grey, long-haired pussycat and a rather attractive young German-Canadian woman, whom he was now using as a chauffeur, as he had recently had an automobile accident himself on driving a new Citroen into the street immediately after taking delivery. ("My thoughts were not on terrestrial matters," he had explained to a mystified Yaoundé policeman, as the wreck of the long-awaited new car was removed.) When the cardinal sat down in a plain wooden chair, his cat sat immediately underneath the seat of his chair, facing in the same direction and with equally regal bearing. We moved on to the cardinal's porch and spoke for several hours that evening and on the two subsequent evenings, staring at the broad and tattered African sky with frequent, distant, almost horizontal bolts of lightning zigzagging across scores of miles. On the second night, my arrival was delayed fifteen minutes as about twenty automobiles and a few buses waited respectfully for a gigantic but lethargic constricting snake to cross the road. I was the only motorist who found the episode in the slightest noteworthy. The last night was a graciously improvised celebration of my twenty-seventh birthday.

My visit was timely as the director of the charity that had built the cardinal's hospital at Yaoundé had suffered from "an excess of optimism," and Léger was becoming concerned that, as he put it to me a few months later, he might have to retire insolvent, to a monastery "to sing for [his] sins." In the circumstances, he spoke quite freely, describing one of the most prominent cardinals as "the Pope's letter-box," and several of his ecclesiastical brothers in somewhat sarcastic terms, e.g., "Our Lady of" this or that city. He spoke of the popes he had known with unblemished respect, especially Pius XII, whom he defended against the routine suggestions of indulgence of Nazi Germany with a detailed grasp of the subject that made it obvious he had often dealt with this argument before.

He spoke very insightfully of de Gaulle. He admired him, was grateful for the prestige he restored to French-speaking people throughout the world, and was gratified by de Gaulle's commendation of him when he spoke at the University of Montreal in 1967, but he was suspicious of his activities in Canada. His brother, Jules, having been rather discourteously received by de Gaulle when he presented his credentials as ambassador, was a notorious appeaser of France in Canada's External Affairs department. He had played a murky role in failing to advise Ottawa of how explosive de Gaulle's 1967 visit could be.

The cardinal acknowledged that de Gaulle had let it be known in 1958, prior to the election of John XXIII and immediately after conferring the Grand Cross of the Legion of Honour on the cardinal, that a French-speaking pope would be a most welcome development, though he denied any effort by de Gaulle to sway the election, at least in Léger's favour. (It is generally believed that Léger received a few votes in the conclave that elevated John XXIII.)

His comments on Quebec then and in succeeding years were naturally a good deal less guarded. Duplessis had been brilliant but overbearing, cynical, and oblivious to forces for modernization. Léger was always unimpressed with those public figures who failed to excite public imagination continuously. He was intellectually a bit trendy though always a brilliant expositor. Léger, almost alone of the Quebec bishops, had had little fear of secularization of education, the bugbear that Duplessis used to frighten the bishops, and couldn't get out of the University of Montreal quickly enough. Lesage was talented but had a "juvenile ego" and was prone to commit "*Bêtises et sottises.*" Paul Sauvé, his old classmate at the St. Sauveur Seminary, was his favourite Quebec politician, followed by Johnson. Bourassa was an unknown and unprepossessing quantity, Lévesque and Trudeau very forceful and authentic popular leaders. Léger omitted to express a clear preference for the constitutional option of either, though he appeared to entertain a slight preference for federalism. His parents had lived in Michigan before returning to Quebec to avoid assimilation. Léger and his brother were brought up in Valleyfield, near the Ontario border. It was clear that he expected Quebec to endure difficult days.

His reminiscences of his days in Japan, 1933–9, were presented with the unmistakable air of a man who thought he had been prophetic, as he thought also of his mission to Africa. He felt keenly the conscientious ravages of affluence and my impression was that he wanted to expiate his own prosperity and simultaneously to cast his lot with the future of the Church with his dramatic move to the Third World. There were, in fact, almost no lepers in that part of Africa, and the cardinal didn't seem overly burdened by the fact that most Quebeckers thought he was personally wrapping bandages in a leper colony. The hospital, when completed, was a fine facility for helping handicapped children of all kinds, but was always staffed with French and Canadian doctors, because whenever a Cameroonese became qualified he emigrated to the country where he had studied.

Even at this point Léger offered a foretaste of his subsequent warnings that the West could not "hide behind a curtain of wheat" with impunity, and that his role was to "alert the West to the plight and dangers of the Third World." He had a great talent for the astonishing gesture, but became somewhat impatient with a failure to follow or appreciate his pathfindings.

On one of the evenings I spent with him in Africa, he washed the dishes. He was at this time a formidable but slightly haggard and disoriented man. When he returned to Montreal in the autumn of that same year, he was in serious financial straits and asked me, among others, to assist him. I became a vice president of his charity, Le Cardinal Léger et Ses Oeuvres, and helped organize a substantial donation for him from my friend Charles Gundy, chairman of Wood Gundy, who found the cause and the man interesting.

There were generous responses from a number of other prominent Montreal and Toronto Establishment figures. Léger called successfully upon Trudeau and Gérin-Lajoie. The Canadian

International Development Agency was forthcoming, as were several orders of nuns. I accompanied the cardinal on a couple of these visits; his ability to mesmerize interlocutors, especially women, was unique in my experience. The histrionic gestures, achingly tired voice, deep-set eyes both playful and piercing, and the incomparable talent for unbroken sequences of *mots justes*, all overpowered any but the most sceptical listeners, and aging nuns accustomed to thinking of Cardinal Léger as their archbishop were far from the most sceptical. His organization was soon back on a sound footing, and he was never unappreciative of the need to render unto Caesar. On one occasion, Charlie Gundy apologetically said to the cardinal that he had to talk to me about money: "Dollars are important, too, Your Eminence." The instant reply came "With great respect, Mr. Gundy, that is not a lesson I have failed to learn up to now."

He was always studiously under-respectful of Anglo-Canadian institutions, as when he fell asleep at the dinner for Queen Elizabeth in Montreal, or when he kept Governor General Vanier waiting needlessly in his anteroom. Yet he was the only prominent French Quebecker to denounce Bourassa's repressive Bill 22 in 1974, which eliminated English as an official language and prescribed language aptitude tests for seven-year-olds to determine whether they would enter the French or English school system. The cardinal did so in an address that was brilliant even by his standards, in receiving an honorary degree from the University of Montreal, where he had been the chancellor for seventeen years. He reminisced about his arrival in Paris as a young priest in 1929 and warned that language could not be protected by laws, but only "by speaking it with such clarity that those hearing it will wish to speak it also."

His penchant for the theatrical did not decline with the passage of time. When in 1979 he (with Roly Michener) was briefly my (and Marcel Masse's) co-chairman at the Canadian Foundation for Refugees (which Pierre Trudeau correctly described as an effort by Joe Clark and Immigration Minister Ron Atkey to dump the issue on the private sector), his all-consuming interest was to take a 747 to Bangkok, to bring back "500 children," an episode that he would not have wished under-publicized.

When his brother became governor general in 1974, he set up a determined and fortunately, unsuccessful agitation to become

Bishop of Hull Quebec, an insane enterprise. His brief tenure as a parish priest for the first time in Montreal at the age of seventy-one, was a fiasco. When I interviewed him for my book on Duplessis, their correspondence in hand, I had the impression he felt under interrogation, especially when I asked about his written accusation against Trudeau of "cowardice," yet his verbal panache never deserted him.

Despite his hypochondria, nervosity, posturing, publicity-seeking, and hauteur, he was undoubtedly a great man, brilliant, galvanizing, fundamentally benign, and one of the most intelligent and articulate people I have known (which is why I cite his opinions at such length). His extraordinary personality reconciled an active spiritual life with an acute worldliness. It was sometimes possible to detect these perspectives warring within him, like dogs fighting under a blanket, but he was no less interesting for that. Nor was he altogether lacking a sense of humour. One morning in 1973, when he was in Montreal, he telephoned; I answered groggily and my companion could be heard sneezing and rustling her bedclothes in the background. When he expressed the hope that he hadn't disturbed me, I assured him I was preparing myself for *les oeuvres de la journée*, and he replied that it is usually alleged to be more difficult to recover from *les oeuvres de la nuit*.

I returned from Yaoundé to Douala at the end of August 1971, on an Air-Cameroon plane whose door could not be closed. Inconvenience was reduced by holding the altitude to about 1,000 feet. I went on to Paris more expeditiously and by car to Normandy, the day begun in equatorial jungle ending by the Deauville Casino.

When Cardinal Léger died in the autumn of 1991, aged eighty-seven, I was in England and unable to attend his funeral, but I arranged for our company's airplane to take Cardinal Carter to the funeral and return him to Toronto. Cardinal Carter wrote me on November 18, 1991: "Although your physical presence was regretted, I made sure that your spiritual presence was active, since I joined my thoughts and prayers to yours for the repose of the soul of our friend Paul Emile Léger. His coffin was left open during all of the Mass, and he looked very peaceful. Even more than when he was alive, those piercing eyes came at us from under his beetling brows. I am sure he was conscious of your feelings." I hope so.

I also attended the Hudson Institute at Croton-on-Hudson, New York, a couple of times in the spring and summer of 1971. It was (with Rand) one of the original and ultimate think-tanks and had been made famous by Herman Kahn, a giant futurologist who was part scientific genius, part presentational genius, and part shameless flim-flammer. As the think-tank industry was just gathering strength, I thought it a potentially useful exposure. I found the sessions too pedagogical, too heavily peopled by well-to-do but ponderous businessmen, or excruciatingly dull Mensa members and too given over to vapid theorizing ("Should the United States willingly surrender its entire steel and automobile industries to Japan?" or "Should the Amazon be dammed and the rain forests turned to grain agriculture?") to be abidingly interesting.

Parallel to my Duplessis research and psychological reading, I read a good deal of basic theology. I do not claim and have never claimed any particular insight into this subject and my pursuit was not of rigorous comprehension but of a comfort level that I knew what I was doing. Reading Newman persuaded me of his "convergence of probabilities" of the "illative" sense of the likelihood, though not the certainty as Newman saw it, of God's existence. I have never been able to state, as Newman did, that I was as sure of God's existence "as of the existence of my own hands and feet."

I read the principal assaults on ecclesiology, too. Freud's *Future of an Illusion* was a sophomoric and presumptuous work, and the only work from that author that vindicated his own uncharacteristically modest criticism of his "sloppy Viennese" prose style. Edward Gibbon's apostrophization of the "Holy romances" of the apostles was better written and more historic, but equally biased and fundamentally inconclusive, since God's existence doesn't depend upon the meticulous accuracy of the authors of the New Testament, and Christian belief is easily reconciled with a high level of biblical allegory, indeed is probably dependent upon it.

My favourite of these works was *The Pathetic Fallacy*, written in an appealingly robust style by Llewelyn Powys, a friend of the renowned American agnostic barrister Clarence Darrow: "This moribund religion interferes with a clear and enlightened vision of life.... Christianity is but a dream of savagery and pitifulness.... The wide, drifting stars of the galactic stream know naught of it. I have stood under a minaret in Turkey and heard the *azan* called in the empty blaze of noon. In the elephant forests of Africa I have seen negroes occupied after the same manner. Narrowly, on more than one occasion, I have watched our Western priests holding up the Host. The Indian, the men of China, none of them has known better than to raise sinew-lean arms to the heavens. It does not avail."

I concluded that all great triumphs of the exploratory intellect, Copernicus's overthrow of the earth-centric theory of the universe, Darwin's discovery that man is descended from a lower order of animals, Freud's assertion that we do not control our own subconscious, the development of nuclear fission with its constructive, destructive, and self-destructive possibilities — all were magnificent advances that yet expanded upon man's vulnerability and diminished or threatened our relative position in the universe. The whole process of acquiring knowledge debunked the theory that there was only a finite amount of knowledge and that every day we approach a plenitude of knowledge, a childlike academic adaptation of the Coué system.

This theory was Bertrand Russell at his most fatuous, the philosophy of the quavering decrepit dupe who led the witless disarmament marches on Aldermaston. (He was better when calling, in the late forties, for a pre-emptive nuclear strike against Stalin.) Newman's most interesting argument, though not his most persuasive, reserved to the penultimate page of *A Grammar of Assent*, was his lengthy quotation from Napoleon "the wonderful man with the special interest in glory who swayed the destinies of Europe in the first years of this century."

It was attributed unspecifically to Lacordaire, and Napoleon was held to have stated that since "palaces sumptuous, innumerable" were not raised up to him and it was not Napoleon's image that was "triumphantly displayed in the proud city, in the open country, in the corners of streets, on the tops of mountains," nor "worn next the heart in life" and "held before the failing eyes in death," and it was not Alexander the Great or Julius Caesar, nor Napoleon himself who "has done without effort what others with lifelong struggles have not done. Can He be less than Divine?" "He," of course, is "the One who passed His years in obscurity, and who died a malefactor's death. Eighteen hundred years have gone by since that time," but "the Owner of that great name reigns.... It has possessed the world, it maintains possession.... Who is He but the Creator Himself; who is sovereign over his works, towards whom our eyes and hearts turn instinctively, because He is our Father and our God?"

Eric Voegelin and Oswald Spengler, though not principally writing on ecclesiastical matters, were magisterial theists. (I almost discouraged my first wife from marrying me by reading Spengler throughout a trip we took together to Hawaii in January 1978.) I came to look upon atheism with intellectual disdain and with fear of the potentialities of the human ego when unleashed from any sense of cosmic proportion and spirituality. I never expect to hear disenthralled voices, but I accept Newman's view that our conscience, "powerful, peremptory, unargumentative, irrational, minatory and definitive," is God speaking in our minds.

It was not until 1986 that I formally converted to Roman Catholicism and began going to church regularly. I eventually reasoned that from belief in the existence of a deity it was a comparatively easy step to believe that that deity had heavily influenced Christ (though not Christ alone) and that Christ invited St. Peter to found a church and that the Roman Catholic Church, "for all its inanities, vulgarities and compromises" (as Léger once put it to me) is the legitimate continuator of the early Christians.

Logically, once launched on this course, it was not possible for me to avoid the conclusion that if I wished to communicate with the creator of the universe, the surest means, though neither a sure means nor the only means of doing so, was to receive the sacraments from the Roman Catholic priesthood. Once intellect and intuition united to convince me that spiritual life was real and useful, I was resistless against the benign temptations of religious practice, though my adherence was delayed for seven years awaiting the annulment of my first wife's first marriage and has been well short of zealous since.

I read the relevant thoughts of many other prominent converts besides Newman, including Edith Sitwell and Evelyn Waugh, and especially Chesterton and his desire "to be rid of my sins," and discussed it with Muggeridge. I did have some sympathy for Rebecca West, who gave up her Catholic preparations when she tired of being sermonized to by homosexual priests. I even found

Marshall McLuhan's comments on the same subject, unlike most of his reflections, rather profound.

Fortunately, my Catholic religious instruction consisted of countless pleasant evenings over fine claret in the home of Emmett Cardinal Carter, reciting Newman and others to each other. "I looked in the mirror and saw a monophysite," said Newman, the cardinal reminded me in one of his Christmas cards. I eventually concluded that I believed in the occasional occurrence of miracles and that if a miracle can happen, logically any miracle can, even the virgin birth and the physical ascension of Christ. But I couldn't go further than to acknowledge that they and other such scientifically improbable events might have happened.

The cardinal assured me I was still eligible, as long as I accepted the resurrection, "without which," His Eminence unequivocally averred, of his entire personal faith and professional life "it is all a fraud and a trumpery." Dear and deeply respected friend though Cardinal Carter already was, I could not fail to admire him even more as a highly learned and talented person who had frankly gambled his entire life on an intelligent and precise act of faith.

I was finally received with my elder son in Cardinal Carter's residential private chapel, June 18, 1986. It was not a wrenching change and I renounced nothing.

I had never been seriously encouraged to consider Protestantism otherwise than as a congregationalist gesture by those who found agnosticism imprudent or unsustainable. This has usually been my experience of practising high-church Protestants. Most have been best defined as Christians who aren't papists, with almost as much doubt as faith, as much goodwill as eternal truth, and often, as much fear of atheism, popery, and the rabbinical persuasion as intellectual sectarian attachment.

Caught between a limited need for spirituality and fear of surrendering too much authority to an autonomous or even internationally directed episcopate, orthodox Protestantism is generally too heavily conditionalized to be more than congregational national churches. Sailing, as Newman wrote 150 years ago, and despite the sincerity of many intelligent adherents, "through the channel of no meaning between the Scylla and Charybdis of yes and no . . . They can not go on forever standing on one leg, or sitting without a chair, or walking with their feet tied, or like Tityrus's stags, grazing in the air." Not forever, perhaps, but for at least another century and a half from when Newman wrote.

Nor are they the party of legitimacy. Luther's and Knox's schismatic endeavours are more commendable heresies than Henry VIII's desire to plunder the monasteries and divorce his unoffending wife in order to marry another whom he shortly executed on a trumped-up charge of adultery and for failing to produce a male heir (though the heir she had produced, Elizabeth I, became the greatest monarch in British history). The followers of none of them have really deposed the incumbent as the true Catholic Church.

The evangelists and fundamentalists are inaccessible to my academic interest, though not to my respect for their faith. I continue to be entirely tolerant of the full range of beliefs and disbeliefs, of intense religious observance and complete abstention. With religion, as with sex, people should do what they want, avoid what they don't want, be discreet, and respect the views of others. I had never been altogether happy with my Anglican confirmation by my principal at Upper Canada College, the ineffably unspiritual Cedric Sowby. I was equally unpersuaded by the nihilistic atheism of my father. I have no desire or standing to proselytize, but I concluded that atheism is barren, unremitting, and illogical. Of course spiritual forces exist; of course there is a God by some definition, before whom humility is appropriate, if not required. The world is not just an accident and life is sacred in general and valuable, though not inviolable in all cases. "Can He be," asked Napoleon of Christ, "less than Divine?" I think not, and by 1986 I had lived in evasive apostasy long enough.

Like any institution that tries to unite the celestial and terrestrial, the Roman Catholic Church is partly enshrouded in the haze of human error, as in the absurdity of its professed prohibition of birth control, divorces, and some of its socialistic nostrums. I have on two occasions been severely discountenanced by divorce provisions, but no institution based on universality, permanence, and eternal truth exists chiefly for the convenience of any individual. Such episodes may affect my practice but not my beliefs.

The spectacle of septuagenarian celibates endeavouring to overmanage the world's sex life, like the foolish economic preachings of clerics beatifically ignorant of the material world, if taken too literally, can demean the institution and trivialize the faith. They are counsels of perfection, like the Sermon on the Mount.

In 1987, I was commissioned by the Canadian Jesuit publication, *Compass*, to review the published social opinion of the Canadian Catholic Bishops since World War II. They evolved from robust counsels of self-help and strenuous opposition to fixed equality of income through to the late sixties to, in 1971, the equation by the Social Affairs Commission of the bishops, which proved not to be representative of the episcopate, much less the faithful, of affluence to "violence." The Social Affairs Commission asserted in 1971 that Canadian "economic and political injustice" was "worse" than "terrorist aggression" and, in 1972, launched an unholy assault on the "narrow prison of individualism."

All the problems of the Third World were the fault of advanced countries; Julius Nyerere was an economic genius; the Sandinistas were wholly benign; the Western deployment of Euromissiles was mistaken and would achieve no concessions from the Russians. The suppression of Solidarity in Poland and the Russian invasion of Afghanistan, when they occurred, were unexceptionable. Technology and capital were the principal "enemies" of social progress. Ronald Reagan's ambition was to wage nuclear war unilaterally, the Korean airliner KAL 007 might as well have crashed as a result of spontaneous engine failure, and, in 1969, most distressingly of all, "the Church is called to be a gadfly . . . in the manner of ancient prophets, Jesus Christ, and such modern martyrs as Martin Luther King and the Kennedys."

As I wrote in the *Globe and Mail Report on Business Magazine* in 1987: "None of the above was a gadfly, Jesus' role in particular is usually considered to be more exalted, especially by Christian ecclesiastics. The Church has a higher role to perform than the Kennedys (the comparison with that family, given some of the Kennedys' better publicized antics and proclivities, is bizarre). And who is it that calls the Church to this banal and possibly heretical destiny?"

The answer was a few silly and contemptible Canadian bishops, but the problem of trendy clerics mouthing socialist platitudes and depicting God as our pal jogging along beside us is quite widespread.

Obviously, if this sort of bunkum had to be taken seriously rather than as incandescently fallible, neither I nor any other serious person could continue in the Faith. Man is rarely God and fadishness is only occasionally eternal truth and it doesn't normally require superhuman intuition to distinguish them. (This, predictably given its tenor and subject, was the one piece I have written that was nominated for a National Magazine award. It lost out to Elaine Dewar's monstrous libel of the Reichmanns.)

The shortcomings or excesses of the clergy do not make God's existence and supremacy and entitlement to the adherence of people less clear. I do commend Catholicism to those so inclined. It is not a panacea, but it is sane, rigorous, and consoling, and the human spirit and intelligence can be comfortable within it.

My father used to cite the French philosophical aphorism that life leads "to suicide or the foot of the cross." I believe the choice need not be so stark, but he and others of my acquaintance who avoided any serious intellectual effort to reconcile themselves to the unkind limitations imposed in the nature of life paid a heavy price in mental strife.

These were pleasant days in Quebec, touring around the provinces and researching its recent history with Rumilly, pursuing my course at McGill, which consisted of my own studies and an occasional monologue to undergraduates about Duplessis and helping to build our company. Almost all my guiding principles were in place. I believe in God and human freedom, including economic freedom, the right of people to most of their incomes, other than during great national or social emergencies. The only basis for a successful economic system was individual incentives. The process of taking money from people who had earned it and giving it to people who hadn't earned it in exchange for their votes had to be approached with great caution. I respected almost all nations, admired many, and loved a few, especially my own, but Canada's future and even survival depended, I was sure, on the relationship of the English and the French becoming a source of strength and not of weakness. I had the beginnings of both a purpose and an occupation.

CHAPTER FOUR

THE TWILIGHT OF *BONNE ENTENTE*
1972–1974

I HAD MOVED INTO THE PORT ROYAL BUILDING in November 1971. It was the tallest and one of the most comfortable buildings on Sherbrooke Street. To someone in my position, something approaching a seventies update on *La Dolce Vita* was not hard to come by. I lived within walking distance of scores of fine restaurants, bars, and nightclubs. Permissiveness and promiscuity, symbolic of liberation from everything from puritanism and lack of spontaneity to the "people who gave you the Vietnam War," were an endemic contagion.

The social and (in Quebec) clerical humbugs of restraint and self-sacrifice were rejected. The medical dangers of too intense or undiscriminating a sex life were unsuspected. Women of all shapes and ages up to the threshold of senior citizenship seemed to join a febrile competition for contraceptive use. For those of us who had started out on the long, often pathetically funny track to adulthood, pursuing the Sisyphean burden of the obligation to seduce, it was a pleasantly unexpected experience to be almost aggressively sought out as a sexual partner, and not always, to my humble astonishment, by unseemly claimants. The fashion was rebellion, in couture as elsewhere. It was an intoxicating time and place. Montreal was a unique intersection of North American and French life, of intense Quebec nationalism and lingering Canadian fraternalism, a haven for the fugitive U.S. left, and the beleaguered fortress of ancient

French-Quebec isolationism. It was a shore on which lapped many ebbing and flowing tides. It wasn't in international terms an important place, but it was fun.

In any less sexually energetic era, I would not have had the ample experience I did. Certainly my natural heterosexual aptitudes, while rather ardently motivated, were limited by natural shyness: a residue of private-school awkwardness, sundry minor inhibitions, and a formalism of dress and manner that were at first so ludicrously uncontemporary as to be judged by a merciful few almost alluring. While never much to write home about at any stage of social intercourse, I made what my preparatory school teachers would have called "steady progress."

Agreeable though this rather sybaritic life of publisher, historian, post-graduate student, political dabbler, and self-help analysand was, Quebec, and Montreal in particular, inspired growing doubt about the permanence of these arrangements. I went in 1972 to a performance of the movie *Cabaret* with a planturous, whisky-swilling French-Canadian securities block-trader, who was my usual companion at the time, and suggested there were some parallels between Berlin in the early thirties and Montreal forty years later, *toute proportion gardée*.

Obviously, there were not organized or uniformed gangs of street toughs in Montreal. I knew Quebec well enough to know how decent and well-adjusted most French Canadians were. Yet there were a good many violent strikes with overtly racist and heavily ideological overtones. The labour minister had been sadistically murdered in 1970, martial law imposed, a British diplomat kidnapped, and there was a good deal in the rhetoric of the separatists, now the province's second largest party, to excite legitimate fears.

In the spring of 1970 I objected so vocally to striking Post Office demonstrators burning the Canadian flag in Dominion Square in Montreal in protest against federal institutions that I was challenged to settle the issue in a *bousculade* (punch-up), but proposed rational discussion instead and eventually repaired with my adversaries, most amiably, to a tavern, in the very best French-Canadian tradition of contestation settlement.

In 1971, Peter White and I had occasion to call upon Paul Desmarais at Claude Wagner's request to pursue the possibility of Wagner as the Union Nationale leader. Paul was in the midst of a *La*

Presse strike and a supposed boycott of Power Corporation products and services. A woman had been killed a few nights before at a demonstration at *La Presse*. Paul was gaunt and haggard, though not defeatist. Also at Wagner's request, we went on to see Claude Ryan in his publisher's office at *Le Devoir*, to discuss the same subject. Seated under a portrait of the newspaper's founder, Henri Bourassa, and an immense crucifix (the Archdiocese of Montreal was then effectively the co-owner of *Le Devoir*), Claude Ryan was immeasurably fatigued.

Both Desmarais and Ryan were unbowed by the difficult political climate in the province, but neither was a reassuring figure of strength or optimism either. Desmarais favoured Masse; Ryan was already leaning to Lévesque, whom he endorsed in the 1976 election. We went on to see Mayor Drapeau, who was his usual energetic but somewhat paranoid self and tended to regard Montreal as a seething hotbed of subversives and latent terrorists. When he took off his glasses, I noticed for the first time that he was easily transformed from the humorous bespectacled little round head who so delighted the caricaturists to a table-pounding Francoesque authoritarian Latin leader.

The only prominent Quebecker we encountered on that day who seemed rested, optimistic, and in top form was Jean Beliveau, the hockey star who throughout his brilliant career had combined elegance, virtuosity, and sportsmanship. (We parked next to each other in the Place Ville Marie garage.)

At about this time I encountered a rather sodden Doug Harvey, the great retired Canadiens' defenceman, at the Montreal Men's Press Club. To make conversation I asked whether, when Maurice (Rocket) Richard had retired, the vote to succeed him as team captain had been close between Jean Beliveau and Bernard (Boom Boom) Geoffrion. Harvey replied, "There was the Rocket and there was me. The rest were jerks. I followed the Rocket." He did no such thing, but waterlogged though he was, with his muscles rippling out from under his T-shirt, I didn't pursue the point with him.

By 1972, the shining goal of *bonne entente* was becoming rather problematical. Too often I had seen people enter a store in Montreal and, if they spoke no French at all, be addressed in French. If they spoke French haltingly or with an English accent, they would be addressed in the shopkeeper's usually rather irksome and laboured

English. An ever-growing number of French Canadians seemed to be addicted to the notion that bilingualism was impossible as well as undesirable. It was, said one of my French-speaking Laval law school friends, an "assimilationist Trojan Horse." For me, as a bilingual person who had invested a good deal of effort in becoming so, the implications of this drift were most unwelcome. I had thought we were assuaging, not inflaming the proverbial insecurities of our French-speaking compatriots, Maria Chapdelaine's "race that knows not how to die."

My nationalistic French acquaintances were almost always gracious to me personally, but seemed to regard my arrival from Ontario and prolonged immersion in the French fact, not as evidence of the pan-Canadian phenomenon that in fact had motivated me, but as confirmation of their narcissistic self-assurance that Quebec was a uniquely and endlessly interesting place. These French-Quebec nationalists tended to blame "English money" for all Quebec's shortcomings.

The old type-casting and myth-making had not been adjusted to account for the facts. English corporate political contributions and an almost ultramontane clerical hostility to social reform were held to have riveted a reactionary regime on the back of Quebec for centuries and the French province had been unable to aspire to more than survival. In fact, it was only the Church that preserved the French language from the Plains of Abraham to the rise of Duplessis. What was most eerie about these people was that I never met one who could imagine that there existed such a person as an English Canadian who could think about Canada as these Quebeckers thought about Quebec.

Canada, they apparently unthinkingly assumed, was a mere stratagem of the Anglo-Americans to anaesthetize Quebec by smothering it in the embrace of this lumpen English-Canadian excrescence of the two (admittedly) great Anglo-Saxon powers. Some even had the effrontery to claim that it was Quebec's misfortune not to be harnessed to the British or Americans, but rather to their pallid Canadian replication. I pointed out, with some piquancy, that all of French Quebec would sink without a ripple in metropolitan Chicago.

Their rhetoric was becoming increasingly tiresome also. René Lévesque had taken to referring to the six constituencies his partisans had won in the 1970 election as "liberated counties." I went in 1972, as the guest of a very intelligent French-Canadian woman lawyer I was going with at the time, to a talk at the Cercle Universitaire in Montreal given by Lévesque's parliamentary leader, Dr. Camille Laurin, a psychoanalyst. In his address, every organ of the body and every conceivable sexual and scatological maladjustment was trotted out in allegorical parody of Canadian politics, from minor pubescent problems to the most severe psychoses. Glib, racist, and relentlessly mocking of anyone who didn't share his irredentist fervour, Laurin was a singularly unappealing spokesman for his profession and for his preferred political option, which, for all its cranky intolerance, seemed inexplicably to gain support.

By the spring of 1972, Claude Wagner had become a figure of topical interest again. Eddie Goodman, with labour lawyer Brian Mulroney as his local operative, and others, approached Wagner to become a federal Conservative candidate in the general election that was expected in the autumn. Brian Mulroney had gone through the Laval law school in the same year as Peter White, Michael Meighen, and George Maclaren and had been intensely active at successive echelons of Conservative Party affairs, starting with his leadership of St. Francis Xavier University's Youth for Diefenbaker movement at the 1956 Conservative convention. He was a sixteen-year-old freshman then and was held up as an example of commendable fervour by the Youth for Diefenbaker elders, Hal Jackman and Ted Rogers, Toronto law seniors who sent him out at four a.m. to put up more Diefenbaker signs in the snow. Mulroney returned, almost frost-bitten, at six a.m. to find his chiefs slipping into the arms of Morpheus, heavily assisted by brandy, but everlastingly impressed by his zeal.

Wagner had expressed concern about his financial security if he abandoned the bench again, having been a Liberal appointee originally and a Union Nationale appointee in 1970. Goodman, a remarkably effective political organizer, corporate director, and builder of a large law firm, combined the arts of political backroom work with an extensive knowledge of British political and parliamentary history.

He was able to assemble a fund widely estimated at $300,000 for Wagner, a fact that was duly leaked and that gave rise to an eventual storm of allegations about a "slush fund," even up to militant Liberal

Claude-Armand Sheppard's spurious book suggesting that Goodman and Wagner had violated the Criminal Code prohibition against suborning a judge. It was all relatively innocuous, in fact, but Wagner suffered from his inability to accept any question touching upon his own probity without becoming so peevish that he was incapable of substantively addressing the question.

I always felt that he would have been much more useful in the provincial arena, and his limitations much less glaring. He frightened Bourassa and could have inconvenienced Lévesque, but Trudeau took little notice of him. If his eventual backers had supported him for the Union Nationale, I doubt that the Parti Québécois would have been elected. It won in 1976 only when the English Quebeckers, disgusted at Bourassa's discriminatory language legislation, bolted to a slightly rejuvenated Union Nationale led by Rodrigue Biron, an amiable charlatan from Lotbinière who eventually defected to the Parti Québécois.

Quebec could have been satisfied with a non-separatist alternative to Bourassa in 1976 just as Ontario in 1990 would have been happy with a less than ultra-socialist alternative to David Peterson. There was none. Wagner was clearly available in 1971, but the Quebec political establishment had less financial muscle and practical astuteness, at least in assessing the potentialities of Claude Wagner, than its Toronto federal analogues (though it must be said that political fixers are a dime a dozen, but, in Canada, there is only one Eddie Goodman). I didn't, in those times, possess the ability materially to influence such developments.

Wagner really only had two ideas, Law and Order and Federalism but since, unlike Bourassa, he at least believed unambiguously in that, he would have defended and promoted those concepts, as the polls indicated, with a great deal more credibility and panache than Bourassa. In his first term, Bourassa was just a mealy-mouthed manoeuvrer manipulated by his hangers-on and always appearing to be a fugitive from a CEGEP model parliament, a poltroon masquerading as a *chef*.

I spent August 1972 in Prince Edward Island, having an enjoyable first sojourn in the Atlantic provinces, and I came back from Prince Edward Island to be present at the announcement of Claude Wagner's election candidacy in September in Montreal. David Radler was gratified to find all his old stalwart Union Nationale friends from the Renaissance Club present at the Queen Elizabeth

Hotel "like a row of vacuum cleaners," as he said. Claude spoke well and it was hoped by Conservatives that he could bring to an end the long-standing tribal one-party system in federal elections in Quebec.

It was practically impossible to win a general election without significant support from Quebec. Not counting the coalition of 1917, the federal Conservatives had won only three parliamentary majorities since the death of Sir John Macdonald in 1891. They had turned out Sir Wilfrid Laurier with the connivance of Henri Bourassa in 1911, electing twenty-four Quebec MPs out of sixty-five. R.B. Bennett took twenty-five MPs from Quebec in 1930, riding the Depression and the Beauharnois scandal to victory over Mackenzie King. In 1958 Maurice Duplessis had turned his party and its prodigious treasury and organization inside out to avenge himself on the federal Liberals who had intervened against him in 1939. Duplessis was chiefly responsible for sending fifty Conservative MPs from Quebec to Ottawa in 1958.

I was reasonably supportive of Trudeau, despite his extravagant liberal economic policies and his vulnerability to almost any fad that surfaced in the world. From zero economic growth to the Third Option (which conspicuously failed to de-emphasize trade with the United States), to the Second Track, his sophomoric arms-control plan (which he earnestly discussed with such unspeakable personalities as Nicolae Ceausescu and Erich Honecker), and North-South, which purported to group Brazilian jungle dwellers, Arabian nomads, the teeming urban poor of India, and Bushmen of Africa, as the "South," who thus bundled together, could then be helped; almost all such specious notions could be assured of Trudeau's enthusiastic support.

His incitement of ethnic, occupational, regional, and sexual groups debased public policy and ultimately almost bankrupted the country. He, more than anyone, turned Canada into a people of whining politically conformist welfare addicts.

I was even prepared to rise above Trudeau's foreign policy misadventures: his fraternization with left-wing Third World leaders and flattery of the Russians with whose authoritarian methods he appeared to be more at home than with the chronically disorganized Americans. I never thought he was anti-American; he was appalled at its chaos and didn't get on well with its leaders, except for Carter, whose manifest unsuitability to the presidency he never understood.

I used to see him in New York, where he loved the celebrities, the glamour, variety, and irrepressible energy of the city. He wasn't anti-American, he just didn't know or understand the country.

I was able to assimilate what I considered Trudeau's appalling policy shortcomings, because on the greatest issue he had to face, relations between English and French Canadians, he was creative, tenacious, and, for many years, indispensable. I was at this time such a devoted federalist and so committed to my vision of co-operative French-English relations, I was more concerned with the preservation of the federal state than with its mismanagement.

Canada's *raison d'être* as a country independent of the United States had long consisted of a patchwork of attachment to the British connection, the existence of the French fact, and a fear, sometimes diffuse, sometimes virulent, of the Americans. René Lévesque said to me in 1974 that no English Canadian could explain Canada, and I tested his theory on many prominent English-speaking Canadians. It was not long before they descended into platitudes about alleged Canadian friendliness, the burning of the autumn leaves, migratory birds, the great outdoors, the Canadian shield — everything but Mounties in red tunics.

Since I read the first volume of de Gaulle's wartime memoirs in 1955, I had been convinced that there could not be any rigorous or durable reason for Canada to exist if the English and French Canadians did not fundamentally think they were fortunate to have each other to share a country with. If Quebec did not believe that, it would probably go its own way, eventually, after riffling through every benefit the Canadian Treasury could be badgered into conferring upon it as an incitement to remain in Confederation.

Trudeau had addressed precisely this lacuna, this collapsed lung of Canadian federalism, by his program of a bicultural country whose functioning would be guaranteed by a federal state with an adequate jurisdiction to do so. When he said in his address to the Liberal Convention in April 1968, "*Maîtres chez nous mais pour tout le Canada,*" it was the most brilliant political formulation I had ever heard in that country.

I used to say to my separatist friends at Laval University that every vote for the secession of Quebec was a vote to make me a citizen of an expanded United States, a not altogether disagreeable fate.

Yet it was unhealthy for Canada to be, federally, a one-party state with a greater resemblance, in that respect, to Mexico, which had had the same governing party since 1928, than to the United States or the United Kingdom, each of which alternated governing parties with some frequency. For decades the principal opposition to the government of Canada had come not from the forgettable sequence of Conservative leaders who had been put up against Mr. King (Manion, Hanson, Bracken) but from the premiers of Quebec, Ontario, and to some extent, Alberta. Johnson, Robarts, and Lougheed had bulked more heavily in constitutional matters than Robert Stanfield. It was especially important to have an alternative to the Liberals because their performance had, in almost all other respects except defending federal prerogatives, been abominable.

Because the government of the country was conducted in a welter of concurrent jurisdictions, jurisdictional strife was constant. No one was really satisfied with the division of constitutional powers; no one had much faith in the institutions of Canada's federal state, except for a few eccentrics who made their livelihoods from it, such as the amiable crank Eugene Forsey, with whom I maintained a sporadic correspondence on constitutional minutiae for some years.

Into this vortex of indifference, confusion, and jurisdictional abrasions, Trudeau alighted like Prometheus, but for the system to work, both parties must have a chance to win. Jack Pickersgill told me in 1962 that "the Liberals are the party of government; the Conservatives are like the mumps, you get them once in your life." The Conservatives were not, in conventional parlance, a party at all; they were a hodgepodge of disparate elements who weren't Liberals — disgruntled prairie farmers, grumbling Bay Streeters, and a few add-ons.

For the Conservatives to become a viable alternative, they would have to have the possibility of gaining some constituencies in Quebec. There was no Henri Bourassa or Maurice Duplessis to make sizeable depredations for them. For that to happen, they needed a candidate who could appeal to Quebec. Claude Wagner was the man, since he couldn't be fitted into the role of the non-separatist alternative to the provincial Liberals. This second prize was the source of my interest in Wagner, not any illusion that he was endowed with an exemplary aptitude for great offices of state.

It had been arranged for Wagner to succeed John Diefenbaker's former junior minister Théogène Ricard, as candidate in St.-Hyacinthe, a constituency that had been kept relatively safe for him by the late provincial member, Daniel Johnson (as Brome-Missisquoi had been for Grafftey by Jean-Jacques Bertrand, and, in his time, Trois-Rivières for Léon Balcer by Duplessis himself).

Peter and I drove out to St. Hyacinthe with Wagner to get his campaign rolling, and we drove around the constituency with him, from the market to the plants of several of the big employers, and back to Montreal. Wagner seemed to expect that Quebec would rally to him by virtue of his presence alone. He was "the tip of the lance" of public opinion composed of the average man and not the state.

Peter made the point, after travelling up the North Shore with him, that Wagner was "a Frankenstein monster"; he had been assembled from a Candidate Kit (a Jewish-German father, a Franco-Ontarian Catholic mother) but if the doctors were not careful, he would arise from his table and lurch about uncontrollably. He was temperamental, sluggish, and unco-operative and frequently refused to adhere to his schedule for no apparent reason other than to show he was indifferent to his minders.

My brother was never a particularly politically involved person, but he had his likes and dislikes. One of those public figures whom he found not at all to his liking was Robert Stanfield, whom he regarded as a drab red Tory who was inordinately vain in ever imagining that he could defeat Trudeau. One morning at the start of October, there was a news report from Montreal that Stanfield had spoken at a large political dinner, recognizing specifically Claude Wagner and Senator Jacques Flynn, but not Heward Grafftey, who, according to news reports, had to be restrained from assaulting his leader.

My brother was usually an earlier riser than I was and telephoned me at seven a.m. to say, "I'm sorry to awaken you but I just wanted to ask you to tell your friend Heward Grafftey that if he goes ahead and actually punches Stanfield, in the presence of authenticating witnesses, I will personally contribute $10,000 to his election campaign." I transmitted the message but Heward never earned the incentive.

I was a poll captain for my friend Michael Meighen, who ran as a Conservative candidate in Westmount against veteran Liberal minister Bud Drury. I was mainly responsible for the Port Royal building poll and I canvassed vigorously, but it was obviously a heavily entrenched Liberal district. English-speaking Montreal was helplessly attached to the view that it owed its language and everything else to the Liberals. (In fact, the articulate, bilingual Michael Meighen was a good deal more likely to defend the English language in Quebec than Bud Drury, a unilingual appeaser and fugitive from the province who now lived full time in Ottawa.)

On election day, 1972, Michael cut Drury's 1968 lead (over my father's old university classmate Murray Ballantyne) in half; Wagner and Grafftey won and were the only Progressive Conservatives from Quebec. Wagner had held a safe constituency but his coat-tails had been snipped off at the waist band. Trudeau had been badly shelled in other regions and limped in with 109 MPs, including, for the first time, Jeanne Sauvé and Marc Lalonde, and Stanfield had 107. We had the makings of an overall two-party system, but the clearest division there had been since the First World War between the party preferences of French and English Canadians.

In early 1972 David, inspired by his consulting work with some of Quebec's native people, and by statistics showing Sept-Iles as the most prosperous city in Canada, bought the local semi-weekly newspaper, *L'Avenir*. The vendor was a former helicopter pilot, Norman Despard, a virtually unilingual English-Canadian north-country pioneer of the old school. He ran a bilingual newspaper and always saw off the competition because of the rock-solid loyalty of the English fifth of the population.

Sept-Iles owed its transition from a sleepy whaling village and Indian post to a bustling city of 25,000 to the iron ore business, and specifically the Iron Ore Company of Canada. The initial ore bodies had been owned and rented by Hollinger Consolidated Gold Mines Ltd. and its subsidiary, Labrador Mining and Exploration Company, which were controlled jointly by Argus Corporation and the Timmins, Dunlap, and McMartin families, but in which the McMartins' cousin and then Argus Corporation Chairman, John A. (Bud) McDougald, was the leading influence.

In the late forties, when the Mesabi iron range in Minnesota and Michigan was running down, and before the beneficiation process had been discovered to extend its life, a group of major American steel companies, led by Bethlehem and National and co-ordinated by the M.A. Hanna company in Cleveland and its chairman, George M. Humphrey (subsequently President Eisenhower's secretary of the Treasury), organized the Iron Ore Company of Canada.

This was one of the world's most ambitious industrial projects at the time and involved constructing a railway 320 miles north from Sept-Iles over tundra to the new mining town of Schefferville, and building huge ore and concentrate processing and handling facilities in Labrador City and Sept-Iles.

Sept-Iles was, in fact, in Duplessis county. In deference to the fact that Duplessis had developed the area and died in Schefferville, city councillor Pierre-Julien Cloutier and I led a campaign, with the encouragement of Robert Rumilly's letter to *L'Avenir*, to unveil Duplessis's famous statue on the Vieux Quai at Sept-Iles in 1972.

Sept-Iles had some of the attractions and all of the shortcomings of a frontier town. It was the most northeasterly point on the North American mainland to which it was possible to drive. Beyond it, across the Moisie River on the lower North Shore of the St. Lawrence, were isolated, desolate, picturesque fishing ports: Natashguan, Kegaska, Havre-St. Pierre, Blanc Sablon. Even a helicopter trip along this rugged fortress was enough to explain Jacques Cartier's alleged comment on first seeing the same landscape in 1534: "It is the land God gave to Cain."

I had become a devotee of the less remote bank of the St. Lawrence, from Baie St. Paul to Tadoussac, when I was a student at Laval University, and particularly liked to watch from the point at Tadoussac where, 600 feet deep, the Saguenay rushes into the St. Lawrence, frequently, from May to September, causing whales to surface in bewilderment.

Sept-Iles is on the Gulf of St. Lawrence, is frequented by 100,000-ton ore carriers, and retains only a few evidences of the explorers' or coureurs de bois past; the old lighthouse, an Indian church, and a few remnants of whaling times and the *Vieux Post des Montagnais* (which had gone broke as a restaurant several times, but which David had been well-paid by the federal government for trying to make viable; when he and I went to dinner there in 1973 his first words were, "They still have those lousy uncomfortable chairs").

The population, except for a few English managers like Despard, and a few French-Canadian professionals and small-businessmen, was a rough-and-ready catchment of labourers, busted-out adventurers, hucksters, and street-wise women who had fetched up at this last-stop end-of-the-earth to make their last stand. Winters were unimaginably cold, the people rumbustious, there was more sand than soil (when the snow had melted), the drinking water was discoloured, the principal architectural feature was the mobile home, and the quality of spoken French was the most raspingly uneuphonious I have ever heard.

Yet the region had its attractions. The houses I visited were the homes of sturdy, hospitable people, with jovial and witty conversation around the dinner table, crucifixes proudly and prominently displayed. Many had interesting stories of the growth of the region from howling wilderness to its then tenuous state of civilization.

By May 1972 Sept-Iles was riven by internecine strife between Quebec's labour unions. The C.S.N. and the F.T.Q., heirs respectively of Quebec's Catholic (Confédération des Syndicats Nationaux) and international (Fédération du Travail du Québec) union traditions, were warring for control of the local steelworkers. The C.S.N. was then led by Quebec's most accomplished rabble-rousers, Marcel Pepin, and the Jew-baiting former monk, Michel Chartrand. The F.T.Q. was led by Louis Laberge, who in those days was comparatively lucid. Gangs of partisans roamed about Sept-Iles, attacking each other with lengths of pipe and construction tools, tens of people were injured, and pandemonium reigned.

Our publisher in Sept-Iles had to hire a pontoon plane to fly *L'Avenir* to Rimouski to have it printed there and returned to the North Shore. When I flew to Sept-Iles in the midst of these problems, and boarded the daunting Quebecair seven a.m. flight from Montreal to Sept-Iles, a very intoxicated, dumpy, smelly, dishevelled little French Canadian bumbled on to the plane just before the gate was closed and persuaded the stewardess, in best libertarian Quebecair manner, to open the bar. When we arrived in Sept-Iles after almost two hours, which this little habitant had whiled away, sozzling and belching, he could hardly walk, but he insisted, because of his mission of *salut national*, on deplaning first. He did, but, after weaving along the aisle, he fell down the ramp, broke his leg, and was conveyed away to hospital in an ambulance. He had the consolation of reading, the next day on the front-page of *Le Devoir*, if he had dried out sufficiently by then for his eyes to focus, that he had been "gloriously injured in the service of Quebec."

I had my own labour problem in Sept-Iles in early 1973. We moved into a new building, bought our own press, and were contemplating going daily, but our publisher lost control of events and the journalists announced they were forming a union. I flew to Sept-Iles and after a brief discussion with the editor, who was the ostensible leader of the union certification movement, concluded that the paper, which was already losing money, could not afford either accommodation of union demands or a strike. The editorial product was mediocre and was not retaining paid subscribers in numbers adequate to prevent steady inroads from a competing free sheet. The journalists involved were quite explicit in their intent to run a crusading separatist socialist paper to help the C.S.N. in the local squabbling with the F.T.Q. Accordingly, I fired the entire editorial department of four people, purportedly for cause (professional incompetence).

Naturally, in the parlance of labour law, they grieved, i.e., took out a grievance against me. The publisher and I did the reporting for a while and then gradually scabbed it. We went to the Quebec Labour Board, sitting in the Superior Court in Sept-Iles, in June 1973. My counsel was Philip Matthews, an understudy of Brian Mulroney's at Ogilvy, Cope, and a most genial and entertaining character. I took most of our remaining personnel out to dinner in relays; they certainly had no interest in a union and a number of them testified convincingly to that effect. There were considerable demonstrations around our building and I was greeted with a hail of racist slurs by union thugs at each coming and going for a couple of weeks, but responded good-naturedly. The majority of the employees were not impressed with either the billingsgate or the Marxist rhetoric of the C.S.N. stooges.

Opposing counsel was the brother of my old law dean, Louis Marceau. His name was Robert, but Philip Matthews, assumedly confusing him with the famous mimist, continually called him Marcel. When I suggested that wasn't his name, he loudly exclaimed, in open court, "I don't give a damn what his name is, but the dumb son-of-a-bitch answers to Marcel!"

One evening, after the fourth day of the trial, I bought a case of beer to distribute among loyal employees, but Philip and I stopped at our hotel, drank the beer ourselves, sinking into armchairs in front of my hotel window and watching the northern sunset descend on Sept-Iles.

Philip was so antagonistic to our opponents and to the town generally, that he changed from Quebecair to a later Air Canada flight to avoid travelling with Marceau and left a stool unflushed in the toilet of his bathroom in the hotel as a parting salutation. We eventually wore down the C.S.N., paid one and a half times normal severance to the dismissed reporters, and carried on uncertified. Yet despite the support of most employees and Philip Matthews's fine advocacy and exquisite companionship, the whole episode, written up in overtly racist terms in Quebec's *Le Soleil* and *Québec-Presse*, and kindly covered on the French CBC (Radio-Canada), was another blow to my fading dreams of Anglo-French-Canadian co-operation.

We were being continually harassed by advertisers who acknowledged that they were racially and politically motivated (the North Shore was notoriously separatist). It was a constant struggle with such companies as Hudson's Bay and Steinberg's, intervening at their head offices to have their local managers "persuaded" to advertise with us.

While I was fighting it out in court in Sept-Iles, David was trying to sell Sterling Newspapers to Power Corporation. At one point, I entertained the hope that I could announce to my pretentious little labour tribunal that henceforth they could deal with Paul G. Desmarais (by now Quebec's most famous businessman). The Power Corporation offer eventually came in at $2.5 million. Since we had been asking $6 million, I only said to John Rae, Paul Desmarais's able and genial assistant at the time, that that wasn't "a serious offer." He was too polite to respond that we didn't have a serious company either, and we soldiered on. (These discussions took place in our little office in the Peel Centre building where we had two desks and four folding chairs. One day when Fred Eaton and Douglas Bassett visited us with the Baton treasurer, Joe Garwood, Joe had to sit on the window sill.) Our motive in thinking of selling was that we were increasingly dubious about Quebec. When this deal fell through, we resolved to de-emphasize Quebec but continue to build our business elsewhere.

We started with Granby, where we owned the little English language weekly *The Leader Mail*, which had seemed so large when I was the editor of the *Knowlton Advertiser* and which Peter White and Brian Stewart and I had tried to buy from Paul Desmarais and Jacques Francoeur in 1967. We also owned *La Nouvelle Revue*, a free-distribution weekly that we had bought in 1971. David became pessimistic about *La Nouvelle Revue* when we produced a forty-eight page paper and lost money. So he kept raising the required advertising ratio and shrinking the paper. One day in 1973, when we were visiting Paul Desmarais to have one of our periodic political discussions with him, bailiffs acting for Desmarais's local manager stormed into our office in Granby and seized "everything down to the pencils" in respect of an unpaid printing bill. It was an entertaining coincidence.

The next week David and I visited the Granby office, and when a salesman complained that other sales people were stealing his accounts and asked for *"une liste de réstriction,"* David responded in his awkward but comprehensible French that it was difficult to have such a list when *"on a un journal de six pages."* We sold it a few months later to the former Union Nationale minister of public works, Armand Russell. David correctly predicted that the acquisition would bring down in shambles Russell's entire range of business interests. So it did. (Russell's indictment on various counts of ministerial misconduct didn't help his career either.) David moved a few months later to British Columbia to build our company and with the briefest interruptions has lived there ever since.

A couple of years later we bought control of a small chain of motels in British Columbia, and David spent his summer vacations driving between them reducing staff almost until he would have to say "David and Rona [his wife] welcome you to our Slumber Lodge." In the first days of our control of the company, David phoned me and said, "There is prima facie evidence our motels aren't doing well; the president of the company committed suicide yesterday." (In fact, that tragic event appeared to be linked to acute health problems.)

David operated this company with his usual efficiency to the point where, when we set out to sell it in 1990, no one could imagine making as much out of it as we already did and no satisfactory offer emerged. In early 1978 we even looked at a package tour hotel in Waikiki (Honolulu), which I would have proposed we rename "David Radler's Blue Hawaii Palace." We were discouraged, among other factors, by two girls from Winnipeg, guests in the hotel, who, when asked by me if their room was clean, replied, "Shall we tell him about Herman?" My first fears were of an aggressive rodent. Herman turned out to be only a roach but we thought better of the idea.

For a year from the spring of 1973, I toiled to sell *L'Avenir de Sept-Iles*, which was steadily losing money and sapping my divided energies. I had prolonged negotiations with the mercurial Pierre Péladeau to this end. He philosophized, discussed religion, literature, women, politics, sport, but never really came to the party. Finally, after beating the bushes, in one of the happier moments of my career, in February 1974, I managed to off-load it on Raymond Bellavance of Rimouski.

The sale was suitably farcical, as the head of the Quebec Weekly Newspapers Association (Hebdos A-1), inserted himself into the middle of events demanding commissions and double-dealing in all directions. I finally gave him one-quarter of his claimed reward and explained why he wouldn't receive more. Crestfallen and mystified, he explained that all brokers were "treacherous swindlers, otherwise they wouldn't be able to feed their families."

In the summer of 1975, when I drove down to Prince Edward Island, I stopped to pick up back cheques from Bellavance and found his office picketed by some of the same union militants who had picketed me in Sept-Iles two years before. They groaned and snorted their lack of appreciation at my arrival, and I solemnly assured them I was there to give Bellavance advice on how best to deal with striking malcontents. Raymond subsequently told me that my presence for one hour short-fused the strike and lightened the burden of the settlement, such was the reciprocal affection between the Quebec newspaper labour unions and me.

I have never had much regard for organized labour, other than when it has taken on heroic proportions as in Poland, despite my friendship with a number of labour leaders such as Cliff Pilkey and Lynn Williams. George Black had never ceased to revile labour leaders as self-seeking frauds who cared little for the workers and often were gangsters or communists. As with people in other occupations, he was also irritated by their syntactical inelegance, as with the head of the Brewery Workers Union who variously accused him during negotiations of "deviating pretty low," seeking to have him "rooneyed" (i.e., ruined), and of living in luxury in a "suit of rooms in the Royal York Hotel."

Once laws existed to protect workers against capricious or exploitive employers, most unions became enemies of productivity increases through automation, advocates of feather-bedding, and a mortal threat to any sense of community in an enterprise. In later years, with the Retail, Wholesale, and Department Storeworkers Union at Dominion Stores, and with the journalists and newspaper production unions in London and New York, I found mainly corrupt Luddites among the leadership, who were less concerned with the welfare of their membership than I was. As our company expanded in British Columbia, we had few union difficulties, especially after David Radler bought up the mortgage on the ski chalet of one of the union officials who regularly negotiated with us.

As our little drama unfolded in Sept-Iles, lesser combat erupted at McGill when my thesis on Duplessis from 1927 to 1939 was challenged by the external examiner, Ramsay Cook. Laurier LaPierre championed me vigorously, but I agreed to make some revisions along the lines Cook suggested. His letter of comment was very gratuitous and Laurier showed it to me with the letterhead and signature removed.

These external thesis readers were supposed to be anonymous, but this letter was so offensive I made it my proverbial business to find out who wrote it. Cook made some worthwhile points, but his real grievance was against any comparative rehabilitation of Duplessis or any undermining of his unicultural social democratic model for English and French Canada that, if followed, he evidently believed, would cause Quebec nationalism to be subsumed in the benign alchemy of pan-Canadian moderate socialism.

Since I had to pretend I didn't know who the outside evaluator was, I devised a reply in which I quoted some particularly fatuous comments of Cook's, without indicating that I knew of Cook's involvement in my own case. I did incorporate some of his stylistic improvements and added to the bibliography the sources he stated, though they added precisely nothing to my analysis and were only convenient reeds supporting Cook's wishful, Torontocentric, fairyland view of Quebec. Despite a desultory effort by Cook to block my M.A. degree, it was awarded in the autumn of 1973. My formal education was finally over after twenty-two often tempestuous years of scholarity, and three earned degrees.

A Quebec provincial election was called for October 1973. Bourassa's slogan was "Bourassa builds, the Opposition tears down (*Bourassa construit, L-Adversaire détruit*)." It wasn't bad. Bourassa himself was thoroughly unimpressive. Trudeau allowed that Bourassa ate "too many hot dogs"; one of his own advisers acknowledged that he had "nervous hair." Indecisive and underwhelming, he seemed a mere fabrication of the Ottawa Liberal leadership.

However, he was running on an acceptable platform of renewed federalism and continued official bilingualism while sustaining the old Johnson formula that all parents could decide their children's language of instruction, and all students would study French. The overtly separatist vote had gone from 6 per cent in 1966 to 24 per cent in 1970. The Union Nationale and the Créditistes were headed for the last round-up without Wagner or any other leader of stature.

I was in Sept-Iles for almost the last half of the election campaign, trying to supervise the installation of the new press. (This task was not made easier by the eccentricity of the Goss Company's press erector, who on one memorable evening crossed wires, igniting an electrical fire, and extinguished it by urinating on it.) We had a good time with the election in Sept-Iles. All my local opponents ardently supported the Parti Québécois candidate, the local head of the Steelworkers. Our reporting was fairly balanced for most of the campaign, but we did an editorial sand-bag job on the P.Q., complete with publication of a poll indicating a Liberal victory. There was no indication of the number of people sampled so the fact that I consulted only seven people (including myself) never came to light.

Because of my numerous appearances on local television and radio, I had been recruited by the CBC in Montreal in mid-1973 to debate with Laurier LaPierre each Monday morning, but it was a condition of work that we were to apply every effort to be there in person rather than by telephone. The subjects were presented a day before, and Laurier and I usually took absurdly extreme positions for our own amusement and were generally in foul mood at seven a.m. on Monday anyway. We raged at each other in a manner that listener response indicated was thought to be entertaining. My favourite bugbear was the teaching profession and if all else failed, I normally railed against the shortcomings of most of those who purported to teach. Less than three weeks before the election, the industry and commerce minister, Guy Saint-Pierre and I, debated Laurier and Jacques Parizeau on the question of separation and, by general agreement, we won handily.

Election day, October 29, 1973, was my last hurrah as an enthusiastic Anglo-Quebec federalist. Bourassa carried 55 per cent of the vote and 102 constituencies of 110 (including Duplessis county, Sept-Iles). The Parti Québécois increased its share of the vote from 24 per cent to 30 per cent, the Créditistes, now led by the preposterous former federal Liberal Yvon Dupuis, declined to 10 per cent, the Union Nationale to 5 per cent, and all three opposition leaders, Lévesque, Dupuis, and Loubier were defeated in their home constituencies. It "was a famous victory," but it had the slightly hollow ring of L.B.J.'s landslide before disaster of 1964 and Richard Nixon's 1972 victory before the fall.

With Bourassa in 1973 as with Duplessis's victory of 1936, it was not long before, in T.D. Bouchard's phrase "victory had its morrow and joy gave way to tears."

Quebec's endless preoccupation with assimilation, which they were supposed to have overcome with the Quiet Revolution, popped up again. Despite repeated studies showing the status of the French language more secure in Quebec than it had ever been, in the shopworn and implausible name of *la survivance*, Bourassa jettisoned his election promises to English Quebec (who provided over a third of his party's votes on October 29) and abolished English as an official language. Under his Official Language Act, Bill 22, presented in early 1974, only the children of people who were educated in English-language schools in Quebec would be eligible to attend English-language schools in the public system. The children of immigrants to Quebec would be given language aptitude tests at age six or seven, on the basis of which the government of Quebec rather than the parents involved would decide the language of instruction. Anyone hanging out a commercial sign or presenting a restaurant menu or wine list in which the French characters were not at least as large as those of any other language was subject to a $3,000 fine.

Bill 22 was a measure of dazzling illiberality. The percentage of Quebeckers who spoke principally French was increasing. The quality of spoken French in Quebec and the strength of French-language cultural institutions, such as universities and media outlets, were also steadily improving. There was orchestrated concern about immigrants assimilating to the English-speaking community, but this was absurd since, by this time, almost no one did immigrate into Quebec, so notorious had its political fractiousness and suspicious attitude to outsiders become. Virtually all immigrants to all parts of North America (north of the Rio Grande) assumed they were arriving in an English-speaking continent, not on a French-speaking postage stamp.

Ever since Quebec had followed the script so ardently wished for it by Toronto universal liberals, it had, in its lust for secularization, literally thrown the baby out (almost literally) with the bathwater and the French-Canadian birth rate, formerly legendarily prolific, had collapsed with no natural population growth and no assimilable immigrants (except a few Vietnamese, North Africans, and Haitians whom not all Québécois, for obvious reasons, rushed to welcome).

Quebec concocted the myth of being culturally endangered, resorted to Duplessis's old flim-flam of "collective rights take precedence over individual rights" and turned the screws on an economically advantaged minority. (Duplessis had invoked this dubious concept only against Jehovah's Witnesses and Communists, and then only to revoke a liquor permit and briefly padlock a few warehouses.)

Since there was no danger to the French language in Quebec in 1974, the real motive of Bourassa's Bill 22 was assumedly to squeeze the non-French out so the French-Quebec élites could take over their Westmount homes, cushy offices, and exalted socio-economic status. The objective was understandable, but it was a disappointing dénouement for the brave new world of 1960. In one of our radio debates, Laurier LaPierre genially volunteered: "We believed we were bringing light to Quebec after 1960 so we had to believe there was only darkness there before." To a *bonne ententiste*, Bill 22 was a cruel immolation of naïve but creditable dreams.

Apart from being offensive in itself, Bill 22 betrayed all those Canadians outside Quebec who had espoused French-English conciliation. Quebec, whose leaders from Duplessis onward, through the Laurendeau-Dunton commission of 1963 and the pages of *Le Devoir*, had espoused reciprocal bilingualism rather than French Canadians alone having to learn English for reasons of economic necessity, had now set itself up as Canada's most implacably unilingual jurisdiction. The ground was cut from underneath all those hundreds of thousands of English Canadians who had sent their children to French immersion schools and defended bilingual packaging and French-language television in places where there were no French-speaking people (most of the country, in fact). It was particularly painful to see the King Lear impotence of English Quebec and to watch formerly moderate French Canadians fall silent or even click heels in obedience to the tribal loyalty oath of unilingualism.

The French-Quebec nationalists could snivel and cavil as they might, but a Québécois would have to be brain-dead not to see the huge transfers of money Ottawa was making to Quebec. Trudeau would never address this issue directly, as he ostensibly objected to the entire line of reasoning, wishing to have Confederation endorsed on the intellectually higher ground of Laurieresque abstract virtue of two founding races sharing half a continent from sea to sea in Canada's century. His principal reason, I have some grounds to believe, was fear of an English-Canadian backlash when the long-suspected proportions of the fiscal inducement to Quebec became known.

It was inexpressibly galling, fifteen years later, to hear Jacques Parizeau accuse Ottawa of mismanagement for piling up a $400-billion deficit and ask rhetorically why Quebec would wish to remain in so profligate a country. Given that a large part of the debt had been incurred buying the affections of Quebec, with rateable amounts of tribute dispersed among the other smaller "have-not provinces," who never would have heard of equalization grants if Duplessis had not forced St. Laurent to recognize Quebec's concurrent right to direct taxes in 1955, Parizeau's remarks had some of the character of traditional blackmail. No sequence of payments would still the blackmailer, until the victim had paid over everything he had and then the original threat would be carried out.

When Duplessis, who headed the only provincial government that had not "rented" its right to direct taxation to Ottawa, announced in 1955 that there would be double taxation, and that St. Laurent would pay the political price for it in Quebec, the federal government allowed provincial concurrence up to 10 per cent.

In its nervosity over its *raison d'être*, Ottawa took unto itself the role of equalizer and stabilizer of regional fiscality, services, and ultimately standards of living, and the equalization grant was born.

Diefenbaker raised the provincial share of direct taxes to 13 per cent. Pearson was "bulldozed" (as John Robarts frequently said to me), by Jean Lesage (who didn't dispute the description when I asked him), to concede 50 per cent. As I wrote in my book on Duplessis, "What Duplessis, the Union Nationale rebel, was asking, Lesage, the Liberal modernizer, would take. And what St. Laurent, the Liberal defender of Canadian national integrity attempted to withhold, Pearson, the Liberal saviour of Canada, would acquiesce in gladly, in the higher interests of Canada (and of the Liberal Party)."

In the early seventies, the nightclub comedian Yvon Deschamps, had developed a routine in which he parodied the habitant worker, a French-Quebec Archie Bunker, and espoused the formula "an independent Quebec in a strong Canada." It was humorous and original, but life imitates art, and economic advantage was the only interest most French Quebeckers had in Canada.

Yet Quebeckers are not a rabble of impressionable Latin Americans waiting to be swayed by a demagogue from a balcony. They are canny and sensible people, descended from Normans and Bretons, frugal and arithmetically adept. They might drink too much in Herbert Radler's restaurant and march around the tables singing *"Il a gagné ses épaulettes"* and complain about the Queen's picture on coins and banknotes. But would they, sober, do anything financially impetuous?

Quebec wanted independence with continued fiscal transfers from Ontario and Alberta. Trudeau would force Quebec to choose, confident it would choose the money.

The bourgeois spirit of the Québécois had always prevailed over the temptations of nationalism, as Duplessis had discovered when he called the 1939 election on the issue of participation in World War II and lost. "What spoiled child, given chocolate ice-cream, doesn't demand vanilla?" John Robarts asked my brother and me of Quebec one day when he came to lunch with us in 1975.

Stanfield, Clark, and perhaps even Mulroney, I thought, would allow Quebec de facto independence, as long as it wasn't too openly proclaimed, and they would buy discretion with continued subventions, Stanfield from sincere conviction as a former (and well-respected) provincial premier, Joe from sincere naïveté, Brian, I suspected from a realistic assessment of the best reconciliation he could make of personal, provincial, and national interests. Brian, as a labour lawyer, was prone to compromise. Trudeau, as a didactic intellectual, preferred to adopt a principle and remain immovable. On these issues, whether my policy hypotheses and imputations of motives are correct or not, the Trudeau Liberals were a good deal more robust than the Conservatives.

I have always believed that Trudeau's judgement was correct, as long as Quebec could be convinced it would have to make a stark choice, that the ultimatum was real, that English Canada wouldn't pay unlimited blackmail. Quebec had to understand that it wasn't pushing on an open jurisdictional door that English Canadians unconvincingly represented as closed. I had thought for many years that there were two political options for Canada that were invested with any grandeur or interest: either a bicultural country made to work, based on mutual respect, not coercion to learn someone else's language, or a well-brokered arrangement with the United States. The latter would only arise if Quebec actually seceded, but I thought it useful to make the case that English Canada was approaching the point where it could make a better deal with the Americans than with the Québécois and had a greater ability to go it alone than Quebec did. Sovereignty-Association was a political fairyland and Quebec's separatist leaders shouldn't be allowed to suck and blow simultaneously for ever.

Not just Quebeckers, but all Canadians, are eventually going to have to decide what they want as political institutions. I believed in 1976, and still do many years later, that Canadians could accept an exchange: a wholehearted English toleration of a French fact appropriate to its numbers throughout the country, entrenched and secure, for an unconditional and irrevocable Quebec adherence to an adequately endowed federal Canadian jurisdiction.

Because it is sensible as well as idealistic, and vastly preferable to Balkanization, it should and can happen. Canada cannot have a national *raison d'être* without Quebec, and Quebec has little incentive to confer that *raison d'être* upon it if it can have all the benefits of Confederation without fully participating in Confederation and while simultaneously enjoying more and more of the pleasures of sovereignty. The version of independence on offer from Lévesque and Parizeau, all the benefits of Confederation and all the benefits of sovereignty too, was bound to attract a good deal of support.

I never took the Quebec pretence to "social democracy" too seriously. It was, despite the histrionics of some of the union leaders, journalists, and academics, just an intellectually presentable method of squeezing out the English and the Jews and taking their places.

A few weeks after Cardinal Léger's comments at the University of Montreal objecting to the spirit of Bill 22, I attended the convocation at the University of Sherbrooke for the twentieth anniversary of Duplessis's founding of that university, where both Cardinal Léger and his brother Jules, recently elevated to be governor general, received honorary degrees. The Légers were delayed because of airplane problems and had to complete a good portion of their trip from Ottawa by car.

When they arrived, the cardinal gave his customary brilliant address. A Quebec university audience in 1974, far removed from the intensely Catholic traditions of its forebears, was not, on an overly prolonged and very warm Saturday afternoon, a naturally attentive audience for a septuagenarian cardinal. We sat, rapt, without murmur or movement as he held us with rich, rapid, and stirring prose, in praise of traditional values and in precisely the lucid faultless French he had commended at the University of Montreal a few weeks before, as preferable to the restriction of other languages, "as clear as the splashing of the fountains and the chirping of the birds that descended from the branches" above the Luxembourg Gardens when he had discovered them in 1929. Thunderous and prolonged applause followed the cardinal's address.

It was very late and really uncomfortably warm when the governor general followed him to the rostrum. Unlike his brother, he was not renowned as an orator and not too much was expected. It was one of the most affecting speeches I have heard. Referring to the cardinal as *"care fratello,"* he said, "There was a man who had two sons; while they were still young, they departed, one in the service of the Church, the other in the service of the State. Their occupations took them to the ends of the earth, but always they returned to the great river on whose banks they were born, partly to renew their dreams, but mainly to catch their breath. Lacking fortune, position, and formal education, this father could only equip his sons with faith and hope, but he felt that that was all they required to make their way in the world. The honour you have done his sons, and him, today, indicates he was correct. Thank you."

Unfortunately, this was the last manifestation of the civility of traditional Quebec that I was to enjoy as a resident of that province. The fine occasion did not end well, as, just after I had been discussing, during dinner, the recently returned and elected President Juan Perón of Argentina with the governor general, who had known Perón when they were both attachés at the end of the thirties in Santiago, Chile, Jules Léger suffered a stroke. He manfully attempted to leave the dining hall under his own strength, but could not walk, and slumped onto a crate, where his brother endeavoured to comfort and encourage him, pending the arrival of an ambulance. Some surmised the governor general was intoxicated and made generous excuses for him. (The cardinal eventually administered extreme unction. His brother survived and served his full term as governor general, but never fully recovered the capacity of speech.)

English Quebec adopted its now customary division over Bill 22: half sat in the decrepit clubs and watering holes crabbing about the uppitiness of their French-speaking compatriots, but didn't actually do anything, such as leave Quebec. English Montreal tended to be rather anti-American, condescending towards the rest of Canada, and violently contemptuous of Toronto; it purported to identify with London, an affection, as far as I know, unrequited by, and unknown to, its ultramarine recipient. The other half of English Montreal pretended this assault on the English language wasn't happening, was a bore and a side-show of no significance. The first group were gin-swilling grumblers of no consequence; "noses pretty far up in the air and pretty far down in the sauce," as my father used to describe much of Westmount. The second group amply fulfilled Peter Brimelow's subsequent description of them as "dogs pathetically licking the vivisectionist's hand on the surgical table." I could not identify with either group and was now virtually a Quebec ethnic group to myself.

In May 1974, the opposition parties in Ottawa voted down the government, precipitating a general election. ("The government, yesterday, fell," said a pompous consul in the Canadian embassy in the Netherlands to Peter White, who was travelling there and who needed to know so he could return to be a Conservative candidate in London, Ontario; his slogan was: "If the price isn't right, vote White"; he won 17,000 votes and went down to honourable defeat.)

Michael Meighen ran again in Westmount, and this time I wrote several speeches for him, in addition to serving as one of his many campaign co-managers. My first speech-writing effort, the inaugural address delivered in the presence of the party leader, Robert Stanfield, has led to much subsequent mirth between us, as I denounced "the dead hand of the fatuous linguistic bureaucracy" created by Bill 22, the so-called "language police." Michael insisted we had to drop either the "dead hand" or "fatuous" and kept only the latter. The incumbent in Westmount, Bud Drury, now a carpetbagger who had decamped his residence to Ottawa, had mockingly referred to the "celebrated Bill 22," and Trudeau had no more interest in attacking the outrageous measure than King and Lapointe had in attacking or revoking (as they had the right to do) Duplessis's Padlock Law in 1937.

I was convinced the only way to make a race out of it for Michael was to attack Bill 22 and denounce the Liberals for selling out the English-Quebec bedrock of their support. My leitmotif in Michael's acceptance speech was welfare bums, and Stanfield was visibly horrified when Michael attacked "the 137,000 unemployment insurance recipients who didn't bother to pick up their cheques during the recent Post Office strike." Michael and his leader were not promoting a very robust version of conservatism and the candidate shrank from the sort of shrill measures that would alone close the gap against Drury, the incarnation of Liberal lassitude, cynicism, and inertia. Drury's majority was appreciably reduced but the reflexive Liberal herd put him back safely enough, and Trudeau regained his majority.

In the interminable hearings that droned on all spring and summer in the National Assembly committees over Bill 22, Jean-Louis Roy, the head of Quebec's civil liberties Union (Ligue des Droits de L'Homme), a position Trudeau had once held, testified in some detail. I had known him well as the head of the French-Canada Studies Centre at McGill and lent him a considerable mass of documents from the Duplessis files, which he used in a book then in progress (without bothering to acknowledge my role in providing them). Given his apparent liberality of mind, the identity of his employer, and the traditions of the group on whose behalf he testified, I dared to hope that he might dissent from the mass of petitioners and suggest that Bill 22 was disrespectful of acquired rights and liberty of expression.

Instead, he proposed that English be abolished as a language of instruction in Quebec schools one scholastic year at a time. Orwellian newspeak was ascendant, in both the outlawed and the continuing official language. (Eleven years later, when, as publisher of *Le Devoir*, he came to see me in Toronto to ask for an investment in his impecunious newspaper, I reminded him of his appearance on this occasion, and he replied that I had "a terrifying memory." I suggested that some memories of Quebec, not my memory, were the real source of terror.)

I had moved to Quebec in 1966, a refugee from the boredom and philistinism of Toronto (as well as from the vagaries of my own academic career), to make my modest contribution to enhanced mutual respect between English and French Canadians. To that end I learned French, became learned in the law of Quebec, learned and wrote about much of modern Quebec history, became a publisher of English- and French-language newspapers that were uniformly supportive of French-English conciliation, served some of Quebec's most prominent public figures in the interests of official moderation, and became a radio and television exponent to the same effect.

Now there seemed only French extremists, English Colonel Blimps, and the vast mass of the indifferent and complacent of both cultural groups. Quebec alternately commended itself on its generous treatment of its "minority" and lightly oppressed that minority. French Quebeckers were so accustomed to thinking of themselves as a beleaguered minority that they were for the most part sincerely incapable of imagining that anything they could do to the English could be unfair. English Canadians, in Quebec and elsewhere, alternately grumbled and yawned, not wishing to address the real implications of Quebec's language laws. It was time for me to go. In Quebec hypocrisy, narcissism, and obfuscation prevailed, in French and in English. As long as I remained in Quebec, I would be hostage to the government's endless provocations of the English; every week my ideal of *bonne entente* would be tormented and mocked. The only way to maintain my affection for Quebec was to leave it.

I did not regret my years in Quebec, only the investment of such an excess of youthful hope in them. I had taken qualified spokesmen for the province at their word when they claimed to welcome bilingualism.

It would have been hard to foresee that Quebec's demographic insecurity and burgeoning jurisdictional self-confidence would infelicitously combine to cause it, with little discernible Francophone dissent, to assault the rights of the English. It would perhaps have been easier to foretell that the English in Quebec would be too defeatist and English Canadians outside too complacent to respond.

It was well-known that Quebec had written off French Canadians outside Quebec as assimilated, but I assumed they placed some value on a French status outside Quebec, which clearly could not long survive suppression of English in Quebec. When Daniel Johnson had pledged not to build a "great wall of China around Quebec" and when Pierre Elliott Trudeau, "on a day when it seemed the cheering would never stop," aspired to be "*maîtres chez nous mais pour tout le Canada*," they inspired credulity because they were strong leaders saying sensible things.

Enhanced pride in Quebec was commendable and I shared in it while I could, but provoking the local representatives of the continent's overwhelming cultural majority, driving them out, and writing off the durable access of the French language to a trans-continental status, though popular for a time, is a cul-de-sac.

As a democrat and a believer in national self-determination, I couldn't dispute Quebec's right to choose its course. As a formerly ardent lover of Quebec who had been lured, perhaps partly by my own romanticized vision of Canada, to spend eight splendid but ultimately disappointing years there, I could, and do yet, resent and regret their parochialism. De Gaulle had suggested that he loved France but didn't particularly like the French. The French Canadians were ever likeable but Quebec was so less and less.

On July 26, I lunched with my friend Gérald Godin, an ardent separatist best known as companion of the strident chanteuse Pauline Julien, who two years later defeated Bourassa in his own constituency and became a minister in Lévesque's government. (Our next exchange was when he came on radio in Quebec City in 1989 during the Bill 178 controversy to denounce me as an "imbecile" for asserting, along with the Supreme, Appeal, and Superior Courts, that suppression of bilingual commercial signs was a restriction of liberty of expression.)

After lunch, I supervised the loading of my belongings onto an independent East Montreal moving van (whose owner had never been in Ontario before), took leave in another poignant parting with my (French-Canadian) girlfriend of two years of ever pleasant memory, and drove to Toronto, after delivering this reflection over the airwaves at the CBC building, where I had so often appeared in earlier days of happier residence: "The present government of Quebec is the most financially and intellectually corrupt in the history of the province. There are the shady deals, brazenly concluded, and the broken promises, most conspicuously that of last October to retain Bill 63 (right of parents to retain choice of language of their children's instruction). But above all we remember the agitation of the political and intellectual leadership of French Quebec in the fifties and sixties for greater bilingualism, particularly among the English. Now that this is occurring, we learn almost every day in *Le Jour*, *Le Devoir*, and even from the government that bilingualism is the means *par excellence* of assimilation. Moderation, then, is no longer possible, under the leadership of the province's technocratic élite personified by Robert Bourassa — scheming, emotionless, dull, and amoral.

"The government dragged out the ancient and totally fictitious spectre of assimilation to justify Bill 22 and its rejection of the right of free choice in education, its reduction of English education to the low echelon of ministerial whim, its assault upon freedom of expression through regulation of the internal and external language of businesses and other organizations, and its creation of a fatuous new linguistic bureaucracy that will conduct a system of organized denunciation, harassment, and patronage. At second reading, the minister of education withdrew the assimilation argument and revealed what everyone already knew: that the French language in Quebec is stronger in every way than it has ever been.

"There is a paralytic social sickness in Quebec. In all this debate, not a single resident French Quebecker has objected to Bill 22 on the grounds that it was undemocratic or a reduction of liberties exercised in the province. . . . The Quebec Civil Liberties Union, founded by Pierre Trudeau, from which one might have expected such sentiments, has instead demanded the abolition of English education, and this through the spokesmanship of Jean-Louis Roy, who derives his income from McGill University.

"As for the political leadership of the English community, where Jonathan Robinson (Duplessis's mines minister and father of my friend, then chairman of McGill's philosophy department), and George Marler and even Eric Kierans once sat we now have the painfully naïve Dr. (Victor) Goldbloom, and the quislings, (William) Tetley and (Kevin) Drummond.

"It is clear that Mr. Bourassa, having persuaded Mr. Trudeau and Jean Lesage to help him cheat Claude Wagner and Pierre Laporte out of the Liberal leadership, having eliminated the non-separatist opposition by turning two consecutive elections into referenda on separation, is now going to try to eliminate the Parti Québécois by a policy of gradual scapegoatism directed against the non-French elements in the province.

"It is clear that the only significant difference between Mr. Bourassa and René Lévesque is that Mr. Bourassa knows how to count. He is content, for the time being, to milk the other provinces in order to dispense patronage in Quebec. This is his idea of 'profitable federalism.'

"Instead of *bonne entente* there will be cat and mouse. The English community here, still deluding itself with the illusion of Montreal as an incomparably fine place to live, is leaderless and irrelevant, except as the hostage of a dishonest government.

"Last month one of the most moderate ministers, Guy Saint-Pierre, told an English businessmen's group, 'If you don't like Quebec, you can leave it.' With sadness but with certitude, I accept that choice."

It was re-broadcast six times on the entire trans-Canada radio network and aroused considerable comment.

CHAPTER FIVE

CLOSING THE NURSERY DOOR
1974–1976

S I DROVE TO TORONTO THROUGH THE NIGHT of July 26–27, 1974, my itinerant contemplations were rudely interrupted when I was only a few miles from my parents' house. A thick fog and acute fatigue combined to produce an accident with a car ahead. Damage was not too serious, but I returned to Toronto as a permanent resident after an absence of twelve years, in the cab of a tow-truck.

I had been largely absent from Toronto for so long that among a large number of acquaintances, I had relatively few friends, and among those, very few women. I had exchanged apartments, my suite in the Port Royal building for a smaller unit in the Lonsdale building, directly across from the Preparatory School of Upper Canada College, "*un retour aux sources*" Cardinal Léger called it when he visited me in 1975. I had less of a sense of coming home than of starting over again.

For my second weekend in Toronto I went to my brother's extensive cottage at Muskoka, where I watched the tasteful resignation of Richard Nixon. Years later, without putting on the airs of a psychiatrist, I suggested to Henry Kissinger (whose office of Secretary of State included the responsibility for receiving the resignations of high public officials: he had already received Spiro Agnew's) that Mr. Nixon was a case illustrative of the truth of the old adage that for every ten men who can stand adversity, only one can stand success and that, in some profound way he was uncomfortable with himself. I referred to his brilliant speech on Vietnam on November 3, 1969, as I had thought of it the night of his resignation. He had said that only the United States could defeat and humiliate the United States. In the end, only Richard Nixon could, and did, defeat and humiliate Richard Nixon.

Henry Kissinger agreed but added that there were five more-or-less distinct sides to Richard Nixon's personality, which coexisted easily most of the time. He was at times an inexplicably nervous man; at times a rather non-descript southern California bourgeois suburban professional; then an obsessive and very suspicious political manoeuvrer and even dirty-tricks specialist; withal a pretty smart Wall Street lawyer; and ultimately a great statesman quite at home with de Gaulle or Chou En Lai. He said that sometimes Nixon would phone him late in the evening and speak for over an hour, and two or more of these aspects of his personality would sequentially prevail.

The American liberal establishment had only fleetingly forgiven him, as when he re-opened relations with China and initiated the Strategic Arms Limitations process, for his having been right in the Alger Hiss case. When he offered live and lethal ammunition to his enemies in the wake of the Watergate burglary, his opponents executed him, patting themselves on the back for their constitutional probity and the triumph of a free investigative press as they did so. Nixon's careerist and ideological enemies, seeing the possibility of tearing down their ancient foe, were resistless against the temptation, even though they should have foreseen that they would de-stabilize the entire American political system, hobble the United States before the intercontinental designs of the Kremlin for almost a decade, and unleash the destructive power of a regicidal press corps.

The press was now immune from being sued for the civil tort of defamation in consequence of madly liberal Supreme court judgements and would be encouraged to believe that it was the cutting edge of truth, the conscience of the nation, the loyal opposition and, in Kay Graham's bone-chilling phrase "the rough first draft of history." Removing presidents became an intoxication to a Democratic Party unable to put up serious candidates for the presidency itself but in permanent control of most of the Congress. Criminalization of policy differences was the foreseeable result of Watergate — sanctimonious pseudo-legalistic putschism.

Richard Nixon's resignation was not, as it has been frequently represented, a triumph of the free press, it was a triumph of Nixon's neuroses and his enemies' vindictiveness over the national interest.

De Gaulle wrote of Pétain, "Old age is a shipwreck; that we might be spared nothing the old age of the Marshal was to become identified with the utter shipwreck of France." It is equally true that an acute professional (though not physical) self-destructive tendency in a statesman is likely to lead to the annihilation of the political authority of his office and of his country as well as of himself. No one in 1974, except possibly and far too late, Nixon himself, seemed to be thinking of that.

As I watched him throw in the towel, from the bucolic majesty of Muskoka, I wondered at the strength and perseverance of a man who, ungregarious, inhibited, awkward, out of sheer determination, intelligence, and courage, had been, along with Franklin D. Roosevelt, the only person in American history to stand for election to national office for a major party five times, and, like Roosevelt, to have been successful four times.

Obviously, by the summer of 1974, Nixon had so squandered his political capital and apparently dishonoured his office that he had to retire. Along with my admiration for his triumph of human will, and my hopes for yet another comeback for Richard Nixon to the esteem of his countrymen, went yet more foreboding for the American political process.

November 22, 1963; March 31, 1968; August 9, 1974: these were not the best methods of changing the chief of state of the world's greatest nation, "the head of the American people," in Franklin D. Roosevelt's phrase (uttered in reference to himself). Gerald Ford had apparently been chosen in succession to Agnew by Nixon as the vice president most likely to win confirmation yet discourage (by his mediocrity) the Senate's removal from office of Nixon. The greatest political agony of the American state since the Civil War was not over.

When I eventually got to know Richard Nixon fifteen years later, he had become a figure of transcendent durability, startlingly intelligent, surpassingly skilful in his analysis of international affairs and domestic politics, "his soul serene, all passion spent," and especially, a considerate, courteous, unselfconscious, humorous, even pleasant, or at least generous, man. (I met him first when I visited him in his wildly improbable and rather nondescript office above a travel agent on a suburban New Jersey highway.)

The American nation has seen off its unworthy adversary. The American presidency has recovered its coequal status with Congress and the judiciary; Richard Nixon has regained the respect of his countrymen. Truly, as Brendan Behan once said to George Black in one of those platitudinous after-theatre dinners at the O'Keefe Centre (whose construction my father commissioned when he was head of Canadian Breweries), the strength of the instinct for self-preservation "is a creditable thing."

I had the good fortune in the summer of 1974 to fall into the company of my old friends in the Eaton and Bassett families. When my family moved to Toronto in 1945, we lived behind the Eatons in Forest Hill and I went to school with the four brothers. We have always been friends. In the sixties, and seventies, I often visited their group of island cottages in Georgian Bay and had many hilarious conversations with John David Eaton, an intelligent but shy man, who had never wanted to run a department store company but persevered out of duty and bequeathed a great trademark though a slightly financially imperilled one to his sons, who brought it to a high level of prosperity. When I was in Vietnam in 1970, I sent Signy Eaton, the elegant and unaffected matriarch who fancied herself something of a liberal, some rather jingoistic postcards, which she somewhat mischievously recalled for many years.

For my 30th birthday, August 25, 1974, I returned to enjoy the hospitality and friendship of the Eatons in the magnificent landscape of Georgian Bay, so engraved in the consciousness of all who know Precambrian Canada, immortalized in the canvasses of Tom Thomson and Goodridge Roberts and the Group of Seven. From the political environment of Quebec to the generous hospitality of Canada's ultimate Establishment family was a great socio-cultural leap, but was no less agreeable for that.

I set up a Sterling Newspapers office in the old Bank of Commerce building on King Street, but couldn't bring myself to bear the cost of hiring a secretary, and I was usually at home in the Lonsdale, working on my Duplessis book with an interest undiminished by my disembarkation from the province; indeed, given Bourassa's antics, Duplessis was looking better every day. Having a less hectic and particularly a more celibate social life, at least for a time, than I had had latterly in Montreal, I usually sat on the phone through the late morning, keeping in touch with my "division," essentially Sherbrooke and Summerside (P.E.I.), put in a cameo appearance downtown at or shortly after lunch time, maintaining and building contacts, usually at the Toronto Club, and then returned and smashed off Duplessis on my typewriter until three or four a.m.

Membership in the Toronto Club, the supreme seat of the Toronto Establishment, was very useful. My father had bought the building next to it on Wellington Street for a headquarters for the United Appeal. When the organization determined that it couldn't use it, he offered it at his cost, despite a sharp increase in value, to the Toronto Club to be turned into a parking lot. The longtime chairman of the management committee, John A. (Bud) McDougald, whose control of access to the membership was legendary and real, demonstrated his gratitude by having delivered to my parents' house on my twenty-first birthday a letter welcoming me as a member of the Toronto Club. My brother was admitted the same day. I don't believe that either of us had ever made out an application. It was nearly fifteen years before there was a member of that club as young as I was and by then I was a relatively senior member.

McDougald reviewed membership applications as zealously as Duplessis had orders-in-council. On one occasion I was sitting with him at his corner table in the dining room, when the manager presented a list of candidates. When Bud got to John Robarts, the former premier, and John Turner, then the former minister of finance and justice, he expressed his almost unvarying disdain for politicians by exclaiming, "Oh no! Tell them if they want to join a club to try Kiwanis."

Bud McDougald was the survivor of the quadrumvirate who founded Argus Corporation in 1945. The principal founder was E.P. Taylor, who modelled it on Atlas Corporation in New York and acted on the beliefs that, after fifteen years of deflation in the private sector, prosperity was around the corner, and that with 10 per cent of the shares it would be possible to obtain a board seat in almost any company and thereafter to infiltrate and dominate that board. He was proved correct in those assumptions, at least for the first fifteen or twenty years and he and his associates and their companies occupied a huge place in Canadian corporate life. Throughout Canada, E.P. Taylor was synonymous with capitalist sufficiency, the ultimate beer baron, fat cat, conglomerateur, race horse owner, and royal social climber.

The initial package of assets of Argus Corporation was an unimpressive grab-bag of E.P.'s pre-war accumulations: a job lot of largely clapped-out breweries, soft-drink bottling plants, coffee shops, and the unpretentious malting business he had bought from the eccentric Montrealer Howard Webster in 1943 in Winnipeg; a block of shares in a modest chemical business and a few per cent of the outstanding shares of Massey-Harris, one of the world's largest farm equipment manufacturers and one of Canada's most famous companies.

In this era, before rigorous rules governing related party transactions or capital gains, the technique devised for upgrading from Argus's founding position was for the Argus principals to buy blocks of stock personally, vend them to related companies or to Argus itself at handsome profits, and, where necessary, retire the associated debt incurred by issuing rafts of non-voting shares. This practice is commonly called toll-gating, and Taylor and his early partners had engaged in it very extensively.

For his early partners, Taylor had recruited Colonel W. Eric Phillips, a brilliant but rather acerbic man. He had been one of the British Empire's youngest colonels in the First World War, co-owner with Pilkington's and Pittsburgh Plate Glass of Duplate, from which company he sold a great deal of auto glass to his father-in-law, R.S. McLaughlin, co-founder of the Buick automobile and chairman of General Motors of Canada. That marriage eventually broke down and Phillips married the sister of Bud McDougald's wife. Phillips was for many years the chairman of the governing body of the University of Toronto. He was a considerable intellectual and an outstanding corporate administrator.

McDougald was a dapper, elegant, droll, cunning, feline man, almost completely uneducated, proud of his ignorance, an entertaining if languorous raconteur, and a childless teetotaller. The last partner was M.W. "Wally" McCutcheon, a hard-nosed and hard-drinking lawyer and actuary.

Taylor himself was a large, blustery man with a friendly and forceful manner. He often started to put a question before his previous question had been answered and was said to start leaving a meeting before he arrived. Hearty and gregarious, he was an inexhaustible storehouse of ideas. His true passion was horse racing, and his chairmanship of the Ontario Jockey Club saw horse racing in Ontario elevated from spavined milk-wagon horses in fixed races in tumbledown tracks transformed to the highest standards of horse breeding and racing. My father had been recommended to Mr. Taylor near the end of the war by C.D. Howe as an accountant with some experience in the brewing industry and a good record as an administrator. Taylor, Phillips, McCutcheon, and McDougald were undoubtedly an effective combination.

At Argus, the brewing assets were consolidated into Canadian Breweries Limited, from 1950 to 1958 under my father's very successful direction, when it became the largest and most profitable brewery in the world. The Massey-Harris position was rounded up to about 10 per cent and eventually all four of the Argus leaders became directors of it. They grew dissatisfied with the performance of the Massey chairman, James S. Duncan, an intelligent and vain martinet, who eventually provoked Phillips and Taylor into firing him in 1956. When he was sacked and forced to retire to his homes "in Bermuda, Jamaica, and Spain," James Duncan had been making six times the salary of the next senior executive, the president, A. Albert Thornbrough. Thornbrough soon made up for lost time and money.

Toronto in the fifties and much of the sixties was, as has been described, a dreadfully drab and unstylish place and much of what little flair there was was provided by these men. They served wine at dinner and were driven about in cars that usually had some high-quality coach work on them. Their rites of the Establishment helped to give the city a patina of taste and refinement: Phillips at the University of Toronto, McDougald at the Toronto Club, and Taylor at the Jockey Club, where almost every year, he accompanied the Queen Mother or some other Royal to the winner's circle at Woodbine, which he built and where, in effect, he, as chairman of the Jockey Club, gave the trophy to himself as winning owner.

Almost every year we used to go as his friends to this ceremony, and my first exposure to the full-throated sound of Canadian envy was to hear the tremendous chorus of brickbats that rained down on Mr. Taylor when he went out to the winner's circle each year. (It was a relief when my wife and I returned to Woodbine, to the last Queen's Plate that E.P. won as owner, rather than breeder, in 1979. The Queen Mother did the honours yet again, but, when E.P. was announced, all the touts and derelicts in the lower grandstands gave him a prolonged ovation. My father used to say, "If you can hang on long enough, you command respect.")

McDougald bought control of Dominion Stores from Rumilly's fellow fugitive from France, François Dupré in the late forties and vended it, in the already well-established manner, into Argus Corporation. He did the same with blocks of Hollinger Consolidated Goldmines, sizeable chunks of which were owned by his cousins, Allen and Duncan McMartin. McDougald was also responsible for picking up the large Toronto radio station CFRB at a knock-down price at the end of the Second World War, securing political approval for a drastic increase in the kilowattage to 50,000 (the Board of Broadcast Governors, predecessor to the CRTC, was unabashedly political), and selling control of it on to Argus Corporation for the customary vertiginous mark-up.

Taylor had masterminded the assembling of chemical-related assets for resale to Dominion Tar and Chemical Company. His *pièce de résistance* was St. Lawrence Corporation, in which he bought a large position for his partners and himself cheaply, scalded its stock price upwards, and sold across to Domtar (as it eventually became) for almost ten times his cost. He also took a position in British Columbia Forest Products of about 10 per cent and exercised significant influence in that company jointly with the Mead and Scott paper companies, who had roughly comparable shareholdings.

The interest in Canadian Breweries, whose competitive position had declined considerably after my father's retirement in 1958, was sold to Rothman's in 1968, who sold it on to Elders IXL in 1988, which merged it with Molson in 1989. Argus was unceremoniously dumped as a controlling partner in B.C. Forest Products in 1969 by the Mead and Scott paper companies in favour of Noranda. For the first time in the Argus experience, a supposedly strategic shareholding was exposed as an imposture.

By the mid-sixties, relations between the Argus founders had become very attenuated. After the death of Phillips in December 1964, many exploratory sessions took place, attended by Taylor, Bud

McDougald, Colonel Max Meighen, who had accumulated a sizeable shareholding, Doris Phillips, my father, and, on occasion, me. My father had been a director by virtue of being president of Canadian Breweries. When he retired from that position, he was retained as a director in recognition of the large shareholding he had accumulated. He behaved with judicious neutrality in the early stages of the Taylor-McDougald squabbling. Relations between Mr. Taylor and Colonel Meighen were particularly abrasive, E.P. bellowing in one scene at our house, "Don't shout at me!" and Colonel Meighen shouting back, "I'll shout at you if you shout at me!" The dialogue between these fabled captains of industry was not always terribly elevated.

The Taylor, Phillips, McDougald, and McCutcheon interests had been pooled in a company that gloried in the pastoral name of Meadowbrook Holdings. Taylor, for reasons that have never been explained, agreed to make the interests equal in four parts, thus forfeiting the advantage he had previously enjoyed as the largest voting shareholder as well as, by far, the largest holder of participating, non-voting, preferred shares.

After McCutcheon left for the exotic inspiration of joining Mr. Diefenbaker's government in 1962, McDougald effectively blocked his return in 1963 when the Pearson Liberals were elected, as he and Phillips could outvote Taylor in such matters, and he blocked him again in 1968 after McCutcheon's sixth-place finish at the leadership convention in 1967 and narrow defeat in the 1968 general election. McDougald was thus the most influential Argus shareholder after the death of Phillips in 1964. He effectively directed the Phillips shares through his sister-in-law, Doris Phillips, through the corporate trustee, Crown Trust Company. He controlled Crown Trust, through a combination of his own shares and his formal and informal influence over blocks of shares held by other McMartin cousins of his, cousins also of the Hollinger McMartins in Bermuda.

These Crown Trust McMartins operated a resort motel and sporting goods complex in the Adirondacks. The McMartins had scattered their attentions quite widely since their fortunate ancestors left Timmins at the start of the century when the Hollinger Mine was founded. This is not unusual in wealthy families, and some of the McMartins were rather colourful. Allen and Duncan between them had nine wives, including one against whom Allen instituted divorce proceedings the day after his wedding, which he professed not to recall. Apart from big-game hunting, they were best known for prodigious feats of consumption, including one Bacchanalian epic at the conclusion of which Duncan flattened an equally sodden and belligerent Errol Flynn.

McDougald had played his political cards with great skill and patience. Frequently derided by Phillips as a "know-nothing," a "hatchet man," and a "jumped-up bond salesman with the ass out of his pants," he had endured the colonel's unflattering attentions more or less without riposte, survived him, and assumed his voting position, if not his moral authority or intellectual eminence, by homogenizing his interests with the consortship of the family he and Phillips had married into: Doris, "Jim" McDougald (her real names are Hedley Maude), and Cecil Hedstrom, the third sister, who were the so-called "three wives of Bud McDougald."

As young women they had been attractive, sporty, and mannerly. Their parents, the respected but impecunious Colonel and Mrs. Eustace-Smith, had urged them to "marry up economically-speaking." Doris took two bites of the matrimonial apple, her first husband, Adair Gibson having committed suicide. Cecil's two marriages, the first to a member of the Gooderham family, were unmitigated fiascos.

The next phase of the history of this much mythologized corporate group unfolded in this fading, slightly sissified atmosphere, part *Auntie Mame* and part *Suddenly Last Summer*.

The struggle between McDougald and Taylor was an uneven one, a little like that between Stalin and Trotsky. Taylor, brilliant, mercurial, but unfocused and almost apolitical, offended the management directors and second echelon. His well-founded criticism of the ill-conceived extravagance at post-Phillips Massey-Ferguson, the indolence at Hollinger, the chronically poor returns at Dominion Stores, alienated the managements in those companies, whom McDougald, with Stalinesque thoroughness and cynicism, had totally suborned by perquisites and preferments and unlimited use of the corporate plane; even, in the case of Albert Thornbrough at Massey, Al Fairley at Hollinger, and ultimately Alex Hamilton at Domtar, seats on the board of the Canadian Imperial Bank of Commerce. Phillips in his last days had favoured breaking Argus up and liquidating its blocks and expressed scepticism about McDougald's aptitudes, like the dying Lenin warning about Stalin.

George Black, though he always admired and liked E.P. Taylor, had never been very pleased about the unceremonious manner in which he left Canadian Breweries, nor about Taylor having, as he explained to McDougald, Phillips, and Meighen at McDougald's house in 1964, "systematically wrecked the breweries." McDougald's largesse to us, such as the effortless admission of my brother and me to the Toronto Club, and Bud's gift to me of the colonel's painting of Napoleon ("I know I am speaking for the Colonel too, when I say that Napoleon will be far happier in your library than he was at St. Helena," he wrote) were generous and intelligent favours that were certainly not unappreciated by our family.

Meighen, an irascible character at the best of times, was not any more highly esteemed by McDougald than by Taylor, but McDougald was at least prepared to be motivated by his own sure grasp of tactical expediency. Meighen was more intelligent than his usually humourless, ill-tempered, monosyllabic, and bigoted conversation would lead one to believe. He had worked hard to escape from the shadow of his famous father (Arthur Meighen was prime minister of Canada from 1920 to 1921 and in 1926) and his gracious brother Ted, and he was grateful for McDougald's sprinkling prestigious Argus group directorships over him. He had been ignored by the previous regime at Argus.

General Bruce Matthews, a well-liked old Toronto gentleman, who had been recruited by Taylor to succeed him as chairman of Canadian Breweries in the mid-sixties, essentially to be the fall guy for the avalanche of bad news that Taylor's policies made inevitable after my father retired, was not pleased to be hung out to dry by being sent to assure the company's personnel that it would not be sold, shortly prior to its sale, in 1968. The general's irritation was understandable.

When Taylor, ever the master salesman, concentrated fiercely, he was persuasive. His last great feat of one-on-one salesmanship was to persuade Paul Desmarais, who saw the Argus Corporation opportunity and the somnolence of the post Taylor-Phillips direction, that the future of the company was his, and Paul eagerly accumulated stock, believing at least part of Taylor's assurances that the founder of Argus could deliver control.

I had been present at the founding of the Ravelston Corporation in May 1969 in one of the ornate meeting rooms of the old Bank of Commerce building, when Meadowbrook had been dissolved and was replaced by an association of McDougald, Phillips, Meighen, Matthews, and our family; the association initially had 47 per cent of the voting shares, but quickly assumed an absolute majority. Meadowbrook had had 38 per cent. Ravelston was the name of the home of McDougald's influential uncle Senator Wilfrid Laurier McDougald, and presumably was inspired originally by the suburb of Edinburgh. The Senator had been cast away by Mackenzie King during the Beauharnois scandal in 1931.

Bud McDougald appeared to have a slight partial motivation to vindicate his uncle, or his family generally, and there was perhaps an element of this in the founding of Ravelston, a McDougaldization of what had been generally perceived as Taylor's company.

The opportunities were obvious enough; Desmarais and the equally opportunistic Harry Jackman (Hal's father) had been buying Argus shares for years, but not for as long as George Black, though he had been motivated by the dazzling quadrumvirate at its peak, not by the prospects opened up by its decline, and had no visions of assuming control. By 1976, he had succumbed to the old Phillips argument and was a liquidationist. Taylor, who had incited Desmarais and to some degree Jackman, was a spent force.

Seeing them all in action at close quarters over many years, it was obvious to me that McDougald would control the play but by 1974, he was sixty-six and slowing down. As Sir Thomas More said, "Nothing will change in England while Wolsey lives," so no movement was possible at Argus while McDougald reigned. The future of Argus Corporation was a race between the natural erosion of the businesses and McDougald's undertaker; if the mortician preceded the liquidator, we would have a chance, possibly a great chance. There was no game for Desmarais and only a bit-play for Jackman (but he was well-accustomed to those); unlike Desmarais, he didn't mind taking crumbs if there was money in them. This was the developing drama that I entered on returning to Toronto in 1974; English-Canadian corporate politics were to prove a good deal more fulfilling than the arid furrows of Quebec electoralism.

It was high time I returned to Toronto for other reasons. Ever since he retired from Canadian Breweries in 1958, my father had fussed over his portfolio. He was, in his own words, though he wouldn't have wished to apply them to himself, "a run-of-the-mill millionaire." He spent almost every evening to a very late hour "brooding," as he put it. He called our modest network of private companies "the system." The cornerstone was Western Dominion Investment Company in Winnipeg, which my father and grandfather bought from Lord Rothermere. We owned 56 per cent of this company and my double cousins, the Rileys in Montreal, owned the rest (my father's sister married my mother's brother). In this company were 22 per cent of Ravelston and a few odds and ends.

Control of Western Dominion was held by an awkwardly acronymic family company, Bemocoge (Betty was my mother's name), which was owned equally by my father on one side and my brother and me on the other, though in keeping with succession-duty avoidance schemes of the time, capital appreciation accrued to my brother's shares and mine. There had not, in fact, been a great deal of capital appreciation and federal estate taxes (though not provincial succession duties) had been replaced by capital gains assessments at death.

A problem with George Black's contemplative approach was that everything had been running down for fifteen years. The only active business we had was the timeless Dominion Malting Company, the very same one that E.P. Taylor bought from Howard Webster then sold to Argus Corporation in 1945, which moved it on to Canadian Breweries and which we bought out of Canadian Breweries in 1968 when control of that company was purchased by Rothmans. (I sold it on to Dwayne Andreas of Archer Daniels Midland in 1990 at yet another profit.) After paying interest on its entire purchase price, it made between one and two million dollars annually, most of which had to be applied to reduction of debt or capital improvements.

My mother had about half a million non-voting C preferred shares of Argus Corporation and a million dollars or so of shares in the general insurance company that her grandfather, father, and brothers had directed for many years. My father had two blocks of stock that he had purchased and married with borrowed money, I.A.C. and Westcoast Transmission, a walk-up finance company and a gas utility. There was virtually no movement nor much likelihood of any in these stock prices, and the positions were a cash-flow drain. He also had a piece of his brother-in-law's successful tanning business, a good business well built up by my uncle Conrad, but no great cash generator for the shareholders.

Father was too out of touch and physically immobile to be either an operator or a stylish and dynamic market player. He didn't know the current crop of financial stars and the market and professional advice he was getting was not at the cutting edge of what was available. This was what motivated him to write pathetic wails of appeal to McDougald at the end of 1975 to wind up Argus and distribute the proceeds. Knowing we would be entirely opposed to such a negative strategy, he told my brother and me nothing of it. McDougald, with $10 million in the bank and gambolling in the role of Canada's supreme corporate director, ignored the suggestion entirely. We discovered it in my father's papers only after he died. He had long since lost his financial nerve, and fears for his physical and financial health gnawed at him constantly. The position, though not tenuous, was far from optimal and the patriarch was slowly running out of money.

Next to the Argus position, the best asset we had in our family by 1974 was my 44 per cent of Sterling Newspapers, which even on Power Corporation's unacceptable low-ball valuation of 1973 had increased one hundred fold in value in five years and was all we had that was appreciating. My brother had tied up his capital, and some of that he had borrowed, in a picturesque stock-broking business, Draper Dobie. When his partner ran into financial difficulties, we bought control of the firm, but these were not great times in the business and it was an industry on a long-term secular trend to contraction. My brother had a flair for the business and had worked in it for over ten years, but it was a cash drain at this point. I had been focusing on my own business and was slightly disconcerted to find such disarray when I returned to Toronto.

I riffled through all this fairly thoroughly in the fall of 1974 and introduced a second and more aggressive opinion of both legal and accounting advisers. I recommended we sell all the publicly held shares except Argus and my mother's family's businesses. Sterling would continue to be a build, Malting a hold, Draper a hold to merge or sell, and Argus, without being morbid about it, a hold to await what might euphemistically be called "developments," i.e., a change in control produced by the natural effluxion of time. George Black was not enchanted with my proposed abandonment of his daily vigil at I.A.C. and Westcoast. He followed these shares like an aging falcon scouring the ground for mice, having the closing market newspaper rushed in to him every afternoon, but there was never any appreciable change.

More worrisome than his slowly deteriorating limbs and sight was my mother's condition. She had always been very robust, but had had bowel cancer surgery in 1974. She appeared to have recovered completely and it was almost never mentioned, but we were all too familiar with the incidence of recurrence of that pernicious disease not to be worried about it. With good reason, as it turned out.

Shortly after Christmas 1974, I went to the Middle East with my Montreal girlfriend. Beirut was magnificent. Exotic, unexpected, rich, original, crowded with beautiful women with copper skin, doe eyes, and comely thighs, a bit of everything, Saigon, Paris, Istanbul, a sort of Near Eastern Hong Kong made to work by the commercial acumen of the Lebanese.

The only rumour of war I saw was when visiting the Canadian deputy ambassador, Raymond Chrétien (brother of the eventual federal Liberal leader), when four planes of the Israeli Air Force conducted a surgically precise attack on a PLO hostel about two miles from his balcony. We watched, drinks in hand, like the matrons of Washington at the First Battle of Bull Run.

The traditional sights of Egypt are well worth a view, though for someone accustomed to the St. Lawrence, the lower Nile is an absurdly slow and narrow course of tepid brown fluid.

Our trip to Istanbul had to be scrapped because of the utter incompetence of the personnel in our roach warren of a hotel and at the airport. It was a classic of Third World ineptitude, worthy of Evelyn Waugh's famous trip up the Amazon — elaborate plans breaking down, each initiative starting out attended by much hopeful pomp and ceremonious leave-taking, but gradually crumbling in a ludicrous débâcle. As a rebuttal to one's own Western self-importance, it was useful; as an exercise in logistics, it was harrowing.

In desperation, we finally crowded onto an Air France plane taking pilgrims back from Jeddah and Mecca to the Maghreb via

Paris. Never did I admire French sang-froid more. The passengers (we were almost the only Westerners) filled the plane to a depth of half a foot from the floor with litter; the lavatories were quickly rendered unusable. The little man next to me had the disconcerting habit of continually removing and reinserting his artificial left eye. The flight crew were almost whimsically unflappable, though the passengers surged through the aircraft, oblivious to seat-belt advisories and the international Civil Aviation Organization's prohibition against sitting on the floor of an airborne airliner.

I had the pleasant sensation of having crossed the great cultural divide to more familiar and welcoming terrain when, in the currency-exchange line at Charles de Gaulle airport, my erstwhile neighbour with the artificial eye, ignoring the queue, bustled ahead of me, burrowing into the flank of a giant of a man from the southern United States, who looked amusedly down at this commotion and said, "Where are you going, little stud?" The one-eyed pilgrim retreated without debating the issue. We visited Colombey-les-Deux-Eglises, where a wreath from Mao Tse Tung was on de Gaulle's grave.

In April 1975, a contest for control of Argus Corporation erupted between Paul Desmarais of Power Corporation and Bud McDougald and his incumbent friends, including us. It was half low farce and half high corporate drama. Paul had visited Bud in Palm Beach and offered the enticements usually shown to aged or unenterprising managements to move them out of control of stagnating businesses. Bud could use the corporate jet when he wanted. This was not a serious analysis of the self-esteem of the Argus controlling group. McDougald already used the airplane when he wanted it.

McDougald's interest in Argus, by Desmarais's valuation, was worth only about $8 million, and McDougald had more than that, as he worked into many conversations, in his account of the main branch of the Canadian Imperial Bank of Commerce. He gloried in the chairmanship of Dominion Stores and Standard Broadcasting (which owned CFRB and some other radio licences). He published his photograph in Dominion Stores newspaper advertising ("We will not knowingly be undersold") and was the subject of deferential references on CFRB. The chairmanship of the executive committees of Hollinger Mines and Massey-Ferguson enabled him to be a perceived leader of Canada's mining community and a social leader of the international squirearchy, from the presidency of Toronto's Royal Agricultural Winter Fair to hobnobbing with the landed nobility of Britain (the Duke of Wellington, Marquess of Abergavenny, and Lord Crathorne were Massey directors).

Desmarais had nothing to offer him and McDougald found the bid insulting, as it exposed the flimsy foundation under his socio-economic eminence and implied that he was a mere time-server, keeping warm the chairs of Taylor and Phillips (a not unreasonable conclusion by Desmarais and thus a hurtful one). This was the view that Taylor had retailed, and Desmarais, the enthusiast who had met the more accomplished salesman, like the spy being turned by the more determined spy for the other side, bought the story, although McDougald apparently gave him a studiously ambiguous reply in their last substantive discussions of the fate of Argus Corporation.

Desmarais had appreciated the sham quality of the Argus reputation, but not the pride and unshakable self-esteem of McDougald. Ravelston had 51 per cent of the 1.69 million voting shares, and the partners (mainly the Meighens and Blacks) had just over 20 per cent of the participating (non-voting) preferred shares. Since the Power Corporation offer was conditional on receiving at least 80 per cent of both classes, fulfilment of its conditions was impossible.

It was bizarre. The Ontario Securities Commission, advised discussions were taking place, required revelation of their existence. McDougald denied there was any serious discussion between him and Desmarais, who apparently believed that controversy would propel the sixty-seven-year-old, childless McDougald to chuck in his hand. Power Corporation brought forth its offer. McDougald was a toady, a snob, a bigot, an elegant anachronism and an unlearned reactionary, but he was also tough, purposeful, and crafty and he was a good deal more adept at public controversy than Desmarais, a charming and dynamic man and a much more creative financier than McDougald, but shy and inconvenienced by a slight speech hesitation.

McDougald heaped ridicule on Desmarais's offer, calling it an episode "from Alice in Wonderland." He finished a Massey-Ferguson preferred underwriting only by threatening to take the whole $50-million issue himself unless Greenshields, Power Corporation's co-agent broker, were excluded. This was splendid bravura, as he had no means to do anything of the kind (and those who did buy the issue had ample reason to regret it within-two-and-a-half years). When Desmarais's talented associate, Jean Parisien, said he had never in his "career heard of treating a firm like Greenshields in this way," after the underwriting group caved in to McDougald's threat, McDougald replied, of Parisien: "His career? What career? I never heard of him before and don't expect to hear of him again."

Desmarais was bidding up from his official $24 per common share price to $30 for blocks, and we spent part of the June 1975 Hollinger annual dinner sitting in a darkened room upstairs in the Toronto Club (as not even McDougald could find the light switch), buying the McCutcheon shares, which were now controlled by his sons. The Hollinger dinner was started by the Timminses and McMartins as a rollicking outing for prospectors and mining promoters, but under McDougald it became a rather genteel Establishment affair. McDougald also negotiated a first refusal arrangement with Harry Jackman and an Argus board seat for Hal, so he had shored himself up to 68 per cent of the voting shares. My father was in hospital at the time, unconscious after severe complications following a hip replacement operation.

It was a surprise when Desmarais took up the stock tendered to him, thus becoming the owner of 51 per cent of the equity, but only about 26 per cent of the voting shares (after the passage of another year enabled E.P. Taylor the freedom from a prior Ravelston arrangement to sell his shares to Power Corporation).

It was assumed that Desmarais, seeing his path blocked by a group of elderly men (McDougald, Meighen, Matthews, and my father were all between sixty-four and sixty-eight), professed to believe that time was on his side. "I'm waiting at the door," he said to the Bryce commission on corporate concentration, which this bid had given rise to. "He'll have a long wait," McDougald said to the same commission. So he did.

I had already played a role in helping to build the McDougald mystique. In 1974, I persuaded a pleasant reporter from the Montreal *Gazette*, Henry Aubin, to write an extensive series on McDougald's spidery corporate influence. (Ironically, for someone who was one of the founders of Canada's Centre for Investigative Journalism, he was unable to find my home, the venue for the interview, though it was the tallest building on Sherbrooke Street, and he had to telephone for supplementary directions.) I also fed a good deal of laudatory information to Peter Newman for his first book on the Canadian Establishment, where McDougald took up the first chapter. This was not entirely embellishment; McDougald was a talent. He was an asexual Casanova, or even an undebauched Cagliostro, the furthest thing from a rake but a grand, impeccable actor, and this was his finest role, and on a national stage. He finally emerged from the shadows of Taylor and Phillips and developed an instant mystique as the ultimate Canadian tycoon, discreet but apparently unlimitedly wealthy and influential. He played the role to perfection, but it was to be his swan-song.

Desmarais had seen through the Argus legend and probably exaggerated the underlying share values, so great was the extent of the corporate rot by 1975. He explained his defeat by attributing it to the racial and religious prejudices of the Toronto Establishment, thus avoiding any great opprobrium in Montreal. McDougald had asserted some influence, but the McCutcheons went to the highest bidder, Jackman saw a greater prospect of capital gains with McDougald and a better deal than in selling out to Desmarais, and religion had nothing to do with it, as McDougald was a Jacobite. Desmarais was very skilful in holding himself out in Montreal as a French-Canadian success story to the French and precisely the sort of French Canadian to be encouraged to the English.

Having helped to launch the McDougald myth, I eventually became so tired of being unable to set foot out of doors without hearing of the inevitability of Desmarais taking over Argus Corporation, when the mortician would have called at Toronto Street, that I set out to give some publicity to a visible alternative, particularly my brother and myself, though not exclusively so, as I got some attention for Jackman also. It worked, but in achieving some national media notice for myself, I breathed life into an image, which danced, flickered, and, as years went by, lurched syncopatedly about taking on unpredictable shapes and attitudes that often tended to have little relationship with facts.

The fall of Saigon in May 1975, and the military subjugation of the whole of South Vietnam by the Hanoi regime, was a depressing event. The international forces of anti-Americanism had their greatest victory of all. The joyous shrieks of the left were deafening. The

Communist powers and committed fellow-travellers had somehow earned their hour of brutish triumph. More annoying were the numberless legions of complacent trendies, and they were pandemic in such a place as Toronto. I could take it from the cadaverous and intense left, but corpulent hedonists flashing V-signs from their Mercedeses and BMWs and embracing with look-alikes in their Yorkville wine bars and trattorias were very trying.

To be subjected to the gleeful antics of such people while Nguyen Van Thieu fled from Tu Do Palace to Surrey, and the whole world watched approvingly, and obloquy rained down on the incapable Gerry Ford as he dispensed "Whip Inflation Now" buttons, was discouraging.

The leader of the Quebec Teachers' Union, Raymond Laliberté (frequently parodied by use of the American popular song-line "Freedom's (*la liberté*) just another word for nothing left to lose"), called for and received from his annual convention of those responsible for the formation of Quebec's golden youth a minute of atheistic silence in thankfulness for the "communist liberation of South Vietnam." This was the coruscation of the post-Duplessis Quiet Revolution. Even the limousine liberals of Toronto seemed comparatively palatable.

It will forever be debated whether the Nixon-Kissinger policy of holding the club of renewed bombing over North Vietnam would have deterred the North Vietnamese from violating the Paris accords if the executive branch of the U.S. government had not dissolved in scandal. At time of writing, those men certainly believe so and, as in the days of their incumbency, make a powerful case for their views, though I am personally unpersuaded; I suspect that Saigon was too corrupt and the South too undermined and unstable to resist such an onslaught as was coming, even with close air support.

The conventional wisdom has ceased to lionize the Stalinist regime in Hanoi with the passage of time and the pitiful and desperate flight of millions of Vietnamese by land and sea, where their chances of physical survival, much less of reaching an unpromised land of plenty, are slim. (One of my few disagreements with Margaret Thatcher fifteen years later was when she proposed to deport Vietnamese boat people from Hong Kong. This was, I wrote in the *Sunday Telegraph*, "an evil policy.") U.S. motives in Vietnam are now generally seen to have been benign, even if the strategic judgement was faulty.

I never doubted that the forces of political repression would fail or that the strength of the United States and particularly of its presidency would be re-established. No one could foresee then that the Communist alternative would collapse early, as it has, though I never worried about the ultimate outcome of the Cold War. Yet, in the spring of 1975, the forces of good sense and good taste, as I perceived them, were passing through the valley of humiliation.

In Canada Robert Stanfield, who had thrice been defeated by Pierre Trudeau (albeit 1972 was an effective draw in all respects except post-electoral parliamentary tactical skill), announced his retirement as leader of the federal Opposition in 1975, and a leadership convention was called for February 1976. It seemed to me that the logical candidate to replace him was Claude Wagner, with whom I had kept steadily in touch towards just this eventuality. While thoroughly aware of Wagner's limitations, his petulance, superficiality and indecisiveness in particular, my objective was a functioning two-party system, not the perpetuation of a governing party, a truncated official Opposition that was just a catchment for dissident non-Liberals, and a whining unofficial opposition. For the Progressive Conservatives to have a chance of victory, they had to put down roots in Quebec, and for that to happen, they probably needed, at least against Trudeau, a Quebec leader.

Once again, Wagner was the one.

I was Wagner's chief initial contact in Toronto and had the obligatory (reasonably well-attended) dinner for him at the Toronto Club. Douglas Bassett, Fred Eaton, and I set about rounding up money and support for Wagner in Toronto and creating the hilarious myth that we operated a sophisticated political machine. It was a splendid fraud. Douglas and I flew to Ottawa in March to concert plans with Wagner. There was a considerable blizzard in progress in Ottawa and the airport was announced to be closed as we de-planed. We each ruined a $150 pair of shoes trudging to and from taxis and had to rent a car and drive through very difficult conditions back to Toronto in the afternoon. As the launch of a political organization, it contained almost slapstick elements that were to prove a mere foretaste of much of what was to come.

The first problem was sanitizing the $300,000 paid to Wagner when he abandoned the bench for the second time to stand as a federal candidate in 1972. I suggested that, on the understanding that it would be replenished later as required, we constitute the money as a fund and make modest, anonymous contributions from it to Wagner's chief leadership opponents, revealing the fact when it would be tactically useful. This proposal failed to account for Wagner's morbid paranoia, especially where money was involved.

There was never any question about whether Wagner would contest the leadership, and he was clearly a strong candidate. None of the contenders from the 1967 race was a candidate again: Diefenbaker, Fulton, Hees, Roblin, Fleming were all absent from this contest. Ontario's outstanding ex-premier, John Robarts, would not run, nor would Alberta's Peter Lougheed. Robarts's successor, Bill Davis, having lost his majority in 1975, was not in demand. Thanks largely to Stanfield's enlightened attitude to Quebec, Conservative opinion was relatively susceptible to an argument for a Quebec breakthrough, and the timing for the victory of a presentable Conservative leader was right.

Mackenzie King had won his greatest victory of six as Liberal Party leader in 1940. Louis St. Laurent had won an even greater victory in 1949 and served as Uncle Louis in that era of Eisenhower, Churchill, Adenauer, Leslie Frost, Duplessis, when, at one level and another, avuncular grey-fringed or silver-haired leaders were in vogue. John Diefenbaker won an even greater victory in 1958, Pierre Trudeau a less one-sided but still heavy one in 1968. Every decade or so, Canada prostrated itself at the feet of a new political suitor, desperate to be rid of its frustrations and inhibitions as a passenger in the Anglo-American bandwagon, yet desirous of avoiding any course so enterprising that it would put the benefits of those relationships at risk.

Though Canada evolved profoundly, this pattern could be taken back to R.B. Bennett in 1930, Mackenzie King's first election in 1921, Sir Robert Borden's first election in 1911, and Sir Wilfrid Laurier before that. Soon after the elevation of the new or recycled political chieftain, rancorous disillusionment would set in and in a tribalistic rite of sacrifice, the king would have to die (politically only, fortunately) and be replaced by a new, instant, ephemeral messiah. Canada was ready to deliver a new majority to a new leader.

Wagner was a talented speaker, a very presentable candidate who always made a good first, second, and third impression. Like the original General Boulanger, Claude was initially hugely attractive; closer acquaintance revealed him to be chronically indecisive and temperamental. Wagner never really remembered a favour or forgot a slight, even an imagined one.

The wild card was my old friend, Brian Mulroney, who was under great pressure from the most powerful and partisan friends of Trudeau to run. Paul Desmarais, a former law client of Mulroney's, Ced Ritchie, chairman of the Bank of Nova Scotia, Ian Sinclair, chairman of Canadian Pacific, all good friends of Trudeau's, all urged Brian Mulroney to make the race. The Liberal plan was to split the Quebec and pro-Quebec vote between Wagner and Mulroney and to ensure the victory of a candidate who would not be able to threaten the Liberal hold on Quebec.

Brian Mulroney, I always felt, was too sophisticated a political operator not to know who was trying to use him and not to use them instead. I visited his house in Montreal in the summer of 1975 and had a most pleasant dinner with him and his charming, poised, and intelligent wife, Mila. I urged Brian to run with a view to establishing himself as the heir to the leadership, as John Turner had for the Liberals in 1968, or John F. Kennedy had in seeking the vice-presidential nomination for the Democrats with Adlai Stevenson in the hopeless race against President Eisenhower in 1956. I made it clear that having pledged my support to Wagner, I would have to stick with him, though Brian was a much better friend personally.

I made the point, over *digestifs* and as delicately as I could, that I didn't really take his candidacy seriously, other than as a blocking move by the Liberals and a tactical self-advancement for himself, a neat trick in using Liberal money to make himself the next leader, if all worked out. He had little chance of actually winning, had no demonstrable qualifications, and was serving chiefly as a spoiler to deny the nomination to a strong and politically seasoned rival to Trudeau for Quebec's affections.

Wagner had had two provincial and two federal election victories and an eventful and distinguished stint as solicitor general and

Quebec's first justice minister, starting with the famous "night of the truncheon," maintaining order when Queen Elizabeth came to Quebec in 1964. (I was in Quebec on a Thanksgiving motor holiday on that occasion. It was not a pleasant spectacle, though Quebec's police beating up demonstrators was one I later became familiar with. Several times when I was a student at Laval, I saw them charge out of the basement of the National Assembly to attack demonstrators, shouting *"Aux arrestations!"* Their field formation was not impressive.) Brian professed, though not too strenuously, to disagree with my analysis and felt he had a good chance and was not unqualified. It was difficult to evaluate the extent to which he was motivated by self-inflating blarney, drink, and cold calculation. He was and remains a boon companion, more spontaneous, yet not entirely relaxed, in those days before he abandoned the bottle, though accounts suggesting Brian Mulroney was just a drunk are wildly exaggerated. Like Duplessis in 1944, he did gain the inner strength of the reformed alcoholic.

Through all of the twenty-five years that I have known him, Brian Mulroney has always been attractive, capable, fiercely motivated, loyal to his closest friends, and cunning at all times and has relentlessly pursued the morning star of his political fortunes wherever it led him. By 1975, he was probably Quebec's most prominent labour lawyer and had served effectively on Robert Cliche's commission of inquiry into labour violence in Quebec. (He had also given me the only advice I had needed in winning my only "cases" in legal practice in rehearsing the ladies who physically inserted sections in the *Sherbrooke Record* to repeat the mantra to the Minimum Wage Commission: "We are casual labour.")

In those days he still felt himself quite keenly to be the underprivileged lad from Baie-Comeau, son of the foreman in the Chicago *Tribune*'s newsprint mill, who identified more with the French than the English in Quebec, and more with the lower economic echelons than with the scions of wealthy Westmount whom he met for the first time through Michael Meighen, George MacLaren, and Peter White at Laval and with whom he was in frequent contact in his practice.

He had the attitude to money of someone who didn't have any himself but had seen others scatter lavishly: he appreciated it more in the spending than in the accumulation, the latter a process he tended to over-simplify. And politically, he had the attitude to money of someone who came to maturity in the last years of Duplessis, when the tangible fruits of a long incumbency were being extravagantly dispersed. He had the heart of a working man but was developing the tastes of the rich. His irrepressible and bonhomous optimism, love of intrigue, and insight into the thinking of both sides in a management-labour dispute equipped him marvellously for his work, though like most people in the field, he tended to err on the side of generosity with the employer's (i.e., client's) money.

Ever since his Youth for Diefenbaker days nearly twenty years before, when he had so impressed Ted Rogers and Hal Jackman, Brian had been almost frenetically active in Conservative Party affairs, ceaselessly attending conventions, raising money, supporting lost causes, and involving himself in the obscure and squalid manoeuvrings within the fissiparous perennial opposition. Thus did he become involved in the Claude Wagner fund issue and become one of the Conservative Party's best known insiders.

Brian had been preparing himself for years to be the Conservatives' saviour in Quebec. The arrival of Wagner, though he eagerly facilitated it, could put an end to such hopes, and the rejection of Wagner, which was rendered fairly likely by Brian's well-funded assault on his natural sources of support, could indeed establish Brian as tomorrow's man. Brian had never been particularly adept at explaining to me, at least, even when thoroughly plied with drink, why he was a Conservative, beyond family tradition and the belief that they were more malleable clay, i.e., more fertile ground for his advancement than the Liberals. Ideology certainly had nothing to do with it. He had seemed content to be Wagner's promoter as someone fourteen years older than himself, but when Wagner produced no appreciable change in the province-wide Conservative vote in 1972, the virtues of the present for a direct political launch became irresistible.

Given his ambitions, it would have been madness for Brian not to make the race. His campaign, when it came, was rather vapid and revealed his lack of concern with "country running," as he had contemptuously called the process of government for years. At thirty-five, never having faced an electorate, he was an implausible alternative to Trudeau and was a good deal less substantial even than Wagner. The Pollyanna flippancy of many of his positions disconcerted his friends, including me; I wanted him to do well, though the thought of him as party leader this time was pretty far-fetched. But he performed well enough to make a respectable showing. Unfortunately, Brian started drinking his own bath water and reacted violently to evidences of wavering among some friends.

After the convention, when he returned home to Montreal (the heights of Westmount, in fact) and found presents for his newly arrived child from a couple of old friends who had not supported him, he kicked the boxes down the walk. I always found the vagaries of Brian's personality rather endearing, including the bursts of mad egotism with which most politicians are encumbered, without which they could not constantly ask people for favours that are clearly a monumental presumption and inconvenience.

Brian's mastery of personal political techniques, of how to position himself athwart any circumstances involving useful acquaintances, of how to be helpful and ingratiating to anyone who could be of the slightest utility to him, of how to extract and amplify gossip, of how to enhance his own status in any situation, easily outstripped his executive talents. His knowledge of how to get ahead was geometrically greater than any notion he had of what to do when he reached his destination.

Although he did a conscientious and competent job in every position he held, from director of Standard Broadcasting arguably unto prime minister of Canada, whether his electorate was a single patron or the whole country, there was always something disquieting in Brian's hyperbole, glibness, and prevalence of wishfulness over convictions. He has always been an authentic admirer of the United States, an American political junkie, in fact, but beyond that his ideas of government consisted of a few platitudes about French-English relations and labour-management co-operation. It was pretty thin gruel for an aspiring prime minister. But to be companionable, interesting, and a rewarding friend, it is not necessary to be a political scientist of limitless virtuosity. It is as a fairly reliable friend, and as a political fixer, rather than as a statesman, that I have principally known him.

While I gave some support to Brian, I, with Douglas Bassett, Fred Eaton, and Steve Roman, worked hard to hold a fair section of

Toronto-area money and delegate support for Wagner. We made a contribution, though not on the mythic scale that Douglas and I implicitly claimed most humorously in an interview I had with former Pearson cabinet minister Judy LaMarsh, right after the convention. I had actually worked closely with Hugh Segal and John MacNaughton to build the Wagner organization in southern Ontario. As Douglas Bassett discreetly pointed out to Wagner after the fact, when Wagner had run out of money on convention eve, "We were the people you called when you needed 'one last $10,000,' and you got it."

I flew up to the convention in Ottawa in February 1976, with John Robarts, and paid my respects to the Wagner and Mulroney campaigns.

Steve Roman and I had been among those who had helped cooper up an arrangement whereby Claude Wagner, Jack Horner, Paul Hellyer, and Sinclair Stevens all agreed to support the strongest among themselves as each ballot required a narrowing of the field towards a majority for one candidate. Funding we gave and raised for all these candidates was on this basis. I had not known Stephen Roman before but quickly developed an appreciation of his rough, earthy, loyal, arch-conservative approach to most people and subjects. After my original conversational gambit, inquiring about the Masaryks and Eduard Beneš, whom Stephen dismissed as "whores," I didn't blur the distinction between Czechs and Slovaks again, and we had the pleasure of supporting many political and ecclesiastical causes together in the future.

My old friend Heward Grafftey was a candidate, though he received only a few votes from his "foot-soldiers" but he was subjected to Stephen's personalized techniques of political finance. With his pen hovering over his trust account chequebook, Stephen interrogated the applicant, filling in the date and even the signature before the amount. Heward did not excel in this examination, declined to join our delegate-vote-consortium, and obtained only a token contribution from Stephen.

Shortly after I arrived at the convention, I became convinced that the delegates were not going to accept either Mulroney or Wagner, the first as too inexperienced and unprepossessing and Wagner because too many questions had been raised, and inadequately answered by the sulking candidate, about the famous trust fund of 1972 and about Wagner's alleged propensity to unleash the police on demonstrators.

Peter White fired the final and decisive salvo on the trust fund. Speaking tendentiously from his personal knowledge of it, he implied a lack of financial probity, to which Wagner responded with his usual combination of mindless bluster, self-pity, and complete absence of imagination. Peter delivered this blast in the *Toronto Star* to the rather left-wing Quebec correspondent, Bob McKenzie, who ghoulishly bannered it on the front page just as the convention opened. Peter referred to a briefcase full of money, which he in fact had picked up from Eddie Goodman. It only contained $15,000 and was for legitimate campaign purposes but Peter insinuated cleverly.

I did my best at damage control with McKenzie, but with a candidate who became catatonic when the press was around, it was difficult, especially as I was not prepared, for obvious reasons, to attack Peter personally. In fact, there was nothing particularly distasteful about the so-called fund that Brian and Peter had helped to raise but Wagner was just incapable of coping with questions about his own conduct. I asked Bud McDougald if Wagner's fund bothered him. "Good God no!" he replied. "It's politicians who won't take a bribe that frighten me." There was no point trying to suggest it wasn't a bribe to such a cynic as McDougald. When asked for political contributions, McDougald usually declined and said, "I have found it more effective and economical just to buy a politician. It's not very hard, you know." (This was just more of Bud's bravura. His political contributions in the years I knew him were niggardly, uncontroversial, and ineffectual.)

Wagner's address on the eve of the vote was fully equal to his brilliant performance at the Quebec Liberal convention six years before. Mulroney's speech was a model-parliament tired pastiche of sophomoric clichés with John F. Kennedy airs.

Paul Hellyer's speech was a worse disaster and he was roundly jeered. There were two suspenseful questions: one was whether Joe Clark or Flora MacDonald would emerge as the stop-Wagner candidate (I thought Joe won that one when he claimed a physical resemblance to Sir John Macdonald, thus turning his physical appearance into an asset). Sinclair Stevens was the only one of our group who bolted; Paul Hellyer and Jack Horner were faithful to their word, but Sinclair went to Clark, probably providing the margin of victory. The second question was whether the emergent stop-Wagner candidate would stop Wagner, as I suspected. It was Joe Clark, and he did.

Joe won 1,187 to 1,122, passing Brian on the third ballot. Brian didn't have to declare on the last ballot, since Wagner, with typical spitefulness, decreed that Brian couldn't be a Quebec delegate. Brian came an honourable third and was well-positioned to be the next leader, an excellent result since he had in six months achieved a position that usually requires years or even decades of parliamentary and electoral slogging to achieve, and he was free to return, enhanced, to the private sector.

Brian, at first, didn't seem to appreciate his good fortune. He never expressed any hostility over my support of Wagner.

The personal highlights of the convention were when Gisèle Wagner, overcome by unimaginable suppositions or magic emanations, kissed me vigorously (a first and last), in front of Fred Langan's CBC television camera, and when John Diefenbaker in his peroration claimed that Trudeau had announced in Moscow that the United States was a military threat to Canada. Mr. Diefenbaker was much in evidence and he supported Wagner throughout. I had a couple of entertaining conversations with him in which he reminisced about Duplessis and about Cardinal Léger. (He had been most helpful in my Nobel Prize nomination of the Cardinal in 1972.)

The bands fell silent, the delegates departed, and the Progressive Conservative Party had to face up to the implications of having chosen Joe Clark as its leader. In my next conversation with Mulroney, about a month later, I told him that I thought he was odds-on as the next party leader, since I didn't believe Joe would last, or that Claude would stay even as long as Joe. Both my candidates had done well, and all those predictions came to pass, though Joe had a teasing flirtation with durability.

Not since the Sherbrooke convention of 1933 that elected Maurice Duplessis leader of the Quebec Conservatives in succession to Camillien Houde, with tacit support from L.A. Taschereau, had there been such covert Liberal influence on a Conservative convention through discreet backing for the Mulroney campaign. Their efforts were well-served for a time; Mulroney denied victory to Wagner, and Trudeau lived on politically, though only barely, into the eighties. Wagner would have swept the country in 1979, and Don Macdonald would have restored the Liberals after a Diefenbaker-like Conservative interlude.

Trudeau's friends thought they were using Mulroney, as Taschereau thought he was using Duplessis in 1933, but Mulroney (like Duplessis) was using them.

By the end of the convention, my family was already well advanced on a terrible ordeal; in September 1975, our worst fears had come to pass and my mother was diagnosed as terminally ill with liver cancer. She bore up magnificently; her composure was majestic and unwavering and she outlived doctors' projections, but it was depressing beyond anything I had experienced. Perhaps, in the abstract, it might have been possible to be philosophical about this relentless illness, and to see even her jaundice as an inexorable process like the turning of autumn leaves. This was not the abstract. The spectacle of that vital person, always so active, slowly, sadistically enervated by this dreadful illness was heart-breaking.

For ten days after Christmas, I accompanied my parents and a very experienced nurse to Bermuda, a place my mother had never been to and the place she most wanted to see. We drove all around the island, ate our meals in the room, and pursued a leisurely pace. I proofed some chapters on Duplessis that were almost ready for galleys and played a lot of chess with my father. When I won twenty-five games in a row, he paid me my agreed winnings with a solemn expression and the statement that "I look upon this as a distribution." As he advanced his last pawn, he pathetically intoned, "The little soldier plods on." Our return from Bermuda on the Argus airplane, a Falcon that McDougald had festooned with his heraldic arms (although he owned less of it than we did), was delayed for two days while it flew Doris Phillips's household and dogs from Toronto to Palm Beach.

There had never been any significant problem of communication between my mother and me, and there was no remaining task of explanation, apology, or exegesis. She was worried about my father but professed great faith in my brother and me. Despite being a bird in a gilded cage for many years with a sedentary and, in any case, not very serviceable husband, her life was her family and she would die serene. The memory of her that predominates, that never abates or ceases to be inspiring, is her burning partisanship for us. The power of her fine example is even strengthened by the excruciating end. When we had our last conversation, two days before she died at home, but when conscious moments were becoming rare, it was intense, difficult, and brief, but we did actually say goodbye, and it helped; at least it helped me.

She died in the early morning of June 19, 1976. I returned to my parent's home within an hour of her death. My mother's ravaged remains had already been removed. I endeavoured to give my father a word of encouragement: "We must turn a new page," etc., but it wasn't a huge success. My brother and I had bought the most prominent plot available at Mount Pleasant Cemetery. Father expressed relief that it was well removed from Mackenzie King's and was happy enough to be near J.Y. Murdoch, the founder of Noranda Mines, but he was alarmed to be told that the wife of a former competitor was nearby, presaging the eventual interment of the widower. "I always liked and respected Jim Murdoch but if I'm supposed to go through eternity next to that thieving hypocrite, I won't go."

He wasn't robust enough to go to the funeral, but went to within sight of the graveside, which he viewed through dark glasses from the back of his car like a Mafia gang lord, driven by his multi-purpose Catalonian houseman.

Back at the house, he received some of the guests upstairs and finally, when most people except a few relatives and friends had left, he descended the stairs and made a valiant try at being amusing, a talent that did not desert him even on this occasion. When Douglas Bassett asked him if he was planning a trip during the summer, he responded that yes, he would be visiting his dentist on Yonge Street in late July.

I was extremely worried about his own physical and psychological condition. The death of my mother had been a crushing, excruciating experience. All my father's tendencies to melancholia and loneliness could be expected to be accentuated, as well as his sense of helplessness at his immobility and poor eyesight. My brother and I visited him frequently to try to buck him up, and I set out, without being tiresomely energetic, to attract his thoughts to new horizons.

My brother came to see me June 28 to say he had had a very difficult session with him the night before, that Father was quite low and even prey to dark thoughts, that he had little will to live and was there anything I could do? Burdened with a heavy summer cold, I went out to see him in the early evening of the twenty-ninth, and did my best.

In surviving my mother, I said, he had at least spared her the sadness he was now experiencing. Even after all he had achieved and endured, especially this latest and heaviest deprivation, his life still had meaning, and there were few practical limits to the happiness he might yet attain or recreate if he could look past, without being disrespectful, the gloom of recent events. I even suggested that, if his morale was insupportably low, he could have a psychological consultation that couldn't do any harm and might even prove beneficial.

He wasn't enthusiastic on this point and was of that generation that found any such recourse demeaning and even stigmatizing. After he died I discovered some books in his library about sadness that he had heavily interlineated: it was the only evidence, and posthumous at that, of a gallant but unnecessarily lonesome effort to cope with a phenomenon many people face, and for which much help is available. As he was absolutely fixed in his materialist view of our "pecuniary society" and addicted to snide remarks about "invisible means of support, God is the noblest work of man," there was no point even raising theistic avenues of encouragement.

Still, I thought I was having some effect, especially when I suggested that we try to co-ordinate our reading so that we could discuss our current books more comprehensively. He responded well to this suggestion and started upstairs to get the book he had just started, a volume of humour by H. Alan Smith. I watched him from the garden room move determinedly up the circular stairs in the front hall. He had a formula he had developed over many years when he retired very late of declaiming Shelley's "Ozymandias," matching lines to steps. I was thinking of this, though he didn't do it in daylight hours, but I had accompanied him as a steadying hand many times, when there came the unnerving crack of straining and breaking wood, followed by the descent of my father backwards through and over the bannister to the floor about ten feet below.

The houseman and I reached the scene simultaneously and carried my father into the library and set him down on the couch. He was not altogether coherent, and though there was a certain amount of blood around, it wasn't obvious that he had broken or ruptured anything important. I called an ambulance as well as the endlessly patient neighbouring doctor and my brother.

My father, when he came around a bit, spoke of having lost his balance on the stairs and of having no desire to live. The ambulance took him to Scarborough General Hospital, where an elderly woman in good and very disgruntled voice was moved from her room to the hall to make way for this new patient. All through my stay at the hospital of several hours, she was audibly grumbling about being downgraded; she was unappeasable by doctors and orderlies assuring her that it was an emergency and that she would get her room back shortly.

My father and I had a little conversation, one more effort to bridge the gap of years and pathos that separates a man from his son. He called me "a good son." It was a deeply affecting exchange. I tried to be hopeful in my words and thoughts, but he had sustained a terrible shock and had practically no will to go on. He began to lapse in and out of consciousness, and I was taken out by the presiding doctor and warned in the most unambiguous terms that he might not make it. I went home, passing Bud McDougald on Lawrence Avenue in the back of his Rolls-Royce Phantom V, had a mahogany-coloured glass of Scottish whisky and settled in to watch a Charlie Chan movie. Charlie Chan was just boarding the *Queen Mary* when the doctor phoned again. My father was dead.

I went to my brother's house, and when we settled into comfortable chairs, he looked up, apparently startled at the thought, and said, "Holy Jesus! We're orphans!" We thought of holding a very private funeral, but at the welcome suggestion of my sister-in-law, we resolved to try to recreate the days of his prominence. As honorary pallbearers, I recruited Bud McDougald, E.P. Taylor, Nelson Davis (an old friend, who fervently avoided publicity but had just been revealed by Peter Newman to be one of Canada's wealthiest men), Charlie Gundy, Max Meighen, Bruce Matthews, Alex Barron, and even John Bassett, who, when Douglas asked him, replied that he hadn't "seen George Black in ten years," but accepted. Grace Church was almost full, July 2, 1976; we sang the ecclesiastical version of

"Danny Boy," "My Own Dear Land," "O God Our Help in Ages Past," and the "Battle Hymn of the Republic." It was a moving tribute and a poignant hour, capped by the industrialists' prayer at the graveside that I had first heard when my mother and I attended the memorial service for Neil McKinnon in 1975, the former chairman of the Bank of Commerce. "May God's mercy come to those who serve him, by expanding the commerce of the nation."

As part of our high state of solidarity with Bud McDougald, I conferred upon him in the printed program of the funeral the minor honour of chief honorary pallbearer. His discussion with E.P. Taylor in the centre of our dining room after the funeral reminded Brian Stewart, who shares my bemusement at comparing great events to local ones, of the meeting of L.B.J. and de Gaulle at J.F.K.'s funeral. As he left, Bud gave my brother and me his famous two-hand handshake, which my brother called, in reference to the coach-and-four event that McDougald sponsored at the Royal Winter Fair and named after his home, "the Green Meadows Four-in-hand."

My brother and I went to see him at Green Meadows ten days later. There was no question of our Ravelston partners exercising their right to buy our shares. Bud McDougald welcomed us most graciously. He was an elegant and considerable figure. His patronage to young men in our position was invaluable and his friendship, though cool and never presumed upon, was appreciated, and for what it was worth, reciprocated. He left it to us to divide up Father's positions as director of Argus, Ravelston, Dominion Stores, and Standard. My brother and I elected Argus and Ravelston for me and the others for him.

The coroner's report, obligatory where death was not from natural causes, spoke of an "accident in the house," which, it was suggested privately, might have been caused by an arthritic seizure in the knee causing him to fall through the bannister. Obviously I would prefer to take that explanation over a self-inflicted cause, but his life had drained away, almost as cruelly and over a longer but less precisely diagnosed time than my mother's, and they had succumbed almost symmetrically, after the proverbial "long illness, quietly at home," in her case, and "suddenly" in his.

With strong feelings of sadness, loneliness, and injustice, I felt also that just enough had been put in place by my ascendants to build into something substantial and extraordinary, yet continuous to what they had done. And I believe that they might, generally, have foreseen what was coming, with some confidence and satisfaction. As my mother said, of the deaths of her own parents, it "certainly closed the nursery door."

CHAPTER SIX

Financier in Waiting
1976–1978

A FEW WEEKS AFTER MY FATHER'S FUNERAL, I went to Europe for a leisurely restorative and contemplative tour of some of France's most commodious watering places.

One evening in Biarritz, after pausing for dinner in the Pyrenees near Pau, my companions and I settled into an ambitious night of fiery Armagnac and nostalgic reflection. We were staying in the Hôtel du Palais, built as Napoleon III and Eugénie's summer palace, which I had first visited in 1963, when the Duke of Windsor and the Emperor of Ethiopia were staying there. We fumbled through the lobby in the early morning, where Edward VII had installed H.H. Asquith as prime minister in 1908 and retired. (There had been no thought in that august era of the monarch cutting short his philandering holiday when illness required the incumbent prime minister, Campbell-Bannerman, to resign.)

The next morning, I felt, as a friend put it, "like an amputated leg." I slowly stabilized my battered metabolism by spending nearly five hours standing in about four feet of water with the Atlantic surf breaking over me. I expressed measured awareness to my friend M. Lafarge, the chief concierge, of the excesses of the previous evening and the hope that his attentive colleagues were not "scandalized." He professed not to know what I was talking about, and he assured me he had seen the "crowned heads of Europe pass out in the fountain and crawl through this lobby on their hands and knees. I respectfully urge you, sir, not to utilize the word 'scandal' lightly."

M. Lafarge had a long pointy nose and a quick, alert face like Duplessis, and he took great pride in his contribution to the war effort, which he spent as chief bartender at the Biarritz Casino. His self-designated role was to induce German officers to alcoholic excess. His finest hour was the night of June 5–6, 1944, when, he claimed with unfeigned pride, that he had spiked the drinks of the German regional commandant and his senior officers with straight alcohol, immobilizing the regional command with an epidemic of head-splitting hangovers.

I returned to Toronto a director of Argus Corporation and settled into my new regime as a "financier." In October I responded to an invitation from John Craig Eaton to come to the Eaton office. When I arrived, it was all four brothers who greeted me, somewhat formally, so I said, in an attempt at humour, "I accept." They did, in fact, invite me to become an Eaton's director. Without inquiring into the condition of the company, I said, "Of course, I'm honoured to be asked and of course I accept." The venerable T. Eaton Company was at this point somewhat beleaguered, but it was a great trademark and the owners had effectively bet the company on the Toronto Eaton Centre.

This was a bold move and Canada being the country it is, it was impossible to avoid for long the knowing advice that Eaton's was circling the drain and that the Eaton Centre would bomb. In fact, the Eaton Centre was a success from the start. Contrary to the conventional wisdom, Toronto did like stores open to nine o'clock every week-night, and I realized for the first time (vicariously) the pleasure of calculatedly gambling everything, and winning. Almost as agreeable as the self-enrichment is the confirmation of judgement. For a proprietor, the second will inevitably lead to the first.

The Eatons eventually decided to take direct control of their own business, probably for the first time effectively since the death of Sir John Craig Eaton in 1922. They did so with their customary suavity and determination, and the improvement in the company's results that shortly ensued completed the renewal of the Eaton family and its fortunes. In letting go a vice president who had sponsored an agency advertising campaign based on the slogan "At Eaton's you're more than welcome," Fred Eaton imparted the news of the executive's imminent departure in the words: "At Eaton's you are no longer welcome."

My natural sympathies are with the proprietors, whose own money is at stake. Too often I have seen non-proprietorial managers focus on keeping others at bay, expanding their companies unwisely and steadily improving their own financial condition irrespective of performance. The proprietor-manager implicitly accepts the responsibility for his actions, the consequences of his mistakes, the reward for his successes. The buck literally stops with him. It has been a particular pleasure to see some of Canada's leading financial families renew and multiply their fortunes in a way that the usual leftist caricature of the hereditary rich doesn't provide for. Less satisfying, but no less an affront to the leftist conviction that the rich (inevitably) get richer (as if there were anything wrong with that), has been the evaporation of many recently accumulated fortunes.

There is not, and should not be, any safety net for the rich. The Eatons, Westons, Bronfmans, Thomsons, Jackmans, McCutcheons, and others have built solidly upon ancestral attainments. That the fact of having successful antecedents doesn't deprive people of all possible merit brightens the horizons for all those aspiring to continuity and seeking to avoid the treadmill of clogs to clogs in three generations. Nor does this durability of deserving families imply any inaccessibility to newcomers. Paul Desmarais, the Reichmanns, Ted Rogers, Jimmy Pattison, and many others assumed their rightful positions as successful and respected leaders in their fields without being constrained for an instant by the presence of "established" socio-economic families.

It is a myth of the left and one of the well-springs of the pervasive Canadian spirit of envy that the success of a person implies the failure or exploitation of someone else. Our economic system is not based on single-combat war or a zero-sum game. It is a dynamic process where the greater the number and effort of economic participants, the greater the transactional velocity of money, the greater the general prosperity, given a reasonable legislative and regulatory framework.

In furtherance of my campaign to become a plausible corporate player, I set out to attain the principal criterion of that status, to become a director of one of the major Canadian banks. My strategy for this minor undertaking was to convince my generous and enthusiastic friend Bill Twaits, the long-time chairman of Imperial Oil and board vice president of the Royal Bank, that I would be a welcome addition to the board of that bank. Since it would not be the height of propriety for me to make the case myself, I got my old friend John Hull, who had done a good deal of work for my father and was intimately associated with Twaits in some projects at the Business Council on National Issues, to lobby for me.

(I did not know then that most of the directors of Canadian banks run their businesses more efficiently than the banks themselves are run and that there is an air of self-important unreality in much of bank board proceedings.)

Bill Twaits rose admirably to the cause and set on the Royal Bank's chairman, Earle McLaughlin, to the same effect. Earle had me to lunch with some of his directors and officers and duly invited me onto his board. Out of courtesy, I advised McDougald, who was rather miffed at the Royal Bank for having bankrolled the Power Corporation bid for Argus. He reacted very vigorously and said I couldn't accept McLaughlin's invitation because the Royal Bank was a hostile institution.

I had not foreseen the extent of his reaction and remonstrated with him to the effect that I could start to rebuild our relations with that bank, where Taylor, Phillips, and Meighen had all been directors, but he was adamant. I pointed out that I had some desire to be a bank director and the Royal had proffered the only invitation I had in hand at that point. He said that he would produce an invitation for me to the Commerce board at once. I replied that McLaughlin had said I couldn't join the Commerce board because the Bank Act forbade more than 25 per cent of the directors of any public company being directors of the same bank.

McDougald fumed that he didn't "need any lessons from Earle McLaughlin on the Bank Act." He said that he would expand the board of Argus to twenty-one from sixteen, to enable me to accept the CIBC invitation (McDougald, Thornbrough, Fairley, and the president of Domtar, Alex Hamilton, were already Argus and Commerce directors). He added that he would consult me about some of the five new Argus directors but that if I accepted the Royal invitation, he would not re-elect me an Argus director.

I had to give way at this point and declined Earle McLaughlin's invitation with sincere regret and thanked Bill Twaits for his efforts.

I hinted to both of them what the source of the problem was. (One of Earle's successors, Alan Taylor, has advised me that I am only the second person in history to decline such an invitation. I did so with reluctance. I believe John Robarts was the other.) Russell Harrison, the new chairman of the Canadian Imperial Bank of Commerce, telephoned promptly the day after my climactic talk with Bud and asked what I was doing for lunch. I replied that I was obviously planning to lunch with him and there began a very agreeable and sometimes close relationship with him.

Bud proposed as new Argus directors an Eaton as, he surmised (correctly), someone I would recommend and he would welcome, and I suggested Fred (who accepted "with gratitude and humility"), Harry Edmison and Jim Wright, the long-time secretary and treasurer of the company, Trumbull Warren, and Bud Baker. Trumbull was honorary colonel of the 48th Highlanders, chairman of Rheem Canada Ltd., current president of the Royal Winter Fair and had been an aide to Field Marshal Montgomery. I barely knew him but thought he would be an excellent candidate. I could scarcely have imagined how helpful, insightful, and valuable a director he would prove to be.

I had known Bud Baker for many years. He was the chairman of the Ontario Jockey Club in succession to E.P. Taylor and had owned an outdoor advertising company. He was a well-regarded person whom McDougald recommended because he had once held the tail of a horse throughout a trans-Atlantic air flight, preventing the animal from kicking a hole in the side of the aircraft. I liked Bud Baker but suggested we were in danger of becoming a little too gentrified and too far removed from finance and industry. I added that I thought the qualification he mentioned a trifle esoteric for the task at hand.

I suggested instead Nelson M. Davis, the very wealthy owner of a multiplicity of small and medium businesses. He was a friend of Bud's and had just retired as a director of the CIBC, and would, with Fred Eaton and Hal Jackman, who had joined the Argus board in 1975, bring some visible financial muscle to the board at a time when we were facing the "inevitability" theory being propagated by Desmarais's flacks about his ultimate status at Argus. Bud agreed. In the immediate future of Argus Corporation, the election of these five directors, especially Nelson Davis, was to prove critically important.

The next day, Dick Thomson, the president of the Toronto-Dominion Bank whom I had come to know as an Eaton's director, came to see me to invite me on his board. All my intrigue and politicking were thus unnecessary, as this was a spontaneous visitation from a man who had not been badgered or bullied into extending it. I was grateful for the invitation, though I couldn't accept it. When I joined the CIBC board, I was represented as the youngest director, at thirty-two, in the bank's history.[†]

The former chairman of the CIBC, Page Wadsworth, was the chairman of Confederation Life and invited me on that board, where George Black had also been a rather infrequent attender. It was a powerful group of directors, despite being a mutual company whose officers effectively occupy sinecures.

Not long before the Confederation Life invitation, I became a director of Carling O'Keefe, the successor company to Canadian Breweries. This really was a sentimental journey, though an expedient one also, as we supplied this brewery with a good deal of malt. It also brought me into close and regular contact with Jean Lesage, with whom I had many illuminating discussions about Quebec, especially in the run-up to the Quebec referendum. We re-enacted some of his debates with Duplessis to our high mutual amusement.

Quebec voted, November 1976. When Bourassa dissolved the National Assembly after just three years, it was generally expected that he would be re-elected comfortably. As the campaign progressed, it became clear that the Parti Québécois and a revived Union Nationale, which was pitching for the English vote, were gaining. I made my modest contribution by writing the editorial recommendation for the *Sherbrooke Record*, in which I described Bourassa's government as corrupt, hypocritical, unworthy of support from English Quebeckers, and "an embarrassment and a disgrace to all Quebeckers."

[†] My attendance record has exceeded my father's at the same bank. He once lamented that the famous Alberta oilman, Eric Harvie, "outsmarted me. I managed to attend one meeting in five years, but Eric got to none in six." This comment was at the most unsocial stage of his career. He offered his resignation to McKinnon every year but it was always declined.

After Gabriel Loubier had led the Union Nationale to extinction in 1973, Joseph Maurice Bellemare, Duplessis's neighbouring assemblyman from Cap-de-la-Madeleine, and Johnson and Bertrand's labour minister, stood successfully in a by-election in 1974 and kept the flame alive.

Peter White, Robert Rumilly, and I had had an unforgettable meeting with this, perhaps the most colourful of all Duplessis's lieutenants except for Camillien Houde, in April 1975, in the Windsor Hotel. Leaning forward in his armchair, fist thrust heavenwards at one moment, pounding the floor the next, only occasionally striking the *juste milieu* of the arm rest, Bellemare swore to revive the once great party he had served with such originality and faithfulness. (At times he was so demonstrative he reminded me of Field Marshal Guderian's description in his memoirs of an aroused Hitler.) When the Duplessis bridge collapsed between Trois-Rivières and Cap-de-la-Madeleine in 1949, it was Bellemare who instantly concluded that it had been sabotaged by communists. Even Duplessis had trouble chinning himself on that one, only discreetly determining the bridge had been named after his father and not himself.

On Quebec election night 1976 I was sitting at the head table of the annual dinner of the Canadian Council of Christians and Jews, under the chairmanship of Earle McLaughlin, who advised the dinner of the decisive victory of the Parti Québécois. I rounded out the evening with a sequence of nightcaps at one of the Eaton residences and left mumbling about the need "to amputate the gangrenous limb."

The overtly separatist vote in Quebec elections had gone from 2 per cent in 1962 to 9 per cent in 1966 to 23 per cent in 1970 to 30 per cent in 1973 to 41 per cent in 1976. In the same period, the Union Nationale had gone from Duplessist "autonomy" to Johnsonian "equality or independence" to crypto-sovereignty, and the Quebec Liberal Party had gone from integral federalism to Bourassa's advocacy in Paris in 1975 of "an entirely French, uniquely sovereign Quebec in a Canadian common market." It was a long way from the *alliance-cordiale bonne entente* that had attracted me to Quebec exactly a decade before, but a logical conclusion to the process that had helped propel me out of Quebec in July 1974.

Trudeau was severe, asserting that Quebec's new government was caught between its independentist ambitions and the undertaking to hold a referendum it couldn't win. What little argument there had been for voting for Clark against Trudeau, given their disparity in personal stature, and the fact that Joe was not appreciably to the right of the incumbent in economic matters, vanished with Lévesque's election, as it was not conceivable to me that Clark could do a better job than Trudeau of defending the integrity of the federal state. We were shortly to hear Joe's whingeing about "community of communities." No matter how earnestly uttered, this always sounded to me like sovereignty-association, Quebec's independence while continuing to receive equalization grants and transfer payments.

In any case, I welcomed Lévesque's victory because I thought it brought us closer to a revelation of our political future, and it punished a loathsome regime of financially corrupt, compulsively cowardly, poll-addicted nerds and tinkerers. It was a choice between Lévesque's second-rate Danton and Bourassa's fourth-rate Talleyrand. Mirabeau (Daniel Johnson perhaps) was dead.

My book on Duplessis was finally ready for publication at the beginning of December 1976. One of my last interviews was with the co-founder of the Union Nationale, Paul Gouin, who owned and operated a *boîte à chanson* in Old Montreal. He was philosophical, and rather generous to Duplessis. He was one of the many elderly Québécois, once prominent, whom I interviewed shortly before they died and who remain a precious connection to a traditional Quebec that preceded them to the grave by several decades.

My assault on the conventional wisdom over Quebec and its recent history was so extensive that I felt it must be meticulously documented with reference to the papers that only Rumilly and I had seen. The result was a 684-page book with over a thousand footnotes.

My basic thesis was that Duplessis exploited the paranoia of the Roman Catholic bishops to convince them they had to continue to staff and operate the schools and hospitals to avoid the agnosticisation of Quebec (only Charbonneau, Léger, and a couple of other bishops were suitably wary of this reasoning). He was thus able to pay comparatively risible salaries to teachers, nurses and other hospital workers, to devote most of the budget to schools, hospitals, rural electrification, and other elements of infrastructure in which Quebec had been notoriously deficient, and to keep taxes low, political contributions high, and avoid deficits.

He had also advanced programs of day care, aid to home-ownership and pensions, and the highest minimum wage in Canada. And his legislated generosity to workers, although discouraging strikes, kept the political loyalty of the province's working class, despite the frenzied hostility of most union leaders, and attracted unprecedented capital investment. Quebec was modernized in all respects except political methodology, and much of the Quiet Revolution was cosmetics, extravagance, and puffery. The secularization of education led to the collapse of the religious orders and an explosion in costs with no commensurate improvement in standards, facilities, accessibility, or choice in education.

Lesage conceded to me that he couldn't have won against Duplessis or Sauvé. Quebec had to change and Lesage was in many respects a good premier, but his government was dumped in 1966 in favour of Duplessis's most assiduous disciple (Johnson). High taxes, labour chaos, discrimination against the English, and a collapse in investment accompanied Quebec's deindustrialization and the drift towards independence.

Rumilly's opus was, unfortunately, but as was widely predicted, something of a white-wash.

Stung by my quotation in my book of some of his more obsequious letters to Duplessis, Rumilly even stirred up a campaign of vilification against me in the letters section of *Le Devoir*, although the newspaper published two highly favourable reviews of my book and the publisher, Claude Ryan, referred to it very positively on many occasions. I carried on a considerable slanging match with Father Jacques Cousineau, who alleged that I had dramatized Duplessis's death and been disrespectful of Quebec's clerical right generally.

I had scarcely seen him off (I described him, not inaccurately, as, *inter alia*, a "quasi-fascist Jesuit myth-maker") when I was attacked in the same pages by an even more bizarre opponent, Duplessis's old valet at the Château Frontenac, Charlie Lamarre. It was not hard to discern Rumilly's gnarled and clumsy hand in this improbable enfilade also. Lamarre subsequently wrote to me, apologizing for having allowed himself to be pushed by Rumilly into questioning the accuracy of my book. I then regretted that I had included in my response to *Le Devoir* the comment that Lamarre was an "illiterate bootlicker" (*"flagorneur illetré"*).

Exchanges of such vitriol are not uncommon in the press of Quebec but were a mere prelude to what was to come in normally more staid Toronto. I had heard from friends who had been doing research at the National Library in Ottawa in the summer of 1976, that Ramsay Cook, working in the same place, had repeatedly said that he had requested the review of my book in the *Globe and Mail*. He had, he said, unfortunately been unsuccessful in his endeavour to block my M.A. degree at McGill, but he would do a shredding operation on the book. There was no question of his waiting to see the finished product — it was a premeditated onslaught.

I spoke to my friend Dick Malone, publisher of the *Globe and Mail*, who told me the review had been requested by and assigned to Ramsay, and that I should await the review to which I would have a full right of reply. He said that if he were to reassign the review, "Cook will only write an even nastier one elsewhere."

I awakened, Saturday, December 18, to discover a dreadful review in the *Globe and Mail*. I read it, wrote a five-paragraph response on my typewriter, and took it over to Malone's house at eleven a.m. When I started up the walk in front of his house, he flung open his front door and said, "I've been expecting you."

He sent me down to the newspaper office to see the assistant to the editor, Cameron Smith, to avoid any possibility of defamation. The letter, printed on the twentieth, pointed out that Ramsay had tried unsuccessfully to block my degree, had devoted a significant part of his career to propagating myths that were exposed by the research in my book, had requested the review for the *Globe and Mail* and that "we are all familiar with the elemental rule of justice that people are to be judged by their peers. The *Globe and Mail* is not to be commended for departing from that rule and entrusting the review of a serious work on an important subject to a slanted, supercilious, little twit."

I had taken the precaution of lining up a good deal of academic support for my book, which was not, in any case, easy to attack for any lack of rigour or literacy, dense though it is. Cook's chief complaint was that it was "unjustifiably long." Had I been much shorter, he would undoubtedly have complained of superficiality. (Five years later, when it was my job to reorganize a sclerotic group of companies, financial analysts sometimes objected that my deals were too complicated. Financial analysts were supposed to be able to understand complex transactions, just as historians were supposed to be able to face up bravely to a book of 684 pages, at least if it were in their fields of specialty.)

It was Cook's prejudgement of the book that infuriated me. I never minded spontaneous criticism. Jack Pickersgill objected to my treatment of federal-provincial relations and André Desrosiers, one of the anti-Duplessis members of Michel Brunet's panel at the University of Quebec in Trois-Rivières in 1971 where I met Rumilly, objected that my book tended to justify an "outworn ideology." Both wrote in learned journals. A professor from the University of Victoria wrote an ideologically hostile review in the Vancouver *Sun*. I replied dismissively to him but much more gently than I had to Cook. Norman DePoe, the veteran news commentator, objected in some of the Thomson newspapers to complicated language in Duplessis. (I had wanted to call the book *Render unto Caesar*, but Jack McClelland said we had to name it after the famous subject to promote sales.) There were several dozen positive reviews, including all the Quebec newspapers, Jack Granatstein in *Quill and Quire*, Ken Adachi in the *Toronto Star*, in Canadian Press, and in *Maclean's*.

Ramsay Cook had not known that I was aware he was my external examiner at McGill, and his feeble reply to my letter, published one week later, amounted to an ungracious retreat from the field. He was particularly upset that I referred to him with "contemptuous familiarity as 'Ramsay'," which is why I did it. (As far as I can recall, we have never met.) If his reply had been feistier, I had prepared a "bench-clearing brawl," for Jack McClelland, John Robarts, John Bassett, and distinguished historian Robert Bothwell were all prepared to support me in writing. As it was, Douglas Bassett voluntarily wrote a generous letter of support to the *Globe and Mail*, for which I was grateful as the sort of help always hoped for but not always received from friends.

There was no doubt, from the subsequent reviews, the authoritative status *Duplessis* achieved in the bibliographies of other books, the large numbers of purchases from universities, schools, and libraries, that I won the battle for a revised view of Duplessis. The documents I used went back into inaccessibility at the Trois-Rivières Seminary, though I microfilmed and photocopied the principal items at my own expense and gave copies to McGill, the Glendon bilingual campus of York University, and the University of Windsor. I considered the French-Canadian academic treatment of Duplessis so shabby that their universities were undeserving of such a collection. (I gave them to Windsor when that university's chancellor, Richard Rohmer, awarded me an honorary doctorate of literature in 1979.) I had been a governor of York University for a time but retired when the governors' choice for an administrative post was passed over in favour of a faculty nominee, and when the university's able president, two years into a five-year term, had himself reelected for five years, starting in three years. The governors weren't governing anything, but I retired in better spirits than one of my colleagues, who quit, advising that York University be turned into an industrial factory.

George C. Scott said of General Patton, whom he so masterfully portrayed in the famous film, and I felt similarly about Duplessis: "He was a splendid anachronism and I rather enjoyed the old gentleman." The book was brilliantly translated into French by my friend Monique Benoit, who had helped in the research. It was published in two volumes in French and sold a remarkable 10,000 copies. To be attacked by Rumilly on the right and Cook on the left reassured me that I had been, as I had hoped, fair. Auréa Cloutier, Maurice Bellemare, and Duplessis's elegant and charming niece, Berthe Bureau Dufresne, came to the gala French launch in 1977, but I regretted the end of my friendship with Rumilly. We did not communicate again, except for my eightieth-birthday greetings, to which he replied cordially enough on stationery emblazoned, defensively perhaps, with his new device *"J'ai recherché et écrit la vérité."*

The greatest encomium *Duplessis* received was from Bernard Landry, Peter White's former law partner and then Lévesque's economic development minister. At one of the new government's first cabinet meetings, the subject of the famous Duplessis statue came up, and Landry resolved the debate over what to do with it by reading from my book: "Successive governments of Quebec made themselves appear ridiculous by seeming to be afraid of Duplessis' statue."

Lévesque, as he recounted to me himself a couple of years later, brought his fist down on the cabinet table and said, "He's right! I hated Duplessis, but he was the prime minister for eighteen years, and I'm not afraid of his goddam statue. The people have paid for it; we'll install it outside this window." An imposing and somewhat graceful likeness looks enigmatically down on the calèches and busloads of tourists that pass beneath it, through the St. Louis gate adjacent to the National Assembly.

My brother and I moved to strengthen our financial position by selling Draper Dobie to Dominion Securities. I again called upon McDougald and suggested he use his influence with the chairman of Dominion Securities, Doug Ward, to promote the advisability of such a move. Bud was an excellent facilitator once again, and my brother successfully negotiated with Dominion Securities' president and our childhood acquaintance, Tony Fell, who was brought up on the same street we were (and is still my neighbour there). Dominion Securities gained some very capable people from Draper Dobie and we made a good gain on the cash and shares deal while insulating ourselves from the vagaries of the brokerage business and reducing our exposure to that shrinking industry. My brother and I moved our offices to DS and it was to prove a most pleasant and profitable association.

My brother suggested we sell our parents' house, but in fact we would never replace the property, seven acres and only about a mile from the demographic centre of metropolitan Toronto. I suggested he take it, since he had the family to fill it, but when he declined, I took it for myself and moved in in February 1977. A hawk flew majestically around the tree-tops at the back of the property for the several hours required to move in my furniture. I had a sensation of setting my possessions with some permanence in the house where I was brought up. It required twelve years for me to succeed in buying the property from my father's estate, in the course of which time I almost completely rebuilt and extended the house and added four adjacent acres (through the neighbourly co-operativeness of Murray Koffler and Tom Bata).

I spent 1977 establishing my candidacy as a plausible alternative to Paul Desmarais and Hal Jackman when the McDougald era might end. The first step was to establish credibility in the Establishment manner, become known, pick up a few directorships, especially a bank. After three years back in Toronto I had done that and had some believability as a vigilant investor, though my aptitudes as a manager had not been put to much of a test since I left Sherbrooke. My initial approach was just to develop excellent working relationships with the principal likely survivors of Bud McDougald within the Ravelston control block, Meighen, Matthews, Barron, Chant.

I made a point of acquainting myself fairly thoroughly with the Argus Group operating personalities as well. The Standard Broadcasting management team, led by H.T. "Mac" McCurdy, were competent, quality radio people who could be relied upon to protect their franchises. Alex Hamilton, the president of Domtar, appeared to be thoroughly capable. In Montreal, and in the Meighen-Barron, as opposed to the McDougald, orbit, as McDougald had given Meighen the Domtar chairmanship as a consolation prize for withholding the Massey chairmanship, Hamilton was not corrupted by the Toronto Street jet-addicted decadence. Argus controlled just 14 per cent of Domtar. The forest products industry was in a severe cyclical recession in 1977.

Dominion Stores was more problematical. The president, Tom Bolton, was an honest career supermarket executive, but the company had missed the bus on real estate and most of wholesale, where profit margins as a percentage of sales were two to three times the retail figure, and was showing the first signs of obsolescence in store layouts and marketing techniques. Rumours were already rife that there were irregularities in the company's purchasing techniques. Where there are so many large suppliers in a business so infested with notorious crooks and such huge inventories of resaleable products passing through so many hands, "shrinkages," i.e., theft by employees, are generally about 1.5 per cent of total sales, $30 million in the case of this company. In Dominion Stores, there appeared to be a lot moving under the floorboards.

Hollinger Mines didn't mine anything. It owned 60.5 per cent of Labrador Mining and Exploration Co. Ltd., which also didn't mine or explore; it secured a royalty on ore and concentrates mined by the Iron Ore Company of Canada. The president of Hollinger and Labrador, Al Fairley, was one of the least enterprising executives I have ever met. He exuded, at first, the charm and the vocal self-confidence of an assertive Alabaman. He had by 1977 reverted to being an Alabaman and commuted to Toronto on the Hollinger plane every so often when it served him to pretend that he had a job and an office. Fairley also had less fighting instinct than almost anyone I have met. He once left the directors' room of the Canadian Imperial Bank of Commerce as having a conflict of interest, because he was an American citizen when the unnamed target company in a takeover it was proposed the bank finance was identified only as an American corporation.

When the government of Newfoundland conducted an inquiry into the mining industry, looking at, among other things, the arguments for and against a provincial tax on royalties, Fairley promised the inquirer that if any such tax were imposed, he would personally assure a reduction in Newfoundland's bond rating. The predictable occurred, and the royalty tax imposed raised Labrador's tax rates to the highest corporate rate I have seen in Canada, about 60 per cent. Apart from collecting royalties, bank interest, and dividends on its 12 per cent of Noranda stock, sending out the occasional prospector, and holding a rather geriatric annual dinner, Hollinger conducted almost no business.

Bud and his friends made occasional belligerent noises about pursuing Noranda and called for the shareholders' list every few years, but no plans survived post-prandial coffee at the Toronto Club. Hollinger and Labrador had about $60 million in cash and of Argus's interests had the greatest opportunity for growth and reapplication of funds. Argus had about 20 per cent of the shares and McDougald's cousins, the McMartins, and the Dunlaps and one or two groups of Timminses had another 20 per cent or so. Hollinger was a sleeping princess who had not felt the kiss of a serious manager for so long that she was almost comatose.

Finally, there was Massey-Ferguson. In the fall of 1977, the famous farm equipment producer ceased payment of preferred and common dividends and published a heavy loss. McDougald had himself elected to the chairmanship, which had been vacant since the death of Phillips in 1964. The president, Albert A. Thornbrough, was an intelligent and interesting man, who had been a colonel during World War II, owned some oil wells, and had a presentable academic background. He had held the presidency for nearly twenty-five years at this point. His residence was Boca Raton, and he spent three or four days of every week there, operating his business from a converted, windowless garage at his house. Thornbrough had an expressionless, Grant Wood, American Gothic face, and in his impetuous, debt-financed expansion into the Third World, fleeing from the insuperable competition of John Deere in the United States, he became a prisoner of his dreams. It was a corporate *Apocalypse Now* and by 1977, Now was then.

It was an uncertain and deteriorating climate in the worn-down Argus Group that was further confused by the news that McDougald had contracted pneumonia in England in September 1977. He was in St. Michael's Hospital in Toronto for over a month but appeared to be recovering.

Having observed him over many years and after working closely with him for a couple of years, I had had ample opportunity to appreciate his personality and techniques. He was a rather handsome man, impeccably turned out, though with a tendency to ostentation — chandeliers in his extensive garages and gold dinner ware; his cars had miniature rear-windows, stylized hub-caps emblazoned with his heraldic arms and race-horse hood ornaments; the pinstripes of his lapels always exactly met those of his collar.

Bud played the role of tycoon to perfection. Following his 1966 coronary, he prevailed upon the Duke of Edinburgh to open the Royal Winter Fair and rode with him on the brief trip from the Toronto Club to the Royal York Hotel. When the *Toronto Star* mocked the Duke for not walking after all his emphasis on fitness, Bud cancelled several million dollars of Dominion Stores advertising in the *Star*. When he and Nelson Davis were stopped for not wearing their seat belts while driving their customized Cadillacs, they lectured the startled police officers on the supremacy of the Criminal Code's prohibition against any assistance to suicide over the Highway Traffic Act's insistence on seat belt use. He and Nelson were always threatening to sell part of their property to Saudi Arabia for a consulate unless some zoning change or other were approved. Bud, Nelson, and Steve Roman all claimed at one point or another to have bought parking lots in order to fire impudent parking attendants. Much of this may have been apocryphal but it was the stuff of Bay Street legend.

Bud McDougald's most attractive characteristic was his loyalty. Jean Lesage, then premier of Quebec, visited Bud in Palm Beach in

1964 and urged him to dump Géreld Martineau, Duplessis's party treasurer, as a Dominion Stores director as he had been indicted for wrongdoing in dispensing patronage. Bud replied: "No, Jean, he was a fine director when he was riding high. Even if you send him to jail I won't forget him, and when your voters tire of you you'll still be welcome in my house." After Lesage had been defeated he was still sometimes McDougald's guest.

In corporate terms, "he could always think of a hundred reasons for not doing anything," my father had said, and this immobilized torpor became more rigid with advancing years. He had become a great figure of Canadian business and society and had even carved out a cameo position in London as chairman of Massey-Ferguson, patron of the Queen's race-horse trainer, and owner of the King's Clere stable where she kept some of her horses. He was also a doyen of the Palm Beach set as president of the Everglades Club, a sumptuous facility whose membership comprised mainly indolent inheritors with a slight leavening of rising meritocrats such as Paul Desmarais (who Bud managed to kick out of the club in 1975 after his attempted takeover of Argus Corporation; he did not rejoin until after Bud died). Non-whites and Jews were not allowed in, even as guests for lunch or golf. Bud cheerfully retained this repulsive regime even though Jews had been among the club's founder-members and were excluded decades later only when the moribund descendants became frightened at Jewish economic advances, like rich white trash fearful of the emancipation of blacks.

Behind this imposing façade there still existed the seamy and meanly cynical Bud of old whom his acquaintances of youth had never forgotten. "I like depressions; I always make a lot of money from them," he boasted. "If these bankers had any brains, we'd be lending them money and they'd be getting rich, instead of the other way around." In fact, though he did baffle and gull the bankers, especially the CIBC, he was too cautious to borrow.

His $10 million in the main branch of the Canadian Imperial Bank of Commerce came from selling most of the property around his house in Toronto to an improbable middle-European financial adventurer, Rifet John Prusac, who covered the land with tacky, jerry-built houses in which, according to Bud, the "Third World" festered. Prusac was (and assumedly still is) a tall, wavy-haired, obsequiously polite fop, boutonnièred, bobbing and bowing and clicking heels, but a cunning enough operator despite being somewhat ridiculous.

Bud conducted a good deal of business with Prusac but always concealed this relationship from his respectable friends. He wouldn't bring Prusac to the Toronto Club but did receive him privately elsewhere and had no difficulty dazzling the garish real estate developer with his rich and self-confident demeanour. As I construed it as my business to be somewhat vigilant of McDougald and his entourage, I became aware of Prusac's presence, of his adulation for Bud, and of his desire to succeed him at Argus, which became common knowledge in the developer community.

It was a manifestation of Prusac's shameless ambition that he sought to enhance his candidacy to succeed to the airs, dignities, and honoraria of Bud McDougald by taking up with Bud's sister-in-law, Cecil Hedstrom, who was at least fifteen years his senior. Prusac had made $50 million or more in the development business, and Cecil, whose judgement often was notoriously deficient, apparently thought this Ruritanian liaison would put her upsides with Doris and Jim, who had married so wealthily while she, twice divorced, had had to flounder about selling real estate.

McDougald had intervened in the proposed sale of the Massey-Ferguson experimental farm by trying to sell the property without calling for bids to Prusac, who was going to give Cecil his side of the commission of the deal. The company's former secretary, Wally Main, who embodied the finest traditions of that corporation, refused to submit to this corrupt practice, and McDougald tried to bully Thornbrough into firing Main. In a typical Thornbrough compromise, he only froze his salary; I unfroze it when I came in and called Wally "the Captain Dreyfus of Massey-Ferguson."

Bud's chiselling was also unseemly for someone with such a hefty bank balance. It was unbecoming for him to make his trips to London on contra tickets from CFRB (tickets the radio station obtained in exchange for advertising) and to snitch Massey-Ferguson's Rolls-Royce Phantom V at an artificially low, depreciated value. (When I bought the other one, it was at market value.) Such was his cynicism that he had no policy but to pocket loose change as it appeared, albeit with as much pomp and sanctimony as possible. McDougald's lassitude, greed, and vanity were not constructive influences in the Argus Group.

Wally Main's successor as Massey secretary, Derek Hayes, had me to lunch early in 1978 with Victor Rice, formerly Massey's comptroller and now personnel vice president and generally recognized as the company's rising executive star. My worst fears of what a shambles the grand old company had become were confirmed. It was an appalling yet humorous tale of venality and self-delusion.

McDougald, to preserve Argus's position, had forbidden the issuance of more equity. Thornbrough, unable to develop a big tractor (over 100 horsepower) that would work, or to update the small tractor that did work, kept sustaining the company's sales by plunging into Third World countries, where sales and profits were chronically unstable and often unremitted. At the end of 1977, everything collapsed at once, but Thornbrough and his senior colleagues, like defeated generals in an overwhelming rout, were issuing orders to units that hadn't been formed or had long since been pulverized. The convalescent McDougald was like the eighty-four-year-old Pétain in 1940, called to lend the prestige of past (perceived) glory to the repulse of irresistible adversity.

McDougald went early to Palm Beach in November 1977, almost directly from release from his treatment for pneumonia at St. Michael's Hospital. We spoke a few times on the telephone in December and January; on one occasion, when the newspapers reported that Paul Desmarais would lead an officially sponsored group of Canadian businessmen to China, Bud phoned cheerfully to say I should tell Paul that he should find out how the Chinese "stole birds' nests out of trees and sold them soaked in hot water as soup for ten dollars each." Doug Ward, chairman of Dominion Securities, visited him in Palm Beach and Bud acknowledged that he felt let down by Thornbrough. Alex Barron also visited him and thought he was recovering. After early February there was an ominous silence, followed by more ominous rumours.

Bud turned seventy, March 14, 1978. I sent the now customary letter, flattering, but sincere in its gratitude for most of his attentions. On the fourteenth, he had himself driven to his farm in West Palm Beach which he had bought from the Norris family. He was very proud of it and had shown it to me and many other visitors. Now only a death's head in an oversized sports jacket, he would have reflected on this symbol of his progress from the little fellow in the wake of Taylor and Phillips to the supreme leader of the Canadian Establishment.

It had been a tenacious, crafty, and stylish exercise, but now it must end. The barbarian, in the form of Desmarais, was at the gate. The most famous interest, Massey-Ferguson, was circling the financial drain. The senior comrades, the old moustaches and true believers, Meighen, Matthews, Thornbrough, Fairley, McCormack, and Bolton, were beyond the point of having any possible purchase on the cascade of events. It had been a boffo performance, but it was only an act and the curtain descended on it on the Ides of March, 1978.

Bud had gone from his farm to the Good Samaritan Hospital and died peacefully there the day after his birthday. (Phillips had died in the same hospital just over thirteen years before.) His timing, like his tailoring, was impeccable. I was sitting in my office at Dominion Securities when Page Wadsworth phoned with the first rumour, followed quickly by John Eaton, who had heard from a friend at St. Michael's Cathedral, followed, a minute later, by Doug Ward, who was going to his farm "to soliloquize," followed two minutes later by Bruce Matthews, who imparted the news officially.

The following night Alex Barron, much the most capable of the Argus executives, came to dinner at our family home with my brother and me. Alex had caught the eye of Arthur Meighen when he was an investment dealer at Fry and Company and had been engaged by him to come into the family business, Canadian General Investments, to work with his son Max Meighen. The two together had done well, and Alex was a font of interesting ideas about managing the Argus Group to better health. He was particularly critical of Thornbrough and Fairley and wanted Ralph Barford and me to be Massey directors.

I had known Ralph Barford from the premier's Advisory Council and knew him to be an accomplished manufacturer and an outstanding businessman. Alex promised to get heightened representation for us in Argus councils. He didn't think Colonel Meighen wanted anything in the succession and anticipated that General Matthews would be the chairman and he (Alex) the president and me a vice president. He could not envision financial engineering and legerdemain as a method of strengthening Argus's position, but he was determined to sharpen operations. We all assumed Bruce Matthews was a McDougald executor and that he would effectively vote Bud's shares. I had been studying the Ravelston shareholders' agreement and left it on the table in front of me before and after dinner as a reminder to Alex of how fluid the company's affairs could become in the event of discord.

The following day, my brother and I went to McDougald's house to pay our respects. The coffin was open, "in the barbaric Toronto custom," as my father said of the same rite when Colonel Phillips died in 1964. My brother had severed an Achilles' tendon playing tennis and was hobbling about on crutches with some agility. Standing beside Fraser Fell, who was substantially bald, Bruce Matthew's nephew and senior partner of lawyers Fasken & Calvin, we stared for a few moments at the waxen face of Bud McDougald. My brother stepped back from the casket and pivoted on his crutches. As I looked upon Bud McDougald for the last time, I heard Monte say, "This is too much for me! Let's have a drink. Hello, Fraser, you're balding a bit! Must be grief." It added a useful note of levity to a solemn occasion.

The funeral the next day at St. Michael's Cathedral was adequately organized. The archbishop, Philip Pocock, who had quarrelled with Bud over the boycott of non-union grapes sold at Dominion Stores, had been bullied by Senator Joe Sullivan in particular to take the chair, though he was not the celebrant.[†]

The Duke of Wellington had been staying with Bud in Palm Beach and was present. So was E.P. Taylor, who had come from Lyford Cay to be sure that Bud was truly dead. Mrs. McDougald professed to be relieved not to find Paul Desmarais there. We sang "O Canada" and departed to Mount Hope cemetery, where John Prusac eerily materialized after most of the other mourners had departed and stood theatrically at the graveside for a long time in his camel-hair coat in the bitter cold. It was not a good augury. My own sadness was genuine. Remembered now were Bud's kindness to my parents and me; his strength up to a point and beyond that point; his surpassing

---

[†] Max Meighen claimed afterward that Peter Newman had taken communion (though of Jewish origins, the Newmans apparently changed during the thirties and Peter did produce a baptismal certificate for admission to the Order of St. Lazarus, but I certainly didn't notice him making his way to the communion rail).

skill as a charlatan. As Hal Jackman said, "He enriched our lives," by which Hal meant, for once, not so much materially as dramatically.

At the McDougald house afterwards, the plot thickened further when Doris volunteered to my brother and me that she was executrix with Jim and the Crown Trust Company of Bud's estate. Even she thought it was bizarre. There was no position in the estate for Bruce Matthews, Doug Ward, or any other friend of Bud's with any commercial acumen. Dixon Chant, as surviving Phillips executor with Doris and the Crown, and as vice president of the Crown, was emerging as a key player, whether he was yet aware of it or not.

I didn't know Dick Chant well. The year before, he had suffered a heart attack and missed the Argus annual meeting. (At the following organizational meeting, Bud explained, "It's only his first coronary and we don't worry about the first two or three." Bud claimed to have had five, but E.P. Taylor professed to believe that all but one were "indigestion from too great a consumption of ginger ale.") Dick had recovered completely, and I had often conversed with him most agreeably at Argus meetings, but I didn't have any idea what his view was of where we should go from here. As I left Green Meadows — never to return as events would have it — I resolved to find out. Argus was crumbling, and we couldn't wait for any more high-priced funerals before taking drastic restorative measures.

The Argus executive committee, to which I had been elected a week before McDougald died, in an intersection of McDougald's desire to have more factions directly in play and Barron's to have an activist ally, met March 22 at ten a.m. It may have been a final preferment by Bud to elect me, but considering the size of our shareholding, and the condition of the company, it would not have been easy or prudent to exclude me much longer. Bruce Matthews took the chair. I arrived at 10:04 because of a monumental traffic snarl on the Don Valley Parkway. Not having heard from Alex Barron since our dinner of March 16, I had assumed that he had achieved the necessary concurrence of Max Meighen and Bruce Matthews to what Alex and my brother and I had agreed March 16, that I would become an officer of Argus Corporation with an office in the company's headquarters at 10 Toronto Street, as well as a Massey-Ferguson director.

When I joined the meeting, with Bruce Matthews, Max Meighen, Alex Barron, Hal Jackman, and Dixon Chant, the committee had elected Max chairman, Bruce president and chief executive officer, Alex executive vice president. (There were a lot of references to business execution bandied about, for a company that had no income except dividends, had taken no initiatives in years, and showed little aptitude to do so now.) There was nothing for Dixon, nothing for me, and no indication at all that Alex even remembered what we had agreed six days before, much less secured the agreement of the others to it.

I stated that there could be no possible objection to the nominations that had been agreed but that especially in the aftermath of Bud's death and given the circumstances at Massey and the incursions of Power Corporation, we should be showing a high degree of solidarity and there should be some recognition of the other Ravelston shareholders. The implicit reference to Dixon was obviously deliberate, but the self-exalted triumvirs saw it only as an attempted thrust by me. Max Meighen replied that I was "rushing [my] fences." (Max subsequently claimed that he added that I wouldn't have long to wait, but he offered no such elaboration at the time.) A deathly silence from Alex was unbroken throughout the brief meeting, and he never offered an explanation afterwards.

In order to satisfy myself that there was certainly an element of spite in their desire to avoid conferring any recognition on me, I said that the press would regard the company's announcement as a slight to me in particular and did we need such intimations of factionalism. Max took the bait with uncharacteristic swiftness and growled that "we are running this company, not the press." I said no more, and the meeting ended.

I could hardly believe that whatever they thought of me, Max and Bruce and Alex would be so antagonistic at such a delicate stage and would do nothing to reinforce their position, as together they had only about 30 per cent of Ravelston (which had 60 per cent of Argus voting stock). Ravelston and its shareholders had about one-third of Argus's participating equity, against 50 per cent for Power Corporation. As I said subsequently to Peter Newman, "I couldn't even have an office at Argus. I could only go there and pay court to this triumvirate. It was a declaration of war. I don't know how they could claim to be so astounded by what happened after that. It's like the Japanese saying, 'We didn't expect the Americans to sink our carriers at Midway. All we did was bomb Pearl Harbour.'"

On my way along King Street after the meeting, I encountered an old friend and allowed that I was "in my eighth day of mourning and manoeuvring."

I went directly to my office at Dominion Securities and began implementation of a strategy for which I had already done some contingency planning in the event that had now come to pass that my brother and I were left out in the cold. It had been indicated at the executive committee meeting that Bruce would replace Bud as chairman of Dominion Stores, Massey-Ferguson, and Standard Broadcasting, and I surmised that the triumvirs had consulted no one but themselves on this subject.

The core of the strategy was to share with the ladies and their representatives a sense of irritation at the high-handedness of Max and Alex, Bruce being assumed to possess too much goodwill with Jim and Doris for that; to make a firm alliance with Dixon Chant and with the redoubtable P.C. Finlay, a permanent officer of Hollinger and who in advising the McMartins and Dunlops influenced almost as many Hollinger shares as Argus owned; and to cement an alternative coalition by taking a sizeable interest in the Crown Trust Company, the corporate trustee in the McDougald and Phillips estates. I also began massaging Al Thornbrough of Massey-Ferguson and Al Fairley of Hollinger, who were thoroughly irritated by Alex Barron's (well-justified) criticism of them. Most importantly, I spoke to Nelson Davis in Arizona and after testing the water I offered the view that he should be the Argus chairman. He did not dissent.

Nelson was a shy and private man, but a tasteful owner of classic boats and private golf courses, his perfectly reproduced federalist house a museum-quality repository of Gainsboroughs, Romneys, Wedgwood ceilings, and magnificent antique furniture. (The crushed meteorite driveway produced no dust, but wasn't great for melting snow.) In a variety of mainly private companies — trucking, oil-drilling equipment, automobile dealerships, shopping centres, and even a card-laminating business — he had amassed a fortune somewhat larger than Bud's, but neither Bud's celebrity nor prestige. The idea of becoming chairman of Argus could not have been unappealing to him, as it was, in a sense, the only type of prize that had eluded him.

I early opened discussion with Dick Chant, who shared my fears about Argus operations and had the impression our new leaders were more concerned with filling Bud's offices than with addressing the accumulating problems. Following the April 4 meeting of the Argus directors that approved the executive committee's recommendations without comment, Dick had a chat with Bruce, who declined to consider aligning his shares with the Phillips and McDougald interests. Bruce added that Dick was probably surprised not to have been made an officer of Argus, but that if they had done it for Dick, they would have had to do the same for me.

Bruce Matthews, the proud owner of 3.9 per cent of Ravelston, apparently thought this a clinching argument, oblivious to the fact that such offices are customarily distributed in some relationship to shareholdings. Both Bud McDougald and Bruce Matthews had promised Dick Chant an Argus vice presidency but Bruce made no reference to this long-standing commitment. This conversation convinced Dick that Max Meighen was envisioning taking effective control with Bruce's collusion (Bruce was a director of Meighen's company) and treating the other Ravelston shareholders as a captive minority. This was neither an unreasonable conclusion nor an inconvenient one for me.

The position of the Crown Trust Company was pivotal, as the corporate executor for the Phillips and McDougald and various McMartin estates. Obviously no fiduciary relationship could ever be compromised, but gathering that company into friendly hands, our hands, could be quite stabilizing to the alliance I was endeavouring to assemble and would also get the attention of the triumvirs, unless they had taken complete leave of their senses, which, on the evidence, was a possibility.

Almost 30 per cent of Crown stock had been assembled by Reuben Cohen and Leonard Ellen, controlling shareholders of Central and Nova Scotia Trust Co. Reuben was, next to K.C. Irving and Harrison McCain, New Brunswick's most prominent businessman, and he and Leonard were accomplished and charming men. They had tended to be overly deferential about gaining admission to the Toronto financial establishment and were especially susceptible to the wiles of McDougald, who, exuding his considerable charm, was looked upon by them virtually as one of the family.

Cohen's talented and beautiful wife, Louise, even painted Bud in his antique Alfa Romeo on a plate and presented it to him. But Bud kept their overtures for control of the Crown at bay and finessed the importunate maritimers. Bud had been chairman and president of the trust company until the Bank Act revisions forced a choice between being a bank or a trust company director.

Almost 25 per cent of Crown Trust was held by the Crown itself, for McMartin cousins, Jean Mulford in New York City and the eccentric Rita Floyd-Jones of Saranac Lake who sat, according to accounts, on a throne in the decrepit hotel where she lived. Reuben and Leonard sent a telegram to the Crown offering to buy this 24.8 per cent block but were unspecific as to price. I precisely offered $34, $13 above market price, and the company's management secured the approval of John McMartin's descendants. It cost us $6.3 million, which Sterling Newspapers could afford to carry. Voted together with over 10 per cent owned by the McDougald estate and the Canadian Imperial Bank of Commerce's block of 10 per cent, we were in effective control of Crown Trust. The deal was completed May 4. Relations with Dick Chant, the Crown's vice president, grew correspondingly closer.

Alex Barron and my brother and I had agreed, March 16, that Hollinger was "the centre of the line," the cash-box that could be intelligently deployed to rebuild the tottering Argus structure. The key to Hollinger was not the Alabaman windbag, Fairley, but the timeless Percy Clair Finlay, then seventy-nine. He had been an officer of Hollinger for forty-three years, a law partner of J.Y. Murdoch (a founder of Noranda Mines), and legal representative for most of the McMartins, Dunlaps, and Timminses, founding families of Hollinger. He was a cantankerous martinet who considered most modern phenomena, from pensions to conflict-of-interest rules, to be effete botheration. (A couple of years later, he presented the Hollinger directors with the proposal that the chairman and chief counsel of Hollinger and of a mining company, Goldale, work out between them a takeover of Goldale. P.C. was chairman and counsel of both companies and Goldale's principal shareholder.)

He looked, and with his mangled English, sounded, like Casey Stengel, always claimed to be on the brink of penury, although he obviously had a net worth of ten to twenty million dollars, and used to buy the bottom-of-the-line Ford, with only one sun visor, until he inherited a Hollinger Cadillac from Fairley, which he kept clean by leaving it outside his garage when rain was forecast. During the tremendous blizzard and hurricane in Toronto in April 1975 (so powerful that a couple of the large windows in the Toronto Dominion-Centre were torn loose), P.C. was crossing King Street when the wind blew him down and a passing automobile drove over his briefcase. He remonstrated so fiercely with the bewildered driver, despite his seventy-six years and having cracked two ribs, that the motorist bought him a new briefcase and a new hat the next day.

By advising or voting a little over 20 per cent of Hollinger shares, P.C. was, as I said at the time, "the Mayor Daley of the Argus group" (referring to the Kennedys' comments on the mayor of Chicago's status as a kingmaker in the Democratic Party in the sixties). P.C.'s son, John, a talented and affable lawyer and businessman, was not too reminiscent of his frugal, teetotalling father but had been a good and sage friend since we both had been inductees at the Hollinger dinner in the late sixties, sitting at the back of the Toronto Club's dining room with the pilots who flew Fairley back and forth to Alabama. John shared a good deal of his father's legal work.

Fairley was retiring and Max Meighen, to his great credit, had refused Fairley's bid to go on full pension, funded by several million dollars deposited in a special fund, while continuing to receive his full presidential salary as vice chairman. It quickly became clear that Fairley would not vote in a board struggle at Argus between the developing factions, so I evoked Hollinger succession politics by suggesting that the new president should be P.C. Finlay, instead of Bruce Ross, an outstanding mining person who had persevered through all the years of Fairley's well-paid aspic immobility and had an activist, but traditional, mining view of the company. P.C. was receptive, and he expressed the view that he not be required "to spend my declining years working for Demaree (Desmarais) or Barron."

At the same time, my brother and I laid out to his son John Finlay a role at Argus and a modest Ravelston participation. The overture to both Finlays was based rigorously on merit, but the political consequences could be reasonably assumed to be useful should feverish manoeuvring give way to internecine warfare.

Al Thornbrough was a man of considerably more weight than Al Fairley. Hard-working, passionately devoted to the international global mission of Massey-Ferguson, his most grievous mistake had been to reconcile McDougald's conservatism over issuing equity with his own fervour for expansion by insouciant debt-financed expansion. He was well aware of Alex Barron's hostility to the continuance of any influence of his on the Massey scene. It was, accordingly, not too challenging to convince him that the elevation of our emergent faction would be, for him, a comparatively welcome development.

One of my Massey informants advised me of a meeting at the Prince Hotel in April, organized by Alex Barron with Victor Rice and Bruce Matthews, for Victor to explain to Bruce how desperate Massey's condition was. Alex was right that the company's condition was desperate, but this was a rather amateurish and circuitous approach, which was helpful to me in my relations with Thornbrough. Alex had followed through on one March 16 promise and I was elected a Massey director in April. Jackman and I walked back to his office after my first meeting and Hal showed me his calculation that, over the last fifty years, Massey had made no cumulative net profit at all. It was a famous but fundamentally unprofitable business.

On April 20, Alex had had his fiancée to dinner with my fiancée and me at Napoléon's restaurant. It was a perfectly pleasant occasion, but as a peace overture, it was too little, too late.

Throughout this period Jim McDougald, Doris Phillips, and Cecil Hedstrom were sitting in Palm Beach reading of the relentless elevations of Bruce Matthews, Max Meighen, and Alex Barron to positions left vacant by the death of their companion and good shepherd, John A. McDougald, without their ever having been consulted. They were not amused.

My newly hatched colleagues at the Crown Trust Company, Ainslie St. Clair Shuvé and Bill Ritchie (president and vice president), reported to me that they found the antics of the Meighen-Matthews faction presumptuous and displeasing. The Crown Trust board was about to include my brother, David Radler, Peter White, and our lawyer, Igor Kaplan, as well as Nelson Davis and Dick Chant. Shuvé was a trust officer of the old school whom one could easily imagine approaching a widow with a handkerchief up his sleeve, sniffling and advising what "he" would have wished. His unctuousness and worldliness combined in a manner that was rather entertaining, and Ritchie was a tough, principled Scot. They did not require very intensive prompting to suggest to the clients that a shareholders' agreement with us was the best way to ensure the respect of the rights of the Ravelston majority. Parallel discussions with Dick Chant led to the same inexorable conclusion.

The matter was referred to Bud and Jim's lawyer, Lou Guolla, who drew up a draft agreement that required the Phillips, McDougald, and Black interests to vote together, by a process of each group polling itself and casting a unitary vote on any given issue. My brother and I thus bound ourselves to support the women, but in exchange for this concession, in view of the ladies' age and distance from commercial preoccupations, we were conceded the right to determine if and when a compulsory transfer notice requiring a shareholder to sell his shares would be issued against another shareholder. (Under McDougald's 1969 agreement, such a notice could be issued by a bare majority of Ravelston shareholders. This group had almost 70 per cent of the stock.) When signing of this agreement was completed May 10, my brother and I were in a position to blow the Meighen and Matthews factions away when we wished.

The tide had turned swiftly and, to the languid denizens of Toronto Street, imperceptibly, since they didn't bother to consult the majority of the shareholders, who, they impetuously presumed, would comport themselves as grieving disinterested widows and deferential young men habitually did.

Lou Guolla, Ainslie Shuvé, Bill Ritchie, and Dick (Dixon) Chant walked Doris, Jim, and Cecil through the Ravelston supplementary agreements clause by clause. The whole arrangement was requested by the rapacious ladies, vetted by them, explained laboriously to them in monosyllables and with examples adapted to the mind of a child of ten, and they understood and approved every letter of every word of the agreement.

By May 12, the date of the annual Hollinger dinner, all was in place, and the triumvirate was slumbering in its high seats in the ancient Greek temple in Toronto Street oblivious to the trembling of the earth beneath them. Following the dinner, which I spent largely in conversation with E.P. Taylor, the first in many years that he had attended, I came home and typed on my maternal grandmother's ancient typewriter a rationale for pulling the Ravelston trigger soon — immediately, in fact.

As always in a revolutionary situation, the momentum is steadily towards the most radical party until Thermidor and ultimately Brumaire, Robespierre gives way to Fouché and Talleyrand, Lenin proclaims the New (i.e., old) Economic Policy, and Napoleon or Stalin restores order. My manifesto of May 12 was rather moderate. I wrote of the restoration of collegiality, of retaining an important but reduced Meighen shareholding in Ravelston, of keeping Barron and Matthews as officers, of redistributing powers in accord with the correlation of forces and not the candy-shop fairy-land the triumvirate was wallowing in, and of my moving to 10 Toronto Street (and into McDougald's office, but only with Jim's agreement).

Nelson, as I had suggested seven weeks before, would replace Max as chairman, Bruce would be vice chairman, I would become president, Alex would stay as executive vice president, Dick Chant would become a vice president, and my brother would fill Bud's vacancy on the board. My suggestions were agreed to by the addressees, my brother, Nelson, Dick, and the McDougald and Phillips entourages.

In practice, I suspected that, when the time came, Alex would loyally wish to share Max's hard regime of principled retirement, but the continuation option was available for them. General Matthews, I suspected, would soldier on under a change of commanders-in-chief, as he had in earlier corporate and military times.

Ritchie, Shuvé, and Guolla reported to me on the thirteenth that the ladies wanted "to teach Max a lesson" and asked me to pull the trigger and execute against him the compulsory transfer notice. I did not demur. Ritchie and Guolla returned on the Argus plane to Palm Beach May 14 and with Thornbrough, who had come from Boca Raton for the return trip to Toronto, explained in excruciating detail the compulsory transfer notice to the ladies, who were eager to spur me into action and to decapitate the enemy, Max Meighen.

I cannot claim that I did not find their mindset convenient, but at this point, before the intense focus of public interest was brought to bear, they were advocating not a mere warning, but an exemplary execution. I would have been happy enough with a milder sanction but if my associates were screaming for the financial death penalty and for Max Meighen to be delivered trussed up like a partridge to their guillotine, I would not fidget and fumble with the blade levers. I was certainly not washing my hands of the trial; I was prepared to carry out but not decree the maximum sentence. The ladies would not hear of moderation. Off with his head.

I had absolutely no confidence in the integrity or staying power of these partners, and I suspected their blood lust could be capriciously redirected, spontaneously or by the operation of Mephistophelean influences, but I believed that the presence of the Crown Trust as corporate executor in both estates and of Dick Chant as Phillips's executor and Crown vice president made it unlikely that the Dowager Committee of Public Safety could proscribe or attaint me, whatever sanguinary remonstrance might be inflicted on the unsuspecting Colonel Meighen.

Dick Chant and I attended upon Max Meighen at 2:30 p.m., May 16, as Bruce visited Nelson and my brother at Nelson's office (Alex Barron was on his honeymoon, his first wife having died in 1977). Dick and I explained, unreproachfully, and, admittedly rather discursively, that we were handing Max a compulsory transfer notice, a feature of the Ravelston shareholders' agreement whose existence he appeared to have forgotten. (On reflection, I think Bud McDougald's greatest contributions to Canadian business were the restoration of the Toronto Club, the compulsory transfer notice, and prolonged retention of the cash board attendance fee.) I said that the signatories of it were not pleased at two months of complete non-consultation and that I, as the ultimate owner of more voting shares than he (he owned one-third of the control block of his company), didn't enjoy being told I was "rushing [my] fences."

I also made it clear that we were prepared to negotiate an adjusted level of shareholdings and influence rather than take all his shares if he wished, and that we would not make any public reference to the service of this notice. He looked in astonishment but said nothing. I broke the awkward silence and commented on the paintings on his office wall of Arthur Meighen, Alex Barron, and their company secretary, Louise Morgan, and Max opened the door and Ms. Morgan appeared. Dick and I, shaking hands unperfunctorily with them, made our exit through the open door. As we reached the elevator, I said, "Let's get out of here before Max realizes what we said," and Dick replied that his opinion of Max had risen considerably (not a gravity-defying levitation) by virtue of the equanimity with which he received our message.

I telephoned my brother at Nelson's office. Nelson's preamble was just ending but it contained enough of the flavour of what was afoot for Bruce to be "panting like a cart-horse."

Alex Barron returned from his honeymoon May 17 and telephoned me in amazement at what Max had told him of the previous day's events. We had an entirely civilized and courteous discussion May 17. I explained our motives and grievances and emphasized that compromise was still possible. In my experience, the fall of a long-prepared and unsuspected fate awakens the slumbering victims to a brief death throe of wild activity, like a housefly buzzing violently about for half a minute after receiving a blast of insecticide.

Thus Alex, a man of high but uneven abilities, who couldn't bestir himself to tell me between March 17 and March 22 that our March 16 agreements making me an officer and giving me an office at Argus Corporation, would not be given early (or any) effect, launched himself into a furious round of negotiations with Hal Jackman and Paul Desmarais. It took him (but not them) several weeks to realize that he had no bargaining position, no power to dispose of or deploy the Meighen Ravelston shares as they were under a compulsory transfer notice.

When these lengthy deliberations came to nothing, he then issued a letter in the first week in June to Canadian General Investments' public shareholders referring to our Ravelston transfer notice. He undoubtedly hoped that this tactic would stir up an immense public controversy, as it did; would shake the fragile resolve of the widows, as it did; and would erode the determination of Nelson, Dixon, my brother, and myself — it did not. At this point, we had 22 per cent of Ravelston and had issued a compulsory transfer notice on Meighen's 26 per cent. The ladies were technically in control under our arrangement.

The three ladies and Nelson Davis came to my house for tea, May 27, just before the public controversy erupted. I suggested that there was no need to treat Max unnecessarily roughly and that perhaps something could be patched up that would preserve his dignity while achieving our ends. Doris commented, almost to herself, "He has egg stains on his ties." Jim added, "He wore yellow socks to our house in Florida." Cecil referred to his "thin lapels," and Nelson to his "gold Mercedes." (Nelson would have preferred that he buy Cadillacs from him, as Bud and Eric Phillips and my father and I had). My tea party guests looked to me, as Max's sponsor in the conversation and the only one who hadn't yet opined. "He does become boisterous after a couple of drinks and I could do without the pansies in his buttonhole but are these valid criteria for throwing him out bag and baggage?" I asked neutrally. Doris rendered judgement with the severity of a Committee of Public Safety prosecutor: "We can dispense with him." Doris and Jim wrote to me words of fulsome appreciation the next day, and Doris had a wooden Napoleonic figure delivered to me, to go with Colonel Phillips's painting of Napoleon that Bud had given to me in 1968.

When Alex blew the cover off the Argus story the first week in June, by sending a notice to Canadian General Investments shareholders referring to Ravelston matters, the press began telephoning all the principals in their homes. It didn't take long for the ladies to scurry into the tall grass, claiming innocence, naïveté, and virtual senescence, in an agile arsenic-and-old-lace public relations handspring. It was an utter fraud but they played their roles with as much aplomb as Bud had always played his, and I was typecast as the lean and hungry aspirant.

Nor did it take long for the ineffable John Prusac to bubble to the surface of this witches' brew. When the story blew, Dick Thomson, chairman of the Toronto-Dominion Bank, wrote me expressing a desire to help us with banking arrangements. A few weeks later, my brother was elected a director of the TD Bank. This was one of the first indications of our upwardly mobile status in the Canadian corporate world.

I had what was intended to be a placatory session with Bruce Matthews in early June. It was clear, unfailing gentleman though he always was, that he was not well-pleased by our initiative, and, as an older man, his lack of enthusiasm was understandable and unexceptionable as such. But in these circumstances, if the ladies wobbled, Bruce's actions could be vital. He assured me with all his usual gravity that he wouldn't do anything rash with his shares.

His opening words to me, in reference to Western Dominion's co-signatory with me on the transfer notice to Max, were "Who's Waters?" (sic) He was referring to Shirley Walters, Western Dominion's corporate secretary whose status as a co-signatory of the compulsory transfer notice had been publicized as "S. Walters." She was also now my fiancée, our romantic and corporate relations having advanced somewhat in tandem. She had removed to this position from Dominion Securities, having come with us from Draper Dobie. We couldn't marry until her divorce was decreed absolute, which occurred only in May 1978 (she got me out of a Bank of Commerce board meeting to tell me about the final decree from a court-house pay phone). We officially became engaged in the course of this hurried conversation, and I bought her an engagement ring that evening.

It didn't serve anyone's interests to be overly public about these complexities, and I spent some time petitioning the Anglican Church for permission to marry, which was graciously accorded. Conversion to Roman Catholicism, which I desired, had to await her annulment from her first marriage and the regularization of our relations. It was all sorted out eventually; I naturally gave Bruce Matthews only a fragmentary answer to his question.

A June 26 cover story in *Maclean's*, headlined "The Argus Grab" and using a promotional shot for the launch of the French version of my book, caused a considerable sensation and Jim and Doris back-pedalled more furiously in their remarks to the media. In order to bring in some heavy reinforcements, I gave the *Globe and Mail* Nelson's telephone number at Dromoland Castle in Ireland, where he was attending a meeting of one of Jim Pattison's companies, with the Argus counsel, Don McIntosh. Nelson was splendid, as usual. "You can't do business with anyone who walks down the street. You have to pick your partners and stick with it." Nelson and Eloise Davis returned to Toronto June 18 to be greeted by Jim McDougald, who phoned Eloise, announced "Nelson's a double-crossing rat," and hung up, ending a friendship of nearly forty years. Nelson called John Robinette to take out a derivative slander action against Jim but was talked out of it by learned counsel.

Max and Alex were finished, but Alex had placed a fragmentation grenade under my coalition. Bruce was obviously not to be trusted, as he had no loyalty to us and had not navigated through his long career by unshakably resisting pressures from all sources. For a few days, the atmosphere was like that in the old western movies when a beseiged good guy looks out his cabin window and says, "It's too quiet out there to suit me."

My informants in Crown Trust and elsewhere advised me that Doris was convening a meeting of Phillips and McDougald executors with Bruce Matthews and John Prusac at midnight June 25–26, at the colonel's old house on Teddington Park. Prusac was at his most ludicrous, strutting about in a cape, barking instructions, and generally simulating a cross-impersonation of Count Dracula and Adolf Hitler. The fate of some of Canada's most famous companies now unfolded in an atmosphere of almost unrelenting buffoonery.

My faith in Dixon was not misplaced. He refused to agree to a transfer of Bruce's shares to the Phillips and McDougald estates. The general dutifully sat down on command from Prusac, put his briefcase in his lap, and signed over his stock to the ladies. The Crown Trust company did not ratify the arrangement, either as executor or transfer agent. I personally found it humiliating that a mountebank developer and virtual slum-lord could so bully and intimidate a retired major-general who had commanded 200,000 Canadian soldiers with some distinction in northwest Europe.

The next day, June 26, Prusac was surging up and down Bay Street, stock certificates in hand, unsuccessfully seeking the transfer of Bruce's shares and proclaiming, virtually from the roof-tops, "The transaction is consummated." A febrile atmosphere settled on the proceedings. Nelson, Dixon, Monte, and I, with various counsel, Lou Guolla and Igor Kaplan in particular, met the afternoon of the twenty-seventh and virtually all day of the twenty-eighth at the antique boardroom of the Crown Trust company, under a portrait of Bud McDougald.

We resolved on the twenty-seventh to serve Bruce with a compulsory transfer notice, with Dixon and Crown Trust providing the majority votes for the Phillips estate which, together with my brother and me, could exercise the May 10 agreement. It was also agreed to sue the widows, the meddlesome Cecil, Prusac, and Bruce Matthews for conspiring to violate both the May 10 and 1969 Ravelston agreements. (I was also loudly threatening a suit against Jim and Doris over their mental competence as executors but this was bravura and sabre-rattling, as success could have invalidated the May 15 agreement and the following day's service on Max.) Finally, Nelson and I exercised our rights under the Argus by-laws to call an Argus directors' meeting for June 30, at which we intended to fire the officers elevated at the trumped-up executive committee of March 22, when I had arrived four minutes late and found the elections closed.

I handed Bruce his compulsory transfer notice with Page Wadsworth as my witness in the middle of the June 27 Massey-Ferguson directors' meeting (in which Bruce snapped angrily at Alex Barron and accused him of lacking "originality of thought," which wasn't Bruce's strong suit either). I told Bruce it was a preventive measure but that there would be a U-Haul of writs along in the next few days if he didn't withdraw his shares from sale. He repaired to the rest room for ten minutes. I spent the balance of the day rounding up support for the upcoming directors' meeting.

The chief go-betweens on our behalf were Doug Ward, with the ladies, and Lou Guolla, with Prusac. Guolla threatened Prusac so repeatedly with a massive lawsuit that Prusac concluded June 28 by pouring his heart out to Peter Harris, Bruce Matthews's son-in-law and chairman of stockbroker A.E. Ames, finally bursting into tears at the impending failure of his coup, like Robespierre at the Paris City Hall the night he was condemned by the convention.

The same evening, June 28, I had dinner with my fiancée at Winston's but absented myself to call Doug Ward, the seventy-eight-year-old Dominion Securities chairman and perhaps Bud's best friend, who reported the failure of his mission to the ladies and advised me to "be tough with those women." I didn't need much encouragement in that direction. Doug had participated in yet another low farce at Doris's house, as he left three times, to be pursued to his car and invited back in by a loping albino domestic of Doris's. Doug was accompanied by the chairman of Crown Trust, Harold Kerrigan, causing, as Dick put it, "Harold's confusion to be added to Doris's!"

Earlier that day, as Igor Kaplan and his Aird & Berlis legal team were returning to their offices from lunch at the Cambridge Club, a client of one of them, who also did legal work for Consumers' Gas, was accosted on Adelaide Street by an acquaintance who loudly and insistently demanded a free gas heater (the temperature was 85 degrees). As the lawyers retreated, the stand-in for the Ancient Mariner shouted after them to the astonishment of numerous passers-by: "If it wasn't for me, you'd be shovelling shit in Islington!"

I had met Igor Kaplan through Dave Smith, MP, subsequently a minister in the Trudeau government, then a member and ultimately president of Toronto City Council, and my old friend from model parliament days at Carleton University. I introduced Igor into my family's legal work when I arrived from Montreal in 1974 and felt a second and more aggressive opinion was needed. He certainly provided it. When he was only eight, he and his family had escaped from Memel, Lithuania, the day Hitler annexed it in 1939, and travelled across Russia on the Trans-Siberian Railway. They went on to Japan before gaining entry to Canada as farmers (which they had never been), and they settled near Brockville. Igor had had an adventurous career as a lawyer and a businessman. The Argus work was undoubtedly a major boost to his career, and he discharged it with great determination and imaginativeness.

I spent most of June 29 organizing support for our ejection procedures at Argus the following day. At the previous regular Argus directors' meeting several weeks before, I succeeded in getting my brother elected to fill the vacancy created by Bud McDougald's death, Alex Barron graciously seconding my motion. The five directors Bud and I had chosen at the end of 1976, Nelson Davis, Fred Eaton, Trumbull Warren, Harry Edmison, and Jim Wright, were all solidly with us and thus decisively changed the balance of power in the company. With Dick Chant, Al Thornbrough, Don McIntosh, and my brother and me, we were certain to carry any vote, no matter how sharply formulated the question.

McCurdy of Standard, Fairley, Alan McMartin of Hollinger, Tom McCormack and Tom Bolton of Dominion Stores, were expected to be absent or to abstain. It was impossible to predict what the company's senior director, the eighty-nine-year-old Harry Carmichael might do, and Jackman, the ultimate conservative, would vote for the new slate but not the removal of the old, as he saw any such action as a form of regicide and all his sympathies were with Charles I (as they were a few years later with Joe Clark).

I surmised that Jackman's chief interest in being there at all was to raise his shareholding in the business at an advantageous price, or to magnify his own influence in the most factionalized conditions possible. I expected him to abstain. Apart from Max, Alex, and Bruce, only Alex Hamilton was almost certain to vote against us, as he had worked closely with Max and Alex at Domtar when Bud gave them the chairmanship of that company. The vote was likely to be 10–4 with six not present or abstaining and Harry Carmichael hard to predict. Without my brother and the five directors who came in to enable me to become a director of the Bank of Commerce, no such vote would have been possible. It was not a flattering comment on either the executive or political abilities of the competition that they couldn't drum up any appreciable support despite their relative seniority.

On the evening of June 29 I went to Tony Fell's party at the Toronto Club to celebrate Doug Ward's sixtieth anniversary at Dominion Securities. (Signy Eaton's sixty-fifth birthday party was the same night at the York Club.) Doug was always a good after-dinner speaker and he made some amusing references to Draper Dobie and the connection with my brother and me. (We were now among Dominion Securities' largest shareholders.) I ducked out a couple of times to have a final try with Jackman by telephone, but he would not move off the fence.

We convened a rump meeting the next morning at Eaton's boardroom. Nelson spoke first, in terms of extreme vituperation against Bruce. Doug Ward followed, describing Bruce's behaviour as "completely unethical and utterly reprehensible." Dick Chant described the midnight June 26 meeting at which Doris was the hostess, dwelling upon some of Prusac's more ridiculous mannerisms. Trumbull Warren came snorting down Highway 400 from Muskoka, arrived in the midst of our meeting and before even taking his seat announced, of the ragged and polyglot opposition, "They're not wanted and they all have to go." The corporate secretary, Harry Edmison, and the treasurer, Jim Wright, whose jobs were on the line, threw in entirely with us. They had not appreciated Max's abruptness or Alex's somewhat smarmy intrusions. Don McIntosh, who had been the corporate counsel since Phillips and Taylor's falling-out with J.S.D. Tory nearly twenty-five years before, was a powerful and convincing ally. There was never any doubt of the stance of my friend Fred Eaton. They were all magnificent.

We went on to Toronto Street. Bruce called us to order. It had been agreed April 4 that while Max was the chairman, he wouldn't chair anything, neither directors' nor shareholders' meetings. I spoke briefly and the meeting adjourned while Nelson, Dick, and Don McIntosh closeted themselves with Max in Bud's old office upstairs and suggested that Max think seriously about retiring. With some justice, Max announced that he knew nothing of Bruce's attempted sale to the women, disapproved of it, and had never heard of Prusac. He said, "If you want me out, you will have to throw me out." He met briefly with me and repeated the same comment. I suggested that I would face up to that challenge gamely.

I had already met with Bruce during the adjournment and told him we would sack them all and sue him, that he was very vulnerable legally as he must have been advised, and surely there was a more seemly way than this of achieving a transition. I offered him a place on our slate as vice chairman, with Nelson as chairman, myself as president, Dick Chant as executive vice president, and Jackman as vice president. I said that if he would promise to all the directors that he would cease in his efforts to sell his shares, we would suspend execution of our compulsory transfer notice on him, would stay other litigation, and would adjourn this meeting to July 13 to enable all the parties to "contemplate the implications of the situation" and seek a more orderly resolution of it. Bruce accepted emphatically, effectively deserting all his erstwhile allies. The meeting reconvened and Bruce asked me to speak.

I was deferential to Max. "Nothing that has happened," I said, "implies any lack of respect for him as an individual. There have been some policy disagreements that a majority of us believe can best be settled by a change of officers, but we do not wish to inflict indignities on anyone and would not ask Colonel Meighen to consent to anything indecorous."

It was hard for me to be quite as polite about Bruce Matthews, but I gave him the benefit of the doubt that in "the confusion of recent days, some inadvertently extremely destabilizing" initiatives had been commenced, but "the general wishes to clarify matters satisfactorily." Bruce spoke with commendable dignity. He said he would not be able easily to explain his actions and didn't wish to try, but he would promise to all his colleagues that he would not sell his

Ravelston shares. Don McIntosh read our revised slate and the meeting adjourned.

The tide was now flowing decisively to us, but our advantage had to be pressed.

I returned to Winston's that evening, then a salon at the height of the gastronomic and political renown of the owner, John Arena, with my fiancée and Tom Birks from Montreal. As we moved determinedly towards *digestifs*, the ever-fecund Igor Kaplan rushed in with his "Lithuanian Triangle" in which Bruce (whose malleability was notorious) was to sign a compulsory transfer notice against himself under the 1969 agreement along with the Phillips majority and Western Dominion. I pointed out that Meighen and McDougald between them had a slight Ravelston majority and gave him full marks for imagination and a tumbler of cognac. (Meighen had 26.76 per cent, McDougald and Phillips 23.47 per cent each; we had 22.4 per cent and Matthews had 3.9 per cent, so the "Lithuanian Triangle" would have had only 49.77 per cent.)

The next morning, Saturday and Confederation Day, Monte and I went to see General Bruce Matthews at his house. As we drove up, my brother said, "We've nailed one of Bruce's feet to the floor, but he's still hopping around in circles so we'll have to nail down the other one." We made it pretty clear we wanted his Ravelston stock and would revive our valid compulsory transfer notice if necessary. Bruce hedged and prevaricated (Al Thornbrough regularly referred to him as "the Vicar of Bray"), and my brother leaned forward and said, "General, we'll have those shares." Bruce replied forcefully, "I won't be bullied," to which my brother immediately responded, "Oh yes you will!"

The meeting was inconclusive, but the following day, Sunday, July 2, came the first overtures for sale from the ladies, who, with Prusac's antics and the general's defection, must finally have realized that the jig was up. Discussions between lawyers continued throughout the holiday third and fourth (Bill Somerville of Borden & Elliot had replaced Lou Guolla, a faithful and competent lawyer whom Jim McDougald defamed outrageously and whom I have occasionally engaged since as a gesture of appreciation for his steadfastness under great and unreasonable pressure).

It was arranged for a climactic session to take place at my home at 10:30 on the evening of the fourth. Prusac, Somerville, the very capable Jack Geller representing Crown Trust, Igor, Monte, and I, and a couple of junior counsel met in my parents' old dining room. Somerville began with a droning and wildly fictionalized litany of his clients' grievances and then said they were prepared to sell for $20 million. I responded that I didn't think there was any need to reply to his obligatory but inaccurate preamble, describing events that occurred before he was on the case, implying he didn't know much about it, as indeed he didn't. I countered at $18 million and we quickly settled at $18.4 million. Since most of the stock was being laid off on Nelson Davis and Fred Eaton, I was prepared to go to $25 million if necessary. Junior counsel wrote out the sale; Prusac took it to the ladies for their signatures and returned them signed.

In the meantime, I telephoned Russell Harrison, who was watching the Miss Universe contest. I said that I had just completed a deal with "two prime candidates for that honour" and asked for $18.4 million the next day at five p.m. This would not be a problem, Russell assured me, but expressed regret that the drama was ending: "I've been enjoying it," he said. Prusac, whose behaviour had been exemplary that evening, returned at midnight and departed after a few minutes. "Your reputation has preceded you," I said with studied ambiguity as we shook hands. Igor stayed until 4:30 a.m., offering a soliloquy from *All's Well that Ends Well* as he left, a recondite feat given his state of fatigue and alcoholic consumption. He transferred the Phillips and McDougald Ravelston shares at nine a.m.

On the morning of the fifth, I advised a number of people of events of the previous evening, and in some cases of wedding plans and parental status. When I told Jackman of the purchase from the widows, he instantly referred to the "young Bolingbroke who in the first act of Richard II arrived with 20,000 soldiers to repossess his father's estates, and in the last act is crowned King of England. Congratulations. This has been high drama."

The Argus board meeting had been scheduled for July 13, because I had already arranged my wedding for July 14, and was determined to have the Argus question settled by then and to wrap up both these tortuous subjects on consecutive days.

The closing at the Crown Trust head office at five p.m., July 5, was uneventful. The final act began when my brother said to me: "We must be near the end of this foolishness; there's that cantankerous old idiot, Pete Elliot." The senior partner of Borden & Elliot was at pains to tell me that the ladies had been very scathing in their references to Bruce Matthews.

My brother's descriptions of these personalities were often entertaining. One of the figures in the minuet just ending was bald with the peculiarity of a vertical tag of baldness in the middle-back of his head, dipping below the line of a hat were he to wear one, a phenomenon that my brother called a "hat-extractor." He referred to the bearer of this minor anomaly as "the hat-extractor" for years afterwards.

When he thought my position was unravelling, Max Meighen called a Ravelston meeting for July 11. By then, Doris and Jim had sold out and retired, and I attended as representative of a large majority of the shares and advised Max and Alex that there would be no gloating or cheap shots but that if they didn't retire on the thirteenth, they would be fired and they couldn't doubt that. They took this in apparently good spirits.

On the thirteenth, I went with Shirley (she changed her name to Joanna in 1990) to City Hall to get our marriage licence. Mayor David Crombie recognized us from his office window and waved jauntily. I drove through Mount Pleasant Cemetery, past my parents' graves, on the way to Grace Church, where I picked up the ecclesiastical marriage licence. Then I went to 10 Toronto Street for the resumption of the Argus meeting adjourned from June 30.

Max Meighen and Alex Barron, isolated and demoralized, accepted their defeat with grace if not sportsmanship and resigned their offices without acrimony. Bruce handled the chair with his usual diplomacy. Max and Alex refrained from voting on the election of the new slate, which, when achieved, gave the chair to Nelson, who expressed the optimistic hope that we were "entering an era of good feeling." I went home to celebrate my impending marriage with the Whites, Radlers, and Brian Stewart and his girlfriend, who were all staying in our house.

Max, Alex, and Bruce Matthews were not bad people. But all three were like generals fighting a war by the methods of the last one. They could not conceive of any corporate alternative to trench warfare, attrition, and promotion by seniority. They were completely over-confident, though only Alex among them possessed any stomach for a fight and only Bruce for an intrigue.

Tactical surprise was total and the first inkling they had that they were in combat, and in very unfavourable circumstances, was when Dick Chant and I handed Max Meighen the call on his shares. He was thus like "the unhappy General Mack" at Ulm, the Austrian commander in the Austerlitz Campaign, who suddenly found that Napoleon had surrounded him. The ant-like movements of my corporate equivalent to armoured reconnaissance were so stealthy and insidious that their position had been completely eroded, riddled, and honeycombed before a shot was fired in anger. "The regime was revealed by the light of the thunderbolt in its ghastly infirmity," wrote de Gaulle of the fall of France in 1940, "as having no relation, and no proportion to the honour, dignity and future of," in this case, the corporation.

Nine years later, I wrote Max Meighen a note of condolence when his wife died, and Alex Barron a letter of encouragement when he was in hospital with cancer. The generous reply I received from Max and the long and friendly telephone conversation I had with Alex, not long before he died, constituted, I hope, a partial reconciliation. Whatever their limitations, they were fine and successful men. Though I always regretted that conflicting interests brought us into rancorous disagreement, I have never doubted that their handling of the succession to McDougald constituted a *casus belli* and that perseverance in their form of administration of Argus and its affiliates would have led us all to disaster, themselves first of all.

Bruce Matthews and I enjoyed uninterruptedly good relations. He was a timeless and indestructible gentleman. Behind a slightly bumbling exterior lurked an instinct for self-preservation of astonishing acuity. The general and the colonel soldiered uneventfully on into their mid-eighties, dying in 1991 and 1992, having become in Housman's words "runners whom renown outran and the name died before the man," other than in the most geriatric regions of the Toronto Club.

A less likely subject of a peace of the brave is the jaded phalanx of the three sisters, incited by the saturnine and oleaginous dandy, Prusac. Where Max, Alex, and Bruce had, at least in the case of the colonel and general, in good faith ignored and underestimated me and the faction I headed, the women had attempted to use me and became spiteful and obstructive when their plans went awry. One (verbal) element of our settlement with them was that the women could go to Florida on the Argus plane one more time. They did but quarrelled so violently with each other that the pilots became alarmed and one of them came back to find the source of the commotion. Cecil was being taken to task (belatedly) for her championship of Prusac.

A Wagnerian blitzkrieg in May gave way to a Flaubertesque bourgeois salon farce in June. The lessons of May were the lessons of 1940 and countless other débâcles: avoid obsolescence, particularly intellectual obsolescence; seek out and reflect the real correlation of forces; and don't pretend to be an unassailable holder of a position if your status is in fact precarious. In finance, only proprietors can consistently act like proprietors.

The lesson of June is to be wary of setting out in the most cynical way to use people who you may have underestimated. The pickpocket whose pocket is picked receives, and deserves, little sympathy. I prefer to think of Doris and Jim and Cecil when I first knew them, as beautiful, glamorous, and whimsical, even eccentric, and unvaryingly pleasant, far removed though this idyll is from my last and most intimate experience of them.

Prusac doubtless deserves some credit for having, by dint of his own efforts and ingenuity, advanced from a very humble position to one of considerable financial success. His motives and methods in this case were fairly transparent and whatever virtue he may possess was not on display in these events. If Prusac had ever gained control of Argus Corporation, as he almost did, the result would have been a denigration and a mockery of the entire corporate and business community of Canada.

CHAPTER SEVEN

REBUILDING ARGUS CORPORATION: FROM TRACTORS INTO OIL
1978–1981

THE ARGUS MYSTIQUE HAD BEEN BUILT ON the showmanship of Taylor and McDougald, and their success in ruling companies in which the interest they controlled was between 10 and 25 per cent. The fact that we bought almost half of Ravelston, or a quarter of the voting shares of Argus, for the relatively mundane sum of $18.4 million illustrates how weak and precarious the financial pyramid was. And of the underlying assets, as has been described, Massey was virtually insolvent, Dominion was sluggish and in decline, Hollinger was slumbering, Domtar had thrown off the Argus yoke, Alex Hamilton making it clear that Barron, Matthews, and Meighen were the Argus representatives at Domtar. With 14 per cent of the stock, we were unable to assert an influence; Domtar was *in partibus infidelium*. Standard Broadcasting was a good company in which we had more than a token control position (47 per cent) but it was comparatively small and showing the first signs of McDougald era decay.

To turn this mess of pottage to profit was conceptually quite simple; it was a straightforward matter of buying in shares at the discounted prices holding companies usually command because they are at one remove from operating profits and are generally unpopular with investors anyway. This condition was aggravated in the Argus group whose stocks had attracted no investor interest for years. Argus was legendary but interest in it was folkloric and not financial. We would pay for our share accumulation by selling assets aggressively at full prices and improving performance in what was left. More challenging would be the task of repositioning Argus in real control of growth businesses. A three-fold task awaited us: shoring up the management of the existing investments; upgrading the quality of the assets by trading up to better companies in better industries; and building a real proprietary interest in the company, instead of the tottering cantilevered and jerrymandered structure of tokens and transparencies that we inherited. We had to look to the day when the non-executive Ravelston partners would prefer to redeploy their investments. Nelson Davis, Fred Eaton, and the others were there mainly out of friendship and confidence that we could make money for them. If the managing partners, myself in particular, wished to become and remain proprietors, rather than proprietors of Bud's fading proprietary impersonation, we would have to flush up to Ravelston significant amounts of cash with which to accumulate stock from some of the proceeds of asset disposals.

If we accept Napoleon's definition of force as mass times velocity, our strength would have to reside for the foreseeable future in a high-multiple equation: we had no mass but I was determined that we would develop considerable velocity. Our commercial position was slightly analogous to Napoleon's when he took command of the army of Italy in 1795. It was a shabby, demoralized, largely unarmed and wholly undisciplined rabble, but he moved it about the river valleys of Northern Italy with such dexterity that he bundled the far superior Austrian forces right out of Italy while giving battle only in the minor engagements of Rivoli and Castiglione.

Of the five investments that we had, only Hollinger-Labrador had the potential to attempt a takeover on a scale that would lead the group in a new direction. In order to gain some Napoleonic mass for ourselves, we would have to peddle our non-strategic interest in Domtar; fix up Massey-Ferguson as best we could and dispose of it; disassemble and liquidate Dominion Stores, a beached whale in a labour- and capital-intensive industry that never made more than one cent for each dollar of sales but whose elements might still fetch premium prices, and apply the proceeds to consolidating our equity interests; and activate Hollinger and Standard.

The interest in Crown Trust was now disposable, and the proceeds should be reapplied to paying for enough of the Meighen, McDougald, or Phillips shares to give Western Dominion over 50 per cent of a Ravelston rebuilt with new and more congenial partners. The first priority was to resolve the impasse with Desmarais and Power Corporation. Second, the Rileys should move from Western Dominion (WDI) to Ravelston, and David Radler and Peter White brought into WDI essentially by merging it with Sterling Newspapers, which with Dominion Malting would give WDI operating income of over $4 million that could be offset against interest on borrowings incurred to take up our Ravelston position.

For the Rileys to be partially exchanged for Peter White and David Radler, Sterling Newspapers brought into Western Dominion, our Crown Trust shares sold to pay for our increased Ravelston position, Domtar shares and Dominion Stores assets liquidated under Argus Corporation for an increased equity interest by us in the remaining Argus companies, Massey disposed of and Hollinger activated, we would have to achieve a greater velocity than Argus Corporation had had since Taylor founded it thirty-three years before.

In acquisitions, our strategy would be Captain Liddell Hart's inter-war theory of the expanding torrent of air and mechanized offence. We would go where resistance was least as, in Liddell Hart's preferred analogy, water poured onto the top of a hillock makes its way to the bottom but by an unpredictable course. We couldn't be confidently precise in advance of our investment targets when we would be in a position to have any, but as in Liddell Hart's championship of modern warfare, logical objectives would commend themselves at the appropriate time.

Peter, David, and I wanted to redirect the group towards the newspaper business, as the industry that we knew and liked best, but the overhaul of Argus and its affiliates that would have to be achieved before any such step could be taken was so comprehensive it could not even be believably hinted at outside a circle restricted to four or five people.

To fulfil my hopes for it, Argus would have to be wrenched loose from its past of reliance on dividend income from token control positions in undermanaged companies in mature industries and set on a new path disenthralled of the restraints of a third of a century, a corporate Long March. I aspired to nothing less, but before taking the first step there was the pleasant leitmotif of my marriage, Bastille Day, the day after the elevation of the new slate at Argus Corporation.

All my adult life I had wished to avoid a large wedding thronged with beaming relatives and gushing family friends and retainers, and resonating with well-disposed platitudes. The ceremony was at Grace Church, where my parents' funerals were held, and where my brother and I donated the heraldic grant of arms from London's College of Arms. John Erb, who presided at my father's funeral, took the service. We invited only twenty guests of whom only a few, including my brother, and Sterling partners, Nelson and Eloise Davis, Igor Kaplan, Douglas and Susan Bassett, and Brian Stewart, figure in this narrative.

At dinner at our house afterwards, my brother spoke very amusingly of the secondary role the media had awarded him in the Argus drama, and Peter White spoke graciously of the occasion and the setting being associated with important recent events. I referred to my parents and thanked several of the guests, particularly Nelson Davis, who, I said, "the *Globe and Mail* referred to yesterday as a great and powerful ally, which is nothing less than the truth." It was a poignant occasion and a splendid summer evening, but the events of recent weeks caused me to tire early and I turned in at about ten, leaving my wife and guests to celebrate to an advanced hour. The events of the previous weeks, culminating in my own wedding, left me thoroughly exhausted.

Implementation of the Argus strategy began on the first business day after these festivities. I set out to sell the Crown Trust company on the eighteenth when Reuben Cohen came to lunch at my house. It was sold by us, a couple of months later, at a profit of about $2 million, but to Izzy Asper and Gerry Schwartz of CanWest Capital, when Reuben declined to increase his bid. He doubtless assumed that my representation that we had a higher bid than his was just chiselling.

Reuben and Leonard then sued the CIBC, who sold their shares with us, when I told Russell Harrison that the Asper-Schwartz bid was the highest, for acting in a manner harmful to the interests of a client, themselves. I testified in the bank's favour and the defendant won at first instance, but lost on appeal, an unjust verdict but a testimony to the barristerial skill of my old schoolmate Alan Lenczner.

I recruited Power Corporation directors Michel Belanger and Bob Scrivener (who was also a director of the CIBC) as intermediaries with Paul Desmarais, and Bob Scrivener, my brother, Paul Desmarais, and I met most amicably for dinner in a suite in the Ritz-Carlton in early September. A deal was struck in October between Paul and Peter Curry (Power Corporation president and an ancient friend of my father's) and Dick Chant and me at a meeting at my house.

Paul and Peter wanted their book value out of their Argus position, which was $87 million. We settled on $65 million cash and $22 million in a note, whose interest rate was adjusted downwards (to nothing in fact) to provide the difference between book and current market value. The discussions could not have been more agreeable or have produced a more satisfactory outcome, and the hatchet that Argus and Power Corporation had been wielding against each other was durably buried. One of the first lessons I learned while assembling Sterling Newspapers was never to embarrass a vendor. To do so is both ungracious and inexpedient.

I worked out with Don Fullerton, president of the CIBC, as my brother did with Dick Thomson of the TD Bank, the sale to those banks of $65 million of non-participating and redeemable equity, which paid off Power Corporation. The next year we bought in the note owing to that company at a discounted price. Thus did 51 per cent of Argus participating equity come into our possession, giving us about 75 per cent of the total (after the pending purchase of the Meighen Ravelston and Argus preferred shares). The era of pretending to be owners was over. (The $65-million term preferred shares were eventually converted into about 15 per cent of Ravelston as a permanent holding for the CIBC, such was the eventual rise in our underlying asset values.)

Another subject requiring immediate attention was our position at Hollinger. In any perceived vacuum, the mischievous as well as the predatory are attracted. The ineffable stockbroker Harold Crang, who, as the chairman of Hanna Mining Company, Bud Humphrey, put it, "ran a bucket shop with style," and who had an awesome wardrobe and an engagingly buccaneering view of corporate life, had a window on Hollinger affairs by virtue of having married Peggy Dunlap, who, with her sons and daughter, had an inherited interest from one of the founders.

Harold and his associate John Churchill Turner, a bluff and voluminous speculator, started nosing around the various pools of Hollinger stock being watched over by P.C. Finlay. I proposed a right of first refusal for Argus over those shares, in exchange for a right for those shareholders of a little over 20 per cent of the stock to put their shares to Argus at $42.50, a median recent price. This was a contingent liability of about $40 million, but my reasoning was that, if necessary, we would be prepared to sell any other asset to trade up into Hollinger. Harold Crang gave his dissuasive powers a good work-out, but he was no match for P.C. Finlay as a lobbyist. When one lady who was involved asked P.C. why she should take his advice over that of her present husband, P.C. responded, "Because you and your late husband and father-in-law have been profitably taking my advice for forty years and this is no time to stop." All the McMartins, Timminses, and Dunlaps signed. When I saw Harold Crang next, a few weeks later at the York Club, and gently suggested to him that he had been a bit of a nuisance, he assumed the righteous air of a gentleman huckster and uttered the inevitable words: "I was only trying to help you."

In December 1978, Al Fairley retired as president of Hollinger at the customary age of sixty-five and was replaced by P.C. Finlay, just turned eighty. It was a step forward in every respect and was universally recognized as such in the Canadian mining community where P.C. was surpassed as a beloved figure only by the legendary prospector and mining engineer, Bill James, Sr.

My initial attempt to sell Domtar was to Paul Desmarais as it would fit well with Consolidated-Bathurst, which Power Corporation controlled, but that was unsuccessful because we "couldn't deliver the board" (an understatement). I then opened up two fronts with apparently acquisitive forest products companies, one with MacMillan Bloedel, via Page Wadsworth, a director, and one with the Krugers, from whom I had bought newsprint at the *Sherbrooke Record*. Joseph Kruger didn't bring forth a serious offer, but MacMillan Bloedel did. At our December 1978 Argus board meeting, Nelson and I urged Alex Hamilton to remain in the room while we discussed the sale of our Domtar shares and invited him to produce a preferred buyer if he had one. We reached a conditional agreement to sell to MacMillan Bloedel a few days later, which I immediately reported to Alex Hamilton and which he purported to approve. (The condition was gaining 90 per cent of the company in a follow-up bid which was announced at once.)

On the same day, we handed over to Canadian General Investments our cheque for all their Ravelston and Argus shares and five minutes after this transaction was physically completed, Alex Hamilton phoned me back to announce that Domtar was making a takeover bid for MacMillan Bloedel. I took Alex's call at Don McIntosh's office at Fraser & Beatty in First Canadian Place, and when I announced this news, John Turner, the future prime minister (and not to be confused with Harold Crang's sidekick), who was acting for MacMillan Bloedel, said, "Don, let's break open the scotch!" This was Alex Barron's final salvo, and it was a feisty gesture. I told Cal Knudsen, chairman of MacMillan Bloedel, what was afoot before he learned through the normal channels, and after a few minutes he phoned back and said that his company would get a flying start on the upcoming battle with Domtar by going unconditional on their purchase of our Domtar shares.

A heavy snowfall had begun in Toronto and the various technicalities required some hours to complete. As Labrador Mining had 300,000 Domtar shares in addition to Argus's 2.5 million, we sold those too, and the newly elevated P.C. Finlay eventually arrived at the Fraser & Beatty office at 10:30 p.m., long after his normal bedtime, his hat, including the brim, supporting three inches of snow, a herniating mass of stock certificates in one hand and the corporate seal in another. (Given his eighty years, it was suggested that we hire a chauffeur for him, but his son pointed out it might be hard to find a responsible driver willing to report for work at 4:45 a.m. every day, only a slight advance on P.C.'s customary time of departure for his office.)

We exited at $27 per share, a price that Domtar has rarely approached since. A couple of days later, Ian Sinclair, chairman of Canadian Pacific, the largest shareholder of MacMillan Bloedel, piled in with his own takeover bid for the company. In the ensuing free-for-all, the premier of British Columbia, Bill Bennett, convened the combatants and asked that control of MacMillan Bloedel remain scattered, and the three pugilists returned to their corners. We had a last antagonistic exchange of press announcements between Argus and Domtar just before Christmas. It was the final volley in the skirmishing with the Meighen faction.

We were out of Domtar satisfactorily, with $75 million in hand, and the chairman of MacMillan Bloedel (Cal Knudsen) had enjoyed our negotiations so well that he invited me on as a director of his company in 1980. I accepted, but before being elected, control of the company passed to Noranda Mines, and I was replaced as a candidate for the board by a Noranda nominee.

When Canadian Pacific, MacMillan Bloedel, and Domtar accepted the premier of British Columbia's ceasefire, they agreed to a standstill, so our block of Domtar was not useful to MacMillan Bloedel and was on the market again. Alex Barron told me several years later, when civility at least had been restored to our relations, that this stock was offered to Canadian General Investments with Alex Hamilton's blessing. Alex Barron said that he wanted to buy and to take their position in Domtar up to 20 per cent or 25 per cent, which they certainly had the means to do, but that Max Meighen declined to assert himself and Ted Meighen opposed the move because he felt that they "didn't have the horses."

Alex Barron lost interest, he told me, in the Meighen companies after that. Passing on Domtar was an unfortunate decision for everyone. It would have been a brilliant investment for Canadian General; it would have usefully prolonged Alex Barron's career in a role where his considerable talents would have been well-deployed. And Domtar might not have fallen under the control of Quebec's Caisse de Dépôts et de Placements, whose chairman, Jean Campeau, told me he had largely been motivated to buy heavily into Domtar by irritation when the head office of the Sifto Salt division was peremptorily moved out of Quebec. If Alex Barron and Alex Hamilton had remained in charge, the calamitous acquisitions that almost ruined the company a decade later would not have been undertaken.

Massey-Ferguson had been a major preoccupation since the first days of the new regime at Argus. I was constantly receiving delegations of bankers from Massey's huge and perplexed banking syndicate, asking for reassurances about our plans for the company and specifically whether we were prepared to invest in it. I gave them no comfort at all, other than that we would modernize the management and review the prospects in due course. It was clear from the bankers' comments that they would not continue to support the company unless both Bruce Matthews and Al Thornbrough were replaced by younger men. Bruce was only too pleased to hand over the chair and there was, effectively, no one else to take it but me, so I did, Max Meighen abstaining, at the directors' meeting of September 1978.

I convened a meeting of the senior management, an aging, inexplicably unembarrassed and rather self-interested lot: Thornbrough; his smooth English minder, Tim Powell; the very beefy and jovial American, John Staiger; the long-suffering and stoical Wally Main; and the Stalinesque personnel director, Jack Belford. Victor Rice was the obvious candidate. He was the only leading candidate to succeed Thornbrough that I knew, and I suspected he would have the imagination, ruthlessness, and unquenchable ambition to take the most radical measures and, if necessary, as I suspected would be the case, to be a credible continuator of the company if Argus had, perhaps abruptly, to take leave of it.

The son of a chimney sweep from Barking in East London, Victor was a man of high intelligence and vivacity of mind. His irrepressible enthusiasm and almost relentless though hardly impenetrable guile would, I hoped, see him through the rude shocks that were surely coming. Through some very difficult moments, and across many years, including a few when we did not meet or speak at all, Victor and I have essentially been united by a constant recognition of the absurdity of much of the corporate drama and the orthodox comedy of much of the rest of normal experience. As with Hal Jackman, so with Victor, the ironic and the cynical are never far from mind. Completely insubordinate, compulsively scheming, a better manoeuvrer than an executive, Victor is a great talent, a delightful man, and in that, in his fashion, a good friend.

When I was on my honeymoon in Nantucket in August 1978, Bill Wilder, the former president of Wood Gundy and head of the Canadian Arctic Gas Pipeline project, telephoned and asked if I would see Sir Siegmund Warburg in Toronto in early September. Obviously, I was delighted to meet the renowned financier, probably rivalled only by André Meyer and Sidney Weinberg of Goldman Sachs as the world's greatest merchant banker, but Bill went on to ask me if I would promise not to make Victor or anyone else president of Massey-Ferguson in the interim. I told him that we would run our companies and I wouldn't uphold the normal course of business out of breathless anticipation of what Siegmund Warburg or anyone else might have to say, but that if he had an interesting proposal, we would be happy to act on it no matter who the president was. I took the tone of the question, like Harold Crang's shenanigans with Hollinger, as indicative of the thin credibility of Argus generally, but particularly of the financial establishment's scepticism about the ability of the new group, myself in particular.

With the huge amount of attention the media gave the Argus takeover, there came also a good deal of envy and resentment, and healthy, normal, neutral wait-and-see dubiety about whether we really knew anything about running a business. It was a legitimate question that could be answered only by events, but it wasn't as relevant as it seemed, given the general strategy that was already developing of getting out of most of the existing assets in favour of better ones. Even though the strategy could not be publicly revealed, it was emerging as a merchant banking operation of profitable asset upgrades requiring skills of trading and finance more than industrialism.

Having had a good deal of experience with the media, I knew how boring and marginal the working press tended to consider business to be. I set out to be reasonably accessible to the media, to make three points: that business can be interesting and that some businessmen are reasonably articulate, both of which were blinding revelations to most of the Canadian media, and that financial success is nothing to be embarrassed about, in the same measure that it should not be the subject of boastfulness or ostentation.

This course was such a radical departure from dour Canadian practice and from the soporific formulations of most Canadian businessmen, that I suspected I was starting ticking a public and press relations time bomb. In a general way, I was able to monitor the rising antagonism of the forces of envy, both the disgruntled yuppies suffering the frustration of obscene ambitions and the trunkless bull walruses in lairs of the geriatric establishment, as well as those whose hostility was, intellectually at least, more consistent, on the soft left of Toronto. Those who simply didn't like me for legitimate reasons of ideology or taste I always embraced virtually as a loyal opposition.

I invited Nelson Davis to join Sir Siegmund Warburg and me at our first meeting in September 1978, as a reinforcement in terms of both financial means and personal longevity. Siegmund Warburg was a striking physical and conversational presence. A fine leonine head, bright, intelligent eyes; large, well-formed teeth; an accent that, though pronounced, evoked film characterizations of intelligent Germans speaking English: syntactically correct but courteously formal.

Given the eminence of our visitor, I was doubly at pains not to be unreceptive to his overture, even though it became evident early on that, doubtless encouraged by Bill Wilder, Sir Siegmund was eager to believe that I was desperately anxious for any initiative that seemed to relieve us of the insupportable burden of reviving the palsied Massey-Ferguson. I explained to Sir Siegmund, in the most explicit terms, that our investment in Massey was the fifth most valuable that Argus had, was historically less than a third of what we (justifiably) hoped to receive for our Domtar shares, and that we could play our hand at Massey in a mood verging on complacency.

Siegmund obviously was trying to steal the company's most desirable asset, the Perkins Diesel division that Colonel Eric Phillips had purchased in the fifties and by virtue of which Massey was still the world's largest unit producer of diesel engines. Once I got to know him better, since we were both interested in psychology, I was able to ascribe to Siegmund Warburg a desire to reingratiate himself with his native land in wishing to relieve Massey of its most desirable asset at a risible price and deliver it up to a leading German company.

His interest in psychology, as I particularly understood when I visited him at his home near Montreux, Switzerland, in 1980, when he showed me his books, tended to a facile imputation to people of sexual motives and an unusual faith in graphology. He had everyone's handwriting "professionally" evaluated and set great store by trivial indications of vanity, such as monogrammed shirts, one of the several reasons he professed to write off Victor Rice, though the real reason undoubtedly was Victor's refusal to be seduced by Siegmund's professions of helpfulness.

I drew Siegmund out in successive conversations in Toronto in September 1978, in London in December, in Paris, New York, and Switzerland in the succeeding two years to the effect that he, like the Iron Cross-winning Jewish passenger on Katherine Anne Porter's *Ship of Fools*, had not, at first, believed that Hitler was as anti-Semitic as his rhetoric would indicate. He was an authentic German patriot, and his neighbour in his country house in Bavaria was Baron Konstantin von Neurath, Hitler's first foreign minister, who assured the thirty-one-year-old Siegmund in 1933 that Hitler's blood-curdling polemical attacks upon the Jews were apt to be followed through in policy. Siegmund emigrated at once and arrived in 1933 in London, a suspect German, and eventually became the doyen of British and then of all European merchant bankers.

His influence spread by degrees throughout the world; he was decorated in 1978 by the Emperor of Japan for his role in the internationalization of the yen. In the autumn of his days, he sought a tangible *rapprochement* with the country of his birth. In particular, it seemed to me, he sought to extract and transplant for a bagatelle, the heart and lungs of a great Anglo-Saxon Canadian company to Klockner Humboldt Deutz, Mercedes-Benz, or Bayerische Motoren Werke, whichever would pay the house of Warburg most handsomely for this redress, both symbolic and real, of the German and Jewish cultural contradiction of Siegmund's remarkable career.

He sent me a copy of Chancellor Helmut Schmidt's address at the Cologne Synagogue in November 1978, marking the fortieth anniversary of the infamous Kristallnacht anti-Jewish pogroms. The chancellor's remarks began: "We meet at the place and on the anniversary of the beginning of our national descent into hell."

Obviously Siegmund Warburg's motives didn't all emerge in our first meeting. Compelling figure of great authority as he was, Siegmund Warburg had no difficulty convincing Bill Wilder that what he wanted was to revive this great Canadian company. He was, in fact, in our dealings, the most elegant, the most believable, the most subtle as well as the most prestigious of all shop-lifters.

We started an extensive correspondence that continued until his death in the autumn of 1982. He was, to a limited degree, a mentor. He was also, by any reasonable definition, a great man. He maintained his network of contacts by having a group of approximately fifty people with whom he spoke regularly by telephone, in some cases, at least once a week. After early 1980, he did me the great honour of making me a "candidate-member" of that list, which was headed by Egyptian president Sadat, Henry Kissinger, and Austrian chancellor Kreisky. He was one of the most brilliant and interesting people that I have known. However it was apparent, even in September 1978 on Toronto Street, that he was unlikely to be of help to the existing shareholders of Massey-Ferguson. Massey's year ended October 31, 1978. The year turned out to have a trick-or-treat hallowe'en loss of $278 million. With plants and inventories honestly valued, there was no shareholders' equity left.

All through the autumn of 1978 we had been working on a new Ravelston shareholders' agreement. The 1969 one provided for a very impractical valuation procedure in the event of a sale of shares between partners. The company auditors who were charged with the evaluation in the Meighen case went to the Supreme Court of Ontario to seek instructions where their counsel alleged, *inter alia*, that there was some doubt about whether Western Dominion would pay our share of the valuation fees. We were represented by John Robinette, who had no difficulty persuading the court of the weakness of that argument, but we found it all so irritating that we replaced the opposing law firm as counsel to Standard Broadcasting and advised the auditors that they would not be re-elected as auditors for any of our companies. They then forgave their fees (were re-elected), and Canadian General Investments' counsel negotiated the price of the Meighen's shares directly with Igor Kaplan in the usual way.

Buying the Rileys' shares in Western Dominion and taking Western Dominion's shareholding up from 22 per cent to 51 per cent of Ravelston cost about $17 million net of our gain on the resale of Crown Trust Company shares. The interest on this borrowed sum was easily supported by the operating income of Sterling Newspapers. As Western Dominion shares my brother and I bought from our father, not long before he died, were paid for from Dominion Malting income, and that company had been bought from Canadian Breweries in 1968 on a straight leveraged buy-out, the only money we had really committed to this investment was my original purchase price for half of the two little Eastern Townships newspapers (Knowlton and Cowansville) — $500 in January 1966 (less a rug of minimal value).

The company that owned those newspapers (Eastern Townships Publishing Company) bought the *Sherbrooke Daily Record* for $18,000 in 1969, and the *Record* founded Sterling Newspapers in 1971 and expanded it on the basis of borrowing half the purchase price of acquired newspapers and retiring the rest of the purchase prices as declining balances of sale in the hands of the vendors. I was like the man who went to the horse races and kept winning, parlaying up his initial $2 bet by re-enlisting the winnings in each subsequent race. Apart from years of effort and personal credibility, I was not gambling more than my original $500 in 1966 on the Argus project.

As it worked out, the Rileys took 10 per cent of Ravelston, Nelson Davis 16 per cent, Hal Jackman 12 per cent, Fred Eaton 8 per cent, and Dick Chant, Douglas Bassett, and John Finlay 1 per cent each. Western Dominion had 51 per cent. About 12 per cent of WDI was held by each of David Radler and Peter White. My brother and I had the rest, with more in my hands after the merger between Sterling Newspapers and WDI. Various different requirements existed for the different Ravelston investors, especially Jackman, who was partially dealing with the funds of an insurance company, and the new agreement, without a compulsory transfer notice, was still not finalized at the end of 1978. On the day before Christmas, an executive from N.M. Davis Corporation arrived at 10 Toronto Street with a handwritten cheque for $7.5 million and a note from Nelson reading: "Dear Conrad: When you have an agreement ready to sign, send it over and I'll sign it; if it's good enough for you, it's good enough for me. In the meantime, here's my money. If you want more, call me. Merry Christmas, Nelson."

Partners of such quality are rarely found and almost impossible to replace, as we were reminded ten weeks later when Nelson drowned in his swimming pool in Arizona aged seventy-one, almost exactly a year after Bud McDougald's death. His funeral was not an Establishment outpouring like Bud's or even George Black's, but it was a moving tribute heavily attended by people who had worked for Nelson — a mailman who had delivered parcels to him many years before and obscure but loyal contacts from far-off days. Eloise Davis, in reply to my condoling letter to her, wrote that "for me, Nelson will always be the eagle at the top of all of his mountains"; and for me, also.

The hot pursuit of strategic objectives continued at an accelerated pace, with the briefest pause for necessary personnel changes. I succeeded Nelson as chairman, my brother succeeded me as president of Argus, Bruce Matthews retired as an Argus director, and we bought his modest Argus shareholding at the same price per share as the Meighens'. I spent most of my time at the brocaded office of Colonel Phillips at Massey-Ferguson at the corner of Simcoe Street and University Avenue; it had been unoccupied and unfurnished for fourteen years.

Victor and his hastily re-built management group, with my intermittent participation, were working feverishly to peel off the encrustations of chronically unprofitable, ill-considered investments left over from the Thornbrough era. The worst was Hanomag, the construction equipment division, which had cost $300 million, all raised from debt, and which had lost staggering sums almost from the day of purchase. The idea was that Massey would make short work of Caterpillar and other established companies in the field and to that end purchased a huge production facility, which had originally been built as a submarine construction yard, in Hanover.

For making the sale to Massey-Ferguson, Toni Schmuecker, the vendor, was named industrialist of the year in Germany and became head of Volkswagen as a reward for his talents as a marketer. (It is perhaps small wonder that Siegmund Warburg had such an unconvinced opinion of our staying power in this business.) Victor Rice's final instructions to our negotiating team over the speaker phone from our executive committee meeting were: "Get us out of this f—-ing awful business!" Mercifully, they did; they sold to Dieter Esch, an evanescent German industrial high-flyer, who was packed off to prison a few years later by German prosecutors after extensive fraud convictions, but re-emerged in the nineties as flamboyant owner of a group of American fashion modelling agencies.

My wife and I toured the Massey-Ferguson plant near Compiègne in April 1979, and when the manager, speaking in French, said the axles produced were shipped to Detroit, she said, "Did he say Detroit? Michigan? Get out of this business! There's no hope!" She was prescient. Victor kept the tenor of our deliberations light-hearted: he arrived at my home for yet another watershed strategy discussion one Sunday evening with a stuffed bear, which, when he pulled its ear, shouted from within, "I'm going straight to the top! No one can stop me!" His sense of humour was a great but unquantifiable asset.

Henry Schacht, head of Cummins Diesel, Dr. Thomée, vice chairman of Volkswagen, Sir Leslie Murphy of Britain's National

Enterprise Board, and Bodo Liebe, Siegmund's candidate and head of KHD (Klockner Humboldt Deutz) all surfaced to relieve me of Perkins Diesel, the one unambiguously valuable asset Massey possessed. To all of them, I indicated a preparedness to joint-venture the asset to add value to it, from which the Massey shareholders would benefit, or to admit them to the whole company as sizeable shareholders, to help give stability while we dispossessed ourselves of the most dreadfully undesirable assets and to strengthen the continuing core of the business. I was not prepared, in Bud McDougald's old phrase, "to sell the carcass and keep the feathers." None of them would touch what I offered, they were all vultures however costly, and I was concerned with the preservation of corporate life, not the distribution of financial carrion.

By the spring of 1979, we were ready for the first of what proved to be a series of Argus reorganizations, in which we realized cash and applied it both upward to raise our level of ownership, and outward to upgrade the quality of our assets. The plan that emerged from a good deal of contemplation and discussion with Igor Kaplan on securities and tax law implications was a simple and slightly elegant manoeuvre: Argus would declare a special dividend of all its Hollinger shares in specie out to its shareholders rateably with a cash alternative dividend for those who preferred it (meaning Ravelston would opt for the Hollinger share as opposed to the cash dividend and receive at least 75 per cent of the Hollinger control block), and Ravelston would then sell Hollinger its Argus shares, making Hollinger the senior public company in the group and putting Ravelston in useful funds. P.C. Finlay was enthusiastic to be set at or near the head of the corporate structure with which, in earlier times, he was not always thoroughly co-operative. Argus shareholders, who had indirectly been Hollinger shareholders through Argus, could be direct shareholders of both companies, accept cash instead of shares from Hollinger, or sell their Argus shares for cash to Hollinger; or a combination of responses: a complete choice, all cash, part cash, continuing shareholding in one or both companies. Ravelston took shares and not cash from Hollinger and cash from Hollinger in exchange for Argus shares.

The straightforwardness of the revolution appealed to many, and it had the effect of starting a lengthy division of institutional opinion on our company and methods. Ned Goodman came to see me and said, on behalf of the noted fund managers Beutel, Goodman, that "this Hollingerization procedure was so smooth and added so much value so fairly, that we decided we want to be sizeable shareholders with the author of such a plan."

Eventually, some of the other best-performing fund managers and institutional investors also became our largest and most loyal public shareholders, in particular, Stephen Jarislowsky of Jarislowsky, Fraser, and Tullio Cedraschi of CN Investments. (Through the last half of the eighties and into the nineties, those two individuals represented over 15 per cent of our stock and joined our boards of directors, Tullio at Hollinger and Stephen at UniMédia and ultimately at Southam. This did not deter several elements of the financial press from intermittent efforts to portray Steve Jarislowsky as an implacable adversary of mine.)

Some other institutions and (generally less astute) investment analysts became morbidly and reflexively suspicious of the "campaign of manoeuvre" we conducted from 1978 to 1985 and noisily recommended sale or avoidance of our shares. Given that an important part of the "campaign of manoeuvre" was the purchase, for cancellation or accumulation, by us, of those shares, the antagonism of much of the institutional community was far from unhelpful since it made our shares cheaper. While we were always accessible to shareholders' inquiries, and I personally dealt with any shareholder concern that was expressed up to 1986, when I started being away from Toronto for much of the year and the direction of the company had become obvious and unchanging, we did nothing to tout or glamorize our shares. Nor did we respond directly to analysts' public criticisms, other than in occasional caustic disparagements of their abilities by me, which tended to incite them further to encourage an artificially low price for our shares.

Hollinger, after becoming the overwhelmingly controlling shareholder of Argus Corporation, was renamed Hollinger-Argus, and with the proceeds to Ravelston we discounted and paid out the note owing to Power Corporation on the previous year's Argus purchase. We also massaged down Ravelston debt and effectively reduced the new Ravelston shareholders' cost of investment with a special dividend. Ravelston had almost 50 per cent of Hollinger plus the first refusal agreements negotiated to stop Harold Crang's shenanigans and transferred from Argus by the Finlays' clients, and Argus had applied much of the Domtar proceeds to increasing its shareholding in Dominion Stores, which we continued to regard as an underperforming but undervalued company, a fine asset play in a sluggish industry. A year after the Argus takeover, progress, if not Napoleonic, had been swift and gratifying.

In June 1979, Joe Clark's Conservatives narrowly defeated Pierre Trudeau and formed a minority government. I entertained no hopes whatever for the new team. Joe Clark is a principled and diligent man who has made the most of his abilities, but I never believed that he possessed sufficient of the arts or abstract qualities of leadership to execute the office of prime minister of Canada successfully, or even unsuccessfully, for a full term; I was not especially surprised, six months later, when he charged into a parliamentary confidence vote despite clear indications that the government would be defeated.

After the June election, I wrote both major party leaders. To Trudeau I quoted Cardinal Villeneuve's letter to Duplessis after his defeat in the 1939 Quebec election: "Who is to say that the future does not reserve to you a return to power? You would come back to it with the strength that adversity alone can give." He wrote back that "of all the roles I have ever played, my Duplessis to your Villeneuve was the most delightfully unexpected." As events unfolded, he had occasion to compliment me on my prophecy.

The fact that Joe formed a government at all confirmed me in my view that with Wagner, the Conservative sweep would have been as great as its decennial precedents in favour of Trudeau, Diefenbaker, St. Laurent, King, and Bennett. Joe had a minority because he was, at first glance and thereafter, a more unprepossessing leader than those predecessors. Claude had second thoughts about languishing as a Liberal appointee to the Senate and publicly offered to join the government. The suggestion was received with the coolness it deserved. A few months later he died, apparently of leukaemia. I corresponded amicably enough with Claude until near the end of his life. He was a puzzling and in some respects a disappointing but not a bad man.

Trudeau's rescission of his resignation, confining Don Macdonald to one of the briefest leadership campaigns in recorded history, and his subsequent re-election in February 1980, completed a particularly silly interlude in federal affairs.

More astonishing to me was Joe Clark's view that this most humiliating squandering of electoral victory in Canadian history did not materially reduce his suitability to continue to lead his party. The ignominy of his defeat conferred no discernible sense at all of people taking real responsibility for their actions. Brian Mulroney was the only other person I knew who never wavered in his view that Joe would not last as party leader. He heartily agreed with, and somewhat embellished upon, my comment in the summer of 1979 that "whatever his office, Joe *n'est pas un chef.*"

Brian had arranged for me to receive an honorary degree from his undergraduate alma mater, St. Francis Xavier, in June 1979, a few days before the election. Malcolm Muggeridge addressed convocation and, at the pre-graduation luncheon, found himself sitting next to Allan MacEachen, the local MP and Trudeau's deputy prime minister. As we walked into the convocation hall, Muggeridge, with whom I had corresponded desultorily since my initial interview with him over Duplessis in 1972, said, of MacEachen: "Am I to understand that this man is the deputy prime minister? And that there is an election next week?" "Yes." "Well, surely the voters will put that right!" They did.

As the convocation wore on and an interminable number of graduates for such a small college came forward to receive their degrees, Malcolm turned to me and said, almost in desperation, "Do you suppose they failed anyone?" Malcolm and Kitty came back to Toronto with us on our airplane and we were in rather more frequent contact after that. (Brian Mulroney offered my brother an honorary degree from another maritime university, St. Joseph's, but was politely rebuffed as Monte had no academic pretensions. Brian astonishedly reported back to me that my brother was "a truly modest guy.") I continued on the honorary degree circuit for a time and was always impressed by how presentable the graduating students appeared, compared to those of my era, ten years before.

By the late summer of 1979 it appeared likely that Massey-Ferguson could be managed to a break-even or slight profit in the year to end October 31, coming off the previous year's $278 million loss. The lending group of over one hundred banks, including the syndicate banks, had been clamouring for more equity almost every day since the initial announcement of losses in the autumn of 1977. Their desire to strengthen a debt-equity ratio of one to one was understandable, especially as the resale value of much of the fixed and inventory assets was doubtful and the equity figure correspondingly very soft.

Although Victor had made good progress in divesting us of some of the poorest quality assets, many potential buyers were clearly holding back in the hope that the condition of the company would erode, forcing bargain or even bankruptcy sales of desirable assets. The only division attractive enough to bring forth reputable buyers with real money voluntarily was the diesel engines group, which I would rather have kept while selling everything else.

Illustrative was the Argentinian business, a chronic and perennial loser. At the beginning of 1979 a representative of Mme. Fortabat of Buenos Aires, allegedly one of the wealthiest people in Latin America, came to see me and offered, on her behalf, to buy the Argentinian division of Massey-Ferguson if we would pay her $10 million (U.S.). I politely declined. Exactly a year later, the same person came back to see me exciting my premature hope that Mme. Fortabat was prepared to raise her offer, given demonstrable improvement in the company's fortunes. Her proposal was identical to the original one except that we were to pay an exit price of $20 million (U.S.). I again politely showed him the door but the overture was indicative of the implacable problems the company faced. (Almost a decade later I had occasion to see Mme. Fortabat from time to time at the Americas Society and we exchanged a few pleasantries about these bizarre discussions, which she claimed dimly to remember.)

Victor and I did succeed in selling Motor Iberica, the Spanish company in which we had an interest of just under 40 per cent, to Nissan. This prompted the Duke of Wellington, who was a director of Motor Iberica and hereditary landowner of large estates in Spain, to devise the novel idea of directors' severances. I did, at the Duke's behest, write the chairman of Nissan asking for compensation for His Grace, but received a very tardy and unenthusiastic reply.

It was to combat Fortabat-style bottom-fishing and to accelerate positive momentum that we announced, August 24, 1979, our preparedness at Hollinger-Argus (whose financial credibility was obviously already a good deal higher than that of the cadaverous old closed-end holding company Argus Corporation, out of which it grew) to participate to the extent of $100 million in a $500-million equity issue by Massey-Ferguson. Our share of $100 million would be uniquely convertible into voting shares, a sizeable portion would be debt-conversion by existing lenders into comparatively attractive preferred stock, and all would be contingent upon the recommendations of a comprehensive due diligence team from the five-member underwriting group that was struck.

But if this issue could be justified and taken up, the strengthening of the company's balance sheet and of its bargaining strength in asset dispositions would be almost miraculous. Jackman warned me that the dividend payment would be too unreliable and Siegmund Warburg treated the whole idea as an hilarious pipedream whenever it was mentioned (no doubt in part because he was so wedded to his own elaborate shoplift), but I thought the idea had a chance. Massey-Ferguson did report a profit of $30 million for the year, and although there was a good deal of latitude in the inventory and foreign exchange figures among others, progress was real. My idea was to have Dominion Stores be our investor; as a heavily taxed company, it could receive high-yield preferred investments tax-free.

Hollinger had sporadically coveted Noranda since J.Y. Murdoch, P.C. Finlay's senior law partner, was unceremoniously removed as president of Noranda in the mid-fifties. The state of friction between Hollinger and Noranda worsened a few years later when Holden, Murdoch, Finlay, and Robinson were replaced as Noranda's law firm, partly by hiring in-house several of the firm's partners. Relations deteriorated further in 1969 when Noranda induced, as McDougald and Taylor saw it, the Mead and Scott paper companies to replace Argus with Noranda as the associate controlling shareholder of British Columbia Forest Products, exposing for the first time the old Argus formula of the "controlling" 10 per cent to 20 per cent shareholding as the charade that it was.

I didn't inherit any of the McDougald regime's grievances against the Noranda chairman, Alf Powis, any more than I had with Paul Desmarais. I did think that Powis had used his frequent rifts with Bud McDougald and Percy Finlay to create an unjustified mystique of corporate invincibility. I gently accused him of confecting the myth that he had ever really been under threat from Hollinger, just as Montgomery had been the principal author of the Rommel myth, presumably, subtly, to exalt his own reputation.

Noranda certainly had its attractions; it was a superb resource company, which Powis had broadened into oil and gas and forest products, but he was not able to reduce the company's acute vulnerability to cyclical collapses of earnings. A takeover of a company whose capitalization then exceeded $1.5 billion was well beyond Hollinger's means, so I entered into discussion with the Caisse de Dépôts et de Placements, then presided over by Marcel Cazavan, a likeable old *routier* of the Duplessis-era type, with a view to making a joint takeover bid. My most frequent interlocutor in these talks was André Saumier, the former assistant minister of natural resources, who had been seeking to compel Hollinger and Labrador to invest more of its royalty income in mining exploration in Quebec before he removed to J.A. Richardson, investment dealers.

Almost nothing had been done in Canada in large-scale joint venturing between the public and private sectors, and I thought there was an opportunity to design a useful association that might have considerable applicability. I thought it might also be useful in showing nationalist Quebec that collaboration with Bay Street, towards whom their rhetoricians and polemicists had been rather abrasive, was possible and potentially very desirable.

Alf Powis had invited me on to the Noranda board, on the understanding that I not appreciably increase our shareholding. Since that would have left us short of the ability to equity account, it made no sense and I declined with thanks. In his fierce ambition to remain independent of any influential shareholder, he had issued rafts of stock in acquisitions, and Hollinger would not have the means to sustain its percentage of the shares indefinitely. Noranda, as I said to our directors was, "potentially a corporate Vietnam into which we might pour more and more resources and never win." Even with corporate allies such as Amax (American Metal Climax), with whom we had some conversations, the same risks existed. The risks were compounded by the fact that Noranda would remain hostage to a welter of unpredictably fluctuating commodity prices.

We could certainly have won with the Caisse, and André Saumier reported that Jacques Parizeau, then the finance minister of Quebec, was not at all averse to my suggestion of an order-in-council enabling us to waive the normal notice period for a takeover bid and go straight to the floor of the Montreal Stock Exchange. Such a move would not have been the apogee of fair play, but what was the point of having a government as a partner if its powers were not applied to the support of defined public policy? As usual in Quebec, with governments of the left or the right, arguments of eminent domain on behalf of the national government of French Canada go far, even if the implications ramify in rather authoritarian ways.

When the Noranda stock price passed above the point where I could possibly justify purchase, we sold the block, which had a historic cost to Hollinger and Labrador of about $35 million, for a $163-million note, high yield and bankable, which deferred capital gains tax over ten years. This generous monetization of a passive non-strategic asset illustrated the truth of our initial view in taking over Argus the previous year that there were extensive undervalued assets in the group that could be liquidated advantageously, and that their proceeds could be strategically reapplied.

I handed over the Noranda shareholders list and our extensive correspondence with the Caisse de Dépôts to Trevor Eyton and Jack Cockwell, who eventually did go into a successful joint takeover bid with the Caisse on Noranda. Alf Powis and others, with Adam Zimmerman in admirable dissent, distinguished himself on this occasion by selling Noranda shares into a high market sustained by takeover fever just before negotiating an arrangement with Brascan, whereby Brascan would buy a good deal of stock from Noranda's treasury, sharply reducing the stock take-up. It was an egregious case of inside trading and the Toronto Stock Exchange rapped the knuckles of the senior Noranda executives. (Later still, Trevor, Jack, Alf, and I served cordially together as directors of Brascan and a couple of related companies.)

With this further strengthening of our financial reserves from the Noranda sale, the first phase of the "campaign of manoeuvre" was successfully concluded. Argus was now subordinate to Hollinger. Hollinger and Labrador had $250 million in cash plus an annual pre-tax iron ore royalty of $45 million. Ravelston was a real rather than a pretend owner, Massey was under believable management, and Dominion Stores was still a potentially rich source of asset dispositions and was effectively controlled after application of some of the Domtar proceeds, so increasing our shareholding to over 30 per cent. We had graduated to a corporate combat potential:

from the penurious General Bonaparte in Italy, we were now MacArthur setting out from Guadalcanal, with an amphibious assault capability, provided we island-hopped with agility.

The first opportunity that arose fell in our traditional and preferred newspaper business. The *Montreal Star* had taken a strike for several months and finally settled it very unfavourably. As usually occurs in a competitive newspaper city where only one paper is struck, the *Star* returned having lost the competitive advantage it had enjoyed over the *Gazette* almost since Lord Atholstan founded the *Star* in 1869. All through Atholstan's era and that of his successor, J.W. McConnell, the *Montreal Star* had been a pre-eminent and very profitable newspaper.

In October 1979, the *Star* folded. It was owned by FP Publications, which was a pooling of interests between Victor Sifton, owner of the *Winnipeg Free Press* (the source of the corporate name, FP) and the *Ottawa Journal*; Max Bell, owner of the Calgary *Albertan*, Victoria *Times-Colonist*, and Lethbridge *Herald*; and Howard Webster, owner of the Toronto *Globe and Mail*. In 1973, the McConnell interests vended in the *Montreal Star*. The resulting share-ownership structure bore some resemblance to the post–McDougald-Ravelston scene, as J.W. McConnell had died in 1963, and Victor Sifton, his son John, and Max Bell had all died since FP was founded.

The McConnell family was represented at FP by Derek Price, who was married to J.W.'s granddaughter and had been the publisher of the *Star*. I had known him well when we were both members of the Quebec Daily Newspaper Publishers' Association. He was an English-Montreal gentleman of the very best type: urbane, affable, completely ethical. When I telephoned him following the announcement of the closure of the *Star*, he said he was "staring out the window trying to decide whether to jump or not." For someone who had worked for so long to promote goodwill in Quebec and to be a spokesman for an enlightened and conciliatory English-Quebec view, it was a cruel fate to have to preside over the closing of the *Star*. The McConnells were certainly receptive to an offer for FP as they had over 20 per cent of the stock, but their principal direct interest had gone.

The Sifton interests were effectively represented by Brigadier Dick Malone, Victor Sifton's old sidekick and a veteran editorial executive. I had known Dick for many years, first socially and then at Canadian Press, where we had both been among the leaders of those calling for a vigorous resistance to the demands of the Guild. During World War II, he had been a Canadian liaison officer to Field Marshal Montgomery and directed the Canadian Armed Forces publicity effort. He concluded the war as an official liaison from Mackenzie King to General MacArthur, which he parlayed into a couple of meetings interestingly described in his memoirs. For all his subsequent life, Dick Malone was an inexhaustible storehouse of famous names and more or less reliable anecdotes linking himself to them. He had a few shares of FP himself, rather like Bruce Matthews at Ravelston. As he spoke for the Siftons, despite June Sifton's (Victor's daughter-in-law) often almost frenzied litigious attempts to depose him, and had been the president of the company as well as publisher of the *Globe and Mail*, he was a figure of considerable influence at FP. He also had a disproportionate number of voting shares.

I had often had lunch and dinner with Dick at his home in Forest Hill, exchanging military history books, swilling scotch, discussing current affairs, and playing croquet. His relations with Howard Webster were poor, as Howard considered Dick's profit performance to be inadequate.

I had also come to know Howard Webster quite well, partly from knowing many of his nephews, and partly from serving with him as a trustee of the Confederation Arts Centre in Charlottetown. He was a famously eccentric character who had married briefly at a rather advanced age. His wife found his erratic and often drink-taken behaviour taxing. He once left her in London for "a day" to go to Ireland, was waylaid by drink and affairs, became alarmed at the passage of time, and flew directly back to Montreal, leaving his uninformed bride to await him with mounting impatience and disappointment in London.

Drink could indeed be a problem. On one occasion in 1969, I was sitting with Bud McDougald at his table in the Toronto Club when the club manager approached and said that Howard Webster was on the landing of the stairs but that his trousers had fallen down. Bud helpfully suggested that Howard be assisted in pulling his pants back up, and in a minute or so Howard came unsteadily into the dining room with his jacket largely tucked in under his belt, but slogged through his lunch uneventfully and with some aplomb.

We came back together from Charlottetown to Toronto in July 1977, and Howard carried a suitcase that was bound tight with twine. In my experience, he was rivalled as the most shabbily accoutred prominent Canadian only by P.C. Finlay, the handle of whose briefcase was fastened with glue and Scotch tape.

Howard Webster was deceptively inarticulate and desperately shy. Even with people he knew reasonably well, such as me, he needed a few drinks to speak with any confidence at all, but generally was unwilling to contradict or disagree, preferring to mumble and prevaricate, nod and grunt, and then proceed as his highly developed financial instincts recommended. He had his own language of grimaces, grasping his chin and emitting apparently insensible noises to indicate amounts of money, usually denominated in many millions. On one occasion he sat at an FP meeting that approved a program of market share purchases of the FP-controlled but publicly listed Sun Publishing Company in Vancouver, and then put in a personal buy order for the stock, competing against the bid of a company of which he was an insider: both a director and a co-owner.

When he was sued for wrongful dismissal by an ex-employee in a terminal elevator business he owned in Detroit, he ignored the award the plaintiff eventually won from the court for increased compensation and for two years could not set foot in, or even overfly, the United States because of an outstanding warrant for his arrest for civil contempt of court. On another corporate adventure in the United States, he arrived at the annual shareholders' meeting of a fountain-pen company and asked a sequence of questions in his halting and almost inaudible manner. The management, considering his shabby appearance and diffident manner, thought he was a tiresome odd-lot shareholder and treated him with increasing disdain, until he revealed the fact that he owned the majority of shares and fired the entire board of directors.

At one time or another he controlled an astonishing variety of assets, including Dominion Malting Limited, the Lord Simcoe and Windsor hotels, the Scripps Estate in Detroit, the St. Raymond Paper Company, Quebecair, 45 per cent of the Toronto Blue Jays, and large chunks of Burns Foods (with Arthur Child) and Maclaren

Power & Paper Company. In addition to his great financial prowess and original personality, he was also very generous and dispensed countless millions of dollars to a great range of worthy causes. By 1979, he realized he had made a mistake putting the *Globe and Mail* into FP. He had made an even greater mistake not securing a first refusal agreement with the other shareholders and had compounded that error by antagonizing virtually everyone associated with FP. His nephew, Norman Webster, was the London bureau chief for the *Globe and Mail*.

The Max Bell Foundation was directed by a group of trustees including George Gardiner, Roland Michener, James Richardson, Joe Sedgwick, and George Currie, the management consultant who had been put up to replace Dick Malone as president of FP, when Dick finally retired in 1979. I knew them all quite well.

Immediately after the announcement of the closing of the *Montreal Star*, I spoke first to Derek Price, then to Brigadier Dick Malone, who had been buffeted by charges of sexual indiscretions against his son, Richard, the publisher of the *Winnipeg Free Press* (and widely known as Bombardier Malone). Dick urged me to make an offer for FP and allege a preparedness to relaunch the *Star*. I spoke next to George Gardiner, to sound out the Bell group of FP directors, and to Howard Webster. Everyone acknowledged that something had to change, that the company was in an unsatisfactory state, and that a bid from me would not be unwelcome.

In addition to the shambles in Montreal, the *Ottawa Journal* was sinking. Long a near equal rival to Southam's *Ottawa Citizen*, the *Journal* had re-equipped at its ancient downtown location with letter-press equipment and had fallen steadily behind the *Citizen*, which went offset and to the suburbs. The president and editor of the *Journal*, Norman Smith, was an old friend of my father's from their days together at the British Commonwealth Air Training Plan in Ottawa in 1940. He was an excellent writer, a man of immense integrity, and a faithful friend, but not a man of commerce. The Calgary *Albertan*, which had never done well with Max Bell, was a chronic loser, and the *Globe and Mail* had seen better days, with steady inroads being made on it by the *Sun*, founded on the remains of the old *Telegram*, and the *Star*. Victoria, Vancouver, Lethbridge, and Winnipeg were all doing well.

It emerged from my conversation with George Gardiner that he and John Bassett were preparing a bid for FP. We agreed to meet and George put the question at once: "Are we allies or competitors?" I assumed that George, one of Canada's most brilliant financiers, would bring his fellow trustees at the Max Bell Foundation, and that John, through Baton, was essentially acting for the Eatons, a powerful support in any case, but one that would be divided if I proceeded without these associates, as Fred Eaton and Douglas Bassett would be involved in both bids. I was delighted to be in business with men of such talent, congeniality, and substance. We had many meetings, some at my office but most at George's house. Those at his house invariably concluded with John Bassett and George Gardiner taking each other's blood pressure with a do-it-yourself sphygmomanometer. They courteously invited me to submit to the same metabolical self-examination, but I didn't think it necessary.

John and I met with June Sifton and her lawyer and with Howard Webster. John, Howard, and I had a pleasant lunch in a private room at the Toronto Club. Howard professed to be entirely in favour of what we proposed and was motivated by extreme hostility to Malone (because of what he regarded as inadequate profits), as was June Sifton (who thought she should vote the Sifton shares). John Bassett shared their low regard for the brigadier for reasons going back to World War II. At one point, when we met at my office at Massey-Ferguson, he exclaimed, like one of Napoleon's grognards, to June Sifton and her lawyer: "The only powder Malone saw during the war was on a woman's face, or perhaps a woman's ass." When we left the Toronto Club after the lunch with Howard, who went out the front door of the club, John and I walked down the corridor to the parking lot and he exulted, grasping me by the forearm: "Do you realize you're the only living person who's on speaking terms with all these fruitcakes?"

We constructed a two-tier offer that put a large premium on the small number of voting shares, thus giving the greatest possible incentive to Dick Malone who was, however, rarely influenced by thoughts of his own maximum gain. Derek Price and Howard Webster professed support, and Dick, though non-committal, was friendly.

In early December 1979, I went to John Turner's luncheon for Peter Lougheed at McMillan Binch in the Royal Bank Plaza and found myself sitting next to the publisher of the *Globe and Mail*, Roy

Megarry. He had heard rumours about our bid and expressed the fear that if matters continued on their present course, the *Globe and Mail* would be called upon to bail out the parent company from its self-inflicted wounds in Montreal and Ottawa. I ended up giving him a ride back from the Royal Bank to the *Globe and Mail*, and we sat in front of his building in my car while I answered his questions frankly. (I was driving the car so we were not in the back seat as has been suggested in Roy's published recollections.)

My reasoning was that as we might be associated soon in important events, I should not give evasive answers to legitimate questions. I endeavoured to satisfy him that we were not at all opposed to his expansion across the country by satellite (though John Bassett was sceptical, I thought him not beyond persuasion), that FP's other problems had to be solved where they originated, and that his own position shouldn't change appreciably, though I couldn't insult his considerable intelligence with the ludicrous untruth that John Bassett, George Gardiner, and I would be quite so passive and disinterested as Howard Webster and George Currie had been. Roy got out of my car with the words, which I noted carefully and tentatively believed at the time: "This isn't a negative and could be a positive development for us. I'm not opposed to you."

It emerged that he went straight into his office and threw himself into the task of blocking us, with the cyclonic frenzy he intermittently applied to the management of the *Globe and Mail*. Over the years he lurched from expedient to expedient: "the national newspaper" (when it was largely chased out of Toronto by the *Sun* and *Star*); the (disastrous) all-day newspaper that drew the *Star* entirely into the morning field; the "élite" newspaper that temporarily ceased to audit its circulation; the plethora of magazine inserts (all but one terminated after a couple of years); eventually, the firing of the editor and managing editor and a belated lurch to the right, and ultimately, Roy Megarry's own withdrawal, in 1992, to dispense aid in the Third World, an admirable calling better suited to his talents than running the *Globe and Mail*.

Roy's version of the conversation in my car, especially the claim that I opposed satellite trans-Canada editions, is self-serving fiction. I cautioned him only against trying to fight Toronto's battle in Winnipeg or Vancouver. John Basset was admittedly less than enthusiastic about the satellite printed editions, but I assured him we would be open-minded about them.

Roy Megarry is a red-headed Irish immigrant, a self-made mature student and devotee of good causes. Whatever his shortcomings as a manager, he is not an ineffectual agitator. He started on this occasion by organizing Norman Webster to lobby his uncle Howard, whom he also approached directly, to detach him from his tacit association with us. Howard had been the ultimate non-interventionist owner, making Roy Thomson's ownership of the *Times* of London seem like Northcliffean autocratic meddlesomeness in comparison. Megarry set out, directly and indirectly, to convince Howard that we would do unimaginable things to, as I put it to one Toronto reporter at the time, "the holy virgin of Canadian journalism" (the *Globe and Mail*).

A few days later, George Gardiner telephoned me with the news that a mutual friend had heard from Howard Webster that the price we were offering was insufficient, though it was exactly the price John Bassett and I had suggested to him ten days before in the Toronto Club and that he had approved. Although Megarry was much more plausible and effective, his role in this drama was somewhat analagous to that of Prusac in the Argus takeover.

A few days after George Gardiner imparted his intelligence, Howard, without any warning or notice, as he didn't want to be accused of skulduggery or bad faith (and would have no defence against the charge), put down an opposing bid at a slightly higher price. I was pretty philosophical about Howard's desertion of us, because I made allowances for his oppressive shyness and eccentricity. We quickly topped Howard's bid and I had no fear of him as a competitor. However great Roy Megarry's enthusiasm for Howard's absentee chairmanship of the *Globe and Mail*, Malone and the other shareholders had had quite enough of Howard's bizarreries. I was sure we could see him off, but the danger was that the Ravelston-like advantage of "interior lines," an inside job, was lost, and Howard's defection put the company publicly in play at a time when Dick Malone's antipathy to John Bassett eroded the sympathy he would have had for us and did originally have for a solo bid by me.

Douglas Bassett and I visited Dick to assure him about Douglas's father's vote as best we could, but it was clear that he had insurmountable misgivings about our offer, though he was very well-disposed to Douglas and me personally. In vain did Douglas urge him to adjudicate the bids "for the right reasons and not the wrong ones."

The ominously expected second shoe dropped, and Thomson made a bid. I did a little research and it was clear that the fix was in. Clair McCabe (Thomson's brilliant and colourful North American head of newspaper operations) had sold Dick Malone a full bill of goods that Thomson, as it had shown with the *Times* and *Sunday Times* of London (which they were about to peddle at what proved a risible price to Rupert Murdoch), would protect the *Ottawa Journal* and might even be able to revive the *Montreal Star*. (Thomson folded the *Journal* and interred the *Star* a few months after this deal ended and then asked me to give what amounted to character evidence at the resulting Combines Act pre-trial, which I did. Thomson and Southam were exonerated.)

Dick Malone was forthright and friendly to me as always but had set his most Churchillian cigar-wielding countenance against any bid but Thomson's. Derek Price was still receptive to us and generously thanked me for helping to precipitate an auction that, a few weeks after the dreadful and traumatizing close of the *Montreal Star*, was going to yield them a very large gain on their FP shares. The McConnells would go to the highest price, as would the Bell shares.

When the bidding went towards the outer limits of what we were comfortable with, given the fix in Thomson's favour and my partners' relative lack of interest in the properties other than the *Globe and Mail*, I made a verbal arrangement with Howard Webster. If he were victorious (which possibility didn't really exist given Malone's mindset), we would buy Vancouver, Victoria, Lethbridge, and Winnipeg from him for the percentage of the quantum of the overall deal that these newspapers had of FP's circulation (about 40 per cent, considering the public minority shareholding in the *Vancouver Sun*). Verbal deals with Howard, as the recent past demonstrated, were nothing to bet the company on, but he might have honoured it, though John Bassett and George Gardiner might not have been interested. The final offers were tendered to Roly Michener, and Thomson won at about $170 million, a brilliant deal for control of 950,000 paid daily newspaper circulation, over 800,000 of it in profitable newspapers and one of the best deals Thomson had made in a great many years.

It had been worth a try and I bore no one any ill will, except Roy Megarry, and not for his opposition, but for his disingenuousness. While Roy had been undistinguished at good-faith follow-through, so had most of the people implicated in the decline and fall of FP, and Roy had been a very effective player at his chosen game, starting the rockslide away from us. Our *échec* at FP ultimately facilitated a more advantageous position at Southam. The patient pursuit of good assets at reasonable prices usually has its rewards.

David Radler's comment was that "Conrad wasted an awful lot of time playing croquet with the brigadier." In fact, I had enjoyed my interludes with Dick Malone, and they continued almost to his death in 1984. He was a name-dropping old water buffalo, but interesting, intelligent, and a good friend. I never forgot the exceptionally fine letter he wrote me when my parents died, including the line: "Life has many bumps but it must go on, and the 'Lord loves a bonny fighter.'"

By the time the FP drama ended, I was in Palm Beach, where, for the second year, my family and I rented the house formerly owned by Neil McKinnon, on the same street as Jim McDougald and Doris Phillips. By this time I was so disgusted with the irresolute performance of President Jimmy Carter that I cheerfully paid $2,000 to go to candidate Ronald Reagan's dinner when he came to Palm Beach in February. I normally am a supporter of whoever is the president of the United States and generally hoped for Democratic victories until that party lost its nerve after the disastrous 1968 convention, wrenched the nominating process out of the hands of the party bosses who, in the smoke-filled rooms, had elevated Roosevelt, Truman, Stevenson, Kennedy, Johnson, and Humphrey, and handed it over to Gay Liberation, Jane Fonda, Shirley MacLaine, the eco-geeks, militant abortionists, and assorted rabble-rousers. These elements gave the nation and the world the singularly unpresidential sequence of McGovern, Carter, Mondale, and Dukakis.

At one point in early 1980 I said to my venerable neighbour, Charles Wrightsman, who owned one of Palm Beach's greatest houses, that I thought Carter was "the worst president since Harding." "I knew Warren Harding," Charles replied, "and he wasn't this bad." (President Harding died in 1923.)

Jimmy Carter was the real-life enactment of Jimmy Stewart's *Mr. Smith Goes to Washington*, as, after two talented presidents,

Johnson and Nixon, who had led the nation astray, the country, without ever articulating it, went for a God-fearing, under-qualified outsider. The only people of any consequence Jimmy Carter knew outside Georgia when he was elected were those in the Trilateral Commission (they were still there when I became a member of the Commission in 1982), with whom he stocked his administration: Zbigniew Brzezinski, Harold Brown, Richard Holbrooke, Henry Owen, Joe Nye. They were competent people, exceptionally so in Brzezinski's case, but the administration was blunted by Carter's widdering indecisiveness.

The Western alliance would have the neutron warhead for deployment in Europe in February, but it was withdrawn in April. The Russian military advisers at Cienfuegos, Cuba, were "unacceptable" on Tuesday, but acceptable on Friday. The aircraft carrier *America* was leading a task force to the Persian Gulf from Monday to Thursday, but then, for no apparent reason, on the orders of the commander-in-chief, the ships executed a 180-degree turn. He confessed to have learned a good deal about Soviet foreign policy from the Soviet invasion of Afghanistan and negotiated a Strategic Arms Limitation Treaty that would have entrenched the military supremacy of the U.S.S.R, no small feat given the swift subsequent crumbling of the Russian challenge in response to Reagan's defence build-up. I had concluded that he was correct when he told the country in the summer of 1979 that it was suffering from a "malaise" and that the most obvious and easily corrigible symptom of the malaise was his presence in the White House.

His ultimate indignity, in my view, came in March 1980, when he called a press conference at 7:30 a.m. to announce that the Iranian president, Bani Sadr, in an address the previous evening, had taken a position on the release of American hostages quite reconcilable with U.S. views and that a breakthrough had occurred. Only one to two days later, when private-sector translations of Bani Sadr's remarks became available, was it clear that the president had grossly misrepresented the Iranian's remarks. I never have objected to minor political chicanery but dishonouring in this manner the headship of a great nation by grovelling before a psychopathic, fundamentalist Third World regime was at least as offensive to me as the tawdry and excruciating psychodrama of Watergate. It did Carter little good in the Wisconsin primary. Party cross-overs are permitted in that state, and Ronald Reagan swamped all the candidates, Democratic and Republican.

In subsequent years, I have several times met and spoken at length with Jimmy Carter, including during and after a tour given him and his wife and me of the Jerusalem Citadel by Jerusalem mayor Teddy Kollek in 1990. He is a pleasant, intelligent, and idealistic man. His love of peace, financial honesty, and humility before God are admirable but his high scrupulosity was flawed by desperate and sanctimonious partisanship as was demonstrated in March 1980.

Beyond that, he had neither the instincts nor panache of a natural leader. The United States and other countries have flourished under unexciting leaders before — Coolidge, even Eisenhower. Mackenzie King was far from exhilarating and became interesting only when his diaries were posthumously opened up and his peccadilloes and neuroses revealed. At bottom, Jimmy Carter failed as president because he couldn't lead consistently, he couldn't inspire the American people with lofty but comprehensible goals, and he didn't satisfy the American public that he gave the United States the benefit of the doubt that its strength in the world was a positive force or that its future would be, or even always deserved to be, benign.

Ronald Reagan I remembered from "Death Valley Days," the 20 Mule Team Borax advertisements, "General Electric Theater," and a few movies. I first took him seriously as a political leader when he refused to move the board of regents' meeting of the University of California from riot-torn Berkeley and on arrival ignored the surging masses of demonstrators and shook hands individually with the beleaguered line of state troopers who were with difficulty restraining them. He went further and ordered the National Guard to clear the main square of the campus with fixed bayonets, which they did, without inflicting or sustaining a single casualty.

The country was coming to him. Improbable though it might seem to his detractors, Reagan had the intuition of what the people wanted, and the mastery of the technique of moving public opinion towards him. After Vietnam, Watergate, and the inanities of the Carter era, the presidency had to be restored to a position of natural leadership, and the United States, which had suffered the most precipitate decline of influence of any great power since the fall of

France, was to be restored to its rightful place of world leadership. Carter was the problem, Reagan the solution. The office seeks the man.

On this occasion in Palm Beach, I was able to speak only briefly with him and to remind him that his last visit to Canada had been on our airplane to address a gathering of kindred spirits in Mississauga and to appear on CFRB. He was in vintage form, but so was the arch-conservative, violently rich community he visited. The three youngest people in the room were, in ascending order, my wife, myself, and Ronald Reagan, and together we lowered the average age perhaps from eighty-three to eighty-one (and probably the average net worth commensurately).

The dinner was billed as informal, but that did not deter the lady on my left from wearing a diamond stomacher and a remarkable series of diamond bracelets. She excused herself to leave some of these mighty baubles with the chauffeur. When she returned, we were standing for an invocation by a fire-breathing clergyman from Jupiter, Florida, who was calling for divine intervention on behalf of a galaxy of patriotic American causes. "They're praying for us now, my dear," said my gravelly-voiced and rather deaf neighbour's husband. "What?" This exchange was repeated four times in rising voices. On my right was a retired air force general, advertising agency head, and friend of Alexander Woolcott's, who, in the mad fashion of Palm Beach, actually believed that General Dwight D. Eisenhower was a "card-carrying communist."

Reagan gave one of his vintage, tub-thumping speeches. No one would "use the U.S. flag as a door-mat when (he was) president," and so forth. At the end of it all, a mighty procession of Palm Beach's most ostentatious automobiles awaited at the front of the Breakers Hotel. As far as the eye could see were Mercedes Benz 600s and 900s, Rolls-Royce Phantoms, Silver Clouds, Corniches, Shadows, and Spurs, many elongated or transformed from saloons to dropheads in proof of their owners' ingenuity at devising methods of spending an additional $100,000 on a $200,000 automobile.

To the front of the line came the portable hospital donated by the former mayor of the town, former, and last, U.S. ambassador to Cuba (and one of my sponsors at the Everglades Club, overwhelming Jim McDougald's attempted blackball), Earl Smith. This ambulatory hospital was usually engaged in picking up cardiac victims on Worth

Avenue, the so-called Fifth Avenue of the South. Two people on stretchers were hurried past me, and I said to one of Reagan's security unit that I hoped it was nothing serious. "Oh no," he replied, "the governor's always a little too much for some of these old-timers." It was my first foretaste of the power of the Reagan Revolution.

The failure of the FP initiative did not reduce our appetite for a sensible acquisition. Labrador, thanks to Fairley's negative persuasive powers, was paying an astronomical rate of tax and as emerging public policy in Canada facilitated the sheltering of income for re-application to oil and gas exploration, an energy acquisition appeared desirable. A committee of Hollinger directors, John Finlay, David Dunlap (Peggy Dunlap Crang's son), and Bruce Ross, the outstanding former mining director at Timmins and president of Labrador Mining and Exploration, had studied the possibilities for several months and concluded that Norcen Energy Resources Ltd. was the best prospect.

There was a tremendous premium on oil assets at this time, and we wanted to be sure not to buy at the very height of an oil price that could not have escaped altogether from the vagaries of commodity price cyclicality. Norcen had not advanced as spectacularly as some oil stocks, because it was still widely perceived as a gas utility, the old Northern & Central Gas Corporation, whose name had been changed after the Northern Ontario Natural Gas scandal, in which the then chairman, Ralph Farris, was sent to prison for perjury over a bribe to the former mayor of Sudbury, Leo Landreville, who, when it all came to light, was a federal Supreme Court justice.

The succeeding management of Spencer Clark and Ed Bovey changed the company's name, accumulated one of Canada's major corporate art collections, and made it a serious patron of the arts. The energy-exploration aspect was steadily emphasized under the brilliant leadership of Ed Galvin and Ed Battle, whose talents as acquirers of assets exceeded the company's record as an explorer. By 1980 it was a superb company, 80 per cent in the energy-exploration and development business, but still somewhat undervalued by contemporary energy industry standards because of its reputation as a utility.

In December 1979 I had asked Trevor Eyton if, as had been rumoured, his group had any Norcen shares. He didn't, but phoned me back four minutes later with the advice that he could lay hands on two million shares, 10 per cent of the company, with which Gordon

Securities was in touch. I bought. The next morning, at 9:01 CFRB time, I telephoned the Norcen chairman, Ed Bovey, a delightfully urbane and good-humoured man whom I knew well from our service together on the board of the Canadian Imperial Bank of Commerce. He took the phone with the words "I hope it's you!"

After some discussion we took our position up to almost 40 per cent in February, in a routine stock-market floor bid that we called Operation Catapult, the launch of our group onto a new level of ownership of an asset of unprecedented quality for Argus. (The World War II action of that name, the British smashing-up of the French fleet at Mers-el-Kebir in July 1940, was not an inspiration.) The bid was at a fairly full price and was not contested.

This was only the first and easier step towards the repositioning of Labrador's iron ore royalty under Norcen, so that maximum tax efficiencies could be achieved by it. The purchase had cost $320 million, of which about $200 million had to be borrowed. (When the Toronto Stock Exchange had required evidence of the means of Hollinger and Labrador to take up shares tendered to the proposed bid, P.C. Finlay came back a few hours later with guaranties of credit for the full amount from three different banks.) After a year and a half of manoeuvring, we had finally assembled the critical mass to make a serious acquisition and had done so cleanly. A thoroughly agreeable association began with an excellently managed company.

René Lévesque finally held his referendum on a complicated question of whether the government of Quebec would be authorized to enter into negotiations with the federal government to achieve sovereignty with association with the rest of Canada, in the spring of 1980. Pierre Trudeau's interventions in the campaign, and especially his last (of four) speeches, at the Paul Sauvé Arena, a few days before the referendum day, were the most effective political campaigning I have observed in Canada. In the last speech, he responded, appropriately scornfully, to Lévesque's allegation that Trudeau didn't understand French Quebec because his middle name was Elliott. The vote was about 60 per cent against, or about an even split among the French-speaking Quebeckers, not an overwhelming rejection, but a breaking of the momentum of the separatists, who polled slightly less than the Parti Québécois itself had in the three-party general election of 1976.

In order to achieve this result, Trudeau had promised (Quebec) a charter of rights and an amending formula. Ever since his strenuous debate with Daniel Johnson at Lester Pearson's last federal-provincial conference in early 1968, Trudeau had countered jurisdictional arguments by asserting that what was important were not the prerogatives of different echelons of elected officials, but the rights of all citizens. It was a beguiling Rousseauesque argument that his opponents both of the separatist and unreconstructedly common law varieties had great difficulty dealing with, but now Trudeau would have to produce something for Quebec's constitutional delectation. (Unfortunately, his relentless truckling to special-interest groups and his fetishistic attachment to regulation, transfer payments, and zero economic growth substantially limited the relevance of his apparently sincere attachment to individual liberties.)

The condition of Massey-Ferguson deteriorated steadily through 1980. After our announcement in August of a $500-million equity infusion, which Argus would lead with a $100-million participation, the cumbrous and exacting process of due diligence unfolded in a traditional way with teams of researchers from the underwriters examining the company's principal operating units. Victor had reduced the number of employees by about 24,000 and had done an admirable job of disposing of the most gangrenous divisions.

But in late 1979, the oceanic tide of events turned against us. The nature of Massey's operations ensured that a rise in the value of the British pound and a decline in the U.S. dollar were very destructive of Massey's earnings. The opening of the Thatcher era and the twilight of Jimmy Carter's bumbling regime created exactly those conditions, as the pound sky-rocketed and the dollar crumbled, shored up at all only by interest rate increases that were also ruinous to so debt-ridden a company as Massey. The United States sank into recession, compounded in the U.S. agricultural sector by Carter's grain embargo in ineffectual reprisal against the U.S.S.R.'s invasion of Afghanistan.

My hope had been to improve operations to the point where an orthodox refinancing could be achieved, led by Argus, which would then become a real and not token controlling shareholder of a properly capitalized Massey-Ferguson. We could then dispose of our shareholding at the top of the merciless agricultural cycle and redeploy to more rewarding businesses. As farm income and spending plummeted and the currency whipsaw lacerated us, it became clear in early 1980, even as the underwriters toiled, that a different approach would be necessary.

We would have to refinance the company in order to achieve the improved performance, and not in consequence of having already achieved it. None of the potential buyers or investors that had been conducted to my doorstep by Siegmund Warburg or who had arrived spontaneously were interested in doing more than stripping out the diesel engine division at a knock-down price and leaving us with disembodied limbs.

Attracting investors in these circumstances was going to be quite a challenge, and by the early spring of 1980 Victor Rice and Russell Harrison (CIBC chairman) were both talking about approaching the government of Canada for financial assistance for Massey. The prime rate was moving inexorably upward through the teens and it was not going to be possible or ethical to disguise the impact of the economic environment upon Massey past the second quarter of the year.

As long as I was chairman of Massey, the serried ranks of the banks in the lending group, which had never ceased to claim an intimate connection between Massey and Argus personified by my position in both companies, were going to assume that Argus would backstop Massey's operational shortcomings, specifically the bone-cracking burden of its interest charges. I was also already hearing from Hollinger-Argus shareholders, and even some directors, that we must not throw good money after bad. The diluvian moment was almost at hand; I was called upon to serve and placate both those who purported to feel it was my responsibility to save Massey-Ferguson and those who felt it was my duty not to commit a cent to it, whether it went under or not.

If an equity issue could be raised, Argus's participation in it would carry more weight and be perceived as a more voluntary investment, if I were not the Massey chairman. We had ten times as large an investment in Norcen as in Massey-Ferguson. The book value of the investment in Massey was $39 million and the banking group had advanced the company over one billion dollars. They had the problem, not I, and anything that brought forward the hour of their recognition of that problem was a constructive step.

I explained all this to the Massey directors, May 23, 1980, and retired as chairman. When I installed Victor as president in September 1978, I had hoped that he would have the credibility and motivation to carry on without an Orwellian Argus overlordship and he leapt to the task with relish. I explained that I had prevented the discussion the CIBC had wished to have with the federal government about Massey's financial condition because I had no interest in asking for government assistance and there would be no possibility of achieving any if Massey were perceived to be a ward of Argus. The time-honoured method of dealing with problems of this kind, if the company were judged to be of sufficient interest not simply to be put into receivership, a threshold I hoped Massey had crossed with Victor's operational improvements, was for the senior lenders to convert to preferred shares, and the preferred shareholders to common equity.

I didn't see that there was much likelihood or even necessity of government involvement. Victor, chronically optimistic (he couldn't have endured the ensuing year otherwise), set out to use the underwriting group to raise equity in large private placements. The underwriters reported generously on the company's progress, but an equity issue on the public markets was now out of the question. Victor set out to persuade ten international investors to provide $50 million each. I was confident that we had deteriorated from the point that companies such as Volkswagen, KHD, and Cummins Diesel wanted to buy our best assets for a bagatelle, to the point that any interested companies would rather wait for the expected opportunity to buy our more desirable assets from the receiver.

I would do what I could to be helpful, but not to the point of mortgaging everything that we had built up at Argus over the last two years. In my remarks to the directors, May 23, I made a point of crediting Alex Barron with foresight as a Massey director and ensured that that comment was in the minutes. I sent an extract to Alex, who had sold Canadian General Investment's Hollinger stock because he was concerned that we might go in over our heads at Massey. He need not have worried.

Discussions with governments were facilitated by my departure as chairman, and Victor pursued them energetically. I attended a couple of rather pleasant meetings with Bill Davis and another in

Ottawa with the Treasury Board president, Don Johnston, where Victor, Russell Harrison, Tony Fell, and I were received by a teeming mass of senior civil servants. I had endeavoured a couple of times to generate some enthusiasm for government involvement and originally proposed a joint venture with the governments of Canada and Ontario with Chrysler for diesel production.

As Massey's diesel engines were entirely produced in England, international profit margins practically evaporated when sterling was comparatively highly valued, as it was in 1980. Building some engines in Canada would provide a good deal of flexibility and would also make some of the more reasonable schemes for selling at least part of the British engines company more interesting to us. I wrote to Herb Gray, the federal industry, trade, and commerce minister to this effect, on July 4, 1980. I was greeted by a glazed pall of official prevarication.

Victor was naturally pressing me to know what we were prepared to do: "You show me yours and I'll show you mine," he called it. Throughout the summer of 1980, pressure on the company mounted as lenders from all over the world pointed out imminent defaults on covenants and agitated for repayment. At one directors' meeting in this period, I was sitting between Hal Jackman and Page Wadsworth and they both handed me notes at the same time. Page's read: "What would you think of the CIBC investing $100 million in Massey equity?"

Hal's read: "The only way this company will make it is for the banks to convert three-quarters of their loans to common shares." Rather than reply to either, I passed on the notes to the alternative author.

By September, Massey was *in extremis*. Events had overtaken our ability to resolve the issue with dignity and I had written to Herb Gray, August 27, asking the government for "favourable noises," while Argus and CIBC led an equity issue. I still believed I could justify such an initiative if the overall package were large enough to assure that we would, in fact, receive our preferred dividends. I wrote that in the absence of such "favourable noises" with some possible modest, tangible sequel to them, we should all prepare ourselves for a corporate débâcle with no Canadian and few international precedents.

At the September CIBC directors' meeting, Russell Harrison, the company's counsel, Alex MacIntosh, and I absented ourselves to meet with Victor and Tony Fell over the composition of a press release on the status of an equity infusion. Victor had prepared a wildly optimistic press release on behalf of the CIBC, Argus Corporation, and the underwriters, the imminent arrival of all three being the financial equivalent of the Seventh Cavalry. Alex MacIntosh demurred on behalf of the bank. Tony Fell diplomatically expressed reservations for his part, and I tried to tone down our commitment without rendering the draft meaningless. Russell said nothing until he suddenly stood up and exclaimed, "This is bullshit! There isn't going to be any new equity. I'm going back into the meeting to get approval for a $100-million bad-debt write-off," and he swept out of his office like a grim tornado, having considerably dampened Victor's parade. (Six months before, Russell had shown the same panache in the same place over a U.S. bank's threat to call its Massey loan. He announced that the CIBC would immediately call its loans to the then troubled Chrysler Corporation and the U.S. bank backed down. Russell was a steadfast and delightful man to deal with in all seasons.)

The CIBC took the write-off. Argus had notionally and for internal purposes written down our position to zero in early summer. Later, on September 5, 1980, at the Massey-Ferguson directors' meeting, Al Thornbrough effectively confirmed that he had lost touch with corporate reality: he proposed we transfer loans from the CIBC to the Royal Bank. I pointed out that the Commerce had authorized its chairman to take a $100-million loss on its Massey position that morning and that the Royal hadn't been the most profitable bank in Canada for forty years by taking on loans in that condition.

More uplifting was the Duke of Wellington's exhortation that "we must not fail." It was, as Dick Chant put it, "a pretty good charge to the troops though probably more for his own benefit than for ours." When he finished his call to arms, I said that I was working on a proposal to protect the Canadian, U.K., and U.S. banks and to make an orderly retreat in other countries, though the French, German, and Italian banks would find it a bit rough. "F— the frogs and huns!" bellowed His Grace, with a blood-curdling clarity entirely worthy of his illustrious ancestor.

My brother, concerned that the creditors could descend at any moment on Massey-Ferguson's assets called the custodian of the Rolls-Royce we had bought from the company, but which was still kept in the yard adjacent to the company office behind Claridges on Davies Street. He aroused the driver from a sound sleep at a late hour and urged him forcefully to remove the car to a garage for unspecified and unnecessary repairs "and tell them to take their time with them." The mystified driver moved the car to his own home instead. (Thornbrough's old Cadillac limousine in Toronto had been purchased by David Radler, who paid someone to drive it to Vancouver and leave it in his driveway, where it would "impress certain types of visitors." David disposed of the car when one of his friends said that he hoped David wouldn't be having over "visitors who would be impressed by an oversized, unwashed old Cadillac with three flat tires.")

On September 15 I wrote my final epistle to Herb Gray along the lines I had indicated to the Duke of Wellington. A "coalition of efforts . . . would emanate from Massey-Ferguson in concentric circles to include the CIBC, the Argus Group, the federal and provincial governments, the Canadian, British and American lenders, until the perimeter is extensive enough that Massey-Ferguson could withdraw within it and rationalize its affairs in an orderly fashion. . . . Without the proverbial favourable noises from the federal government, Massey-Ferguson would not be able to seek such re-arrangements, except on a basis of unabashed supplication. . . . Massey would have to meet its lenders denuded of any semblance of support or assurance of continuity and would have nothing to show them but a corporate begging bowl. . . . Under absolutely no circumstances will we [Argus] inflict further embarrassment upon ourselves than we have already done by maintaining some appearance of solidarity between Massey-Ferguson and ourselves, which is all that has kept Massey afloat for the last two years."

Finally, we were in the end-game. Even allowing for the propensity of people to believe what they want to believe, I was astounded that the press generally and even my interlocutors in the federal government persisted in the view that I had tied myself inextricably to the farm equipment business.

The high road of refinancing on the back of improving results had been narrowly foreclosed by unkind circumstance. (When Ronald

Reagan was inaugurated and the U.S. dollar sky-rocketed, Massey greatly benefited.)

The middle road of orthodox refinancing with symbolic or project-related public-sector support had become a mirage because of the dithering of all those who thought that I was ensnared in a financial trap that would tighten with each day and that I could ransom my way out of only by leading an Argus bail-out of Massey-Ferguson.

There remained only the low road, which I had worked out in the spring with Dick Chant and my brother and which led to the escape hatch: the gift of Argus's Massey shares in equal halves to the Canadian unionized and non-unionized pension plans, and the retirement from Massey's board of the Argus directors.

The company's crisis had become so intractable that some corporate replication of the slicing of the Gordian knot was the only option. I telephoned Herb Gray on the evening of September 30. He said the government couldn't do anything to help Massey as long as Argus Corporation was a perceived beneficiary. I replied, "I understand the problem. I believe I have a solution and you won't have long to wait for it."

I had intended the continued Argus presence as a potential buyer of a new equity issue to be a reassurance and encouragement to lenders, governments, and, even in less desperate times, to underwriters. For a complicated variety of reasons, some cynical, some naïve, our presence had become an obstacle to progress. I would remove the obstacle.

On October 1, I secured the approval of the Argus executive committee to contribute our shares to the Massey-Ferguson pension plans and ascertained that these plans were eligible to receive the shares. Hal Jackman left the meeting rather than approve or vote against the sale for no consideration, because he thought I was giving away an asset, but he sent over his resignation as a director in the hands of a commissionaire accompanied by a clerical, in case the bearer was struck down "by a car or a coronary" in which event, like an Olympic relay performer, he would, in his dying breath, commit the paper to the survivor for delivery.

Hal followed the same reasoning his father Harry had when he violently opposed the expropriation of the Texas Gulf Sulphur

Company by the federal government for the Canada Development Corporation in a letter to the chairman of that company, after he had tendered his stock to the offer at a handsome profit.†

David Radler had left his resignation as a Massey-Ferguson director with Dick Chant in May, when I first bruited this contingency plan. Fred Eaton and Trumbull Warren sent theirs in and on October 2, I sent these resignations, with those of Dick Chant and my brother and myself and certificates for three million Massey-Ferguson shares signed over to the company's Canadian unionized and non-unionized pension plans, to Victor and issued a brief press release that made the point that we might yet be prepared to participate in a refinancing. We were never asked.

Massey did indeed present its "corporate begging bowl" but at this, as at many other unconventional corporate arts, Victor exceeded the imagination of Oliver Twist's creator. The refinancing that ensued was a triumph for Victor and for the smooth, imperturbable and slightly affected treasurer, Douglas Barker.

Victor's management was masterful and piquant: the lenders were all almost washed into shareholders, North American Farm Equipment was vacated, and some of the most hopeless assets dumped on the local lenders somewhat as I had envisioned in my letter to Herb Gray of September 15. The shareholders were put through the wringer, receiving one share for every ten previously held, leaving the number of issued shares not much changed from my day. The business became an auto parts and diversified concern and in 1991 departed the NDP's Ontario for New York State, deserting the jurisdictions that had, with infinite reluctance, helped

---

† Hal came back from overseas a few years later, in the midst of a takeover battle for Union Gas and discovered that his talented chairman of National Victoria and Grey, Bill Somerville (no relation to the Phillips and McDougald lawyer), had, as a Union director, remained loyal to Union management led by the former provincial treasurer, Darcy McKeough. Hal told Somerville to tender National's stock to the offer. Darcy abruptly resigned as a director of Hal's Algoma Central and Hal asked me to persuade Darcy to stay. He abruptly declined to do so and Hal expressed concern that "Darcy's a politician who doesn't understand that political loyalties that don't cost anything don't really exist in business."

rescue Varity, as Victor Albert Rice had renamed Massey-Ferguson (Varity was the name of a plough company bought by Massey in the nineteenth century). Hal Jackman sophistically came and went from the board again. *Plus ça change.* . . .

Argus and Hollinger-Argus converted a perceived and potential open artery into an immediate recovery of our $7.4-million capital gain assessment on the Domtar sale and further larger avoidances in future. The *tricoteuses* who had been joyfully awaiting my arrival at the guillotine were audibly disconcerted when the tumbril arrived empty. I launched a public relations blitz for a couple of days, accepting almost all requests for interviews. At the October 3 CIBC directors' meeting, I was greeted by Russell Harrison with the words: "I didn't expect to see you here," and responded, "I wouldn't be anywhere else."

After the September 5, 1980, Massey-Ferguson meeting, I said to Victor, "I'll be damned if I'm going to have nothing to show for my years here. Send me an invoice if you want" (for the painting of a gun carriage moving past the bombed-out Massey-Harris dealership at Arras in 1918 that I carried out under my arm). He didn't.

In the days immediately following October 2, I received a number of congratulatory telephone calls. Gordon Fisher, president of Southam, was the first, but the most appreciated was from Sir Siegmund Warburg: "Very good, my young friend! Brilliant! What imagination, my dear Konrad! How did you think of it — a liability becomes an asset as if by magic?" Malcolm Muggeridge wrote that I was "well out of it: our neighbour's Massey-Ferguson combine harvester breaks down reliably every autumn." The next time I saw Herb Gray, at Trudeau's party for the economic summit leaders in June 1982, he smiled broadly and quoted Barbra Streisand: "You don't write me letters any more." One pensioner sent me a letter of thanks. I had told Derek Hayes, eventually secretary of the CIBC, and John Egan, later Sir John Egan, chairman of Jaguar, who both left Massey at about the same time I did, that I wasn't abandoning the fight, merely "transferring my flag to a more seaworthy vessel, like the American Admiral Fletcher at Midway" (the American fleet commander). We subsequently agreed that there was "life after Massey."

The *Sun* grossly libelled me in an editorial by Peter Worthington, saying I was personally responsible for Massey-Ferguson's debts, and in a cartoon by Andy Donato, likening me to Willie Nelson's gambler knowing "when to fold" his hand, entitled "Conrad Tricky." After the prompt arrival of my writ, Doug Creighton and I agreed that I would reply in any terms I wished and these would be prominently published on the editorial page without comment by the newspaper. My riposte began: "For the record, not that the *Sun* is a newspaper of record to anyone who does not suffer from severe lip-strain after half-a-minute of silent reading. . . ." Worthington became so perturbed that he wrote an editorial entitled "Mea culpa" and announced his retirement. He was eventually replaced by my glamorous and talented friend, Barbara Amiel. I met her first at John Bassett's house in 1979 and as we were among the few Canadians who regularly took a rational conservative position and could get any audience for one, we always found our fairly frequent encounters convivial. Our relations remained thoroughly cordial, but it was not until many years later when we were both unattached that they became romantic.

At the beginning of 1980, to strengthen the board, I had invited Ralph Barford, who had retired in 1979 out of loyalty to Alex Barron, his original sponsor, and John Turner to become Massey-Ferguson directors and they accepted. Having brought them, in good faith, into what proved a very nerve-wracking situation, I repaid what I perceived as a debt by inviting them both into Ravelston in 1981. Ralph accepted and made a handsome profit. John did not feel able to accept but expressed appreciation for the gesture.

On October 28, 1981, these two (Ralph Barford *in absentia*) held a dinner to honour Victor Rice at the York Club. John Turner toasted Victor, who graciously replied and cited Vince Laurenzo (who succeeded Victor as president after Victor succeeded me as chairman), Douglas Barker, and me as his co-saviours of the company.

Victor had taken Douglas on his overseas vacations while I was chairman, "because he didn't want me left behind alone with the figures," Douglas later explained. Faintly smelling of absinthe, Douglas Barker triumphed in febrile times, his nights rent by frequent calls from our distraught joint-venture associates, especially our fretful partner in Khartoum. One of his desperate tours of outlying banks was rendered even more uncomfortable than it was bound to be by Lufthansa's misplacing of his luggage and well-intentioned but not completely satisfactory emergency issue of paper replacement underwear. Through all this and much more, Douglas Barker persevered unwaveringly.

I was eventually dragooned to my feet to reply and saluted Victor's courage, ingenuity, and perseverance and turned to Alex Barron and expressed my admiration for his prescience as a Massey director, an admiration which easily transcended our well-known disagreements on other subjects. I reflected that throughout the darkest days, no Massey director was heard to give any thought to any interest except the company's and that there was not one that I would not be proud to serve with again. It was a good evening and a happy ending.

Shortly after the Massey drama did end, Igor Kaplan died of the brain tumour and metastatic cancers that had gnawed at him almost incessantly for two years. He was forty-nine. It was a cruel fate and a brave death. The rabbi who presided at his funeral gave the most brilliant and poignant eulogy I have heard, expressing the tragedy of the occasion without being maudlin or platitudinous. Igor's former law partner, John Aird, had recently been sworn as lieutenant-governor of Ontario and attended in a private capacity. At the end of the service we were both too moved by the sadness and eloquence of the occasion to speak or even shake hands properly, and only lightly grasped each other's forearms. To Igor's mother Nadya, a beautiful and timeless woman, I wrote an apposite quote from Newman, and Ravelston funded a distinguished lectureship in Judaic studies at the Toronto School of Theology. I described him to the Law Society's *Journal* as "a great lawyer and a dear friend."

The reverberations of the Massey-Ferguson dénouement were just quieting down when the federal government introduced its National Energy Program. It was predicated on the assumption that the world oil price, which had advanced from $3 to nearly $40 per barrel under the influence of the OPEC cartel, would double again in the next decade. There was a massive increase of taxes on extracted oil, and the management function was largely usurped by the government offering "petroleum incentives" for frontier exploration. For Hollinger-Argus, although our most palsied asset had gone, our newly acquired prize, Norcen, had been significantly undermined by this ill-conceived legislation. Norcen's reported income would be cut about in half. The cash flow wouldn't be too much changed, but about a third of it would be misspent government hand-outs squandered in such places as the Arctic Islands, where oil was uncertain, inaccessible, and uneconomic.

We had been working on a complicated plan to sell our iron ore properties and Dominion Stores and Standard Broadcasting shares to Norcen and retire the debt in Hollinger and Labrador that had been incurred to buy control of Norcen. It was a refined form of self-dealing and had already attracted criticism from elements of the financial press that thought they had smelled blood at Massey. Press opinion, like the envious hordes of middle management and the snuffling walruses of the geriatric establishment, was becoming hostile. It was not only the public relations atmosphere that was turning. Interest rates were above 20 per cent and, as Jackman gleefully pointed out in early 1981, Labrador had to borrow a little to pay its dividend.

The energy minister, Marc Lalonde, his parliamentary secretary, Roy MacLaren, his executive assistant, Michael Phelps, the deputy minister, Mickey Cohen, and the senior assistant deputy minister, Ed Clark, all intelligent and affable people who went on (or back) to some distinction in the private sector, could never in subsequent years remember their enthusiasm for the NEP. Nor, inexplicably but fortunately for them, given their successful subsequent careers, were they much held accountable for it either.

It has not been my experience that the private sector is necessarily better managed than the public sector, only that it is more swiftly punished for its errors and indisciplines. Nor has it been my experience that the learned professionals conduct themselves with greater probity or even intellectual lucidity than mere men of commerce. Humbug and pretention are no substitute for practical intelligence. The entire National Energy Program episode was a disgrace for which its principal authors were never forced to assume real responsibility. The minister of finance, Alan MacEachen, was amenable when I and others approached him to substitute exonerations from tax for the exploration grants envisioned in the NEP, which would help the oil companies' profits without costing the federal government anything because grants were not treated as income for accounting purposes, but reduced taxes were. The government could have made the tax exonerations conditional on frontier exploration activity in an appropriate proportion. The accounting professions, however, sandbagged the initiative at the Ontario Securities Commission, claiming political infringement of professional self-regulation and resisting de facto alteration to accounting rules by collusion between government and industry. Any such initiative as we were proposing was seen as a transparency to subvert the profession's ability to determine what the clients' incomes were. It was hopeless.

In taking over Argus Corporation in 1978, I had sought tactical inspiration from the blitzkrieg methods and swarming infiltrations of the German tank commanders of 1940. In the sequence of sales and shuffles with Crown Trust, Power Corporation, Domtar, and Noranda, a successful war of manoeuvre was conducted to acquire some critical mass. This series of actions, though hardly worthy of a great strategist like Napoleon, aspired, at least pallidly, to apply some of his precepts. Force was achieved through transactional velocity and was translated into advantageous acquisition of control of an excellent asset, Norcen.

The next phase, which I had ambitiously hoped would be a MacArthur-like island-hopping sequence of selective inexpensive amphibious assaults, had got off to an unimpressive start. FP had failed, but no one had been lost on the beach. In that sense it wasn't even a Dieppe. Norcen's prospects for increased income and a rising share price had been gutted by the federal Energy department. We had escaped from Massey as painlessly and with as much dignity as possible, but, as Churchill said after Dunkirk, "Wars are not won by evacuations." The proposed reorganization of the old Argus group under Norcen now had to be abandoned. Strains would assumedly be reduced with declining interest rates but in the meantime we were suffering from and had no active remedy for financial overstretch.

The reorganization would have put the debt in Norcen, which could certainly have managed it and would have resulted in the sheltering of the Labrador royalty income and its intelligent re-application in energy exploration. The reorganization had been cumbersome and had more of the tactical qualities of the disastrous Japanese plan for Leyte Gulf than the luminous simplicity of some of MacArthur's actions, but its termination left us awash with interest charges, with a principal asset of uncertain and reduced value, listening to the jubilation in the ever more numerous camp of my critics.

However trivial they might be personally (and the few that found voice for their grievances in my presence were trivial), they had an influence on financial community opinion, including at the securities commission, slowly reducing the climate of receptivity to my apparently endless campaign of corporate manoeuvre and reorganization.

Before settling into trench warfare, I explored the possibility of a lightning exit somewhat on the model of, though more lucrative than, our departure from Massey-Ferguson. Some Ravelston shareholders had occasionally indicated some interest in liquidating or reducing their positions. I entered into discussions with Paul Reichmann about selling Ravelston's Hollinger-Argus shares to him. Paul and his brother were now, on the heels of their tremendous bonanza in the New York real estate market, setting out to build, as Paul put it, their "own Canadian Pacific," without the railroad. The natty, astute, and extremely affable Latham Burns assisted us.

I had first met Paul Reichmann when he endeavoured to buy the old Crown Trust head office on Bay Street from me in 1978 to add it to his First Canadian Place. I was prepared to sell the building in exchange for an equity interest in his massive project but not for cash. We did not reach agreement and it became academic when we sold our Crown Trust shares, but the conversations were very amicable.

He is an impressive man. Dark eyes, hair, beard, and complexion, a tired voice but unfailingly courteous, learned, and civilized in the attractive Talmudic manner, his decisiveness, swiftness, imagination, scholarship, and reliability are all remarkable. Through all the years that I have known him, I have always considered him one of the most interesting and brilliant businessmen I have dealt with, in a category with Siegmund Warburg, Dwayne Andreas, Jimmie Goldsmith, Kerry Packer, Rupert Murdoch, Leslie Wexner, Warren Buffitt and a very few others, and that judgement is unchanged by his eventual liquidity problems at Olympia & York. Money is only money. Paul Reichmann, because of his vision, majestic stoicism, whether in financial ascent or retreat, and the quality of the monuments he has conceived as well as his integrity and scholarship, is in these respects at least a great man.

We came within a few million dollars of agreement. His proposal would have given me about a $75-million profit for two and a half years of fairly high-pressure work, and a net worth of rather more than $100 million. I thought I could probably make more money more quickly by reinvesting it, probably in the United States, and working again with David Radler and Peter White on expanding a new version of Sterling Newspapers with drastically increased means. But making money was not my sole or even principal motivation. Any such course would have had about it the air of an orderly but cynical retreat. I had made a good many comments about rebuilding Argus Corporation. Shuffling it around and peddling it to Paul Reichmann was not going to fit any definition of reconstruction.

I never doubted that Ronald Reagan would rout the hapless Jimmy Carter, that his tax cuts would reinvigorate and ultimately reindustrialize the U.S. economy, that his defence build-up would ultimately bring the Russians to heel, and that he would restore the presidency's place in the U.S. political system and America's place in the world.

Alluring though re-emergent America was, irritated though I was by the envious back-biting, mediocrity, crypto-socialist governmental tinkering, and national ambivalence of Canada, I was not prepared to seem to be driven out by it. I might choose to leave some day, but on less ambiguous terms than these. Hal Jackman said, "It's all a question of what you want to do with the rest of your life." Cutting and running for a mercenary profit was not the answer. I explored the possibility in good faith with Paul Reichmann as a sensible examination of alternatives. If he had raised his offer sufficiently, the temptation and the agitation of some of the other Ravelston shareholders might have been irresistible, but he didn't. I remained to fight on, to be a financier at least, perhaps even an industrialist, and not a mere parvenu.

CHAPTER EIGHT

FINANCIAL ENGINEERING: FROM OIL INTO IRON ORE
1981–1983

THE NEXT STEP IN THE RECONSTRUCTION OF our business was the dismemberment of Dominion Stores. That ramshackle company had been atrophying peacefully for years; it had largely avoided the profit potential of real estate and it rented almost all its locations. Dominion had almost entirely avoided the wholesale business, where margins were a good deal higher than at the retail level. It had a late and mediocre entry in the convenience store business (Min-a-Mart), and apart from a controlling interest in the marginally profitable General Bakeries, Dominion had avoided the food manufacturing business also. It bought from suppliers and sold through unionized outlets at rented locations. From 1978 on, sales increased less than the inflation rate despite steadily increasing volumes of selling space due to new stores added each year. Market share was slipping, though this inescapable fact was militantly denied by the management.

The company had many good locations, but its management had a reputation for excessive conservatism and lack of imagination, as well as questionable financial ethics. Many of the recent leasehold arrangements were inexplicable unless lessees' representatives had had private incentives. More worrisome, each year's accounts were materially altered after the year-end by Earned Cost Reductions, a bulk-purchase discount system that was zealously guarded by the senior vice president, John Toma, and that was never properly audited. The temptation was obvious to buy according to the kickback arrangements, disclosed or otherwise, and with insufficient regard to the wishes of the customer. Toma had a tenuous attachment to the truth in almost any conversation I ever had with him. His sallow complexion and evasive manner gave him a faintly sinister air.

The outgoing president of Dominion, Tom Bolton, was a distinguished and honest man of an earlier era of food retailing. Apart from him, the Dominion Stores management was composed almost exclusively of unprepossessing and virtually uneducated people. They were known as "good company men," an annoying euphemism for slavish conformity to Toma's obscurantist orthodoxy. When gathered together informally, as at a baseball game or a golf tournament, the Dominion management all wore white shoes, huge belt buckles, and loud shirts and told each other ribald stories of an unusually banal kind.

They weren't hired for their social graces, but what concerned me was their lock-step refusal to contemplate anything new; their arrogant insistence, as if constant repetition would make it true, that they were the North American continent's greatest food retailers; and their inability to explain the numbers. When I started as a Dominion Stores director in 1979, there were quarterly financial statements of one page, the figures rounded to the nearest $5 million. As time went by, the quantities of paper became more extensive, but the figures reported were neither more satisfactory nor more believable. Not one of Dominion's financial officers could ever remember one number, no matter how central to the company's fortunes, such as the previous year's published profit (or loss), without rummaging around through reams of papers to inform himself.

Even when they could be believed, the company's figures did not make very agreeable reading. At its greatest extent, Dominion Stores had sales of $2.7 billion for a net profit of $27 million, 1 per cent of sales. This was not an abnormal return for the industry, and the unexplained annual inventory shrinkages attributable to employees, i.e., theft by employees from the company's inventories, were steadily $30 million or so; customers' thefts were about another $10 million. When I revealed this fact in 1986 in the midst of a controversy over pension surplus entitlement, although other companies in the industry privately confirmed my findings for their own businesses, I was pilloried for my defamation of the unskilled workers of Ontario. There was a conspiracy of embarrassed liberal silence, such as long operated in the United States to prevent the media from reporting that over 70 per cent of violent crime was by and against (i.e., within) the 11 per cent of the American population that was black.

Such profit as there was was never sufficient to pay more than a modest dividend, build and stock new stores, and replenish existing ones. The income was neither extensive nor reliable enough to justify sizeable borrowings and the disposable cash flow, after dividends and maintenance of plant, was a negative figure.

Under the division of interests that my brother and I agreed with Bud McDougald in July 1976, my brother became a director of Dominion Stores and Standard Broadcasting when I joined the Argus and Ravelston boards. Ultimately, he succeeded to Bud's and Bruce Matthews's positions as chairman of those companies, and I focused on Massey-Ferguson, Hollinger, and Norcen. There were some limits to what I could practically achieve at Dominion as a non-executive director.

I agitated constantly for the company to become a source of cash for us, as all the other Argus holdings had been (even Massey-Ferguson when we recovered tax after disposing of our shares). My proposals that we either radically change the company, i.e., to a franchise and wholesale business, or sell off chunks of it were not unsympathetically received by my brother and Dick Chant, who had become a vice president of Dominion Stores, but they approached the question less single-mindedly than I did.

I managed by early 1981 to enlist everyone's agreement for the notion that we should dispose of the Quebec operations, which on $600-million sales had never made as much as $3 million. The first discussions with a Quebec buyer were with a co-operative called Coop-Prix, brought in by André Saumier (the former deputy minister of mines of Quebec with whom we had discussed a joint takeover of Noranda). The dickering with Coop-Prix motivated the Dominion management, headed jointly now by Allan Jackson, a pleasant but somewhat limited and hypochondriacal ex-butcher, and Tom Bolton (now vice chairman to my brother) to enter into substantive conversations with Provigo, a franchise food-store company that had enjoyed a considerable success in Quebec and was now imbued with the missionary entrepreneurial self-confidence that animated Quebec throughout the eighties, until the bubble burst.

Bolton and Jackson handled the discussions very competently and the result was that we sold four outlying stores to Coop Prix and all the remaining Quebec stores to Provigo. The two stores in the Lake St. Jean region, as well as one in Rimouski and one in Abitibi, effectively drove Coop-Prix into bankruptcy in just two years.

Provigo, one of Quebec's most confident and successful companies, after the predictable bellows of triumph over the Anglo-fossils, wrote off the entire $78-million purchase price of our stores and eventually sacked the senior management, with this transaction generally recognized as one of the principal contributing factors.

It was not the brave new entrepreneurial Quebec's finest hour, but the $78 million Dominion Stores received enabled us to resume the steady corporate reorganization that had been severely interrupted by the National Energy Program. We produced a sequence of steps that retraced the Hollingerization of Argus in 1979. On that occasion we distributed Hollinger shares in a special specie dividend from Argus and sold over control of Argus to Hollinger, applying left-over cash in the hands of Ravelston (the controlling shareholder first of Argus and then of Hollinger) to reduce the debt incurred in buying half of Argus's participating shares from Power Corporation and to increase our real equity interest in Hollinger.

In 1981, my brother and I designed a symmetrical sequel: Hollinger declared a special specie dividend of all its Argus shares and with them control of Dominion Stores and Standard Broadcasting, and Ravelston sold the control position in Hollinger to Dominion Stores for 1¼ Dominion shares and $14 for each Hollinger share with an instant follow-up offer to all Hollinger shareholders. In this process the McMartins and others with Hollinger put-rights to us exercised them, and Dominion became the owner of about 92 per cent of Hollinger. Ravelston made a further cash realization of about $30 million, which was employed to issue a special dividend of $10 million and further reduce debt, now well under control.

My brother, as originating co-author of this plan, was a memorably flamboyant defender of it. When one of our Dominion Securities advisers said it was a "big" deal for Dominion Stores, Monte exclaimed, "Big, shmyg! We'll get Hollinger as tightly under

Dominion as a jock-strap." The financial adviser, unfamiliar with the sports metaphor, was too astonished to reply. When a lawyer suggested there could be a securities problem, my brother responded, "We will build a stone wall around the transaction, with two slits in it, through which we will peer at Henry [Knowles, the Ontario Securities Commission chairman], pots of boiling oil in hand." It was eventually judged that the correct legal response was to be a little more forthcoming than that.

There was some grumbling from institutions. Sun Life was making very litigious noises about this related party transaction, especially after seven Toronto law firms in succession declined to act against us because of their relations with us. Sun Life senior management felt the minority shareholders of Dominion Stores, and not just the independent directors, should be consulted. I visited the chairman and president of that company and addressed their concerns satisfactorily but not before Brian Mulroney insinuated himself as a go-between. He had become the president of the Iron Ore Company and we had had him elected as a director of Labrador Mining and Exploration and Standard Broadcasting, and I had successfully championed him as a director of the Canadian Imperial Bank of Commerce.

The presidency of the Iron Ore Company of Canada had originally been proposed for Brian by Bill Bennett, the outgoing president, before Brian's PC leadership campaign interlude. When he returned to the subject after the election of Joe Clark, the principal shareholder and contractual manager of the Iron Ore Company, the Hanna Mining Company in Cleveland, accepted him, though Bennett, C.D. Howe's long-time assistant, was now less than enthusiastic. His job was essentially one of labour and government relations, important fields to be sure, especially so given the Iron Ore Company's often poor relations with its radicalized North Shore work force, but sales and administration were conducted in Cleveland and the operation of the mines and processing of the ore were managed by Hanna appointees in Sept-Iles.

Brian did his job well, though it was not an orthodox corporate presidency. In the years between the 1976 and 1984 Progressive Conservative leadership contests, he evolved from a visceral champion of practically all working-class causes to a more balanced socio-economic view. He was not one to forget or abandon or ever be other than aggressively proud of his modest origins; if anything, he exaggerated them. But he had rich tastes, admired the style of the industrious wealthy, and sympathized with constructive businessmen; indeed, he became one himself. When I was lobbying the most influential directors of the Bank of Commerce in his favour as a potential member of that board, he took an uncommonly intense interest in the process, even telephoning me in New York on one occasion to give unnecessary advice on how to pursue the objective. He was duly elected, and there as elsewhere was a capable and well-appreciated director.

Brian was always vitally, almost morbidly interested in gossip of all kinds, and when he heard indirectly from Pierre Genest, the brilliantly genial counsel at Cassels, Brock, that Sun Life was exploring the possibilities of suing me, he rushed to insert himself, as helpfully as possible, in the counter-strategy, but he wasn't really necessary, didn't tell me anything I didn't already know, and it was, in any case, a momentary problem that I easily defused by clarifying a couple of points to the Sun Life management. It was, however, an illustration of the Mulroney technique I had often witnessed from the other side but never before from this perspective, of the eager volunteer fixer amassing due bills for the future account, though he didn't accumulate any on this occasion.

The Dominionization of Hollinger proceeded smoothly after that. I had no difficulty convincing institutional Dominion shareholders, whom I met in several groups, that the proceeds from the Quebec sale were better invested in assets of the quality of Norcen, Hollinger, and Standard than in more food stores striving for a 1 per cent margin against the nibbling, shop-lifting depredations of our own work force.

It would require the sale, as I said to the *Globe and Mail*, of "undreamed of quantities of tomatoes and radishes" to produce the sort of cash flow Dominion was buying into without paying any control premium. Though the financial press was becoming sceptical about my repeated complex related party transactions, and the Securities Commission brought in policy guidelines after this one that made multi-step transactions more difficult, there was absolutely no, and no possible, shareholders' complaint on value and I continued to deal personally with all shareholders' queries. Our stalled MacArthuresque "island-hopping" progress towards a fundamentally stronger company had resumed after a nine-month hiatus.

I had always assumed that Hal Jackman joined us in the hope and flickering expectation of bagging the whole Argus basket at a knock-down price. He recognized that it had to be taken from the inside as my partners and I had, and not from without, as Paul Desmarais had attempted it. Hal's father, Harry, died in 1980, and Hal had had a rather unceremonious and unequal financial tussle with his sister, Nancy, and brother Eric. On one occasion, Eric asked me if I would buy some shares in one of their semi-private companies at something better than the savage discount to book value Hal was offering. I instantly agreed, but four minutes later, Hal phoned and beseeched me not to complicate his family life, so I desisted. The third brother, Eddy, when he abandoned Protestantism and announced his intention to become a Dominican priest, was temporarily disinherited by his father with the aphorism: "There are two vows I have always had a lot of difficulty with: poverty and chastity." It is a colourful family.

By the early eighties, Hal was alternately despairing of getting control of Argus and working himself into a panic that I would lead the whole group to bankruptcy. His own techniques were profoundly conservative. He controlled an array of funds and semi-private companies, with "independent" quora, consisting invariably of stockbrokers Bill Corcoran (formerly E.P. Taylor's executive assistant) and Chris Barron and lawyer Alex Langford. Capital dividends came in free of tax to Hal, and the other dividends were recycled around as Hal gradually accumulated stock at grossly discounted, slumbering, odd-lot prices.

Insider rules governing such things are rather porous, so there were no audible guffaws (other than my own) when Hal went to the chairman of the National Trust Company and said that he had "just discovered" that he had 44 per cent of National Trust Stock in his group and that he would have to sell it "to Sam Belzberg" unless National wished to merge with Hal's Victoria and Grey. Hal was suggesting a conflict in his shareholdings of competing trust companies and in Belzberg was evoking the most frightening possible spectre for conservative trust managers. To the *Globe and Mail*, he said, "I don't own any National Trust shares, but interests close to me own 44 per cent of it." It was an artful performance, and he is an extremely talented man, though his unrelievedly cynical view of the world can irritate almost as often as it amuses.

I went to a ship-launching of his Algoma Central Railway at Collingwood in 1977. Harry Jackman had been the trustee in bankruptcy for one of the categories of bond holders of Algoma Central and had, with Charlie Burns (Latham's uncle and co-founder of the family business) and John Aird, held the company in bankruptcy for many years until they had scooped up enough certificates to be controlling shareholders when it was refloated. The mayor of Collingwood in his chains of office and virtually with tears streaming down his cheeks gave an emotional luncheon address complimenting Hal and John Aird (his chairman at Algoma Central) on "putting their money where their mouth is." I whispered to Hal that I thought the construction was heavily grant-assisted — "How much of the shipbuilding cost did the company put up?" I asked innocently. Through a pall of cigar smoke, he smiled slightly and replied, "Five per cent."

Hal is one of the most intelligent and entertaining people I know. Most of our conversations over nearly twenty years and many of our exchanges of correspondence reduce us both to convulsions of laughter, as he masquerades as a person concerned only with the public welfare. He is, in fact, a generous supporter of good causes and is sincerely interested in public affairs, having run as a Conservative MP in Rosedale unsuccessfully against Don Macdonald three times. The conventional Toronto view was that Hal was awkward, unsuccessful, and somewhat boring. All the journalists who came to see me when I was a current flavour in the late seventies I sent on to Hal, and gradually his strong personality as a man of high culture, vivid sense of humour, financial acumen, and worldliness worthy of a Borgia came to be noticed and celebrated. (He told me on more than one occasion that his interest in charitable causes was partly due to a fear that if he didn't busy himself with non-business matters, he might overpay for something.)

For years when we met, even in private, he would pretend to kiss my hand like a pilgrim at the court of a medieval pope.

Because of him, the myth has persisted that I am a collector of toy soldiers. In fact, he is, and on a grand scale. The walls of his bedroom were covered with shelves stocked with thousands of toy soldiers, until he gave them, on an appropriately advantageous tax basis, to the Royal Ontario Museum, and every shelf had on it a card displaying the cost price and current value of the soldiers on that shelf. Gifts such as the Bahamian Police Band, which was a present for his fiftieth birthday in 1982, had the cost inscribed as zero, in gold. (I am a collector of model battleships.)

Though I like and enjoy Hal enormously, he has not been an easy partner, and when I called him in 1981 to see if he would pick up some of the Argus Corporation preferred stock that was floating around, he typically brushed off that suggestion and proposed instead that I buy half of all his Ravelston shares. Bill Corcoran, a thoroughly charming man, always handled Hal's most delicate negotiations, as with his family. I reached agreement with him at a price that subsequent events proved risibly cheap, and Ralph Barford and various members of the Webster family, represented by Ben and Lorne, sons of my old colleague at Massey-Ferguson, Colin Webster, and nephew of my newspapering acquaintance, Howard Webster, succeeded Hal as to half of his shares.

After one exceedingly liquified evening in 1984, at about four a.m., while I was plying Hal with his own liquor in his own home surrounded by his books and toy soldiers, he produced a paper which by applying a lot of Jackmanishly pessimistic modifications to underlying values purported to show that Ravelston's rate of accretion of shareholders' value had been less than I had suggested. I bought him out, for Ravelston's account, and confirmed it later in the morning. He came and went as a director of our senior public company, but we eventually made an agreement that he would stay on the board, and I would be a director of his troubled railroad, Algoma Central. The agreement lapsed when he became lieutenant-governor, and I had essentially moved to England.

The directors' meetings of Algoma Central, heavily attended by retired politicians, were mainly hilarious discussions of ways of bringing more grants or rich expropriations from one level or another of government. The railway was saved from insolvency in the midst of the 1990 provincial election campaign by a hastily accorded grant from the Peterson government, writhing in its death throes. Hal has a deadly instinct for buying value cheaply and patiently, but no gambler's instinct, and no financial imagination to help him see how assets can be transformed or how anything more ambitious than incremental accumulation can be achieved.

I did, in February 1981, recruit Siegmund Warburg as a friendly buyer of Argus Corporation shares. Despite his seventy-eight years and the fact that he was "listening to gramophone records" when I telephoned him at home in Switzerland, he sprang at the opportunity to be an investor of ours. He said, "This sounds like something for our Luxembourg company."

I bought the shares at a profit to the holding vehicle, and not by any pre-arrangement, after he died in the autumn of 1982. It was the last transaction I had with him, though our correspondence and conversations on current events continued right to the end of his life. By that time he thought the world's only well-managed countries were "little Switzerland and big Japan" and told me there would be no limit to my success when I "had a few more grey hairs."

At a luncheon Siegmund and our wives and I had in Paris in 1979, I had drawn Siegmund out on his faith in psychoanalysis and handwriting analysis and his slightly prurient curiosity about the sex lives of others. It happened that the night before, my wife and I could not have avoided overhearing in the restaurant at the Ritz a rather voluminous woman discussing her relations with Siegmund Warburg, his offer of employment and, it was strongly implied, other attentions.

My wife accurately but somewhat mischievously shared this information with Eva Warburg, and when we returned to our hotel room in the evening, an agitated Siegmund telephoned and asked for "your dear wife who said she overheard someone discussing my sex life." She factually explained what this confident candidate for employment had said to the evident interest of many of the Ritz patrons. She did not join Warburgs, to the considerable relief as I eventually discovered, of many of Siegmund's colleagues in the firm.

In May 1981, thanks to Don Macdonald and Tony Griffin, I attended the first of many annual Bilderberg meetings. (Don had held many senior government positions but was now a prominent Toronto lawyer. Tony had gone to Appleby College in Oakville with my father and had been the head of Siegmund Warburg's interests in Canada.) Don was a member of the Sterling Committee and Tony of the advisory board of the Bilderberg meetings, and they had the

FINANCIAL ENGINEERING

authority to invite Canadian attenders. This group was set up in the mid-fifties by Prince Bernhard of the Netherlands and was designed to strengthen understanding between prominent people in the North Atlantic community. It met at the Dutch resort hotel that gave the group its name. About 120 or so people meet from every full-fledged traditionally non-communist European country, as well as Canada and the United States. They normally include senior officials of the governments of all the countries represented, with a wide swath of enlightened business, academic, media, and military leaders. There was also always a group of international officials, led by the NATO secretary general and military commander and the head of the OECD (Organization for Economic Co-operation and Development).

The key to the unique success of the Bilderberg meetings has been to hold them in remote places almost entirely without spouses or aides, to discourage prepared texts, to rigorously impose tight time deadlines, and to confine discussion as much as possible to English.

Although I had first met Henry Kissinger in Palm Beach in 1979, and then at a luncheon in Toronto jointly hosted by the *Economist* magazine and our company in 1980, and later socially in New York, it was at Bilderberg that I got to know him and a number of our other, future, directors and advisory board members. These included Gianni Agnelli of Fiat, Dwayne Andreas (controlling shareholder of the giant agri-business Archer-Daniels, Midland), Zbigniew Brzezinski (former national security adviser in the Carter administration), Lord Carrington (former British foreign and defense secretary and secretary-general of NATO), Andrew Knight (editor of the *Economist*), Richard Perle (former U.S. assistant secretary of National Defense and one of the champions of the Strategic Defense Initiative ["Star Wars"] and Euro-missile deployment), Paul Volcker (former Federal Reserve chairman), and George Will (U.S. conservative columnist and commentator), as well as many other interesting people.

Not having very satisfactory recollections of school days, nor being a very enthusiastic or observant university alumnus, Bilderberg has been the closest I have known to that sort of camaraderie. The animated social sessions, as much as the stimulating cut and thrust on the principal strategic and economic issues faced by the

Atlantic community, have given me, and many other regular participants, a powerful and entirely agreeable sense of community with some very talented and prominent people. After 1986, I became the co-leader of the Canadian group and effectively chose most of the Canadian participants.

Providentially, the world became more accessible for me as Canada became less commodious. It was from Bilderberg that our company's eventual vocation as an international newspaper organization arose.

Emboldened to revisit the issue of how to retire the debt contracted by Labrador and Hollinger to buy control of Norcen, my closest associates and I carefully considered how best to implement the Norcenization that was on the verge of achievement when the National Energy Program struck down the 1980 initiative. The Labrador iron ore royalty had to be united to the Norcen exploration activity and the greater the influence we would be able to exert on the Iron Ore Company, the better.

Hanna Mining Company owned 20 per cent of Labrador. The Norcen management was as interested as I was in expanding our business in Ronald Reagan's America. Hanna was not especially cooperative with our reorganization ideas. Bud Humphrey had died in 1979, the longtime chairman having effectively inherited that role from his father, George M. Humphrey, President Eisenhower's secretary of the treasury. Neither his widow, Louise, nor his sons, George and Watts, were well-pleased with the antics of the new chairman, Bob Anderson, a hard-rock miner from Hibbing, Minnesota, who was a little short on gentility by the standards of the Humphreys.

I went to dinner with Bud Humphrey and his senior executives, including Bob Anderson, in Cleveland in January 1979, and said that when we got the Argus Group re-organized we hoped to develop some business in the United States and looked to Hanna as natural allies. He was a valued Massey-Ferguson and Labrador director and professed to be receptive.

In June of that year, I telephoned him in Cleveland from the main Dominion Stores warehouse in Toronto to explain how our "Hollingerization" would affect Labrador and the Iron Ore Company. He reminisced a little and said that his father had told him at the end of an annual meeting of the American Iron and Steel

Institute that "what this industry needs is a few high-priced funerals." Two days later, he died, at Pebble Beach, California.

The Humphreys and their relatives had about 25 per cent of the Hanna stock diffused among many dozens of aunts and cousins. I had seen enough of this sort of thing to know when family heirs were being cuffed around by hired managers. In July I had a chat with George Humphrey, one of Bud's sons and a Hanna vice president, who, almost within earshot of Bob Anderson, held forth to me on the evils, ingratitude, and incompetence of Bob and his colleagues. He spoke, as I subsequently testified, "with great bitterness and vituperativeness."

In April 1981, my wife and I went to a Canadian night at the Metropolitan Opera House in the Lincoln Center in New York. This too had its surrealistic aspects. As the guests awaited the arrival of Pierre Trudeau, John Roberts, at that point one of his ministers, stood a few steps up the grand staircase, straining for a glimpse of his leader when he would arrive. He was wearing some sort of celebratory sash over his dress-shirt for the occasion, and I set out to test his concentration by saying that he looked "like Wallenstein on the march." No reaction. "You should complete the ministerial dignity with epaulettes the size of fruit tarts," I said. He grunted, heedless of the bait. "John, if you don't mind my saying so, you look like a perfect asshole." "Here's the PM," he responded excitedly.

After the operatic divertissement, I found that I had been assigned a dinner place next to Louise Humphrey, a Metropolitan Opera patroness, Bud's widow and sister of R.L. "Tim" Ireland, another Hanna director, whom George had advised of his talks with me. She wasted no time plunging into a business discussion. With a discordant orchestra alternating with an endless sequence of loquacious Opera officers in providing background noise, Louise attacked Anderson, criticized various others, and urged me "to buy some shares" (my expression). Trudeau was at the next table and from time to time, we more or less bumped into each other and exchanged amusing asides about the bizarre ambiance.

Bob Anderson assured me in August 1981 that he wouldn't mind at all if I decided to "buy some shares" in Hanna. Since he showed no curiosity about how many shares we might buy, I saw no reason to enlighten him at that point. Norcen did "buy some shares" in

August 1981, and on September 9, the executive committee, consisting of Ed Battle, Ed Bovey, Ed Galvin, Dick Chant, my brother, and me, approved the purchase of up to 4.9 per cent of the shares.

The directors were of several minds about the investment. Some were reluctant to invest at all, and most were reluctant to get into anything hostile, especially given the company's close connection with the Bechtels, Graces, and Mellons. Ed Battle spoke of ultimately achieving 51 per cent control under certain hypothetical circumstances. Bill Kilbourne, the company secretary, was also legal and administrative vice president and was rather overworked. He wrote up the minutes of the meeting as approving the acquisition of the 4.9 per cent interests in an unnamed U.S. NYSE-listed company "with the ultimate purpose of acquiring a 51 per cent interest at a later date." This was fairly ambiguous but not accurate, as such an "ultimate purpose" was mentioned only along with other possibilities.

Being in the habit of assuming that all such minutes were, in the Argus tradition, which Norcen generally followed also, completely innocuous ("a general discussion ensued"), I signed the minutes without reading that part of it.

Kilbourne didn't remember or reread the minutes as our relations with Hanna management deteriorated. Jimmy Connacher of Gordon Securities produced a block of 575,000 shares for us, which we bought at $37 (U.S.), October 28, 1981, taking us up to 8.8 per cent. I telephoned Bob Anderson, but he was in Brazil, and I spoke instead to his rather agitated vice president, Carl Nickels, and explained, to his obvious incredulity, that we weren't a hostile shareholder.

George Humphrey phoned the next day and was supportive, provided he wasn't "blind-sided and I'm sure we won't be." I thought I grasped the football metaphor but, in any case, looked upon the Humphreys as friends rather than potential enemies.

On November 4, Ed Battle and I went to Cleveland and met Bob Anderson and Carl Nickels at the Sheraton Hopkins Hotel at Cleveland airport overlooking the hangar where Hanna kept its two corporate jets. (This does not include the Iron Ore Company jet that Brian Mulroney insisted upon after one particularly long and turbulent trip on the company's rather dated G1 turbo-prop.)

Our hosts were very antagonistic and would hear nothing of compromise and demanded we "peel off" our stock. I got a little tired of Nickels's implying that I was incompetent and had nothing to show for four years of perpetual corporate motion. I invited him to compare Norcen to the old Hollinger and Ed Battle to Al Fairley, apart from their accents (Ed Battle, though a naturalized Canadian, was a Texan and has almost as broad a southern accent as Fairley). I also mentioned that the Ravelston shareholders had had a rather handsome capital appreciation. Our SEC (Securities Exchange Commission) filing of November 9 described our shareholding as an "investment," which was accurate.

Just before Christmas 1981, at the recommendation of Louise Humphrey, Ed Battle and I visited her son Watts at his home in the up-market Pittsburgh suburb of Sewickley. He was Louise's second son and an officer of National Steel (whose chairman, George Stinson, was a Hanna director). He was very friendly and forthcoming. I stressed that we didn't want any hostilities, that we would be happy with a significant minority position, and that although we probably had a higher opinion of Anderson than Watts's next of kin did, our natural identification was with the owners and with younger people like his brother and him. I elaborated an idea for a pooling of Hanna-Humphrey-Mellon interests with Norcen to exercise a controlling influence on Hanna and elevate George Humphrey to the presidency of the company. This was in contemplation over the New Year's holiday. On February 5, 1982, Ed Battle and my brother visited Watts again and were received more coolly than we had been in December, but not negatively. On February 8, Watts phoned my brother to announce that they weren't interested in any variation of our proposal.

Brian Mulroney, in his capacity as a Hanna director, gamely tried to assure Anderson and his cronies that our shareholding was a benign development after I asked him to tell his colleagues that I didn't "have cloven feet or wear horns." By the spring of 1982, the idea of ignoring Anderson's tedious pleas to us to "peel off" our stock, and of bulldozing our way into a position of influence at Hanna, including getting them out of Labrador, had a definite appeal.

Ed Battle and I had sporadic discussions with Bob Anderson into the spring of 1982, but Bob never had any other proposal than that we sell our Hanna shares at a loss and adjust to whatever they, as 20 per cent Labrador shareholders, commended to us, the 63 per cent shareholder. They were prepared to sell their Labrador shares but not at a realistic price and only in partial exchange for all our Hanna shares. This emerged at a February 16 meeting with Bob Anderson in Toronto, where I again expressed a desire for a 20 per cent interest in Hanna. (This was the percentage that would enable us to equity account, i.e., take 20 per cent of Hanna's income into our own accounts.)

My mental resistance to a straight takeover fight, unimaginative a course though it was, costly and acrimonious though it was certain to be, was slowly evaporating in the glare of Cleveland's condescensions. Hanna had always considered itself, with some justice, the builder of the Iron Ore group of seven big U.S. steel companies, and the builder and operator of the great Ungava project, and Hollinger as a sclerotic concession company, an impression not much contradicted by Bud McDougald's and Al Fairley's medieval sedentariness.

Our associates in Cleveland showed little recognition of the fact that Hollinger was under new management and that, with Norcen, I had five times the cash flow of the old Hollinger or the present Hanna. A chicken game was in progress. The presentation by Bob Anderson of a solid front with the old families was an imposture I endured countless times without contradicting, because I didn't want to blow George's cover. Sometime in 1982, somebody would have to move.

In the inner counsels at Norcen, a good deal of talk, some of it from me, was heard of "rolling the cannon up to Bob's cheek-bone." This temptation was accentuated by the disingenuous waffling of the younger Humphreys. Ed Battle and I had difficulty explaining to ourselves why we should acquiesce in being so dismissively treated by rather underwhelming people. Their behaviour did not, we felt, represent the correlation of forces between us.

Bob and Carl Nickels met with Ed Battle and me at my house in Palm Beach in mid-March. They expressed their preparedness for a Hanna-Labrador swap arrangement, though not at satisfactory prices. We assumed that was negotiable, but it wasn't really the point. We had not bought into Hanna as a greenmail gesture, though their unco-operativeness with some of our reorganization proposals was galling and would obviously be eliminated if we bought them right out of Labrador. Ed Battle and my brother and I had actually generated some enthusiasm for the possibilities of

FINANCIAL ENGINEERING

Hanna and didn't care to be bundled out of our position quite so cavalierly. We had a couple of legal strategy sessions in Palm Beach, including one attended by the famous New York takeover lawyer Joe Flom, who subsequently phoned me and followed up with an invoice for the telephone call for $10,000. I enjoyed him and his advice was probably worth it.

On April 2, 1982, as I flew to Palm Beach with Rupert Hambro, a merchant banking acquaintance from London, Monte and Ed Battle attended upon Bob Anderson again at the Sheraton Hopkins Hotel at Cleveland airport and advised Bob of Norcen's intention to launch a takeover bid for 51 per cent of Hanna on Monday, April 5. A vigorous but civilized exchange followed, and Ed stated that we would accept a minority position with proportional representation on the board of directors and certain safeguards. Thirty per cent was stated as our alternative target, but Ed Battle made it clear that that was negotiable. Discussion was adjourned to Sunday, and both sides professed to be hopeful of avoiding open warfare.

I spoke to Bob Anderson on Saturday. He urged me to come to Cleveland the next day. My wife was well along towards the birth of our second child; I feared that my colleagues might interpret my return as a lack of confidence in them, so I declined but promised Bob that I would concert carefully with the Norcen representatives and that we would pursue a compromise. Given the stakes and the subsequent complications before we achieved our goals, it was probably a mistake not to have gone.

The Sunday, April 4, meeting was not a success. Versions of what occurred differ but the Norcen account was that Hanna offered no safeguards for a Norcen minority shareholding, against either dilution or capricious decisions by the incumbent Hanna directors. The Hanna position was that Norcen wanted 30 per cent of the votes and the directors and a requirement for an 80 per cent majority for most categories of important board decisions. I don't doubt that the Norcen account is closer to the fact.

Peter Newman, in his otherwise rather fair description (*The Establishment Man*, pp. 241–257), clearly fed by Mulroney, espouses most of the Hanna line. If Ed Battle and Monte Black took any such intractable position as that imputed by Newman, it was not what they agreed with me in advance, or told me afterwards.

It was a foregone conclusion that Hanna would be successful in getting a temporary restraining order against our offer proceeding, as the federal court in Cleveland was not going to renounce its own jurisdiction against a party from Canada seeking control of one of Cleveland's most famous companies.

In preparing the material required to be produced as evidence, Norcen's U.S. counsel, Cravath Swaine & Moore uncovered the September 9 executive committee minutes, referring to an "ultimate purpose" of acquiring 51 per cent of Hanna, which Bill Kilbourne had left behind like a grenade with the pin pulled. When it was handed over to Hanna's counsel, it was immediately described as "the smoking gun" and we were smugly invited to the whole proceeding before they blew us away. Inside the Norcen camp, there was a determined effort, led, for obvious reasons, by Kilbourne, to minimize the consequences of this fiasco. Ed Battle, Kilbourne, and most of our legal team came to Palm Beach for a strategy conference April 8. It was a grim session.

I quoted de Gaulle and said, "It has begun as badly as it could, and so it must continue." Hanna's lawyers were incredulous when we elected to proceed despite the September 9 minutes revelation and prepared briefs and press releases righteously describing me as a criminal, a racketeer, and a recidivistic fraud specialist. This sort of pyrotechnics is routine in the United States and not taken too seriously, but the financial press of Canada made no effort to contain its enthusiasm for the painful public relations trip to the whipping block that the Cleveland venture immediately became for us.

I couldn't personally be too critical of Hanna for availing themselves of all the ammunition we handed them. Nor could I engage in self-pity: I should have been a conciliatory influence at the climactic session in Cleveland, whether it would have had any effect or not, and I should have read the September 9 minutes, certainly before I signed them, but, at the least, once trans-border litigation became a clear possibility. Kilbourne had botched it, but Kilbourne wasn't the chairman of the company. To get the SEC off our backs, the Norcen senior management agreed to sign a consent decree admitting no wrongdoing but promising to abide by U.S. securities laws.

As someone who revelled in somewhat glib references to Napoleon and other great historical figures, it was doubly humiliating

FINANCIAL ENGINEERING

to be implicated in such an appallingly amateurish launch. My lack of thoroughness had propelled us into the mess; only I could resurrect our position by a powerful court appearance. The potential equalizer with which we could surprise our opponents was the degree to which the Humphreys had encouraged our interest in "their" company. I could not imagine that George would have confessed to Bob Anderson more than a fraction of his early indiscretions. We had a grenade to throw back if we could survive the opening barrage.

This would not be any conventional notion of "island-hopping," by which I had meant the avoidance of unpromising obstacles (as MacArthur bypassed the 250,000 Japanese soldiers at Rabaul) and advance by swift and inexpensive assaults on unsuspecting targets. This would not be Attu and Kiska. This would be the jungles of Guadalcanal, the beaches of Tarawa, the sands of Iwo Jima, the caves of Saipan; hand-to-hand combat ending only with the incineration of the enemy by flame-throwers.

I rationalized that constant manoeuvre, to be effective, must be punctuated from time to time with real combat. Sometimes, to defeat the enemy, you have to inflict casualties as well as inconvenience. Norcen was a much stronger company than Hanna. Certain elements of the Canadian financial press and its devotees who were exulting in my discomfiture would learn, I resolved, not to discount me in open combat any more than in corporate manoeuvre.

I gave my deposition, under very intense questioning in Palm Beach over twenty-four hours, on the Thursday, Friday, and Monday bracketing Easter. The opposing counsel, John Straugh of Jones, Day, was extremely belligerent but neither his attempts to bully me nor to mouse-trap me into damaging admissions were successful, and the factor of attrition took at least as great a toll on him as on me.

As the trial opened in Cleveland almost immediately after my deposition was taken, Cardinal Carter, who was our house guest in Palm Beach, and counsel, who were preparing me for the trial, conducted a moot court on our patio, with the cardinal as judge. When I responded to one question that Norcen had taken a "collegial decision," the cardinal intervened: "Don't touch collegiality. Several popes have warned against it. If you have the authority, don't pretend you don't. If you don't have it, don't pretend you do!"

On this as on countless occasions, I have been inexpressibly grateful for the friendship of Cardinal Carter. Our relations began with reflections on Duplessis, Charbonneau, and Léger and proceeded through my time as a patron of Sharelife (Toronto's Catholic charities) before I was a Roman Catholic, from which I retired when my efforts to reunite Sharelife at least partially with the United Way failed because of shifts of opinion among the parties I was attempting to conciliate. They flourished through my lengthy, cautious, and stately paced personal progress towards Rome and have been immensely gratifying for me for many years.

Despite the differences in our ages, professions, and backgrounds, or possibly in part because of them, our relations are intimate and without rancour. His culture, from Irish folkways to Thomist theology, is inexhaustible; his humour vivacious but gentle. He is one of the very few people I have ever known who successfully combines worldliness with idealistic sincerity. He is always confident but never arrogant, serene in the face of his declining years and life's approaching end.

In the abstract, his composure is inspiring, but when I contemplate the actuarial probability of life without him, the sensation of sad loneliness is profound. (However, Andy Warhol wrote in his diaries of the party we had for him at the Art Gallery of Ontario in 1981 that the cardinal, who was just recovering from his stroke, appeared pretty parlous, yet he has soldiered on for many years after Andy's final curtain-call; Emmett's endurance should not be underestimated.) As he wrote in an inscription of a book he gave me about himself, we came together when his "sun was setting," but his friendship has been one of the greatest pleasures and privileges of my life, and it is a brilliant and, thankfully, prolonged sunset.

I testified in Cleveland for twenty hours over four days in a court room jammed with lawyers, journalists, and the curious. It was scarcely a week after the end of my deposition so my earlier testimony was fresh in my recollection, which I supplemented with a systematic memorization of every relevant part of my vast pre-trial record. This was a mnemonic feat for which John Straugh had not allowed, and I felt the tide turning as, with each pre-selected question, a junior thrust up the appropriate sheet from the deposition and Straugh handed it back, unable to find a discrepancy. I often quoted verbatim from my deposition, which clearly disconcerted Straugh. At one point, he caught the lining on the back of his trousers on something, and they abruptly opened, revealing his underwear as he returned to his table from a conference at the bench. He was unaware of the light entertainment he provided.

I had not realized how different U.S. laws of evidence are from Canadian rules, but after about half an hour, I came to enjoy the joust. Over 90 per cent of Straugh's bombastic, repetitive, and accusatory questions, and of my self-serving, exculpatory, and often equally combative answers, would be ruled out of order in a British or Canadian court.

I was able to reveal the Humphreys' duplicity with considerable effect. With each question for a whole day, I took the tompion off another gun and was able to riddle George Humphrey's deposition and to a lesser extent his brother's and turn them into a very well-ventilated Swiss cheese. Straugh was persistent and cunning, but four days of intense single combat broke the momentum of the case.

The murderers' row of Bob Anderson, Carl Nickels, Jim Courtenay, and Dick Pogue, the much-respected senior partner of Jones, Day, sat in the front row facing me on my right. The *Wall Street Journal* commented that there appeared to be no reason to prevent our offer from going ahead. Even the *Cleveland Plain Dealer* criticized the Humphreys editorially for their conduct. The arbitrageurs held the stock price up fairly close to our indicated offering price of $45, showing their growing confidence that the bid would proceed despite the litigation. The Toronto reporters, Jack Willoughby of the *Globe and Mail* and Eric Evans of the *Financial Post*, both honest and capable professionals, gave much more sympathetic coverage of the case once my testimony started.

When I finished testifying, the presiding judge, John M. Manos, invited me into his chambers. He was a formidable berobed physical presence of about six feet, five inches, looking like Daddy Warbucks, as he was as bald as a billiard ball. He had impressed me as a martinet during the trial. He excoriated any whisperer or shuffler of papers in the court, and although counsel of neither side seemed in awe of his legal scholarship, he was a figure of considerable authority.

Judge Manos volunteered that "in twenty years as a judge, you are the finest witness I've ever had in my court. Whatever my verdict, from what I've seen this week, it won't reflect unfavourably on you as a witness." Somewhat more ominously, he advised me of "the superhuman ingenuity of the American lawyer." He went on to warn me of RICO, which, he said, was named after the former mayor and police chief of Philadelphia. I was well familiar with the career of Mayor Frank J. Rizzo and with the Racketeering-Influenced and Corrupt Organizations Act (RICO), which it was then fashionable for almost all civil plaintiffs to invoke as a tainting procedure and with the lack of any connection between the mayor and the statute. But I thanked the judge (despite his imperfect sense of jurisprudence) for his kind words and returned to Palm Beach.

I wasn't greatly reassured either, when our counsel visited the chief judge of the federal court in Cleveland at his auto-parts business, where his activities were under grand jury investigation. Opinion of counsel, and other qualified observers, was that we were back as serious contenders in the case, which would now be judged on its merits and not turned into a kangaroo court on the basis of a mistaken reading of the September 9 minutes. My own guess was that we would lose the legal case in Cleveland on the issue of lifting the temporary restraining order, but without the judge sandbagging our ability to appeal and that, at that point, serious discussion with Hanna could resume.

I was more concerned at this point with Hanna seeking a white knight interloper and asked Trudeau's former principal secretary, Jim Coutts, to advise Mulroney that transfer to a foreign company of ultimate control of the Iron Ore Company would be subject to serious scrutiny by the Foreign Investment Review Agency, which he did. I doubted that any other Canadian company would want to contest Hanna with us, and so was reasonably confident that Bob Anderson would have to deal with us eventually, and responded good-naturedly to his torrent of abuse of me through the press. I felt I had redeemed myself from the earlier oversights and had shattered the self-righteous Humphrey-Hanna façade. The trial closed after George Humphrey and Bill Kilbourne were given about equally (and very) rough treatment by opposing counsel.

Bob Anderson came to the Labrador annual meeting, stood up like a student on prize day in front of P.C. Finlay, and announced he was casting his 20 per cent of the votes for his own re-election but against the Hollinger nominees. We re-elected the Hanna representatives despite their antics. Brian Mulroney had the good sense not to be present at this fatuous interlude.

I was sitting at the head table at the annual Hollinger dinner at the Toronto Club, between Cardinal Carter and the chief justice of Ontario, Bill Howland, engaged in the usual convivialities on such occasions, when one of the many lawyers present whispered to me that a warrant had been issued and served on Norcen's counsel in a criminal investigation arising from the September 9 minutes. Norcen had subsequently circulated an issuer bid document, which didn't mention the alleged material change of the "intention" to take control of Hanna. An issuer-bid circular, the information package on the basis of which shareholders decide whether to tender their shares to the issuing company for cancellation, has the same obligation to accuracy as an underwriting prospectus, and the deliberate withholding of material facts would be an infraction of the Securities Act and, at worst, a fraud case.

The warrant was issued in respect of the forgery provisions of the Criminal Code, i.e., circulating "a false document, knowing it to be false," a category designed to deal with counterfeiting and the like, not with a flawed prospectus (which Norcen's wasn't). Two journeymen sergeants of the Metropolitan Toronto Police Fraud Squad had served the warrant on Norcen's counsel, Fred Huycke, joint senior partner of Osler Hoskin & Harcourt and a Norcen director.

Whoever in the Crown law office had authorized or, more likely, incited these gasconading dupes in the fraud squad to swear out and exercise the warrant must have known that Norcen would have to refer to its existence in its written court pleadings in Cleveland, enabling Hanna's counsel to make public the fact of a "criminal" investigation. The obvious objective was to create some semblance of plausibility for the most extreme allegations against us in the eyes of Judge Manos, who could not be expected to have any familiarity with a foreign jurisdiction.

One of the officers had been somewhat drawn out by Fred Huycke when he served his warrant upon him and had volunteered that he had "always thought Black was a crook after he bailed out of Massey-Ferguson." Here was the destructive complex of envy at its most ignorant and visceral, in the hands of constabulary with no aptitude for exercising such power. The two sergeants were, in fact, suggesting that all the Norcen directors, since the executive committee minutes were circulated to all the directors, were implicated in a criminal fraud.

Apart from Battle, Bovey, Galvin, Chant, Huycke, Radler, and both Blacks, this board included Douglas Bassett; distinguished Montreal lawyer Jacques Courtois; Robert Després, former president of the University of Quebec and current chairman of Atomic Energy of Canada; Fredrik Eaton; P.C. Finlay; John Finlay; the former lieutenant-governor of Manitoba, Jack McKeag; and the longtime former chairman of Imperial Oil and dean of the Canadian oil industry, Bill Twaits. The idea that any of these people, let alone a combination of them, should be engaged in a plan to defraud shareholders did not bear thinking about by anyone not motivated by malice who had an intelligence quotient in at least double figures.

It was obvious that it was a tainting procedure and that the law-enforcement system was being manipulated. After a ten-minute legal consultation, I rejoined my after-dinner guests. I launched my counter-attack against this new salient the next morning at nine o'clock.

It quickly emerged that these policemen often and, in this case, had, worked under the guidance of an assistant Crown attorney whose career at the Ontario Securities Commission had been intimately entwined with that of Sam Wakim, Brian Mulroney's old undergraduate room-mate and the lawyer to whom Brian had entrusted such legal work as Hanna and the Iron Ore Company had in Ontario. It did not require Hercule Poirot to assemble the pieces of the puzzle.

It was clear from the testimony in Cleveland that no case could possibly be made for a wilful misrepresentation in our issuer-bid circular, and it shortly came to light that the senior staff at the Ontario Securities Commission, led by its endlessly patient and fair director, Charles Salter, had asked the police to stay out of the matter unless any evidence was unearthed indicating a possible criminal infraction.

I made an appointment the morning after the Hollinger dinner to see the attorney general of Ontario, Roy McMurtry, whom I had known casually but cordially for many years. He saw me that afternoon. Some of our New York lawyers were visiting Toronto to

FINANCIAL ENGINEERING

prepare contingency plans for the various possible legal scenarios in Cleveland, and I took one of them, Paul Saunders, with me to see the attorney general, who had his deputy minister Rendall Dick, a well-regarded veteran civil servant, with him. Roy's immediate reaction was: "You have to question the motives of the people behind this investigation." I hardly needed to be told that and it was reassuring when Roy added, "Even if I accepted that material information was withheld from your issuer-bid circular, this wouldn't be the offence." (It would be a Securities Act fraud, not a Criminal Code forgery.)

I made it clear that I wasn't asking for any investigation to be stopped; I just didn't want an important financial initiative involving the interests of tens of thousands of Canadian and American shareholders and a possible patriation of the country's largest mining company to be compromised by a smear job like this. I wanted it noted I was not seeking any preferments and if there was the slightest possibility of an impropriety in my visit, he must tell me. There was none, he assured us emphatically, and the deputy attorney general nodded in agreement.

Since Roy was a good friend of Brian Mulroney's and had been one of those urging him to make the federal leadership race in 1975, I thought a return of fire might be timely. I said that there was a political sensitivity and that since we were both friends of Brian's, Roy should be aware that "the powder trail from this trumped-up charade of an investigation leads straight to Brian's door. I understand he has to please his employer, but powder trails can burn in both directions, and before the summer's over, I could be his employer." Roy nodded and blinked non-committally.

Paul Saunders and I left, and a few days later Sam Wakim's friend in the Crown law office (Brian Johnston) was removed from the case by Rendall Dick who was critical of what he considered insensitive handling of an important commercial matter (Rendall Dick's description to me many months later when the matter had been concluded). Thenceforth he and other senior officials were in direct touch with it themselves, virtually eliminating, it seemed, the possibility of a frivolous, vexatious, or malicious prosecution. For good measure, I telephoned the chief of police of Metropolitan Toronto, Jack Ackroyd, whom I knew slightly, and said that, while I obviously couldn't assert any influence on an investigation in progress, this was a completely spurious matter and he might want to keep an eye on it. The conversation was brief.

Manos's judgement came down June 11, 1982. As was foreseen, he found Norcen's explanation of the September 9 minutes "strained and unpersuasive" and said there was evidence of "manipulative violations" of the Securities and Exchanges Act, but made it clear it was not a fraud case and said nothing inflammatory about any Norcen individuals. We were confident of winning an expedited appeal from the U.S. Circuit Court of Appeal, the second highest in the United States, sitting in Cincinnati where the judges would not be so accessible to the entreaties of the Cleveland establishment.

Bob Anderson and Pierre Trudeau were among the honorary doctoral graduates at St. Francis Xavier University that spring, as Muggeridge and I had been three years before. Bob liquored himself pretty thoroughly at the graduation eve soirée and uttered a tremendous stream of King Lear-like curses and accusations against me, which were duly reported to me. They doubtless reflected his state of mind at the time.

Without an expedited appeal, we could be two years waiting to be heard, so Hanna's lawyers vigorously contested the issue, repeating all the hackneyed polemics against me of "recidivism" and "racketeering." The circuit court confirmed our hopes about the points made in the trial in Cleveland, ignored Hanna's plea, and agreed to hear our appeal at once. Finally, we had the upper hand. It would be a straight legal question in an eminent court and if Hanna lost, Anderson and all his chums would be unemployed a month later, possibly including, depending on his performance, the heir apparent to the leadership of the federal Canadian Opposition. Hanna would also have to publish some results soon and we knew from our position at the Iron Ore Company that its profits had collapsed. Hanna would not, I pointed out to the *Globe and Mail*, "make enough to pay the chairman's salary."

I expected an overture from Hanna, and it came quickly. Peter Newman had been preparing a sequel to his 1975 book on the Canadian Establishment for several years. He had interviewed me many times and had said it was a book about all the leading business figures a generation younger than Bud McDougald and the other principal figures in the earlier book — Hal Jackman, Fred Eaton,

Galen Weston, Ted Rogers, and others, including me. Only well along in the project did he give me to understand that the volume would be a good deal more directly focused on me.

A few days after the Cincinnati verdict Peter Newman asked to see me, which was not at all unusual, and came in the next day. He did not follow his normal routine. He said, "As your biographer, I am concerned that you are endangering your reputation in the battle with Hanna and want to urge compromise on you." He had, he said, been urged to play the role of go-between by the inevitable Brian Mulroney, in narrow preference to Russell Harrison and John Turner, who might have conflicts, Harrison in his banking relationships and Turner as chairman of Bechtel Canada.

I replied that I had always been happy to compromise, had never failed to indicate that, and had been defamed and now persecuted by the police for my trouble. I understood that Bob Anderson blamed me for assaulting his company, but that I had a different version of events and if he had any interest in a settlement that wouldn't be just a capitulation by us, as his previous proposals had been, he should call me.

I added that I would absolutely never make any concessions to the existence of this police investigation, that it was an outrageous grotesquerie, and that when it had run its course, and our innocence of any wrongdoing had been established, we would investigate the investigators. I told him the Hanna case was like the Yom Kippur War of 1973. We were Israel and had got off to a bad start but had crossed the Suez Canal and enveloped one of the enemy's armies.

In his book, which came out later that fall, and was more than generous to me, and thus a certain aggravation to all the forces of envy that lurked in Toronto, Peter modestly omits his role in resolving the Hanna problem. (Hal Jackman and I conducted an informal competition to see which of us could get the more pretentious quote into Peter's book. I won with an aeratedly pompous comment that Jackman and I were in constant debate over whether we were philosophically more Nietzschean or Hegelian. In fact, Nietzsche was a brilliant but deranged epigrammatist and I'm only superficially familiar with Hegel's work.)

I was in general agreement with the many people who said that I was an unworthy subject of such an extensive and flattering work.

My favourite in this category was the man who wrote the *Toronto Star*, which serialized the book, that he would have more respect for me if I "had ever coached a pee-wee ball team."

The day after Peter Newman's visit, Bob Anderson telephoned. My imperturbable secretary, Joan Avirovic, was for once nonplussed and thought it was a prankster. I had no such concern and took up the phone with the old line from the end of the Prohibition era (allegedly uttered by one of the Carolina governors to the other: "It's a long time between drinks"). We met the next day in the Hanna suite in the Carlton House on Madison Avenue in New York where Bob Anderson assured me George M. Humphrey had once entertained President Eisenhower and Vice President Nixon. A few days later, we met at the Bristol Place Hotel in Toronto airport. Ignoring the bellicose advice of one of our New York lawyers (who went on to some renown years later by joining in the chorus of advice to Bob Campeau to "dare to be great" in the department store business), we reached a general agreement.

We bought enough stock out of treasury at $45 to take ourselves up to 20 per cent and retire almost all of Hanna's long-term debt. Battle, my brother, and I became Hanna directors: I joined the executive committee; Bob Anderson became a Norcen director, and Norcen bought Hanna out of Labrador, Hollinger North Shore, and Hollinger-Hanna at fair prices. We had an eight-year standstill. It was a good deal closer to what I had proposed at my Toronto meeting with Anderson on February 16 than the Hanna counter-proposal in Cleveland, April 2, but in any case was a satisfactory compromise.

The next morning my brother announced to the Dominion Stores annual meeting (the ultimate public parent) that a settlement had been reached and that "the atmospherics and pyrotechnics are over." At our first directors' dinner in Cleveland, Bob Anderson graciously introduced me, and I said it was a pleasure to say a few words in Cleveland "without being under oath." They were a very intelligent and interesting group of directors, and this proved the first of many convivial meetings. It went on to a late hour with my brother improvising a stirring harangue on American economic prospects, which he rendered upliftingly to the droll chairman of National Steel, George Stinson, concluding "The road to recovery is paved with steel!" George blinked and replenished his glass.

Since we settled at 20 per cent, which had always been our ambition, I dared to hope that the sleuthing marionettes in the local fraud squad would be persuaded by this powerful evidence of what our "intention" at Norcen towards Hanna had really been. I spoke to Paul Godfrey, the Metropolitan Toronto Council chairman, in his capacity as a member of the police commission and asked him to find out (i.e., confirm) how this investigation got started. He came back a few days later and said that his information was that there was no evidence to justify an investigation but that the policemen involved were so adamant about it that it would be impossible to shut the investigation down without causing a political furore.

On June 28, 1982, I was in the expectant father's room next to the delivery room at the Wellesley Hospital, having the first of many discussions with Peter Atkinson about the iniquitous police investigation of Norcen, when my wife and new-born daughter were conveyed into the room. Arana, as she was named, has been a constant source of pride and happiness to us from that first day. No little girl could ever give a doting father more pleasure than she has always done.

Paul helped to broker an arrangement with relatively senior people in the Crown law office. If this foolish proceeding had to go forward, it should go forward as quickly as possible. We would cooperate entirely, providing anything they wanted, without warrants (and motions to quash the warrants) and they would proceed as quickly as they practically could. The existence of the Norcen investigation was now public and both sides, it was agreed, would maintain an absolute silence about it.

This agreement had not been concluded two days before it became obvious that our co-contractants had no intention of honouring any of their undertakings. Their "intention" was that I should refrain from saying (as I wrote in the *Financial Post* when the story broke) that the perpetrators of the Norcen investigation were themselves a more fit subject for an investigation than the exemplary directors and officers of Norcen. They further intended, as their conduct made clear, to take the whole year the Securities Act permitted before reporting, despite their promise to proceed as quickly as possible.

Two days after we handed over reams of minutes, correspondence, and other documents all carefully indexed, they began chattering to the press about this "criminal investigation." When this was pointed out by Peter Atkinson and Paul Godfrey, the officers were "reprimanded" with the result that they now held a continuous not-for-attribution press conference on their "intention" to send me to prison.

The Crown law office muscled the Securities Commission into a joint investigation, even though the commission expressed the view that it was not properly a police matter and that it could be resolved quite quickly. Charlie Salter told me after a few months that he was satisfied there were no grounds for further action and that the policemen involved were "New Democrats who had been manipulated and were Black-bashing." The Crown law office, by forcing the OSC into a joint investigation, managed to prolong the defamation of the Norcen directors, and me in particular, for many months beyond what would otherwise have been possible.

I encountered for the first time the fascistic mentality of an element of the police. They were unaccustomed to their quarry doing anything other than hiding behind a legalistic "no comment" and cowering. The greater the evident irritation of the subject of their attention, the more unshakeable was their conviction of his guilt. When I finally met the two officers, after they had interviewed most of the other Norcen directors, they were rather affable and plodding and smirked knowledgeably at each answer I gave to their rather simple questions.

As Paul Godfrey said, "They had dreams of sugar-plums dancing in their heads" and had built up a self-image as single-combat warriors struggling with a master criminal, a formidable (i.e., worthy) adversary. I was a Moriarty of commerce. The thought that they might be mistaken, pawns in a larger plot that had now been discarded, would have overloaded their limited imaginations. My friend Barbara Amiel wrote in the *Toronto Sun*: "The Toronto police have imposed basic height requirements on the force. What about basic intelligence requirements?"

I had never really had anything to do with the police and always assumed that they were like the rather pleasant men and women who answered false burglar alarms or even handed out speeding tickets. Most of them surely are, but I found this experience so disagreeable that in the autumn of 1982 I bought, on Ravelston's behalf, into a security company, to ensure that I wasn't totally reliant on the palookas that were oppressing and defaming us to guarantee the safety of my home and family. (They were, with only a few exceptions, rented meatballs who spent most of their watch at our home sleeping or, as my wife said, "staring at their feet." I was delighted when Dick Chant skilfully sold us out of this, as he correctly described it, "pissy business" at a modest profit in 1986.)

Brian Mulroney regularly telephoned to give advice on how to deal with the police, offering as the source of his inside knowledge officials of the Quebec Provincial Police whom he had met when a member of the Cliche Commission. I suggested that he need not engage in such absurd subterfuges since the real channel of his information was well-known. I was somewhat philosophical about Brian's role in the initial incident because I was quite conversant with his foibles. In the early stages, after the September 9 minutes surfaced, he assumed we were dead meat and knew nothing of the extent to which the Humphreys were implicated. He was far enough along in the chain that generated the Norcen investigation that his fingerprints wouldn't be on the knife. He helpfully assured his masters in Cleveland that the *coup de grâce* would be administered. As the trial unfolded, though his exact role was shadowy, the most believable conjecture is that he advised his employers of the existence of a tactic for recovering the initiative that we had regained.

Knowing Brian as I did, I had had plenty of experience of his propensity to truckle to the desiderata of those whose goodwill was most important to him. Up to a point, I had always admired his singleness of purpose in advancing his lot from the fabled modesty of Baie-Comeau to 24 Sussex Drive and have, at times, helped him a little along that road. I didn't take his activities personally. Though the nature of these activities is clear, the exact extent of them is not. For many reasons, I prefer to give him some benefit of doubt. He was, as he said, "the jam in the sandwich." I have always got along well with him and, in general, we like each other. But his protestations of helpfulness and innocence on this and a few other occasions were hard to endure, not so much for their smarminess as by their implicit presumption of cavernous naïveté on my part.

In the spring of 1982, I was also receiving some attention from the most prominent of all Canadian politicians, Pierre Elliott Trudeau. My friends Jim Coutts and Tom Axworthy, successive principal secretaries to the prime minister and ever fecund political schemers, determined that I, like Brian Mulroney and Jack Horner and a few other prominent ostensible Conservatives, should become a Liberal government minister. (Jack accepted and vanished into oblivion. Brian, obviously, declined the invitation.) Trudeau invited me to dinner at his home, following a meeting with leading businessmen on the federal government's plan to reduce inflation with compensation increases of 6 and 5 per cent in the immediately succeeding years. (The highlight of that meeting was when Bob Campeau said, "We shouldn't ask what the government can do for us, but what we can do for the government." I suggested he was the only person in the room who had made $200 million from the government of Canada.)

I had known Trudeau casually for some years. I had always been sceptical about his limousine-liberal interventions in Duplessist Quebec (driving his Mercedes-Benz 300 SL around the Murdochville strike site in 1957) and his trendy opposition to economic growth and the incentive system and to an adequately vigorous prosecution of the Cold War. His relentless incitements of special-interest groups, multi-cultural, regional, and sexist organizations, did terrible and perhaps irreparable damage to the social and fiscal structure of the country. He imposed a ruthless economic egalitarianism, especially in such areas as medical care. Yet, withal, I had always supported his championship of federalism, biculturalism, and national unity.

He lived like a Benedictine monk in 24 Sussex Drive. There was very little furniture in the house, except for the dining room, which had to have a table and chairs to function at all, and it more resembled descriptions of Ezra Pound's house at Rapallo than the usual version of the official residence of a head of government of a serious country.

Trudeau kindly expressed astonishment at the defamatory procedure my associates and I were being subjected to and, as a former professor of civil liberties, inquired how such a thing could have been made public in the first place. I avoided the political aspects of the story, but expatiated a little on the spirit of envy. His was the most brilliant star in the country; he was better qualified than anyone to know that the destructive fixation of the envious English-Canadian mind required that the highest, happiest, most agile flyers be laid low, as a cat, faced with a garden of birds, pursued the most swiftly flying and brightly feathered, the one whose destruction would most frighten the others.

It was, I suggested, a sadistic desire, corroded by soul-destroying envy, to intimidate all those who might aspire to anything in the slightest exceptional. Trudeau added that he was well familiar with the phenomenon and invoked a sports metaphor to say that what made Canada especially difficult to govern was that French Canadians "like a winner and mercilessly boo a loser, and English Canadians indulge a loser and, for reasons I have never understood, lustily boo a winner." (He obviously meant himself, but it was an insightful comment.)

He asked if I thought he should retire before the next election, due in two years. I said that my impression was that Canadians deeply respected him, whether they liked him or not, but that they now preferred to think of him as an important part of their history rather than an overwhelming current presence. I doubted whether Joe Clark could hang on as leader after the 1979 fiasco (and despite the best endeavours of Trudeau and others to raise Joe's prestige by endlessly speaking respectfully about him), that Mulroney, who was much cleverer, would probably replace him and that it would be hard, after sixteen years as prime minister, to persuade the people to resist the temptations of change.

Tom Axworthy, who was also present at dinner, said there had been some discussion of my being a Liberal candidate. I gently interjected that I thought it had been suggested I might be offered a Senate seat, though I had never expressed any interest in one. Electoral candidacy, I added, was "a little like Henry Kissinger's reference in his memoirs to Richard Nixon's suggestion, the night before his resignation, that they pray together in the Lincoln bedroom in the White House. Henry professed not to recall actually kneeling, and I don't recall talking about running in an election." In any event, it was clear that I was not enthusiastic about seeking political office, but it was, as always with Pierre Trudeau, a most stimulating discussion.

The Norcen investigation dragged on through the fall of 1982, an autumn made more sombre for me by the deaths, in rapid succession, of six old friends whose advice, in some measure or another, I had been in the habit of seeking and often following: Siegmund Warburg; Doug Ward (Dominion Securities); Charlie Burns (Burns Fry); Bob Dale-Harris (Coopers & Lybrand and a man who had equally observed my rather bumbling pursuit of his glamorous daughter, who sensibly married the tennis champion of France in 1968); Bob Chisholm (Confederation Life director and veteran of the food business), who always warned me against "blandishments"; and, most tragically, of self-inflicted gunshot wounds, John Robarts.

We put through our corporate reorganization, two years after the National Energy Program torpedoed the original effort. Labrador Mining and Exploration was sold to Norcen in exchange for as many Norcen shares as Labrador held in Norcen and the Norcen shares in Labrador were then contributed up to Norcen and cancelled. Effectively, Labrador sold its iron ore assets for the cost of the Norcen control block and yet retained control of those assets through control of Norcen. The adjusted cost base on our Norcen control position was thus reduced to about $7 per share. Norcen retired the debt by splitting its stock into voting and non-voting shares and issuing preferred shares convertible into the new class of non-voting stock.

Many institutions, by mid-1983, were vocally opposed to the issuance of non-voting stock and a two-thirds majority is required for the issuance of a new class of shares. By a considerable feat of last-minute arm-twisting, I brought in just over 70 per cent approval at the special shareholders' meeting. Trevor Eyton on behalf of the Royal Trust Company and Ced Ritchie, chairman of the Bank of Nova Scotia, were particularly helpful with discretionary stock when I canvassed them. A large turnout of the financial press departed the meeting audibly disappointed that the stock split carried. I was still one full jump ahead of my opponents.

The reorganization was achieved without significant dissent. Steve Jarislowsky, who had or represented about 1 per cent of Labrador's stock, proposed some changes that, after amicable negotiation and adjustment, were agreed to, despite strenuous efforts in parts of the financial press to portray me as an oppressor of minorities. In fact, Stephen was a large and supportive shareholder.

Just before Christmas, 1982, I read Jock Ferguson's account in the *Globe and Mail* of Roy McMurtry's appearance before the legislature's judicial affairs committee. Under close questioning from one of the

NDP members, Jim Renwick, Roy declared that the removal of the original assistant Crown attorney in the Norcen investigation was effected because he was not a specialist in that sort of case and vigorously debunked what he had privately admitted of the irregular and dubious origins of the Norcen investigation. He did a full tap dance to Renwick's tune, implying that it was improper for me to have visited him when the initial warrant had been served. He also expressed reservations about my intermittent public comments on the case.

Considering that the police and the Crown law office had violated every agreement we had made, had publicized, retarded, and misrepresented the proceedings that they had, as subsequent events would prove, no valid reason for undertaking in the first place, I could not allow this back-pedalling of the attorney general to pass without comment. Even allowing for political exigencies and the practical need to support his officials, this was a shabby performance by someone who was obviously incapable of withstanding any pressure. I telephoned Jock Ferguson, apparently awakening him, and told him what had really happened — the real reasons for the change of Crown law officers and the real discernible motives of the Crown in the case, at least at the outset.

I also dwelt on the illegal wire-taps that sweeps of the telephones regularly turned up at our office. We never received the advice of telephone intercepts that the law requires, and for a time, I began all conversations with vulgar expletives against police eavesdroppers, including one occasion when a startled David Rockefeller telephoned. I generated a fairly provocative story by Ferguson in the *Globe and Mail* on the subject on Christmas morning, my Christmas greetings to the attorney general.

Early in the New Year, *Maclean's* ran a cover story of me with a stubbly face like Herblock's McCarthy-era Richard Nixon, entitled, "Power in High Places." The principal reporter, Linda McQuaig, whom I eventually described (accurately) in the *Financial Post* as a "weedy, . . . and not very bright leftist," had not the slightest interest in fairness, much less the presumption of innocence. It was a corruption-of-the-rich, abuse-of-privilege, class-war story, but cleaned up just enough not to be clearly libellous.

From here on, public exchanges degenerated. Roy regularly arose in the legislature in answer to a question and affirmed, "The criminal investigation into Mr. Black and his activities is ongoing" (syntactically, as well as substantively, offensive). I regularly referred to "Roy and his performing fascists." Whenever the subject came up, I denigrated the Norcen investigation as the travesty that it was. Douglas Bassett and Fred Eaton loyally wrote to the premier, Bill Davis, objecting to the police burlesque.

As the OSC's one-year deadline approached, the eight commissioners, with two sets of advice from independent counsel, voted unanimously that "Norcen and its officers have handled a difficult compliance situation correctly, and have complied exactly with the law." Roy and several of his officials lobbied the OSC to lay a charge (any charge) under the Securities Act to preserve the fiction that there had been some justification for the year-long Star Chamber. The commission, in the first week of May 1983, declined to be bullied and publicly announced that an exhaustive investigation with which we had fully co-operated had revealed no evidence of wrongdoing.

The next day was Norcen's annual meeting, and I described the police element of the Norcen investigation as "a cowardly and disgusting smear job that can have had no other purpose than to defame innocent people regardless of the impact this would have on the interests of Norcen's shareholders. It has been the work of an insolent prosecutorial élite who believe they can persecute whomever they wish for as long as they want."

The day after that, my wife and I left for Rome for the Trilateral Commission meetings. To my astonishment, I was telephoned in our hotel there and advised that the "tawdry little farce" (another of my publicly quoted descriptions of it) had taken on yet another life. Ms. McQuaig was having some sort of personal relationship with the lawyer, in another matter, of one of the investigating policemen. The policeman, through this channel, fed Ms. McQuaig the story that the attorney general's department had asked for a prosecution but it had been declined, because the OSC chairman (succeeding Henry Knowles), Peter Dey, was formerly at Osler, Hoskin & Harcourt and once worked on a Norcen debenture issue. Peter Dey, a distinguished lawyer of unquestionable integrity, was alleged to have fixed the decision in Norcen's favour. *Maclean's* returned to the charge with a cover that defamed the OSC and was not overly flattering to me, since it implied I was guilty of bribery as well as defrauding shareholders, though it was again cleaned up enough not to be clearly libellous of me.

When I returned from Rome and London five days later, my brother allowed that it had been "a good week to be away." I launched my most vociferous attack yet, defending the commission as distinguishedly composed (including a future Supreme Court of Canada Justice, Frank Iacobucci), and demanded to know why a "criminal" investigation was "ongoing" when an exhaustive inquiry by qualified people at the OSC for a year had failed to produce evidence of even a civil infraction of the Securities Act. (One of the younger OSC investigators did suggest some experimental action to set some guidelines on the correct legal interpretation of corporate "intention," i.e., when it would be deemed to have emerged and become obligatorily disclosable.)

An underling at the commission sent us some material "accidentally," including a letter to the consumer and corporate affairs minister, Dr. Robert Elgie, to whom the commission reported, declaring that the commission no longer could trust or work with the attorney general's department or Roy McMurtry. I delightedly sent it at once to the Opposition leader, David Peterson, who read it in the provincial parliament to the intense embarrassment of Roy McMurtry, who was even more inarticulate than usual.

Emmett Cardinal Carter, Paul Godfrey, Alan Eagleson, and John Aird, all of whom had been magnificently supportive throughout this ordeal now spluttering into its second year, all made discreet interventions with or around the premier, Bill Davis. I raised it directly with the premier only when I encountered him in the washroom of the York Club during a retirement party for Don Hartford of CFRB with Wally Crouter singing sentimental songs in the background. I suggested that he jog his attorney general. He smiled and winked enigmatically, his customary response to all direct comments.

Finally, on June 9, 1982, Jack Ackroyd announced that there would be no prosecution, that there was insufficient evidence (in fact, no evidence as he eventually acknowledged). I had been on my way back from a trip to Halifax where I was helping to preserve the last remaining World War II corvette as a memorial to the Royal Canadian Navy's anti-submarine work in that war. Ed Bovey and George Mara were with me and I successfully predicted Brian

Mulroney's congratulatory and advisory telephone call (not a triumph of clairvoyance).

Whispering in French, as was his wont in particularly delicate matters, he advised "*un mutisme parfait*" — no comment. I replied that that was "*une option valable*," but I would await Roy's statement. Parliaments were adjourned for the federal conservative convention and I asked Brian, Julian Porter, and Paul Godfrey each to tell Roy at the convention they would all be attending that if his sign-off in the legislature were conciliatory, my final comments would be also.

Even this was too much for Roy. He waited until the last day before prorogation and regretted that Norcen had not been prosecuted. I took the press's calls and produced a new avalanche of sulphurous epigrams. To Diane Francis of the *Toronto Star* I said that "Roy had scrambled about through our records like an asphyxiated cockroach for over a year and come up empty-handed."

The renowned criminal lawyer, Ed Greenspan, wrote that he almost regretted the non-prosecution because of the pleasure we would have had shredding the Crown law office.

It had been a singularly taxing episode. The police had behaved like Kafkaesque, Orwellian, Koestlerian thugs. The attorney general was wholly spineless. The incoming leader of the (federal) Opposition, though perhaps not unpardonable, had been, to say the least, undistinguished or possibly even contemptible. His most irritating affectation was the pretense of having intervened to prevent a prosecution of me, after Norcen had been cleared by the OSC. Despite our good, though wary, relations, I icily reminded him that he had more to do with the beginning than with the end of this shameful affair.

True friends, the cardinal, the Bassetts, Eatons, Paul Godfrey, John Aird, John Turner, were an inspiration, but many others were palpably eager to believe the worst. I was fairly experienced but it was disappointing to see how easily social group-think warmed to the notion that I might just be led away in handcuffs to what I called "the Harold Ballard Memorial Suite at Beaver Correctional Camp." I would have found it less bothersome as I also said at the time, "if I had actually done anything wrong."

One of our many counsel, after reviewing all the relevant material, said of my performance, almost entirely in jest: "To have been so meticulously honest was, in itself, a form of deviousness." It was annoying to find our driver and housekeeper urgently whispering rumours in the kitchen when I came down for breakfast, to drive by an illuminated advertisement for *Maclean's* on Lakeshore Boulevard proclaiming my legal problems, to receive regrets from the provincial chief justice at his inability to attend the Hollinger dinner for evident concerns of respectability. (His absence in 1983, the anniversary of the start of the investigation, was more than compensated for by the presence of Henry Kissinger, David Rockefeller, Jack Heinz and Tony O'Reilly, chairman and president of the H.J.Heinz Company, who dropped by on their way to the Bilderberg meeting at Montebello, Quebec.)

When Leonard Rosenberg, the final buyer of the Crown Trust Company in a transaction that was eventually judged fraudulent, suffered a pre-emptive seizure of his assets, telephoned to say he had a rich dossier on Roy McMurtry, I invited him to our office. His information, as I expected, was rather insubstantial. We did not meet again, but I did admire Rosenberg's chutzpah in arriving in an elongated Cadillac limousine festooned with stickers proclaiming "Rosenberg's right, It's time to fight!" and quoting Hitler (to illustrate the injustices he was suffering). Peter Atkinson joined me at the meeting but our long-serving receptionist, an observant and conscientious woman, when Rosenberg left, said, "We're not accustomed to having people like that here! I'm glad you didn't meet him alone."

The two sergeants and the Crown officer who originally worked with them certainly did not enhance their careers with this affair. There was no point suing Roy McMurtry as he had already filed a defence in the Susan Nelles case of an absolute Crown immunity. (A nurse at Sick Children's Hospital in Toronto had been charged with poisoning children to death, had been released at preliminary hearing on insufficient evidence, and was suing for malicious prosecution.)

Once again, our great liberal media were sound asleep. I wrote a piece for the *Globe and Mail's ROB Magazine* decrying this outrageous concept of an absolute immunity, which would have disenthralled the Crown attorneys from any discipline or responsibility at all in the exercise of their vast powers, but *Maclean's*, the *Toronto Star*, the NDP, and the compulsive do-gooders such as June Callwood and Clayton Ruby, observed *un mutisme parfait*.

Roy had not prosecuted me, though he had been malicious as well as pusillanimous and incompetent, so I contented myself with a contribution to the Susan Nelles defence fund. Her case was ably argued by John Sopinka, who was upheld by the Supreme Court of Canada when it got there, though he had to recuse as he was appointed to that bench after the Nelles arguments. I was proud to have played a modest role in at least securing that right.

Events took their usual course, and I made some sort of peace with the prominent players and am unlikely to encounter any of the bit players again. Jack Ackroyd apologized for what happened and Roy acknowledged it had not been well-handled and that I had been a "victim." The editor of *Maclean's*, Kevin Doyle, apologized to me for the damage the story had caused me and professed not to have regretted Ms. McQuaig's departure to the *Globe and Mail*. It was the best possible end to a year of needless defamation and harassment.

The Argus reorganization was another mighty and essential step forward for our group as Norcen was fully possessed and the debt associated with its takeover was crunched down. However, it was achieved at great psychological and public-relations cost. There had, I thought, to be an easier way to make a living than this. I was reasonably robust, but I was endeavouring to inspirit myself with the less sanguinary campaigns of Bonaparte and MacArthur, not with the adventures of King Pyrrhus.

CHAPTER NINE

ARGUS BECOMES HOLLINGER: FROM GROCERIES INTO NEWSPAPERS
1983–1986

THERE WAS A STRANGE SYMMETRICALITY IN Brian Mulroney's elevation as leader of the Opposition a few days after the final collapse of the spurious investigation against Norcen (i.e., me). At the annual convention of the federal Progressive Conservatives, Joe Clark allowed himself to be manoeuvred into agreeing with Brian's friends in the media that if there wasn't a 70 per cent vote for his confirmation as party leader, he would call a convention.

Meeting in Winnipeg, 69.5 per cent of the delegates voted to confirm Joe. He duly ignored the wishes of the heavy majority and, faithful to his pledge, called for a leadership convention at which he would be a candidate. Hal Jackman described to me, with his usual comic brilliance, the arrival of the Quebec delegates, "stuffed into buses like sardines, having no idea where they were, what they were doing, or what the Conservative Party was, taught only to vote yes for a convention." (This sort of endeavour was called *un concours de paquetage* in the Duplessist Quebec where Brian Mulroney first was politically active.)

This avalanche of questionably motivated Québécois, a costly operation to which I made a significant contribution, provided just enough support to push Joe under his self-imposed 70 per cent threshold. I tangibly supported this initiative not because I thought it was a brilliant exercise in reform politics or because I had anything particularly against Joe, but because people must accept responsibility for their actions, and he subjected his party and country to an electoral fiasco with, to my knowledge, no valid precedent. To have ousted the opponents after sixteen years, and so bungled the parliamentary tactics as to be needlessly rebuffed after six months, was more amateurism than I thought any party, even the Progressive Conservatives, riddled with generations of self-inflicted wounds as they had been from Meighen and Bennett through Diefenbaker and Stanfield, should be asked to endure.

Hal was, above all, a legitimist. The same reasoning that propelled him to avoid a vote against Max Meighen or Alex Barron, but to vote to elevate their successors, caused him to support Joe loyally, even fervently. Any involuntary change of leader of any organization smacked to him of revolution. In the same measure that he wished not to share the figurative fate of Charles I himself, he wouldn't vote to inflict it upon others. A vote against Joe Clark was tantamount, in the mind of this *ne plus ultra* of high Tory cynicism, to a vote against Hal's re-election as chairman of Empire Life, the National Victoria and Grey Trust Company, or the Algoma Central Railway. (I was sent a video of Hal at the Winnipeg convention, standing on a chair at the front of the hall, waving a coat over his head as a cheerleader for Joe, and for my own amusement and in keeping with the general tenor of our relations, had Ravelston consider a corporate resolution criticizing him for bringing "embarrassment, disrepute, ridicule, and obloquy" down upon all of his colleagues by his behaviour.) It was at about this time that Fred Eaton asked our commissionaires to remove a jalopy from our parking lot on Toronto Street during a board meeting he arrived at while it was in progress. He couldn't imagine that such a vehicle could be driven by an Argus or Hollinger director. It was a wreck of Jackman's that was one of his many send-ups to the conventional attitudes of the Toronto Establishment. He professed great umbrage.

Immediately after the convention, Brian Mulroney came to Florida on a holiday and visited me in Palm Beach. Sitting in my library, he asked me if I would intervene with some of my "wealthy Toronto friends," in particular Hal Jackman and the Bassetts and Eatons, to try to detach them from the Clark camp. I said I would do my best but without great optimism, that most of the Toronto

Establishment didn't really want anything from any government and, insofar as it took any interest in politics at all, it tended to be for completely unopportunistic reasons. This was not a culture or political motivation with which Brian had had a great deal of experience.

I took this opportunity to probe into his motives in a way I had not been able to do since the liquefied evenings ten years or so before when we were both bachelors, or he was a comparative newly-wed, when he would amusingly disparage the naïve devotees of "country-running." I said that my impression was that he was interested in being prime minister, and in politics generally, "so that henceforth Paul Desmarais and Charlie Bronfman, and humble folk like myself would have to call on you rather than the other way round." There was that aspect to it, he acknowledged, but he also wanted to do some things.

I asked if he now considered himself a "policy-oriented candidate." "Not exactly," he replied with some agility and offered a few general notions of French-English *bonne entente*, better relations with the United States, especially the Reagan administration, and a better deal for the private sector in taxes, foreign investment, and general atmosphere. I assimilated these commendable velleities easily enough but returned to sociology.

"I'm all for that, as you know, and I know you are too, but, if I may take liberties as an old friend, don't you, and there's nothing wrong with this, or with ambition generally, really want, in Disraeli's phrase, 'to get to the top of the greasy pole'?" He stared at me thoughtfully and neutrally for several seconds, pondering, I assumed, not what the real answer to the question was, but whether he was prepared to answer it truthfully. "Yes," he said evenly, "but I want to do something useful when I get there, and I won't forget my friends."

I said I would make the calls he asked, that I thought he would win the leadership and probably the election, but that "then there will be millions of Canadians expecting you to do something personally useful for them. You know how Canada invests unreasonable hopes in incoming leaders, except for Joe who was just too uncharismatic for that, and then heaps unjust disappointment upon them. Are you ready for all that?" He said that he was, I wished him well, and I meant it. As predicted, Jackman declined to desert the leader for philosophical reasons. The Bassetts, John (Sr.) and Douglas, detest disloyalty in any form and wouldn't transfer their allegiance from their preferred candidate, no matter how beset he was or how obscure their reasons for supporting him in the first place.

The Eatons' political activities were at this time in the hands of John Craig Eaton, who was Bill Davis's co-chief fund raiser with Joe Barnicke. John Craig was taking his cue from the premier, who was under pressure from some members of his entourage to run himself. In the circumstances, Bill Davis, who was one of the most inscrutably capable Canadian politicians I have known, and who by this time, after twelve years as premier, having lost and regained his majority, had Ontario comprehensively in hand, purported to be leaning to Clark while deciding whether to pull the rug out from under him. Even if there were a stampede among their peers to Mulroney (there wasn't), the Eatons weren't about to join it.

As the campaign progressed, our companies supported Brian not only with large donations, but also in picking up Peter White's bills as he travelled and worked with the candidate. As a second choice, we gave a significant contribution to John Crosbie, the irrepressible former finance minister, and, for old times' sake, a modest contribution to my brother's and my former associate, Michael Wilson, to whose political launch I had been able (and delighted) to give a helpful shove. As the convention drew nearer, Brian telephoned somewhat urgently asking for supplemental contributions. He managed this ancient and fundamentally undignified politician's rite with a good deal more panache than Claude Wagner, Jean-Jacques Bertrand, and others whom I had observed (and heard from), when similarly occupied, and I was fairly obliging.

His victory was not unexpected nor unwelcome. Joe lost narrowly and with great dignity. The decennial juggernaut of disaffection, regicide, and elevation of a new chief was rolling and could be stopped only if the Liberals made a clever change as they did in 1968 and the new leader, assumedly John Turner, performed as cleverly as Pierre Trudeau had then. Failing that, the landslide that would have been given to Wagner in 1979 would be given five years later to Mulroney.

I thought Brian would be a good prime minister, sensible if equivocal in policy matters, unoriginal in carrying on with the backbreaking quango of Canada's equalization and transfer payment systems, but favourable to the private sector, capable at dealing with

Quebec, and sure of instant success in making the most out of our relations with the United States. Since the federal government's principal *raisons d'être* are to keep Quebec in the country and to maintain a positive climate in the American relationship, Brian was well qualified, even if his formal credentials were thin. Politically, he was an alley cat.

The long succession of losers, distinguished ones such as Meighen and Drew, and not so distinguished ones, Bennett, Manion, Hanson, Bracken, Stanfield, Clark, punctuated by the unqualifiable and volcanic John Diefenbaker, had left the Liberals unprepared for the onslaught of partisan determination, chicanery, and professionalism that I was confident Brian would mount. The one-party federal system with the real opposition coming from the principal provincial premiers was over, and unlamented by me.

At a personal level, my relations with Brian had always been cordial. Whatever misgivings I may have had about his role in the outrageous Norcen investigation, I was always satisfied that his customary zeal in serving his current chief sponsor (Bob Anderson at the time) swiftly gave way to genuine (if also possibly expedient) concern that matters were out of control and bad results could ensue. If it was not always easy to determine where sincerity and expediency intersected in Brian's thoughts, if he blurred the edges of truth more than most people I knew as well as I knew him, his opportunism was almost majestic in its single-mindedness and sometimes its ingenuity, but rarely, in my observations, reduced him to being unnecessarily nasty or completely unethical.

As Brian Mulroney, by dint of his own political aptitudes and good fortune climbed sure-footedly towards the highest political office in the country, I resumed the humdrum reformation of what was still generally known as the Argus Group. Standard Broadcasting was sold from Argus to Hollinger at the end of 1982. There was the usual light squawking in parts of the financial community that this was abusive self-dealing. This was not a durable complaint, as the control of Standard Broadcasting within a few years fetched Hollinger almost four times what it paid Argus for the shares.

There was at this time a good deal of snide disappointment abroad that I had not been a more orthodox, and apparently industrially successful, successor to Taylor and McDougald. The criticisms, at least the more benign formulations of them, were not unfounded. Massey-Ferguson, as it turned out, had been a lost cause; Dominion Stores was an unrewarding one. Managing our way through the operational problems would have been a constructive approach that could have been frankly explained and easily followed, but it wasn't the fastest, most direct, or most profitable exit from the neuralgic corporate tangle ambiguously bequeathed to us by Bud McDougald. Nor, it must be admitted, was it the role for which I was best suited. As my many critics were not reluctant (nor should they have been) to point out, I had never managed anything larger than the *Sherbrooke Record* (and there David Radler had done a good deal more managing than I had).

Having accorded myself the complex mandate of upgrading the Argus assets, attaining to real proprietorship of those assets, and putting a somewhat more articulate and flamboyant face on at least our small part of Canadian commerce, I could not (and rarely did) complain when my performance was ungenerously judged. I endeavoured, not always without success, to be more of a stylist than the garish materialists of the latter eighties that for a time became my caricature. I sometimes felt acute embarrassment at reading my own comments. I do not like boastful or overly materialistic people, but I had put myself in a position where I had constantly to justify my record as an executive and could only do so on the basis of enrichment of the shareholders, myself first among them.

There is nothing reprehensible in that, but it was not exactly attractive, especially in Canada, where money making comes well behind "caring and sharing" in general esteem, even in the business community, and the model of a business leader would resemble Alan Alda, if not John Denver. Leaving out my friends, and fortunately they were numerous and often influential, and leaving out the ravenously envious and misanthropic, I could often understand why much reasonable opinion would have been delighted to see me fall and would have felt it a fate I richly deserved. I could understand that view, but obviously I could not share or accommodate it. There was nothing for it but to finish the reconstruction of the business and capitalize on the antagonism that existed and to do so by continuing to exploit our relatively low share price.

Many of the stock analysts had confected the theory that a "Black factor" existed that had to be applied to our stock prices as a discount, because it was impossible to predict how the group would develop or what complex, related-party transactions it might pursue. It was not generally alleged that I was either incompetent or dishonest, though both of those were sometimes hinted at, only that investing with us was a crap shoot on how I could trade, shuffle, and strip, rather than predictably manage, our way to higher values for the shareholders.

The more discerning institutional managers, in particular Tullio Cedraschi and Stephen Jarislowsky (our second and third largest shareholders), were less concerned with the step-by-step process than with the steeply rising progress of shareholder values. They were happy enough to be passengers on the mystery tour I would conduct. They construed their task as pursuit of accretion of asset values, not identifying the perfect industrialist.

In the circumstances, the "Black factor" became an opportunity. It was usually applied to Norcen, which was particularly absurd since Ed Battle ran the company with great skill and absolute probity, and I had almost nothing to do with it. If our stocks were to be systematically undervalued, we must buy more of them, either for accumulation or cancellation (thus distributing the ultimate unrealized value among all continuing shareholders).

A new game was afoot and, in furtherance of it, in 1984, we made the traditional Dominion Stores a 100 per cent-owned subsidiary of the parent, which also owned 50 per cent of Standard Broadcasting, 93 per cent of Hollinger and Labrador, and through them almost 40 per cent of Norcen. The holding company was called Argcen Holdings Ltd., the most unglamorous name we could think of, an acronym of Argus and Norcen. One of our counsel humorously suggested it include Dominion in the anagram and become Arcend, a deglamorization so extreme that it descended to slang scatology.

The suggestion was not advanced seriously, but the principle of unmanipulatively accentuating the undervaluation of our shares possessed an admirable logic. The issuer bid at Norcen in 1982 that was the pretext for the subsequent investigation was the first of many that we did around the group, interspersed, within the permissible delays, with accumulative purchases usually paid for by occasional special dividends from the proceeds of sales of poor quality assets at inflated eighties' prices.

Most fundamentally difficult policies, from high interest rates by a central bank, to discount prices by a retailer, have to be pursued longer than had been foreseen and with a tenacity that becomes almost as unbearable to him who imposes them as to the public involved. Even I became rather uncomfortable tearing companies down and cutting and pasting unrelated assets. But the more vitriolic the financial press and general business community group-think became, the more determined I was to carry it through to the natural end of its utility.

The uncompetitiveness of Dominion Stores was becoming chronic. In 1981, after we sold the Quebec assets to Provigo and Coop-Prix and were "Dominionizing" Hollinger, Ray Wolfe (chairman and owner of the voting shares of The Oshawa Group) had his counsel call the Toronto Stock Exchange and ask them not to shut down our stock, pending our announcement of our plan to sell Hollinger to Dominion, as they wished to bid for Dominion. It was a rather inept overture and the exchange pointed out that it customarily took its advice on cessation of trading from the management involved. On the basis of Ray's proposal, we would have received about $90 million for our interest in Dominion. As my brother and Dick Chant and I were convinced we could do a lot better than that, and as we had $85 million in the Dominion treasury from the Quebec sales, I declined Ray Wolfe's overture.

In 1983, I reopened discussions with Ray Wolfe about Dominion Stores, and with the direct competitor Steinberg also, after receiving an expression of interest from the Dobrins (Mitzi Dobrin was Sam Steinberg's daughter). Neither Ray Wolfe nor Arnold Steinberg (with whom I mainly dealt) was the most decisive negotiator I have met, though they were both among the most frugal. Ray asked for more and more detail every meeting we had, invariably early in the morning at his house, which was only about a mile from mine. His accountant, Marvin Kates, attended and he concluded almost every session with the routine assertion that they had a "laundry list" of further information that they wanted.

For the Steinberg discussions, I brought in John Turner as counsel. While Trudeau was in office, it was unlikely any foreign purchase of Dominion would be allowed, but I thought it might be politically useful eventually if John Turner was at least conversant with the subject. I received an overture from A & P in 1984, through a friend in New York, Arthur Ross of Central National Bank Corporation, another discerning and loyal Hollinger shareholder.

Through 1983 and 1984, it gradually became clearer that Ray Wolfe and the Steinbergs were helplessly addicted to the decline of Dominion Stores, which made their competitive progress easier every year. Cautious men in a backbiting, high-volume, low-yield business, they reasoned that as long as Dominion continued to erode, they were secure; if any dedicated food retailer bought it, the beached whale of the industry would no longer be there to slice chunks from. If either of them bought it, it would no longer be there for all to enjoy, and the buyer would have to clean up our mess. It was a sign of my lack of credibility as a supermarket operator that the thought that we would actually clean up our own business was not seriously considered.

Tom Bolton's successor, Al Jackson, took early retirement in 1983, pleading health reasons, plausibly, as he was a notorious hypochondriac, but also because of the deteriorating position of the company and of his inability to do anything about it. John Toma took his place, but my brother prudently retained the position of chief executive officer for himself. Toma was regarded with a good deal of suspicion already, but he was Jackson's and Bolton's choice and the proportions of the company's slide, in early 1983, were not clear to me as a non-executive director. Since I fundamentally disliked the business anyway, and our Quebec dispositions had been so profitable, although the business was even more unsatisfactory there than elsewhere, I wasn't too concerned. Even when the impossibility of a sale to Canadians at a serious price became clear in late 1983, I wasn't as alarmed as I should have been.

When Toma took over, he set about convincing the directors that he would be embarking on a radically new plan to increase sales and customer satisfaction. Implicit in this was the admission, confirming our suspicions, that instead of being demand-driven, the merchandising policy had been determined by Toma's murky relationships with some suppliers. A study had been commissioned from a recognized retail consultant, practically all of whose recommendations for reforming buying practices, improving stores, upgrading personnel from the quagmire of mediocre cronyism it had become, diversifying into vertical integration, and taking advertising up-tempo ("Mainly because of the Meat" had become a little passé at a time when everyone was eating pasta) were suppressed or discarded by Toma. In his quest for confirmation as CEO, Toma frog-marched in the trained reptiles of his management group and presented a slick package of changes that replicated most of the recommendations of the external consultants.

We were generally, though warily, disposed to accept the grace of conversion. In 1983, the results appeared to improve, though profits seemed significantly higher on almost unchanged volumes. In response to intensive questioning, Toma and his managers insisted that they weren't just raising prices and margins and sacrificing volume at the company's best locations, where resistance to higher prices would be less. There were unverifiable claims of operating efficiencies and stocking with higher margin products. Not without general misgivings, Toma was given the dignity of chief executive officer with a generous management contract, on the considered recommendation of Monte and Dixon, over the outright disagreement of John Finlay, in 1984.

By late 1984, the chickens had come home to roost; Toma's manipulation of suppliers' accounts could no longer conceal the eroding market share. Profits had evaporated and the discreet expectations of Ray Wolfe and the Steinberg executives had been fulfilled. Under prodding from some of the directors, Toma had finally set up some franchised stores. The company's policy with losing stores had been to conduct a local price war, and when losses increased, as they were sure to do, close the store. There was no flair, fighting spirit, flexibility, or imagination, just rote, defeatism, and the type of perverse arrogance defeatism sometimes engenders.

There was also, we suspected, and would shortly confirm, the profligate corruption of looters in a deserted city or even a doomed ship. (It would be unfair to blame employees exclusively. They accounted for three-quarters of the theft, but customers took another $10 million. In one quarter, a Protestant minister, a Roman Catholic priest, and a rabbi, each in a different province, were apprehended for shoplifting.)

The attempt at franchising stores was carried out with the advice of a member of a well-respected labour law practice. Unfortunately this particular counsel, as it materialized, was probably the only lawyer in the firm who was likely to have the knack of rendering completely mistaken advice. I and others continuously asked Toma and his industrial relations director about the progress of the first test case of our Mr. Grocer franchised outlets, and we were invariably assured of almost certain success in the pending process before the Ontario Labour Relations Board, which aroused my profound suspicions. When the verdict came, in late 1984, it was worse than even I had imagined.

An academic interloper from British Columbia who sometimes applied for Ontario Labour Relations Board cases wrote a florid verdict, replete with references to "the brooding presence" of Dominion Stores and other such sophomoric forays into colourful writing. His judgement was that none of the Mr. Grocer employees had a right to take up their jobs and that the Dominion Stores employees who worked in the same location before the store closure and reopening as a franchised store were wrongfully laid off. This was not too surprising, but he also found that the existing Mr. Grocer workers were, in any event, represented by the Retail, Wholesale and Department Stores Union. Thus, although the verdict did not purport to address the financial consequences at all, Dominion owed back pay and job restoration to the laid-off workers, and the franchised employees retained their entitlements and had them enhanced by virtue of being represented by a union they did not want and remunerated at the same levels as the previous employees at the same location. The very wage-cost structure that contributed importantly (in addition to the company's general incompetence) to the store closing in the first place would be more than doubled.

The province's press generally rejoiced in my perceived discomfiture and naturally failed to note the slight incongruity in the RWDSU being declared to represent workers who the union claimed (and the board agreed) had no right to a job. Cliff Pilkey, the long-time head of the Ontario Federation of Labour, and one of my friends on the moderate left, had told me that under Bill Davis, nineteen out of twenty supposedly neutral nominees to the Ontario Labour Relations Board were, in fact, organized labour appointees. (Under David Peterson it became thirty-nine out of forty; under Bob Rae forty out of forty.)

My opinion, after hearing counsel's view that we had a strong case at appeal based on the Charter of Rights, apart from the fact that we should dismiss our foolish lawyer and claim back the fees we had paid him, which we successfully did, was that the judgement was so preposterous we should just ignore it, appeal, and go on closing and converting stores at an accelerated rate.

As the company's condition deteriorated, I took to visiting our competing stores on Saturdays. On one occasion, I encountered a gaggle of elderly ladies in a Loblaws store entranced by watching Dave Nichol, the company president, as he prepared, on a closed-circuit video, some sort of barbecue recipe. It had never occurred to me until that moment that anyone could have considered his bumptious self-advertising as an inducement to shop anywhere other than with a competitor. I was mistaken.

At about this time, John Finlay visited the Dominion Store at the corner of Bayview and Eglinton avenues, which we had already agreed should have been a museum of how people bought groceries thirty-five years before, and discovered Galen Weston, himself, walking through the store, rubbing his hands and excitedly telling John, "This is a good store!" Good for him, certainly. (One of my few achievements at Dominion was to get that store replaced by a rather attractive new one.)

The ultimate store-visiting demoralization came for me in November 1984, when I visited the Knob Hill Farms store in Etobicoke. I knew and admired Steve Stavro, who had built the business up from a fruit and vegetable stand. He had no union and huge stores, and his office was in his car, or wherever else he was. (In a political discussion I had had with Steve and George Eaton some years before, he exasperatedly said that the government of Canada should be handed over to "that bookkeeper," by which, I eventually ferreted out, he meant the auditor general. He eventually performed a high public service by restoring the Toronto Maple Leafs to much of their former distinction as a hockey franchise after the demeaning antics of Harold Ballard.)

As my seven-year-old son and I walked down the aisles of this huge-volume, low-price, thinly manned store, there was a commotion; large doors opened in an exterior wall, and a railway boxcar was shunted slowly into the store, right inside the selling area, and workers started to unload it directly onto the shelves. How were we to compete with this, with smaller stores feather-bedded by clock-watchers paid $40,000 per year for stacking bags of frozen peas? I asked myself. Answer came there none.

Almost as depressing was my visit to Dominion's cavernous warehouse, where the shrinkage of inventory would have embarrassed the legerdemain artists portrayed by W.C. Fields. A forklift swept around a corner dumping on the floor a load of goods, which had then to be declared damaged and auctioned at 90 per cent discount, presumably to the enterprisingly lucky forklift driver.

The whole company was rotten, and to preserve our hoped-for asset values, we would have to bring in a serious manager, at least put on a believable show of turning around the company, and broaden sale discussions to include foreigners. This was now reasonable because Trudeau had been succeeded by Mulroney who, as former head of an American-controlled mining company, had a much more relaxed view of foreign ownership than Trudeau had.

My brother had John Toma to my house in Palm Beach and in the same room where the previous year I had inquired into Brian Mulroney's political motivations, we handed Toma his proverbial bus ticket, with the minimum of *obiter dicta*. He took it quite civilly and my brother wrote in our visitors' book: "Two coffees and a firing!"

David Radler had already become a director of the company and had, with John Finlay, conducted an inquiry into Toma's tenure on the basis of which the directors voted unanimously to dismiss Toma and to engage forensic accountants to investigate his activities. Dick Chant described management as "fiendishly dishonest," *le mot juste*.

David Radler became the new president of the company and set about cleaning it up. At his first luncheon at the head office, he asked how long it would take to dispense with the extravagance of the executive dining room. The vice president for finance asked if he had finished his dessert. David nodded and the vice president quickly announced, "It's closed." It did not reopen. It was unearthed that Toma had made side deals with his son to sell dollhouses in the stores (a bit off the beaten track for a food store chain) and had hired one chum as an advertising co-ordinator, another as a non-consulting management consultant, and a lady friend, whom he chivalrously flew around on our plane and housed in a condominium in Fort Lauderdale that the company thoughtfully bought, as an executive in an inchoate bottled-water business. He forgave almost a million dollars owed by a friend who supplied the company plastic bags, and the whole pattern of company operations was an anthill of dubious activities. One of Toma's henchmen became so alarmed at our new regime that he abruptly joined the Salvation Army. David made rapid progress but it was a distressed company.

We unilaterally revoked Toma's severance package, and the day before his lawsuit was to go to trial, he settled, surrendering the supplement payable to him as an ex-CEO, retaining only his contractual rights arising from years of service, which we had never wished to challenge.

Our companies contributed somewhat generously to John Turner's campaign to succeed Pierre Trudeau in the summer of 1984. It was not so well organized as Brian's had been (though Brian was, after all, trying to unseat an incumbent party leader).

I had first met John Turner in February 1963 when he was a freshman, back-bench MP just before the collapse of the Diefenbaker government. In May of that year, he married Geills Kilgour, my father's god-daughter, whom I had known all my life. She was a rather controversial political wife, frequently exasperating people with her peremptory manner. I always defended her against all comers until I suddenly became the victim of one of her neurotically ill-tempered outbursts when she effectively disinvited me from John's sixtieth birthday party in 1989. My championship of her became rather more muted after that.

I encountered John fairly often through his years in cabinet. He took me to a performance of the Montreal Symphony Orchestra in Ottawa's Capital Theatre in 1964 and participated in the final ovation by bellowing: "Attaboy, Zube," in reference to the conductor, Zubin Mehta. He always combined a sort of locker-room exuberance with real intellectual gifts. At the time of his wedding, he was a Canadian Kennedy, intelligent, well-educated, attractive, Catholic. (No non-French-Canadian Roman Catholic had been elected prime minister of Canada prior to Joe Clark in 1979, although J.S.D. Thompson did briefly succeed to that post in 1891.) John Turner was deemed to have a brilliant future. So he would have, had he not been unkindly confined to only a few months at centre stage between a Trudeau who was reluctant to leave it and a Mulroney who was implacably determined to ascend. John went almost overnight from tomorrow's man to yesterday's without ever enjoying the day in which he actually lived.

Without taking excessive psychological liberties, the difference between Brian Mulroney and John Turner was largely that between the Irish and English Catholic cultures. Brian, cunning, not overly conscientious about means, though worthy enough in ends, feeling keenly a desire to avenge past sociological grievances, would not scruple unless it was absolutely necessary. John, guileless, spontaneous, and full of good intentions without ever being unctuous or outwardly pious, was bound to have difficulty with Brian's intense and relentless drive for the highest office.

In the campaign of September 1984, John was unable to look the voters in the television eye and believably say that the Trudeau government, from which he had resigned in 1976, should be re-elected merely because he had replaced Trudeau. He was too respectful of the truth, too untouched by the egomania that enables many politicians to ask routinely for immense favours.

For eight years, he had been a prime minister in waiting. Peter Newman even demeaned the great name of General de Gaulle by writing in his column in *Maclean's* that Canada's Colombey-les-Deux-Eglises was John Turner's corner banquette at Winston's restaurant. This was a terrible metaphor, but it illustrated John's success at remaining as apparent heir throughout nearly a decade since his retirement as finance minister. I was a regular attender at his boardroom lunches and dinners in Toronto, and he appeared ready to take Trudeau's place at any time. When his moment came, it became instantly clear that the years away had dulled his politician's desire, instincts, and sense of entitlement.

When the wheels started to come off his election campaign, he soldiered stoically on. In what must have been a nightmarishly difficult time for him, he did not, as the real chief resident of Colombey wrote of Paul Reynaud in the spring of 1940, "through days without respite and nights without sleep, cry out, complain, lose his temper or blame those around him."

Whatever John Turner's other shortcomings, he was magnificently philosophical as the greatest enterprise of his life swiftly became a prison of self-humiliation. His God wasn't deserting him;

He was testing him, and John, in the terms that mean most to him, the anticipated opinion of the Supreme Elector, passed magnificently. That this criterion is ultimately more important than the caprices of the Canadian voters is almost certainly true and reflects credit on John Turner as a man, but the Liberal Party did not elevate him to succeed Trudeau for theological reasons.

On election night, 1984, I rejoiced for the winner, felt for the loser, and looked forward, a bit sanguinely perhaps, to good government and intelligent Opposition, and I did not write off John Turner's political future. I voted Conservative, partly out of loyalty to my old schoolmate and local MP, John Bosley, and partly because I heard Geills Turner on election morning urging some American tourists to vote for Walter Mondale. (Not many did, as Reagan took forty-nine states six weeks later.)

My only unusual participation in the campaign was when the short-lived Montreal tabloid, the *Sunday Express*, reported that Brian Mulroney, as a director of Standard Broadcasting, had been involved in the distribution of pornographic films through a video sales and rental business Standard had invested in. The story had been partially confirmed by a flippant comment from a junior spokesman in that division, and Brian called me one Sunday morning in mid-campaign from Sept-Iles. I got out of the swimming pool to take his call and stopped the story from getting into serious media outlets with a thunderously self-righteous press release that I wrote and then gave to Mac McCurdy, the president of Standard. It was a cameo role, to be sure.

I, unlike almost everyone else, thought John Turner could still become a formidable opponent for Brian, because confessed, humbled, and absolved, John would be just as determined as Brian, though not as tactically agile, and some of Brian's mannerisms could, I reasoned, grate on his countrymen. John would have felt he had paid his penance (for offences he probably didn't commit anyway), I thought, and henceforth could resume being a winner again, as he had been all his life. I wrote to this effect in my column in the *Globe and Mail*'s *ROB Magazine*, concluding with the reference, from Newman's sublime *Second Spring* to "the revolution of the solemn circle that never stops and that teaches us in our height of hope ever to be sober and in our depth of desolation never to despair." As with

Claude Wagner, my apologia tended to require more virtuosity than the subject possessed. (George Radwanski, then editor in chief of the *Toronto Star*, when I gave him the case for Turner, offered to put my name up for the Leacock Medal for Humour.)

In the fall of 1984, I was working fiercely to sell Dominion Stores, preferably to foreigners. My idea of the retail business was now to wholesale the retail assets. I was following my able colleague, Ralph Barford's advice to "run, don't walk, to the nearest exit." By the end of the year, conversations with Jim Wood of A & P had reached a fairly advanced stage. In order not to have all the eggs in one basket, I did my best to keep a parallel track functioning with Ray Wolfe, but he was more of an amiable scavenger, hoping to pick a prone carcass rather than negotiating with a vendor who didn't have to sell.

In February 1985 Jim and his entire senior management group came to Toronto in the midst of a howling blizzard and together we worked out a deal. They took 115 stores, the warehouse, the office "tower" (of six floors, a matter of relativity; these were two of Toronto real estate's most prodigious white elephants), and left us thirty Ontario stores plus another forty in the West and the Atlantic provinces, the wholesale business, the pension surplus, convenience and general stores, gas bars, bakeries, a dairy Toma had overpaid for and, such as it was, the left-over real estate.

There was no goodwill factor, but there wasn't a great deal of goodwill left in the Dominion trademark. We pocketed about $150 million and estimated that we could ultimately realize up to $200 million on the other assets, and the main sale to A & P would end the serious operating losses and transform the remaining dispositions from a buyer's to a vendor's market.

As news of a deal with A & P circulated, Dick Currie of Weston offered to buy our thirty best locations. Ray Wolfe good-naturedly accused me of floating the rumours to prod him into an end to his endless requisitions of "laundry lists." Before and after the deal with A & P was consummated, Ray expressed incredulity and then astonishment that Dominion could extricate itself so (apparently) painlessly from the mess it was in.

The remaining assets were disposed of steadily over the next couple of years. We requested that store managers protect their most deserving employees; this was the best we could do at job security. The company had been so ineptly managed for so long prior to David Radler's arrival that Solomonic wisdom would be required to distinguish the deserving from the undeserving, the honest majority from the gluttonous pilferers who leached $30 million per year from the shareholders. I recommended that a scythe be taken through the ranks of the low-lives at the warehouse, and it was. "It is a long lane that knows no turning."

The RWDSU, which had been completely intractable, unlike the United Food and Commercial Workers who were accredited with most of our competitors, now heard persistent intimations of its own mortality. It had refused to consider any compromise on franchising, on part-time workers, on flexibility in job definition, on enhanced disincentives to employee theft, serenely arrogant in its belief that there would always be a Dominion milch cow to fatten on. The union leader was a monosyllabic little man who had arranged the succession in his moribund organization for his son. He and his union were about to be largely subsumed into its rival at A & P. The war to the (commercial) death between the union and Dominion had one violent exchange left.

We sold most of the Atlantic provinces' stores to Ray Wolfe, now refreshingly expeditious and even casual; the Atlantic wholesale assets went to an excellent management buy-out group. An orderly liquidation of assets proceeded through most of 1985 and into 1986, one of whose highlights was Weston's purchase of General Bakeries. At an analysts' meeting shortly after, Galen did me the honour of saying that, indeed, his company had overpaid us, but that "anyone who buys anything from Conrad will be sucking gas."

Less satisfactory, initially, were David's efforts to dispose of Epletts Dairy. One visitor from Quebec, introduced by my friend, the distinguished lawyer, Fraser Elliott, made an offer like Mme. Fortabat's representative in trying to buy Massey-Ferguson, Argentina, in 1979: we could pay him to do so. David invited him to leave, with a minimum of ceremony, but telephoned me to acknowledge that his just-departed visitor might unfortunately be right. (A year later, he did succeed, in a masterpiece of iron-nerved negotiation, in getting us out of the dairy with a handsome profit.)

As the full enormity of the former management's incompetence and venality emerged, my brother, a meticulously honest person, felt a heavy responsibility for the disgraceful conduct of those who were officially reporting to him. In fact, so uniform, seamless, and unconscionable had been their concealment of what was really going on below decks at Dominion, that the chairman's responsibility was notional, like that of the honourable government minister accepting responsibility for his underlings and doing the gentlemanly thing. After mature consideration, he decided to dissolve our partnership, completely amicably, and withdraw.

He had not always found the role of president of Argus Corporation easy or enjoyable, and it rarely *had* been easy or enjoyable. I sustained myself through these tumultuous years with faith in finding a more serene vocation for a repositioned group. He never lost that faith but saw less of a role for himself and, shaken by qualms about his own overlordship of Dominion Stores, and perhaps by the acrimonious end of his marriage, elected to take a very handsome profit and carve out a new role for himself away from intense publicity and invidious comparisons with his brother. In the next year or so, there would be many days when I would envy him. Our excellent relations were never interrupted, and our close association happily continues in a number of private and family concerns.

With this development came two others that enabled me to see the end of the long road of corporate manoeuvre and reorganization. An intricate series of steps would be required to complete the seven-year process, but my brother's retirement and the production of large sums of money in the dispositions of Dominion Stores' assets enabled me to envision buying out most of the other Ravelston partners, and two large newspaper investment possibilities emerged that justified the hope that we could finally focus on the newspaper business, where my own tortuous commercial career had begun nineteen years before, in Knowlton, Quebec.

The corporate objectives had been identified in 1978 as becoming real rather than token owners of sharply higher quality assets and generally to improve standards of management in the group. All of these goals had already been achieved to a significant degree, but I owned 50 per cent, with my brother, of the company (Warspite Corporation; I replaced most of our private numbered companies with World War I Royal Navy capital ship names), which owned 70 per cent of Western Dominion (Peter White and David Radler owned the rest), which owned 51 per cent of Ravelston. (Glen Davis, Nelson's son; Fred Eaton; Ron Riley and his sister; the Websters, in replacement of Hal Jackman; Ralph Barford, Douglas Bassett, Dick Chant, and John Finlay still owned the minority.)

In a word, I owned 18 per cent of Ravelston, or between 8 and 9 per cent of Argcen, a useful and strategic block, but not the sort of thing great fortunes or even real proprietorships are made of. I proposed to all the Ravelston directors (other than David Radler and Peter White) that if they wanted to withdraw, this was the time; that I intended to issue a special dividend from the Dominion proceeds in sufficient amount to pay them out at more than triple their net original investment cost six and a half years before. None was asked to go; I had no power or desire to force anyone out, but some had been a bit restive from time to time and indicated they had alternative uses for the money. For my part, I didn't want the ability of all of them to put stock to Western Dominion hanging over me like a sword of Damocles.

After much deliberation among themselves, all of them went except Dick Chant, who worked actively in the business. My brother accepted, volunteered, in fact, that the others could negotiate his price for him. Including the special dividend, Ravelston was valued at a little under $200 million, and my share of it jumped to about 70 per cent, though significant debt remained from this series of transactions. It had been very close to a perfect association. Everyone made a fine profit. Everyone had been entertained — "best theatre tickets in town," Ralph Barford called it — and not a brusque word had been exchanged among any of us throughout our association. They all remain friends and, in many cases, colleagues.

As real and potential debt mounted, the necessity of selling more assets mounted. Standard Broadcasting was a splendid company, but it had never been able to achieve any investor interest and the stock price lagged at one-third to one-half of its real value. I particularly enjoyed the Toronto FM station, whose announcers frequently referred to me in very humorous terms, but Mac McCurdy was anxious to retire and there was no one of comparable stature to replace him. CFRB, though a uniquely successful station in Toronto, was becoming more and more a station for elderly listeners. The purchase of the cable system in Los Angeles had been a fiasco to date, and the federal government had served notice of its intention to issue an independent television licence in Ottawa, which could not fail to cut into the market of CJOH, the Standard CTV station in Ottawa.

This was not Domtar, in which I had had no interest at all, nor Massey, from which in the desperate circumstances of late 1980 I had to extricate us, nor Dominion Stores, which had long since rotted from the top of operating management down into the bowels of the business. Although CFRB had gone farther than was advisable with an aging audience, and the investment in a Los Angeles cable system had not been explained properly (the shareholders saw only the decline in reported earnings, not the sharp cash-flow increase as the soft costs on the system wiped out taxable income), and there were some questions about the competence and competitiveness of the television management in Ottawa, it was a fine and endearing company. I got on well with all the well-known on-air people, such as Gordon Sinclair and Betty Kennedy; it was in every respect an enjoyable company to be a large shareholder of and was recognized as a high-quality radio and television operation.

There were some of the signs of traditional Argus Group erosion; the new president was significantly less authoritative than Mac McCurdy, who had become vice chairman. The California system had just been taken under David's control a couple of months before he rushed to the salvation of the disintegrating ship at Dominion. In the circumstances, the financial vice president of Standard, a competent and diligent Englishman, was, as much as anyone was, running the company, and the company doctor, who was also the family general practitioner of most of the Argus and Ravelston principals, was the de facto vice president of human resources (i.e., personnel). With entire good faith, these two individuals rushed to fill a partial management vacuum.

Determined not to replicate the Dominion fiasco of going too long with inadequate self-generated management, we were receiving and interviewing prospects, but the buy-out of my brother and other Ravelston partners and the requirements for a special dividend and probably for some form of issuer bid to ensure that the reduced Ravelston retained control of the swiftly shrinking Argus Group created irrefutable arithmetic in favour of an advantageous Standard sale.

John Finlay opened discussion with Allan Slaight, owner of a Toronto AM licence and another FM station, though less well-established ones than Standard's. Allan was highly interested from the start. I had known him since 1975 when we had had extensive and almost successful talks about merging Sterling Newspapers with the Global Television network, of which he was then the president. He had always been a most convivial interlocutor and companion, and he quickly produced an offer of $21 per share for what had generally been an eight to ten dollar stock. Inevitable indiscretions occurred, rumours circulated, the stock price came up a couple of dollars, and competing buyers came out of the woodwork, Raif Engle of Selkirk Broadcasting being the most persistent. It was quite a contrast to hustling the clapped-out assets of Dominion Stores, much less giving away the Massey-Ferguson shares, like, as one of the *Toronto Star* commentators wrote, "the booby prize in the neighbourhood bridge game."

At one well-advanced point in the discussions with Allan Slaight, he came to a luncheon party at our house in honour of Marietta Tree, the gracious and glamorous New York hostess and businesswoman, perhaps best known for having once been the chatelaine at Ditchley Park and the companion of Adlai E. Stevenson. She had introduced us to our architect, Thierry Despont, who redesigned and heavily rebuilt our house and went on to considerable and well-earned renown, and she was anxious to see the finished home. After lunch, I took Allan aside in my library and advised him, *digestifs* in hand, that I was under such pressure from competing bidders, he really should raise his offer. He did, by 50 cents per share, and wrote my wife the next day thanking her "for a splendid and most enjoyable lunch, it only cost me $3,000,000!"

As the negotiations came to an end, the Selkirk bid was ostensibly higher but conditional on CRTC approval that was more problematical than the almost certain approval Allan would get, since he was undertaking, and had already negotiated, to sell the radio stations he then owned. Allan would wish to be able to "put" the California cable system back to us at the company's historic cost, and both he and his banker, the Bank of Nova Scotia, confidentially indicated that he was almost certain to do this, an advantage for his bid as far as we were concerned, as we were confident that its real value was a good deal higher than the bargain-basement price we had paid for it from its temporarily improvident former owner, who had been under heavy pressure from the Toronto-Dominion Bank.

On the night the bidding would end and the deal would be consummated, Latham Burns telephoned to announce that Selkirk was prepared to go unconditional on its offer, and that if the CRTC disapproved the transaction that would be the buyer's risk. It would have been a tempting and probably a winning offer had it been made earlier. At this point, as we were committed to Allan Slaight in all but the most extreme circumstances, and the slightly higher quantum of the Selkirk offer was, in our judgement, offset by the likelihood of Allan putting the California cable system to us at an unrealistically low price, we elected to stick with Allan.

He telephoned a few minutes after Latham had and, when advised that I was reading my children bedtime stories, asked my wife to interrupt me and tell the children that "Uncle Allan will read to them." When I took the phone, he said, "I am sitting here with a lot of high-priced counsel looking for someone to sue. Can I sue anyone?" I suggested that would not be necessary and returned to the perils of Frederick the Mouse and Garth Pig.

Allan Slaight did exercise his right to require us to buy the California cable system from him, handing me the notice with his usual sense of occasion, at a luncheon I held for the new American ambassador to Canada, Tom Niles, at the York Club in September 1985. We resold 90 per cent of it at a profit of about $30 million less than two years later, for over $1,200 per subscriber, one of the highest prices ever paid for an American cable system at that time. We retained the tax-loss vehicle of the former owners and used it to shelter our eventual U.S. newspaper operations from tax. All in all, we netted about $40 for each of our 3 million Standard Broadcasting shares, from four to five times their apparent starting value in the early summer of 1985. We miss the association but know at least that Standard is in good hands with Allan Slaight.

We netted from dozens of asset realizations over several years almost $60 per share for Dominion, which never traded above $24, and Argcen (which later became Hollinger) got the entire proceeds of nearly $500 million, as Dominion was a wholly owned subsidiary at the time of its sale. These two dispositions, Standard Broadcasting and Dominion Stores, carried out in many piecemeal transactions, enabled David Radler, Peter White, Dick Chant, and me to become genuine proprietors of an operating company focused on a business we understood.

This last step, the repositioning of the company in the newspaper business, pursued two principal routes in 1985. Through the spring of that year, there was great agitation in the Southam share price. About one-fifth of the company's shares was owned by a diffuse group of about 200 Southam, Balfour, and Fisher relatives. Successive generations of all three families had directed the company for a century. I knew many of them cordially. Their franchises were splendid — broadsheet monopolies in Calgary, Edmonton, and English-language Ottawa; English-language monopoly in Montreal; and absolute monopolies in Vancouver, Windsor, Sault Ste. Marie, Kitchener-Waterloo, North Bay, Moose Jaw, Medicine Hat, Prince George, Owen Sound, Barrie, and Kamloops — all good towns. The company had adopted the policy that, since foreign ownership of Canadian newspapers was effectively prohibited, it would not purchase foreign newspapers, a righteous but strategically insane conception.

The Canadian properties were accordingly awash with money; in almost every Southam town, the newspaper building loomed up on the horizon like a Taj Mahal, a monument to the feckless lack of imagination of its owners in the art of reinvesting earnings. Nor were the earnings adequate, never more than 12 per cent pre-tax cash flow on daily newspaper revenues, less than half what we wrung from very mediocre franchises such as Sherbrooke, Quebec, and Prince Rupert, British Columbia. Nor, contrary to fervently propagated mythology, were they very distinguished newspapers. With the rarest exceptions, Southam newspapers tended to be illustrative of the bland worthiness, inhibitedness, and derivative impersonality of much of Canadian life. The general air was of banal sanctimony, "Proudly participating in the Canadian experience," as one annual report boosterishly put it, beside a majestic west-coast colour photoscape.

The senior management, Clair Balfour and Gordon Fisher, who was then tragically dying of cancer, were gentlemen of high quality not apparently disposed to effect very radical changes to the product in the hands of either the shareholder or the reader. As the agitation in the Southam stock price intensified, with very large volumes of shares changing hands, it was widely assumed that I was mounting a takeover bid. In fact, I had not bought a share, and apart from hearing from brokers blue-skying, especially my old friend Jimmy Connacher, and from a couple of institutional investors, I had no involvement of any kind in the activities that were convulsing the market.

I telephoned Clair Balfour and offered myself as "an honorary Southam," meaning that I was prepared, with the incumbent management's blessing, to take a position in Southam stock and vote it in a co-ordinated way with the shares of the traditional families. He thanked me for my interest most courteously, but, with what I subsequently described as a "gentlemanly doffing of his cap," rushed past me into the arms of the *Toronto Star*, with whom a large reciprocal share issue was arranged, without the regulatory approvals for issuance of new stock required by the Toronto Stock Exchange. This was a bold, not to say impetuous, move for such proper companies, prim old Southam and squeaky-left, stridently moralizing Torstar.

The *Star*, which regularly apostrophized non-voting shares, undeterred by the minor inconvenience that almost 90 per cent of its own shares didn't vote, issued a full 30 per cent of new equity, without voting rights, in the dead of night without any but board approvals in a massive affront to the Securities Act, to Southam, the recently discharged co-defendant with Thomson in the post FP monopolies *cause célèbre*. As compliance companies, the regulators understandably thought Torstar and Southam left much to be desired. Southam paid with almost 20 per cent of normal voting shares to Torstar, subject to a comprehensive voting agreement with the Southam, Fisher, and Balfour families, who reassembled their shares over the next few months, in nine groups confederated into one master group for the purposes of voting and exercising control.

It was an ingenious enough arrangement, and I never had any standing or disposition to criticize it, but they shouldn't have infringed the Securities Act. In doing so, they showed an unbecoming attitude of panic, left themselves wide open to attack from the federal Consumer and Corporate Affairs Department, who ultimately forced them to dissolve most of the formal connections between Southam and Torstar, though not to cancel the shares they had issued to each other.

Not least, it outraged many thousands of shareholders, some virtual arbitrageurs who bought in the hope of a takeover contest, but also others, such as Steve Jarislowsky, who were supportive long-term holders who had been promised by the Southam management that their interests would be protected. They were unceremoniously put over the side but, as we were not shareholders, it was no concern of mine. The aggrieved official assault on the Southam-Torstar arrangements kept alive the possibility that that marriage might never be consummated and that Southam might yet be a candidate for our attentions.

More promising, more imminent, and much more bizarre were the possibilities opened up by the London *Daily Telegraph*. The editor of the *Economist*, Andrew Knight, a fellow Bilderberg attender, told me at the Bilderberg meeting at Westchester, New York, in the spring of 1985 that the *Daily Telegraph*, the Western world's largest circulation broadsheet general newspaper, was seeking equity and asked if I might be interested. (In Britain, Sunday newspapers are considered to be separate titles. The *Sunday Telegraph* went with the *Daily*.) I had known Andrew since the *Economist* and our company had staged a program in Toronto in May 1980, at which Henry Kissinger spoke. Apart from Bilderberg, we had met from time to time since, usually when I was passing through London. I said that we might be interested in such an opportunity.

Andrew Knight, an ever youthful and attractive-looking man, enjoyed a huge prestige as editor of the *Economist*. He had probably sharpened its already excellent contents and drastically increased its circulation with a well-conceived push into the United States. He was almost universally respected and very influential, but he had a modest salary and no accumulated means.

Andrew telephoned me a few days later at 6:00 a.m. on the Victoria Day holiday (which is not observed in the UK) and said that the underwriter, Evelyn de Rothschild, who was also the chairman of the *Economist*, and whom I had also met at Bilderberg, would send me the *Daily Telegraph* prospectus and that he would be calling. The prospectus revealed that an £80-million debt facility was conditional upon the raising of £30 million of equity, which had been only half-subscribed; i.e., before the lenders would provide the money necessary to finish the new plants under construction, shareholders had to be found to subscribe £15 million. It was clear that the whole underwriting was in serious difficulty and what stood out like a pikestaff in the prospectus was that the huge off-set printing plants had been commissioned for the *Daily Telegraph* without any systematic thought about how to pay for them or how to capitalize on them.

The owners of the *Daily Telegraph* had literally ordered the construction of giant facilities that resembled nothing so much as hangars for the great Zeppelins and airships of the thirties and paid the contractors' invoices as they came in until the inevitable call came from the banks. A usurious arrangement with a lending group was worked out that would leave the Berry family (principally Lord Hartwell and Lord Camrose) in control with 59 per cent of the stock. It was a little hard to take the prospectus seriously since it foresaw a miraculous increase in revenues without any appreciable wage savings.

What made the timing interesting was that one Eddie Shah had won a battle with print unions in a provincial city where he owned the newspaper and was about to launch a national daily in London with the so-called new technology (direct inputting from the journalists' word processors to typesetting, with the journalists making their own corrections on their own screens — no copy boys, no hot metal, no typesetters as such, and huge manpower savings).

Rupert Murdoch, whom I had met through Marietta Tree in 1980, had built just east of the Tower of London a very large new-technology newspaper plant that had been unoccupied for five years except for sanitary and security personnel. It was well known that Mrs. Thatcher's regime had imposed significant disciplines on British unions in other fields, most notably the coal miners. My intuition told me that this prospect might be arising at a providential turning in British newspaper history.

I was adequately familiar with the history of the *Daily Telegraph*, founded in 1855 for the purpose of opposing the continuation as nominal commander of the British Army of Queen Victoria's incompetent cousin, the Duke of Cambridge, after the shambles in Crimea, and as Aberdeen was replaced by the more purposeful Palmerston, as in other British wars Rockingham gave way to Pitt, Asquith to Lloyd George, Chamberlain to Churchill. It was a conspicuously unsuccessful corporate mission and the Duke continued in that role for another twenty-five years.

The *Daily Telegraph*'s most famous moments were in the celebrated interview with the German emperor, Wilhelm II in 1908, in which the Kaiser fantasized about his role in the Boer War and about Anglo-German relations generally, and the publication, in 1917, of Lord Lansdowne's letter calling for a negotiated peace. In the thirties, when the Chamberlain government had prevailed upon Lord Beaverbrook to dispense with Mr. Churchill's services at the *Express*, the *Daily Telegraph*'s proprietor, Viscount Camrose, employed him. During the appeasement crises of the late thirties, when the editor of the *Times*, Geoffrey Dawson, was head of the Anglo-German Friendship League and pulled negative comments about Hitler from the tray himself, the *Telegraph* was honourably sceptical about the entire appeasement policy.

I was dimly aware of most of this, having read about the great British newspapers and some of their famous proprietors. I was much more certainly aware of its pre-eminence in circulation among London's broadsheet newspapers, at over 1.1 million, or significantly above the combination of the *Times* and the *Guardian*. If the *Times* was the paper of the Establishment, corporate, political, academic, episcopal, and military, and the *Guardian* was the paper of the thinking left in all walks of life, the *Telegraph* was the faithful voice of the British bourgeoisie — frugal, sober, prurient, diligent, principled, numerous, and not without a sense of humour.

The *Daily Telegraph* had enjoyed tremendous success under Viscount Burnham in the late nineteenth and early twentieth centuries, declined until it was brought back to phenomenal success by Viscount Camrose in the twenties, who sharply increased his circulation by reducing his cover price and forced his chief competitor, the *Morning Post*, into an unequal merger with him.

The key to the *Daily Telegraph*'s immense success was a formula devised by Lord Camrose and faithfully continued by his son, Lord Hartwell, consisting of an excellent, fair, concise, informative newspaper; good sports coverage; a page three in which the kinkiest, gamiest, most salacious, and most scatological stories in Britain were set out in the most apparently sober manner, but with sadistically explicit quotations from court transcripts; and extreme veneration of the Royal Family. Generations of travellers on the verandahs or in the public rooms of the hotels in Russell Square feverishly read of the flagellators, deviant clergy, errant politicians, psychotic criminals on page three of the *Daily Telegraph* with relish and without embarrassment. It was in some measure a brilliant confidence trick: a titillating chronicle, wrapped in a good but almost featureless news and sports paper.

By 1985, in addition to the financial overstretch, there were management and editorial scleroses that had tipped the title into what some regarded as an irreversible decline. When Rupert Murdoch bought the *Times* from Ken Thomson in 1980, he announced that he was seeking "the sons and daughters of *Telegraph* readers," and to that end brought the *Times* somewhat down-market in design and promotional aspects, running contests and rather more racily presented stories that caused some of the traditional clientèle to grumble about a "yuppie bingo sheet," but which did produce steady circulation gains.

Despite the erosion of the *Telegraph*'s absolute pre-eminence, if it were capitalized correctly, it would not lose money; it was not conceivable to me that its competitive decline could not be arrested before its lead of nearly 600,000 on its nearest competitor evaporated; and this opportunity was arising at a fascinating time in the history of London newspapers.

Evelyn de Rothschild telephoned to ask if I could come to London in the next week. I could not. He called back a few minutes later to ask if I could meet his clients at Kennedy airport, and this was arranged. I arrived at the agreed room of the J.F.K. Hilton, a thoroughly undistinguished hotel, a few minutes after the British visitors, Lord Hartwell, his managing director and deputy managing director, merchant banker Rupert Hambro (whom I had engaged to advise on the personalities and the corporate politics), and a Rothschild's representative. They were apparently surprised that I was alone.

I was relieved when, after I had told Lord Hartwell that I had read his prospectus and thought I could probably top up his equity issue but that we would need a pre-emptive right on sales of shares out of the control block or material issuances of treasury shares, he answered at once, "I don't think we can resist that." My first impressions of him were quite positive as he made no effort to lecture me on the historic value of the newspaper or even to tout its future. Anyone in his right mind in my position would have requested what

I had, so it required more though not excessive intelligence for him to concede it graciously and confidently than for me to have asked for a pre-emptive right at all. I felt at once as I had when the Phillips and McDougald estates entered into the May 1978 Ravelston shareholders' agreement with us. After years of retreat and regrouping an amazing prospect was opening up. In corporate life as in other spheres, Fabian tactics eventually produce results.

As an administrative team to achieve the ambitious targets outlined in the prospectus, Hartwell and his companions had a substantial credibility gap. His managing director, H.M. Stephen, a pleasant and experienced man with a fine war record and considerable personal exposure to Lord Beaverbrook and Lord Thomson, had no background in industrial relations and relayed my questions over demanning to his deputy.

His deputy managing director, Hugh Lawson, was an extraordinary character. With straight dark hair, a rotund, monocled face, immense elliptical girth, he gambolled about the hotel room. One inhalation in three yielded a disconcerting stertorous noise as he bellowed "Sir!" to Hartwell (and all within distant earshot, including, as it turned out, the quizzical black couple from Detroit in the next room who were on their second honeymoon). He snorted at frequent but unpredictable intervals like an endomorphic Terry Thomas and fetched up randomly on chairs and other surfaces like a one-passenger hovercraft. His attempts to answer my questions on demanning and competitive positioning were unconvincing.

Hartwell, himself, was well-dressed, appeared to have once been a rather good-looking man, handled his cigarette holder with almost Rooseveltian assurance, and had a sly, even pleasing smile. He was also quite deaf and mumbled a great deal, so it was hard to be confident when talking to him that either side was receiving the message ungarbled. In order not to seem too eager or overly decisive, I excused Rupert Hambro and myself and walked around the hotel a couple of times conducting a light pantomime as airliners roared determinedly overhead. Having met the senior management, I was profoundly sceptical that they could avoid another massive capital call or outright sale.

Rupert, being operationally unfamiliar with newspapers and, for obvious reasons, more naturally respectful of the talents of the

British hereditary upper classes than I was, thought the prospectus might be achievable. I didn't tell him this too emphatically, as I wanted his emollient personality deployed entirely to the reassurance of our interlocutors, but it seemed to me that an option for control of one of Europe's greatest newspapers was on offer at a once-in-a-lifetime price. On a worst case, Hartwell and I between us should be able to find some egotist or chump in the long Fleet Street tradition who would take us out at, in my case, no, or minimal loss. We went back upstairs, I loudly and monosyllabically reconfirmed our understanding to be sure Hartwell had grasped my condition and agreed subject to minor due diligence.

I sent them back to the British Airways terminal with the driver I had hired, watched them from the hotel room we had used as their Concorde took off for London, where they returned just twelve hours after leaving, and I went back to Toronto. Subject to legal drafting, a tremendous opportunity and challenge were opening up. I confidently left the legal work to Dan Colson and the agreements were finalized in about six weeks, triggering the cascade of £30 million of equity and £80 million of debt, and I looked forward to my first directors' meeting in September.

The *Telegraph* opportunity arose just as the Ravelston buy-out was being completed. The process of transition was accelerating from a miscellaneous holding company with significant but not really proprietary interests, to a real proprietorship of an operating business in an industry where the owners had some track record.

When I went to London in September, I visited the *Telegraph* and formed my own assessment of the management, which confirmed my original impressions. Hugh Lawson intruded on each session like an overbearing Colonel Blimp, inhibiting the responses to my rather basic questions. The head of production, Alan Rawcliffe, was obviously an outstanding executive, the industrial relations manager had possibilities, the advertising director was at least workmanlike, and it tapered down from there. Rawcliffe showed me through his clacking, deafening, desperately overmanned, pre-war press room.

I called the classified number the next day from my hotel purporting to want to take out an ad and was shirtily advised by a very flustered woman that I could wait several weeks or phone the

Times or the *Guardian*. I even got her to give me the *Guardian*'s classified telephone number but she balked at performing the same favour on behalf of the *Times*. It was not an encouraging start for a 14 per cent shareholder, other than in the May 1940 sense that the more swiftly the slope became a fall, the sooner would be the inevitable change of regime to one where I was pre-eminent.

I was entitled to name two directors to the *Daily Telegraph*'s board. I took myself, with Rupert Hambro as an alternate. Andrew Knight's suggestion for the other place, when I asked him, was Frank Rogers, former managing director of the *Daily Mirror*, when it had had a daily circulation of over 5 million, and chairman of East Midland Allied Press, which he had helped to guide from £200,000 annual profit to over £20 million. The three of us had dinner at the *Economist* office, at the top of their building in St. James's, looking out over much of central London.

I liked Frank at once. Physically he was a shorter and less rumbustious E.P. Taylor. His Staffordshire diction was at refreshing variance to the standard *Daily Telegraph* public school resonances, and his vocabulary was the unique product of a very intelligent and original autodidact. I was advised early and often to "divest" myself of some notion or other. "Nauseating rubbish" was frequently encountered, and dispatched, by Frank.

His most memorable utterance came after I had asked him to be our second director at the *Daily Telegraph* and had described the status of the *Telegraph*'s management, prospects, and ownership as I saw them. When Frank asked whom, if I should gain control of the *Daily Telegraph*, I proposed as a managing director (H.M. Stephen was at retirement age), I replied, "Our genial host, Andrew S.B. Knight, Esquire, peerage anticipated." Frank uttered a portentous "Ah hah," leaned back, and said, "Then this most convivial occasion brings together a potential proprietor of the *Daily Telegraph*, a potential managing director of the *Daily Telegraph*, and a potential director of the *Daily Telegraph*. Let us delete the word 'potential' and decide what WE are going to do with OUR newspapers."

So it swiftly came to pass. Before our first *Telegraph* directors' meeting, I had lunch with the other newcomers, Rupert Hambro, David Montagu, and Lord Rawlinson, at Jacob Rothschild's office where Montagu was a vice chairman (J. Rothschild and Company, not to be confused with N.M. Rothschild, the famous merchant bank controlled by Evelyn, later Sir Evelyn Rothschild). Lord Peter Rawlinson, a former solicitor general and attorney general of the United Kingdom, dapper and gracious, a brilliant barrister, was a reassuring colleague in the difficult days just ahead of us.

Montagu is a sly and urbane man, whose ingenuity and sense of humour never deserted him and were to prove invaluable. Our relations have always been excellent. David Montagu had his family business, Samuel Montagu, sold out from under him to the Midland Bank and had been chairman of Orion Bank, a consortium bank composed of the Royal Bank of Canada, Chase Manhattan, and three others, before moving on to Merrill Lynch in London. I had met him once, at a race track, when I was in Britain on Massey-Ferguson business in 1979. David had been a very active race-horse owner and once, when queried by telex from Merrill Lynch in New York why he had flown first class from London to Paris (to watch one of his horses at Longchamps), telexed back, informatively, "Chartered jet not available." He shortly moved on to the more agreeable culture of Jacob Rothschild and, under the *Daily Telegraph* prospectus agreements, was the chairman of the audit committee (a new function).

He was given considerable investigative powers and was appalled at what he found. He said at our luncheon that he thought I either had made a good minority investment or would gain control of "two outstanding titles." He shortly replaced the ancient little accounting office that had been producing the audit with Coopers & Lybrand, as there were no discernible controls or real auditing procedures in place and the figures, including those in the prospectus, were mere guesswork. "An unutterable shambles," he called it. I was neither surprised nor astonished. The house of the Berrys (Hartwell and Camrose) was shaking from the basement to the rafters. David Montagu beseeched me to come to the October meeting. "I'll feel naked without you," he said. I promised to come, "if only to spare you the fate of Cardinal Wolsey."

Lord Hartwell had about thirty people connected to the refinancing to his house for a most agreeable dinner in September. I was sitting next to his abrasive and raffish younger son, Nicholas. Apart from a couple of sentences at the October board meeting, these were the only words I would exchange directly with him, and they were perfectly civil. When his father finally told him the facts of our arrangement, he became cyclonically antagonistic and vituperative. Dan Colson bore and rebutted his infantilistic aggressions without difficulty.

I left London after eight days. When I returned a month later, the difference was like that between Churchill's visits to Paris and Briare in May 1940. In the interval, Andrew Knight visited me in Toronto with a madcap scheme for leaving the *Economist* to work for Tiny Rowland at the *Observer*, and then, after a year or two, coming across to the *Telegraph* when I might have attained to some influence there. It revealed two of Andrew's traits: a tendency to ludicrously complicated and impractical schemes — the idea of moving by pre-arrangement between senior posts at serious publications like the *Economist*, the *Observer*, and the *Telegraph* was preposterous; and his penchant for being an ardent courtier to powerful and wealthy men who suffered from some incompleteness in their relations with the British establishment. (He claimed that the only person apart from his wife with whom he had discussed his prospects was Mohammed Haikal, the Nasenite Egyptian newspaper editor and propagandist, an exotic source for career advice.)

Rowland was a controversial German Rhodesian of great talent and suavity who had been more or less ostracized by the proverbial top people because of his maverick, murky, and rough-house business and political style. He had already been deemed to have turned the virtuous *Observer* of Kenneth Tynan and the Astors into a flying carpet for his own vendettas, especially over the Al-Fayeds' transformation of an apparently passive investment or even warehousing arrangement in the House of Fraser, including Harrods, into a successful takeover.

I advised Andrew that events were moving more quickly than that and that it wouldn't be possible, corporately, or probably even physically, to get out of the *Economist* before the Hartwell regime ended at the *Telegraph*. He was slightly incredulous but shifted quickly, for the next six weeks or so, to proposals for an approximately even-share split between Hartwell and me, so that he could replicate his insubordinate position at the *Economist*, where Pearson owned half the shares but couldn't really vote them and Evelyn de Rothschild represented the others and the editor was immunized against both by the bylaws devised by Brendan Bracken. When he controlled the *Economist*, Andrew was autonomous and virtually life-tenured.

Naturally I ignored Andrew's advice as self-serving and in an area where he was no expert. Having just disentangled myself from a very complicated but amicable partnership at Ravelston, I was not about to reassociate with Hartwell and his fissiparous family, especially Nicholas, who was becoming a public nuisance.

I similarly ignored Andrew's poor wails of appeal for me to come to London during November or December. (This didn't stop him from telling the *Telegraph*'s historian, Duff Hart-Davis, that he had advised this course. In fact, he beseeched my presence before the fall of the *ancien régime*, but wisely counselled absence while the demanning arrangements were being negotiated in 1986.)

I arrived in London on the evening Concorde the night before the October meeting and met at the Inn on the Park with Andrew, Dan Colson, and Frank Rogers, who would be attending his first *Telegraph* directors' meeting the following day. Frank had come from chairing a Press Association dinner for the head of the Trades Union Congress. He warned that in his experience of Fleet Street dynasties, which was considerable, their tenacity was Homeric. Andrew added that while we discussed the future of the *Daily Telegraph* "Lord Hartwell is sleeping soundly beside a coal fire."

I awakened early the next morning, and, as I was in the final approaches to conversion to Roman Catholicism, I walked purposefully over to Cardinal Newman's London church, the magnificent Brompton Oratory. (He may never actually have been in the existing church, though he was eulogized in it.) At the unecclesiastical hour of 7:00 a.m. there were only four other communicants. I would never commit the profanation of invoking His assistance in merely commercial matters and was thinking appropriately pious thoughts as I knelt before the priest and he placed the host on my tongue (which I technically had no right to receive). My stupefaction was considerable, then, when the elderly nun next to me whispered, "Good luck with the *Telegraph*. We all read it."

David Montagu and I met with Hartwell at mid-morning. David outlined the gravity of Coopers & Lybrand's revelations and we urged on him the necessity of steadying the banks' nerves (often a difficult assignment even for someone more vigorous and numerate than Hartwell), by naming a new managing director to replace the retiring H.M. Stephen. David had already thought of Andrew Knight and put his name forward on behalf of both of us. Hartwell agreed, almost without comment.

The banking group, headed by National Westminster, but including Security Pacific and Hongkong and Shanghai Banking Corporation, asked to see me over a sandwich lunch. I did my best to reconcile loyalty to my chairman with reasonably candid answers but was emphatic in answering a hypothetical question that new buyers could be found to keep the banks whole if it came to that. I responded more non-committally when asked if I might head such a group. Agility was already required to bridge Hartwell's dynastic tenacity and the mounting perplexity of the lenders. The danger of catastrophically dropping the great and venerable newspaper in passage between grasping pairs of hands was growing every day.

Frank took his place at the afternoon directors' meeting, graciously introduced by Lord Hartwell. David Montagu outlined the perilous conditions in which the poor old company was gasping. (We met in a heavily panelled room, with a 1939 map of the world on one wall and a miniature statue of Salisbury on the mantelpiece.) Dan Colson and Rupert Hambro attended by invitation.

H.M. Stephen proposed to dismiss up to seventeen doormen and effect various other similar economies and asked for a supporting resolution. Frank, in what was to prove the first of many apposite interventions as a *Telegraph* director, after pausing for comment from other directors, of which there was none, said, "This is the first time in my experience that a company managing director has asked for a resolution authorizing him to do his job." I went directly from Fleet Street to Heathrow after a few jocularities with David Montagu and telephoned Andrew Knight from the Concorde lounge: "Your hour of destiny has struck. Hartwell will call you tomorrow." He did, but Hartwell would prove reluctant and indecisive, until events forced his hand.

In the ensuing weeks, Nicholas Berry importuned almost every monied person of his acquaintance anywhere in the world to buy into the *Telegraph* and represented our agreement as of no legal value. Montagu finally asked Rawlinson to read the agreement and give his opinion, as Colson and I were satisfied it was airtight. One of Britain's most distinguished lawyers, Lord Rawlinson read it overnight and reported the next morning that Dan Colson's drafting was "inviolable, unassailable, and bulletproof."

Nicholas would not desist. Lord Hanson, one of Britain's most talented and powerful industrialists, phoned Evelyn Rothschild from the House of Lords and said that he was "ready, willing, and able to buy the *Daily Telegraph*," and was on his way to N.M. Rothschild's office. When he arrived, without taking off his coat or even sitting down, he read our agreement with Hartwell, said, "It seems we have nothing to discuss," and went to another part of the Rothschild offices to talk with other partners about an acquisition in an unrelated industry.

The Australian raider, Robert Holmes à Court, called me in Toronto one day to announce he was considering a competing bid. I politely told him to be my guest and offered to send him a copy of our agreement. With the speed of an impala, he jovially determined not to make a competing offer. We maintained an intermittent but cordial relationship up to his untimely death. Fairfax, the Australian newspaper group, was another suitor, briefly. Hartwell's preference for almost anyone but me, despite my unfailing courtesy to him ("magnanimity," his brother, Viscount Camrose called it), was becoming tiresome.

Nicholas Berry planted some rather nasty stories in the London press. Some of them were condescending to Canada generally and actually stirred up a small backlash in my favour in the Canadian media, which had been highly critical for the last two or three years. (Even Peter Newman, momentarily inconsolable at the break-up of Dominion Stores, defected noisily, but briefly.) John Ralston Saul, Adrienne Clarkson's companion, with whom I had always had rather good relations, wrote an extremely hostile piece in the *Spectator*. I decided that, lest the contagion grow to serious infection, a robust reply was called for, despite Andrew Knight's fear that I would "alienate the entire British aristocracy and intelligentsia." He wanted to be the sole spokesman for the administration-in-waiting, and later, in office.

I produced a comprehensive and caustic refutation, concluding that he "should confine himself to subjects better suited than this one was to his peevish, puerile, sniggering . . . talents." The "aristocracy and intelligentsia" appeared to enjoy it. Saul's response a few weeks later was as damp a squib as Ramsay Cook's in similar circumstances nine years before and was written, as *Punch* magazine used to put it in Victorian times, "in a voice grown mighty small." Newman, whom Saul had quoted, I dealt with, without naming him, as "an unrequited Canadian Establishment groupie," though as our corporate strategy was seen to succeed, he resumed his positive attention to me and our good relations were quickly restored. Press attention was more careful and balanced thereafter and has been generally benign in London ever since.

The lenders formally advised Hartwell of the requirement for an equity infusion. Rothschilds (N.M. Rothschild, acting for the *Telegraph* and the Berrys, as they had when they recruited me) entered into negotiations with Dan Colson on the amount and pricing of the rights issue we would be prepared to underwrite. Evelyn was in a delicate position. His firm was not insusceptible to serious criticism over the *Daily Telegraph's* prospectus earlier in the year. Montagu dramatically claimed that it had offered me "the Berry family's balls on a silver salver." Evelyn was advising the Berrys and the *Telegraph* that the best interests of both would be served by a deal with us, correct advice, as subsequent events have shown, but a difficult position to adopt serenely at the time.

Intense meetings with lenders and merchant bankers were almost continuous. In one such session, Michael Richardson, one of Rothschild's leading deal makers, noted that it was snowing outside. Dan Colson instantly added, "It will be snowing writs if we don't agree this price, Michael." At one point, Richardson called me and suggested that I was "moving the goal posts" by insisting on control. "The goal posts are moving faster than the players," I replied. "They are a blur. I'm the only party whose position hasn't changed. I didn't write that fictitious prospectus. You did." I heard no more of moving goal posts.

Nicholas Berry had become a pestilential irritation to us and erupted into many of the meetings, accusing Colson of being "a colonial mouthpiece" and using other terms of endearment. At one point, he shouted that he would not serve as a director of a company controlled by "that predator" (me), and Colson assured him that, indeed, he would not have the opportunity to do so for longer than the statutes required for us to call a shareholders' meeting and fire undesirable directors. Finally, after denouncing his own father as mentally incompetent, Nicholas was almost physically ejected from one meeting at Rothschilds, leaving shouting and swearing. His disappointment was understandable, but his behaviour was difficult to excuse.

The November *Telegraph* directors' meeting, at which I was not present, was tragicomic. Hartwell fainted, gasping, gurgling, and foaming, and many of the directors feared he was taking a coronary. Nicholas was mercifully out of the room, having made his churlish exit prematurely, but Hartwell's other son, Adrian (a fine, if idiosyncratic, man with whom I have had an uninterruptedly cordial relationship), shouted, "Daddy! Daddy!" in the English manner down the table as others called for an ambulance. When paramedics arrived, Hartwell's loyal secretary, faithful to what might have seemed the last, to the dignity of the *Telegraph* and its beleaguered chairman, defiantly announced, "I will not allow just anyone to lay hands on Lord Hartwell!" (It was only a fainting spell.) It had become surrealistic, as tenacious resistance to the inevitable eventually always does, the surest sign that the end-game was finally afoot. Evelyn de Rothschild regularly visited Hartwell, who understandably felt that the fabled House of Rothschild had not served him too distinguishedly.

Although his daily waffling and fishtailing, reported to me by Rothschild and Montagu and others, was irksome, especially after he had received the dervish-like visits of his younger son, it was hard not to sympathize with Hartwell. He had cared passionately about his newspapers, maintained their editorial integrity zealously, bravely, if impetuously, commissioned splendid new plants, and had toiled assiduously through mounting crises. He had endured widowhood, worsening deafness, the loneliness of the elderly, deepening financial problems, the bilious antics of Nicholas, who had thrown down the filial mask and violently accused his father of mismanagement (Nicholas, whose principal qualification for directing the *Daily Telegraph* seemed to me to have been surviving childbirth), and the ridicule of the irreverent — "Lord Fartwell," *Private Eye* invariably called him.

Personally he is sometimes mean and generally unrepentant, but neither unconscientious nor contemptible. I have rarely heard Lord Hartwell say anything positive about anybody. ("Churchill was a sponger," Mountbatten "bogus," and none of his fellow newspaper proprietors found any favour at all.) He is one of the ultimate misanthropes of my experience, unlike his dapper and affable brother, Lord Camrose, but he is neither a bad man nor inaccessible to sympathy, though affection is somewhat more problematical. Certainly, I would do what I could to protect the alluvium of his dignity. Camrose and his flamboyant wife Joan, formerly married to Lowell Guinness and to the Ali Khan, and mother of the present Aga Khan, live in considerable luxury at Hackwood Park, near Basingstoke. The first time I was there, I said to Andrew Knight as we left that "Joan is an energetic and dynamic person." Andrew, who is rarely given to such drolleries, responded pensively: "Energetic, yes; dynamic, yes, but as mother of God she's a hard sell."

By the end of November, the lenders were threatening to call in the receivers, and the auditors had advised Montagu the company was on the verge of technical insolvency, which would have to be revealed. Hartwell had twice advanced over a million pounds of his family's money under tight and insolent ultimata from junior echelon bankers. David Montagu had performed prodigies, going over the heads of the snotty little bank functionaries, even pretending at one heavily attended meeting to be in telephone conversation with the governor of the Bank of England, when he was really talking to a clerk.

"Yes, governor, you have made it clear that it would be a national shame and a tragedy if these great titles failed because of the impatience and incompetence of a few bankers," he po-facedly intoned to an astonished secretary at the other end of the line. Unfortunately the principal banker, an unsubtle American from Security Pacific, knew and cared nothing about British protocol and rightly asked if the "governor of the central bank is going to guarantee my loans." David's bandying about of the names of the good and the great was artful but ineffectual in this case.

By then, I had accomplished my due diligence: a one-page summary from Colson on changes to British labour laws and enforcement under Thatcher, and an emissary to Rupert Murdoch, Marietta Tree, gamely asked him what he proposed to do with his five-year-old unoccupied printing plant at Wapping. Rupert declined to be precise but said he wouldn't put up with this much longer. "I'm going to take Draconian measures." That was reassuring enough and I didn't realize that Murdoch would prove an over-achiever and fire his entire production work force of 5,500 without bothering to pay them any severance as he did so.

On December 6 agreement was reached. Thirty million pounds would be injected, underwritten by Hollinger. (Ravelston, unfortunately, had insufficient means for this phase. I was roundly criticized by a few analysts for laying off my own hobby horses on Hollinger, but that charge was little remembered a couple of years later when the financial harvest came in.) The share price would be down to 50p, from £1.40 six months before, assuring Hollinger and Ravelston of at least 50.1 per cent even if all existing institutions subscribed. Nicholas Berry resigned, depriving me of the pleasure of throwing him out. Hartwell would stay indefinitely as chairman and his family could have four directors, H.M. Stephen replacing Nicholas while Camrose and Adrian Berry continued.

Andrew Knight's appointment as chief executive was also announced. Hours before the announcement, he held us to ransom so inflexibly that Dan Colson wanted to send him packing. Andrew explained to me that he was being asked to leave "a cozy bath for a very cold one," and so he asked for (i.e., demanded) an option on 5 per cent of the *Telegraph*'s equity at £1 per share. I agreed to most of his terms because I believed Andrew would quieten the lenders with his articulateness and self-confidence and the prestige he had earned at the *Economist*, while fronting my ownership opposite the various London establishments. And I believed he would identify the new executives that almost every key position required. A hecatomb was urgently needed throughout the upper reaches of the *Telegraph* gerontocracy.

I wasn't so offended by his avarice. He had identified the prospect and if it succeeded, we would have more than ten times as many shares as he would, and a 100 per cent capital gain on his option shares.

Andrew's impenetrable arrogance, however, was irritating. Just before the antics of Nicholas Berry became entirely frenzied, Andrew assured me that Nicholas "admired" him. He was flustered when I replied, "So do we all, Andrew, but can you translate that well-founded admiration into civilized behaviour by Nicholas?" When Dan Colson finally and reluctantly gave way to Andrew's demands, and only because I asked him to as I didn't think we could afford at this point to launch a search for a new chief executive, Andrew phoned Evelyn de Rothschild in his role as chairman of the *Economist* to advise him formally. "This is a sad day for the *Economist*," Andrew modestly averred. When he left us nearly four years later, Andrew wrote that the press release should say, *inter alia*: "Mr. Knight is the greatest thing since sliced bread."

Those statements would have attracted sufficient dissent that Andrew's reluctance to leave such judgements to others was understandable. But in between those two clangorous Andrewisms, we had many more good days than "sad" ones and would not have been there at all but for him. This was the greatest gamble I had taken, but so unambiguous was my intuition on the subject that I little worried about it as I went to Palm Beach on Boxing Day 1985. This was fortunate as 1986 would shortly be freighted with other concerns.

CHAPTER TEN

A TRANS-ATLANTIC NEWSPAPER COMPANY
1986–1989

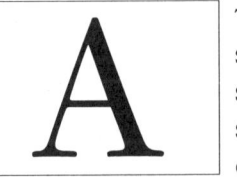T THE MOMENT WHEN THE EIGHT-YEAR struggle for real proprietorship of assets with some prospect for growth and which we had some aptitude to manage was on the verge of completion, yet another crisis developed. Buying out most of Ravelston, despite the special Argcen dividend, led to a peak debt level of $154 million in that company at a time when Hollinger's cash-raising abilities depended on more asset dispositions, especially of the old rump of Dominion Stores. The utility of the unsonorous name of Argcen having been exhausted, Hollinger re-emerged after the special dividend. The most interesting of these realizations, it was hoped, would be the surplus in the Dominion Stores' pension plan, which we expected would come in at about $75 million.

That surplus had accumulated over seven or eight years, and subsequent close analysis revealed that a small share of the surplus came from lay-offs of employees of slight seniority whose company pension contributions had not vested. Inflation was helpful, but only because of the instructions given by the pension committee, chaired by Dick Chant, to the pension managers, on liquidity levels. Dick had an uncanny intuition on the course of interest rates, and this, more than anything else, led to huge accretions of surplus. The shareholders were responsible for any shortfall in pension benefit and the shareholders' representatives were the creators of the surplus. All precedent and legal advice uniformly told us that the surplus was rightfully available to the shareholders despite some public relations perception problems in the circumstances of Dominion Stores' wind-down. It was obviously not going to be universally popular to remove pension surplus while the company was effectively being liquidated.

This realization did not prepare me for the earthquake that ensued after the Pension Commission of Ontario routinely authorized a withdrawal of almost $60 million of pension surplus. The union representing the present and former Dominion employees affected (and representing also, according to the Ontario Labour Relations Board, the employees of the franchised Mr. Grocer stores whom the union claimed had no right to their jobs) litigated against the Pension Commission itself, claiming it had failed to give plan members the required notice of withdrawal.

While this litigation, which counsel did not take seriously at first as we assumed the Pension Commission knew what it was doing, started into the courts, the credit squeeze at Hollinger and Ravelston became steadily more acute, aggravated by belligerent attitudes in secondary echelons of the CIBC credit structure, of which I was blissfully unaware for some weeks. I had naïvely assumed that fifteen years of profitable lending and ten years as a director with that bank and excellent personal relations with four consecutive chairmen provided some fire wall against sudden inflammation.

I had met with Henry Kissinger when passing through New York in December and he had told me that in recent contacts with Saudi leaders, including the king, he had been advised that the world oil price would decline from the mid-twenties to under ten dollars a barrel. It seemed clear enough that supply was outstripping demand and that a decline in the world oil price, perhaps a fairly sharp one, was inevitable. I had thought Norcen could endure that without too much effect on its performance, so skilful was Ed Battle's management.

A decline on the scale Kissinger was forecasting was less easily assimilable, and, as our status as a borrower came under more intense scrutiny, as we took over the *Daily Telegraph* and the Los Angeles cable network that Allan Slaight put to us, it became necessary to contemplate parting with Norcen. As the *Daily Telegraph* discussions entered their most hectic phase, I had several sessions with the CIBC chairman, Don Fullerton, to ensure that the money was available for the London and Los Angeles purchases, and also with Trevor Eyton, Jack Cockwell, and other Brascan figures about a sale to them of our Norcen shares. These discussions, after the briefest respite at New Year, resumed in January, and I was hoping to complete them before the expected oil price collapse.

At the end of January 1986, I suffered a sudden recurrence of acute back pains from a ruptured disc that sent severe shooting pains down my legs and throughout my back and chest. It was impossible even to sit up without pain so intense that I fainted after a few seconds, and I continued negotiations with Trevor Eyton and Jack Cockwell in my room in the Wellesley Hospital where they visited me twice, bringing helpful books on backaches, as the oil price started to slip seriously. We reached an agreement that was ratified by the Hollinger directors in early February, with a suspensive reinvestment obligation to protect the buyers somewhat from too steep or durable an oil price decline. Hees International, the financial colossus Jack Cockwell had created from George Hees's old venetian blind company, was the buyer.

The consideration was a little over $300 million, of which only about $130 million was in cash, being the adjusted cost base for tax purposes of our original Labrador shares, for which our Norcen shares were exchanged in the complex transaction of 1983. We took the balance in Hees shares at an issued price of $27, which we sold a few months later at almost $35 per share, adding almost $50 million to our real proceeds of sale, which we sheltered from tax with Dominion Stores' tax loss.

We balanced the reinvestment clause by a cross-reinvestment obligation of Hees in Hollinger, with an option for Ravelston to buy those shares. Thus, Hollinger invested $25 million in the company that bought our Norcen shares; that money was immediately reinvested in Hollinger preferred shares convertible into commons at $8. Ravelston bought this instrument with a fixed-rate loan costing only slightly more than the dividends on the shares purchased and enjoyed an early unrealized capital gain of nearly 100 per cent on it.

It was a successful but difficult exit from a splendid company in an industry whose pricing was beyond private-sector influence and accurate prediction. I became a Brascan and a Hees director and was able to appreciate Jack Cockwell's great financial virtuosity. At one point in a difficult period in 1991, marvelling at Jack's ingenuity in finding a Brascan profit to report from a subsidiary's capital gain, I handed my neighbour at a Brascan director's meeting (Alf Powis), the admiring note: "We're a manufacturing company. We manufacture profits!"

I was still hobbling from back problems when I was laid low by bronchitis. Flat on my back at home, my bedroom reduced to a fantastic scene of swirling steam from several vapourizers, I was particularly lacking in robustness when the Ontario Provincial Court ordered us to repay into court the $60 million in surplus we had legally withdrawn from the Dominion Stores' plan. The judge initially seized on the case of Robert F. Reid.

Reid went through a little charade of offering to recuse — because we had both briefly been members of the Toronto Commanderie de Bordeaux — before legitimizing the union claim against pension surplus distribution because the Pension Commission of Ontario had not required an adequate prior consultation with the plan members. He and other first instance judges wallowed in their fleeting moments of press attention and achieved prodigies of populist posturing and solicitude. The initial judgements were unreasoned, reflexive, and polemical, including the vapid requirement of an undistinguished journeyman judge, Hollingworth, that the entire surplus withdrawn be returned at once, as if $60 million were a mere bagatelle. These judgements were entirely procedural and had nothing to do with the issue of ultimate ownership.

The leader of the Ontario NDP, Bob Rae, in a burst of defamatory demagogy that would resonate and ramify for some years, swaddled himself in his parliamentary immunity and accused me, in effect, of theft, graciously describing me as the "symbol of bloated capitalism at its worst." I replied in the *Sun* the next day, saying in my reedy and congested voice that Rae, on his way to becoming "a game-ending trivia question" was "the symbol of swinish socialist demagogy at its worst." In mere terms of slinging invective, I had, as I usually do, broken at least even, but Rae's privileged slander caused public relations problems that would not recede from one week to the next.

One of my comments to the *Sun* was that the NDP had been kept alive only by the former Davis government to split the opposition and that Davis's advisers, Eddie Goodman and Hugh Segal, had "breathed fetid air into the limp sail" of the NDP. I promptly received, from a very demonstrative bailiff, what purported to be a writ from Eddie Goodman alleging defamation in the implicit charge against him of having "fetid breath." It was a welcome humorous interlude and I returned a mock defence citing all sorts of imaginary cases ("*Listerine v. Encyclopedia Britannica*, British Statutory Reports [BSR] 1947," etc.).

Conditions escalated further in the next couple of days, when I pointed out to the *Globe and Mail* that although "nobody [felt] very good" about lay-offs at Dominion and that, regrettably, "sadness [had] come to many homes," we were discussing a work force a minority of whose members had, since time immemorial, stolen more each year than the profit attributable to the shareholders. This stirred the pot furiously as the entire Ontario wimpocracy charged to the ramparts of defence of the province's wronged working class. There was a deafening chorus of scandalized self-righteousness, which I ignored, not only because it was almost entirely hypocrisy and grandstanding by the faddish groupies to Ontario's "yuppie-ridden lumpen proletariat" (as I described them at the time in the *ROB Magazine*) but also because my voice and strength failed completely.

The Toronto business community zipped itself into its usual cocoon of mute pusillanimity. When telephoned by the press, the senior executives of the major food retailers, although advising me privately that their experience of employee theft was identical to ours, expressed scepticism about my remarks on the subject. Though we were fighting a battle for virtually every company in the province that had a successfully managed pension plan, I received not one word of public or private encouragement in the litigation we were defending on the issue. As the infamous drum-head kangaroo court of the Ontario Labour Relations Board decreed that a union with no voluntary adherents among people that it claimed had no right to their jobs in fact represented them, Ontario's employers maintained a pristine silence.

I never laboured under any illusions that I was a popular favourite with the staid, conformist, and rather inhibited closed society of Toronto's senior business community. That many of them regarded me as opinionated, bumptious, and, in executive terms, at best unproven, was neither surprising nor necessarily entirely unjust, but some of the issues in which I was then involved affected many of them at least as materially as they did me. However consolable they might be at my discomfort, their silent spectatorship did not evidence a very vigorous sense of self-preservation.

Five years later, after I had financially evacuated the province and Bob Rae had become premier on a platform of labour union usurpation of the commanding heights of the private sector and confiscatory taxation, I did not reciprocate the earlier complacent *schadenfreude* of my industrial peers. My inveighings against Rae's official kleptocracy achieved wide approbation, but even then, some dissent from the most determined appeasers.

When I was physically prostrate and severely enfeebled, my wife gave birth to our third child, James, and the Canadian Imperial Bank of Commerce, through a rather excitable credit officer, consummated a long-escalating dispute with David Radler and called one of our key Dominion loans. David himself abruptly resigned as president of Dominion Stores and, in accord with our understanding, called Peter White back from Brian Mulroney's office to take his place. David and I (when my health recovered) would devote ourselves entirely to liquidating non-core assets and cleaning the financial house. In mid-February 1986, with political and media obloquy cascading down upon me, with respiration laborious and painful and conversation almost impossible, I watched, not undismayed, as our bank withdrew in one direction, calling for a $40-million loan repayment, while the courts were demanding the restoration, on the other hand, of $60 million.

At the very moment when my oldest associates and I had become real proprietors of what was largely a newspaper company, our solvency was under severe pressure and I was completely immobilized. Debt levels were excessive and asset values were uncertain, as our primary lender, through junior officials, analogous to those in Britain who had hounded Hartwell so relentlessly, had taken to telephoning me in my sick bed and agitating for a fire sale of Hollinger.

I croakingly called Don Fullerton, made an appointment with him, and as soon as I was strong enough (about a week later) was conveyed to his office to deliver a simple message: I pointed out that if the CIBC's loan portfolio were as sceptically valued as Hollinger's assets, the bank would have no shareholder's equity; if the lender thought the Hollinger loans were in any sense uncertain, then Hollinger's management must remove that doubt, but the bank would have to give that management a fair chance to put matters right. I handed over a summary of drastic debt-reduction measures I planned. Don Fullerton did not need my gentle reminder of the Bank Act's requirement that directors act in the best interests of their bank and instantly assured me that I would have the opportunity to clean up the company. My physical and our financial recoveries began at once and accelerated more or less steadily, but it was one of the most nerve-racking periods I have known.

Paul Desmarais came to see me at home at one of the lowest points and offered words of encouragement. Less helpful were his immediate indiscretions, which led a wide swath of prominent people, including Brian Mulroney, to the unhelpful conclusion that I was on the verge of bankruptcy. Fortunately, the financial press got no hint of it.

I was self-reproachful rather than self-pitying that, after eight years of strenuous effort, our fortunes were so parlous. Logically, I was sure that the strategy had been correct, and whatever tactical errors I had committed they did not, in sum, vitiate our strategic progress. Logic is of questionable utility in the face of clamouring lenders and hostile courts, yet my morale did not flag, and David Radler, Peter White, Dick Chant, our urbane and indefatigable legal vice president, Charlie Cowan, and I developed an intrepid spirit of defiance. Everyone did his part.

David, quickly recovering his equilibrium after his harrowing days as operating head of Dominion Stores, performed brilliantly. He explicitly threatened shopping centre owners who wouldn't release us from our covenant to operate with a reasonable penalty with the bankruptcy of the lessee and in a couple of cases had employees put rotting vegetables out in front of the stores to reduce the general ambiance of the shopping centres and to encourage a greater desire by the landlords to see us off as tenants. Virtually all the landlords came around fairly quickly. Head-leases, which had been accorded no book value, he hastily reassessed and bargained some away, always for undreamed-of prices.

Dick Chant disposed advantageously of the security business I had bought into when Roy McMurtry's persecutions in 1982 and 1983 made me somewhat mistrustful of the police. He also got rid of our Challenger jet, of which Bud McDougald had been inordinately proud (though he didn't live long enough to ride in it) for more than any of us thought it was worth. Some months later, when our prosperity was returning, the spread of our business required an aircraft, and Jack Cockwell's aversion to them caused Norcen's G2 (Grumman Gulfstream, a very comfortable and reliable aircraft) to be offered as shares of the single-purpose company, Bud's old Sugra Ltd. (Argus spelled backwards), Dick Chant picked this up on a very favourable basis also.

Peter White was unflagging and imperturbable at the melting iceberg of Dominion Stores. Every week we closed more stores, converting them into Mr. Grocer franchised stores. We reasoned that it was the best method of bringing the union to a reasonable compromise before the implacably one-sided Labour Relations Board, which required nine months to adjudicate a single store, could impose itself oppressively on us. My hope was that, as our old union was being subsumed into A & P's union, and the continuing Dominion workers were being relentlessly laid off as the stores were closed or franchised, the union leaders, to preserve their own nepotistic sinecures as much as their members' jobs, would be disposed to compromise and that the compromise could be extended to the pension surplus question as well.

To this end, I entered into negotiations with Dick Currie, the exceptionally able operating head of the Weston-Loblaw group, and at the end of the summer of 1986, he thought that a deal was at hand. My hope was that the prospect of the end of combat and the appearance of a durable employer would induce the union to be generally amenable to settlement of all issues. The details and approvals continued through the autumn and into the New Year, but the old Dominion union, whose rapacity and cynicism had so effectively complemented the failings of the management to ruin the company, to avoid complete extinction (i.e., the extinction of the income and perquisites of the union leaders) agreed to accept the franchised store workers, to purport to represent them. And we, to complete the charade, discounted our sale price to Weston's of our wholesale business to allow for paying three years of union membership fees for the employees.

I have my doubts about the ultimate destination of this Danegeld, but we certainly owed it to the replacement workers not to ask them to pay directly to the shiftless union they had contributed so importantly to bring to heel.

The pension surplus case would be settled in equal shares between the shareholders and plan members. Given the political climate that obtained at the time, this was a fair reconciliation of the conflicting interests at play. It must be said that the RWDSU did, for once, achieve something for its members. As the surplus continued to grow, we received about three-quarters of what we had originally sought and were happy enough to set up a benefit fund for former workers to ease their path to more solid employment than the stricken, pillaged Dominion Stores had proved to be. The proceeds from the wholesale business sold to Weston and the pension surplus recovery netted us another $80 million.

One element of the recovery plan we formulated was to complete the assembling of a highly professional team at 10 Toronto Street. Dick Chant made a giant step in this direction when he recruited Charlie Cowan, who had been the managing partner of P.C. Finlay's law firm to be legal vice president and secretary of Hollinger. The financial vice president, Wendell White, was perfectly adequate at keeping the books and sending royalty invoices to Cleveland, but he tended to become flustered and to stammer or giggle when questioned by bankers. He was about to retire, and I invited my long-time tax adviser, Jack Boultbee, who was head of tax at Coopers & Lybrand, to take the job.

I made no secret of the difficulties Hollinger was facing, but believed Jack Boultbee, who was a daring gambler, sometimes literally betting on his poker hand without picking up his cards, would not be intimidated by them. An aggressive tax planner, he was as bold and imaginative an accountant as I had ever met and was introduced to me by Igor Kaplan, a nostalgic factor of no real relevance, but psychologically a reassurance of continuity. He did accept and started in May, and his appointment was doubtless one of the smartest moves I have made at Hollinger. He achieved wonders in lender and shareholder relations and immediately gave Hollinger's accounts an imaginative attention. He has proved inexhaustibly resourceful.

Through 1986, if a military inspiration were required for our company, it was a defensive war on interior lines, such as Frederick the Great's in the latter phase of the Seven Years War, Napoleon crossing the Berezina in 1812 in the face of three Russian armies on both banks of the river, with a combined strength triple his own, or, more upliftingly, the Battle of Britain. Like the squadrons of RAF fighter command, the proceeds of the Norcen sale were zealously guarded and deployed, at least rhetorically, to pacify lenders and, where necessary, buyers, concerned about our continuity. (It was sometimes difficult to separate these from Dominion Stores landlords, whom David had been threatening with the spectre of our default, at Dominion, not Hollinger, if they were too greedy in stipulating terms for our lease withdrawals.)

At the lowest point, in early February, I had actually listened to overtures from Don Cormie, who wanted a respectable corporate cover for his investment activities, which crashed spectacularly a couple of years later. Our position was at one point so precarious that I feared that if our partner in the little security business we owned put his stock to us, as he had a right to do, the whole structure could come down. It required a Ciceronian act of persuasion for me to get the Bank of Commerce to honour my promissory note in favour of my brother, finishing my purchase of his Ravelston shares. I had to mortgage my Palm Beach house to the CIBC for a few months just to pay my debts to next of kin. (I purchased the house in 1980 from a profit in gold trading, a commodity that rises in response to acute political uncertainty of the kind generated by the Carter administration.) I even discussed with Doug Creighton a possible sale to the *Toronto Sun* of part of our *Daily Telegraph* shareholding, so severe was the pressure from lenders. But the timing wasn't convenient for Doug, and our circumstances did not continue to be so strained as to require consideration of such desperate measures for more than a few weeks. It was a harrowing time, but keeping calm and purposeful was an objective and an achievement each day. The horizon narrowed to maintaining progress toward the distant prospect of prosperity, avoidance of indiscretion and concentration on important values, like health, family, friends. I took some comfort from the fact that what was at stake was solvency, not, as in the spurious Norcen investigation, one's ethics and respect for the law. There were, however, many moments of anxiety and self-criticism. Like many unpleasant episodes it was more usefully formative after the fact than while being endured.

Though I made no interventions about it, some of the instigators of this confrontation at the CIBC found it a distinct hindrance to their future career progress. Had it not been for my access to senior bank executives, these fretful and badgering functionaries, such as those who abruptly told me to "sell Hollinger" in February 1986, would have severely destabilized a fundamentally sound account.

By spring, the crisis was passing; by autumn, it was over. It had been a humbling but usefully formative experience. Dominion's war to the death with the Retail, Wholesale and Department Store Union had resulted in the death of both, a fate they both deserved as mismanaged, anachronistic, and useless organizations. The only sadness attaches to the fate of the many innocent and unsuspecting victims. The shareholders large and small, at least, were spared, and most of the employees, the more deserving ones if the managers carried out instructions for once, were retained by successor employers.

Almost all large companies that have been in business for fifty years or more accumulate a lot of hidden value in unrecognized assets. As the program of debt reduction I wheezingly outlined to Don Fullerton in February was implemented, lender confidence returned. The pressure was somewhat alleviated at Ravelston and Argus by our reluctant sale to Hollinger of the celebrated building at 10 Toronto Street (whose front doors Peter Newman used to illustrate the endpapers of his books on the Canadian Establishment), and of Ravelston's initial shareholding in the *Daily Telegraph*. (The greatest financial pressure was at Ravelston and Argus Corporation. The threat to Hollinger was more distant pension liability and vulnerability to Labour Relations Board awards before value could be added to the *Daily Telegraph*.)

Both were transferred at what shortly proved to be knock-down prices, a bonanza to the minority public shareholders but a necessary relief for the controlling shareholder. Among the many minor irritations of the era were the frequent calls I got, some from rash real estate speculators, offering to buy our building. It was clearly believed by many that we were on our way right out of business. I also sold a million Hollinger shares to the CN Pension fund. The astute head of that institution, Tullio Cedraschi, like Stephen Jarislowsky, saw the potential of the *Daily Telegraph* almost as soon as I did.

The steady sale at generous prices of the flotsam and jetsam of Dominion Stores and the growing realization of the potential value of the *Daily Telegraph* started the Hollinger stock on a long upward move. It tripled from where we bought out the original Ravelston partners in 1985 within two years. (Even after the October 1987 crash, it settled at 80 to 85 per cent of its high.) It was an extraordinary roller-coaster year, 1986, in which the opening months were spent in a desperate struggle for financial survival and the last months included ten days in each of which my own ostensible value of investment increased by over $5 million dollars, almost unmitigated by any loss days.

It was one of the most tumultuous years in the 132-year history of the London *Daily Telegraph*. While the statutory period required to canvass shareholders for a rights issue was elapsing, Rupert Murdoch's production employees at the *Times, Sunday Times, Sun,* and *News of the World* were advised that they were expected to report to work at Murdoch's relatively new and hitherto unoccupied East London printing plant. In the time-honoured Fleet Street manner, oblivious to the implications of Mrs. Thatcher's revolution, the unions downed tools and struck, illegally. In accord with the law, Rupert summarily fired all those who persisted in their work stoppage for forty-eight hours. So over-confident were the old Fleet Street production unions that they had no idea that Murdoch had trained an entire alternative work force, partly composed of Australians and Americans, and had qualified them as members of the Electricians' Union.

Margaret Thatcher passionately believed that Britain had to be competitive and this meant disciplining an industrial work force that had long since become addicted to bringing employers to their knees in an almost wholly capricious manner.

Substitute employees arrived for work in buses whose windows were protected by steel mesh, and mobs of hired toughs routinely attacked the gates of Rupert's building with such violence that literally hundreds of policemen were injured in the course of the violence, which erupted several times a week, with the largest riots on Saturday evening, over a period of a couple of months.

The ancient recourse to secondary boycotting, which was also illegal, was relentlessly attacked by the attorney general, and finally the treasury of the principally aggrieved union, the Society of Graphic and Allied Trades (SOGAT), was impounded. In response to one parliamentary question about the Home Office's defence of the Wapping installations, Mrs. Thatcher declared that if "there are 10,000 rioters, there will be 10,001 policemen." The law would be upheld and mob rule would not be tolerated. It was a stark and refreshing contrast to the mealy-mouthed truckling to organized labour engaged in even by our courts in Ontario.

Despite the immense furore, it was obvious after the first couple of days, when Rupert successfully got his newspapers out, that he would win. The implications for us, when we took effective operational control, could not fail to be positive.

Rupert Murdoch is a man of tremendous courage, stamina, and intelligence. He has proved an amiable acquaintance and reliable co-contractant, and his services to the newspaper publishing industry at Wapping and elsewhere have been magnificent. Against this, he has a particularly virulent case of the Australian disapproval of the British, and the tenor of his papers, in their reflections on the world and in their internecine politics, tend to be chippy, backbiting, envious, and often unnecessarily obnoxious.

Rupert commands respect for the remarkable progress he has made in less than forty years from two floundering provincial Australian newspapers to his present eminence. The trajectory of his career has been dramatic and has given me much inspiration at times, though his motives have never been particularly clear; neither money nor influence seeming to weigh as heavily as the artistry of corporate building, the agility of buying and selling, the exhilaration of the tight-rope walk over the debt mountain. Whatever, he is a remarkable and an admirable man, who has needlessly denied himself a full measure of greatness by being, almost wherever he has gone, a debunker, especially of the British Establishment (rather beyond what it deserves), a cynic, a man whose newspapering instincts are almost all down-market, in contrast to his very agreeable personality and that of his beautiful and talented wife, Anna.

Andrew Knight's first tasks at the *Telegraph* were to appoint new editors as the incumbents at both the *Daily* and *Sunday Telegraphs* were retiring. His choices were inspired: Max Hastings, for the *Daily*, one of Britain's greatest journalists and an outstanding military historian, and the legendarily colourful columnist Peregrine Worsthorne for the *Sunday*. I had read Hastings's book on Normandy and was aware of his reporting derring-do in the Falklands. I assumed he was at least in his fifties, but he is in fact younger than I. Andrew naturally made his offer conditional on my agreement, and Max came to see me in Toronto in February 1986. I interviewed him hurriedly between receiving relays of Brascan negotiators over the sale of our Norcen shares. Brascan's technique was to send two Hees officials, followed an hour or two later by two more, followed after another hour by Trevor Eyton and shortly afterwards by Jack Cockwell. They really had only me to deal with and I came to feel rather outnumbered, though not overwhelmed. I spoke to Max Hastings in between these waves of interlocutors.

He was tremendously motivated, appeared to know who the readers were. They were not all "dumpy, middle-aged, middle-class bungey dwellers with campers in their driveways on the road to Oxford," he reassured me, more or less in jest. He was strongly determined to resist the continuing desertion of our traditional middle-class readers. I assured him he had my vote, and he returned to London to finish his history of the Korean War, leaving me to cope as best I could with the legions of Jack Cockwell.

The vetting of Perry Worsthorne for the *Sunday Telegraph* was more picturesque. The only day that could be arranged for his visit to Toronto was a Sunday, so he would come to my home. It was meticulously explained that he should ask his taxi to come up the back driveway, on which the gate would be left open. The message was lost or garbled in transmission. Perry arrived in the middle of a howling blizzard, was disembarked at the front gate, and trudged through calf-deep snow for a tenth of a mile. He shambled like a retreating French or German soldier in the Russian winter, past my security guard, who was, as usual, sound asleep at the wheel of his car, and materialized on my doorstep with flowing mane like Lloyd George, carrying an incongruous carpet-bag in case he should have the misfortune of spending the night in Toronto. (Whenever the threats from displaced Dominion Stores employees reached a crescendo of volume and explicitness, "security" was "reinforced.")

I had read his columns in the *Sunday Telegraph* ever since I first went to Britain in the summer of 1963 and well remembered the first of Perry's columns that I read, advocating federal union between Britain and the United States. I was heavily biased in his favour, notwithstanding a rather condescending piece he had just written about me in the *Spectator*, inspired by my demolition of Ralston Saul. I made no reference to this but started by saying, "You should have had this job twenty years ago. What do you propose to do with it?" He replied, "What we're doing now, but I hope to do it better."

I assured him he would have his chance and he asked for aspirin. As I didn't have any, it gave me the greatest pleasure to rouse the security unit from his slumbers and send him out to a pharmacy to buy a headache remedy. That, plus a couple of stiff glasses of whisky and a vigorous discussion of nineteenth century British history cured Perry's headache and he returned to London. My relations with both editors have been uninterruptedly excellent. They have performed splendidly, and Andrew Knight deserves great credit for their appointment.

Illness, childbirth, and financial crisis as well as tactics delayed my first visit to London as proprietor of the *Daily Telegraph* since October 1985, until the following April. On the second day of that London visit I went to Chequers for lunch with Margaret Thatcher.

Mrs. Thatcher was at this point in one of her troughs of public disapprobation. The defence secretary, Michael Heseltine, had quit over the silly issue of whether the helicopter manufacturer, Westland, should be taken over by an American or European company. (Heseltine is boringly anti-American.) The American raid on Libya occurred on the day I arrived in London, and I made one of my rare interventions in the *Daily Telegraph*'s editorial policy by telling Max not to take up a policy that would give aid and comfort to Gaddafi and that would strain the Anglo-American alliance.[†]

[†] Two weeks before I had attended David Rockefeller's dinner in New York for Lord Carrington and when the guest of honour, who was then secretary general of NATO, advised caution at counter-terrorism and added, "We have more experience of these people, unfortunately, than you do," I said that "doing absolutely nothing while Gaddafi's goons blow up airliners, discothèques, and other public places and even shoot London policewomen will lead to unlimited experience with them."

I thought the U.S. action was entirely justifiable, as Gaddafi's subsequent, relatively inoffensive behaviour would suggest. Apart from that, if Britain were to take the position that the U.S. bases in Britain could be used by the Americans only when Britain determined and not when the United States considered its own national interest required it, the alliance was over. Max promised "not to be gratuitously beastly to the Americans" and in fact executed a subtle course correction on the issue. Instant British opinion was as reflected in Max's view.

It was against this backdrop that my visit to Mrs. Thatcher occurred. Charles Powell, her secretary in foreign policy matters and an official of almost superhuman versatility, talent, and discretion, joined the prime minister, Andrew, and me. (Denis was at a football match.) Mrs. Thatcher was determined to fight her way back from a popularity rating in the twenties, but volunteered that she would go if she had no chance of leading the party to victory.

I asked the source of her confidence in the British voter. I eventually suggested that the three greatest British electoral issues of the nineteenth century were repeal of the Corn Laws, in which Peel was correct but his career abruptly ended anyway; the Eastern Question, which Disraeli was right to dismiss as a preposterous issue for a British election, but which brought his magical, shamanistic career to an end all the same; and Irish Home Rule, where Gladstone was almost certainly correct, but which ruined his last three terms as prime minister and effectively finished his career also.

She listened carefully and replied instantly, "The reason for my confidence is that recent former governments didn't clearly appeal to the economic interests of the British voters and I do. There was little obvious difference between Ted Heath and Harold Wilson that would affect the take-home pay of the average person. But there is a huge difference between us and the Labour Party now, and the people will know it. But my ultimate faith in the people comes from knowing their patriotic instincts. I saw it during the Falklands War. They want Britain to be respected in the world. They will have nothing to do with unilateral nuclear disarmament."

Her logic was compelling. Of course, she had to be right about Wilson and Heath. If the people couldn't see where their economic interest was engaged, it was like a cricket game, and whoever looked like a plucky underdog would win. It might offend the puritanical, nonconformist conscience of Britain to be so preoccupied with their own material well-being, but Margaret Thatcher was not Tweedledee or Tweedledum.

After lunch I gently asked if, in the unlikely event we had a work stoppage at the *Daily Telegraph* over introduction of the most modern newspaper technology in our new plants, and had to import production personnel from Canada — I got no farther when she said, "I would sign the work permits myself." Her ideological soundness and decisiveness were as compelling as her logic.

As we were leaving, to enable her to have her weekly audience with the Queen, I said that I thought "the revolution you have wrought in this country is more important by far than the episodes in British history that usually enjoy that description. What were the decapitation of Charles the First or the deposing of James the Second compared to what you have done?" She patted me indulgently on the forearm and said, "That's very good. Do come back, won't you?" I assured her she wouldn't have "to ask twice."

It was a splendid launch to what would prove a fine relationship. She impressed me as having little historical perspective before the time of Churchill but a powerful sense of how to make contemporary Britain prosperous and internationally influential. In pursuit of these goals, neither her courage nor her stamina could be eroded by even the sternest or most enervating challenges. Although fiercely determined and forceful with a tendency to be overbearing, she was not at all arrogant, sensed her own vulnerability almost to the point of exaggerating it — "We can't win without you, you know" — and was unfailingly courteous towards the household staff.

She was extraordinarily purposeful but had no discernible interest in holding her great office for enjoyment of incumbency only, unlike most politicians I have known. She liked power, but only for the perfection of her idea of Britain, a strong, pivotal trans-Atlantic lynchpin with a world vocation. And she was obviously feminine, a very strong woman but not at all a mannish one, almost Elizabethan in her cunning, courage, and in the feasts and famines of her likes and dislikes.

I was confident of her re-election. Whatever the polls showed, she was respected if not liked, even if it was the respect reserved for a fair but firm nanny or girls' school games teacher, who rewards generously but wields the rod on misbehavers like Arthur Scargill (the miners' union leader) with a vigour that would impress habitual readers of page three of the *Daily Telegraph* (which regularly recounts the prosecution of flagellators). She was one of the few famous people I have met who were as impressive in person as their public reputations. She effortlessly won and has always retained my admiration, even when she is uttering extreme or simplistic opinions, as is not infrequently the case. Her instincts are sound and her courage, integrity, and stamina are magnificent, almost peerless.

The task at the *Daily Telegraph* was as daunting as the opportunity was tempting.

It had lost 300,000 circulation in five years. This may be better appreciated from the facts that the *Financial Times*'s entire worldwide sale was then 253,000 and that, in the same period, the circulations of the principal competitors had increased in the case of the *Times* by 172,000, or 55 per cent, and in the case of the *Guardian* by 150,000 or about 40 per cent.

From 1975 to 1986, display advertising had increased only 3.4 per cent, much less than the competitors', and classified advertising had declined by some 520 pages annually, against large gains by the *Times* and *Guardian*.

For complicated historical reasons whose sources historians will long debate, pre-Thatcherite Britain had convinced itself that most of commerce as North Americans would define it was crass, garish, avaricious, and just not done. In the last pre-Thatcher years, top personal and corporate income-tax rates were at 98 per cent and 80 per cent. It was understood to be acceptable for individuals to aspire to a country house, three cars, vacations wherever and whenever they wanted, and the best schools and universities for their children. But the accumulation of wealth was unseemly, unworthy, and contradicted the pre-Thatcher culture and ethic of wealth redistribution that Malcolm Muggeridge memorably identified as one of the principal ingredients of what he called "Britain's great liberal death-wish."

Virtually every night there was a debate with the shop stewards and union chapel fathers over whether the newspapers along Fleet Street would come out at all the next day. Publication was secured only by endless concessions, and no London publisher had abstained from making them, certainly not Rupert Murdoch.

Our immediate tasks at the *Daily Telegraph* were to stop the fall in advertising and circulation, which was then running down at 10,000 per month, almost half of that due to the deaths of subscribers. Second, we had to de-man drastically; third, we had to refinance and replenish the personnel and the asset base; and, finally, we had to reduce printing over-capacity.

The parlous condition of the enterprise required that these goals be undertaken immediately. There was no time for mature contemplations, as the *Daily Telegraph* was losing over £1 million per month and the debt-equity ratio was over four-to-one, when we became the majority shareholder in February 1986.

As soon as the company's means allowed, we added more editorial pages. The new plants greatly enhanced our editorial presentation, and the new editors, building on the solid base of *Telegraph* supporters, gradually rejuvenated the product. The results were that, despite a 40 per cent increase in our cover price and the successful launch of a new competitor, the *Independent*, by former *Telegraph* employees, and despite the death of more than 150,000 of our subscribers in three years, our sale rose by 20,000, while the *Times* lost over 30,000 and the *Guardian* lost 90,000. Thus, the *Independent* drew almost even with the *Times* and the *Guardian* but our lead over our nearest competitor widened from 580,000 to nearly 700,000 daily.

Display advertising rose in three years, as a percentage, by five times the *Times*'s performance and fifteen times the *Guardian*'s. Classified advertising rose by more than 600 pages in three years. In 1990 I went to Brussels to address the *Telegraph*'s advertising sales personnel. Our boat deposited me at the lower Thames dock that the driver assured me was adjacent to the London City Airport. In fact, I discovered as the boat disappeared into the night, the dock was locked off from the land and was adjacent only to the empty parking lot of a brewery. The airport was several miles away. I threw my suitcase over a fence, climbed over it myself, almost spraining an ankle, and walked half a mile to the brewery where I paid a night watchman to drive me to the airport. The rest of the trip to Brussels was uneventful, but I wondered, as I trudged through the gloom towards the brewery, like a peddler with my suitcase in my hand, if

Rupert Murdoch or Vere Rothermere ever suffered such indignities. It made a good opening to my remarks to the salesmen the next day.

The two new printing plants were joint-ventured first with Murdoch's *News International* and then the *Guardian* and *Evening News* in Manchester and with Express Newspapers in London, where, since 1990, we have produced over 2.5 million newspapers per day, making West Ferry Road the second largest newspaper printing plant in the world outside Japan, after Wapping.

None of these improvements would have been possible without de-manning on a historically unprecedented scale. The new technology, direct inputting, would mean that copy boys and linotypists and all who worked with hot metal were eliminated. To some degree, I bought into the *Telegraph* because I was betting in industrial relations matters on Mrs. Thatcher and Mr. Murdoch as much as on myself, and they proved not to be bad people to bet on.

The *Daily Telegraph* had no contributory pension scheme; workers who retired received half a pound per week for each year's service, i.e., £20 per week after forty years' employment. Many employees wished to retire but couldn't afford to. We ignored the national and district offices of the production unions and dealt directly with the forty craft units.

The principal architect of the de-manning strategy was Joe Cooke, a consultant known to and engaged by Frank Rogers. As the workers became more visibly tempted by our tax-free pay-outs of up to £45,000, the union leaders resorted to ludicrously desperate measures, such as demanding secret ballots, a recourse they had vehemently opposed for decades. Our own labour relations personnel were at first sceptical that Joe Cooke's targets could be achieved, but gradually the desire of many employees to retire comfortably and the fear (unjustified though it was in fact) of a Wapping-like slicing of the Gordian knot, brought the craft units over, one by one. Full agreement was reached in the last weeks of 1986. After eight months of arduous day-and-evening, six-day-per-week negotiations, we agreed generous pay-outs to 2,500 of 4,000 printing and publishing personnel, reducing our work force in those areas to under 1,500, despite combined increases of over 100 in the editorial and advertisement-selling departments. Each employee has an individual contract of work, with clear and drastic sanctions for any derogation including the risk of being dismissed with cause and minimal compensation. There has not been any formal union presence in our plants since 1989.

At this point the return to profitability of the *Daily Telegraph* became inevitable. The *Daily Telegraph*'s loss of £15 million in 1986 became a pre-tax profit of £800,000 in 1987, a profit of £29 million in 1988, and £40 to £46 million annually through 1992 despite the onset of Britain's worst recession in decades. With revived earnings, and some windfall gains, the debt-equity ratio went from four to one in 1986 to one to ten in 1992. The protection of the franchise by broadening the base and rejuvenating the profile of the readership would be a prolonged and implacable struggle, yet the position of the *Daily Telegraph* was enviable. It was swiftly restored to its status as one of the world's greatest newspaper franchises and one of Britain's most profitable newspapers.

As the profitability of the *Telegraph* became firmly predictable and then imminent, the long march of Hollinger, Ravelston, my close associates, and myself towards the threshold of real ownership of high quality and profitable assets that we had some aptitude to manage ended suddenly, given the tortuous ineluctable struggles of the previous eight years, and even the last eight months. Henceforth, the struggle would be for orthodox asset and profit growth, pulled forward by the powerful engine of the *Daily Telegraph*.

My family and I spent the summer of 1986 in London. It is part of the British culture that owners of the great newspapers are greatly deferred to, more, undoubtedly than their own merit justifies. I was a beneficiary of this and there is no one, in my experience, more agreeable than the British upper echelons setting out to be ingratiating to those whom they consider can be of use or importance to them. For my part, I had to steer between the Scylla and Charybdis of seeming another Commonwealth social climber rushing across the Atlantic with my coat-tails trailing behind me in search of a peerage, and of seeming another asset-stripping North American with no knowledge of or interest in British institutions.

Neither caricature had much applicability to me so both were easy to avoid, but most British are unshakably attached to their parodies of North American economic man, and some subtle effort is required to overcome the powerful will to typecast. I have always thought Roy Thomson was popular in Britain partly because he made no pretence to interest in anything except making money, confirming the British view of the North American businessman. He didn't muddy the waters with claims to culture or even altruism.

The Thomson executives graciously had Frank Rogers and me to dinner at the Savoy with senior executives of the other London newspaper companies, including Viscount Blakenham, chairman of Pearsons, which owns the *Financial Times* and Robert Maxwell, controversial owner of the *Mirror*. I developed excellent relations with both, different as they were. Michael Blakenham is a rather shy man, who loves to sit on a rockpile off the Scottish coast in the most rugged circumstances and watch sea birds, a delightfully understated and completely honest gentleman, nobleman in fact.

We had had some discussions with Bob Maxwell about joint-venturing our plant in Manchester, and Andrew, Frank Rogers, and Dan Colson went to see him at his Oxford headquarters on January 2, 1986. In a remarkable act of stamina, Bob phoned the SOGAT leader, Brenda Dean, at half-past midnight on his speaker phone, beginning "Brenda, I hope I haven't awakened you — I'm sure I haven't" and ending "Brenda, I trust you not to breathe a word of this to the *Telegraph* people" (three of the most senior ones sitting with him as he spoke).

He was endeavouring to wring pre-emptive concessions from her in the event of joint-venturing the plant. This was a technique of Bob's, one that he often tried with me subsequently, a routine and even prideful manifestation of his deviousness. "I trust you not to tell Conrad about this," he would sign off several future telephone conversations as I sat with him, amused by his accompanying facial and digital signals.

When I visited him at home in Oxford, Bob told me once of the provenance of his formidable dinner service displayed in an immense cabinet. He unembarrassedly told me that, when in the British army of occupation in Berlin in 1945, he spent much of his time pillaging and plundering. One day, in the French zone, he unearthed this splendid dinner service, which he alleged had belonged to a czar, and was loading it onto his trucks when a representative of the French commandant arrived and told him to put it back. "I think I have a better idea," Bob triumphantly exclaimed. "You designate someone to assist my men to divide it exactly in two.

I'll deliver one half to your attention anywhere you want in the three Western Allied zones, and I'll take care of the other half." "Very good idea, Captain," came the reply. It never occurred to Bob that he didn't have a perfect entitlement to anything he could lay his hands on, as became shockingly clear shortly after his death in 1991.

On the night I met him for the first time, under Thomson auspices at the Savoy, in July 1986, with his bushy black dyed eyebrows, slicked-back dyed hair, dark eyes, and immense girth, he seemed sinister, even satanic, and not a bit affable.

He was part Middle Eastern bazaar rug-trader and part an eastern European, multilingual conspirator. Every day for Bob was a celebration that he was no longer a fugitive from the Nazis nor an undischarged bankrupt apostrophized by the Department of Trade and Industry as unfit to be a director of a public company. He lolled on his sofa in his theatre-set office in Holborn Circus like Jabba the Hut, a behemoth of about 300 pounds. A sincere family man, legitimately generous to many causes, he was, I thought, after I got to know him, a likeable rogue, compulsively devious, yet reliable if there were elements of vengeance and subterfuge in what was afoot.

The same man who held himself out as the protector and model for all Jews had written in the *London Jewish Chronicle* many years before that he was not, in fact, Jewish. This was the Bob Maxwell who, when asked in John Aspinall's casino how he reconciled his support of and caucus membership in the Labour party with his presence in the casino, replied, "How do I justify myself? By having you thrown out! Throw him out!" He announced he would underwrite the Edinburgh Commonwealth Games in 1986, but never advanced a farthing.

He endeavoured to cajole us into printing an evening newspaper, the London *Daily News*, which he launched against Rothermere's *Evening Standard*, without a printing contract. Andrew Knight pursued him around his launch party from room to room at the *Mirror* headquarters. The motif of the party was a real circus with acrobats, wild animals, astounding displays, freakish occurrences, and rides, and Andrew finally told Bob he would stop the presses if Bob didn't sign. The contract was signed in the palm-reading tent, which Bob abruptly appropriated, to the astonishment of the reader and her clients.

I declined to give the annual address at the Quebec City Chamber of Commerce in 1989 after Quebec's repressive language legislation, as I didn't wish to fan further controversy on the issue. Bob spoke there instead and scurrilously attacked me for opposing the prohibition of bilingual commercial signs. The publisher of *Le Soleil* sent me his text and I replied on page one of *Le Soleil* the next morning that Bob's expressed view was "hypocrisy and buffoonery." He faxed me back a rather wan reply, and I published this and another withering response on page one of the following day's *Le Soleil*. Bob abated for several days and then meekly suggested that we go back to corresponding without recourse to publication. It was an amusing exchange that was well-publicized in Quebec.

Bob Maxwell claimed to have said to Konstantin Chernenko, in response to a question of how the world would have been different if Nikita Khrushchev rather than John F. Kennedy had been assassinated, that "it is unlikely Mr. Onassis would have married Mrs. Khrushchev." That witticism is usually credited to Mao Tse Tung. Bob almost certainly did not say it first but he surely said it most. His obsequious grovelling to the most loathsome communist tyrants, especially Ceausescu ("Why, Mr. President, do your people love you so?") and Erich Honecker ("These people from East Germany aren't fleeing: they just want to visit their relatives in West Germany," he explained, two weeks before the tearing down of the Berlin Wall) was especially nauseating.

But it was Bob, the prodigal son of Czechoslovakia, who spoke, Bob the social climber, Bob the publisher who had a profitable trade with eastern Europe, Bob the ex-Labour MP all in one. He was a sincere, if misguided European, ante- and post-Cold War man. Rupert Murdoch, whose success obsessed Bob, thought him, as he told me in 1987, "a crook, a thug, a buffoon, and probably a KGB agent." He was certainly in part the first three, possibly the last, but what counted with Bob Maxwell was not what he said or did, but the spirit, the ebullience, and the cunning determination that propelled this corrupt, courageous, and clever mass of idiosyncrasies out of poverty, persecution, combat, obscurity, adversity, and opprobrium to wealth and fame.

As Max Hastings generously wrote when Bob died (November 6, 1991), "The nation's headlines will be much the poorer for his passing, and the length of his journey from the place and circumstances of his birth demand respect from all of us who have had to travel much less far, to rise much less high."

I was naturally disappointed and shocked at the revelation that he had grossly abused his fiduciary position and misappropriated hundreds of millions of pounds of his employees' pension funds to prop up his company's own shares. His talents as a huckster on a grand scale did not translate easily into orthodox administration, and when his extravagance led him to the financial precipice, he didn't have the self-confidence to convene his bankers, as Murdoch did, and outline the proportions of the problem and a plan of action to deal with it, as, on a very modest scale, I did in February 1986.

An endomorphic, shameless gadfly, poseur, fugitive, and confidence trickster, he tried to embezzle his way through his problems. He deferred the hour of reckoning by his leonine perseverance at mendacious bluster and outright theft. It was typical of Bob that when the end came, he thought, finally, of his admirable and attractive family, and did so by apparently committing suicide, disguising it as an accident and perhaps fraudulently trying to snaffle the insurance pay-off for his heirs.

He could have been a rogue on a mighty scale but with redeeming virtues, but will be remembered instead as one of history's greatest swindlers, a crook of Dickensian (*Little Dorrit*) and Zolaesque (*L'Argent*) proportions. Rupert Murdoch called me a few weeks after Bob died (and had been hastily given an honoured funeral in Jerusalem just before the revelation of his skulduggery), ostensibly to talk about Australia, where I had just invested. It shortly emerged, however, that he really wanted to exult about the fall of Maxwell, some of whose personal belongings were being auctioned that day. When I asked if he didn't have any sympathy for Bob's family, Rupert paused for a few seconds and replied, "I have sympathy for anyone who was related to that son-of-a-bitch."

Reprehensible and ultimately disgraceful though his conduct was, I always liked Maxwell, after he told the New York Society of Financial Analysts of the *Daily Telegraph*, even before I met him, that "Mr. Black has landed history's largest fish with history's smallest hook." That proved to be substantially true, but Bob Maxwell realized it before I did.

The day after the Hollinger dinner in May 1986, where Bill Buckley gave a rather entertaining address, David Radler and I had flown to Hornell, New York, to explore the possibility of buying a group of eighteen little American daily newspapers with a combined circulation of under 100,000. This was the only echelon of American daily newspapers that had not been fished out by the larger chains or at least had their perceived values scaled up to unsustainable heights. Adapting a perspective from the cable business, David and I reasoned that eventually the value of these units, cumulatively, would approach that of a metropolitan monopoly newspaper of the same aggregate circulation. We negotiated through the summer and autumn.

We reached agreement on the purchase of the eighteen little American newspapers and launched American Publishing Company on the last day of 1986. A representative property was the *Punxsutawney (Pennsylvania) Spirit*, in the town that is the home of the famous groundhog that comes out every February 1 from its glass-walled home under the town hall (familiar to those who saw the film *Groundhog Day*). The purchase of these modest newspapers began implementation of what I described to incredulous big-city publishers like Kay Graham (*Washington Post*) and Punch Sulzberger (*New York Times*), as my "Mao Tse Tung strategy": we would surround the great cities and mystify their besieged journalistic occupants.

I never wavered in my faith in Reaganomics, in the revival of the Rust Belt, and in the determination and competence of the American industrial worker. I had "In rust we trust" translated into Latin as a device for the division. Over the next six years, the performance of American Publishing as it expanded steadily through more than eighty daily newspapers in nearly thirty states justified that faith. Rupert Murdoch eventually told the *New York Times* that he didn't "have the time to visit newspapers in a lot of little towns like Conrad Black does." I don't either, but David Radler does.

While we were at it, we sold Sterling into Hollinger at the end of 1986 on the same pricing formula as we bought the American newspapers out and had a letter from John Tory, president of Thomson's, upholding that approach, which yielded us $37 million for Sterling (slightly ten times profit before interest and taxes). We had started nearly twenty years before, with $18,000, which came from the *Knowlton Advertiser* (the enterprise in which I purchased a 50 per cent interest in 1967 for $500 less a cheap rug, ultimately my only investment in Sterling or Hollinger). As a capital-gains tax-deferral measure, $15 million was in convertible preferred shares, convertible into Hollinger common shares at a little over $8. At time of writing, such an exercise and such a conversion would yield the vendors of Sterling a total of $46 million.

Both the past and subsequent performances by Sterling would fully justify that price, but after the directors approved the purchase, David, for the first time in our seventeen years together, congratulated me. I congratulated him; he, more than anyone else, deserved the credit for running Sterling and thereafter American, with a fanatical determination that regularly produced margins more than twice those achieved by Southam in its comfortable metropolitan monopoly markets. At the very end of the tumultuous year 1986, we had a functioning and slightly profitable newspaper company in Canada, Britain, and the United States. It was something to build on.

Our proceeds from asset disposals rolled in all through 1987. Another of David Radler's inspired moments came when he sold the California cable system in late 1987 for $30 million more than we paid Allan Slaight for it a year before (retaining only a sliver of it to assure our tax status). As the pension surplus question moved towards resolution and the spectre of foregoing all of those resources was lifted, and as we liquidated Hees shares at large increases on their issue price free of tax, in Dominion Stores, the cash proceeds on the Norcen sale, which I had been conserving as a *masse de manoeuvre* to hurl against any front that might be collapsing at the time, became available to emerging acquisition plans.

At the *Daily Telegraph*, as the company's prospects brightened swiftly, we ran another rights issue and exercised our option to buy half of Lord Hartwell and his family's shares. In the United States, there appeared to be a practically unlimited number of these small daily newspapers available and our initial experience with American Publishing confirmed our long-standing history with Sterling, that these smaller units could be successfully managed by recourse to careful and constant electronic monitoring of pay roll, advertising, and circulation, which had not been possible until recently, and by maintaining a flying squadron of fixer-counsellors, who travelled around between the centres on our airplane, encouraging, advising, imposing controls or conducting surgery, like frontier marshalls.

When David and I founded Sterling Newspapers in 1971, only the Royal Bank could provide a rudimentary cash-management scheme that would assure that a current account balance in one place would be offset against an overdraft in another. By 1986, it was possible to micromanage a far-flung business of small units from one centre, including centralized despatch of cheques and invoices. The traditional criterion of Roy Thomson and Roy Park and other owners of large numbers of small newspapers, that beneath 10,000 daily circulation, or at the least 7,000 with some prospects of growing to 10,000, was not worth bothering about, was now obsolete. David Radler was undoubtedly the world's greatest authority on newspapers of this size and when he told the Kent Commission on newspaper ownership in 1980 that our greatest contribution to Canadian journalism was "the three-man newsroom and two of them sell ads," he wasn't speaking entirely in jest.

Thomson had generally ignored "shoppers" (free sheets) and put their publishers under such pressure to produce high margins that franchise erosion resulted and competing shoppers sprang up like dandelions.

Technology had touched our end of the industry just enough to make central management of so many small units possible, but not enough to be as threatening as it was to metropolitan newspapers. It was rarely practical to wire-cable our towns. Unions were rare and reasonable. Our readers could not discover who beat whom at the bowling or the church bingo by reading the *Chicago Tribune* or *New York Times*, nor could the local grocer sell his products through those media and, strategically, they could not invade our markets for the same reason that Hitler didn't invade Switzerland, the cost would be far too great to be justified by any possible resulting gain.

We applied rigorous ratios to purchasing and worked hard to improve the editorial product at minimal cost, even using the *Daily Telegraph* news service, and American Publishing grew steadily, by about 100,000 paid daily circulation per year, through the eighties and into the nineties.

In Canada, the first serious growth opportunity that presented itself was UniMédia, Jacques Francoeur's company that owned *Le*

Soleil, Le Quotidien, Le Droit, Le Parole, and a rag bag of other assets, including some free distribution newspapers in Ville Laval. I had known Jacques Francoeur for many years, since Peter White and I tried to buy the Granby *Leader Mail* from him in 1967. I got to know him better after we bought the *Sherbrooke Record* and we met often at Quebec Publishers' Association meetings. I had interviewed him for my book on Duplessis, as his father, Louis Francoeur, one of Quebec's sensational characters, had known Duplessis well.

Louis Francoeur had been studying to become a Benedictine priest in Belgium when World War I began, and he spent the war as an Allied spy of great courage and efficiency. He returned to Quebec as a journalist and became one of Quebec's best known faces and voices as a radio announcer, introducing much of the world to Quebec in a way somewhat comparable to René Lévesque's television role a generation later. Louis Francoeur was an early champion of Duplessis, a co-author of the hilarious *Catéchisme des Electeurs* in 1936, and an uproarious political candidate a couple of times.†

Louis Francour's premature death in an automobile accident in 1941 shocked the province, and his funeral somewhat recalled the extravagant thirties obsequies of Hollywood stars.

Jacques Francoeur, too, had had an interesting though not quite so amazing career. He started *Dimanche-Matin*, a ground-breaking Sunday picture newspaper in the fifties, distributing it on the steps of Montreal's churches. Action photos from the previous winter night's hockey game at the Montreal Forum were developed in the back of a station wagon on the road to Granby where the newspapers were published. In 1972, he succeeded in buying the Quebec newspaper, *Le Soleil*, after Bourassa had intervened to prevent its sale by the Gilbert family to Paul Desmarais.

For many years, *Le Soleil* had been a rabidly Liberal newspaper, with the masthead slogan "L'Organe Libérale," but when Jacob

---

† He was even considered a candidate for the leadership of the Quebec Conservative Party after Camillien Houde and against Duplessis in 1933. When the possibility was broached by eventual federal cabinet minister Noel Dorion with the words, "If you want to stop drinking and living like a bum," Francoeur interrupted with, "You can keep your job of leader; I wouldn't touch it."

Nicol sought Mount Orford as the site of his television tower for the independent licence he had just obtained in Sherbrooke, Duplessis arranged for him to have the location, in a provincial park, and a new publisher, Colonel Oscar Gilbert took over, and became at the same time, a Union Nationale legislative councillor, in the highest traditions of disinterested Quebec publishing.

Peter White and I both contacted Jacques Francoeur in 1987, and he expressed an interest in selling his company for $50 million, which he acknowledged was more than Paul Desmarais was offering. Jacques was a Québécois of the (by then) old Duplessist school, in outlook, diction, and vocabulary. Eventually we struck a deal with him that included an element of continuation for him to accommodate his tax convenience.

A considerable controversy ensued, as Parti Québécois members of the National Assembly demanded we be prevented from buying Quebec newspapers, as outsiders, it was euphemistically asserted, rather than as non-French. I was grateful for the support Peter and I received from a number of prominent Quebeckers, including Claude Ryan, who was reported to have said in the National Assembly that "Conrad Black could teach many Quebec journalists and editors a good deal about their occupation and about the history of Quebec."

The lobbying against the sale was led by Paul Desmarais. Notwithstanding our long cordial relations, he had always coveted *Le Soleil*, as an addition to the other newspaper properties he owned in Quebec, *La Presse*, *La Tribune*, *Le Nouvelliste*, and *La Voix de L'Est*. Paul attended upon Bourassa with great persistence. Bourassa telephoned me after each major visitation in which he asked, as was his usual technique, for the pressures he was under to be countered in some effective way by pressures or inducements in the opposite direction.

Peter White worked out with the Quebec communications minister, Richard French, an undertaking to offer *Le Soleil* and *Le Quotidien* of Chicoutimi in the event of resale by us to Quebeckers first, and I promised Bourassa to recruit "*Québécois prestigieux*" as directors of UniMédia. To this end, I recruited a strong group in the forty-eight hours he gave me, including, as president of UniMédia, Pierre Des Marais, former Montreal Urban Community chairman and my chairman at Carling O'Keefe, whom I described when I telephoned him as "*sous-employé*" and with whom my first contact had been fifteen years earlier when I urged him, at Robert Rumilly's request, to seek the leadership of the Union Nationale.

Bourassa, the pressures from Paul Desmarais and the nationalists adequately assuaged, telephoned to thank me for my "*ouverture.*" He dismissed the P.Q. opposition as the ineffectual work of "*une brave femme,*" Carmen Juneau, a minor opposition figure. The most outrageous conduct was that of Roger Landry, the publisher of *La Presse*, who accompanied his employer (Paul Desmarais) to Bourassa to second the agitation against us as buyers of *Le Soleil*, while conducting an intense negotiation on the telephone and on two occasions in person with Peter and me for the position offered to and taken by Pierre Des Marais as head of UniMédia. Even by the most *opéra bouffe* standards of Quebec business, it was a pretty shameless performance, though certainly not an unamusing one.

What awaited Pierre Des Marais was a prodigious task of management. Under Francoeur a mishmash of non-performing assets had proliferated and they all had to be sold or drastically overhauled. Almost all the units required new managers, and over a couple of years Pierre did find new managers for them. The Montreal-area weekly newspapers, which had never been significantly profitable as a group, although the Laval papers had been somewhat profitable at times, Pierre and I sold to Philippe de Gaspé Beaubien. Peter White and I had originally approached Philippe Beaubien as a prospective partner in UniMédia but abandoned him when he solemnly assured us we would not be permitted to own UniMédia and therefore he must own 51 per cent of it. Counting all forms of consideration, including some free advertisements on Philippe's radio stations, we realized $20 million on this transaction.

The unprofitable old Montreal Granby Press, where *Dimanche-Matin* and the Granby *Leader-Mail* had been printed, Pierre Des Marais sold (presses and building separately), for about $10 million. A knottier problem was Litho-Prestige, a magazine printing facility at Drummondville, which federal and provincial government grants had largely paid for and which printed Rupert Murdoch's *New York* magazine. Litho-Prestige had been in a desperate condition after Rupert's executives abruptly revoked the printing contract. Jacques naturally sued him, and I went to lunch with Rupert in New York at his office in September 1987 and settled the lawsuit at $4.5 million.

Pierre closed the regional sales offices, which hadn't effected any significant sales, hired a plant manager who won some substantial wage give-backs from the workers, and eliminated the $3-million operating loss. He negotiated extensively with Southam for most of the first year of our ownership of UniMédia, but Southam declined to buy Litho-Prestige because "we might as well let you go broke, Pierre." Three years later, after the losses at the Drummondville plant had been eliminated, Southam closed down some of their printing operations and came back to us for Litho-Prestige, paying $14 million for an asset they could have had a year earlier for one dollar. Eighteen months later, after a drastic shakeup at Southam and some severe financial setbacks, Litho-Prestige was again offered for sale with other printing assets at a sharp discount to what had been paid to us.

An even harder and more sensitive nut to crack was *Le Droit*, the Ottawa newspaper that had been founded by the Oblates to combat the infamous Bill 17, which banned French-language instruction in Ontario at the time of the First World War, and to promote, along with the University of Ottawa, the culture and interests of Franco-Ontarians. Cardinal Villeneuve, who contributed more than any French-Canadian except perhaps Louis St. Laurent to the unity of the country during World War II, in the full fugue of his nationalist youth in the twenties had been one of *Le Droit*'s star polemicists.

The Oblates had conceded the softest and richest contracts to production workers I have seen in the newspaper industry (not excluding Fleet Street and New York City) and Francoeur had not made any progress in the fourteen years of his ownership. Pierre developed and implemented an intricate plan, worthy of the most Byzantine French-Canadian political tradition, a tradition in which he had been thoroughly schooled. He bought an off-set printing business in Hull, Quebec, that had an unaffiliated union and could print *Le Droit* very economically. The journalists of *Le Droit* struck in early 1988, a serious tactical error, as we produced the newspaper without them and achieved the settlement we sought. Journalists at a Franco-Ontarian newspaper that had lost money for forty years were not the most intimidating work force to deal with.

In 1989, we transferred *Le Droit*'s printing to our plant in Hull, a move that would have been more difficult were it not another province; moved our journalists, advertising sales personnel, and administrative staff to rented premises in Ottawa; and sold the old press and the old building eventually for $5 million each. Extensive demanning was achieved and generously paid for. In 1991, for the first time since the twenties, *Le Droit* made a modest profit. We thus realized on disposals of unprofitable assets almost $60 million (including settlement of the lawsuit with Murdoch), or $10 million more than we initially paid for the company, and UniMédia's cash flow increased between 1987 and 1992 from $2 million to $14 million.

Between Litho-Prestige and *Le Droit* alone, $5 million of losses were converted to cash and disposable assets of $25 million and a modest additional operating profit. Progress in demanning at *Le Soleil* was slow, as Quebec journalistic and production unions had to be approached with caution and at a statelier pace than in Britain and other jurisdictions where we were active. UniMédia's Novalis division produced parochial summaries of prayers and masses for much of Eastern Canada and the north-central and eastern United States, with the editorial co-operation of St. Paul University in Ottawa.

Cardinal Carter admonished me that the homilies contained in Novalis's material were often rather tendentiously socialist, so, when he retired as Archbishop of Toronto, I invited him to become a UniMédia director, with particular attention to Novalis. He has proved an outstanding director, for his knowledge of Quebec and his administrative talents. I am not qualified to judge his gentle quest for more supplicative balance in Novalis's offerings.

From our first days as owners of UniMédia, we resumed acquaintance with Pierre Péladeau, the vital but eccentric proprietor of the tabloids *Le Journal de Montréal* and *Le Journal de Québec*, which competed with *Le Soleil*. His initial success at *Le Journal de Montréal*, during one of the *La Presse* strikes, was based on his astute judgement of the urban French-Quebec working class's taste for crime ("*Hold-up au Snack Bar — Voleur Audacieux Prend $2.79*," proclaimed one headline when I was a student at Laval) and for the star system, in entertainment, sports, politics, and elsewhere. Péladeau had had a frenetic sex and romantic life, which he rarely hesitated to talk about with astonishing and graphic candour, although he professed to be a born-again Christian of considerable fervour (once when I was visiting him in the early eighties he interrupted himself in mid-sentence as if about to undergo an epileptic seizure and began intensely mumbling prayers, as he subsequently explained them to be).

He had occasional attacks of severe nervosity and ruled his company by recourse to a system of honeycombed squealers and *dénonciateurs* worthy in their numbers and garrulousness, though perhaps not the sophistication of their mission, of Richelieu. Withal, his achievement has been considerable and he is an entertaining companion and formidable competitor. Being rarely offended by people's foibles, I always respected and liked him, but this did not propel me to wish to participate in his planned Montreal English tabloid daily, though Pierre held forth at almost constant press conferences that I would be joining him.

In the end, it was Robert Maxwell who came in with him, partners who were in many ways well-suited. I was never optimistic about the paper's chances for success in the shrinking Montreal English market, but I rejoiced for my friend George MacLaren, who had bought the *Sherbrooke Record* from David and me in 1977 for $865,000 and sold it to Pierre Péladeau ten profitable years later for $3 million, in order to become publisher of the new Péladeau-Maxwell Montreal daily.

The Bilderberg meeting in 1987 was in Como, Italy, where Gianni Agnelli, controlling shareholder of Fiat and a world-admired paragon of taste and corporate ingenuity was our de facto host.[†]

As Don Macdonald had retired from the Steering Committee of Bilderberg, it was principally my task to choose the Canadian attenders; one member of our group was Norman Webster, editor of the *Globe and Mail*. I had known Norman, like many others in his large family, for many years, and always admired his talents as a writer and his journalistic integrity, whatever my reservations about his rather uncritically soft-left tendencies and despite his duplicity in Roy Megarry's plot to deprive us of control of FP and the *Globe and Mail*.

[†] In the course of this meeting Gianni Agnelli gave me one of the most memorable lines I have heard. When I asked him how he had arranged some political concessions for Fiat, he stared into the middle distance for a few seconds and said "You must remember we are the country of Machiavelli." He is a far more considerable prince than the indifferent Borgia to whom Machiavelli dedicated his book.

Norman and I travelled together between Como and Milan airport in a luxury police sedan with a military escort, which Gianni Agnelli's interventions produced for all the Bilderberg participants (his evident influence easily recalled vivid descriptions of Renaissance Italian princes, few of whom would have exceeded his power, prestige, or munificence). Norman had owned *Saturday Night* magazine for some years, and I asked him as we sped past crisply saluting Italian soldiers, as splendid in their uniforms as Mussolini and Ciano reviewing a parade of the "conquerors of Abyssinia," if he could be interested in selling the magazine to me. "Yes" was the instant reply, and I referred the detailed negotiation, after we had reached immediate tentative agreement on a valuation procedure, to Peter White.

This turned into a slight fiasco, as Norman imagined his working capital had deteriorated less than it actually had, but, despite a semi-public hiccup, our purchase of *Saturday Night* at nominal cost was consummated in the summer. I reasoned that *Saturday Night* could be transformed into a somewhat authoritative publication, should that be our wish, but that it would be useful at the least in neutralizing or rallying opinion in the rather conformist Canlit fraternity. I had in the back of my thoughts a possible bid for Southams and, in that event, would not have wished English Canada's entire published intelligentsia becoming too vocally hostile.

As it turned out, having accumulated 5 per cent of Southam's stock, I concluded that nothing could be done without the collaboration of Torstar, who, with the hydra-headed Balfour, Fisher, and Southam families and the employee pension and stock incentive plans, had about half the shares. I sold our Southam position on New Year's Eve, 1989, to Dominion Securities having got Tony Fell out of the York Club's annual luncheon, just as he was calling for a second cognac, at $31 net to Hollinger, a modest profit, whereupon the share price descended steadily over the next eighteen months to about half of our exit price. The Southam management had been loudly claiming to have added value to the share price. Although they had made a few positive changes, they had really only bruited the possibility of a bid from us in order to keep some speculative froth on the stock price.

The Southam newspapers in 1988 made their all-time high percentage of gross income of 15 per cent, against 26 per cent and

27 per cent at the vastly inferior franchises of Sterling Newspapers and American Publishing. The Southam management was pouring borrowed money into the printing business, which is fundamentally unprofitable. The excellent company had been directed for too long by good people whose exemplary gentlemanly qualities were unleavened by either strong commercial acumen or any discernible aptitude for professional journalistic excellence. Southam would have done better to decry the unjust law barring foreign ownership of Canadian newspapers, as Thomson and we did, while buying foreign newspapers, as Thomson and we did, rather than pouring an inordinate proportion of retained earnings into publishing palaces in every Southam city across Canada.

I admired Robert Fulford as a writer and invited him to lunch with Peter White and myself to ask him to remain as editor of *Saturday Night*. He did not consider our meeting a success, as he has recounted in his memoirs, and he resigned. It was heartening that our relations developed with time and he consented to become a *Saturday Night* contributor again. John Fraser indicated some enthusiasm for the position, and when I called him in London, where he was *Globe and Mail* bureau chief, to suggest it might be available, he said, "I'd kill for it." I hadn't encountered such fervent expectations since Max Hastings.

There were a few resignations from less venerable figures than Bob Fulford that were less regrettable. Sandra Gwyn, the voluminous wife of the *Toronto Star*'s London correspondent, Richard Gwyn (both are talented writers, if, in Ronald Reagan's phrase, "haemophiliac bleeding hearts"), informed me breathlessly on the steps of the Royal Opera House, Covent Garden, "I'm resigning." I wasn't sure of what she had said or to whom she said it, but she laboriously explained that she was resigning as, in Fraser's expression "a non-contributing contributing editor" out of (misplaced) fears of editorial interference by me. I faced manfully up to this defection.

Less noticed, though ultimately more consequential, was the withdrawal of Ron Graham, with whom I had had cordial relations for almost ten years. He withdrew his (in practice minimal) services.

Eventually, Allan Gotlieb became the publisher, after his retirement as Canadian ambassador to Washington, and we settled on a strategy of distributing the magazine in the more prosperous areas served by the *Globe and Mail* and the Vancouver, Montreal, Ottawa, Edmonton, and Calgary Southam newspapers. The contents were rendered more contemporary and, at time of writing, commercial viability was in sight for the first time since Jack Kent Cooke's time as owner in the early sixties. John Fraser described *Saturday Night*'s first profitable month in decades, in November 1992, to the *Globe and Mail* as "the greatest miracle since the early days of Lourdes." (This after losses of over $5 million, more placation than Canlit is worth, but a public service all the same.)

In July 1987, the *Globe and Mail* published an article about me in which it was alleged that my habitually unnamed critics considered that I had "milked" corporations and institutions, oppressed minority shareholders, pocketed other people's pensions, "destroyed" public companies, and had been caught with my "hand too close to the cookie jar." The article conceded some positive aspects and concluded by acknowledging that I had unshakable control of Hollinger, which I had at least managed with some degree of financial success.

Cardinal Carter was staying with us in England in the house we rented for the summer when the piece was published. When I showed it to him, he said it was certainly libellous. Peter Atkinson told me there would never be another opportunity so inviting as this one to give Canada's financial journalists a powerful disincentive from defaming me. An identifiable group in the *Globe and Mail*'s *Report on Business Magazine*, including John Partridge, the author of this article (to whom I did not speak for the article, but a number of my friends did, including Hal Jackman, Peter White, Roy MacLaren, and Michael Meighen) had been regularly debunking me as a business failure of doubtful ethics for some years. The first part of that description was a matter of opinion and fair comment; the second, if too explicitly formulated, was clearly actionable. This time the goose had cackled once too often and too loudly, and I sued with no intention of accepting less than an abject apology.

I had known for nearly ten years that of those who were implacably hostile to me, the hard-bitten political left was irreconcilable and the grumbling detritus of the Establishment Old Guard in the billiard room of the Toronto Club was slowly melting in the hands of the undertakers, and both were irrelevant. The forces of contemporary envy were more antagonistic and more capable of doing real damage, and for less presentable motives, than those who saw me as an ideological fiend or a precocious usurper.

The vintage Canadian spirit of envy was at its most sulphurous with the young journalists. Their discomfort at being chroniclers rather than the chronicled was energized by a self-righteous awareness that I had made lateral financial movement, especially related party transactions and licit asset stripping, work to my considerable profit. Along with my spiritual and legal counsel (Carter and Atkinson), I saw Partridge's piece as an impetuosity for which my opponents could be painfully punished.

So it proved to be. I spent many happy hours of bed-time reading with transcripts of Peter Atkinson's examinations for discovery of Partridge and his co-calumniators. "What is your authority, Mr. Partridge, for this allegation about Mr. Black?" "Well, you know." "No, I don't know, Mr. Partridge, but that's why we're here, you're going to tell me, aren't you?" Eventually, the witness would reluctantly volunteer the name of an ROB colleague who had alleged dishonesty in some activity of mine, and we would add him as a defendant. The *Globe and Mail* would claim delays had expired and defendants could no longer be added. We would respond that we added defendants as soon as we had any reason to be aware of their involvement in the publication of the remarks objected to. In each such instance, the newspaper challenged the judge's ruling in our favour, appealed to the master, and had a reporter ready for the master's decision. And on each occasion, our victory in the master's judgement went unreported. We gradually went through the ROB newsroom like a blotting paper, taking contradictory evidence from journalists, sweating them under oath, exposing malice, and adding defendants.

The extent to which the smears of yesteryear, Bob Rae's in particular, had been effective was revealed in the discovery comments of well-disposed opponents, especially Norman Webster and the *Globe*'s counsel, Bruce MacDougall. It was obvious from Norman's responses and Bruce's questions that they really believed that I might have done something dishonest in the Hanna takeover and in the Dominion Stores pension surplus affair.

This furnished additional reasons for a relentless prosecution of this case until the record could be set straight once and for all. After

I had finished four full days of examinations, during which we went through the minutiae of Massey-Ferguson, Hanna, Dominion Stores, *inter alia*, it became entirely clear to the *Globe*'s counsel that his client was in a position of great vulnerability. Settlement discussions began in earnest in the autumn of 1988.

The lawsuit was only half of my strategy to return the *Globe and Mail*'s antagonism. The second front was to push for a daily *Financial Post*. Roy Megarry's ill-considered tactical lurchings had drawn the *Toronto Star* from the afternoon into direct morning competition and forfeited an important part of the traditional Toronto upper-middle-class readership. The *Globe* had become dependent on a cross-country business readership and had lost virtually all retail and much display advertising, to the point that it was almost entirely sustained by the high end of jobs and career advertising in the Report on Business.

Under the quaint notions of Norman Webster and the managing editor, Geoffrey Stevens, whom I found an unusually unsympathetic person (more for his smarmy pretentions to profound insight and reportorial excellence than for his dreary leftishness and strenuous hostility to me, disagreeable attitudes to which I never questioned his entitlement), reporters were rotated unpredictably around the newspaper. Thus, some of the most convinced leftists infested the ROB, attacking not only dishonest and incompetent businessmen as they should, but the system in general. This was an unconventional method of building business readership.

I believed that the *Globe and Mail*'s traditional constituencies had been sorely tried by Stevens's toadying to the left, as well as other slippages such as two-day-old sports, Gutenberg-era design, and a steadily more exaltedly pompous tenor, almost unfortified by the traditions of the writers' paper that had built the *Globe and Mail*'s reputation when I first knew it in the fifties and sixties. Megarry and Stevens had gone out on a limb and I set about recruiting allies for a chain-saw party. The *Financial Times of London* was interested from the start. The *Wall Street Journal* was stand-offish, preferring to build its direct Canadian circulation.

Doug Creighton was intrigued by the idea, and when he succeeded in off-loading the *Houston Post* onto Dean Singleton in 1987, the idea of a daily *Financial Post* became his highest priority.

North America's greatest authority on daily newspaper start-ups, as well as one of the international newspaper industry's most affable and colourful characters, Doug Creighton turned my idea, which had gradually evolved from a vindictive to an opportunistic one, from a pipedream to an imminent fact.

He took charge of the exacting preparations, the FT came in for 25 per cent, and Doug graciously offered me 15 per cent (which we took to 20 per cent in 1991). I promised, at the launch party February 4, 1988, "to give new meaning to that nauseating expression, minority rights." In fact it has been an enjoyable association, although profitability will have to await the departure of the recession and the NDP in Queen's Park. Creighton achieved a great deal in bringing the paid daily circulation from a standing start to over 100,000 in scarcely two years.

Norman Webster fired me as a *Globe and Mail ROB Magazine* columnist for my role in the founding of the *Daily Financial Post* and I wrote my final piece regretting this narrow view and pointing out that this ostensibly heavy news fell on me on Christmas Eve. My attempt to put the traditional "30" at the end of my last column was rejected by the editors as flamboyant.

Margaret Thatcher attended and addressed the Hollinger dinner in June 1988 at the end of the Group of Seven economic summit in Toronto. The entire political and financial hierarchy of Canada was present, and I couldn't help reflecting on the sparsely attended meetings of superannuated horse owners and retired miners that Bud McDougald and Al Fairley used to organize on corresponding occasions. Mrs. Thatcher gave her general political philosophy and at one point advised: "Many have admired our achievements without liking our methods. If you don't really believe in our program, don't try it because you won't have the courage to see it through." All eyes were on a slightly fidgety Brian Mulroney, who was then groping half-heartedly towards a couple of partial privatizations.

I introduced Mrs. Thatcher, and Henry Kissinger, who became a director of Hollinger in 1987, thanked her, using Bismarck's famous aphorism that a statesman must "listen for God's footfall and touch the hem of his garment as he passes." Margaret Thatcher, fatigued after speaking for forty-five minutes at the end of an intensive four-day summit conference, had a momentary lapse of attention and said to me, "Whose hemline is Henry touching?" When I explained to her what Henry actually said, she replied, "Bismarck touching God's hemline? Good God! It's time we all went home!"

The next day in Ottawa, Mrs. Thatcher addressed parliament. Brian Mulroney kindly sent me the video and when Mrs. Thatcher praised Paul Reichmann and me as constructive forces much admired in Britain, my immediate and rather rare reaction was regret that my mother wasn't (apparently) able to hear this.

Through much of 1988, David Radler and Dan Colson had been negotiating for the purchase of the *Jerusalem Post*. Started as the *Palestine Post* in 1930, this newspaper had always served the Jewish population of the Middle East with courage and eloquence. The *Post* was the authentic voice of the old Mapai Labour Party establishment, of the intellectual kibbutzim and the followers of David Ben Gurion. It was severely critical of the Likud block under Menachem Begin and Yitzhak Shamir and was relentlessly hostile to every aspect of the occupation of the lands taken over by Israel following the 1967 war.

The difficulty created by this state of affairs was that much of Western reporting from the Middle East, despite the commendably enterprising performance of the local bureaux of the *New York Times*, the London quality newspapers (including ours), and a few others, consisted of rewrite jobs from the *Jerusalem Post*. Many of the *Post*'s staff doubled as stringers for Canadian and American newspapers, and this influence was deployed throughout the Western press in a manner militantly hostile to the Israeli government. I was myself rather critical of the unimaginative and inflexible attitude of the Shamir government, but it was not desirable to have Israel's most authoritative international media source propagating such a virulently one-sided view of the region.

David and I felt that the editorial stance had to be more robust, the reporting scrupulously balanced, and the comment equally weighted between the four main factions on the peace question. These, roughly formulated, were Peace Now, led by the old guard of the Labour Party, Jerusalem mayor Teddy Kollek and former foreign minister Abba Eban, which essentially wanted to return to the 1967 borders except for Jerusalem itself, which they wished to remain undivided; Land for Peace, identified with the right wing of the Labour Party and people such as Itzhak Rabin, with a more restrained notion of territorial give-backs; the more liberal Likud position of substantive discussions of a conservative definition of Israel's security needs, a faction led by the Sephardim foreign minister David Levy; and the no-compromise, no-negotiations group led by Ariel Sharon. Shamir tried to straddle the last two, while the opposition leader, Shimon Peres, tried to straddle the first two. (I have long believed, and my direct experience with Israel has confirmed me in the view, that the future ultimately lies between the second and third schools, essentially the position taken by Rabin in the 1992 election campaign and the 1993 agreement with the PLO.)

The newspaper was for sale because Histadrut, the Israeli Confederation of Labour, had suffered severe economic reversals in many of its assets and the direct parent of the *Post* was insolvent. An auction ensued in which we participated at the urging of Colonel Yehuda Levy, who had known David well when he lived in Vancouver as representative of the Jewish National Fund. David and I discounted what we would pay for such a property in Canada or the United States by about 60 per cent, which we thought an adequate adjustment for the vagaries of doing business in Israel, and put in a bid on that basis.

The myth arose that we overpaid for the *Post*, which is not a sustainable argument on either our normal pricing criteria or the subsequent performance of the property. Our reasoning was that Israel's prospects were actually fairly good, that the Arab threat was subsiding, and that the pressures for Israel to abandon its romantic flirtation with Herzlian collectivism and to adopt an incentive-based economic system towards which almost all the rest of the formerly socialistic world was evolving would prove irresistible. It has always struck me that one of the great ironies of the contemporary world is that the Jewish people are renowned, wherever they are a minority, as a financially and professionally gifted people, disproportionately prosperous and talented, but not especially militaristic, but that Israel, the world's foremost warrior and garrison state, was an economic basket case, sustained from New York and Washington. This would surely change.

The *Jerusalem Post* had 420 employees, more than a quarter of the work force of the *Daily Telegraph*, a newspaper of nearly forty times the circulation of the *Post* (which averaged about 30,000 daily sales with 60,000 for the weekly international edition). Obviously, we thought, economies could be effected, no matter how difficult Israel's labour laws were. Finally, we were, for reasons that have already been outlined, buying a good deal of influence relatively cheaply.

The ineffable Bob Maxwell was one of the principal promoters of the idea that we had overpaid. He had the same protective and possessive attitude towards the press of Israel as Paul Desmarais had had towards *Le Soleil* and accused me of "pissing in my pond." He lobbied most of my Jewish directors at Hollinger, especially Paul Reichmann, Allan Gotlieb, and Henry Kissinger, who called to say, in his unique Katzenjammer accent that often makes him sound like the Marx Brothers imitating Kaiser Wilhelm, "I understand that you and Maxwell are bidding against each other for the *Jerusalem Post* and I just want you to know that you're both welcome to it!"

The Hebrew-language newspaper in which Bob Maxwell had an interest, *Ma'ariv*, professed to find me an unsuitable owner of the *Post* because of my perceived status as "a devout Roman Catholic," a description of doubtful accuracy and no relevance, especially coming from Maxwell, who denied he was a Jew prior to his virtual Napoleonic self-coronation as King of Judea. I threatened to publish his infamous 1950s denial that he was Jewish if any newspaper of his ever wrote such a thing about me again. He was, for once, I believe, sincere in his apology and there were no recurrences.

As Dan Colson, who finished off the intensive negotiations in both New York and Israel, was leaving his hotel in Tel Aviv with executed sale contracts for the *Post* in his briefcase, he noted that Bob Maxwell was holding a press conference in one of the hotel's public rooms. On stepping unobtrusively into the back of the room, he heard Bob announce that he had "canvassed a number of Hollinger directors. This deal has not been consummated. I don't believe Hollinger can complete it. I am here to buy the *Jerusalem Post* and expect to do so." Bob offered me a substantial capital gain on our price the next week and regularly thereafter. I declined, as we are not traffickers in newspapers but did bring him on as a director of the *Jerusalem Post* in 1990, joining Richard Perle, (Lord) George Weidenfeld, and the former chief of Israeli military intelligence, General Shlomo Gazit. (As Dan Colson ended this trip and cleared the intensive pre-boarding security required for El Al flights, he explained that the purpose of his trip to Israel had been to buy the *Jerusalem Post*. The incredulous security official said, "You can't buy it in London?")

Like everything else in the Middle East, our editorial repositioning of the *Jerusalem Post* would not be an easy or effortless process. Itzhak Rabin, then the Labour Party deputy leader and defence minister, called Yehuda Levy when our purchase was announced and expressed the hope that the *Post* would no longer be "a pro-PLO newspaper." In 1989, the long-serving editor, Ari Rath, retired, and late in 1989, his co-editor, Irwin Frenkel, resigned when Yehuda Levy excised from a weekly international edition a clause in a reprinted daily editorial to the effect that the *Post* would "never" approve of the Israeli government's territorial claims. Yehuda had no problem with disapproving the policy but he didn't want to commit us in the international edition to permanent disapproval regardless of future circumstances.

The managing editor, David Landau, who had operated a news service in direct competition with the *Post*, the Jewish Telegraph Agency, out of the *Post*'s office with the *Post* paying the telephone bills, until Yehuda told him that the old regime's indulgent ways weren't in effect any more, demanded that he be named as editor. This demand was unanimously considered by David, Yehuda, and me as unacceptable, so Landau escalated it to an insistence that he be named as editor and Yehuda Levy fired as publisher, or he and a large section of the editorial department would quit. This was an insolence that couldn't possibly be accepted if we wished to preserve any credibility. It was also an opportunity for relatively inexpensive demanning so we peremptorily rejected Landau's demand and happily received the uncompensated resignations of fifteen journalists. Landau was a stringer for the *Toronto Star*, which shortly began to retail his colourful fictions of a bloodless journalistic holocaust at the *Jerusalem Post*.

Elements of the Canadian media, under this false influence, circulated the notion that I was the midwife of a virtual Jewish fascism. Christopher Young, the retired editor of the *Ottawa Citizen*, slavishly wrote that I was the author of a "shame for Canada." When Landau's destabilization strike came, Yehuda was on his annual return to his regiment and he hastily came back to the newsroom in paratrooper's fatigues (he had been on the Entebbe raid and is a considerable physical presence). He discreetly left his machine gun in his office but harangued the journalists from a desk-top: "This is not a kibbutz!" he began.

He and I dutifully rebutted the principal Canadian newspaper stories, including a particularly venomous and dishonest treatment from the *Canadian Jewish News*, and the controversy gradually subsided. Personnel were reduced by one or two a week for the first three years of our ownership, and profitability, which had been as elusive at the *Jerusalem Post* as at Ottawa's *Le Droit*, slowly emerged in 1990 and 1991, severely interrupted by the Gulf War.

When the scuds appeared over Jerusalem and Tel Aviv in February 1991, our readers sat in their basements wearing gas masks and eating soda crackers, and advertising, not altogether surprisingly, evaporated. Enemy missiles overhead proved the most severe challenge to our advertising sales force David and I have faced. When that war was won, the long march to prosperity in Jerusalem resumed and by the spring of 1992 the *Post* was achieving satisfactory levels of profit.

In the autumn of 1988, Brian Mulroney returned to the polls on the issue of free trade with the United States, which I supported because I believed that if Canadians could see they could compete with Americans, I hoped Canada would become a more self-confident, serene, and less envious society. Brian became the first prime minister of Canada to win two consecutive majorities since Louis St. Laurent, and it was an interesting campaign because business leaders such as Paul Reichmann, Galen Weston, David Culver (Alcan), and Alf Powis took a public position and pulled more votes than Stephen Lewis, June Callwood, and Margaret Atwood. I was encouraged. John Turner ran a much more professional campaign than in 1984, though his opposition to free trade and his spending proposals were scurrilous. He more than doubled the number of his MPs but announced his retirement as Liberal leader in the spring of 1989. Brian Mulroney called me and asked me to offer John the post of ambassador to the Vatican, in absolute confidence and retaining the ability to deny the offer if it were treated indiscreetly. It wasn't, but John declined the offer somewhat peremptorily implying he had expected better but wouldn't have accepted it anyway. It was a generous gesture by the prime minister.

I enjoyed writing for the *Financial Post* more than I had the *Globe and Mail*'s *ROB Magazine*, as the three-month deadline required for a magazine gave way to almost instant gratification when writing for a daily newspaper. But the irony was obvious when Roy Megarry suddenly figured out in late 1988 that habitual readers had been thoroughly alienated by the *Globe and Mail*'s Stevens-inspired editorial posture of NDP wolf in the moth-eaten clothing of a spavined old Toronto Tory sheep and fired both Webster and Stevens. I regretted Norman's fall, though at his subsequent post of editor of the Montreal *Gazette* his high talents as an editorialist have probably been allowed greater play than was possible at the *Globe and Mail*. Megarry himself left a few years later.

The new editor, William Thorsell, had been a sequential neighbour as a columnist in the pages of the *ROB Magazine* and had been something of an ideological soulmate. On advice of counsel and unencumbered by Stevensesque hubris, he oversaw the negotiation of one of Canada's most extensive litigated libel retractions, finally published June 30, 1989, and invited me back as a columnist. Loyalty to Creighton prevented that, but the successful end of our libel case brought an end also to the *Globe and Mail*'s sporadic war on me (John Partridge, the original defendant, has proved very balanced and forgiving). Competition and skirmishing would continue, as they should. But peace broke out with a large and boldly headlined page two apology and retraction reprinted in the magazine, composed entirely by the *Globe and Mail*'s editors and counsel on the basis of their prolonged pre-trial examination of me.

The newspaper apologized unreservedly, and generously referred to a poll that had found me to be "Canada's most respected businessman" (though the sample was small and the survey was hardly scientific).

The retraction debunked the ancient falsehoods that I had exploited the widows or acted improperly in pursuing Hanna, reorganizing Norcen and Labrador, or withdrawing Dominion pension surplus. At Massey-Ferguson, "Mr. Black promoted new senior management that has successfully guided the company back to solvency and arranged to have Argus divest itself of its interest in the company on the most satisfactory basis available. Massey management has since confirmed that Mr. Black's action in dissociating

Argus from the company was a material factor in permitting the company to secure the financing necessary for its survival."

At Dominion Stores Ltd., I had "successfully encouraged the company to close or dispose of unprofitable or marginal stores, to sell the rest to franchisers and to dispose of other units in a manner that was to the advantage of all of the shareholders and saved jobs.

"The shareholders in companies influenced by Mr. Black who have followed his fortunes have prospered with him and have been supportive of his stewardship.

"The Globe and Mail accepts the facts set out above as true."

The asset shuffling and stripping and the ancillary financial and public relations crises were over. The more fulfilling work of systematically building a profitable international quality newspaper business was already well-advanced.

CHAPTER ELEVEN

SPANNING THE WORLD FROM QUEBEC TO AUSTRALIA
1989–1991

THE *GLOBE AND MAIL*'S WIDELY NOTED recantation was an agreeable parting notice as I quietly removed my principal residency from Canada.

The cultural bigotry in Quebec, the inexorable erosion towards the left in Ontario, the constitutional quagmire, the pandemic envy, mediocrity and sanctimony, punctuated in my own experience by countless defamations and a public police witch-hunt, had taken a toll. I would never fail to be proud of being Canadian, nor surrender my home or hard-won office on Toronto Street, but residentially Canada and I deserved a rest from each other, though not necessarily a permanent one.

In June, 1989, a controversy had erupted over the role played in the complicated relationships with provincial and municipal governments by the land development company of my neighbours, the Del Zottos. I was a director of the company, Tridel. Political activities of developers are always sensitive, and this fact was compounded in this case by Elvio Del Zotto's status as chairman of the federal Liberal Party in Ontario. I had always personally liked David Peterson, going back to the days when he had the lowest polls recorded in Canada, only about 12 per cent opposite Bill Davis. He had been very helpful during my travail at the hands of Roy McMurtry and the "performing fascists" of the Toronto Police Department.

When it was revealed that one of Peterson's assistants was alleged to have accepted a refrigerator and a free coat of house paint from a Tridel executive, the Toronto press fell into a feeding frenzy at the premier's expense and that of officially unaccused private-sector developers. The lynch mob was led by Linda McQuaig, who six years before had been the chief author of the theory that I had bribed the entire Ontario Securities Commission so that it overlooked my act of "forgery" in Norcen's issuer bid prospectus. I telephoned the premier to encourage him and to urge him not to be bullied by rabid journalists cock-a-hoop with blood lust. He appreciated the call but, the next day, his office asked Elvio's wife to retire as an unpaid director of TV Ontario and Elvio's brother to withdraw as an unpaid hospital trustee.

I wrote in the *Financial Post* of the rights of those who deserved a presumption of innocence, especially where, as in this case, there had not been any judicial accusation (and never was against the Del Zottos or their company). I accused the premier of suffering "an implosion of authority" and of allowing the quasi-judicial process to be determined by the "swarming, grunting jackals of investigative journalism," especially Ms. McQuaig, whom I described with admitted relish as *inter alia* "a weedy, . . . not very bright, left-wing reporter."

On the morning when I left Canada, as the *Globe and Mail* honourably prepared to abandon the long desultory effort to portray me as financially unethical and competent only at self-dealing, the *Financial Post* and the *Sun* ran my assault on the Star Chamber then being inflicted by the press on the Del Zottos.

Unfortunately, where the *Sun* deleted an additional word for reasons of libel (McQuaig, after her performance in 1983, would have had trouble successfully suing me even if I had written that she was a vampire bat specializing in child molestation), the *Financial Post* removed the entire description of McQuaig. This was contrary to Creighton's orders and to promises given to me, and I naturally retired as a contributor to the *Financial Post*, returning after a ritualistic absence of a year.

Echoes of this episode reverberated for some time. The inevitable and bedraggled and still occasionally amusing Allan Fotheringham wrote that I had relieved summer tedium as had some athletes and entertainers who had traded insults with paying customers.

I replied in a letter to the *Sun* (as I was no longer, temporarily, a columnist anywhere), that the presumption of innocence was not really a matter of entertainment and concluded: "I suppose I'm slightly pleased Allan finds me entertaining. I wish I could say the reverse were true." (The last time I had actually seen Allan, almost four years before, I had given him a ride to his hotel at the end of the party celebrating Barbara Amiel's marriage to David Graham. He was drunkenly lecturing me on the shortcomings of Dominion Stores. I was generally agreeing with him, somewhat to his irritation, and when our car pulled up at the front door of the Park Plaza, he declaimed, "I still say you're floundering!", staggered from the car, and collapsed in a heap at the feet of the hotel doorman.)

The Supreme Court of Canada in 1990 threw out the entire inquiry procedure implemented by David Peterson as grossly prejudicial to the rights and reputation of the parties, in particular the Del Zottos. The *Globe and Mail* eventually apologized to the Del Zottos and paid them $15,000 after McQuaig had left the paper to write another of her sophomoric, soporiferous left-wing books. The Canadian system still provides a safety net for the propagation of socialist rap.

The cameo role played at this stage by Ronald Reagan, man of the decade, who attended and addressed the Hollinger dinner, June 29, 1989, was also somehow apposite. From the assassination of President Kennedy through the purgatorial years of Vietnam and Watergate and the righteous inanities of the Carter era, I almost wept for America, an optimistic and generous country gnawed by the liberal death-wish within and the spiteful envy of foreigners, "steel, nor poison, malice domestic, and foreign levy." She was the greatest of all nations, humbled every night in 60 million American living rooms by the liberal media with the magnified facts of racial violence and inequity at home, ineffectuality abroad.

It always has seemed to me that the greatest schism in American life is not between races, regions, and economic groups, but between the imperishable idealism of America's mythologized origins, the virtuous country raised up in the dreams of countless millions of immigrants, the town meeting, the band shell in the park, the white frame churches of New England, Norman Rockwell, Grandma Moses, and Grant Wood; and the tinsel, spangle, gluttony, hucksterism, and mawkishness of Madison Avenue, Detroit, and Hollywood at their tawdriest.

Reagan bridged this cultural gap by yoking the techniques of cynicism to the glorification of ancient virtues, and by embodying both in a personality so abstracted, intuitive, and venerable that it could be the commodious and untroubled host to severely contrary tendencies. He was, as Rupert Murdoch put it to me, a "cunning old peasant" but no less sincere for that. It was no more true that he was "an amiable dunce" than that he was a Grade B actor. As even the waspish liberal misanthrope Gore Vidal explained, "He was one of the greatest actors in world history, who had the misfortune to play in a lot of Grade B movies."

His intellect is not unlimited but in his prime he was far from being unintelligent. On June 29, 1989, as on several prior and many subsequent meetings, Ronald Reagan impressed me as a man of astonishing self-confidence and patriotic optimism, a mighty Claude Wagner who really functioned, who worked marvellously, in fact: courageous, decisive, and positive, mowing down the years with a psychology of Walter Mitty leavened with a home-spun version of the Coué system.

His vague countenance, imprecision, and anecdotal response to almost everything could be disconcerting, but he was a shaman, a magician as talented, if not as intelligent or knowledgeable of his own powers, as Roosevelt or Disraeli. However he did it, he redeemed America: the combination of the 600-ship navy, 19 million net new jobs, virtual elimination of inflation, victory in the Cold War, and a 28 per cent top personal income tax rate qualified him in my estimation for Mount Rushmore. His only serious error was his failure to means-test social security or other entitlements, opening up a mighty chicken game with the Congress over deficits.

When he came to Toronto in 1989, he was in the closing chapter of a sensational career that had brought him from Tampico, Illinois, Eureka College, and his first job as a lifeguard, California-bound in the Great Depression; to Des Moines, Iowa, where as a sports announcer he became one of the most famous voices in the mid-west in his early twenties; to Hollywood, stardom, six terms as head of the Screen Actors' Guild, executive of General Electric, governor, president.

Despite his hyperbole (electing Lyndon Johnson in 1964 was not really "the first step into a thousand years of darkness" and the Nicaraguan Contras weren't really very reminiscent of Washington, Jefferson, Franklin, and Hamilton), and despite his occasional complete mental lapses, as in his famous claim of the relationship between trees and air pollution, the nation and the world vindicated him. His entire public career was based on the incentive economic system, the superiority and legitimacy of democratic government, and the criminal fraudulence of communism.

As Henry Kissinger said, he was "not a chess player, but a poker player, and a brilliant one," and he kept raising the ante until his Soviet opponent was bankrupt. His supply-side economics fed consumerist cravings and incited unsustainable notions of instant gratification. But they addicted the middle class as thoroughly to low taxes as they had already long been to their entitlements and created an impasse with the Congress that ended decades of using taxes on the most productive people to buy the votes of the least productive. The Reagan Revolution won the Cold War, the greatest, most bloodless, most benign strategic victory since the rise of the nation state; it re-industrialized America, re-established the presidency's place in the American system, and removed two fingers of the state's hand from the pockets of the people.

As I said in my introduction of him, June 29, 1989 (following a very tasteful greeting from Brian Mulroney), "He has been judged by his countrymen, to whom alone he was answerable, to have altered for the better the course of American and of world history. No statesman can aspire to more, and few there are who attain so much." As the passage of subsequent years took their toll, his twilight has not been without majesty or poignancy and has taken nothing from the brilliant trajectory of his life and service.

Reagan was eloquent at the Hollinger dinner, especially in his praise of the late P.C. Finlay and E.P. Taylor and of Canada's contributions to the world wars and in his correct prediction of the imminent collapse of the Ceausescu regime in Romania.

I arrived in London June 30, with the stirring words of Ronald Reagan, the condign apologia of the *Globe and Mail*, the thundering furry feet of Linda McQuaig's latest lynch mob, and the banalities of Allan Fotheringham resonating behind me. I found considerable administrative disarray at the *Daily Telegraph*.

The *Sunday Telegraph* had been founded in 1961 by Lord Hartwell when his cousin, Lord Kemsley, had sold the *Sunday Times* to Roy Thomson. In cancelling the *Sunday Times*'s printing contract, Hartwell believed he might impossibly inconvenience the *Sunday Times* as he launched his own Sunday paper. The *Sunday Times* generally held the same readership as the *Daily Telegraph*, with a significant overlay of the six-day *Times* as well. With the exception of the catastrophic strike at the *Times* and *Sunday Times* in 1977 and 1978, the *Sunday Times* maintained an overwhelming advantage in circulation and desirability of readership for advertisers over the *Sunday Telegraph*.

Despite the splendid efforts of Perry Worsthorne, who gave the *Sunday Telegraph* great definition as a high Tory, Little England, eccentric, and reactionary newspaper, the *Sunday Times* maintained this advantage and after the survival and profitability of the *Telegraph* had been assured, the question of what to do with the *Sunday Telegraph* became one of the company's most urgent questions.

Andrew Knight finally determined that the best course was the so-called seven-day publishing option, in which Max Hastings would become the editor of the Sunday newspaper as well, except for a four-page comment and letters section, which would remain under Perry Worsthorne, and all functions except comment would be merged and pooled between the two titles.

On its face, this was a proposal not without merit, but Andrew committed some serious tactical errors. He announced the change with no plan at all to implement it, and he represented to Max Hastings, Frank Rogers, and me rather exaggerated versions of the extent to which each was in favour of it.

When the announcement was made, a crescendo of abuse rained down on Andrew, including from Paul Johnson in the *Spectator*, an experience he found uniquely disagreeable in his career and which clearly demoralized him. In fact, there was considerable duplication between the daily and Sunday newspapers that it was certainly desirable to reduce, but this could have been done (and ultimately was done) without turning the Sunday newspaper into what Paul Johnson called "a pantomime horse."

This issue fell in the midst of another internal debate, over inexorably rising editorial costs. As these costs rose out of any proportion to all other departments where economies were possible and were progressively achieved, I demanded with greater and greater insistence that some restraint be imposed. When I arrived in London in July, I found that Andrew was, in his own words, "a busted flush" at wringing cost concessions from Max Hastings, who ignored him and ran the editorial department as a medieval walled city from whose ramparts he prepared to pour down fire on anyone who approached.

Max ran his department autonomously, as, in Frank Rogers's words, "a management no-go area." Most of the other departments reported in a more-or-less orthodox manner to Joe Cooke as managing director, and Andrew ran a sort of itinerant court of transient favourites, known as "the flavours of the month," who under Andrew's inconstant guidance flitted from project to project like pollinating bees.

Andrew Knight was an intelligent man to whom I owed the identification of the *Telegraph*'s availability originally, and the selection of almost all the senior personnel who guided the company to an astounding success. But his pessimistic, divisive, erratic, and joyless management style had brought a group that should have been celebrating one of the world's greatest newspaper turnarounds to a squalid and demoralized level of constant internecine dispute.

A systems and editorial joint inquiry into ideal editorial manning levels, which Max contemptuously dismissed as "a time and motion study," produced aggressive recommendations and became a flashpoint for virtual civil war between Max and Joe Cooke — Andrew, the chief executive and editor-in-chief, having ignominiously abdicated. By the summer of 1989, the *Daily Telegraph* was like a great ship knifing through the water satisfactorily, her rudder fixed amidships because no consensus for a course correction could be found among the fiercely factionalized and quarrelling flag officers who milled around in shambles on the bridge. Since Andrew Knight had lost all will or ability to assert authority, I had to do it myself.

I eventually imposed upon Max's editorial barons and Joe Cooke's de-manners a median number of employees, a four-and-a-half-day work week with six-day scheduling (i.e., all employees might have to work Saturday or Sunday), and an end to the squabbling and backbiting. I particularly insisted on an end to the more histrionic threats of resignation and vengeance that had resonated through the upper floors of the *Telegraph* building for some months. With these more tiresomely belligerent noises there also drifted away some of the more stylish gambits, such as the suave executive editor, Jeremy Deedes's solemn assertion that if I pressed any further, he would have to lay off "Deedes," i.e., his father, subject of Evelyn Waugh's novel *Scoop*, Harold MacMillan's minister of information, model for *Private Eye*'s "Dear Bill" letters, editor of the *Daily Telegraph* for fourteen years, and still a valued columnist.

There was a thirty-six-hour strike by some of the editorial personnel at the promulgation of the new levels and practices, but Max, who was astounded at this insubordinacy, responded brilliantly and, with his principal collaborators, produced two splendidly newsy and elegant editions of the paper, exposing one of the greatest myths of the industry: that journalists are essential to producing a newspaper. Opposition fizzled.

This was the last initiative of Andrew Knight's tenure. He informed me of his intention to retire, not heart-breaking news in the circumstances that his lassitude and pessimism had created. He undertook not to let any hint of his departure leak out while I put new arrangements in place but blurted it out prematurely at a compensation committee meeting in early September. He was in a desperate hurry to disengage from us, for reasons that were widely suspected and soon became clear.

My wife and I went to Poland with the American Holocaust Memorial Committee, including several U.S. senators, in the late summer of 1989. We were invited by my friend George Will. The visits to Auschwitz and Treblinka were unforgettable, and the balance of the trip rather light-hearted. George, a renowned baseball authority and a director of the Baltimore Orioles, and I bet on the contest between Baltimore and the Toronto Blue Jays for leadership of the American League's Eastern Division. We wagered millions of Polish zlotys on the week's games as reported by the *Herald Tribune*, but at the end, George gave me two cents and an Orioles tie in overpayment. When I pointed out to him that Senator Alan Cranston of California was carrying a tennis racket with him on the bus going to Auschwitz, George advised that Cranston had once lost a lawsuit to Adolf Hitler for breach of copyright on *Mein Kampf* and exclaimed, "Damn it! I'm blind! Cranston at Auschwitz with a tennis racket! That's good for one column at least!"

I was asked to improvise a few words at the Wall of Death at Auschwitz, where 30,000 people were shot. As it was adjacent to the laboratory where CyclonB poison gas was developed and tested, I quoted Sir Winston Churchill's references to "the long night of Nazi barbarism . . . made more sinister and more protracted by the lights of perverted science." It was one of the most affecting trips I have made.

For several years bracketing this period, Hollinger effectively owned the right-wing intellectual magazine *Encounter*. It had been founded at the height of the Cold War, in part, by the C.I.A., and among its editors were Malcolm Muggeridge, Stephen Spender, and Irving Kristol. *Encounter* played a splendid role in defeating the early post-war communist attempt and was also an eminent literary magazine, publishing, *inter alia*, Nancy Mitford's famous essay on what was "U and non-U." For these historic reasons and as a long-time subscriber, I was happy to help *Encounter*, but when I suggested that the Cold War was ending satisfactorily and that it was time to develop an additional *raison d'être* besides anti-communism, the long-serving editor, Mel Lasky, showed he was suffering from a terminal case of Cold War cabin fever and became very abusive. Insolences from beneficiaries were not the goal of our largesse, and I cleaned up the magazine's bank overdraft with cash, hard bargaining, and contra-advertising for the lending bank, and withdrew. Lasky shortly ran *Encounter* into bankruptcy and a fine Cold War institution ended with the conflict it importantly helped to win.

Andrew Knight's abiding admiration for Rupert Murdoch had been clear for years. He was always speeding off to pay court to him, quoting Rupert endlessly for weeks afterwards, suppressing any news in our titles that was less than flattering to the Murdoch interests. I had always sensed that he fancied that Murdoch, like Tiny Rowland, Paul Reichmann, and even Evelyn de Rothschild, suffered a subtle awkwardness opposite the British Establishment which he, Andrew, could fill. His talents as a courtier were not likely to be underestimated by me (having had ample exposure to them).

I told Andrew that if he wanted to work for Rupert, that would not occasion a problem; it would just have to be effected with care to assure a proverbial decent interval and the apparent absence of excessive avarice, given that Andrew was leaving with option rights that had a windfall value of about £14 million. I never begrudged him his financial coup, only the relentlessly devious and unrepentant manner in which he stole away to our chief competitor, denying at every stage that he was doing so.

He started out accepting to be a vice chairman of the *Telegraph*, swiftly withdrew from that, but agreed to continue as a director permanently. It was then when he modestly drafted a press release for his own retirement as chief executive, suggesting I assert that "Mr. Knight is the greatest thing since sliced bread." All through the spring, summer, and autumn of 1989, Murdoch's porously indiscreet entourage reported that Andrew would be joining them imminently. When these reports reached crescendo levels, as they did every six weeks or so, I would remind Andrew that he was welcome to make such a move but should do it with some elegance. He vehemently denied at every stage that there was any truth to the rumours.

His wife lobbied with Dan Colson and me not to put Andrew under "such terrible pressure," i.e., pressure to tell us the truth about his intentions. She interspersed with these pleadings the unqualifiable proposal to me, in my living room in October 1989, to give her the *Daily Telegraph*'s entire charitable donations budget so that she could gradually "abolish ignorance and envy in the world" by producing a creative children's newspaper.

I would reiterate each solemn reassurance Andrew gave me of his indefectible attachment to the *Daily Telegraph* to Max Hastings, Frank Rogers, and others, who would smile somewhat condescendingly and mutter knowing words of scepticism. By now, I was motivated not by faith in Andrew's word, but by suppression of doubt that he would be quite so brazenly provoking as to make an abrupt, pre-planned jump to Murdoch after all his denials. I was mistaken.

Two days before I left London in mid-December for the holidays in Canada and Palm Beach, I telephoned Andrew to ensure that the comment I was then inserting in the Hollinger quarterly report, that he would continue indefinitely to serve as a *Daily Telegraph* director, was accurate. He assured me that it was but three days later he arrived at the *Daily Telegraph* office after an absence of many weeks, removed his files, left an invoice for £5,000 of wine (mainly Lynch-Bages) delivered to his house to be paid for by us, and handed in his resignation as a director.

He also set out to bully the company secretary, whose sadistic Dickensian tenacity on some technical points served him well on occasions such as this, into backdating his resignation to August. This initiative was resisted. He acknowledged to several of our executives what he had denied to me three days before — that he was moving to a senior position in the Murdoch organization. In another couple of days, he sent me a note that "Citizen Murdoch has made me an offer I can't refuse." I did not immediately reply.

Andrew conducted a feverish campaign of self-justification and ingratiation towards senior *Telegraph* personnel. He had had several large meetings with middle-echelon people, complete with flip-charts, Q and A, and a texted speech to help him explain how he had saved the *Telegraph* and that it was now time to move on. He bombarded a few with sycophantic notes and did his best to assure generous coverage from our business reporters by dissembling to Frank Rogers and me that the other favoured moving our financial journalists from the Docklands to the City, which he then unilaterally did, a popularity-booster for him at considerable expense to us. (He had opposed our move to the Docklands from Fleet Street, suggesting instead a hare-brained notion of spreading the *Telegraph* between three buildings in different districts. Dan Colson and I bought a building in South Quay Plaza at Cross-Harbour near Greenwich in 1987 and sold it to Paul Reichmann three years later for a profit of £27 million as part of our move to Olympia & York's massive Canary Wharf project.)

Andrew took an extensive foreign holiday and ostensibly entered into his functions as executive chairman of News International at the beginning of March, though he in fact had an office and secretary there from the beginning of January.

I wrote him a letter from Palm Beach at the end of December, inviting him to reconcile his actions with his countless assurances that he wouldn't jump to Murdoch and would always leave a "decent interval" whatever he went on to. I also asked him to justify having sold a couple of million shares to the Cayzer interests (a distinguished Scottish investing family), to pay for the exercise of his £22.75 million value of options and callable shares on the strenuous guaranty that he would remain at his post, the day after he told me of his intention to retire. (His pre-tax profit on a price underwritten by Rupert Murdoch's company, an unusual gesture from a competitor, indicating Andrew's talents at self-promotion, was £16.25 million.)

Frank Rogers gave my letter to the *Sunday Telegraph* as well as to the *Observer*, and Andrew, whose morbid sensitivity to any criticism was legendary, had a rough ride in the press for several weeks. Perry Worsthorne, Frank Johnson, and Geoffrey Wheatcroft unlimbered their heavy guns and Andrew did not make life easier for himself with his flatulent letters of self-justification in reply to me and his other principal accusers.

In early January, the venerable and widely respected Lord Cayzer, located by the *Daily Mail*, volunteered that his family might not have bought the shares but for Andrew's assurances that he would remain indefinitely as chief executive of the *Telegraph*.

It eventually emerged, though not publicly, that Andrew had tried to sell some of his shares to Lord Hartwell, recruiting the unsuspecting chairman of the *Spectator*, Algy Cluff, as a go-between. This was to pay for the call and option exercise (he could buy one million shares at 50 pence and six million more at £1 and sold two million to the Cayzers at £3.25). In the circumstances of my slightly tenuous relations with Hartwell, which Andrew was trying to exploit, this was a singularly unseemly act.

On January 16, 1990, in an interview with Ray Snoddy of the *Financial Times* and with Andrew cooing at his elbow, Rupert Murdoch announced Andrew Knight as his eventual successor. How Andrew could have imagined that anyone would believe that such a relationship could develop in four weeks over the Christmas and New Year's holidays completely escaped my comprehension.

Having seen through all the years I had known him his energetic courting of the good and the great, I was astounded that he would expose himself as he did to the likelihood of my poisoning those wells, which I frequented as much, though hardly as ingratiatingly, as he did. Our *Daily Telegraph* and Hollinger directors, some of them much attended on by Andrew in the past, shared my disappointment at his antics. David Montagu wrote to Andrew that he had added "new depth, warmth and colour to the meaning of the word 'shit'."

I would not forget or soon pardon Andrew's shabby leave-taking, but I never forgot his contribution to my financial welfare and to the *Telegraph*'s recovery. Our encounters are always affable and often interesting.

In Canada, all through 1989 and into 1990, the ancient bugbears of language rights, the Constitution, and the status of Quebec festered and flared again. Robert Bourassa had responded to the Supreme Court of Canada decision upholding Superior and Appeal Court decisions that declared Quebec's ban on bilingual commercial signs illegal in December 1988, by invoking the notwithstanding clause of the 1982 constitutional agreements to vacate those judgements. He reinstated the legislation while gutting Quebec's charter of rights and freedoms and prevailing upon the so-called national council of the Quebec Liberal Party to alter the party's manifesto over the weekend.

The new legislation, Bill 178, decreed that all external commercial signs in Quebec would be in French only, and that any wording in any other language, no matter how small the character, was illegal and subject to heavy fines and physical removal. As Mordecai Richler subsequently pointed out in the *New Yorker*, this applied even to a chalkboard notice outside a restaurant bilingually stating the daily special. This, as far as I was concerned, was the *ne plus ultra* of betrayals. Bourassa had supposedly learned his lesson after the Bill 22 fiasco of 1974 in which he lost a large share of the non-French vote without picking up any significant number of nationalists. He had made his miraculous return to office in 1985 on a platform calling for restoration of official bilingualism. Even his erstwhile opponent, Pierre-Marc Johnson, expected something subtler from Bourassa.

One of our directors at UniMédia, Johnson came to have lunch with me in Toronto just before the Supreme Court decision, and we agreed that Bourassa would respond to the anticipated decision with some *chinoiserie* requiring unilingual signs in places with practically no non-French-speaking residents, or zoning Greater Montreal street by street, or dictating relative sizes and number of words, but not an abject capitulation to the extremists.

Apart from being, in itself, an obnoxious attack on the liberty of expression, it was the ultimate desertion of the English-Canadian moderates, of all those who had fought for recognition of the French fact throughout the country. We were made to look ridiculous to our less tolerant compatriots, who had always argued that conciliating Quebec would be pushing on an open revolving door, a process that would never stop costing money and incurring humiliating provocations. We were back to Bill 22, which had caused me to leave Quebec in 1974, but with the additional outrage of the legislated overturning of the judiciary's three-layered interpretation of law and equity.

This was the crowning insult to English Canada, Quebec's benefactor, as Bourassa himself acknowledged, to the extent of up to $8 billion annually for Quebec. Quebec would take the money in equalization payments and transfer payments but render the language of 70 per cent of Canadians, more than 90 per cent of North Americans (above the Rio Grande), and nearly 20 per cent of Quebeckers invisible.

It was not to be borne, and as soon as Brian Mulroney replied, the day after the introduction of Bill 178, to questions about it in parliament, in French though the questions were posed in English, and treated the whole subject as a ho-hum, it was obvious that he had made a Faustian bargain with the Quebec nationalists. It was a disgusting spectacle. (Brian rode into the subsequent sunset uttering spurious apologia for Bourassa because of the "pressure" he was under. He also wrote to me, objecting that my version was not in accord with *Hansard* and suggested, perhaps with some reason, that what I had seen on television had been misleadingly edited. The treatment he received from the media was frequently scandalous enough to justify such a fear.)

I considered at once that Meech Lake, the constitutional agreement that foresaw the return of Quebec as signatory to the Canadian Constitution in exchange for a partial devolution of powers, and which Brian had represented as a great achievement, was dead. In any case, I didn't wish to proceed with it myself. I had initially supported Meech Lake despite the ten-province veto over four key constitutional areas and the selection of Supreme Court justices from lists provided by the provinces, in the higher interests of bringing

Quebec fully into the constitutional fold. I never had any particular problem with the Meech Lake description of Quebec as a "distinct" society, as it obviously is one.

But when the ostensible head of a federalist government in Quebec resorted to such illiberalism, it was obvious that his (Bourassa's) version of federalism had not evolved since his mealy-mouthed crypto-separatist casuistry of the early and mid-seventies. I considered that a government capable of suppressing the visibility of all languages except French and treating fundamental liberties so cavalierly was in no sense preferable to an avowedly separatist government. And I believe a constitutional arrangement based on the assumption that such a government's signature contributed durable adherence to anything was worthless. I wrote essentially this in the *Financial Post* and *Le Soleil* and won heavy reader support in English Canada and deafening obloquy in French Quebec. It was on this occasion that my old friend Gérald Godin bustled into a radio station in Quebec City to denounce me as an "imbecile."

The adoption process for Meech Lake did stall, and by the spring of 1990, our "first ministers," who had too long survived from a perennial fix of singing "O Canada" around the old Ottawa railway station, reborn as a conference centre, and while masquerading as latter-day fathers of Confederation, were becoming frantic.

There was one last argument, one last self-righteous rendition of "O Canada" in the old railway station. Then Brian Mulroney commended himself to the *Globe and Mail* for having "rolled the dice" constitutionally, an NDP Manitoba legislator filibustered, the Trudeauite premier of Newfoundland declined to put the issue to a vote in his legislature, and Meech Lake finally evaporated. Although it was unlamented by me on its merits, as I watched mercifully truncated reportage from England, this was the worst of all possible worlds. Duplessis had always warned that the only circumstances under which Quebec would consider seceding from Canada would be if Quebec felt rejected by English Canada. This was the dismal point we had reached.

Because even the reasonable Québécois were incapable of imagining how offensive Bill 178 was to English Canadians, and the Quebec nationalists rejoiced in any provocation of English Canadians, French Quebec was almost unanimous in seeing the failure of

Meech Lake as a gratuitous rejection by English Canada of any notion of Quebec's distinctness.

Because English Canadians had no sympathy for or knowledge of French Quebec's demographic problems, and in any case (correctly) considered the subject of commercial signs to be irrelevant to demography, their sense of betrayal, of Quebec's treacherous response to their conciliatory overtures, was overwhelming and almost indissoluble. And because Brian Mulroney had treated Bill 178 as an unpleasant but unimportant and excusable expedient, French Canadians were encouraged to believe English Canada had rejected them. Because he took no trouble to explain Quebec's case to the rest of Canada, English Canadians had little opportunity to ascertain that Quebec was not acting, however foolishly and outrageously, out of spite alone.

The federal government's failure to discharge its most primordial duty of making English and French Canadians comprehensible to each other assured that almost no Canadians had any notion of the correct cause and effects that had led to the rancorous impasse. Mulroney's attempt to force English-Canadian support for Meech Lake by invoking the separatist ogre merely legitimized the rednecks, French and English, of whom there was no shortage. Bourassa, convictionless placeman and rather decayed servitor that he was, could not accept his responsibility for the imbroglio caused by the infamous Bill 178 and could go no further to damp down overheated spirits than obscurantist apparently non-separatist comments on Quebec's economic interests.

The Opposition leader Jacques Parizeau, uncontradicted by the federal appeasers of Quebec, was bound to be rather successful selling a version of separatism that added the joys of independence to all the benefits of Canadian participation. Since no one was pointing out that Quebec would have to assume its full per capita share of the federal public debt (of $400 billion), or that counties that voted to remain in Canada could do so, or that legally Ungava would revert to Canada, Parizeau had a huge early success with a version of Quebec's independence that included Canadian money, a common market, and even membership in the Commonwealth. It was a challenging political version of simultaneous consumption and retention of the same political cake.

The constitutional issue was now bound to be inflamed for several years. As long as Ottawa, government and opposition, was determined to appease Quebec, and Quebec's official concept of federalism was tokenistic window-dressing over a steady transfer of federal revenue and jurisdiction from Ottawa to Quebec, federalists, nationalists, and the growing ranks of both English and French bigots were sure to be unhappy. This degrading cycle was bound to reach its final stage if, as recurred in 1992, an updated formula of giving everything to every jurisdiction and special-interest group that asked for it were put on offer, especially if accompanied by the customary orgy of governmental self-congratulation. Serendipitously, the United Nations eventually prevailed upon Quebec to consider relaxing its prohibition of visible bilingualism. Quebec could accept such an overture more easily from that organization than from its own courts or the federal government. In 1991 I was one of the financial backers of the 50th anniversary celebrations for the Atlantic Charter of Placentia, Newfoundland, where Churchill and Roosevelt proclaimed the Four Freedoms, including freedom of expression. I reflected, as we re-enacted their ceremony, on how improbable it would have seemed then that any of those freedoms would ever have to be reasserted from outside in any part of Canada.

The constitutional shambles was complemented by the assurance of an economic débâcle with the election of the New Democratic Party led by Bob Rae in Ontario in September 1990. The smug Ontario voters, who had wallowed in effortlessly rising prosperity and notions of their manifest superior "quality of life" for decades, had ended forty-two years of Conservative rule when they became grumpy about fulfilling 118-year-old obligations to the separate-school system.

David Peterson and his Liberals were the beneficiaries in 1985. When he called an election after only three years of a majority term, which he won in 1987, Peterson was dumped and with no apparently serious examination of what the NDP were pledged to do to Ontario, the official Opposition was brought in with 37.6 per cent of the vote. Elections in over-confident Ontario had become a mindless game of Buggins's turn. This was the false romance of dour Ontarians who recognize the real thing is neither romance nor politics. The incoming government was not a coherent party at all in any traditional sense: it was an uneasy and incoherent coalition of single-issue fanatics, militant advocates of organized labour, feminists, abortionists, homosexuals, ecogeeks, all standing and shouting on each other's shoulders, though supported by the bedrock of Ontario's traditional mild do-gooders, forgetting to case their benefactions.

Since they believed that those engaged in commerce were merely scavengers, who, like raccoons riffling through garbage, would take what they could find and go on investing and employing with undiminished energy even if their profit margins were drastically reduced, the thought that capital would depart Ontario and that job-creation would suffer did not arise.

At a dinner Hal Jackman and I gave for the leader of the Reform Party, Preston Manning, at the Toronto Club on the eve of the Ontario election, I jocularly explained in my introduction of Preston that I wasn't concerned about the following day's provincial election because "I can get to the airport before Bob Rae can get to the lieutenant-governor's office!" This was what happened, but I wrote a column in the *Financial Post* predicting economic disaster. As the Rae government handed over all industrial power to the labour unions, as it had pledged to do, private-sector capital investment and job creation were sure to dry up. This process would be compounded by the tax increases the NDP had promised. No one in his right mind would invest a cent in Ontario under this regime, and Ontario's manufacturing, the great majority of Canada's secondary industry and largely connected to the automobile industry, was almost certain to avail itself of the greater flexibility afforded by free trade with the United States to move south.

The accuracy of this prediction was illustrated when the *Toronto Star*, Canada's largest and most successful as well as leading left-wing newspaper, a raddled supporter of every conceivable haemophiliac bleeding-heart cause, announced in an astonishing editorial (September 7, 1991) that it could not guarantee its ability to continue in business if the provincial government's proposed amendments to the Labour Relations Act were adopted.

Under these rules, which were adopted a year later, labour contracts followed work throughout the province (contracted outside work could not be moved to another provider of the work at a lower labour cost), in the event of a strike there could be no replacement work by outsiders or supervisory personnel, and virtually all personnel short of the most senior executives were materially encouraged to unionize. It was, as I wrote in the *Financial Post*, the seizure of the commanding heights of the private sector and the elimination of the shareholders' interest in favour of the employees'. The employers would lose all ability to withhold profit from the workers and remit it to the investors.

The petulance and naïveté of the Ontario voters in delivering over half the GNP of Canada to such a regime of economic thieves and vandals, on the heels of an eruption of the ancient dispute with Quebec, reduced Canadian public life to the lowest point of contumely, mean self-interest, mediocrity of debate, and general economic death-wishfulness in my time.

At a time when most of the rest of the world was celebrating the victorious end of the Cold War, or replacing repressive with liberal regimes, Canada's two largest provinces, two-thirds of the country, were led by mindless stooges of a corrupt antediluvian labour movement in Ontario, and by craven ethno-narcissists in Quebec. Even from the safety and distance of London, it was painful to see so great a country laid so low by the lassitude, fadishness, and philistinism of its own voters.

At the Hollinger annual meeting in June 1991 Hal Jackman sat in the directors' place in the front row, ostentatiously reading a copy of the London *Independent* during my remarks. My response to this amusing diversion was to point out that those, such as Hal, who had prematurely commended the provincial premier on his supposed moderation had made themselves, in Lenin's famous phrase, "useful idiots."

Bob Rae, having no apparent sense of humour himself, ignored the possibility that Jackman and I might be making jokes at each other's expense. He took up Hal's defence and triggered another acidulous exchange between us in the pages of the *Financial Post*. Jackman, having secured a grant for his money-losing Algoma Central Railway and after being gratified by the provincial government's abandonment of its plan for a state takeover of car insurance, was ultimately rewarded for his deference with provincial government approval for his nomination as lieutenant-governor.

I found slightly discouraging the spectacle of Hal leaving the high position he held in the private sector to accept such an antiquarian ceremonial office where he could, as I put it in a roast Mickey Cohen organized for him, simulate the young Bishop Talleyrand voting for the abolition of church property by giving royal assent to Bob Rae's sodomization of the private sector.

Most discouraging of all was the criticism I privately received from some of my wealthiest friends in Toronto for the public jousts I had had with Rae. Although I received a herniating mass of messages of support from small businessmen and employed people throughout Ontario, a few of Ontario's largest and most respected employers privately urged me not to aggravate the premier. The washed-out *fin de la race* pusillanimity of those from whom the rank and file of the private sector had every right to expect clear direction did more than anything to convince me that our corporate leadership had failed as completely as the academic, journalistic, bureaucratic, political, and ecclesiastical élites.

All, with only individual exceptions, had subscribed to the myth of compassionate Canada, of more and more confiscation and redistribution of income in exchange for votes and in the name of fairness. Dour sanctimony: hear, see, and speak no evil; most of it was illusion and illusion was glorified. As Irving Layton (of all people) had written of Canada twenty-five years before: Mediocrity is sanity, philistinism is olympian serenity, and the spitefulness of the weak is moral indignation. UN surveys were doubtless correct in putting Canada and Denmark at the top of advantageous places to live, but not for the most ambitious, exceptional people who give a nation its character. It was a comfortable place but not an exciting one. I did not, at this time, feel I belonged there.

The Britain to which I returned, a few days before Rae's inauguration, in September 1990, was not without its political jejuneries. *Daily Telegraph* chairmen can always play some role in Tory politics if they choose. I have rarely knowingly yielded to anyone in my admiration for Margaret Thatcher, and I was appalled to find the extent to which her caucus had become fractious and skittish under her strong, if eccentric and rather arbitrary leadership. I made my customary calls upon some of the party elders and found a disconcerting reticence about the prime minister.

I felt passionately that she had redeemed her country from vassalage to the thugs of the Labour union leadership and the hobnailed fiscal jackboot of 98 per cent top personal tax rates and had played a role in the world that was indispensable to victory in the Cold War. Her services were beyond estimation, and she had had them translated into the only three consecutive full-term general election victories for a British party leader since Lord Liverpool, before the first Reform Act, which broadened the electorate beyond Disraeli's "very few" in 1832.

My zeal to support the undermined leader was only slightly diluted by her own beatific unawareness when I visited her, and that of her principal supporters, of the threat to her continuation in office.

The parliamentary Conservative Party was infested with people who had no loyalty to Margaret Thatcher, no real comprehension of her program, and no concern for anything except their own incumbency. Interposed among the mass of MPs were about forty whom Mrs. Thatcher had, in the past eleven years, consigned to the back benches from cabinet or ministerial positions. They were obviously waiting for an opportunity to stick the knife between her shoulder blades, and the sound of sharpening metal was audible at Westminster. She had given only a few patronage posts, such as Leon Brittan in Brussels, and generally only loyalists the peerage, leaving most of her militant and implacable caucus opponents, such as Edward Heath, waiting in the shadows in the grim expectation (or ambition) of an assassin.

Nigel Lawson had admirably reduced and reformed taxes but over-reacted to the October 1987 stock-market crash, creating serious inflationary pressures to which his only response was to raise interest rates to 15 per cent. Given that every point in the interest rate represented half a point in the rate of inflation, this always seemed to me like pouring gasoline on the fire. Eighty per cent of British mortgages have floating rates, and the inconvenience caused by Nigel's interest-rate policy, and generally continued by his successor, John Major, when Nigel resigned in the autumn of 1989, was considerable. Nigel had given up working on money supply and turned monetary policy into shadowing the Deutschmark, an abdication of sovereignty and a hazardous escapade as the side effects of German reunification were to prove.

The greatest single bugbear bedevilling the government seemed to be the community charge, the so-called poll tax, under which all adults in a municipality above a minimum income level paid a uniform annual charge for local services, regardless of their means or the value of their residential property. The principle was not without merit: that everyone used municipal services, such as street lighting, park benches, and garbage collection, and everyone should contribute equally, as do those who ride the public transit system. The community charge replaced the rates system, under which fifty-seven criteria were applied to massage money in lump-sum payments from the central government to poorer municipalities with the result that left-wing borough councils routinely made grants in aid to the Sandinistas, the African National Congress, Gay Awareness, and only slightly in exaggeration, the Turkish Lesbian Hang-gliding Society.

Mrs. Thatcher had already responded to the outrages of the extreme left-dominated Greater London Council by abolishing it, firing its civil servants, selling its headquarters — County Hall, Britain's largest building — to developers and effectively placing one of the world's greatest cities under direct rule from the Home Office.

The community charge was designed to eliminate the free-riders. There were more than 15 million more voters than rate-payers, though most were spouses or equivalent or children of voting age living with their parents, as well as tenants whose rents assumedly included an allocation of rates. The charge was also intended to be a rod on the backs of the profligate and antagonistic left-wing local councils.

All of these ends were admirable enough, but the poll tax was poorly conceived and incompetently implemented. The imposition of the new tax was first entrusted to Nicholas Ridley, a perversely abrasive and antagonistic figure. I had met him several times and although he was ideologically reliable, fervently loyal to Thatcher, and an intelligent and dedicated Conservative, I had always found his reactionary brusqueness rather unattractive. In July 1990, Dominic Lawson (Nigel's son) published in the *Spectator* (which the *Daily Telegraph* had owned for two years) an interview with Ridley that included some inflammatory remarks about Germans in general and the federal chancellor, Helmut Kohl, particularly. He was obliged to resign in consequence. He had recently moved from Environment secretary responsible for the poll tax to Trade and Industry secretary and had been replaced at the Environment by Chris Patten, an amiable and intelligent red Tory whose political hero was Stanley Baldwin and who never believed in the poll tax. He gave a couple of good parliamentary speeches debunking the Labour Party's position but never lifted a finger to sell the tax to the British public.

Thus, the most explosive issue in British politics was handed from a secretary with appropriate convictions but negative talents of advocacy to a considerable salesman with no faith in the policy whose implementation he knew when he accepted the promotion to be his principal task. The peculiar British love of the underdog, which fastens itself easily onto so many unworthy economic groups, such as strikers and voluntary welfare addicts, was stirred up against this tax, and its ultimate author, the prime minister. Though Britain is a rather irreligious country, its non-conformist conscience can be roused as surely as it was by Gladstone against the Turks in the Midlothian campaign of 1879, and the country was swept by the unstoppable belief that the poll tax was unfair, regressive, and confiscatory against those who could least afford it.

Most municipalities, and not only Labour-governed ones, jacked up their taxes outrageously and blamed the new charge. Instead of being a fiscal discipline on profligate municipalities, it became a club with which the least reputable municipal authorities savaged, routed, and humiliated the government of one of the strongest and most accomplished prime ministers in British history. It was a monumental fiasco and, in jurisdictional terms, one of the greatest upheavals in Britain since James II was sent packing in 1688 for advocating religious toleration. And not even utilitarian Whig myth-makers like Macaulay or the Trevelyans could consider the poll tax débâcle a "glorious revolution."

The poll tax riots in London in the spring of 1990, where the unruly scum of London's mobs vandalized the area in and around Trafalgar Square, furnished a graphic example of the erosion of support for the government. Although subsequent polls indicated no support for the rioters, nor did they show any reactive enthusiasm for the government.

The one good thing revealed by the riots was that the British, despite a lot of hypocritical pieties uttered to poll-takers about preparedness to pay higher taxes provided disadvantaged people got the benefit of them, didn't wish to have their taxes raised.

I had called upon Mrs. Thatcher and the then party chairman, Kenneth Baker, just before leaving for South Africa, Palm Beach, and Japan in March 1990. Mrs. Thatcher seemed somewhat shaken and fatigued by recent disorders and quite uncomprehending of the nature and extent of public opposition to the poll tax. She was, as always, resolute in her determination to fight on. I had, over the past year, questioned her tactics, but this was the first occasion in at least fifty encounters with her when she seemed out of touch, haggard, and bewildered.

Kenneth Baker was a good deal more realistic and had plotted a municipal election campaign on the slogan "Labour councils cost you more," which actually proved a modest success in enabling the government, as Max Hastings put it in a Dunkirk image, "to get 300,000 men off the beaches." Mrs. Thatcher, for all her leadership qualities, was not always an astute or thorough judge of her political associates. In the summer of 1989, she had finally sacked the amiable Sir Geoffrey Howe, who had rendered past service as Chancellor of the Exchequer, from his post as Foreign Secretary, as he had led Britain too far along the path into an imprecise and utopian integrated Europe. This was not an unfounded concern but there was an element of the scapegoat in his status: Mrs. Thatcher was the prime minister. Geoffrey Howe's irritation at being shunted into the non-post of deputy prime minister and leader of the House of Commons was understandable, and even there she didn't treat him very gently.

From the summer of 1989 on, Geoffrey Howe was a time bomb waiting for his time to explode. So already, and for several years, had been Michael Heseltine, the flamboyant, slightly leftish, former defence secretary who quit the government over the Westland helicopters affair in 1986, but who had maintained an important independent constituency in the Tory caucus. Nigel Lawson, aggrieved at Mrs. Thatcher's repeated hints that he had bungled into inflation and recession (which he had) had abruptly quit as chancellor in the autumn of 1989. In neither sacking him nor wholeheartedly supporting Nigel, she appeared both unsupportive of a respected colleague and yet fully implicated in unpopular policies.

My fear in the autumn of 1989 had been that Heseltine, Howe, and Lawson would combine to assault Thatcher in the annual caucus election of the leader. This was an aberrant procedure set up after Harold Macmillan ignored both the caucus and the constituency associations to put Sir Alec Douglas Home in as his successor ahead of Rab Butler and Quintin Hailsham in 1963.

It was preposterous for an incumbent prime minister to have to submit to so demeaning a procedure as an annual caucus leadership contest, and when the undistinguished Anthony Mayer presented himself against Mrs. Thatcher in 1989 I was about to generate an editorial suggestion for a signed ballot, i.e., that caucus members who didn't sign could be assumed to have supported Mayer with the implicit prospect of being deselected as candidate for their trouble. Mrs. Thatcher telephoned me to say that the ballot had to be free and fair and unsigned. I reminded her that this was "mortal combat, we must take no prisoners. In the words of your most illustrious predecessor [Churchill], 'We must strangle this insurrection in its cradle.'" She commended me on my "spirit" but declined to adopt my methods.

I spoke on several occasions in 1989 and 1990 to Tim Renton, the chief whip, who, it was shortly obvious, had no loyalty whatever to Thatcher, and who was an incompetent machiavellian. Being an honourable person herself, well aware of her ability to dominate and run roughshod over her opponents in and outside her own party, despising treachery and conscious of her mighty achievement in leading her party to office and keeping it there for over ten years, it was incomprehensible to her that those who owed office to her could betray her.

Elizabethan personality as she is, she had, in a non-physical way, fancied younger men and promoted them sequentially. John Major, who had succeeded Nigel Lawson as Chancellor of the Exchequer, was the latest in this series. Her most loyal supporters tended to be the least presentable or compelling figures, such as Nicholas Ridley, and since the caucus included so many disgruntled former office-holders there was a great deal of tinder around waiting for inflammation. This occasion arose when Geoffrey Howe finally tired of Margaret Thatcher's bullying and resigned, landing a deadly blow in his well-crafted House retirement speech a few days later in which he purports to have waited too long before objecting to the prime minister's mistaken European policy and overbearing manner generally.

Apart from matters of personality (Mrs. Thatcher regularly referred to Geoffrey Howe in terms of puddings and other soft, malleable substances), their greatest bone of contention was Europe. This issue threatened to provide the greatest schism in the British Conservative Party since Joseph Chamberlain's turn-of-the-century campaign for Imperial preference, if not since the rending struggle between Peel and Disraeli over the Corn Laws in the 1840s. The British generally seemed to think that Europe was a good thing and that the United Kingdom should accordingly be part of it, but there were great reservations about the utopian ideas of the euro-integrationists. Brussels was seen as socialistic, meddlesome, addicted to high taxes and over-regulation, undemocratic, and *dirigiste*. And most Tory opinion had reservations about stripping Westminster of its powers in favour of unproved institutions that would be dominated by countries that had never developed workable democratic institutions, such as Italy, or only recently, Germany in 1949, France in 1958, and Spain in 1974.

The natural British response was to make conciliatory noises but advance rather tentatively, hoping the Europeans would become more credible or less unitary. Some, including Heath, Heseltine, and Howe, and most of the Foreign Office, wanted to plunge into Europe head first, partly because they subscribed to the grand vision that included the resurrection of "Europe" as the world's political centre, partly merely to escape perceived American domination. Mrs. Thatcher wanted a common market and co-ordinated monetary policies but no further concessions of sovereignty, no common currency or central bank, and certainly no common defence or foreign policy.

I spoke at the Conservative Party annual conference at Bournemouth in October 1990, to the Centre for Policy Studies, under the chairmanship of the distinguished historian Hugh Thomas (Lord Thomas), whose masterful study of the Spanish Civil War I had lugged around Spain as a student in 1963. My basic theme was that European institutions were not adequate to do what they were already tackling, that there was no evidence that further concessions of sovereignty would give Britain better government, that the European Community should be broadened to include emerging Eastern Europe as quickly as was practical, that Britain must never be forced to choose between Europe and the United States, and that the Opposition's views on Europe were fatuous and based chiefly on European Commission president Jacques Delors's comment to the Trades Union Congress in 1987 that all the powers taken from the miners and other unions by Thatcher would be given back in a few years by Brussels.

My remarks were well received by Mrs. Thatcher and her supporters, and even Hugh Thomas, who is more of an integrationist, when I asked him at the end of my remarks if we were still on speaking terms, replied, "Of course, I don't agree with you, but I like you!" I was assisted in preparing the speech by one of our most talented and traditionalist editorial writers, Simon Heffer, who was relatively undismayed by Max Hastings's endeavours to send him to cover the Afghanistan War, where his red hair and tweed suits would have made him rather conspicuous. I dissuaded him from going to the Conservative Party's central office with a call to electoral arms so hair-raising that he stood bolt-upright and solemnly intoned: "This is magnificent. I shall invite Enoch to lunch." This was the highest level of enthusiasm. Enoch Powell, legendary maverick of the Tory right, did come to lunch, but though our relations are cordial, they are retarded by his pathological anti-Americanism and his long-standing championship of an Anglo-Russian alliance as an alternative to NATO.

The Conservative Party and the country generally were getting a little tired of Mrs. Thatcher's tirades at European Community meetings, and of Britain always being outvoted eleven to one at such meetings. After Geoffrey Howe's resignation, concern among Conservative MPs over Europe came to rival dislike of the poll tax, fear of high interest rates and recession, and concern generally that the prime minister was out of touch.

Michael Heseltine expressed support of Howe, and Mrs. Thatcher's belligerent press secretary, Bernard Ingham, told him to "put up or shut up" in the upcoming caucus elections. Heseltine announced his candidacy against the prime minister, who indicated her tenacious underestimation of the strength of her caucus opposition by entrusting her re-election campaign to two fine but very secondary and retiring MPs, Peter Morrison and George Younger.

All through the autumn, I was getting regular bulletins on the state of caucus opinion from our Westminster correspondents, whose ranks were augmented as the crisis deepened and who had no difficulty canvassing a broad section of the caucus almost daily. From all my information, the prime minister was in difficulty, but when I telephoned her aides to ask them what was being done "to suppress this state of insurrection," I was avuncularly counselled on the inadvisability of over-reaction. Our editorial support of Mrs. Thatcher was unambiguous.

Max Hastings advised me of the results of the first ballot — that she had fallen four votes short of the required two-thirds — and I replied at once that she was finished. She had certainly the will to fight on prior to the result, but I doubted whether even she could easily absorb the shock of running so narrowly ahead of a man she considered contemptuously as a treacherous charlatan. Our editorial policy, however, entertained no compromise with our support of the incumbent.

I went to a hastily improvised last-ditch Thatcher defence meeting the next day in the private room at Mark's Club, with the party treasurer, Lord Alistair McAlpine, Thatcher tacticians, Sir Gordon Reece and Tim Bell, and the editor of the *Daily Mail*, Sir David English. John Major, recovering from the extraction of wisdom teeth, was on the telephone.

My advice was to indicate a willingness to take Michael Heseltine back into the government, to undertake to consider retiring gracefully if there were not any appreciable improvement in the government's standing in the country within six months, and to let it be known, through "sources" — and I volunteered to have this printed in the *Daily Telegraph* — that if despite these undertakings, the caucus failed to support her, Mrs. Thatcher would advise the Monarch to dissolve parliament. My comment was that "the prospect of having to get out and work for a living might inspire in our MPs a late recognition of the virtues of loyalty to their leader." My views were thought rather hard line, but Alistair McAlpine undertook to deliver them with the comments of the others to the prime minister at 7:30 that evening.

Max Hastings and I worked out our next day's editorial, which concluded that Mrs. Thatcher had been one of the greatest prime ministers of British history "and as long as she seeks to retain that office, she may count on the support of this newspaper."

By the time most copies of that edition of the *Daily Telegraph* were being read, her intention to retire had been announced, as Max informed me at a few minutes past eight a.m. There had, she told me later, been "evil in the air" the night before, as her cabinet secretaries and ministers proceeded through Downing Street making altogether insufficient statements of support. Heseltine, she told me, was said to be "hoovering up votes."

And great Thatcher fell, as if to assassins.

Partly because of Mrs. Thatcher's inattentions, but particularly because so many of her caucus members were spiteful, cowardly, and narrowly self-interested, it was a lamentable end to a great premiership. It was given a suspensive dignity only by the possibility of saving the government from the anti-Thatcherites and by the prime minister's brilliant response to the Opposition no-confidence motion on the afternoon of her resignation announcement. The greatest applause was reserved for the Tory back-bencher who used a pause in Mrs. Thatcher's magisterial rebuttal of her official opponents to wave at the declared candidates for her succession, Heseltine, Major, and Foreign secretary Douglas Hurd, as well as to the official Opposition and to say, "You could wipe the floor with this lot."

At the *Telegraph*, as elsewhere in Conservative circles, after a hiatus of perhaps an hour to salute the departing leader, the customary febrile manoeuvring ensued. For those who didn't favour Heseltine, the urgent requirement was to blow a wheel off his bandwagon, as with Thatcher's withdrawal he was briefly the only candidate and had achieved considerable momentum. My own meetings with Heseltine had been cordial. He had been a successful commercial publisher and a capable Defence secretary and had a number of endearing attributes, including his undoubted talents as an ornithologist. I could not support him, however, for both tactical and policy reasons.

His victory would be universally interpreted in Britain and outside as a repudiation of Thatcher, not a state of affairs that we could possibly countenance. That the glorious victrix over the Marxists who had brutalized British organized labour, the restorer of the incentive-based competitive economic system and of British political relevance in the world should be replaced by someone as much pledged to demolish as to continue her work was a gruesome and a depressing thought. In straight policy terms, Heseltine had always struck me as far too compulsive a euro-joiner, irresolute in his commitment to low taxes and expansion of the private sector and abrasively anti-American.

I accordingly called my *Telegraph* and Hollinger colleague, Lord Carrington, who is really a cunning and cynical Whig nobleman, and jocularly announced that since he had publicly declared for Heseltine, I was throwing him out as a director. He said he didn't want to spend his "declining years under Labour" and would ask Heseltine to telephone me. When he did so, early on the day of the second ballot, to see if anything could be done to make the *Telegraph*'s treatment of his candidacy more positive, I explained that we could not be a party to perceived de-Thatcherization and mentioned the specific policy differences that concerned me. He denied anti-Americanism but when I asked why, when my friend Richard Perle had given him satellite-photographed evidence of Soviet violation of the A.B.M. treaty with the phased-array radar at Krasnoyarsk he had dismissed it, he seemed to suffer an attack of glottal stops, before stammering something about "supporting [his] officials." I did say that I hoped if Major won, Michael would rejoin the government. Heseltine did so and performed valuable service in dismantling the poll tax without going all the way back to the inanities of the rates system, and he performed brilliantly in the 1992 election campaign. (I should also add, he was extremely helpful to those of us promoting a memorial to Canada's role in both world wars, in Green Park across from Buckingham Palace. Without his help and John Major's the whole project could have been buried permanently in the British cultural and municipal quangos.)

The strategy I worked out with Max Hastings was to promote both John Major and Douglas Hurd in order to chip as many votes as possible from Heseltine and support the strongest of them, assumedly Major, on the final ballot. The *Daily Telegraph* endorsed Hurd, with kind words for Major, and undoubtedly helped Hurd secure the support he did. The *Sunday Telegraph* supported Major with kind words for Hurd. Between Thatcher's withdrawal and the Major–Hurd declarations of candidacy, and the second ballot, the Conservative caucus members returned to their constituencies to hear from their local party association executives.

We made the most of this opportunity, as all indications are that up to 90 per cent of Conservative constituency association executives read the *Daily Telegraph*, and the overwhelming majority of them were loyal to Mrs. Thatcher.

We editorialized that the caucus, in the manner of the lesser murderers of Caesar, might now be asking "What have we done?" and we employed the phrase "political assassination" in a tendentious, but not, I think, inaccurate context. These initiatives, as well as many stop-Heseltine moves, including intensive lobbying by Margaret Thatcher, had their effect, and John Major came, on the next ballot, within one vote of outright victory, his opponents withdrew, and the Thatcher succession passed, at least, to her preferred candidate and the person most likely to continue and defend her achievements.

Beneath John Major's almost impenetrable pleasantness I had occasion already to discover a tough and shrewd operator. The son of a circus acrobat, who did not finish secondary school, spent most of a year as a welfare recipient in Brixton, and worked his way up from bank clerk to prime minister at age forty-seven, John Major was the ultimate mid-market riser. He had managed to attract and retain Mrs. Thatcher's approval, though not by the practice of sycophancy employed by some of her earlier younger favourites, while being the preferred candidate of those who agreed unspecifically with most of what she had achieved but wanted a softer, gentler approach. He seemed an inspired standard bearer for the party of meritocratic assisted self-help for the disadvantaged against the traditional Labour Party formula of righteous income confiscation and redistribution.

In the abstract, the change of leader was a mélange of political opportunism and continuity that would be effective if Major really possessed an aptitude to govern. Major might better satisfy the desire for change than Neil Kinnock, who had already been one of the longest-serving and least prepossessing Opposition leaders of the twentieth century. This faculty for putting a plausible face on a rout, like Mountbatten's representation of the chaotic withdrawal from India as the pre-planned consummation of Britain's long-cherished objective of conferring independence on the sub-continent, couldn't entirely disguise the proportions of the rout and of the treachery that engineered it. After eleven years of rising productivity and competitiveness, half of Mrs. Thatcher's caucus didn't understand or believe in what she had done.

One of the most powerful and purposeful governments of British history had been ludicrously put to flight by a ragged miscellany of local politicians, ranging from the urban guerrilla left to the extreme detritus of Pecksniffian shire Tories. By British standards it was indeed a revolution. Presentable elements managed to put themselves at the head of the mobs just before the collapse descended unmistakably to parliamentary mob rule.

But for someone who had watched closely from near or far, usually with actual or subsequent acquaintance with the personalities, the departures of John Diefenbaker (the only such leave-taking I really approved), Jean Lesage, Lyndon Johnson, Charles de Gaulle, Richard Nixon, it was a gloomy and disillusioning spectacle.

Where Margaret Thatcher had allowed public services to deteriorate while privatizing them and lowering taxes, generally producing a consequent improvement in services and taxpayer morale, John Major would now have to convince his electors that he would produce improved services and less automatic privatization and would continue to be the guardian of lower taxes and fiscal responsibility. It could be a tense, yet hopeful and somewhat artistic struggle to preserve the beneficent heritage of a magnificent regime and a great leader. Obviously, like de Gaulle and Reagan, and Roosevelt in his time, she had moved the whole polity in her direction, and reversion to the disorder, discouragement, and debauchery that preceded and elevated the departed leader was unthinkable. Yet the whole process of scrambling to preserve so manifestly great a record of courage and achievement was becoming familiarly disconcerting.

I sent her de Gaulle's comments on the rejection of Mr. Churchill in 1945, that Churchill's (i.e., Thatcher's) "personality, identified with a magnificent enterprise, (her) countenance, etched by the fire and frosts of great events, were no longer adequate to the era of mediocrity." She appreciated the comparison.

I saw her even more often out of office than I had in, for a while. She had little in her own interests or friends, apart from Denis, never having been especially gregarious or companionable, to fall back upon. Boredom, shock, disorientation, and the rancour of betrayal and of what might have been weighed heavily upon her.

A couple of weeks after her retirement, I had her to dinner with Henry Kissinger to discuss how best to handle memoirs, television appearances, the foundation she was planning, and the problems of adjustment. Henry's advice was given from a platform of great expertise as well as admiration for her, and she eventually followed most of it.

Over the succeeding months, gradually Margaret Thatcher could be seen to recover her spirits. In the darker moments of deprivation and bitterness, her natural bravery and unassailable, majestic dignity banished the unseemly. Disappointing as was the ingratitude and venality of many who owed everything to her, astonishing as had been the atrophication of her own sense of self-preservation, the paralysis of disappointment slowly gave way to new activity, encouraged by the vast army of her unwavering supporters, including me. We were reminders, though rarely explicitly, of the truth of de Gaulle's serene realization that "since everything eternally begins anew, everything we do that is worthwhile will be taken up with new ardour after we have gone."

All through 1990 and 1991, worsening economic conditions produced increasing strain on over-levered businesses. Many famous fortunes that had arisen spectacularly in earlier decades crashed just as flamboyantly. Bob Campeau, Sam Belzberg, the heirs of Steve Roman, Reuben Cohen and Leonard Ellen, Bernard Lamarre, and most breathtakingly of all, Bob Maxwell, and ultimately Paul and Albert Reichmann, were among those whose fortunes evaporated or were severely reduced. Not being envious of successful people, I sincerely regretted all these reversals. As Bob Campeau's difficulties increased, he and Paul Reichmann, who was for a time his principal backer, asked me to become an independent director of Campeau Corporation. I held that post for about six months, but when Bob rejected the compromise that I extracted with difficulty from his directors, that he stay as non-executive chairman but retire as chief executive, and when he became chiefly preoccupied with trying to launch spurious lawsuits against the Reichmanns, I withdrew.

I had wanted to encourage Bob in his move into the United States because I sympathized with his basic premises, that the United States was a more desirable country to invest in and that Canada should develop an awareness of how uncompetitive it was becoming as a place to invest.

When we took control of the *Telegraph* in early 1986, if asked what international businessmen I knew most impressed me as unassailable in their demonstrated ability to foresee and surmount economic vicissitudes, I would have named Rupert Murdoch and Paul Reichmann. By 1991, Rupert was wracked by a severe, though not mortal, liquidity crisis, and Paul was being pestilentially importuned by nervous bankers.

(It was in May 1992 that the Reichmanns sought judicial protection from their creditors. By the end of 1992, Paul had no expectation of salvaging more than bits and pieces from the equity of Olympia & York.)

I gave an address to the Media Society at the Café Royal in London in February 1991, in which, among other things, I attacked Murdoch's critics as largely motivated by "spite and envy." So grateful was he to have something positive said about him (and I ensured that this passage was quoted in the *Daily Telegraph*'s round-up of the address) that Rupert, his exquisite wife Anna, Andrew Knight, and the editor of the *Times*, Simon Jenkins all wrote appreciatively to me. Rupert ultimately had to endure painful debt reorganizations and asset disposals. If his bid for MGM had not been topped at the last minute by an Australian parvenu, Rupert would have gone completely bankrupt (as the winning bidder for MGM did). The Reichmanns' fate was sadder and more shocking. Both endured their ordeals with dignity. I engaged in a modest amount of official lobbying on Paul's behalf with the U.K. and Canadian governments and the CIBC, within the bounds of indisputable arithmetic. It was the best and least I could do for so distinguished, exemplary, and scholarly a businessman and friend.

In our annual Hollinger reports and at our annual meetings from 1989 on, I assured shareholders that if the long-awaited recession came, I was confident that our cash flows would prove resistant to downward pressure and that we would be well-positioned to take advantage of a buyer's market for assets. This proved to be the case. As the recession deepened, our discretionary cash flow was virtually unaffected because of the invincible market leadership and tight management of the *Daily Telegraph*, the tenacious resistance and cost restraint at the American Publishing units, and because our gradual progress with the Quebec assets, easing them out of the hamstrung, overmanned condition we found them in, out-stripped the ravages of the recession. Streamlining operations in prosperous times when generous settlements can be afforded and work is relatively available for laid off employees always saves jobs when the economy slows.

In the enshrouding economic gloom, we looked at a great number of potential acquisitions in related businesses. The most interesting was the very first on a large scale in the newspaper industry to succumb to recessionary problems. The John Fairfax Company in Australia operated the leading newspapers in the country and enjoyed virtual broadsheet monopolies in Sydney, Melbourne, and a number of smaller towns, as well as the country's only financial daily and a range of other assets. In an intra-family dispute, a young scion of the family, Warwick Fairfax, allegedly influenced by his eccentric and slightly delusional mother, Lady Mary Fairfax (who sent out twelve-page Christmas cards jammed with miscellaneous quotations and who bought the top three floors of New York's Pierre Hotel)[†], was advanced A$2.4 billion by banks and junk-bond underwriters and produced a minority shareholder buy-out. The debt equity ratio, of about 2.4 billion to one, was perhaps the highest ever recorded and came just before the October 1987 stock-market crash.

The previous Fairfax management had been among the long list of alternatives contemplated and pursued by Nicholas Berry in 1985 for the *Telegraph*, but they sensibly withdrew when they discovered the terms of our agreement with Lord Hartwell. Two of their senior people paid a courtesy call on Andrew Knight and me in the summer of 1987. Warwick called on me in Palm Beach with his new chief executive in early 1988, seeking a possible buyer for the

---

[†] She claimed she could rent them out to visiting heads of state, but as I pointed out to her one day at Claridge's, such people seem happy to stay at their United Nations legations or at the Waldorf Astoria, and recruiting them as tenants could prove a challenging management task.

Melbourne Age to relieve his acute debt imbalance. They met in London first with Andrew Knight, who advised me to expect "a middle-aged man with a younger man on a leash, and the young man has a long, somewhat vacant face like a latter-day Hapsburg." Warwick proved a courteous and not obviously unintelligent man, whose much publicized tendencies to reclusiveness and evangelical Christianity were not evident.

We did eventually produce a conditional bid for the *Age*, which fell $300 million short of the offer Bob Maxwell had been bandying about prior to being declared an ineligible buyer by the then treasurer of Australia, Paul Keating, who considered Maxwell to be not the most desirable type of foreign media owner. Andrew and Dan Colson and I all had the impression we were being used as beaters in an auction process, as was eventually confirmed to be the case, but we went along with it to pick up the (London) *Spectator*, a lively, literate, and money-losing weekly that we thought could be run more efficiently and used as a pool of excellent writers that could be cycled through the *Telegraph*s.

The *Spectator* was offered for an almost nominal consideration as bait for the *Age*. We took the bait but not the hook. (The *Age* was withdrawn following the fiasco with Maxwell.) A slight irony was perceived in the purchase of the *Spectator* as it had been the forum for the attack on me by John Ralston Saul in 1985.

As had been generally foreseen, Warwick, who removed to Chicago to study the newspaper business at a modest echelon, ran out of money in late 1990, and the Fairfax company went into receivership. Operating results were improved significantly but skyrocketing interest rates, recessionary revenue declines, and an inability to spin out assets quickly and advantageously enough laid the company low and brought Warwick's wild escapade to its sad and widely predicted end.

Australia, with a population of 17 million, does not have unlimited ranks of financially serious people, especially after the economic devastation of the late eighties. All who could still find voice for their ambitions stirred at the prospect of Fairfax.

In June 1990, I had met Kerry Packer, Australia's wealthiest and most colourful businessman (mainly a television and magazine owner) at Jimmie Goldsmith's house in London, and asked him his prediction on Fairfax. He naturally foresaw the arrival of the receiver and expressed an interest in participating in a bid at the appropriate time. We agreed to keep in touch and eventually agreed that it was time to make a move almost a year later.

Kerry Packer is the roughest, toughest, as well as one of the most astute and picturesque businessmen I have met. He is a man of monumental and very uneven qualities, though it must be emphasized that he was a magnificent co-investor in the consortium formed to bid for Fairfax, and that throughout, even when he had been obliged by events to withdraw from our consortium, he was unwavering in his support and vital to our ultimate success.

Kerry Packer's father, Sir Frank Packer, was a legendary womanizer and gambler. Kerry was a familiar and renowned figure at the principal gambling places of the Western world. At a decisive point in our bid for Tourang, he flew to Las Vegas, taking various prizefighters, polo players, and business associates with him, won $7 million in four days, and tipped the croupiers $66,000 each on his way out.

A large man, more interested in polo than anything else, he had the usual Australian male's penchant for sex, salacity, and vulgarity. (One of the shelf companies, an unused incorporation, set up by an articling law student with a good Australian sense of humour, and available to us as a Fairfax bid vehicle, was an acronym for a particularly bawdy act, raunchily described.) Kerry Packer is generous and a bully, brilliant though dyslexic, domineering but convivial, completely without pretence yet a lonely man, fiercely possessive, ferocious and vindictive in dispute, yet strangely gentle and protective at times; Dan Colson and I got along excellently with him.

His vast country home, set on 120,000 acres, has stables for more than 200 polo ponies and several of the best polo fields in the world. His impeccable butler, Brian, served, in striped trousers at the ancestral home in Sydney, splendid meals that Kerry, a teetotaller, usually took in a track suit. Rumbustious, restless, suspicious, coarse, and paradoxical, I always found him an enjoyable companion and associate. When Kerry combined with the almost evangelical Jimmie Goldsmith (a *Daily Telegraph* director) and the urbane Jacob Rothschild (a Hollinger Advisory Board member) to "unbundle" (Jimmie's then incumbent enthusiasm, before ecology ruled his passions) BAT Industries, headed by Sir Patrick Sheehy (one of our

Spectator directors), it was a remarkable and unlikely coalition of talents. (Jimmie Goldsmith is such a hyperactive and agile mind and such a restless personality that he must always believe the world is on the verge of either a triumphant coruscation beyond previous human imagination, or of an unprecedented universal catastrophe. If the perceived alternatives were less extreme, he would be bored if not depressed.) At one point during the Fairfax affair, the BAT corporate aircraft bumped into Kerry Packer's DC8 while being moved in the hangar in Sydney, causing minor damage but considerable irritation.

Kerry Packer telephoned me in May 1991 to suggest we seriously put our heads together over Fairfax, and we met in his commodious suite at the Savoy twice during his annual spring polo trip to England. At the first meeting, I brought with me Dan Colson who would be heavily involved if the project really got going, though no one could foresee just how heavily involved; and Max Hastings who, since becoming a member of the *Telegraph* board of directors, had shown an encouraging understanding of the commercial side of the business. (One of our several objections to the Fairfax charters of editorial independence that we soon encountered was the prohibition against having any editors on parent company boards. In addition to all his other accomplishments, Max Hastings has shown how absurd and harmful such antiquarian segregations are.)

It was a very convivial occasion. Kerry Packer at his most congenial is a very gracious host. We agreed on the general outline of an approach. After lunch was served, Kerry sought privacy from the Savoy footmen who abounded and said so. Unfortunately the Italian captain didn't understand him clearly, and as Kerry asked the attendants to "stop flapping about and go," more and more of them crowded into the room, just like the famous shipboard scene from the Marx Brothers's *Night at the Opera*, until someone whose English comprehension was adequate bustled his cohorts out.

It emerged that a proposal had been assembled in Sydney by a stockbroker, Neville Miles, and by a merchant banker, Malcolm Turnbull, wrapping up the predominantly U.S. junk bondholders (who were in litigation with the banking group and had a paper value of $450 million to defend) into one entity. This entity would participate on an exclusive basis with invited investors in order to secure some value for their bonds. The banks were the principal creditors and they were represented by a prominent Sydney merchant banker, Mark Burrows, who tended to dismiss the junk bondholders as losers under the ancient rule of *caveat emptor*. His insouciant lender clients were naturally, and legally, in a much more secure category.

The reasoning behind the junk bond exclusivity arrangement proposal was that the bondholders had some rights, however subordinate; that they had serious powers of harassment and had engaged a suitable representative for such endeavours (Turnbull); and that only they could bring a termination to the litigation and thus enable a legally clean sale of shares, as opposed to Fairfax assets. This strategy would preserve the huge tax loss Warwick Fairfax had run up and was of considerable commercial value to a buyer. It was an enterprising proposal.

Turnbull and Miles could scarcely have been less alike personally. Where Neville Miles is a rather deferential, quiet, and serenely courteous South African, Malcolm Turnbull is mercurial and volcanic. He is an intelligent and attractive and articulate man, who sometimes has considerable difficulty maintaining his self-control against an onslaught of unimaginable compulsive inner tensions and ineluctable ambitions. Malcolm had immense agility at composing scenarios whose common feature was the happy ending of his ruling the world or whatever part of it was currently under consideration.

Malcolm's fugues were notorious, such as the case when he allegedly punctuated an altercation with a friend by sneaking into her home late at night and putting her kitten into the freezer, transforming a frisky pet into a well-preserved corpse. He became uncommonly belligerent and histrionic, threatening vengeance on people, including occasionally himself.

As usual in the aftermath of such a corporate débâcle as Fairfax where there was real underlying value, the most astute players came forward, picking their way amongst the wreckage in search of advantage for themselves. In contemplation of the wheels coming off Warwick Fairfax's bizarre ultra-leveraged buyout, I asked Rupert Murdoch for his prediction, without referring to any potential interest of my own. "The bottom-fishers will start. Of course, Kerry (Packer) is the most outrageous bottom-fisher of all, but it will get past that stage and it's hard to guess who will emerge until we know who the players are. Foreign ownership and cross-media will be a problem. Even if Kerry becomes serious about price, he will have real political problems." As usual, Rupert Murdoch's analysis proved very accurate. He and Kerry Packer were almost the only Australian businessmen I knew but a few pointers from them went a long way.

It did not take Malcolm long to call upon Kerry Packer, who was predictably doubtful about the financial strength and strategic value of the bondholders. Another of Malcolm's calls had been on Tony O'Reilly, the ubiquitous Irish head of the H.J. Heinz Company in Pittsburgh. O'Reilly had also bought some provincial newspapers in Australia largely through a trust for his children who were all Australian citizens, as O'Reilly's first wife was Australian. He owned newspapers in Ireland and was known to be an active acquirer in the field. O'Reilly had apparently sent Turnbull packing, provoking Turnbull to utter one of the Fairfax saga's portentous comments, that that decision to ignore the bondholders would ultimately cost him Fairfax.

Turnbull and Packer were old friends and colleagues through the stormiest moments of Packer's colourful career. This included a ten-year-old Royal Commission inquiry into underworld connections to the labour movement in Australia that had become a smear campaign against Packer. Having known something of that sort of thing myself, I certainly respected the nature of the relationship and assumed it would prove more durable than it ultimately did.

Packer indicated he would be prepared to pay something for the bondholders, although cross-media rules prevented him from taking more than a 15 per cent interest in Fairfax. When Turnbull had indicated he would be calling on me, Packer advised him not to as he and I were already in consultation. (Turnbull and I had never met but he surmised from hearsay that our company could be interested in Fairfax.)

This set the scene for our second meeting in Kerry Packer's suite at the Savoy, Monday, June 3, 1991. I arrived shortly after 3 p.m. to find my host with Malcolm Turnbull, Brian Powers of the San Francisco fund manager, Hellman & Friedman, Steve Ezzes of New York, chairman of the Fairfax bondholders, Neville Miles, and a couple of others. The meeting had been in progress for several hours.

Malcolm Turnbull reminded me at once of Brian Mulroney, the affable confidence, neat, well-scrubbed appearance, prominent chin, and persuasive fluency. The Spycatcher affair was his equivalent to Mulroney's service on the Cliche Commission. I assumed his relationship with Packer was a little like that between Brian Mulroney and Paul Desmarais, with which I was well acquainted. The similarities would prove to be fragile. Turnbull and Miles were inviting Packer, Hellman & Friedman, and me to lead the equity participation in a consortium which would have an exclusive arrangement with the bondholders and whose additional equity needs would be underwritten by Ord Minett, with banking facilities offered by Westpac. It was a clever one-stop shop well presented by Turnbull.

I was struck at the outset by the coziness of the arrangements. Turnbull was representing the bondholders, taking a fee from Ord Minett, had been counsel to Packer. Except for Packer, I was meeting them all for the first time.

I asked obvious questions about the political saleability of a purchase of the leading newspapers by a cross-media owner and two foreigners. Australia was, at the time, a country I had never visited and didn't know much about. I knew there were rules governing both categories of investors and wondered how this would fly. I had no choice but to rely altogether on the ensuing barrage of assurances that this was easily manageable politically. Packer and Turnbull both had reputations as political operators in Australia.

Three principal agreements arose from this meeting. The *Telegraph* would subscribe for 20 per cent of Tourang Ltd. (our bid vehicle), Hellman & Friedman for 15 per cent and Packer's Consolidated Press for 14.99 per cent, the limit prescribed for cross-media owners. The foreign component was discretionary to the treasurer of Australia but Packer and Turnbull kept repeating that these levels were politically sustainable.

The second and third agreements produced by this meeting arose from one-on-one discussions of proprietorial succinctness between Packer and me in the bedroom of his suite. We agreed to offer the bondholders 28 cents on the dollar, or $125 million. Packer had started at $50 million (fulfilling Murdoch's "bottom fisher" prediction). My initial view was $100 million, but after Malcolm Turnbull's performance, I was persuaded that an additional $25 million for the bondholders could easily be recouped from the banks.

Finally, I had made inquiries of a few friends about a likely Australian managing director for Fairfax. Frank Rogers, who had worked in Australia, was a valued contributor to this exchange. A name that recurred was Trevor Kennedy, Packer's managing director at Consolidated Press. When I asked Packer what he thought, he said he had been considering Kennedy. Subject to my meeting with Kennedy and offering him the post, Kennedy was our candidate.

Obviously the intimacy of Packer with Powers, Turnbull, and Kennedy would create the impression that Tourang was just a Packer front. I made it clear that I wasn't interested in being a fig-leaf and that if this consortium was to have any credibility politically, it would depend on my ability to convince a great commonwealth I had never set foot in that I was not a flag of convenience for Packer. I felt equal to that task as it was nothing less than the truth, but I wanted it understood in advance that I expected to be treated like the senior shareholder and the principal newspaper manager in the Group and not as a witless dummy in an Australian corporate salon farce. With occasional reformulations of this position as we went along, I was confident that all the relevant participants understood the *Telegraph's* role.

Turnbull professed an ambition to be the bondholders' representative on the Fairfax board. Packer and I had no objection. Trevor Kennedy came to see me in Toronto on June 18. I was impressed by his background, his agreeable personality, and his eagerness to direct Fairfax and offered him the post of managing director designate. He accepted. In the meantime, the day following the June 3 meeting at the Savoy, all the participants except Packer came to see me at the *Telegraph*. Powers and Turnbull arrived early but separately, each to caution me about the other. From the earliest days, Turnbull objected to Hellman & Friedman's presence, as Australian equity investors could easily be found, but the problem was obviously personal. Powers objected to Turnbull's status as bondholder representative, commissionee of the underwriter, minor equity investor, and Packer adviser, but his underlying objection was to Turnbull personally. Our serene coalition was showing signs of strain after one day.

Apart from disliking each other, Powers and Turnbull were both apparently concerned about each other's relationship with Packer. I was confident I could establish my own independence of Packer without that fact being irksome to Packer himself, but from Tourang's earliest moments, I was reminded of Marshal Foch's statement that he had "less respect for Napoleon now that I know what a coalition is." When I left London a few days after the meeting at the *Telegraph* to spend the summer in Canada, I left detailed discussions of our participation in Tourang to Dan Colson to conclude. They proceeded smoothly enough for a time.

I made a hectic but rather successful visit to Sydney and Canberra in July 1991, launching our bid. Trevor Kennedy met me at Sydney Airport at six a.m. in Packer's white Rolls Royce. What followed was a whirlwind round of attendances upon Australia's business and political leadership. Trevor had arranged for a telephone interview a few weeks before with one of Packer's magazines. It hit the stands as I arrived and I had the odd sensation of walking around a strange city watching my face peer back at me from magazine covers and billboard advertisements for the magazine. It was an exercise in instant credibility, if not celebrity, creation. I was the bemused guinea pig in a socio-economic experiment as well as consortium leader in a serious takeover bid. The magazine article was an effort to meet most concerns about Tourang by anticipation and this was followed up by a media and political blitz.

I was delighted when Sir Zelman Cowen, former governor general of Australia, agreed to become Tourang chairman. I had met him at George Weidenfeld's house, when he was provost of Oriel College, Oxford, and we shared an interest in Cardinal Newman, as he eventually explained to a mystified young interviewer in Queensland. (When asked who brought us together, Zelman ceremoniously replied, "Cardinal Newman.") He invited me to inspect the Newmania at Oriel and also to attend the ceremony observing the centenary, in 1990, of Newman's death. The presence of so distinguished a figure was designed to assure the Australian public of the quality and probity of Tourang's goals.

On my second full day in Australia, Trevor Kennedy conducted me to Canberra to meet with the Prime Minister, Bob Hawke, the Treasurer, John Kerin, and the Communications Minister, Kim

Beazely. We flew on one of Packer's planes and stayed in Packer's Canberra house. My first introduction to the porosity of industrial security in Australia occurred when I went to look out the drawing-room window of the house and discovered a battery of cameras and newsmen on the front lawn. When we went to the government buildings, it was in an impromptu phalanx of press vehicles from which television cameras protruded like anti-aircraft batteries from the superstructures of World War II battleships.

Bob Hawke was affable, though clearly distracted by the rising challenge to his position following a narrow caucus victory over Paul Keating, the former treasurer whom Kerin had replaced. I emphasized our independence from Packer, which, as it was already becoming clear, would not be an easy point to make. Apart from me, a total unknown in Australia, and Sir Zelman Cowen, and Sir Laurence Street, no one else around Tourang appeared to have much independence of him. The invocation of Sir Zelman's presence was noted though Hawke allowed that he did not consider the former governor general "a barrel of laughs."

I expressed a fervent desire to accommodate any reasonable political concerns the government had and asked the prime minister and the treasurer to indicate what they could wear in foreign and cross-media ownership, so I didn't inadvertently "hand them a political grenade with the pin pulled." It was at this point that Kerin uttered his remark that "up to 35 per cent, concerns for foreign ownership are piffle." He subsequently disputed employing the word "piffle," but that is precisely what he said and I obviously took careful note of it and repeated it. Given Kerin's subsequent conduct, including his dismissal for forgetting some of the basic expressions required of his portfolio, his mnemonic lapse was not surprising. I considered this the most important point in the exchange. Both men professed a desire to encourage foreign investment but they were not much concerned with the banks who had loaned money in unjustifiable amounts to Warwick's mad gasconade. When I suggested they might not get all their money back, Hawke snorted derisively and said that was "a matter of hairstyling," a reference to the current practice of describing financial losses as haircuts. Hawke and I discussed Israeli politics a little and I was able to say friendly things about the Labour Party of that country.

Kerin seemed to me a simple man, plain-spoken, but not very economically literate. Hawke was a charming old political roué. Both were beleaguered, in the polls and in their own caucus. The meeting went well and the informal reports afterward were very favourable, but it was obvious that Hawke and Kerin were not reliable. Their encouraging noises were mere atmospherics that could be blown away with any change of wind, and it did not require a clairvoyant to see that the Fairfax affair could become tempestuous. It was also obvious that they, and the media with whom Trevor and I spoke for the balance of the trip, took the issue of Packer's position in Tourang a good deal more seriously than Packer, Kennedy, Turnbull, or Powers did. With Hawke and Kerin, as with the Australian press, I used Jackman's old line in reference to Packer, that "with 15 per cent he would get a free lunch and a tour of the plant." Australians were not accustomed to thinking of "the big man" in such a passive role.

The same points came up in the luncheon with the communications minister, Beazley, where we spent much of our meal watching television cameras pointed at us from all directions, as the hilltop restaurant where we met enjoys a panoramic view. Beazley and I had some amusing exchanges over military history. At one point, the minister wondered amusingly at the challenges of being a damage control officer on the giant Japanese battleship *Yamato* when she was attacked by 360 American aircraft off Okinawa in 1945. The aspect of the Packer problem that he focused on was Trevor Kennedy's status. After several minutes of this, I turned to Trevor and told him he was "sacked." It was not intended to be a portent.

I was reasonably sanguine because if Packer and I were unable to convince the authorities of Tourang's true character, the option existed of proceeding without Packer. I would be loathe to do so as he was my initial entrée into Fairfax and into Tourang, though Turnbull and Miles would have called upon me anyway. Foreign ownership concerns, within the limits Tourang envisioned, were treated dismissively by the political leadership. There was no evidence at this point that O'Reilly's efforts to portray me as a mortal enemy of independent journalism whose political views made Genghis Khan appear a social democrat, had had much impact.

O'Reilly deployed his prodigious powers of ingratiating persuasion to masquerade as a quasi-Australian and to lobby the Irish-descended caucus members of the governing Labour Party. He had bought some provincial newspapers in Australia from the debt-ridden Warwick Fairfax through a trust of which his sons were the beneficiaries, and had been helped by Murdoch to a substantial instant gain in ownership of some newspapers in Queensland. On the basis of these bonanzas and his ownership of some newspapers in Ireland, O'Reilly, who in Australia described himself as "Dr. O'Reilly" in celebration of a postgraduate degree in marketing economics, held himself out as an ideally qualified and proven proprietor of great and profitable newspapers.

We had a virtual debate over Australian Broadcasting Corporation radio when I was in Sydney in July and he was in Dublin. After saluting his undoubted talents and our longstanding cordial relations, I pointed out that "the Doctor, as he calls himself in the Southern Hemisphere, did not acquire his rich brogue around the billabong," that he was no more an Australian than I was, and that, although he owned some profitable newspapers, that was not his real occupation, which was "manufacturing ketchup in Pittsburgh." He jovially responded that I reminded him of "the Jesuit who, when asked what his order was famous for, said, 'We're tops in humility.'" Later, when our formal exchange was over, I asked him the origin of his doctorate. To the great amusement of the technicians and others still on the line, he responded, "Marketing economics and it's not worth a shit!"

O'Reilly, a former international Irish rugby star, had had a spectacular record building Heinz, but a rather more checkered career as an entrepreneur acting on his own and friends' accounts. His foray into Waterford crystal and Fitzwilton, the Irish venture capital business, were rather unsuccessful. But O'Reilly's irrepressible and affable talents as a lobbyist and courtier when he flew to and around Australia on the Heinz plane (he could spend only ninety days a year in the United States for personal tax reasons) proved formidable. (A couple of months after I visited Hawke, Henry Kissinger called upon him, and though slightly non-plussed when the Australian press questioned him almost exclusively about our bid for Fairfax, rose gamely to the subject and proclaimed my "eminent desirability" as a newspaper owner in Australia.)

My initial impressions of Australia were very positive. It was vast and beautiful. Sydney was a magnificent city with many of the best elements and few of the less salubrious of San Francisco and Vancouver. Melbourne was solid and reassuring, as a Victorian capital should be. Canberra was much of what Ankara and Brasilia were supposed to be but are not; (mainly) graceful monuments in a park. The cultural life of the country appeared vital; literate people were not hard to find. The general tenor was cheerful without being oppressively gregarious. Australians are rather good-looking people, especially the women of Sydney. The Fairfax newspapers and one or two others were of high quality; there were flourishing universities and mighty cathedrals. (I was impressed by the memorialization of Newman in a stained glass window and chapel in St. Mary's Cathedral, Sydney.) It is probably hemispherism to say so but it was all somewhat surprising to find at the end of the earth. I hadn't had such a sensation since I visited Sao Paulo in 1968. (The most truthful thing Bob Hawke said to me was, "It's not true that Australia is not a centrally located country; it's a 24-hour flight from everywhere!") A few weeks later I said to a Canadian reporter, while attempting not to sound overeager to buy Fairfax and so not to excite Mark Burrows's recovery expectations, that I had got through 46 years without going to Australia and could live without seeing it again. The context was clear but this was used by our opponents in Australia to suggest I disliked the country. In fact, the reverse is true. I have never failed to find Australia refreshing.

Two weeks after I left Australia, Kerry Packer returned from his two-month polo trip to Britain, at the conclusion of which he gave his daughter away in marriage at a spectacular ceremony (somewhat snottily reported by the *Daily Telegraph*). When the wedding celebration ran out of one form of libation, Kerry led a delegation to the nearest pub. The owner refused to open up his bar at that hour and Kerry proceeded on to the next pub which did re-open. Kerry rewarded the publican with a very large cheque on the provision, happily accepted, that he show it to the unobliging neighbouring innkeeper.

Soon after his return, Kerry, Brian Powers, and Dan Colson, who had gone there to represent us as the bidding procedure gained momentum, became concerned that cross-media and foreign ownership preoccupations would prevent the principal Tourang shareholders from exercising any influence on Fairfax. The Broadcasting Act would prevent Packer from being a Fairfax director, as he controlled a television network that he had sold to Alan Bond for a billion dollars and in which he bought back a controlling interest (after Bond's financial reversals) at less than half the per-share value he had been paid for it. If these fears were justified, Trevor and Malcolm, using foreigners' and Packer's money, would rule Fairfax and sway the fate of all Australia. Packer, Colson, and Powers did not consider this to be the purpose of our investments.

I was more concerned about Packer's discussions with Powers over Powers succeeding Kennedy as managing director of Packer's company. While this rumour was about, it was going to be impossible to propagate the view that Powers and his principals were really independent of Packer. Dan Colson and I urged them to lay this fear to rest before it became another club with which our competitors assaulted us. They agreed and those discussions were terminated though Powers did take up the post in 1993.

I always found Trevor Kennedy a rather likeable man, and even my relations with Malcolm Turnbull were cordial enough, but the abrasions between them and Packer, Powers, and Colson, grew steadily more grating through the Northern Hemisphere's late summer and autumn. The tensions were aggravated by Trevor's rather cavalier approach to his task for which he was more than generously paid.

Not the least irony in the Fairfax drama was the increasingly intense agitation against Kennedy and Turnbull as lackeys of Packer's at precisely the time when they were gratuitously demonstrating their "independence" of Packer well beyond what was necessary or appropriate. This was doubly irksome as the allegations against Kennedy and Turnbull were fanned by O'Reilly while he assiduously attempted to woo them from Tourang. At the same time, O'Reilly engaged the prominent New York lawyer, Arthur Liman, who had been counsel to the congressional committee investigating the Iran Contra affair, to try to pry the bondholders away from Tourang, while not quite committing the tort of inducing breach of contract. I tried, with declining success, to be an emollient influence on this fractious coalition of Tourang's discordant personalities.

The other principal competitor to surface, apart from O'Reilly, was a group of Melbourne financial institutions who ballyhooed themselves as the all-Australian, pro-journalists' bid and started a mighty political agitation to restrict foreign participation by both equity and debt-holders to a point that would effectively eliminate O'Reilly and ourselves. They recruited Greg Taylor, managing director of Fairfax's Melbourne group and a very distinguished statesman of the country's media, as their managing director designate. This group, Australian Independent Newspapers, (AIN), was led by the ultimate Melbourne establishment opponents of the Labour federal government. The nationalist card was being played by a conservative alliance of rather grey financial institution heads, the antithesis of the average Bob Hawke enthusiast.

O'Reilly, by his relentless schmoozing with Hawke and his entourage, and his ardent courtship of the Irish-Australian members of Hawke's caucus, was the prime minister's preferred candidate. Hawke didn't like the Melbourne establishment and had nothing against me but was terrified out of his hard-pressed wits by Packer. Hawke, like many less prominent Australians, was so frightened of Packer's influence that he wouldn't attack Kerry directly but instead incited endless cavil about the status of Kennedy and Turnbull. It was a general spectacle of cowardice and hypocrisy for which even my long experience of the limitations of political courage had not prepared me.

My sympathies were entirely with Packer. Whatever his shortcomings, he was a distinguished citizen and very astute media owner. He had complied exactly with the law requiring profound separation of newspaper and television ownership and no one was prepared to represent me overtly as a Packer front after I had met the Australian politicians and media. The objections to Packer were completely spurious and were made more contemptible by the inability of anyone from the prime minister down to acknowledge the real source of their fears. It was a gratuitous embarrassment for Kerry and reminded me of how I felt when, in the midst of trying to patriate one of Canada's largest mining companies (Iron Ore Company of Canada, Brian Mulroney, President), I had been knifed by the palookas in the Crown Law Office.

O'Reilly's activities were fiendishly insidious. As he serenaded the American bondholders, he bombarded the Australian Broadcasting Tribunal with outrageous allegations against Packer and Tourang and preyed upon all the rather incandescent susceptibilities of Kennedy and Turnbull. I never object to roughhouse tactics, as my stoicism during the Hanna absurdities demonstrated, and am not slow to respond to them, but systematic defamations amplified by official shilly-shallying are harder to endure.

In mid-September, Hawke told Mark Burrows that the caucus couldn't accept Tourang as long as Packer was in it. At about the same time, Rupert Murdoch, whose Australian sources have always been accurate in my experience, told me that I could win if I dropped Kerry. I naturally replied that I saw no justification for doing such a thing.

Between early September and late October, a consensus of the Transport and Communications Committee opposing more than a 20 per cent foreign interest in a substantial Australian newspaper concern including all forms of debt, was narrowly overturned by the governing party caucus and the 20 per cent limit applied to voting shares only. I telephoned Kerry Packer, not an infrequent occurrence at this stage, and said I probably didn't want to know the full range of his lobbying methods. He replied (in jest) that he wouldn't comment then, other than to volunteer that he had "almost run out of $1,000 bills, incriminating photographs, and crowbars."

From this turn, in late October, AIN's fortunes declined. Their whole strategy had been to wrap all the domestic institutions into their own group, lobby successfully for the exclusion of foreign lenders (relying on the lobotomous parochialism of the left wing of the governing party and the lassitude of its spavined prime minister to subscribe to the notion that loans from foreign banks would infringe national sovereignty and editorial independence, a notion Castro or Franco would have had trouble with), and thus to squeeze out Tourang and O'Reilly. By a hair's breadth, Fairfax was spared yet another undeservedly unkind fate: becoming a branch plant of the Melbourne Club.

Trevor Kennedy had made a serious tactical error in not signing an employment contract early on. When he and Dan Colson got down to this task in October, there had been so many unpleasant encounters between Trevor and Dan and Brian Powers, and Trevor had so failed to impress them with his aptitude to run such an outstanding and managerially challenging company as Fairfax, that serious revisions to the original compensation and tenure package were envisioned. In the ensuing negotiations, Trevor adopted a totally unreasonable posture, demanding exorbitant terms, including unconditional options even if he didn't last as managing director and regularly threatening to "blow up" our deal, marching about the room describing himself as a "bombthrower," and shaking his fist in Dan's face (thus presenting a challenge that only concern for corporate decorum and certainly not his own physical safety prevented Colson from taking up). Dan and Brian Powers removed ashtrays and other possible projectiles from the room prior to their climactic meeting with Trevor.

In the circumstances, our offer fell short of his vertiginous expectations and Trevor huffily withdrew, blaming "McCarthyism" of his independence by the regulatory and media critics. Having, with Turnbull, apparently been contacted by our competitors, and after collecting a multi-million dollar quittance settlement from Packer when he resigned from Consolidated Press, Kennedy was confident he could sink our bid and auction his way into another and winning bid. He and O'Reilly had the same lawyer and O'Reilly wasted no time dangling job possibilities before him but his parting arrangements with us required him to show discretion.

The campaign against Tourang, partly fomented by O'Reilly, had become hysterical. Groups of protesting employees calling themselves the Friends of Fairfax and The *Age* Independence Committee in Melbourne systematically denigrated Packer, staged wildcat strikes, lobbied politicians, and handed out inflammatory leaflets to passers-by on street corners. They had prepared rather puerile and platitudinous "charters of editorial independence," divorcing the management, directors, and shareholders from any relationship with the editorial function. O'Reilly and AIN pledged to sign these charters, and O'Reilly relentlessly represented me as a ravenning troglodyte whose raison d'être as a publisher was to degrade the craft of journalism and stir up public nostalgia for feudal times.

Even more tiresome was the sudden emergence of an unholy alliance of former prime ministers Gough Whitlam and Malcolm Fraser crusading against foreign ownership of Australian media, though they were more ambivalent about O'Reilly than about us. Given their long-standing mutual antagonism, and Whitlam's call to his followers to "maintain the rage" against Fraser as the beneficiary of the governor general's unusual dismissal of Whitlam's government, this really was contrived hypocrisy of a high order.

When I read that Fraser had told the House media committee that it should investigate Murdoch's relations with the Reagan administration, I commented on my regular telephone radio interview with Peter Martin of the Australian Broadcasting Corporation that the last time I had seen Malcolm Fraser, he was urging some well-to-do friends of mine from Palm Beach and me to support the Contras in El Salvador, a dubious enterprise that made him an unnatural source for such self-righteousness. (In fact, I approved of the Contras and thought the congressional legislation prohibiting support of them mistaken as well as *ultra vires* to the U.S. Congress, but it wasn't an appropriate cause for private-sector support and Malcolm Fraser was, as I put it, in the Sydney *Morning Herald*, "a sanctimonious balloon in need of puncture.") Fraser responded to my comments by shrieking like a wounded animal but henceforth his interventions had little weight in the contest. Fraser's supreme fatuity occurred in Melbourne when he told 2,000 people that Tourang's purchase of Fairfax would be "a crime against the Australian people." It was a little-noticed irony that my slanging match with Fraser resulted from my defence of Murdoch on ABC and specifically of his relations with the Reagan administration, which were no business of anyone in Australia anyway.

Packer offered several times to withdraw from Tourang but I urged him to remain. He had done nothing to offend the spirit of the governing laws and regulations and I was against "throwing raw meat to the jackals." Packer and I both appeared, on consecutive nights, on one of his stations' most popular public affairs television programs, "A Current Affair." He debated with three journalists, demanding they read the first article of the Australian Journalists' Code of Ethics, which required impartiality and accuracy. They balked, and Packer won the exchange. I appeared twice, going on the second occasion from Armagnac at Brooks' Club and a *Spectator* dinner to a little studio on Newman Street where I sat in front of a cardboard-backed blow-up of St. Paul's, the Tower, and Tower Bridge, in blazing summer sunlight, and filibustered the rather pulchritudinous interviewer, Jana Wendt. I assured her that, if we were not successful in our bid, "I will not become so discouraged that I jump off the bridge behind me as we speak."

I sued the Friends of Fairfax for defamation and asked counsel to serve the subpoenas on the respondents in their homes so they and their families could appreciate that their shenanigans could have a downside. (As events unfolded, this wasn't necessary.) We also informed Fairfax that injunctive action would be contemplated to prevent the company assisting in legal costs. Their descriptions of me as a fascist and racist were freelance endeavours. In Australia, as elsewhere, it was necessary to make the point that defaming me had its risks. When Dan Colson told Kerry Packer what I was doing, he exclaimed that if I had been defamed, certainly he had been too and a joint notice of intent to sue was sent to four defendants. The Friends of Fairfax were little heard from again until after the takeover procedure was completed, and then in rather more civil terms.

I gave a two-page interview to the Sydney *Morning Herald*, whose New York bureau chief visited me in Toronto. It was published November 2. I denounced in extreme and rather flamboyant terms the hypocrisy of those Fairfax journalists and others who espoused concern for professional standards of fairness in reporting while being grossly unfair in their reporting on the Tourang bid and on Packer's role in it.

The *pièce de résistance* was Kerry Packer's voluntary appearance under oath before the media select committee of the House of Representatives. His nationally televised performance before the committee, November 4, was brilliant. Referring to his near-fatal coronary on a polo field, he said: "I didn't die for long, but it was long enough for me. I didn't come back to control John Fairfax. I didn't come back to break the law. And I certainly didn't intentionally come back to testify before a parliamentary inquiry." It was a masterful appearance. Every one of the committee's usually naïve, and occasionally insolent, questions he batted out of sight like Babe Ruth hitting fungoes. O'Reilly had been lobbying the Australian Broadcasting Tribunal fiercely to mire Tourang in a month-long inquiry into Packer's relations with Tourang, which would effectively have eliminated us. Our exclusivity arrangement with bondholders would expire and it would be difficult to renew it, especially as O'Reilly had finally figured out that the bondholders were of tactical value and he was offering to top our $125 million if he could do so legally. There was great pressure from Burrows, the banks, and the politicians to end Fairfax's receivership as soon as possible. Packer's outstanding defense appeared to assure a clear passage for us at the

Broadcasting Tribunal and to increase pressure for an accelerated timetable out of receivership.

On October 31, to amplify this pressure and complete our counterattack, we delivered Burrows an enhanced offer, raising our bid by $300 million and offering to take out all the banks and unsecured creditors at their face value. Burrows had delivered for his clients. The banks would not suffer a financial penalty for their ill-considered loans to Warwick Fairfax. We reckoned this would expedite the process and flush out O'Reilly, who for all his evangelistic pursuit of Fairfax, was unspecific about how he planned to pay for it.

Burrows had urged the same underwriter on the Melbourne group (AIN) that was purporting to guarantee O'Reilly's offering price to the extent of eight times the underwriter's own shareholders' equity, an implausible arrangement. Even O'Reilly was astounded that the same underwriter would act for two competing bids. Australia's casual commercial methods held a few surprises even for the well-travelled doctor.

We had briefly stabilized Tourang's position but the pressure on Packer did not cease. A petition against increased media concentration, clearly aiming at Tourang as long as Packer was in it, was signed by 137 members of parliament (out of 195 who were not ministers). The most conspicuous abstentions were from the right wing of the New South Wales Labour Party, particularly Paul Keating, who was preparing a decisive blow against Hawke. Keating had told the National Press Club on October 22 that there was no media concentration problem with Tourang and no reason to doubt Packer's status as a non-controlling shareholder. His cool-headed fairness was well appreciated by Packer and me. I had not at this point met Keating but I couldn't imagine that this splendid country could not produce more substantial leaders than Whitlam, Fraser, and Hawke. (I had been informed that Hawke had attempted to sign the anti-Tourang petition until it was pointed out that it might be inappropriate, as it was addressed to him.)

Turnbull was now urging me to put Packer over the side, despite Packer's fine defense of Tourang before the media committee on the television screens of the nation. I indignantly refused. It was through Packer that I had become involved in the pursuit of Fairfax and I didn't treat partners that way. Far greater was the agitation for us to dispense with Malcolm Turnbull. The bondholders were regularly representing that they were dissatisfied with him and we pointed out that that was their problem. The banks and Burrows also expressed grievances against Turnbull, but we were prepared to ignore those. More problematical were the independence questions and the concerns of the Australian Broadcasting Tribunal. But Brian Powers and Dan Colson couldn't work with him. They found him unspeakably difficult and believed that he was leaking inside Tourang information to the press and that questionable conversations had taken place between him and O'Reilly. I had got on well enough with Malcolm, but I was not prepared to countenance disloyalty to the consortium partners who were actually putting up the money, particularly Packer to whom Turnbull owed so much.

Powers and Colson demanded that Turnbull go and Packer and I weren't disposed to resist them. A fierce internecine struggle ensued. A special meeting of Tourang shareholders was called to remove Turnbull but an arrangement was worked out just before that meeting occurred. Colson and Turnbull had a much celebrated stroll in the Sydney Botanical Gardens above the Opera House, with Malcolm raving and fuming amid exotic flowering plants. The former premier of New South Wales, Neville Wran, an associate of Turnbull's, did much of his bidding and attempted to rattle Dan Colson with the spectre of Malcolm's talents as a saboteur, with which we were already well familiar. Malcolm, as is his custom, produced some wordy and self-righteous letters alleging *inter alia* that the only possible concern we could have with him was that he was truly independent. He also, more relevantly, suggested that his departure could arouse the interest of the Australian Broadcasting Tribunal which, after circulating massive questionnaires to the Tourang participants and in light of Packer's testimony before the parliamentary committee, was not expected to hold an inquiry into Tourang. Malcolm was not the type of person to go quietly, especially not from the position of Fairfax director that he had coveted so ardently for so long. Nor did he.

Trevor Kennedy sent the Australian Broadcasting Tribunal a letter enclosing his hastily reconstituted "diary notes" ten minutes before the extended deadline for making submissions. Trevor Kennedy claimed that when he was managing director of Tourang, he considered himself answerable to Packer and to me. This contradicted Trevor's earlier testimony to the print media inquiry and also seemed to contradict Kerry Packer's testimony before the House of Representatives media committee, where he denied he would assert any influence on Fairfax.

As Malcolm Turnbull had implied that his departure from Tourang could have repercussions at the ABT and as he had a Mephistophelian influence on Trevor anyway, it wasn't hard to find Malcolm's fingerprints on this knife. The Tribunal naturally announced it would hold an inquiry after all. Tourang was dead unless Packer pulled out. Speaking by telephone from Argentina, where he had gone to play polo after his brilliant success at the casino in Las Vegas, Packer said: "A good general must know when to attack and when to retreat and this is the time to retreat. I withdraw." He left his considerable political apparatus with us. Our relations were, and remain, excellent. I said to him at the time, and publicly repeated, that as far as I was concerned he would always be welcome as a shareholder, especially in Fairfax. His departure from the consortium eliminated the principal political obstacle to our success but left us without the political muscle that Kerry Packer alone possessed.

When informed of Packer's withdrawal by Mark Burrows, Bob Hawke was inexpressibly relieved and produced from his briefcase a copy of a letter written by the wartime British ambassador in Moscow celebrating the arrival of the new Turkish ambassador who rejoiced in the name, Mustapha Kunt, "We all feel like that . . . now and then, especially when spring is upon us, but few of us would care to put it on our cards." Hawke thought at first that Tourang as a whole was packing up and was slightly disappointed when Burrows explained that only Packer was and that I would fight on. He was also concerned that Packer not think the Labour Party caucus had opposed him, though it had.

Dan Colson and Brian Powers were reminded of the Monty Python character, the Knight, who, as each limb was severed by an opponent's sword, shouted more belligerently, "Come and get me!" Of those who started out in our group on the long march to Fairfax in July, only Hellman & Friedman and the *Daily Telegraph* now remained.

All the cowardly legions of low-life Australian Labour Party caucus members had professed to find Packer's presence problematical but were afraid to confront him personally. Instead they nibbled at the edges by questioning foreign ownership and the independence of Kennedy and Turnbull (ironic considering their conduct). Now they were able to surrender to O'Reilly's insidious blandishments and subornings without incurring the wrath of "the big man."

The atmosphere around the Fairfax dénouement was becoming steadily tawdrier under the relentless influence of O'Reilly, who was oiling his way around the twilight zone of a divided and unpopular government that the polls indicated most Australians felt had wallowed too long in office. There were persistent reports of overtures from the O'Reilly faction to Trevor Kennedy. For several reasons, Trevor was advised that he had violated our parting agreement and that, as a result, we could not honour all its (generous) financial provisions. The departure of Turnbull, meanwhile, was greeted with general relief and enthusiasm, accompanied predictably by King Learesque threats to "blow up" our deal once again.

In his submission to the Foreign Investment Review Board, O'Reilly took the considerable liberty of including a four-page section entitled, "Observations on the Proposed Tourang Acquisition of the Fairfax Group," in which he predicted partisan meddling in editorial matters and "extreme industrial unrest, strikes, and loss of valuable staff" if Tourang were successful. For his part, O'Reilly envisioned shutting the *Sunday Age* and squabbled with Burrows, even threatening to sue him for the way he was conducting the auction. Now that Turnbull was not with us, he and O'Reilly made frenzied efforts to detach the bondholders from Tourang, and O'Reilly redoubled the dangling of job offers in front of Kennedy. He brought every conceivable pressure to bear on the bumbling John Kerin. As treasurer, Kerin would decide on acceptability of bids requiring attention from the Foreign Investment Review Board.

It was clear from the reports we were getting in early December that O'Reilly had suborned or dragooned enough MPs that Bob Hawke, now facing a severe leadership challenge from Keating partly because of Kerin's inept performance, could be easily influenced by the resourceful Irishman, as he now had no resistance to any pressures that arose in his own caucus.

Kerin had decided to reject Tourang, hanging his hat on the red herring of foreign ownership, though in voting shares the O'Reilly bid had an equal level of foreign participation. The Foreign Investment Review Board members divided evenly: two wanted Tourang and O'Reilly approved, two wanted them both rejected. The Board cautioned against accepting O'Reilly and rejecting Tourang, and all the members were sceptical about the Melbourne (AIN) bid as they felt it represented no change, no new expertise, and had almost no newspaper background among the investors. The political fix was in for O'Reilly and Kerin dutifully disqualified Tourang as "not in the national interest" in almost his last act before being fired as treasurer on December 9, 1991. What was "piffle" in July had become unshakeable national policy in December, after a five-month tutorial from O'Reilly.

As we had expected some such treachery we had secured an extension of the deadline for submitting bids, and we were ready with a reformulated offer. O'Reilly had hoped to sandbag us more thoroughly with a rejection half an hour before the deadline for receipt of offers. But Kerin was getting the axe, and it proved even beyond his powers to manipulate the most susceptible factions of the Australian Labour Party. We mounted an immediate campaign of moral outrage, which was widely taken up, even by elements of the media that had been previously rather antagonistic. This corrupt political intervention appalled sensible opinion throughout Australia. I described the official volte-face in an interview with the Sydney *Morning Herald* as "sleazy, venal, and despicable" and the bid process as a "degrading and grotesque charade."

Hellman & Friedman also made useful representations about shabby treatment of American investors. As President George Bush was expected in Australia in two weeks, for the first visit by a U.S. president since Lyndon Johnson came to Harold Holt's funeral in 1967, this was a particularly sensitive point.

O'Reilly, believing he was close to victory, launched an unholy assault on the bondholders, but we raised our offer to them from $125 million to $140 million and beat that off. In fact, O'Reilly was not going to win. Apart from his soft underwriting that papered off the back of his offer, he needed a shareholders' meeting of his Australian company, in which he only owned 28 per cent. Like most of the rest of his proposal and behaviour, this was credible only to the lowest political denominators in Canberra. If we had been unable to clear the political hurdle, Burrows would have gone to the Melbourne group (AIN) who had the money. Burrows was, by now, thoroughly exasperated by O'Reilly's egregious performance. We also engaged the indescribable larrikin, John Singleton, oft-married, hard-drinking, foul-mouthed, the Labour Party sloganeer, and an intimate of Hawke and Packer. "Singo" importuned Hawke ceaselessly, making the point that as Tourang now mirrored Independent (O'Reilly) in foreign ownership, it would be outrageous to deny us. Singo had advised us earlier, while Packer was still involved, and had authored an hilarious advertising campaign suggesting Packer possessed unsuspected humanitarian qualities (which we did not publish).

Dan Colson lobbied some of the left-wing caucus, suggesting we could agree to the journalists' charter with a few sensible changes, and discussing Eric Beecher, a former *Herald* editor as Fairfax chief executive. I had met Beecher before and now spoke with him again. His basic view was that if we didn't announce his appointment at once, we had no chance of acceptance. Dan and I agreed that Beecher reminded us of Andrew Knight and we didn't want to go through all that again. Mark Burrows reminded the new treasurer that nearly 3,000 unsecured creditors would get their money by Christmas under the Tourang proposal, while O'Reilly's had a wait of about a month, with vulnerability to market fluctuations and no deal secured with the bondholders.

Final bids went in December 11. Tourang's reformulated offer was approved by the treasurer on December 13. Burrows recommended Tourang and we closed with the banks December 16. There was one final mighty showdown with the banks on December 15. They were trying to lay $50–$60 million of receivership fees and penalty interest on Tourang. Dan Colson walked out of negotiations for several hours, and Brian Powers negotiated a compromise at about 50 per cent of what had been asked.

I suggested to Dan Colson that my violent strictures against the government might actually have been helpful but he thought not.

It was a great victory. Buying from a receiver one rarely overpays. The equity holders had been handsomely paid off by Warwick Fairfax and no one had any intention of paying Warwick anything.

We paid $1.39 billion for an enterprise that under Warwick had produced a cash flow of $190 million, or seven times best year's cash flow. We were confident this could be improved with systematic management. If a return to prosperity in the economic cycle were factored in, we would be seen to have bought for four and a half times the cash flow that would result.

Our underwriters had no doubt that within a few months a public issue could be brought forward that would trade at about 150 per cent of our share price. This proved to be the case. The stock was brought to the public in April 1992 marked up 20 per cent to $1.20 and rose steadily through the next year to well over $2. The franchises and assets acquired were of the highest quality and the price was more than reasonable. As far as I could determine, it was the best large newspaper deal done in the Western world since the purchase of the *Daily Telegraph*, and it discharged our oft-stated obligation to our shareholders to take advantage of the recession with judicious investments.

I went back to Australia when our success was confirmed, just before Christmas 1991. After this roadshow of just two days, Australia's financial institutions oversubscribed our $420 million follow-up issue by over $200 million. I had all the press into our broker's office for a humorous session that lasted for over two hours, as long as they had questions. It was suggested I had been "uncomplimentary to Dr. O'Reilly." I replied, "That wasn't uncomplimentary. That was neutral. If you want uncomplimentary, I'll give you uncomplimentary." When asked what "most impressed" me about Australian journalism, rather than saying insularity or unprofessionalism, in deference to the formidable array of good-looking women seated somewhat revealingly in front of me, I made a flattering and unchauvinistic reference to the appearance of many of the local women journalists.

Three days after our bid was formally accepted, the inconstant Labour Party caucus finally bounced Bob Hawke and brought in Paul Keating. Kerry Packer's lobbyists and advisers who had served us assumed rather more influence with the new regime than they had enjoyed with Hawke's. Coincidentally, our victory was complete. Hawke became the official greeter at a newly opened hotel in Sydney where we occasionally encountered him in his track suit.

Like most politicians, he was a good deal friendlier out of office than in. Malcolm Turnbull suggested to Dan Colson we might want him as a *Daily Telegraph* director. Trevor Kennedy and his wife sent me flowers. Victory has its rewards.

The receivership ended on December 23 (despite O'Reilly's last-ditch attempt at an injunction, a frivolous and vexatious litigious endeavour that was thrown out of court with a ringing excoriation from the Bench). Dan Colson had spent seventeen weeks in Australia, many of them lonely times of apparently forlorn struggle against seemingly insurmountable problems of political chicanery and bad faith.

When he finally left Australia to join his family in Florida on December 23, he had turned the third-floor lounge of Sydney's Ritz-Carlton Hotel into a virtual court, receiving local dignitaries suddenly become respectful (including senior police officers called to check on the interception and the publication in Murdoch's *Australian* of a rather unflattering description of some Fairfax editors. This description had been contained in a fax to me from Max Hastings that had included an unsolicited memo sent to the *Daily Telegraph*'s foreign editor, Nigel Wade, from a journalist in Australia). We now had beach-heads on four continents, and the sun would never set on our successful newspaper publishing endeavours.

The Fairfax saga had been a front-page story in Australia most days for six months. It was a chapter in Australian history. Large numbers of staff lined the lobby and corridors of our hotel when Dan Colson and I left Sydney a couple of days apart, just before Christmas. Dan's performance had been beyond praise or estimation. It was a gratifying end to an implacable struggle.

It had been the roughest takeover battle I had seen, not excluding Hanna. My contempt for the conduct of many of those involved was mitigated by the fact that we won. The parochialism and bigotry of some of the politicians is probably inevitable in so isolated a country. The hypocrisy of much of the journalistic attention I received is perhaps inevitable from newspaper and broadcasting monopolies where there has been little professional discipline for years.

The country has grandeur. I love to walk around Sydney, reading the plaques recording the views of distinguished literary visitors such as Mark Twain and Anthony Trollope, or those commemorating the departure of Australian troops for foreign wars where they acquitted themselves heroically.

Without a colossal neighbour or a profound cultural schism, which are the chief political realities of Canada, Australia has developed a distinct nationality. This is evident on boarding an Australian airliner in a distant country, or on encountering Australians abroad or hearing a familiar Australian song. Remote and relaxed, inhabited sparsely by bronzed and attractive people from every imaginable ethnic provenance, Australia is a strangely romantic concept that does not disappoint expectations. Flying out across the Pacific, it is possible to imagine what earlier visitors and immigrants of the most disparate circumstances imagined of this vast, lush, and splendid place when they first saw it; an immense antipodean paradise full of promise and hope. Such it remains for me, as for all those who preceded me to its mysterious shores.

CHAPTER TWELVE

DOMESTIC UPHEAVALS AND A WORLD VIEW
1991–1993

As 1991 EBBED AWAY, SO, CONTRARY TO MANY years of hope, work, and expectation, did my marriage. My wife did not enjoy our years in England. Although the social life was interesting, she found herself confined in Highgate, dependent upon drivers to get around a vast, intense, and unfamiliar city, missing her friends and the familiarity of surroundings that she felt her own.

I was prepared to divide my time more equally between London and Toronto. I was not enthusiastic about trading altogether the life I had earned as a London newspaper owner to immerse myself in the suburban life of Bob Rae's Ontario. All my life I had sought a more distinguished, varied, and eventful life than could be provided by the milieu in which I was brought up.

Yet I could have sacrificed much if it would really have saved our marriage. In September 1991, I returned to London and my wife and children remained in Canada. I endeavoured, through September and October, to propose arrangements that could restore the basis of our marriage. Geography was ultimately only a contributing problem.

My wife finally said that despite my fidelity, generosity, and the "interesting life" I had given her, and my general merits that made me "better than 90 per cent of husbands," she wasn't "happy." Our relations had drifted gradually apart for years until we were bound together largely by habit and love of our children. I was not going to perpetuate a "lifeless marriage." What proved to be a mortal blow to our marriage was my wife's almost unquenchable interest in the company of selected members of the Roman Catholic clergy. Our houses were virtually turned into seminaries, where I was not her de facto preferred male company. There was some, though little, acrimony. Almost imperceptibly, excruciatingly, the marriage died. In May 1993, she married one of the clergymen, after he had changed his occupation to environmental studies. Given my long and complicated contemplation of the Roman Church before adhering to it, this twist was richly ironic.

The last lap was the Hollinger dinner and introductory advisory board meeting in London in October 1991. My wife, brother, sister-in-law, and Cardinal Carter flew from Toronto and stayed in our house. For the last time, my wife and I greeted a long procession of the good and the great, at Jacob Rothschild's splendid Spencer House. Margaret Thatcher spoke, and was thanked by Bill Buckley. Lord Carrington proposed the toast to the Queen, David Brinkley to the president of the United States.

The following night we went to Harry's Bar and on to Annabel's. The next day I took Cardinal Carter to Cardinal Hume's house, and in the evening my wife and I went to the last of many elaborate dinners together, Malcolm Forbes Junior's dinner for Ronald and Nancy Reagan. She departed with Cardinal Carter for Toronto the next day.

A week later, I telephoned with proposals to build on marriage, emphasizing that that was what I wanted. We agreed I would call back in a week. When I did so Joanna (she had changed her name from Shirley the year before as she had never liked her name and could change it now without offending her mother, who died in 1987) drowsily commented that she didn't "know what (she) want(ed)." She remained unenthused about my plans for resuscitating the marriage, and considered that we were "separated," with her "living in one of our houses." This wouldn't do and could not last.

I sat for several hours in the encircling gloom of my conservatory in Highgate, yellowed autumn leaves windswept on the skylight, in a house where my children had laughed and played and grown, now inducive of bitter solitude.

Never more than when my connection with them became more tenuous did I appreciate the accuracy of Dr. Freud's famous aphorism that "my children are my joy and my riches." The saddest and lowest moment of all in the unravelling of my marriage came when our five-year-old, James, a brilliant, adorable, and spontaneous child repeated over the transatlantic telephone that was now my principal contact with my progeny, "It makes me sad." All I could say was that it made me sad, too. "Do you still like mummy a little bit?" I did and I do. His comments were heart-breaking and inspired haunting feelings of failure, helplessness, and remorse. We almost wept together.

For a proud and traditional man who believes in marriage and loves his family as I do, this was a harsh fate. The fissure that had always existed at the core of our marriage was that I romantically adhered to the view that the birth of our elder son brought together two people who belonged together. My wife from time to time suggested that the same event might have brought together two people who didn't belong together.[†]

Ours was, I reckoned, a no-fault, or joint-fault, break-down. I had failed to give Joanna the sense of being loved and appreciated to which she felt entitled. She had gradually withdrawn all the ingredients of a functioning marriage — empathy, intimacy, even simple solicitude. Shared parenthood and some degree of disinterested respect were all that remained. It was a time laden with fears, self-reproach, heartaches, and loneliness.

I sat in Highgate for three weeks, venturing forth in the days but generally spending the nights in a sort of *manresa* from which some far-reaching decisions emerged. I did not wish to live alone. This marriage was over, but it must be replaced by an entirely voluntary relationship firmly based on community of interest, purpose, and opinion and intense affection.

[†] My intense attachment to my children did not prevent me occasionally appreciating Jimmie Goldsmith's decisiveness when he became so exasperated with one of his sons that he telephoned the BBC information service, found the nearest town to the direct other side of the world from his London residence to be in the South Island of New Zealand, telephoned information for that town, and negotiated restaurant employment for his son, which Jimmie paid for, and sent the apprentice restaurateur to his new calling with a one-way ticket. It worked.

I sensed, perhaps self-indulgently, that if I devoted myself single-mindedly to my career and enjoyed reasonable good fortune, I might aspire to an obituary like André Laurendeau's for Duplessis: "Viewed from afar, such a career . . . seems brilliant indeed. Examined more closely, it appears much more austere because of the solitude he who exercises authority is condemned to, and because of the renunciations such a career requires."

I was not, I determined, going to accept such renunciations or such solitude. As I observed from my conservatory the twilight of autumn and of conjugality, I scanned the range of women acquaintances in a way I had not over the eleven or twelve years in which I thought I had a reasonably happy marriage. Gradually, tentatively, and then with greater fixity and deepening conviction, and finally with intense determination, my thoughts and hopes settled on Barbara Amiel.

Beautiful, brilliant, ideologically a robust kindred spirit, a talented writer and galvanizing speaker, chic, humorous, preternaturally sexy, a proud though not a religious Jew, tempest-tossed in marriage, disappointed in maternity, a fugitive from Canada assuredly making her way from and towards poles not unlike my own, a cordial acquaintance for many years, she shortly became the summit of my most ardent and uncompromising desires. I was amazed, relieved, and lest it be unrequited, worried, to discover that I was profoundly in love. My amazement at this turn of events was easily surpassed by Barbara's.

She was pondering a move to New York, seeking a more serene life with a distinguished novelist and writer of screenplays. As we were both on our own in London, we had gone twice to dinner and once to lunch together in ten weeks and were scheduled to go to the opera at Covent Garden on Saturday, November 17. I arrived early to pick her up and encamped, "a large Canadian," on her sofa.

Slowly, hesitantly at first, I set out my stall. She was first bemused, then incredulous, and finally she fenestrated with astonishment. She good-naturedly advised me to see a psychiatrist, which I did. I was assured by a distinguished analyst from the Tavistock that my thoughts and conduct were unexceptionable. A regular reader of Barbara's who had often seen her on television, he did not find her attractions difficult to comprehend. I persevered relentlessly and Barbara's scepticism gave way to receptivity and, ultimately, reciprocity. We pursued the new genre of the love-fax.

When matters had reached a point where honour required that I tell Joanna, I did so. Our discussions of separation and arrangements had already proceeded reasonably civilly though there were a few very unpleasant moments. Public indignities were avoided and my legal position facilitated negotiation of a sustainable financial settlement. I was saddened but ungrudging. Counsel agreed that we were separated from when Joanna left England in May 1991 and were eligible for divorce a year later.

In order to preserve some sort of a family framework for Christmas, we had a somewhat mean little holiday, though Joanna and I had our customary Christmas party in Toronto and attended Trevor Eyton's annual outing in North Palm Beach. We were both determined to carry out this unfortunate phase with as much dignity and discretion as possible. I returned to London for New Year's after a singularly difficult parting from my children, and my liaison with Barbara came to light in Nigel Dempster's widely read gossip column in the *Daily Mail* in mid-January.

There was intense interest in the press of Canada, including some exceptionally nasty misrepresentations of Barbara's previous romantic and marital life and a few completely false insinuations that she had broken up my marriage. The editor of the *Globe and Mail* spontaneously apologized for one particularly insolent piece. All those envious of Barbara's great talent and beauty, all those affronts by her ideological solidity, all the forces of professional and "lifestyle" and lesbian antagonism erupted splenetically. The British press was much more able to accept her editorial gifts and pulchritude and much less vulgar and contemptible than the Canadian newspapers. The *Daily Mail*, in particular, speculated rather benignly on whether romantic motivations would prevail over my presumed Catholic aversion to divorces and second marriages.

I had advised Cardinal Carter on Christmas Day of the demise of my marriage and new romantic life and after suitable expressions of concern, especially for our "sweet children," he quoted Thomas Aquinas — "*Primo vivere* — First we must live." He understood my dilemma and asked me to convey his regards to Barbara. As always in important matters, I was inexpressibly grateful for his support.

Barbara and I were married at the Chelsea Registry Office July 21, 1992, fourteen years and one week after my previous marriage. I sent Joanna a note that I ensured was delivered the night before, and she extended warm congratulations. We wished each other well and do so still. The registrar advised us that under the Marriage Act of 1946, any reference to God or simulation of the nuptial wording of any recognized religion, even Muzak from Wagner's or Mendelssohn's wedding marches, was not acceptable. We improvised samizdat references to marital institutions surpassing "parliament and State," enduring and transcending and so forth. It was a dignified service and furnished Barbara a fine subject for a widely appreciated column in the *Sunday Times*, filed from Maine where we went on holiday with my children.

We went directly from our wedding to Walter Annenberg's party for the Queen Mother at Claridge's. His second toast was to us, and it was a fine occasion. I had struck up quite a close relationship with Walter, then eighty-four, whom my father might have described as "down to his last four billion dollars with old age creeping on." His friendship, generosity, and wise counsel are made even more valuable by his Old Philadelphia formality: "The gates of Sunnylands (his palatial home at Palm Springs, California) will never be opened to that individual" is one of his preferred conversational blackballs.

Sometimes unmindful that few are as wealthy as he is, Walter urges me, from time to time, to execute a takeover of a four- or five-billion-dollar company. He is a delightful companion. On this occasion, the Queen Mother thanked me for our tasteful coverage of the marital difficulties of the Royal Family, as the Queen had, when swearing me into the Canadian Privy Council three weeks before.

We had twenty friends in the evening to Annabel's, went to New York the next day and what Bill Buckley called "a chirpy dinner," and on to Toronto and other dinners, including an occasion where Cardinal Carter put himself to considerable inconvenience to attend and toasted us with affecting graciousness. Barbara and I expect to live happily together for a long time.

As I had predicted for years, our cash flow proved practically impervious to the recession that yet battered and made susceptible many had subsided in Australia, I began at once to try to raise our percentage in Fairfax.

I had returned to Australia in mid-January 1992 and went to dinner with the new prime minister, Paul Keating at his Sydney residence, Kiribilli House (signing the visitors' book immediately after George Bush). Where Hawke had been smooth, emotional, yet inaccessible, not to say disingenuous, Keating was straightforward and infectiously humorous, his lip frequently twitching at the temptation of the incipient quip. The difference was between the beleaguered and fretful incumbent clinging desperately to an office to which he had lost his right, and the long-frustrated heir, bursting with the desire to fill the office he feared might have been too long denied him.

On the terrace overlooking Sydney Harbour, Paul Keating was thoroughly philosophical about what he considered his slender chances of re-election. He was almost evangelical in his salacious Australian fashion, about what he had achieved as Hawke's treasurer in deregulating, reducing tax rates, and promoting the interests of the entrepreneurial classes against the excessive appetites of the labour unions, which were his party's traditional bedrock of support. To hear it from Paul Keating in full flight, it was almost possible to believe that Australia was a martyr to the work ethic, rather than as it is more often portrayed a nation of somewhat lethargic, bawdy, and beer-swilling men lurching after the country's uncommonly attractive women.

The prime minister described with hilarious candour the vagaries of the regime whose headship he had just narrowly seized and explained how he couldn't vary the 15 per cent cap O'Reilly's infamies and the antics of the moribund Melbourne group had imposed upon us. It was "shitty and outrageous, of course," but would I leave him six months for matters to settle, whereupon he promised to put things right? Of course I would, having no choice. I came to realize what an extraordinary, powerful combination Paul Keating is of Bankstown (Sydney) cunning — Irish, political ward-heeler, cultural autodidact happy to discuss Nash and antique clocks with the Queen and constantly listening to classical music, and a great comic talent splendidly aware of the absurdity of much activity, including much of his own.

John Major and Michael Heseltine scrapped the poll tax, and the prime minister and Douglas Hurd won an opt-out from the European Community on the outrageous social chapter of the Treaty of Union. Major and Douglas Hurd had gone off to the conference at Maastricht in December 1991, with, ringing in their ears, an editorial of Max's in which I had had a modest input. (My contribution was prompted in part by Barbara reading aloud to refresh our memories excerpts from Orwell's "England, Their England.") We urged them to feel free to come back without an agreement if they thought that would serve the national interest. They did well to negotiate what they did and the worst spectre of all, a profound split in the Conservative Party over Europe, was avoided. There was widespread agreement in naturally Conservative circles that we should do what we could to put the government back and fight for the heart and mind of John Major later. The election came at almost the last possible moment, and the campaign began very rockily for the government, which floundered and waffled through the first couple of weeks.

I was in Florida but got daily bulletins. I put to Max Hastings the quasi-military question: "Is it the French Army of 1914, preparing for victory at the Marne, or of 1940, preparing for cowardice and rout?" It wasn't clear, but John Major remained cool. He campaigned, literally on the soap box he had used when running as an alderman in Brixton many years before and bore up well when pelted with eggs, especially in contrast to a cocky Neil Kinnock, shouting at a rally at Sheffield like a drunken Welsh football yobbo.

Major had told me at the start of the year that he didn't think he had "become prime minister to be an historic triviality, a trophy in someone else's career, particularly not Kinnock's, not having achieved this office at the age I have." This showed something bordering on a sense of destiny, and he kept a firm grip as election day approached, even if his colleagues, except for Michael Heseltine, were demoralized and ineffectual.

The newspapers owned or directed by Murdoch, Rothermere, Stevens, and me consistently warned of the consequences if Labour came in and raised income taxes and National Health Service payments to a total of 59 per cent (from about 45 per cent) as it had promised. The *Sun*, on election day, put a 300-pound topless woman on page three, and headlined: "If Labour wins, the Page Three Girl will look like this." They had already used the headline: "Nightmare on Kinnock Street." On election day, the front page of the *Daily Mail* was taken up by the warning: "Don't Trust Labour!" The corresponding front page on the *Daily Express* was "Don't Throw It All Away!"

The proverbial Tory press, all the London newspapers except the *Guardian, Independent, Observer,* and *Mirror,* did a much better job of warning the people of the implications of a Labour victory than the government did.

We own serious newspapers and reported fairly but went as far as we could in rational editorial argument in favour of the government. In the last *Sunday Telegraph* before the election, Charles Moore, Paul Johnson, Frank Johnson, Sir Peregrine Worsthorne, Ambrose Evans-Prichard, Christopher Booker, most of our most powerful and elegant writers, fired every cannon we had in promotion of the government's cause. (I had called Perry Worsthorne from Florida the week before, after he had virtually endorsed Labour, so colourless and convictionless did he find the Tories. I urged him to contemplate the full horror of a Labour win, and he gamely responded in the last pre-election Sunday with an endorsement of the government because it would not abolish fox-hunting, an activity Perry did not participate in or even particularly approve but regarded as a worthwhile tradition.)

On election night, the *Telegraph*s and *Spectator* revived a tradition of the Berry era, and we had a large party at the Savoy. Barbara and I went to a diverting opera at Covent Garden and arrived at our party just as the first serious results started to come in. (As my dinner jacket was half at home and half at Barbara's, I was one of the most unusually accoutred voters at my local polling station. I lost my vote as Hampstead and Highgate voted for that singularly ill-favoured Glenda Jackson, the Labour candidate.)

The *Telegraph*'s Gallup organization was the only one that predicted a Conservative victory, albeit probably a minority one, and I thought the tax issue and reservations about Kinnock might just put the government across, despite a bumbling campaign. It soon became clear that the Conservatives were running well ahead of expectations, and it was not a particularly suspenseful evening, yet there were some remarkable scenes at our party.

Margaret and Denis Thatcher came straight from the Concorde at Heathrow, and she came up the embankment steps of the Savoy, announcing, "We've won again. We've done it!" The people were voting for Thatcherism, if not Thatcher, I told her, which was doubtless true. The token Labour supporters, such as John Mortimer and former Lebanese hostage Charles Glass, skulked off early, but among relieved Tories an almost emotional scene developed.

People who had quarrelled for years embraced. Max Hastings, not a religious man, had pledged £500 to his local Anglican Church if the government were returned, and he went about the room like a biblical pacificator repairing slights and quarrels from years before. Paul Johnson was so relieved not to feel required to emigrate that he came back to writing regularly for the *Daily Telegraph*, from which Max had unceremoniously dismissed him three years before for writing "disloyal" reflections in the *Spectator*.

The spirit of reconciliation did not bind Lady Thatcher to Max, whom she did not forgive for his dispute with Carole Thatcher. (Max once correctly told our directors that "it would be too much to ask that Mrs. Thatcher would see my firing of her daughter as an example of Thatcherism in action.") Neil Kinnock gave the most ungracious concession speech I have ever heard but uttered the truest words I have heard from him: that the Tory press won the election. Certainly, the government's official campaign was not well-organized.

The government emerged with a majority of twenty-one, well down from Thatcher's huge victories, and John Major graciously wrote to thank me for the *Telegraph*'s contribution to the result. In my first post-election meeting with him, he reiterated his view that European monetary union was undesirable and that he would never commit Britain to it, despite the fact that the wording of the Maastricht Treaty ("A Treaty of Union") is entirely and overwhelmingly a promotion of just such a union. I asked him why, if he was opposed to the achievement of the goals that are the stated *raison d'être* of the treaty, he was, even then, so wantonly risking the life of his government, a few weeks into a new, highly personalized mandate, on its ratification.

He claimed a desire, vocation, and ability to desocialize Europe. Instead of Britain being subsumed in the euro-narcissist world of "rich poor and poor rich" (a phrase of the gracious and intelligent Queen of the Netherlands) in deference to the role played in French and German history by huge masses of discontented workers and farmers, Britain would lead Europe out of its relative fear of the incentive system. Apart from Britain, the European Community has an unbearable over-commitment to social spending, and more than 50 per cent of its collective gross product is in the public sector.

Since he says different things to different people on this subject, it is hard to be sure of the extent to which John Major is confidentially enunciating policy or merely papering over the crevices that divide his partisans. Neither role is contemptible but it is unsettling to be unable to distinguish them.

When I returned to Australia on a semblance of a honeymoon in August, I raised again with Paul Keating the issue of our shareholding in Fairfax, and he deferred matters to November in his usual torrent of four-letter words deluging obloquy on a miscellany of political and journalistic friends and foes.

Fairfax's annual meeting in November was in the picturesque Sydney Opera House. It should have been a love-in over the company's great progress of the previous eleven months, the acceleration out of receivership, a 60 per cent appreciation in the stock price, sharply increasing profits, and a new management team. Instead, Malcolm Turnbull had his final fleeting gasconade. Because of incompetent drafting and legal advice, Malcolm had been able to win the sympathy of a court on the technical point that inadequate notice had been given of the requirement for a special resolution approving options to the directors.

Malcolm stirred up a number of odd-lot shareholders as if what was in contemplation was a rape of the company and not a trivial procedural error. The Australian Stock Exchange, showing the granite resistance to minor agitation that we were already familiar with from Australian regulators, asked us to withdraw the resolution in question. We did so, yet Malcolm harangued the annual meeting like a Nuremberg prosecutor. We had engaged in wholesale deception of the shareholders, had mingled genuine incentives with retrospective unearned rewards, were guilty of "greed and mismanagement," and since the Australian directors included a former governor general and former chief justice of New South Wales, and other industrialists whom Malcolm had "respected all [his] life," they must have fallen under the baneful influence of the overseas directors.

As usual, Malcolm led with his lantern jaw as he gabbled out his preposterous indictment from a typed text. I noted his comments and had the pleasure of replying (as this sort of exchange was not to Zelman Cowen's liking) that the directors were "chastened" at the technical errors that would not be repeated and had at least led to a reduction of legal fees, but that those whom we wished to reward were fully deserving for having "emancipated Fairfax from the degradation of receivership and having so swiftly enriched all of the shareholders." I pointed out that Malcolm had "gouged" $6.3 million from the company and his clients for minimal services "apart from obstructing the consortium of which he was ostensibly a member. Consequently his moralizing to some of the most illustrious citizens of this country is, and to say the least, bizarre." I counted it as a minor vote of confidence that Malcolm had snitched 3.3 million shares from his clients at a founders' price and had hung on to them despite being so critical of the authors of his $2-million capital gain.

The tide turned decisively with my peroration, which denounced as "shameful" Malcolm's "xenophobic attack on foreigners whom he had, in my case, solicited as a Fairfax shareholder, who have come to Australia with unblemished reputations and who are proud to have invested in this country." Heavy and prolonged applause ensued.

Two days later Paul Keating received Dan Colson and me at his Sydney office. He had read a transcript of my remarks and quoted from it at a journalistic awards dinner. We had the usual extremely informal and rather coarse exchange, and he acknowledged he had been delinquent in not acting earlier on the promise of January. He urged us to send an application at once to the Foreign Investment Review Board to raise our share to 25 per cent and he would champion it. He was entirely encouraging of our long-term presence in Australia.

In the course of the year, Keating had drawn about even in the polls, largely by recourse to a sequence of red herrings about the flag, the monarchy, Britain's role in World War II, and other antipodean susceptibilities. More importantly, Hewson was mired in his championship of a goods and services tax. In March 1993, he was handily re-elected and in April he approved our ownership increase application. He impresses me as a more capable leader than any other current English-speaking government head as well as a delightful companion. Rupert Murdoch had advised me we would find the Fairfax journalists "a snake-pit" but Keating's reflections on them are often less charitable even than that. So are those of more conservative politicians. The premier of Victoria called the *Melbourne Sunday Age* "the morning star in drag," while a prominent political clergyman wrote to me complaining of the "Sydney Morning Homosexual." Both exaggerate. In fact, most seem to me acceptable, but as a group they required a serious debriefing from their long bout of disenthralled liberty to be as tendentious or even defamatory as they pleased.

We were on the verge of a great corporate breakthrough. All our research and intuition indicated that Fairfax profits and stock price would more than double in the next four years, having already doubled in the first year.

With the assistance of such vintage characters as the distinguished author Morris West, I had come to enjoy this distant, splendid, rough country enormously.

The missing ingredient to complete implementation of our newspaper grand strategy was an American flagship. It was in contemplation of this step that I moved to slice away Hollinger's debt in the spring of 1992. My strategic investment in Lord David Stevens's United Newspapers had proved to be mistaken.

My initial reasoning, in 1988 and 1989, had been that United Newspapers was an undermanaged and undervalued company, that the market had over-emphasized the perceived inexorable decline of the Express titles (the *Daily Express* had declined from over 4 million daily sales when Lord Beaverbrook died in 1964 to only about 1.6 million twenty-five years and more than ten editors later). A number of aggressive, well-managed publishing companies' chairmen were making purposeful statements to me about a takeover of United, a move that would not have been an unusually bold initiative in the financial climate of the late eighties.

My initial hope was that Lord Stevens would lead a somewhat leveraged buy-out of the national titles himself. We had a number of discussions on this point, but it soon became clear that he didn't wish to make a deal, though he claimed otherwise, and he was less than delighted to have me as a large shareholder. I couldn't entirely blame him, though I thought there were opportunities for collaboration that his suspicious nature excluded from serious exploration.

My eleventh commandment as a London newspaper chairman is never to speak ill of another such chairman and my relations have been almost uninterruptedly cordial with all of them. I always considered David Stevens a shrewd financial operator who had translated himself from a provincial newspaper company non-executive director into a Fleet Street chairman with considerable agility. He had, admittedly, paid a heavy price to break into national newspapers, valuing Express Newspapers at six times our valuation of The Telegraph p.l.c. when we took control of it at about the same time. He deposed Lord (Victor) Matthews, a capable and unpretentious man well-remembered by his newspapering colleagues for the militancy in industrial-relations matters of his household. Telephone callers to his house were generally subjected to the background bellowing of Lady Matthews to "sack them, Victor" and even more belligerently, the family parrot, which screeched constantly, "Sack them, Victor, for God's sake! Sack the lot! Be a man! Out with them all!" The ambiance of Lord Stevens's household, from my observations, is just as purposeful, but less confrontational.

The economic climate had changed more dramatically by 1992 than I had foreseen, the feisty chit-chat of would-be predators gave way to an irritating expectation that I would make a bid, and Stevens skilfully turned his widely regarded limitations as a publisher of the *Express* into a deterrent to others wishing to grasp his company. I was enough of a tactician to appreciate with admiration and entirely without rancour his cleverness in turning a weakness into a strength. The problems of the *Express* discouraged takeover bids while enabling him to imply that United could be a takeover target for me, which he must have known to be grossly improbable, thus fanning his own share price while not incurring any serious worries of a hostile takeover.

While I generally believed during the run-up to the election that the Conservative government would be re-elected, other than about ten days before the election, when they were still showing few signs of life, the catalyst in selling United shares in March was continued widespread polling showing a Labour victory. In such an unbidden event, it would be well not to have 17,250,000 shares of United Newspapers (8.8 per cent of the total) sitting in Hollinger opposite a bank loan.

I negotiated with N.M. Rothschild a disposition of our block in March. (David Stevens was most gracious when I gave him advance notice and kindly invited me to dinner for the first time in several years and to fill Bob Maxwell's vacancy at the head table of his annual corporate luncheon.) At the same time, we announced an impending underwritten sale of enough of our *Daily Telegraph* shares to qualify that company for a full London Stock Exchange listing. We were reluctant to part with any of our *Telegraph* shares, but the growth ambitions of our company required our debt to be cleared away and our cash and credit position to be made ready for new acquisitions.

The London listing procedure proved somewhat more complicated than had been anticipated. The dreadful fiasco of Bob Maxwell, the last controlling shareholder of a media company to list a subsidiary in England, had made the governors of the stock exchange skittish.

The sniggering forces of envy, which are sometimes as easy to arouse in England as in Canada, at least in commercial matters, put in a cameo appearance at our institutional meetings and in the financial press. They claimed that there was no growth in the *Telegraph* and that we were on the verge of helplessly clamping our corporate lips around the gas-pipe in television acquisitions or in New York, where we were negotiating over the *Daily News*.

I pointed out in vigorous sessions that our acquisition strategy had been rather successful up to now, how Hollinger had evolved from a clapped-out mining company into a highly profitable media company in a few years, how successful the *Telegraph*, Fairfax, and American Publishing had been.

I thought I made the case that I was conversant with the vagaries of the newspaper business in New York and with the television business in Britain, but that we had some obligation to look at all serious investment alternatives. Eventually, N.M. Rothschild underwrote the sale of 26 million *Telegraph* shares at £3.25. The pound at this point was worth $2.40 (Canadian), so the combination of the United and *Telegraph* sales yielded almost $320 million and a net capital gain of nearly $50 million.

The backing and filling with the underwriters led to a number of humorous exchanges, not least of them the final pricing discussions, which occurred on a Sunday by conference telephone, when I was at home in Toronto. I was in my dressing room wearing a dressing gown when a persistent ringing and banging at the front door began. I eventually absented myself from all the Rothschild and Cazenove parties I was talking to and discovered on my doorstep an urchin selling stuffed animals in favour of a children's charity he was rather vague about when I questioned him closely.

I said, "This is obviously a scam and I'm rather busy right now but I respect the commercial enterprise of any unannounced young person who comes on foot on a Sunday all the way down this long driveway to sell stuffed animals for a bogus cause." (The last visitor to walk it had been Perry Worsthorne in 1986 in pursuit of the editorship of the *Sunday Telegraph*.) I said I'd give him $10 for a golden bear for my daughter, but when he asked for sales tax I told him I was insulted, that charities needn't pay G.S.T., and that he obviously wasn't remitting tax or anything else. "I don't mind helping to sharpen up a young merchant, but I'm not going to be made a chump of while underdressed on the doorstep of my own house on a Sunday morning. Take it or leave it."

He took it, and when I returned to the telephone and recounted the highlights of this conversation to my interlocutors, we concluded our discussions at the upper end of figures they were comfortable with after a good deal of sabre-rattling by me about pulling the transaction altogether if I didn't get a reasonable price.

Rothschilds had sub-underwriters and were risk-free agents. The competing press responded gleefully when the stock opened at £2.85 but we had our money at £3.25 per share and the price rose nicely in succeeding months on our results and the devaluation of the pound in September. While cleaning house, we moved some Trinity International shares (a provincial British and North American publishing company) from Hollinger to the *Telegraph*, issued a 10p-per-share special dividend at the *Telegraph*, effective before selling down our position from 83 per cent to 68 per cent, and sold the last residue of our California Cable company, which we had retained for tax reasons, raising to $43 our effective per-share realization on the old Standard Broadcasting $8 to $12 stock. The Trinity shares were resold in March 1993, producing a £6-million capital gain for the *Telegraph* on top of a $12-million gain on the same shares for Hollinger.

The incomparable ingenuity of Jack Boultbee also succeeded in putting out $150 million of low-yield preferred shares (3.6 per cent), which constituted a minority interest, in place of the same amount of debt which had been yielding 8 per cent. The total debt reduction in all these steps was $522 million. The balance sheet, which had been the subject of sniffy English comment implicitly and outrageously likening us to Murdoch if not Maxwell, was made over as if by a fiscal Balm of Gilead.

In its post-Maxwell regulatory zeal, the London Stock Exchange imposed some absurd conditions on us. The exchange required that if a venture in Europe or Australasia, such as in Greece or New Zealand, were declined by the *Telegraph*, but Hollinger wished to proceed with it, that Canadian company's right to buy a newspaper or other property in Greece or New Zealand should be subjected to a majority of minority vote of *Telegraph* shareholders (i.e., the controlling shareholder would abstain).

Thus do regulators attract the contempt of the public, especially those whom they directly regulate: by the capricious imposition of ridiculous and unjust measures grossly *ultra vires* to themselves.

Kevin Maxwell came to see me at home at 8:30 a.m. Sunday, November 24, 1991, and offered parts of his father's business for sale just before evidence of Bob's monstrous skulduggery came to light. I told Barbara that I was determined my children would not have to make such a financially embarrassed call on anyone following my death. He didn't specifically offer the *New York News*, but it was obvious that the group was under severe financial pressure even before the legal and ethical problems came to light, a condition I did not try to exploit.

The discussions over the *New York News* went on for almost a year. Less than a month after Bob Maxwell's death, as his corporate group started to collapse, the storied tabloid, the model for Clark Kent's and Perry White's *Daily Planet*, was put into Chapter 11 by its managers. The paper had been losing circulation for thirty-five years, from 4 million shortly after the end of World War II, to about 800,000 when Maxwell died.

It had been 1.2 million before a ruinous strike in 1990 reduced circulation to about 200,000, mainly because of the unsportsmanlike behaviour of the Drivers' Union who selectively firebombed newsagents and shot up delivery vehicles, including, in several cases, their drivers, demoralizing practices for even the most enthusiastic work force.

I considered it an achievement for Maxwell to have succeeded in rebuilding circulation as well as he had. He also achieved the disqualification of employees accused of criminal misconduct as ineligible to return to the *News*. This, too, was no small accomplishment for Bob, given the casual attitude the New York newspaper labour movement has to such matters.

The Drivers' Union leader, Doug LaChance, referred to his years in federal prison as "government service" and when last seen by me, when I asked how he was, responded philosophically: "Terrible. A move to impeach me as president of the union was launched yesterday; my wife sued me for divorce this morning; I expect to be indicted for embezzlement tomorrow or the next day; and I have an awful hangover."

I was in a position, after I met Doug LaChance and the other labour, legal, and commercial personalities in the picture, to identify with Maxwell when he said to a press conference in some astonishment in 1989: "All these people seem to have been invented by Damon Runyan." In the midst of the discussions, when we were named as preferred bidders by the creditors' committee, Rupert Murdoch telephoned and said, "Your timing is perfect in New York, just as it was in London." His evidence for this was that the district attorney, Robert Morgenthau, had finally achieved a conviction against Mafia leader John Gotti.

I didn't find the conviction of a Mafia boss hugely reassuring or even necessarily relevant to industrial relations, although it was well known that the Drivers' Union, in addition to its penchant for violence, delivered almost as much cocaine as newspapers.

The *New York Times* had replaced the Drivers' Union with the Teamsters, considered in this context to be a tremendous move towards reform. I suspected that all the unions — the most corrupt (the drivers); the most Luddite (in this farrago the pressmen, the quintessence of Irish American pig-headedness); the typographers who had lifetime job guarantees, the firemen who represented only two people but made enough noise for 2,000 — that all of them could be influenced by the fact that if the *News* folded, they would get nothing. As long as the *Chicago Tribune* had been the owner, any closing would be generously paid for and all employees would go away having trousered a good deal of cash.

All this had changed. Without the *Chicago Tribune* there to pay severances in the event of closure, with only the empty cupboard of Bob Maxwell's administrators, I thought even the most obstreperous of New York's unions might accept the demanning, work rule changes, and radical alteration to the culture of the work place that alone could make the *News* capable of resuscitation and of interest to us. We would not be dealing with Marxist unions on the old Fleet Street model. Whatever else they may be, the Mafia are capitalists. The *Daily News* operated within what management called "the red zone," a $10-million facility advanced by a bank across 42nd Street whose motto was confirmed by its loan to the *News* and was proclaimed in a large sign in the bank's window: "We lend money to anyone!"

The *New York News* had been founded by Colonel McCormick and his cousin, Captain Patterson, in 1919. It had effectively run William Randolph Hearst's tabloid *Mirror* out of business and had been the evocator and the voice of New York's white working-class Archie Bunker population, especially in Queens and Brooklyn. It had not followed its clientèle out to the suburbs, had moved from its founder's arch-conservatism to a somewhat liberal view, and was pursuing less advertising-lucrative blacks and Hispanics. All these facts created the conditions in which we were the only serious newspaper company in the world to express interest in the *News*.

The *News* had 2,100 employees, or about 700 more than we reckoned it needed. Each job cost the company about $67,000 annually and the *News* was losing, on a cash basis, about $750,000 per month. Our view of the economics was that with the elimination of 700 jobs and various other economies we had in mind ($1 million per month in rent alone on 42nd Street where the *Chicago Tribune* was still the landlord), we could make $50 to $60 million, which would justify a new $125-million printing plant. (I met the mayor of New York, David Dinkins, when he came to London in June; the city was prepared to make generous concessions to keep the *News* printed in the five boroughs.) Liberated from its antiquated work rules, antagonistic industrial relations, and ancient printing process, we believed the franchise could be partly rebuilt, and its decline, at the least, arrested.

Our real involvement began when Barbara Walters, my dinner companion at George Weidenfeld's Chelsea salon in early December 1991, suggested she have the well-known media buyer, John Veronis, call me. He did so and acted for us in the complicated and protracted procedure that followed.

My first idea was to do a joint deal with the *New York Post*, which had prospered during the *News* strike, but whose owner, Peter Kalikow, was personally also in Chapter 11. We had dinner together at John Veronis's house in February 1992 and worked out a means of making a joint bid for the *News*. As John Veronis predicted, "Corporate governance could become a problem."

It became so long before there was any prospect of a corporation to govern. Kalikow early presented the notion that we should put up the money, he would run the business, and all indications were that his motive was to strip the *News* in order to build up the asset value of the *Post* and strengthen his desperate position opposite his own creditors. This was not what we had in mind so we proceeded alone. From time to time, discussions with Kalikow were revived but as months went by, he fell more and more helplessly into the hands of creditors and bottom-fishing new investors. Conversation with him continued to be entertaining but became less and less relevant.

The *Post* had been Manhattan's liberal Jewish high-income evening paper under Mrs. Dorothy Schiff and her leftish-chic editors, but Rupert Murdoch had turned it into a harum-scarum right-wing morning tabloid of very sensational bent. When Rupert had asked Marvin Traub, head of Bloomingdale's, for more advertising to reflect his higher circulation, Traub allegedly replied: "Your subscribers are my shoplifters."

Under Kalikow, who bought from Murdoch after Teddy Kennedy and others forced through tough cross-media rules out of vengeance against Murdoch who owned a New York television station, the *Post* lacked definition and dwindled. It was the flip side of the *News*: often a better editorial product with a severely and perhaps permanently diminished franchise. After late 1991, when Kalikow was proved to have largely padded circulation and the delivery function was decimated with cocaine indictments, the franchise seemed virtually to have died.

Salomon Brothers administered the process of finding a buyer for the *News* but the Chapter 11 bankruptcy judge, Tina Broznan, effectively invited the unions to name the new owner. The former equity holder, the administrators of Bob Maxwell, were excluded as no longer having a viable interest. The lenders and trade creditors and unions were all represented on the creditors' committee, where the *Chicago Tribune* figured prominently as landlord, newsprint supplier, and contingently interested party in pension and other liabilities where Maxwell had superseded it.

All the unions except the International Typographers were in the Allied Printing Trade Council but the different unions, as I could attest from meetings with them, had no coherence. The Drivers and Pressmen were represented by John Connery, a rather surly lawyer from Joe Flom's law firm, who was antagonistic to us at every stage. I called Joe and asked him to impart a little civility, even if impartiality were impossible, to his partner. Connery's behaviour became slightly less obnoxious for a time.

Connery was trying to shoulder aside Ted Kheel, the venerable labour counsel for the Allied, and the Pressmen's union leader, Jack Kennedy, was trying to replace George McDonald as head of the Allied. McDonald's union, the Paper Handlers, like the machinists and photoengravers and even the Guild, was comparatively flexible. The stereotypers, who performed a completely superfluous function even under the *News*'s 1950s technology, were very militant. So were the porters, a recently certified, almost entirely black union of doormen and janitors. There were several lesser unions squawking and chivying in varying states of mindless bellicosity.

The management and directors had only a supporting role in their own fate, as they had fallen on their swords by going into Chapter 11 initially and retaining Salomon Brothers, with a mandate to find new owners. The creditors' committee fumbled away its opportunity to play a role by a complete absence of leadership in its own ranks. A consensus was never achieved and the interests of the different categories of creditors were so distinct that the banks, suppliers, and unions never even went through the motions of seeking a common front.

The directors of the *News* included three respected new outsiders, Arthur Levitt, son of the long-time state controller of New York and subsequently head of the S.E.C., a recent unsuccessful mayoral candidate, Richard Ravitch, and a CBS news executive. One of these were seeking participation in the winning bid, and Ravitch was a co-sponsor of a competing bid, a neo-Fourierist workers' co-operative commonwealth bankrolled by a group of film investors. It never got off the ground.

Meetings were always packed with specialist advisers and were interminable filibusters by an endless sequence of irreconcilable factions inflexibly arguing their interests, usually in the amusing generic manner of their ethnic New York neighbourhoods and occupations.

From April on, it was clear that the only serious alternative to ourselves was Mortimer Zuckerman, a real estate developer originally from Montreal and owner of *U.S. News and World Report* and the *Atlantic Monthly*. At the trilateral commission meetings in Lisbon in April, I suggested to Zuckerman's editor at *U.S. News*, David Gergen, formerly Ronald Reagan's communications director, that we avoid a bidding war.

Mort Zuckerman phoned me a few days after that, and we met a couple of weeks later in New York. He was a type I recognized from my days in Montreal: Snowdon-Côte-des-Neiges, much doted on by his mother, very intelligent, hugely ambitious, a pleasant manner, and a vulnerable ego. His chief associate, Fred Drasner, was a Brooklyn variant, much more cocky and abrasive, but not without the aggressive charm of the New York Jewish businessman. Fred was going to be the publisher of the *News*, as he already was of *U.S. News and World Report*, and he would operate the *Daily News* more or less in his spare time. David Radler, who was more heavily engaged in the direct negotiations than I was, and I both thought that Mort and Fred drastically underestimated the complexities of running a large daily newspaper, especially in the competitive and labour relations environments of New York and with the recent history of the *News*.

Mort and David and I explored several ways of trying to make a combined bid. His opening gambit made Kalikow seem the soul of reason. Since the company was in bankruptcy, they wouldn't pay severances. They would make their big pay-off to Connery, Kennedy, and LaChance and put everyone else to the wall. We could put up such money as was required and we "would be welcome to come to lunch when you're in New York, and we'll tell you how we're getting along" (with your money — this was one of Drasner's bonhomous gems).

David and I tried all manner of formulae with Zuckerman. When he was clearly going to give the store away to the Drivers and Pressmen, I suggested we write in a joint bid combining, from the buyer's viewpoint, the best elements of both his and our offers, and thereafter have a referee, a shotgun buy-sell, or even flip a coin to see who the sole owner was, because "I would rather have nothing for my trouble but avoid stuffing the pockets and egos of the riff-raff you're cranking up to pay off."

My candidate for referee was Henry Kissinger. He assured me that he was prepared to be an adjudicator between Mort and me and that if called upon, he wouldn't serve interests contrary to ours. (Barbara, though an admirer of Henry's who fully appreciates his droll and subtle personality, when I told her of this, said, "That's what he said to the South Vietnamese.") Mort would not accept a referee, neither Henry nor Richard Perle, my other candidate, though he likes and respects both.

Henry Kissinger by 1992 had refined the private-sector state visit to a higher point even than had David Rockefeller, the inventor of it among my acquaintances. When we were detailing the occupations of our directors for an annual report, David Radler and I agreed that Henry's occupation was to be Henry Kissinger.

America had not really had to practise diplomacy as other great powers have, from when Franklin and Jefferson were padding around Europe in support of the Revolution until Nixon's time, so isolated or pre-eminent in its hemisphere and then in its Cold War alliance systems was it. It is a testimony to the country's meritocratic flexibility that when it did have to weigh the interest of states against each other more precisely than was necessary in the long bouts of isolation punctuated by the diplomatic evangelism of a Woodrow Wilson or even a John Foster Dulles, its first two practitioners were a Jewish German and a Polish Canadian, Kissinger and Brzezinski.

Henry had made a fair amount of money without devaluing the originality and disinterestedness of his opinions, despite frenzied efforts on the hard and soft left to discredit him. For the first ten years of the post-Nixon era, the American liberal media, in their febrile hatred of the deposed president, heaped all credit for what Nixon and Kissinger achieved together on Henry. Thereafter, in the post-Carter period, when there seemed a possibility that Kissinger might make a comeback to government, they reapportioned the credit to Nixon and systematically denigrated Kissinger. Serious historians will long debate the allocation of credit for the China policy, the beginnings of the Middle East peace process, and of Strategic Arms Control just as the Nixon-Kissinger Vietnamization plan will long be debated. Nixon and Kissinger obviously both grasped the strategic elements, but, because of his position of ultimate authority, Nixon was the *sine qua non* of making any progress in these areas at all.

Their relations with each other are cordial and respectful, but not without rivalry. When Nixon became a frequent contributor to his old tormentors, the *New York Times* and *Washington Post*, Henry told me, "He's like a prison camp inmate who's fallen in love with his guard." Kissinger's talents are as an historical analyst of foreign and strategic policy, a rigorous academic, a proven executant of bold foreign and strategic concepts in dramatic circumstances, a presentational talent with his piercing sense of humour and sepulchrally Teutonic delivery, an historic figure, a much sought-after personality, a star.

His rhetorical flourishes are invariably entertaining. "We must stop treating foreign policy as a substitute for psychiatry and theology" was long one of his best. He has an inexhaustible repertoire from Metternich, of which my favourite is: "Foreign policy is like a drama. Once begun it proceeds to its logical conclusion, either by the actors reading their scripts or by the audience mounting the stage." (Like Cardinal Newman's quotes from Napoleon, no one really knows whether Henry cites Metternich without embellishment.)

His sense of humour never deserts him in great or small matters. When he attended the bar mitzvah of the son of an underling when he was secretary of state, he was asked by a journalist if the occasion reminded him of his own bar mitzvah in Germany in 1938. "Von Ribbentrop wasn't able to attend mine," he dead-panned. When he became a Hollinger director, we had a dinner for him at our house in Toronto, and I seated him next to a neighbour who favoured a local sewer installation scheme that I opposed because it would be voted per property but paid for by feet of frontage. With 600 feet of frontage, I would have been paying for my neighbour's sewers, which, with a perfectly adequate septic system, I didn't wish to connect to, because, as I said to the local alderman, I didn't want stools jumping like salmon in my basement.

Slightly coached, Henry solemnly intoned to my neighbour that the major world problems were Russian internal reforms, East European restlessness, the Middle East, trade imbalances with Japan, sewer installation in suburban Toronto, and arms control. His dumbfounded interlocutor asked for a reiteration and he nonchalantly repeated the subjects in the same order as originally. Bismarckian determination was required to extract any amusement from such mundane subjects.

Henry Kissinger is undoubtedly capable of deviousness, as was amply recounted in Walter Isaacson's well-written but rather destructive work *Kissinger*. (When I asked Henry what he thought of it after I was invited by both the *Sunday Telegraph* and the *Spectator* to review it, he said, though he had co-operated with the author, "The only thing I like about it is the title.") Henry Kissinger has been motivated by a powerful ambition, above all an ambition to put as much socio-economic distance as possible between himself and the anti-semitic pogroms he fled as a child in Germany. (His motivations would be irrelevant and of no interest were he not a brilliant strategic thinker and a great statesman fully worthy of the traditions that so engrossed his academic interest.) I have always found him frank, humorous, a helpful and reliable friend, an amusing companion. In different ways to the even more complicated president whom he principally served, he is a great and much misunderstood man, but Mort Zuckerman didn't want him as joint-venture referee at the *New York News*.

When the creditors' committee and board of the *News* again declared us preferred bidder, Judge Broznan gave me a fixed period, the duration of her summer holiday, to reach agreement with the unions. I gave their leaders my pitch, new manning levels, new rules, a new culture, their members "coming to work like happy little elves singing "Hi-ho, hi-hi," in exchange for a new plant, a serious marketing budget, the full determination of our company with its track record in London and elsewhere, to turn the tide of decades of deterioration at the *News*, "to chase Archie Bunker into the suburbs," while still serving the newest New Yorkers.

We had tentative agreements with all the unions except the Pressmen, even the Drivers, but at the end of each such session the union negotiators phoned Fred Drasner, who assured them he and Zuckerman would do better. Connery had been suborned and led Kennedy and his knuckle-dragging pressmen by the nose. We almost had a deal with LaChance, until Zuckerman agreed to ban wholesalers, putting himself definitively into the Drivers' capricious hands, and to remove Maxwell's ban on hiring the former strikers accused of criminal wrongdoing. This was a concession of great symbolic significance. Hiring violent felons from a Mafia-dominated union judged morally unemployable even by Bob Maxwell was not what we meant by changing the culture of the workplace.

When Zuckerman's and Drasner's meddling had derailed our discussions sufficiently for us to be unable to reach agreement by the deadline decreed by the judge, our representatives in New York, especially the tireless David Dodd, financial vice president of our American Publishing company, held a very amicable joint press conference with LaChance and Kennedy, who graciously credited us with providing Mort Zuckerman the incentive to make offers they found highly unrefusable.

Mort asked for minimal demanning and didn't accept that the less powerful unions had any right to severances from a bankrupt company. He was putting up only $13 million for an 800,000 circulation paper in the greatest and richest market in the world. Yet his economics were clearly impossible. The demanning he would achieve wouldn't justify the capital expenses a new plant would entail, even with local government incentives, and a new plant is required to arrest the decline of the *News*.

Our relations continued to be amicable and I publicly and privately wished him well, though his closing was delayed for a couple of months when the lesser unions he had expected to bulldoze litigated with partial success. He did score a major success with the Guild, partly vindicating his strategy, but he will have to get massive further cost reductions from demanning and there will not be another opportunity as propitious as the post-Maxwell bankruptcy.

One of the several irritations about our many months of fruitless work in New York was that no one took us at our word that we wouldn't chase the *News* beyond the point where we were commercially comfortable with it. Not the creditors, who phoned up at the end of the process and asked what "WE are going to do"; not the friendlier unions who did the same; and not the securities analysts in Toronto or London who convinced themselves we would pay any price for the privilege of losing money on the sidewalks of New York. I did my best to give the press graphic epigrams, but, as in other spheres, people tend to believe what they want to believe, and many wanted to believe that we were eager to open an artery in New York. Towards the end of the drama, I told the *Globe and Mail* that "we have other things to do beside kissing that comatose princess awake." Nothing availed.

The creditors who, in the words of one of my friends at the Tribune Company, "wimped out," the friendly unions, the management and directors who fussed and plotted like the followers of Big Minh between the flight of Thieu and the fall of Saigon in 1975, were worthless to us as allies. Mort Zuckerman had clearly settled on more robust co-combatants, as Connery, egregious though he was, once bought, stayed bought, and brought the rag-bag of his clientèle with him. (LaChance didn't go the distance, as he failed his parolee's cocaine test and was packed off back to "government service" as his union was overwhelmed with a new raft of indictments.)

The shambles of the *Post* and the final collapse of Kalikow dumped that newspaper into the hands of someone who was immediately indicted for massive stock fraud and then into the lap of a hallucinating parking lot owner. Finally, Rupert Murdoch seemed to return as owner, partly to secure his receivable and partly, no doubt, on the equally useful errand of humiliating Teddy Kennedy. Within a couple of days, the *Post* ran a cartoon of Mort Zuckerman distraught on a psychiatrist's couch. There doesn't seem to me to be much profit for anyone in the tabloid New York newspaper field, other than for *Newsday* on Long Island.

Mort Zuckerman demonstrated again that the bane of the newspaper industry has been the well-to-do amateur making non-economic deals to get into the glamour and influence business, especially in very large cities. In the circumstances, we were well out of it. For David Radler and me, there has never been any glamour or influence in losing money.

Undeterred by this disappointment but still in need of an American flagship, we moved on to other prospects, which had owners, a profit, and good labour relations.

Shortly after the end of our part in the New York drama, a decisive turn finally came in our Byzantine minuet with Southam. After buying *Saturday Night* magazine in 1987 partly to quiet the Canlit set in the event that we assaulted the unholy and uneasy alliance between Southam and Torstar, and selling off in 1989 the 5 per cent Southam shareholding Hollinger had accumulated, my associates and I then watched, not altogether inconsolable, the collapse of the soufflé of the old Southam family pretensions to be adding value to their stock through applied management skill.

At the same time, Torstar was consecrating nearly half a billion dollars to a new plant north of Toronto with ultra-sophisticated German presses. It was piling debt on to the company and leaving almost its entire revenue-earning capacity in the hands of a few highly skilled pressmen armed with all the swaggering praetorian powers conferred by Bob Rae's Labour Relations Act amendments (which the *Star*, home and inspiration to four generations of Ontario's oversuckled left, had already editorialized on September 7, 1990, might drive the newspaper right out of business).

Finally, in the spring of 1992, Torstar had rebelled against what it thought (rightly) an extravagant and complacent indulgence of under-performing assets, including the printing facility Southam had overpaid UniMédia for by $14 million two years before. Members of the old controlling families were effectively forced out as president and chairman. The Southam-Balfour-Fisher era was over, and the vast and disparate array of those who held hands against the imaginary threat of the 1985 takeover began hurling chunks of stock onto a declining market like learned treatises on a roaring book-burning.

All through 1992, Torstar's agents and representatives of the dispossessed and demoralized old families milled about unhappily, seeking a better future. Some made the ritualistic trip to Paul

Desmarais, as I had, at his invitation, on the same subject, in 1989 and 1990. Paul told me he had become rather doubtful about Canada generally and labour relations in the newspaper industry in particular, after his unhappy experiences at *La Presse* and *Montréal Matin* (which he bought from the Union Nationale in 1973 and had to close a few years later). He was much more interested in building his Franco-Belgian connections, which had become a lucrative and socially fulfilling financial hobby. His only responses in respect of Southam were bottom-fishing on a scale that would impress even Kerry Packer.

The Southam road led, eventually, to me. Like a dazed frontier scout, I emerged one day from my encampment to see the approach of an immense host, once minatory but now announced by a vanguard of well-wishers and tribute bearers. Various complicated scenarios were kicked about involving Torstar effectively trading their 22.6 per cent shareholding for a couple of the Alberta and Ontario newspapers. Torstar's position as a rank insider made its status very difficult, and the preposterous poison pill provisions that the management had layered in during their long watch of immobilized vigilance on the ramparts of the stagnating company would require an incoming shareholder to bid for all the stock, which I was not about to consider.

Inexorably, Torstar's impatience mounted. The complexities of navigating the anti-takeover bylaws and carving up the company, in the dismal context of Canada's interminable recession, constitutional disarray, and Bob Rae's lethal injection of lobotomous socialism, finally caused Torstar to look longingly for the exit. Dave Galloway asked if we would buy their block of 14.25 million shares at 15 per cent above the recent market, necessitating no follow-up offer to the other 77.4 per cent of the shareholders. We would.

The Hollinger executive committee approved the $259-million transaction in a telephone meeting, November 13, 1992. The Torstar directors approved the deal two days later, while Barbara and I were on our way to Jerusalem to attend the handing over of the new Supreme Court of Israel building by my colleague Lord (Jacob) Rothschild. It was a noteworthy occasion. I had an opportunity to meet the leaders of the new Rabin government and was gratified to note how much less besieged, unfashionable, and surly the Israelis appeared than they had on my previous visit, two years before, although unrest in the occupied areas appeared considerably more serious.

There was the usual social to-ing and fro-ing, but the highlight of the trip was Sir Isaiah Berlin's interrogation by Israeli security at London Airport. By the time Isaiah had finished his genealogical and cultural summary of his purposes in visiting Israel, the authorities were thoroughly confused. Barbara and I visited the *Jerusalem Post*, including the bomb shelter where the paper had been composed during the Gulf War. Barbara visited Ethiopian refugee camps. We reverently observed the rites at the principal shrines of our faiths and lingered in the most traditional Jewish quarter, replicating seventeenth-century shtetls.

Our trip was steadily interrupted by mounting telephone and fax traffic from Canada praising our Southam purchase. (I shortly heard from Hal Jackman also, writing on his vice-regal stationery to tell me how much Southam stock the National Victoria and Grey Trust company had under administration or officially advised. Life wasn't all cutting ribbons and signing confiscatory legislation for the monarch's disinterested representative in Bob Rae's Ontario.)

To my amazement, my ancient foe, the *Globe and Mail*, on November 17 led with an editorial stating that I was the best thing that could possibly happen to Southam, that the former regime had been self-serving and incompetent, and that I had been unfairly judged because of my "robust political incorrectness." I was virtually urged to clean the Southam house.

This was truly the end of the tiresome era in which Bob Rae's calumnies of 1986 had required me to be rather litigious to blow out of every media organization's computer queue the notion that I had upholstered myself with the purloined social security of widows, orphans, and the hoary-handed working men. All the infantile fussing of John Ralston Saul, Ron Graham, and even the inevitable Pierre Berton, to the effect that the libel laws should be changed to emulate (in this instance only) those of the United States and require proof of intent to defame for successful prosecution, had mercifully evaporated.

A few of the libel chill activists demonstrated against me on Toronto Street when I was unfortunately elsewhere. The Reichmanns were also taken to task for objecting to a murderous piece in *Toronto Life* that suggested the entire Reichmann fortune was based on selling wartime contraband to the Nazis.

As Paul explained to me, "It is as if they called my mother a hooker." Rather more defamatory even than that, I thought. I played a modest role in arranging a settlement based on an overwhelmingly abject apology and a sizeable charitable contribution.

The author of another defamation of me, in a soporiferous volume about pension surplus entitlement, even put it about in her concentric leftish circles that her book's sales had sky-rocketed after the unsold copies (the great majority of the print run) had been pulped in response to my writ. (The book contained the usual allegation that I had pocketed the pensions of the financially defenceless, plus a few other flourishes.)

Apart from the physical and commercial difficulty of increasing the sales of a pulped book, I pointed out that destroying the unsold copies was an inspiration of defendant's counsel, presumably after reading his client's book and taking note of her sales figures. Ron Graham's publisher paid for an apology in the *Globe and Mail* for his charge that I had propagated human misery. The *Star* corrected and apologized. The pension myth was expunged from my file and calm returned to the brackish teapot of Canadian journalism.

Another uplifting contemporary development putting right a good deal of difficult personal history was our decisive victory in the journalists' strike at *Le Soleil* in Quebec City. Having endured a good deal of Marxist agitation and anglophobic provocation from elements of the French-Quebec press over many years, I was proud of the performance of our Quebec management, headed by Pierre Des Marais and the former deputy treasurer of Quebec, Robert Normand, publisher of *Le Soleil*. They skilfully divided all the rest of the work force from the journalists, who finally struck us after working two years without a contract. They refused to be assigned and demanded a sharp increase in average pay to $60,500 for a three-day work week in the midst of the most severe recession in sixty years. Their pickets were ignored; freelancers working and faxing from home and editors produced an improved paper, as polls that we steadily published on page one showed, and we turned the historic tide of industrial relations in the newspaper industry in Quebec.

Some of the strike leaders were long-time antagonists and one was an amiable former editor at *L'Avenir de Sept-Iles*.

The whole episode was well executed by our Quebec management and culminated in a Christmas Eve vote to accept management terms causing the union executive to resign. It was one of my more pleasant career experiences. (I would never, even in my most combative moments, have gone quite as far as Jimmie Goldsmith, who broke a strike at the Paris magazine *l'express*, when he owned it, by haranguing the journalists that "Instead of blood, you have only pus in your veins.")

While the New York and Southam dramas slowly unfolded, we lightly participated in the extraordinary carnival of British television licence applications. It was probably evidence of Mrs. Thatcher's declining judgement that she put all the independent television licences up for renewal with no advantage to those incumbents, almost all of them, in fact, who had exercised their licences faithfully.

We joined a group to bid for the morning weekday licence with NBC who kept telephoning me as a fellow North American to ensure that what appeared to be a ludicrous charade really was happening. It was ludicrous but it was definitely happening. Also with us were ITV itself, MAI, Taylor Woodrow (the construction company), and the talented and energetic Michael Green, head of Carlton, a cleverly constructed and managed production business that he had built up to a capitalization of over £1 billion.

In any disorganized auction for desirable items, the cleverest operators will corner the market. Michael Green, a delightful if mercurial and suspicious man, made a series of fortuitous arrangements with the London Weekend Television head, Christopher Bland. Michael Green discussed our business plan with Christopher Bland in its early stages. When Bland produced his competing bid, it narrowly topped ours, and he won. Green and Bland made a facilities-sharing arrangement between weekend and weekday television (a licence Green wrested from Thames Television; we had a 5 per cent interest in the winning bid). Green was the not-so-surprising final shareholder for the unsubscribed 20 per cent of Bland's company's morning bid. It was all pretty coincidental.

The *Telegraph* had achieved its basic objective of becoming a recognized and serious player in the television sweepstakes, despite being iniquitously confined, like other national newspaper companies, to a single 20 per cent interest. Michael Green called me a few months after the dust settled on this fiasco to ask if I wanted to participate in his bid for ITV. When it became clear he was again offering a 5 per cent interest, I quoted Mussolini to him: "I am not a collector of deserts" (uttered about some obscure border dispute between Egypt and Libya in the thirties). In these matters, at least, Green and Bland were the contrary of Dickensian figures and were not aptly named participants.

A further divertissement was the preparation of a bid for Channel 5. No new licence, in my experience, could have been more skilfully designed to deter buyer interest. London and the South East were largely excluded, all the U.K.'s VCRs would have to be retuned to some unascertainable degree, and there would be great but undetermined problems transmitting from a suitable antenna. Our chief associates were to be Time Warner and the memorable duo of Australian television executive Bruce Gyngell and the television presenter and producer, David Frost.

Our group never addressed the technical problems and we eventually determined not to proceed because the economic variables were too risky and unquantifiable, but we had many amusing sessions. They were usually leavened by Frostie's ebullience, including the occasions on which he invited me on Sunday afternoons to his London home to toast in fine champagne our impending "victory."

Such celebrations proved premature but followed directly my sacramental devotions at the Brompton Oratory and were highlighted by Frostie marching about, Dom Perignon bottle and glass in his hands with his shirt-tail hanging down beneath the back of his jacket. I thought at first that this was similar to Andrew Knight's simulation, under the influence of his former wife, of Pakistani customs as in the red bloomers and long shirt that he wore to Bob Maxwell's sixty-fifth birthday party, but it was Frostie's costume as referee for some benefit cricket match. No real business was done, and in the end the licence wasn't awarded at all, but they were among the most amusing business meetings I have had.

Another deal that wasn't completed was for purchase of some newspaper interests in South Africa. My family and I visited the colourful owner of casinos and private zoos, John Aspinall, at his splendid house near Capetown in the spring of 1991. John was an enthusiastic booster of the leader of the Zulus, Mangosuthu G. Buthelezi and had organized a series of dinners for him, to counterbalance slightly the great foreign success of the African National Congress, many of whose partisans were now unjustly trying to represent Buthelezi as an Uncle Tom.

In fact, Buthelezi had been detained in South Africa in the last several years of Nelson Mandela's imprisonment, because he refused to negotiate with the all-white government while Mandela was imprisoned and refused to consider negotiating a mere homeland Bantustan status for his Zulus. He was opposed to sanctions as a capitalist and considered the "Spear of the Nation armed struggle" waged by the ANC to be both unwise and farcical. (The ANC had blown up a few bridges and killed only a couple of white settlers in years of supposedly unrelenting struggle.)

Gatsha Buthelezi has many of the characteristics of his people: pride, sensitivity, courage, loyalty. Despite the Western media's profound seduction by the ANC, Buthelezi and his powerful tribe are the third force in South Africa after the ANC and the National Party government and will play an important part in the country's future.

I had a dinner for Buthelezi and his entourage and Aspinall at the Toronto Club in November 1990. The lieutenant-governor, Lincoln Alexander, Cardinal Carter, the South African ambassador, and a considerable array of business and media leaders were among those who attended. The dinner was a reasonable success, though its most entertaining aspect was that pro-ANC demonstrators threw blood at the door of the Toronto Club and taunted formally dressed couples, arriving to have their pre-Royal Winter Fair dinner in another part of the club, whom they mistakenly supposed to be Buthelezi's and my guests.

The cultural incomprehension between the ANC stooges and Toronto's mink and manure set was profound. (The Toronto Club's very able manager, Ingo Schreiber, pretended he was a *Toronto Star* reporter and convinced the demonstrators that the dinner had moved to a hotel, so the demonstrators had gone when Buthelezi and I arrived. Left-wing mobs, or other mobs, haven't grown any cleverer in the decades of my exposure to them.)

I also received a very abusive letter from a Canadian black federal NDP MP who accused me of fostering white racism by entertaining Buthelezi. The NDP hasn't grown much smarter in the years of our acquaintance, either.

On Buthelezi's first full night in Toronto, he came with us to Latham and Paddy Ann Burns's annual Winter Fair dinner at their home and actually attended the equestrian show. Galen Weston had been relied on, as president of the fair and a friend of several members of the Royal Family, to fill the Royal Box with a suitable party, but wasn't able to do so. Paddy Ann, a lively soul, shrieked with delight when I sheepishly inquired if we could bring Buthelezi and his party to dinner. "Isn't he a prince or something or other?" I assured her he was indeed a prince of the Zulus, by some reckoning a more formidable tribe than the Hanoverians.

"That's it! You've found us a worthy occupant of the Royal Box!" Gatsha Buthelezi, with the jet-lagged John Aspinall dozing beside him like a clapped-out white batman, took the salute, brandished his tribal chief's baton, and played his assigned role to perfection. We repaired back to the Burnses' afterwards, and the day, on which angry Zulus were reported in the world's press to have "scattered thousands of their ANC opponents in fright before them" (*Daily Telegraph*), ended after two a.m. with Mangosuthu G. Buthelezi and his hostess, Paddy Ann Burns, singing "When Irish Eyes Are Smiling" to the accompaniment of a well-known social Toronto pianist.

Having thus made Buthelezi's acquaintance, and slightly indebted him to me, I was well-placed to visit him with John Aspinall and some of his other house guests in Kwazulu in April 1991. John Aspinall is a vintage character, part Oswald Mosley-style admirer of the strong leader (in his case Jimmie Goldsmith and Kerry Packer as well as Buthelezi); part *Boys' Own Annual* rugged individualist and supporter of tribal values; part British gentleman cynic of the hard-bitten gambling school. Among his best friends was the legendary Lord Lucan, who disappeared mysteriously after murdering his nanny when he hoped he was murdering his wife. "Asper's" comment, when asked by the press, was that "if she were my wife I would have clubbed her to death long before, and there wouldn't have been any mistaken identity."

Some of Aspinall's soirées are especially memorable, including one attended by Sir James Goldsmith, Charles Powell (Mrs.

Thatcher's chief foreign policy adviser), the defence minister, Alan Clark and me, in 1989. It was alleged in Parliament and in Alan Clark's diaries that I had been asked to dismiss Max Hastings as editor of the *Daily Telegraph*, or at least amend our supposedly pro-Heseltine line. The *Telegraph* took no such line and no such request was made of me.

His houseguests in South Africa in April 1991, an unlikely group of British aristocrats, were improbable visitors to Kwazulu. We flew to the Mangosuthu G. Buthelezi airport at Ulundi, and drove down Mangosuthu G. Buthelezi Boulevard to the Mangosuthu G. Buthelezi Parliament building to have lunch with Mangosuthu G. Buthelezi. (The lunch was very efficiently served by his white butler.) At dinner, Buthelezi and his king, Goodwill Zwelathini, and their principal collaborators appeared in their leopard skins and Aspers, on demand, gave them an address whose peroration called upon the Zulus to "burnish your shields, sharpen your spears, and remember Shako the Great."

I whispered to my thunderstruck English neighbour that "we will be lucky if this doesn't bring on civil war," as Buthelezi proclaimed him "a white Zulu" and invited him to speak at Jambulani Stadium in Johannesburg, which he did a month later. Unfortunately, Buthelezi's food was inedible to the uninitiated and we repaired to the Ulundi Holiday Inn for a Texan hamburger.

On this occasion, Buthelezi assured me that the tall, spear-carrying, fierce-countenanced young men who accompanied him and the king were "not warriors. They are boy scouts. We have no warriors." I asked how many "boy scouts" he had. "About 100,000." The ability of the Zulus to strike cold terror into the hearts of everyone in South Africa except perhaps the Afrikaaners is not hard to imagine. These are the descendants of those who helped to bring down Disraeli at the Battle of Isandlhwana in 1879, the British Little Big Horn, where the Zulus appeared "thick as grass and black as hell." It was at the same hands that the Prince Imperial, Napoleon IV died, ending the legitimate Bonaparte dynasty. (On a subsequent visit to Zululand organized by John Aspinall, Kathy Ford, Henry Ford II's third wife, who has an outstanding sense of humour, was greatly amused when a prominent Zulu offered Aspinall 200 cattle for her. These junkets to Buthelezi are interesting as well as informative.)

After some study and research, I concluded that the two strongest groups in the ethnic quilt of South Africa were the Afrikaaners and the Zulus, and that as long as Buthelezi could speak for almost half the Zulus and F.W. De Klerk did not put him over the side in favour of the ANC, there would be no extreme left government in South Africa. The resistance to the imposition of one could be extreme and violent; the vicissitudes could be severe and very distasteful, but South Africa could not be governed by other parties in the teeth of Afrikaaner and Zulu resistance.

The course of some of the township violence clearly suggested that the Afrikaaner government didn't altogether discourage the Zulus from resisting too complete or authoritarian a township takeover by the ANC, a vast umbrella like Poland's Solidarity, encompassing an unruly congeries of tendencies. (In South Africa and in London, President De Klerk assured me that he would produce policies that should succeed in separating the moderate from the communist-inspired elements of the ANC.)

Because the Afrikaaners and Zulus were demonstrably South Africa's most historically and currently important ethnic groups and were capably led by determined men who would not squander what they believed to be the birthright of their constituents, I thought that South African newspapers, properly marked down in price to allow for political risk, could be worth a modest bet. I had known Harry Oppenheimer, South Africa's leading industrialist, for many years, since he attended a Canadian Imperial Bank of Commerce dinner as a former advisory board member and told us about his meeting with General de Gaulle, in which de Gaulle began with "*Que voulez-vous de moi?*" and concluded with advice that the white South Africans represent their task as "*une mission civilisatrice.*"

Harry Oppenheimer had been one of Field Marshal Smuts's moderate MPs, advocating universal suffrage, a bicameral legislature, with one house giving an effective right of veto to each "culture." He had left public life with Smuts in 1948, but had bought practically all the South African English-language press in order to prevent it from being muzzled by the apartheid regimes of the Purified National Party under Malan, Strijdom, Verwoerd, and Forster. Oppenheimer, as controlling shareholder of Anglo-American and its affiliates, including De Beers, one of the legendary companies of the old Commonwealth, along with Canadian Pacific and Hudson's Bay in Canada, and Broken Hill in Australia, was too powerful to be attacked even by the authors of the evil and repulsive system of apartheid.

His underlings at Johannesburg Consolidated Industries, Times Media Limited, and the Johannesburg *Star*, entered into lengthy discussions with Dan Colson and me about a purchase of the company that controlled the Capetown papers, the national Sunday paper, and that had part of joint ventures in Port Elizabeth, Pretoria, and Durban. As time went by, Harry's underlings became restive and chipped and caviled, sought to eliminate political discounts, as if we were buying in North Carolina or Alberta, and wanted to perpetuate exact joint ventures with them in control of management and no liquidity for us. As far as we were concerned, the door remained open.

I suggested to De Klerk at a dinner at Aspinall's Capetown house that he could produce a constitutional package of massive devolution to the States and the judicial districts and an upper house that would have a de facto veto for the principal voting blocs and that the whole package could be sold by including a distribution of shares to the whole population from state-owned enterprises, South African Airways, South African Broadcasting, and so forth. Every citizen of every pigmentation and tribe would receive his stock in an overall yes vote. The idea was certainly not original to me, and De Klerk strongly implied that this might be his method.

The combination of De Klerk, Buthelezi, and Mandela is one of the most impressive and talented groups of national political leaders in the world, though my impression of Mandela when Kissinger introduced us at Davos in February 1992 was that he is a distinguished, virtuous old man, well past his prime and worn down, as well he might be, by twenty-seven years of unjust incarceration.†

---

† After this introduction, Henry, Barbara, and I sat down and started into a pot of tea when Kissinger started grumbling: "Oh no, here comes that goddamned Indian again." I accused him of quoting General Custer but the man he referred to, elegantly dressed and exquisitely courteous, proved to be a very senior official of the government of India, representing the prime minister of that country with whom Henry, as part of his constant practice of private sector state visits, then had a very satisfactory meeting.

In early 1993, I concluded negotiations with Southam's chairman, Ron Cliff, for Hollinger to succeed to some elements of the Southam-Torstar agreement. Initial proposals that in exchange for three board seats we commit in advance to support the slate of directors put forth for election by the majority of the nominating committee, I rejected as "not reflecting the true correlation of forces." (After the evaporation of earnings and shareholders' equity and the collapse of the stock price, I didn't doubt that the shareholders would be happy to elect us and dismiss most or all of the incumbents, if asked, though we preferred to avoid such an imbroglio.) I told Ron Cliff that we declined "to have the honour of paying for the shares while entrusting the voting of them to others."

We eventually reached an arrangement that conceded independent majorities on committees, a 23.5 per cent ceiling for our shareholding for two years, and a promise not to lead opposition to the "poison pill" for two years.

At David Radler's and my first board meeting in February, the dividend was cut in half, I proposed a further $80-million allocation for demanning to remove 1,000 superfluous employees, all in the year-end figures for 1992, and a special committee was struck to consider methods of further collaboration between Southam and Hollinger. Southam's newspaper division employed 7,500 people, clearly a third of whom shouldn't have been there. Our research revealed that from 1981 to 1991, personnel costs as a percentage of overall costs and of total revenues had increased from 51 per cent to 67 per cent and from 41 per cent to 58 per cent. Restoration of profitability required a serious assault on costs above all other things.

This discussion led to an exchange over an equity issue, as the lending banks were threatening to withhold a waiver of technical, covenant breaches if the equity base were not replenished. David's and my suggestions that the banks not be grovelled to and that management focus on producing the conditions for operating improvements and not shovelling out cheap stock at historically low prices was judged divisive.

Further exchanges of the same general tenor at the next (telephone) board meeting drove the most conservative Southam board faction and the lurking bargain shopper Paul Desmarais into each other's arms.

I had known Paul for twenty-six years. He had built up a bankrupt bus company in Sudbury into Provincial Transport and then into a partnership with Jean-Louis Lévesque and on to voting control of Power Corporation, which, when he took it over from Peter Nesbitt Thomson in 1967, was a mess of ill-fitting assets. He shaped that business up with judicious sales and purchases, especially the takeover of Great West Life and the sale of Consolidated-Bathurst and Montreal Trust just before the end of the great boom of the eighties. Along the way, his sequential purchases for cancellation of his own shares in Great West Investor's Group and Power Corporation itself were splendidly timed. I had always found him entertaining and astute, though it required a certain talent to discover in all his energy and effusiveness when he was being serious and when, in an expression he made famous at the Ontario Securities Commission, he was "merely musing."

After the Consolidated-Bathurst and Montreal Trust sales, he was left with around $750 million in cash in Power Corporation, as well as considerable further resources in some of the affiliates. He was always claiming to me to be contemplating some grandiose acquisition but after the recession had set in for a couple of years and he still hadn't made a decisive move, I told him that he reminded me of the cautious first-class passenger on the *Lusitania* in 1915 who was so fearful of being torpedoed that he slept each night in the lifeboat but was almost drowned when the liner was sunk within sight of the Irish coast. He didn't find the allusion particularly apposite.

In any case, he was stirred from his torpor by the spectacle of Southam's eroding share price and the preparedness of some of the Southam board factions to parachute him in ahead of and as a counterweight to us. Even David's and my relatively diplomatic lobbying for serious efficiencies rattled the nerves of the survivors of the *ancien régime*. I heard from Paul Desmarais in my car on my way to London airport to fly to Toronto, March 10, 1993. He said he had been approached to make an investment in Southam and was planning to do so. He didn't mention timing, quantity, or share price but emphasized he wasn't motivated by any unfriendliness towards us.

I responded that I assumed he wasn't unfriendly but that the Southam representatives he was in discussion with certainly were. I wasn't much concerned with people's motives but generally welcomed Paul Desmarais's appearance on the horizon as a certain force for increased profitability. I did not highly appreciate then or subsequently that Paul would join what was conceived as a sand-bag operation against us even if, as I believe, that was not his view of it, but the co-operation with him of the conservative elements of Southam's board indicated they finally were abandoning their entrenched positions that they had defended successfully against Torstar's ineffectual agitations for more intelligent management.

When I arrived at Toronto airport seven hours later, I was handed the notice of a director's meeting the following day containing a proposal to sell Power Corporation out of treasury a larger block of shares than we possessed at $13.50 per share (compared to the $18.10 we had undertaken to pay Torstar by April 15), as well as conferring upon Power Corporation the status of underwriter of a $75-million rights issue at $11.50 per share.

If accepted, this proposal would condemn Hollinger to a secondary status at Southam, dilute all the shareholders by over 30 per cent, and sink our endeavours to sell half our shareholding to the *Telegraph*, which had the cash in hand to buy it but only with the approval of the majority of minority shareholders, who couldn't possibly agree to an $18.10 price after such a development.

We were to be offered our proportionate share of the treasury and rights issues as our agreement with Southam required, but it was well known to our Southam colleagues that it would not be maximally convenient for us to embark on a further $50-million investment in Southam as the *Telegraph* was effectively sent packing as a potential investor. It was a sign of desperation by the old guard, but a serious threat to Hollinger, both an assault on our ability to influence Southam and on the bankability of the investment. There was no suggestion of a shareholders' agreement with Power Corporation such as the one I had negotiated. We could survive the acceptance of the Power Corporation offer but only with significant public relations and financial embarrassment.

I started rallying resistance to the proposal from my car phone as I went to my son James's talent evening at the Toronto Montessori school where I had formerly been a trustee. It was a nostalgic occasion and a pleasant interlude in high-tension corporate lobbying. I dropped James at his mother's house, went home, and continued working the telephone until after two a.m. (seven a.m. in London, where I started the day).

The next morning at Southam, after a lengthy but not overly acrimonious discussion, starting with Jack Boultbee's interim election as our third Southam director, we were upheld and the Power Corporation offer was narrowly rejected. It was a watershed like the failure of Prusac's bid for Bruce Matthews's Ravelston shares in 1978, the collapse of Nicholas Berry's perfervid efforts to find an alternative buyer for the *Telegraph* in 1985, and the political acceptance of our reformulated Fairfax offer over O'Reilly's hydra-headed opposition in 1991. The Southam old guard was finished; it was Waterloo. Paul Desmarais knew that if he wanted in he would have to deal with us, and he telephoned me that afternoon. We agreed to meet in Palm Beach two days later, March 13.

I went to his magnificent house on South Ocean Boulevard a couple of hours after arriving in Palm Beach and explained that I had the management to assist in cleaning Southam up, a comprehensive plan for partially integrating Southam with Fairfax and the *Telegraph* in a peerless assemblage of quality newspapers, and the undoubted ability to remove all the recalcitrant incumbent directors at a shareholders' meeting. I didn't particularly need his presence and I didn't thank him for plunging into our deal to the ostensible rescue of our opponents with no notice to us in a manner we would never have entertained towards him and which violated the well-known protocol we had both often espoused, between real, as opposed to pretend proprietors. With that said, I expressed happiness to work with him in a structured, agreed way — against any lingering culture of inefficiency that might exist at Southam, not against each other.

He pledged fidelity to an alliance he would make with us and said he had some precise proposals. We agreed to reconvene the next day. On that occasion his very convivial son André was present, and we agreed on a system of assured parity between us and a community of objectives, especially profit enhancement and editorial improvements. We would effectively become co-controlling shareholders without either of us paying a control premium. The following day, Monday, March 15, the venue changed to my house, with counsel present personally and by telephone. Faxed, typed agreements were finally exchanged after twelve hours' intensive discussion and Paul's son and his lawyer left shortly after.

One minute later my telephone rang yet again. Paul Desmarais, who had returned to Montreal earlier in the day, spoke in French: in the most flattering terms. "I'm delighted to be in business with you and I promise I'll be a hell of a good partner." I told him I too had admired him over many years and was honoured to be his associate also. In the same city and on the fifteenth anniversary of Bud McDougald's death, the occasion was, at least for me, a somewhat poignant one. Compliments from so eminent a financier and delightful a man are to be highly prized and don't come easily. I thought of our first business meeting, in 1967, when Peter White, Brian Stewart, and I proposed to "rent" the Granby *Leader Mail* from him and he benignly sent us to see Jacques Francoeur.

Since, if he cared to raise his price enough, he could force himself into Southam no matter what I did, it was the best arrangement I could make. His earlier initiative I would have to overlook in the interests of corporate political expediency, like Howard Webster's backflip at FP in 1979, and Brian Mulroney's role in the spurious Norcen investigation in 1982. Sometimes it is difficult to distinguish between pardonable and unforgivable provocations, but this was not such an occasion. Unless Paul had made uncharacteristically profound commitments to his original Southam sponsors, his community of interest with us would be sufficient to ensure that we applied a uniform joint influence in encouragement of the new Southam management. This team was making purposeful noises but in the pandemonium of recent Southam history had not had a full chance to prove itself.

The Power investment would add $2.50 per share to the treasury ($180 million at $14 per share), eliminate the debt-ratio problem with the lenders, and be perceived as a show of strength for the company. Instead of being put over the side, as in the March 11 proposal, Hollinger obtained permanent parity with a larger company as co-controlling shareholder and the only element of the infamous poison pill that was retained was a joint 47 per cent ceiling on our shareholding for two years.

There were a few more abrasions. March 18 marked another Southam board meeting, which I attended by telephone from Palm

Beach. Several of the enthusiasts of the proposal of the previous week had seen Desmarais as a bulwark against us and were distinctly less well disposed to the new proposal, despite reduced dilution and a higher share price, because Southam's long, distracting, and finally pathetic struggle for independence was lost, albeit to a dual alliance.

Three of the independent directors who had been most helpful to us unfortunately retired, thoroughly disgusted with the political backbiting and management errors they had endured and been involuntarily associated with at Southam. Our competitors in the London press attempted to create the expectation of a shareholders' revolt when the minority voted on the *Telegraph*'s participation in our Southam purchase and a Torstar spokesman, presumably motivated by the fact that the prize of control of Southam that had eluded them for seven and a half years had fallen to two successor companies in barely three months, had the effrontery to question whether Hollinger could easily fulfil its obligation to Torstar in respect of the balance of sale of $189 million. In a heartwarming display of support, 97.4 per cent of voting *Telegraph* minority shareholders approved the company's participation in the Southam joint venture with Hollinger and the agreement with Power Corporation, and Torstar was paid on schedule, April 15. (Arrangements were in place to finance it entirely at Hollinger if that had been necessary.) Stephen Jarislowsky succeeded Jack Boultbee as our third Southam director, a further show of strength, given Stephen's influence with the institutional shareholders. He, the Desmaraises, and David and I would clearly represent an overwhelming majority of the shares.

We had bought half a loaf for the price of a quarter of a loaf. A very substantial capital gain was virtually inevitable, whether we would choose to realize the gain or not, and the Southam transaction was a worthy successor to the *Telegraph* and Fairfax. The Southam share price was already above where we bought in at the time of the Southam annual meeting in early June 1993. Patience and adequate tactical agility, as I had predicted, had exploited the recession and produced another splendid opportunity for us. Given where we started, in the shadow of Packer at Fairfax and as successors to unhappy Torstar at Southam, effective control of Fairfax and joint control of Southam were fine tactical prizes economically purchased.

By the spring of 1993, Hollinger was one of the world's greatest newspaper companies, a unique affiliation of quality newspaper franchises, with a total daily circulation, including Southam and Fairfax, of nearly 4.5 million. This is a figure surpassed in the Western world only by Ganett, a middle-brow supplier of newspapers to middle America, and Rupert Murdoch's News Corporation, which, in its newspaper divisions, except for the *Times* of London and the *Australian*, is essentially a purveyor of down-market tabloids.

It was a profound metamorphosis from the shambles left behind by McDougald in 1978, and even from the beleaguered Hollinger that propelled itself into the newspaper industry in London at the end of 1985, from the proceeds of painful but profitable exits from other industries. The Southam purchase also somehow made the rejection of our 1979 bid for FP (including the *Globe and Mail*) more palatable. We could not have done both deals, and Southam is a much better company.

Our corporate destiny is now disclosed, if not manifest, to even the most sceptical onlooker, (though few audible sceptics remain). Newspapers, especially quality newspapers, remain powerful outlets for advertising and information (and political influence). Fragmentation of market, remote-control operating devices that cause television advertising to be muted, and program recorders have made television advertising more vulnerable than it has been, and literacy and the printed word are not as out of fashion as many have feared.

Continued acquisitions, with suitable periods of consolidation, should be possible. Some diversification, sectorally and geographically, will be advisable. The challenge, less formidable than many we have successfully faced over the previous fifteen years, will be balanced growth. The equity base will have to be expanded in tandem with executive resources, to avoid excessive debt and unmanageability. To this end, Dan Colson joined the *Telegraph* and Hollinger full time in 1993, an overdue recognition of his great talents and services.

In the Canadian constitutional imbroglio of 1992 every conceivable special interest group and jurisdictional appetite was appeased with a terminal devolution that would have emasculated the federal government. The completion of the process whose ratification was proposed in the referendum of October 26 would have left the provinces in charge of immigration, nominations to the Supreme Court of Canada, and probably telecommunications, as well as education, natural resources, welfare, property and civil rights, and culture; the Senate regionalized and in charge of the appointment of the governor of the Bank of Canada; and designated native people governing themselves.

I asked Bill Davis, predictably one of the leaders of the Yes Committee what Brian Mulroney or any successor would have left to do apart from printing postage stamps and greeting important official visitors (who would not be numerous). Bill, who has created yet another career for himself advising Bob Rae, a service for which his own management of Ontario's fortunes amply qualified him, smiled enigmatically and said, "The agreement isn't ideal." This is the same Bill Davis who became Ontario's chief fund raiser for the Gorbachev Foundation and who once told me he had "religious objections" to something and smiled typically when I responded, "Surely you mean psephological objections. As far as I can judge, your religious views are those of a lapsed Unitarian."

All three federal party leaders, all the provincial premiers, virtually all the media, captains of industry, and labour leaders urged a yes vote on Brian Mulroney's devolution, October 26, 1992. (The first telephone call I took on returning to my Toronto office a few days before the referendum after six weeks abroad was from Senator Trevor Eyton asking me for $100,000 for the Yes Committee. I declined, for which he congratulated me a few days later.) Brian Mulroney once even accused those who might vote no of "treason" and of being "enemies of Canada."

On referendum day, I gave an address, whose date was arranged well in advance of the referendum, to a heavily attended meeting of the Canadian Club of Toronto. For reasons of personal relations, with Mulroney and Bourassa, whose sincerity on this issue I didn't question, only their judgement, I didn't recommend a no vote, though it was obvious I was no great admirer of the proposed deal.

On referendum night, Canada did finally repudiate its entire political class, except for three of the Atlantic premiers. Jacques Parizeau also was somewhat vindicated, as he persuaded Quebeckers that, in jurisdictional terms, the concession of everything was somehow insufficient.

Setting aside his earlier preoccupation with "treason," Brian Mulroney, who had darkly implied such unimaginable fates in the event of a no win that the Canadian dollar dropped sharply and the Bank of Canada raised interest rates two full points in the middle of the campaign, blandly told his countrymen, 54 per cent of whom had voted no, that it was time to return Canada's attention to the economy.

The Canadian federal system had finally, after gradually approaching such a state for decades, achieved a condition of unmitigated absurdity. The people had said they wanted the circus to stop and the clowns replaced, but, finding the message inconvenient, the poor performers just continued to bore and annoy their involuntary audience.

Brian Mulroney did the honourable, as well as the expedient thing, by retiring in the spring of 1993. Despite his unsuccessful attempts to give away much of the federal jurisdiction he was in policy terms the best Canada has had since Louis St. Laurent. Not overburdened with convictions, seeking always to conciliate the most persistent lobbyists, Brian had shortly fallen victim to the pitfalls of unappeasable public expectations we had foreseen when he visited me in Palm Beach ten years before. Free trade was his triumph but he left high office as he came to it, an indistinct personality. Politically agile to the end, he escaped undefeated, but his departure had nothing epochal about it and was almost universally unlamented. He probably deserved somewhat better. There may have been a possibility that Brian could have been chosen secretary general of the United Nations in 1991 if he had really sought it and he would undoubtedly have done the job very effectively. He will probably not receive the credit he deserves for passing up the opportunity in order to fight for his vision of national unity, any more than Richard Nixon has received the credit he deserved for accepting so philosophically being cheated out of victory in the 1960 presidential election. (Nixon told me that contesting the election judicially would have been "rather irresponsible as it could have left the country without a president for six months.")

As many of his friends had feared, after a lifetime of ardent pursuit of Canada's highest political office, Brian Mulroney was unable to build a real constituency based on a community of national goals. Like some leaders in other countries, including Richard Nixon and Lyndon Johnson, he became the victim of what Dr. Johnson called "the disingenuousness of years." He was excessively mistrusted and given far too little credit for what he achieved. It would be a political injustice as well as inept sociology to consign his public record to *Death of a Salesman*, but there are a few sad traces of just such a political fate. Towards the end of his first year in office, in 1985, he enumerated his governmental achievements and included the application of "a sensitive metric system." There are feet and yards, and metres, but not sensitive metres. All measures have limits and sometimes offend everyone. Shortly after leaving office, Brian was rather embittered, reproachful of his compatriots and unconvinced that they really want Canada to work.

Apart from his real shortcomings and being grossly underappreciated by his countrymen for his genuine attainments, Brian always conveyed to me the impression of greatly exaggerating the importance of his office. The Canadian political system is so jurisdictionally fragmented and the population so regionally fractious, the federal prime minister's role consists chiefly of endless debates with his provincial analogues. Maurice Duplessis took to referring scathingly to federal-provincial *circonférences* in the late forties. By the time Brian Mulroney convened such conferences, the whole Canadian political system had become a ludicrous and demeaning talking shop, massaging borrowed money around a population composed almost entirely of self-proclaimed geographic, ethnic, behavioural, and physiological victims. New categories of victims are eagerly sought out and placated, as each one proves the superior level of caring and compassion of Canada vis-à-vis the United States. Group rights have been handed out so generously that individual rights are infringed upon. Freedom of expression can no longer include any form of disparagement or subjectively perceived harassment. Democratic countries normally get the governments they deserve, but I am not convinced that such an envious, whingeing people as Canada had become in the mid-eighties really deserved so fundamentally well-intentioned a political chameleon as Brian Mulroney. I wish him and his fine and much-maligned family well.

Canada was not greatly less coherent than several more eminent political cultures. While the United States in the Reagan years created 19 million net new jobs, Europe — apart from Britain — created none. John Major well knows what a political and economic myth Europe is, how uncompetitive it is, and how officially dominated its institutions are by the *dirigist* alumni of France's Grandes Ecoles. All the institutions of the French state were devised by Richelieu, Colbert (on behalf of Louis XIV), Napoleon, and de Gaulle and none of them had any respect for, or much toleration of, a private sector. This mad regimental mentality is completely out of control in the European Commission in Brussels. In his first public appearance in many years, at the Palais d'Orsay in June 1958, de Gaulle claimed credit for all kinds of social programs, industry nationalizations, and even tax increases when he was head of the provisional government, 1944–1946. In some important ways, de Gaulle was far from a conservative.

In vain did I suggest to John Major, in July and again in October 1992, that his mission to desocialize Europe, though commendable, is a challenging concept when approached through a treaty designed to achieve precisely the opposite, and that such a program would be subtle even for Richelieu, Metternich, or Bismarck. I respectfully suggested that those three had more experience at diplomatic complexities than my interlocutor (who was foreign secretary for three months, just long enough, as he put it, "to learn where Bukina Fasso is"); that they had each a constituency of one, the monarchs they served, and that two of them were fired eventually anyway.

These British policy incongruities came back to the fore when the policy of shadowing the Deutschmark and trying to pursue a reflationary course while maintaining virtually fixed exchange rates with a deflationary Germany came unstuck in September 1992, as virtually everyone had predicted. One fiscal policy for all or floating rates are the only alternatives, and only an authoritarian, inflexible, academic, continental, bureaucrat or British emulator could imagine otherwise.

The shambles of the British government's credibility in the débâcle of sterling devaluation in September and in the waffling over the Maastricht vote in parliament later in the autumn were painful. Max Hastings ordered a cartoon depicting the chancellor of the exchequer, Norman Lamont, as Sidney Carton running away from the guillotine. And we referred to him as Waugh's Mr. Grimes, from

Decline and Fall, who, after disgracing himself in the Great War, was given a bottle of whisky and a loaded revolver to use on himself. When his judges returned after a decent interval, they found the bottle empty, the revolver still fully loaded, and Mr. Grimes vanished. Norman Lamont finally did go, in May 1993, but in an ungracious exercise in which it was hard not to feel some sympathy for him.

After Denmark's initial plebiscitary rejection of Maastricht and France's wafer-thin vote in favour, John Major's fervent attachment to such a beleaguered policy was the harder to comprehend. Doubts sprang to the minds of all, including the most hopeful, about John Major's true aptitude to govern. His tendency to take utterly obstinate stances in support of causes he is shortly forced to abandon and then to accept no responsibility, indicating no contrition, and to blunder on to the next vulnerable position, is profoundly disconcerting. With a sensibly devalued pound and a sensible work force uncorrupted by Europe's socialist anaesthetic, prosperity began, finally and distantly, to reappear.

John Major is a capable and considerate man who has fought commendably against schism within his own caucus. It would be churlish not to wish him success as the ultimate mid-market riser, risen to the head of an historic party and a great nation. Unfortunately, in seeking to be simultaneously the party leader of low taxes, fiscal responsibility, and improved public services, "at the heart of Europe," yet in important respects outside it, he has taken up an impossible burden. Lacking the primal force of a Thatcher and the magic manipulative skill of a Disraeli, relying mainly on a Baldwin-esque shilly-shallying pleasantness, his success is far from assured.

As the government bumped embarrassedly along, the ultimate British institution, the monarchy, was severely demystified. Tittle-tattle and pirated recordings apparently revealing conjugal coldness, infidelity, banality, and monstrous indiscretions among some younger members of the Royal Family saddened and irritated the nation and adherent elements of the Commonwealth.

More damaging than public disappointment is the spreading feeling among the great Whigs, the cleverest and most dispassionate noblemen in the realm, that the monarch hasn't habitually sought or taken the best advice and has revealed a bourgeois complacency and lack of sophistication.

No one could perform the ceremonious functions of the chief of state more diligently than the Queen, nor with greater attention to the pageantry of the office. I hope and assume the useful anachronism of the monarchy will continue, at least in its home country. Perry Worsthorne only slightly exaggerated when he wrote in the *Sunday Telegraph* in December 1992, that rather than waiting for the London tabloids to bring down the Sovereign, it would be more merciful to take her respectfully from Buckingham Palace and decapitate her on the guillotine. A gentler fate than either of those should await her.

In sum, the ancient British pride in its governmental institutions has been shaken just as the debate over how much jurisdiction to cede to Europe has become disorganized and as the British government is more and more widely thought to be in incapable hands. The country has endured worse crises but the times are uncommonly debilitating.

If Canada and the United Kingdom were wallowing in a post–Cold War political slough, the perspective from the United States was not much more uplifting. Twelve years of Republican rule in the White House ended, as the necessary consequence of George Bush running what Richard Nixon told me a month after the election was "the most incompetent campaign for a serious office I have ever witnessed." Bush had been an adequate president, had done brilliantly in the Gulf War, adequately with the environment and drugs, and pardonably in education.

With Bush, as with lesser politicians such as John Turner and Claude Wagner, my apologia were perhaps too sophisticated. When I told the president that I assumed Saddam Hussein was still in power in Baghdad because he, Bush, wanted him there, totally discredited, yet the only person who could prevent the Iraqi Shiites from adhering to "Greater Iran" and the Kurds from destabilizing eastern Turkey, he looked at me incredulously.

When I tried the same line on Dan Quayle, whose political instincts were often better than his boss's, he roared with laughter.

Bush was defeated because the public sensed that he had no interest in the matters that most concerned them, they were fed up with his "read my lips," "education president," "thousand points of light," "flexible freeze" obfuscation (the Americans would have really loved Brian Mulroney), and because he obviously didn't really passionately want to win. These are all good reasons and the American voters have almost always been right in presidential choices in my lifetime.

The great American people cannot really be faulted for steadily re-electing Roosevelt, who triumphed over his infirmity and saved capitalism, notwithstanding the inanities of the capitalists, who banished the Great Depression by leading his countrymen into and through the ultimate Just War, who bequeathed in nuclear fission and the United Nations the polar destinies of Armageddon and universal brotherhood. They cannot be faulted for elevating Truman, doughty creator of the policies and institutions that eventually won us the Cold War; Eisenhower, the supreme figure of reassurance, elderly, golfing, avuncular, clad in a five-star general's uniform; the glamorous Kennedy; the gifted if flawed masters of the political game, Johnson and Nixon and Reagan, the silver-tongued optimist who let America be America.

With George Bush, the conservative mantle passed to a nonbeliever. Since he was visibly unconvinced of what he was saying about abortion or taxes and gave far too much prominence to religious extremists, he offended the centrists without enlisting the right. To true conservatives, whether of the intelligent or merely fervent varieties, Reagan was the ventriloquist, Bush the dummy, left mechanically uttering platitudes when his master retired.

The declinists have been put to rout and even if Clinton is banal and impressionable, politicians rarely do much real harm or good to the enduring nature and solidly based institutions of a great nation. Harding was a Good Time Charlie, Hoover aggravated the Depression, Carter embarrassed the country with his joyless agonizing about a "malaise," which didn't exist and whose only real symptom was Jimmy's presence in the White House. Yet they did little lasting damage. The current self-inflicted assault of politically correct inverse discrimination and denigration of admirable traditions will break on and not over the good sense, individual self-esteem, and unshakable genius of the American people.

Clinton may at least start to address, with the Congress, some of America's serious problems that Reagan benignly neglected and Bush ignored, especially medical care, education, and crime. As

George Will says, "American children are the only ones in the advanced world who go to sleep to the sound of gunfire." Obviously, this must stop.

With a liberal Democrat in the White House, most of the idiocy about an absolute or relative decline of the United States as a world power, mercifully stopped. This was just the sour grapes of chronic political and ideological losers, like Republican claims forty years before that Roosevelt and Truman had been rolled by the Communists. Roosevelt, more than anyone else (except possibly Churchill) won World War II, and Truman and Reagan, more than anyone else (possibly along with Nixon), won the Cold War. Apart from the period of American nuclear monopoly, 1945–1948, no country since the rise of the Nation state has been so pre-eminent in the world as the United States in the early 1990s.

I had occasion to suggest to both Bush and Quayle that as military units are withdrawn from Europe and Korea, they be retrained and redeployed under local control in the great cities of America. Many large urban areas are now no-go districts to respectable people. The president and vice president listened with alarm as I explained that "if there are 60,000 armed bikers in Los Angeles, insert two divisions of marines. Repossess the streets and sidewalks of your great cities. The armies that won us the Cold War aren't needed in Germany or Korea at their present force levels, but they are needed in Detroit, Washington, and Los Angeles." They were both horrified. Even serious gun control was too radical a concept.

I doubt whether President Clinton is fiscally numerate or sufficiently dextrous in the congressional arts to achieve his goals. Without Reagan's ability to mobilize opinion or Johnson's to manipulate the Congress or Roosevelt's to do both, the American political system doesn't move far and the Congressional barons govern. Early indications are that just this process is underway. At the moment of the supreme triumph of the West, the English-speaking countries, especially, are confused and indifferently led (except for Australia and, to the extent it qualifies, South Africa).

Japan's financial structure has wobbled and its political system has approached a state of disrepute almost as complete as Italy's, but its manufacturing and marketing strengths are durable. Germany will complete reunification but most of Europe is facing a long struggle with the complacency of its welfare-addicted work force. The United States should surge to new heights of productivity and competitive achievement. The identity of the chief occupant of the White House is virtually incidental. Bush, convictionless and without discernible purpose, had to go. If Clinton has empty or mistaken convictions or an unpresidential demeanour, he will go too. America abides, the only truly great nation in the world, endearingly almost unaware of its economic, military, and popular cultural supremacy.

The United States has no rivals but an uncertain purpose. The traditional powers of Europe and Japan have muted and civilized rivalries and are tentatively trying to regain international status lost during World War II. At the traditional fringes, in China and parts of Islam, fierce and probably unacceptable ambitions burn.

Canada is a matter of slight and rare curiosity to the great and turbulent world which it inhabits almost like an unwhimsical Pan among nations. On my returns I realize how far I have moved from the diffident, derivative, envious mood of the country, though I often think of Canada and the miraculous process of a full assumption of national consciousness. This, almost as much as economic reasons, is why I wanted to buy into Southam. Though their ruling élites are exhausted and discredited, the Canadian people are admirable and the country is rich. Salvation is available from their own doubts and shortcomings and status as history's first country to designate practically all compatriots as victims, appropriately, with the irony history often evidences, in this most abundant and fortunate of countries.

The process begun by Trudeau of using the federal treasury and parliament to identify and appease ethnic, regional, behavioural, sexual, and physiological complainant groups has become both dangerous and absurd. Virtually everyone except Anglo-Saxon, able-bodied, middle-aged, heterosexual, male, middle-class Ontarians is now the officially recognized bearer of a subventionable grievance. Organizing society into clamouring categories of self-pitiers is scarcely distinguishable from and just as dangerous as Quebec's old practice, much despised in English Canada, of putting collective rights ahead of individual rights. This is, and has always been, recognized as a matrix for dictatorship, whether we are purporting to protect society from Communists, Jehovah's Witnesses, assorted bigots, wife beaters, gay bashers, office voyeurs, or discriminatory hirers.

As this book is finished, a vastly expensive Royal Commission, the latest in a long sequence of institutionalized orgies of national self-reproach, has produced nearly 500 recommendations for the avoidance of violence to women. These include a universal pledge from the adult male population to avoid violent intent toward women and locally administered neighbourhood violence audits to incite and assess denunciations and tittle-tattle. Because of emergent definitions of rape, consent forms have become advisable between adult Canadians contemplating heterosexual intimacy, even if the parties are married. Freedom of expression no longer extends to many forms of disparagement or subjectively perceived harassment. As Chesterton wrote, the state has gone mad.

The greater the emphasis on charters of rights, the more ambiguous the rights of Canadians have become. Subject only to reasonable statutes designed to entrench and not curtail individual liberties, legally competent Canadians should have a plenitude of rights circumscribed only at the point where the exercise of those rights would infringe another citizen's ability to exercise the same rights.

Almost the entire massive and intricate structure of enforced equalization, other than equalization of the fundamental legal rights of all citizens, should be dismantled with the resulting savings of billions of dollars applied to deficit reduction. It is a Sisyphean and unnatural task to impose a state-prescribed behavioural, economic, and cultural norm for the people. We have reached the final and terminal stage of the fraudulent *raison d'être* of an infinitely caring and compassionate Canada.

When that collapses, the federal government, if it has retained any authority, should use that authority to assure reasonable tax levels and an equitable distribution of reward to workers and investors, labour and capital. It should do this, if needs must, by threatening to tax exorbitantly and rebate to citizens in a manner exempt from provincial taxation, and by threatening to buy from and lease back to its rightful owners much of Canada's dwindling manufacturing sector in order to shield it from communalizing provincial labour laws. (Unless Ottawa succeeds in its apparent recent ambition to implode altogether and give away all its powers to the provinces, the provinces should not be able to tax federal tax rebates or legislate work rules in ostensible federal crown corporations.)

This is the true vocation of the government of Canada: protection of its citizens' rights, including their right to be treated as individuals and not units in a vast grievance pool; their right to their property and all but a reasonably withheld portion of their income; and their right to a functioning country. It's not the federal government's business to pander to every social imperfection, nor to dismember itself jurisdictionally in favour of what John Diefenbaker well described as "ten satraps."

Failing some such measures as these, Canada will continue to wallow, banal, self-righteous, and unable to convince the world or itself of its nationality.

As the referendum of October 26, 1992, showed, the people know that the key is gently to reject and replace almost the entire leadership class. In sum, my evaluation of Canada's governing élites has not changed very much since my unhappy, far-off days at Upper Canada College.

Canada will not be more confident until more Canadians are more confident of themselves as individuals. Only then will Canada be what it never has been, a thoroughly and competitively interesting place. The country can be put back together if the French and English stop fantasizing and accept that each is a worthwhile national cohabitant. The excruciating process of seeking artificial distinctions between Canadian and American society will end.

It will end either by the development of real and constructive distinctions, based on a durable French-English understanding, or by a closer direct association of English Canadians with the United States, which would be a much more important geopolitical event than the reunification of Germany. Either resolution will be preferable to continuation of Canada's paralysing ambiguity. Without the French, English Canadians would have to accept that profound distinctions with the United States do not exist and that we should cease trying to invent them.

Quebec must stop being coy and accept or reject Canada. Canada will embrace either Quebec or, failing Quebec, the United States. North America will be divided geographically or linguistically. Britain and the United States and other coherent nations can muddle along indefinitely, but Canada has yet to decide if it wishes to be a real country. On that question, at least, Pierre Trudeau and Brian Mulroney agree and are right. Patient Canadians wait and the world, for once, mindful of Canada's strategic importance, watches. Earle Birney, in his fine poetic allegorization of Canada as an immature teenager, concluded impatiently: "Will he grow up before it's too late?" The answer is yes, teenagers usually do. I doubt that Quebec, unless it is oppressed or rejected in some unimaginable manner, has any real interest in independence if it costs anything and there is no version of independence that won't be costly.

Duplessis said he had shut up the Quebec nationalists for ten years with the flag of Quebec and would do so for another ten years with a delegation in Paris, and for ten years after that with a world's fair. He used to say that dealing with Quebec nationalists was "like having a ten-pound fish on a five-pound line. It has to be gently reeled in and let out." It is time for this game to stop. After all that I have seen and tried to describe I still believe Canada's time will come.

In extending and exploring my own horizons, I have not deserted my country. It is possible to transcend nationality but very few people are entirely disenthralled from political events, disappointing though political practices and personalities usually are. I await with others in the Canadian dispersion a spark of national self-esteem and renewal: Canada for its own sake and value and not in pursuit of some extravagant fable about being more socialistic than the Americans. If no such renewal comes, I will be consolable, a partial, voluntary, comfortable, and trans-national exile. If it does come, I will rejoice and be present.

INDEX

A & P, 317, 325, 326, 358
Abrams, Gen. Creighton, 59–60
African National Congress (ANC), 493, 496
Agnelli, Gianni, 384, 385
Alaska Highway News, 79
Algoma Central Railway, 261, 276, 277, 310, 416
American Publishing Co., 376, 377–78, 386, 432, 474, 485
Amiel, Barbara (later Barbara Amiel Black), 263, 400, 463–65, 467, 468, 482, 488, 489, 497
Anderson, Bob, 280, 281, 283–85, 290–91, 294, 296, 313
Argcen Holdings Ltd. (later Hollinger), 315, 328, 331–32, 351
Argus Corp., 117, 142–45, 147–48, 149, 151–56, 171, 174, 176, 177–78, 194, 196–97, 204, 209–13, 217–22, 223, 230, 232–33, 237, 239, 253, 254–56, 258, 260, 262, 272, 277, 278, 327, 361, 396–97
Argus Group, 186–88, 190, 191, 192, 313, 314–15, 329
Aspinall, John ("Asper"), 492–93, 494–95, 497
Atkinson, Peter, 387, 388
Australia, 375, 432–59, 466, 470–72, 512
Australian, 458, 504
Australian Independent Newspapers (AIN), 446, 447, 448, 451, 455, 456
L'Avenir de Brome-Missisquoi (Farnham, Que.), 34
L'Avenir de Sept-Iles (Sept-Iles, Que.), 117, 119, 123, 491

Balfour, St. Clair, and family, 80, 332, 333, 385, 487
Bank of Canada, 505, 506
Bank of Nova Scotia, 160, 330
Barford, Ralph, 192, 263, 325, 328
Barker, Douglas, 261, 263–64
Barron, Alex, 170, 192, 194–96, 200, 202, 203, 204, 205, 206, 214, 215, 224, 256, 264
Bassett, Douglas, 163, 183, 244, 246–47, 292, 310, 311–12, 328
Bassett, John F., 66

Bassett, John W.H., 49, 77–78, 81, 170, 183, 244, 245–46, 247, 310, 311–12
Battle, Ed, 252, 282, 283, 284, 292, 315, 352
Beaverbrook, Lord, 338, 472
Beazely, Kim, 441, 442
Bemocoge, 150
Berry, Adrian, 347, 349
Berry, Nicholas, 341–42, 343, 344–46, 349–50, 432, 501
Berry family, 335, 341, 346. *See also* Hartwell, Lord
Bertrand, Jean-Jacques, 34, 55, 93–94, 312
Bilderberg meetings, 278–80, 334, 384–85
Bill 22, 126–28, 133, 410, 411
Bill 178, 410–13
Black, Arana (daughter), 297
Black, Barbara Amiel (second wife). *See* Amiel, Barbara
Black, Conrad: early life, 1–9; formal education, 10–18, 22–25, 28–29, 32, 33, 42–43, 54, 124–25; lives/works outside Canada, 27–28, 45–48; early publishing/writing career, 34, 35–36, 45–48; literary influences on, 35; political influences on, 19–22, 28–29, 32, 39, 40, 44–45; anxiety condition of, 52–54; religious beliefs of, 54, 100–106; researches/writes *Duplessis*, 90–91, 92–93, 106, 124, 141–42, 180–84; marriage to Joanna (née Shirley Walters), 206, 213, 214, 220, 231, 460–62; marriage to Barbara Amiel, 462–65; businesses owned/operated by (since 1968). *See under specific company names*; directorships. *See under specific company names*; travels, 6–8, 10, 25–27, 32–33, 55–66, 94–99, 152–53, 173–74, 405–6. *See also* Australia; South Africa; views of: on Canada, 133–15, 513–16; on Canadian Constitution, 75, 411–14, 504–6; on journalism in Canada, 74–75; on organized labour, 123–24; on politics. *See under specific politicians' names*; on Quebec, 126–31, 135, 136–37, 515, 516; on U.K., 508–10; on U.S., 507–8, 510–12, 513; on Vietnam, 57–66, 156–58
Black, George Montegu (grandfather), 2, 6

INDEX

Black, George Montegu, Jr. (father), 2, 3–5, 6, 7–8, 17, 18, 146, 148, 149, 150–51, 152, 155, 168–71
Black, George Montegu, III ("Monte"; brother), 2, 4, 6–7, 25–26, 116, 151, 170, 171, 185, 193, 200, 202–7 *passim*, 209, 210, 212, 213, 272–73, 292, 296, 316, 317, 318, 321, 326–27, 328, 329, 360, 461
Black, James (son), 356, 462, 500, 501
Black, Joanna (née Shirley Walters; first wife), 206, 220, 231, 460–62, 464, 465
Bolton, Tom, 186, 192, 209, 270, 271–72, 317
Boultbee, Jack, 359, 476, 501, 503
Bourassa, Robert, 52, 54, 178, 379, 380, 381, 410, 411, 412, 413, 505
Bovey, Ed, 252, 253, 292
Brascan, 239, 353, 354, 364
British Columbia Forest Products, 145, 237
Broznan, Tina, 480, 484, 485
Buckley, Bill, 376, 461, 465
Bull, Gerald, 36–37
Burns, Latham, 331, 494
Burrows, Mark, 436, 444, 447, 450, 451, 452, 453, 454, 456
Bush, George, 455, 466, 510–11, 512, 513
Buthelezi, Mangosuthu G. (Gatsha), 493–94, 495, 496, 497

Caisse de Dépôts et de Placements, 238, 239
Camp, Dalton, 75–76
Campeau, Bob, 430–31
Camrose, Lord, 335, 336, 341, 348, 349
Canadian Breweries Ltd., 144, 145, 146, 148, 150. *See also* Carling O'Keefe
Canadian General Investments, 192, 204, 205, 223, 229
Canadian Imperial Bank of Commerce, 189, 220, 256–57
Carling O'Keefe, 178, 380
Carrington, Lord, 366, 427, 461
Carter, Emmett Cardinal, 99, 103, 287–88, 383, 387, 388, 461, 464, 465, 493
Carter, Jimmy, 248–50
CBC, 4, 74–75
CFRB, 145, 153, 190, 328, 329. *See also* Standard Broadcasting
Channel 5, 492
Chant, Dixon ("Dick"), 194–96, 197, 198, 200, 201, 202, 203, 204, 207, 209, 210, 215, 221, 260, 261, 271, 292, 316, 318, 321, 328, 332, 351, 357–58, 359
Chicago Tribune, 478, 480
CIBC, 147, 176, 177, 178, 198, 255, 256, 257, 258, 259, 262, 352, 353, 356–57, 360, 361, 431, 496
Le Clairon (St. Hyacinthe, Que.), 78–79
Clark, Joe, 165–66, 180, 234–35, 309–10, 311, 312, 313, 322
Clinton, Bill, 511–12, 513
CN Pension Fund, 361–62
Cockwell, Jack, 239, 353, 354, 358, 364
Cohen, Reuben, 197–98, 430

Colson, Dan, 43, 52, 339, 342–50 *passim*, 372, 391, 393–94, 407, 408, 433, 434, 435, 440, 444, 445, 447, 448, 449, 452, 453, 456, 458, 471, 497, 504
Connacher, Jimmy, 282, 333
Connery, John, 480, 482, 485, 486
Consolidated Press, 438, 439
Cooke, Joe, 370, 404
Cook, Ramsay, 124, 182–83
Coopers & Lybrand, 341, 359
Coop-Prix, 271–72, 316
Cowan, Charlie, 357, 359
Cowen, Sir Zelman, 440, 441, 471
Crang, Harold, 221–22
Cranston, Alan, 405–6
Creighton, Doug, 78, 263, 360, 389–90, 396, 399
Crown Trust Co., 146, 194, 196, 197–98, 200, 203, 207, 213, 219, 220, 229, 267
CRTC, 330, 331
Currie, Dick, 325, 358

Daily Express, 468, 472
Daily Mail, 409, 425, 464, 468
Daily Mirror, 340
Daily News (New York), 474, 478, 481
Daily News (Prince Rupert, BC), 79–80
Daily Telegraph, 334–50, 352–53, 360, 361, 362–71, 375, 377, 378, 392, 403–5, 407–11, 417, 419, 426, 427–28, 431, 432, 434, 435, 438, 439, 444, 454, 457, 458, 468, 469, 474–79, 491–92, 495, 500, 501, 503, 504
Davis, Bill, 305, 312, 319, 354–55, 398, 505
Davis, Nelson M., 170, 177, 178, 188, 196, 200, 202, 203, 204–5, 206, 207, 209, 210, 211, 213, 214, 220, 230, 328
de Gaulle, Charles, 19–21, 22, 39, 40, 44–45
Del Zotto, Elvio, and family, 398, 399, 400
Desmarais, André, 501, 502, 503
Desmarais, Paul G., 108–9, 121, 148, 149, 153–56, 160, 189, 191, 204, 221, 222, 357, 379, 380, 381, 393, 487–88, 498–500, 501–2, 503. *See also* Power Corp.
Des Marais, Pierre, II, 93, 380–81, 382, 490
Diefenbaker, John, 313, 429
Dimanche-Matin, 379, 381
Dominion Malting Co., 150, 151, 242
Dominion Securities, 185, 206, 208, 210, 272–73, 385
Dominion Stores, 145, 147, 153, 171, 186, 188, 196, 218, 237, 239, 265, 269–73, 274, 314, 315, 316–22, 325–32, 345, 351–62, 364, 377, 388, 389, 396, 397, 400
Domtar (Dominion Tar and Chemical Co.), 145, 186, 217, 222, 223–24, 239, 262, 329
Draper Dobie, 151, 185, 206, 210
Drasner, Fred, 481, 482, 485
Drivers' Union, 477, 480, 482, 485
Le Droit, 379, 382–83, 395
Duplessis, Maurice, 38, 180–81, 184–85, 379, 380, 412, 507, 516; Black's book about, 90–91, 92–93, 106, 180–84

[518]

INDEX

Eastern Townships Advertiser (Knowlton, Que.), 34, 35–36
Eaton, Fred, 78, 163, 174, 177, 209, 210, 213, 244, 261, 292, 310, 328
Eaton family, 141, 174, 175, 244, 310
Economist, 334, 340, 342–43, 349, 350
Ellen, Leonard, 197, 198
English Canadians, 1, 110, 114, 126–28, 130, 132, 134–35, 412–13, 515
Europe/European Community, 423–25, 467, 469–70, 508–9, 510, 512–13
Express Newspapers, 370, 473
Eyton, Trevor, 239, 252–53, 302, 353, 364, 464, 505

Fairfax, Warwick, 432–33, 436, 441, 443, 451, 456–57
Fairfax Co. *See* John Fairfax Co.
Fairfax, Friends of, 448, 449–50
Fairley, Al, 147, 176, 186–87, 192, 196, 198, 209, 252, 390
Fell, Tony, 185, 258, 385
Financial Post, 389–90, 396, 399
Financial Times, 368, 372, 389, 390, 409
Finlay, John, 199, 252, 292, 318, 320, 321, 328, 330
Finlay, Percy Clair (P.C.), 196, 198–99, 222, 223, 232, 242, 253, 292, 402
Fisher, Gordon, and family, 262, 332, 333, 385, 487
Fotheringham, Allan, 399–400, 403
FP Publications, 240–41, 243–44, 245, 248, 333, 384, 502, 504
Francoeur, Jacques, 378–79, 380, 381, 382, 502
Francoeur, Louis, 379
Fraser, John, 12, 386, 387
Fraser, Malcolm, 448, 449, 451
French Canadians, 1, 110, 114, 126–28, 135–37, 412–13
F.T.Q. (Fédération du Travail du Québec), 119, 120
Fullerton, Don, 221, 353, 356–57, 361

Gardiner, George, 243, 244, 245, 246, 247
Gazette (Montreal), 396
Gilbert, Col. Oscar, and family, 379, 380
Globe and Mail, 78, 182, 240, 241, 243, 244–47, 384, 386, 387–90, 396–97, 399, 400, 403, 464, 489, 490, 504
Goldsmith, Sir James ("Jimmie"), 433, 434, 435, 462, 491, 494
Goodman, Eddie, 111, 165, 355
Gotlieb, Allan, 386, 393
Graham, Ron, 386, 489, 490
Gray, Herb, 257, 259, 260, 262
Green, Michael, 491, 492
Guardian, 336, 340, 368, 369, 370, 468
Gulf War, 395, 489, 510
Guolla, Lou, 201, 202, 207, 212

Hair, 66–67
Hambro, Rupert, 337, 338–39, 340, 344

Hamilton, Alex, 147, 176, 186, 210, 222–23
Hanna Mining Co., 280–91, 292, 294–96, 388, 389, 396, 447, 458
Harrison, Russell, 177, 213, 255, 258, 262
Hartwell, Lord Michael, 335, 336, 337–38, 339, 341, 342, 343–45, 346, 347–48, 349, 356, 377, 403, 409, 432. *See also* Berry family
Hastings, Max, 364–66, 386, 403, 404, 405, 407, 421, 424, 425, 426, 427, 435, 458, 467, 469, 495, 508
Hawke, Bob, 440, 441, 442, 443, 446, 447, 451, 453, 454–55, 456, 457, 458, 466
Hedstrom, Cecil, 147, 190, 200, 201, 202, 203, 204–5, 207, 212, 213, 214–15
Hees International, 353, 364, 377
Hellman & Friedman, 437, 438, 439, 454, 455
Herald (Terrace, BC), 79, 80
Heseltine, Michael, 365, 421, 422, 423, 424–25, 426–27, 428, 467, 495
H.J. Heinz Co., 437, 443
Hollinger, 239, 265, 313, 315, 316, 317, 349, 351–55, 359, 360–62, 371, 376–77, 385, 387, 390, 393, 400, 402, 406, 407, 409–10, 416, 431–32, 472, 474, 475–76, 487, 488, 498–503. *See also* Argcen Holdings Ltd.
Hollinger-Argus, 233, 255, 262, 264–65
Hollinger Consolidated Gold Mines Ltd., 117, 145
Hollinger Mines, 153, 186–87, 198, 199, 218, 221–22, 232, 238–39, 253, 272
Hongkong and Shanghai Banking Corp., 344
Howe, Sir Geoffrey, 421, 422–23, 424
Humphrey, Bud, 280–81
Humphrey, George M., 118, 280, 281, 282–83, 290
Hurd, Douglas, 426, 427–28, 467

I.A.C., 150, 152
Independent, 369, 416, 456, 468
International Typographers, 478–79, 480
Iron Ore Co. of Canada, 117, 118, 186, 273, 280, 290, 292, 446
ITV, 491, 492

Jackman, Hal, 155, 177, 194–95, 200, 204, 209–10, 211, 257, 259, 260–61, 275–78, 309, 310, 311, 328, 387, 415, 416–17, 442, 489
Jackman, Harry, 149, 155, 156
Jackson, Allan, 271, 317
Jarislowsky, Stephen, 302, 315, 334, 362, 503
Jerusalem Post, 391–95, 489
John Fairfax Co., 345, 432–58, 466, 470–72, 474, 501, 503, 504
Johnson, Daniel, 34, 37–38, 40, 47
Johnson, Frank, 409, 468
Johnson, Lyndon B., 30, 31, 32, 44, 511, 512
Johnson, Paul, 403, 468, 469

[519]

INDEX

Le Journal de Montréal, 383
Le Journal de Québec, 383
J. Rothschild and Co., 340–41

Kalikow, Peter, 479, 480, 486
Kaplan, Igor, 200, 207, 208, 209, 212, 213, 264, 359
Keating, Paul, 433, 441, 451, 454, 457, 466, 470, 471–72
Kennedy, Jack, 480, 482, 485
Kennedy, John F., 28–29, 511
Kennedy, Teddy, 479, 486
Kennedy, Trevor, 439–41, 442, 445, 446, 447–48, 452–53, 454, 458
Kerin, John, 440, 441, 442, 454, 455
Kilbourne, Bill, 286, 290
Kilgour, Geills (Mrs. John Turner), 322, 324
Kinnock, Neil, 428, 467, 468, 469
Kissinger, Henry, 54, 138, 139, 279, 334, 352, 390–91, 393, 402, 430, 443, 482–84, 497
Knight, Andrew, 334, 340, 342–45, 348–50, 363–66, 372, 373, 403–10, 431, 432, 433, 456, 492
Knowlton Advertiser, 122, 377

Labour Relations Act (Ontario), 415–16, 487
Labrador Mining and Exploration Co. Ltd., 117, 186, 187, 239, 252, 253, 265, 302, 315, 329, 353, 396
L.A. cable system, 328–29, 330–31, 377, 475
LaChance, Doug, 477, 482, 485, 486
Lamont, Norman, 508–9
Lawson, Nigel, 418, 421–22
The Leader Mail (Granby), 379, 381, 502
Léger, Jules, 131–32
Léger, Paul-Emile Cardinal, 94–99, 131, 132
Lesage, Jean, 84–85, 429
Lévesque, René, 85–86, 110–11, 184–85, 253
Levy, Col. Yehuda, 392, 394–95
Litho-Prestige, 381–82, 383

McConnell family, 240, 247
McCurdy, H.T. ("Mac"), 186, 209, 324, 328
McCutcheon, M.W. ("Wally"), 28, 143, 146
McDougald, Hedley Maude ("Jim"), 147, 190, 194, 196, 200, 201, 202, 203, 204–5, 206, 207–8, 212, 213, 214–15, 248
McDougald, John A. ("Bud"), 77, 142–46 *passim*, 147–49, 153–56, 170, 176, 185–86, 188–94, 200, 203, 313, 314, 358, 390, 502, 504
MacLaren, George, 81, 384
McMartin family, 117, 145, 146–47, 187, 196
MacMillan Bloedel, 222–24
McMurtry, Roy, 292–93, 305, 306, 307, 308, 357–58, 398
McQuaig, Linda, 303, 304, 399, 400, 403
Major, John, 418, 422, 425, 426, 427–28, 429, 467, 469–70, 508, 509
Malone, Brigadier Dick, 240–41, 243, 244, 246, 247, 248

Mandela, Nelson, 493, 497
Manning, Preston, 415
Manos, John M., 289–90
Masse, Marcel, 81–82, 98
Massey-Ferguson, 147, 153, 154, 187, 190, 191, 192, 194, 196, 200, 218, 224–25, 227, 231, 235–37, 239, 254–62, 264, 314, 326, 329, 330, 389, 396–97
Massey-Harris, 143, 144
Matthews, Gen. Bruce, 148, 155, 170, 192, 194–95, 196, 197, 200, 202, 205–7, 208, 210, 211–12, 214, 215, 501
Matthews, Philip, 120–21
Maxwell, Robert, 372–75, 384, 393, 430, 433, 474, 476, 477, 478, 480, 485, 486, 492
Meadowbrook Holdings, 146, 149
Meech Lake Accord, 411–12, 413
Megarry, Roy, 244–46, 248, 384, 389, 396
Meighen, Col. Max, 146, 148, 149, 155, 170, 186, 192, 194–96, 197, 199, 200, 202–5, 206, 208, 210, 211, 212, 214–15
Meighen, Michael, 116–17, 133, 387
Melbourne Age, 433
Melbourne Sunday Age, 454, 472
Miles, Neville, 435, 436, 437, 438, 442
Mirror (London), 372, 373, 468
Mirror (New York), 478
Mr. Grocer, 319, 352, 358
Montagu, David, 340, 341, 343–44, 346, 347, 348, 410
Montréal Matin, 488
Montreal Star, 74, 240, 247
Morning Herald (Sydney), 450
Muggeridge, Malcolm, 93, 235, 262, 406
Mulroney, Brian, 111, 160–66, 235, 273–74, 283, 290, 291, 299, 309–13, 321–24, 356, 357, 390, 391, 395, 402, 411, 412, 413, 446, 502, 505–7, 511, 515
Murdoch, Anna, 36, 431
Murdoch, J.Y., 168, 198, 237
Murdoch, Rupert, 247, 335, 337, 348–49, 362–63, 369, 370, 374, 375, 376, 381, 383, 401, 406–7, 408, 409, 431, 436–37, 438, 443, 447, 449, 458, 467, 472, 476, 477, 479, 486, 504

Napoleon, 21–22
National Energy Program, 264–65, 280
National Trust Co., 275–76
National Victoria and Grey Trust Co., 310, 489
Newman, Peter, 156, 193, 294–96, 323, 345, 346, 361
News International, 370, 408
News (St. John's, Que.), 79
News of the World, 362
New York magazine, 381
New York News, 476–87
New York Post, 479–80, 486
New York Times, 391, 477, 483
Nixon, Richard M., 66, 138–39, 140–41, 483, 484, 506, 510, 511, 512

[520]

INDEX

N.M. Rothschild [merchant bank], 341, 345, 346, 347, 474, 475
Noranda, 145, 187, 237–39
Norcen Energy Resources Ltd. (formerly Northern & Central Gas Corp.), 252–53, 264–66, 280, 282–87, 291–96, 299, 301–3, 304, 309, 313, 315, 352–53, 358, 360–61, 364, 377, 396, 399
La Nouvelle Revue, 122
Le Nouvelliste, 380
Novalis, 383

Observer, 342, 409, 468
Olympia & York, 408, 431
Ontario Labour Relations Board, 319, 352, 355, 358, 361
Ontario Securities Commission, 154, 292–93, 298, 299, 301–3, 304–5, 399, 499
Oppenheimer, Harry, 496–97
O'Reilly, Tony, 437, 442–43, 445–48, 450–58 *passim*, 466, 501
Ottawa Citizen, 243, 394
Ottawa Journal, 240, 243, 247

Packer, Kerry, 433–42, 444–54 *passim*, 456, 457, 494
Parizeau, Jacques, 86, 238, 413, 505
Le Parole, 379
Partridge, John, 387, 388, 396
Péladeau, Pierre, 383–84
Pension Commission of Ontario, 352, 354
Perkins Diesel, 227, 232
Perle, Richard, 393, 427, 482
Peterson, David, 305, 319, 398–99, 400, 414
Phillips, Doris, 146, 147, 190, 194, 196, 197, 200, 201, 202, 203, 204–5, 206, 207–8, 210, 212, 213, 214–15, 248
Phillips, Col. W. Eric, 143, 144, 145, 147–48, 149
Powell, Charles, 366, 494
Power Corp., 109, 121, 153, 155, 195, 221, 499, 500–501, 502, 503
Powers, Brian, 437, 439–40, 442, 444, 445, 447, 448, 452, 453, 456
Powis, Alf, 237–38, 239, 354, 395
La Presse, 109, 380, 381, 383, 488
Pressmen [union], 477, 480, 482, 485
Price, Derek, 240, 243, 244, 247
Prince Edward Island Journal-Pioneer (Summerside, PEI), 80
Provigo, 271–72, 316
Prusac, Rifet John, 189–90, 193, 205, 207, 208, 210, 211, 212–13, 215, 216, 501
Punxsutawney (Pennsylvania) *Spirit*, 376

Quayle, Dan, 510, 512
Quebec/Quebeckers, 110, 126–29, 130, 134, 253, 515, 516
Le Quotidien, 379, 380

Radler, David, 50–51, 55, 66, 67, 71–73, 75–76, 121–23, 200, 219, 259, 261, 292, 314, 321, 322, 326–29, 332, 356, 357, 360, 376, 377, 378, 384, 391, 392, 394, 395, 481–82, 487, 497, 499, 503
Rae, Bob, 319, 354, 356, 388, 414–17, 487, 488, 489, 505
Ravelston Corp., 149, 150, 154, 155, 171, 193, 195, 197, 201–2, 203, 204, 205, 207, 212, 213, 217, 218, 229, 230, 232–33, 239, 263, 264, 272, 277, 310, 327–28, 329, 338, 339, 343, 349, 351, 352, 353, 360, 361, 362, 371, 501
Rawlinson, Lord, 340, 341, 344–45
Reagan, Ronald, 248, 250–52, 400–402, 461, 481, 507–8, 511, 512
Reichmann, Albert, 430, 431, 490–91
Reichmann, Paul, 267–68, 391, 393, 395, 405, 406, 408, 430, 431, 490–91
Report on Business section/*Report on Business Magazine*, 387, 388, 390, 396
Rice, Victor, 191, 200, 225, 231, 236, 255–58, 261, 262, 263
Ridley, Nicholas, 419–20, 422
Riley family, 6, 150, 230
Riley, Jean Elizabeth ("Betty"; mother), 3–4, 6, 150, 152, 167–68
Ritchie, Bill, 200, 201, 202
Ritchie, Ced, 160, 302
Rockefeller, David, 365, 482
Rogers, Frank, 340, 343, 344, 370, 372, 403, 404, 407, 408, 409, 439
Roman, Stephen, 163, 164, 430
Roosevelt, Franklin D., 21, 511, 512
Rothermere, Vere, 370, 375, 467
Rothschild, Evelyn de, 334, 337, 341, 342–43, 345, 346, 347, 350, 406
Rothschild, Lord Jacob, 340, 341, 434, 461, 488. *See also* J. Rothschild and Co.
Rothschilds [merchant bank]. *See* N.M. Rothschild
Rowland, Tiny, 342, 406
Royal Bank of Canada, 176, 341, 378
Roy, Jean-Louis, 133–34
Rumilly, Robert, 87–90, 92–93, 179, 180, 181, 381
RWDSU (Retail, Wholesale and Department Store Union), 319, 326, 352, 355, 358–59, 361
Ryan, Claude, 52, 109, 380

Salter, Charles, 292, 298
Saturday Night, 385, 386–87, 487
Saul, John Ralston, 345–46, 365, 433, 489
Saumier, André, 238, 271
Sauvé, Maurice, 29, 30
Security Pacific, 344, 348
Selkirk Broadcasting, 330, 331
Senate Committee on the Constitution, 75
Sheehy, Sir Patrick, 434–35
Sherbrooke Record (Sherbrooke, Que.), 49–51, 55, 66, 68, 70–73, 75–77, 81, 229, 314, 379, 384
Shuvé, Ainslie St. Clair, 200–201, 202
Sifton, June, 241, 244
Slaight, Allan, 330–31, 352, 377

[521]

INDEX

Society of Graphic and Allied Trades (SOGAT), 363–64, 372
Le Soleil, 379–81, 383, 490–91
South Africa, 492–97, 512
Southam, 247, 248, 332–34, 377, 382, 385–86, 387, 487–89, 498–503, 504, 513
Southam family, 332, 333, 385, 487
Special Senate Committee on Mass Media, 73–74
Spectator (London), 403, 409, 419, 433, 435, 468, 469
Standard Broadcasting, 153, 171, 186, 196, 217, 265, 313, 315, 324, 328–32, 475. See also CFRB
Star, Montreal. See Montreal Star
Star, Toronto. See Toronto Star
Steinberg family, 316, 317, 318
Stephen, H.M., 338, 340, 344, 349
Sterling Newspapers Ltd., 80–81, 121, 141, 151, 219, 229–30, 330, 376–77, 378, 386
Stevens, Geoffrey, 389, 396
Stevens, Lord David, 472–73, 474
Stevens, Sinclair, 165–66
Stewart, Brian, 17, 28, 30, 68, 71–72, 502
Straugh, John, 287, 288–89
Sunday Age. See Melbourne Sunday Age
Sunday Telegraph (London), 334, 363–64, 365, 403–5, 409, 428, 468
Sunday Times (London), 247, 362, 403, 465
Sun Life, 273, 274
Sun (London), 362, 467–68
Sun, Toronto. See Toronto Sun

Taylor, E.P., 2, 142–45, 146, 147–48, 155, 170, 193, 201, 313, 402
Telegraph. See Daily Telegraph; Sunday Telegraph
10 Toronto Street, 202, 361
Thatcher, Denis, 366, 430, 469
Thatcher, Margaret, 335, 348, 362, 363, 365–68, 370, 390–91, 417–26, 428, 429–30, 461, 469, 491
Thieu, Nguyen Van, 63–65
Thomas, Lord Hugh, 423, 424
Thomson, Dick, 178, 205, 221
Thomson, Ken, 337
Thomson, Peter Nesbitt, 499
Thomson, Roy, 72, 246, 371–72, 373, 378, 386, 403
Thornbrough, Albert A., 144, 147, 176, 187–88, 190, 191, 192, 196, 200, 202, 209, 212, 225
Times (London), 247, 336, 337, 340, 362, 368, 369, 403, 431–32, 504
Toma, John, 269–70, 317–18, 319, 321–22, 325
Toronto Club, 142
Toronto-Dominion Bank, 178, 205, 331
Toronto Life, 490
Toronto Star, 78, 243, 325, 333, 386, 389, 394, 415, 490
Toronto Sun, 78, 243, 262–63, 360, 399

Toronto Telegram. See Telegram (Toronto)
Torstar, 333–34, 385, 487–89, 498–503
Tourang Ltd., 433, 438–42 *passim*, 444–56 *passim*
Tree, Marietta, 330, 335
La Tribune, 76, 380
Tridel, 398–99
Trilateral Commission, 249
Trinity International, 475–76
Trudeau, Pierre Elliott, 75, 113–14, 167, 179–80, 253–54, 299–301, 312, 316, 321, 322–23, 513, 515
Turnbull, Malcolm, 435, 436, 437–40, 442, 445, 446, 448, 451–52, 453, 454, 458, 470–71
Turner, Geills (Mrs. John; née Kilgour), 322, 324
Turner, John, 142, 223, 263, 312, 316–17, 322–25, 395, 510
Twaits, Bill, 175–76, 292

UniMédia, 378–83, 410, 487
Union Nationale, 49, 54–55, 81–83, 89, 93, 108, 178, 179
United Nations, 414, 506
United Newspapers, 472–74
U.S. News and World Report, 481

Varity (formerly Massey-Ferguson), 262
Vietnam, 57–66, 156–58
La Voix de L'Est, 380

Wadsworth, Page, 178, 257
Wagner, Claude, 52, 82–84, 111, 112, 116, 117, 158–59, 160, 162, 164–65, 312, 325, 510
Warburg, Sir Siegmund, 225, 226–28, 231, 255, 262, 278
Ward, Doug, 185, 192, 194, 208, 210
War Measures Act, 66–67, 68
Warspite Corp., 327–28
Webster, Howard, 143, 240, 241–43, 244, 246–47, 502
Webster, Norman, 243, 246, 384–85, 388, 389, 390, 396
Weidenfeld, Lord George, 393, 440, 479
Westcoast Transmission, 150–51, 152
Western Dominion Investment Co. (WDI), 150, 206, 219, 229, 230, 327–28
Weston, Galen, 33, 320, 326, 395, 494
Weston-Loblaw group, 325, 326, 358, 359
White, Peter, 29–30, 34, 49–51, 55, 66, 79, 81, 116, 165, 200, 219, 220, 312, 327–28, 332, 356, 357, 358, 379, 380, 381, 385, 386, 387, 502
Whitlam, Gough, 448, 451
Will, George, 405–6, 512
Wolfe, Ray, 316, 317, 318, 325, 326
Worsthorne, Sir Peregrine (Perry), 364–65, 403, 409, 468, 475, 510
Worthington, Peter, 262–63

Zuckerman, Mortimer, 481–82, 484, 485–86